Third Canadian Edition

Strategic Management

Competitiveness and Globalization CASES

Third Canadian Edition

Strategic Management

Competitiveness and Globalization CASES

Michael A. **Hitt**
Texas A&M University

R. Duane **Ireland**
Texas A&M University

Robert E. **Hoskisson**
Arizona State

Jerry P. **Sheppard**
Simon Fraser University

W. Glenn **Rowe**
The University of Western Ontario

NELSON / EDUCATION

NELSON EDUCATION

**Strategic Management:
Competitiveness and Globalization—Cases,
Third Canadian Edition**

by Michael A. Hitt, R. Duane Ireland, Robert E. Hoskisson,
Jerry P. Sheppard, and W. Glenn Rowe

**Associate Vice President,
Editorial Director:**
Evelyn Veitch

Editor-in-Chief, Higher Education:
Anne Williams

Acquisitions Editor:
Amie Plourde

Marketing Manager:
Kathaleen McCormick

Developmental Editor:
Tracy Yan

Permissions Coordinator:
Sandra Mark

Production Service:
ICC Macmillan Inc.

Copy Editor:
Wendy Yano

Proofreader:
Dianne Fowlie

**Manufacturing Manager,
Higher Education:**
Joanne McNeil

Design Director:
Ken Phipps

Managing Designer:
Katherine Strain

Interior Design Modifications:
Tammy Gay

Cover Design:
Sasha Moroz

Cover Images:
Brem Stocker/Shutterstock
J. Stan/Shutterstock

Compositor:
ICC Macmillan Inc.

Printer:
Edwards Brothers

**Library and Archives Canada
Cataloguing in Publication**

Strategic management:
competitiveness and globalization:
cases / Michael A. Hitt ... [et al.]. —
3rd ed.

Includes bibliographical references.
ISBN 978-0-17-650082-5

1. Strategic planning—Case
studies. 2. Strategic planning—
Canada—Case studies. I. Hitt,
Michael A.

HD30.28.S727 2008   658.4′012
C2008-90629-8

ISBN-13: 978-0-17-650082-5
ISBN-10: 0-17-650082-0

To all of my current and former students. I am blessed to have the opportunity to teach and learn from you; there is a little piece of each of you in this book.

—Michael A. Hitt

To Jackson Blair Funkhouser, my wonderful new grandson. My hopes for you are that you will always smile, that you will open your heart to those who love you, that you will keep the fire burning, and that you will never forget to dream, baby, dream. I love you, Jackson.

—R. Duane Ireland

To my dear wife, Kathy, who has been my greatest friend and support through life, and I hope will remain so into the eternities.

—Robert E. Hoskisson

To the wisest of counselors: Marnie. I love you and I'm so proud of all you've accomplished. To my other bright lights in this cloudy place: Ben, Bailey and Jesse; to my parents, Rose and Rocky; and to Barb and Harvey.

—Jerry P. Sheppard

To Fay, Gillian and Ryan—you are the most important people in my life. I am very proud of all you do and I love you all so very much.

—W. Glenn Rowe

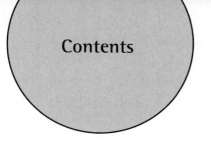

Contents

Case Studies

About This Book

This casebook is intended for use primarily in strategic management and business policy courses. The third Canadian edition of this book features a total of 30 case studies. More than half of these are Canadian cases. Of the 17 Canadian cases, eight deal with some international issues. Of the remaining cases, two cases deal with U.S. companies' U.S. operations, two deal with U.S. firms' international operations, and the remaining 10 cases are international in scope. In total, the cases are concerned with a variety of business and organizational situations representing corporate, business, and global strategic issues. For example, we offer cases representing manufacturing, service, consumer goods, and industrial goods industries.

Importantly, given the 21st-century competitive landscape and the emergence of a global economy, many of these cases represent international business concerns (e.g., Nintendo, Interbrew). Also, this third Canadian edition of this book features cases dealing with high technology (e.g., Blu-ray, Nokia) and service firms (e.g., Cirque du Soleil, YMCA). Some of the cases focus on larger firms (e.g., Target, L'Oréal, Nucor). Some cases focus specifically on strategic issues of entrepreneurial or small- and medium-sized firms (e.g., Med-Eng).

Consistent with the nature of strategic issues, the cases included in this book are multidimensional in nature. Because of this, and for readers' convenience, a matrix listing all cases and the dimensions/characteristics of each one is provided on page X. Furthermore, the matrix lists each text chapter that provides the best fit for teaching that particular case. Given the current challenge within the global economy, more than 50 percent of the cases include some international issues.

In summary, a set of cases that represents a wide variety of important and challenging strategic issues is presented in this edition of our book. We believe that this comprehensive selection of cases yields an exciting and contemporary setting for case analyses and presentations. The Case Notes highlight the details of the cases within the framework of the case analysis guide presented in the first part of this book. The structure of the Case Notes allows instructors to organize discussions along common themes and concepts. For example, each Case Note outlines the time frame, chapters most relevant to the company, company URL, a case summary, teaching objectives, information available in the case, questions to guide discussion, and a chapter-by-chapter set of notes.

Case List	Time Period	CDN	U.S.	International	Mfg./Industrial	Service	Consumer Goods
1 Activplant: The European Opportunity	2006	🍁		🗺	🏭	🛎	
2 AGF Management Limited	2002	🍁		🗺		🛎	
3 AMD in 2005: Coming Out of Intel's Shadow?	2005		★	🗺			
4 Becoming Competitive: An Industry Note on the Canadian Telecommunications Industry	2005	🍁					
5 Bell Canada: The VoIP Challenge	2005	🍁					
6 Blu-ray and HD DVD: Betamax–VHS 'Format Wars' Redux?	2006			🗺	🏭		
7 CCL Industries: Divesting the Custom Division	2004	🍁			🏭		
8 Coach Inc.: From Staid to Stylish	2006		★	🗺	🏭		🏠
9 Compassion Canada	2002			🗺			
10 Cott Corporation, World's Biggest Maker of Retailer-Brand Carbonated Soft Drinks: The Growth Strategies	2005	🍁					
11 DHL Bangladesh: Managing HQ–Subsidiary Relations	2005			🗺		🛎	
12 East Coast Trail Association	2005	🍁					
13 Embraer: The Brazilian Aircraft Manufacturer's Turnaround and Growth	2006			🗺	🏭		
14 Entrepreneurial Search: Growing from a Monopoly Situation—Med-Eng Systems Inc.	2005	🍁		🗺	🏭		
15 The Global Luxury Hospitality Industry and the Four Seasons Hotels and Resorts	2007	🍁		🗺		🛎	
16 GVM Exploration Limited	2005	🍁					
17 Haier—The Chinese Global Competitor	2005			🗺	🏭		🏠
18 Innovation at Cirque du Soleil	2007	🍁		🗺		🛎	
19 The Interbrew–AmBev Merger Story	2004	🍁		🗺			🏠
20 L'Oréal's Business Strategy	2003			🗺			🏠
21 MTV Networks International: Localizing Globally	2006			🗺			
22 The Nintendo Wii: A 'Revolution' in Gaming?	2006			🗺			🏠
23 Nokia and the Global Mobile Phone Industry	2005			🗺	🏭		🏠
24 Nucor in 2005	2005		★		🏭		
25 The Print Shop at Eva's Phoenix: "Training Youth for Life"	2004	🍁				🛎	
26 Ryanair: Flying High at Ryanair	2006			🗺		🛎	
27 Selectpower—Green Energy in Ontario	2004	🍁					
28 Target Stores' Differentiation Strategies	2005		★				🏠
29 WorldSpace Satellite Radio: Fading Signals?	2006			🗺		🛎	🏠
30 The YMCA of London, Ontario	2005	🍁				🛎	

High Tech.	Media/Entertain.	Food/Retail	Social/Non-Profit	Entrepreneurial	Industry View	Emphasized Chapters		
						Input	Formulate	Implement
💻						4	9	
					🔍	3, 4		
💻					🔍	4	5	
💻					🔍	3	6	
💻						3, 4	5, 6	12, 13
💻					🔍	3, 4	5, 6, 10	-
						1, 3	7, 8	11
						4	5	13, 14
			🎖			1, 3	8	
		🏭			🔍	1, 3, 4	5	
💻							10	12
			🎖			1, 4	5, 10	
💻					🔍	3	5, 6, 8, 9, 10	
💻				📡		3, 4	6	
					🔍	3, 4	5	
			🎖			1, 4	6	
						3, 4	5, 7, 9	12
	🏰			📡	🔍	3	5	13, 14
		🏭			🔍		6, 8, 9	11
							5	13
💻	🏰					1, 3, 4	6, 10	14
💻					🔍	3	6	
					🔍	4		12, 13, 14
			🎖	📡		1, 2		
				📡	🔍	1, 4	5	14
			🎖			1, 2, 3, 4	5	
		🏭				4	5, 10	
💻				📡	🔍	3	5, 9	14
			🎖			1, 4		11, 12, 13

Introduction

Preparing an Effective Case Analysis

What to Expect from In-Class Case Discussions

As you will learn, classroom discussions of cases differ significantly from lectures. The case method calls for your instructor to guide the discussion and to solicit alternative views as a way of encouraging your active participation when analyzing a case. When alternative views are not forthcoming, your instructor might take a position just to challenge you and your peers to respond thoughtfully as a way of generating additional alternatives. Instructors will often evaluate your work in terms of both the quantity and the quality of your contributions to in-class case discussions. The in-class discussions are important in that you can derive significant benefit from having your ideas and recommendations examined against those of your peers and from responding to challenges by other class members and/or the instructor.

During case discussions, your instructor will likely listen, question, and probe to extend the analysis of case issues. In the course of these actions, your peers and/or your instructor may challenge an individual's views and the validity of alternative perspectives that have been expressed. These challenges are offered in a constructive manner; their intent is to help all who are analyzing a case develop their analytical and communication skills. Commonly, instructors will encourage you and your peers to be innovative and original when developing and presenting ideas. Over the course of an individual discussion, you are likely to develop a more complex view of the case as a result of listening to and thinking about the diverse inputs offered by your peers and instructor. Among other benefits, experience with multiple case discussions will increase your knowledge of the advantages and disadvantages of group decision-making processes.

Both your peers and your instructor will value comments that help identify problems and solutions. To offer relevant contributions, you are encouraged to use independent thought and, through discussions with your peers outside class, to refine your thinking. We also encourage you to avoid using phrases such as "I think," "I believe," and "I feel" when analyzing a case. Instead, consider using a less emotion-laden phrase, such as "My analysis shows. . . ." This highlights the logical nature of the approach you have taken to analyze the case. When preparing for an in-class case discussion, plan to use the case data to explain your assessment of the situation. Assume that your peers and instructor are familiar with the basic facts of the case. In addition, it is good practice to prepare notes regarding your analysis of case facts before class discussions and use them when explaining your perspectives. Effective notes signal to classmates and the instructor that you are prepared to discuss the case thoroughly. Moreover, thorough notes eliminate the need for you to memorize the facts and figures needed to successfully discuss a case.

The case analysis process described here will help prepare you to effectively discuss a case during class meetings. Using this process helps you consider the issues required to identify a focal firm's problems and to propose strategic actions through which the firm can improve its competitiveness. In some instances, your instructor may ask you to prepare an oral or written analysis of a particular case. Typically, such an assignment demands even more thorough study and analysis of the case contents. At your instructor's discretion, oral and written analyses may be completed by individuals or by groups of three or more people. The information and insights gained through completing the six steps shown in Table 1 are often valuable when developing an oral or

Table 1	An Effective Case Analysis Process

Step 1: Gaining Familiarity	a. In general—determine who, what, how, where, and when (the critical facts of the case). b. In detail—identify the places, persons, activities, and contexts of the situation. c. Recognize the degree of certainty/uncertainty of acquired information.
Step 2: Recognizing Symptoms	a. List all indicators (including stated "problems") that something is not as expected or as desired. b. Ensure that symptoms are not assumed to be the problem (symptoms should lead to identification of the problem).
Step 3: Identifying Goals	a. Identify critical statements by major parties (for example, people, groups, the work unit, and so on). b. List all goals of the major parties that exist or can be reasonably inferred.
Step 4: Conducting the Analysis	a. Decide which ideas, models, and theories seem useful. b. Apply these conceptual tools to the situation. c. As new information is revealed, cycle back to substeps a and b.
Step 5: Making the Diagnosis	a. Identify predicaments (goal inconsistencies). b. Identify problems (discrepancies between goals and performance). c. Prioritize predicaments/problems regarding timing, importance, and so on.
Step 6: Doing the Action Planning	a. Specify and prioritize the criteria used to choose action alternatives. b. Discover or invent feasible action alternatives. c. Examine the probable consequences of action alternatives. d. Select a course of action. e. Design an implementation plan/schedule. f. Create a plan for assessing the action to be implemented.

Source: C. C. Lundberg and C. Enz, 1993, A framework for student case preparation, *Case Research Journal*, 13 (Summer): 144. Reprinted by permission of NACRA, North American Case Research Association.

written analysis. However, when preparing an oral or written presentation, you must consider the overall framework in which your information and inputs will be presented. Such a framework is the focus of the next section.

Preparing an Oral or Written Case Presentation

Experience shows that two types of thinking (analysis and synthesis) are necessary to develop an effective oral or written presentation (see Exhibit 1). In the analysis stage, you should first analyze the general external environmental issues affecting the firm. Next, your environmental analysis should focus on the particular industry or industries in which a firm operates. Finally, you

should examine companies against which the focal firm competes. By studying the three levels of the external environment (general, industry, and competitor), you will be able to identify a firm's opportunities and threats. Following the external environmental analysis is the analysis of the firm's internal environment, which identifies the firm's strengths and weaknesses.

As noted in Exhibit 1, you must then change the focus from analysis to synthesis. Specifically, you must synthesize information gained from your analysis of the firm's internal and external environments. Synthesizing information enables you to generate alternatives that can resolve the problems or challenges facing the focal firm. Once you identify a best alternative from an evaluation based on predetermined criteria and goals, you must explore implementation actions.

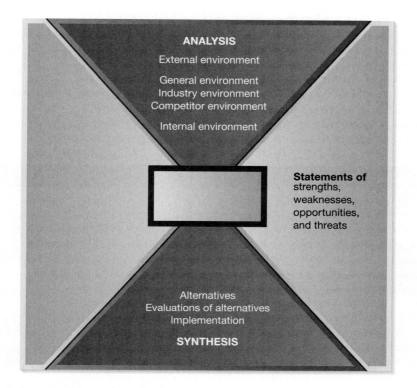

Types of Thinking in Case Preparation: Analysis and Synthesis

Table 2 outlines the sections that should be included in either an oral or a written presentation: introduction (strategic profile and purpose), situation analysis, statements of strengths/weaknesses and opportunities/threats, strategy formulation, and implementation.

These sections are described in the following discussion. Familiarity with the contents of your book's 14 chapters is helpful because the general outline for an oral or a written presentation shown in Table 2 is based on an understanding of the strategic management process detailed in those chapters. We follow the discussions of the parts of Table 2 with a few comments about the *process* to use to present the

Table 2	General Outline for an Oral or Written Presentation

I. Strategic Profile and Case Analysis Purpose
II. Situation Analysis
    A. General environmental analysis
    B. Industry analysis
    C. Competitor analysis
    D. Internal analysis
III. Identification of Environmental Opportunities and Threats and Firm Strengths and Weaknesses (SWOT Analysis)
IV. Strategy Formulation
    A. Strategic alternatives
    B. Alternative evaluation
    C. Alternative choice
V. Strategic Alternative Implementation
    A. Action items
    B. Action plan

results of your case analysis in either an oral or written format.

Strategic Profile and Case Analysis Purpose

The strategic profile should briefly present the critical facts from the case that have affected the focal firm's historical strategic direction and performance. The case facts should not be restated in the profile; rather, these comments should show how the critical facts lead to a particular focus for your analysis. This primary focus should be emphasized in this section's conclusion. In addition, this section should state important assumptions about case facts on which your analyses may be based.

Situation Analysis

As shown in Table 2, a general starting place for completing a situation analysis is the general environment.

General Environmental Analysis Your analysis of the general environment should focus on trends in the six segments of the general environment (see Table 3). Many of the segment issues shown in Table 3 for the six

Table 3	Sample General Environmental Categories

Technological Trends

- Information technology continues to become cheaper with more practical applications
- Database technology enables organization of complex data and distribution of information
- Telecommunications technology and networks increasingly provide fast transmission of all sources of data, including voice, written communications, and video information
- Computerized design and manufacturing technologies continue to facilitate quality and flexibility

Demographic Trends

- Regional changes in population due to migration
- Changing ethnic composition of the population
- Aging of the population
- Aging of the "baby boom" generation

Economic Trends

- Interest rates
- Inflation rates
- Savings rates
- Exchange rates
- Trade deficits
- Budget deficits

Political/Legal Trends

- Antitrust enforcement
- Tax policy changes
- Environmental protection laws
- Extent of regulation/deregulation
- Privatizing state monopolies
- State-owned industries

Sociocultural Trends

- Women in the workforce
- Awareness of health and fitness issues
- Concern for the environment
- Concern for customers

Global Trends

- Currency exchange rates
- Free-trade agreements
- Trade deficits

segments are explained more fully in Chapter 3 of your book. The objective you should have in evaluating these trends is to be able to predict the segments that you expect to have the most significant influence on your focal firm over the next several years (e.g., three to five years) and to explain your reasoning for your predictions.

Industry Analysis Porter's five-forces model is a useful tool for analyzing the industry or industries in which your firm competes. We explain how to use this tool in Chapter 3. In this part of your analysis, you want to determine the attractiveness of the industry or industries in which the focal firm is competing. As attractiveness increases, so does the possibility that your focal firm will be able to earn above-average returns by using its chosen strategies. After evaluating the power of the five forces relative to your focal firm, you should evaluate how attractive the industry is in which your focal firm is competing.

Competitor Analysis Firms also need to analyze each of their primary competitors. This analysis should identify competitors' current strategies, vision, mission, capabilities, core competencies, and a competitive response profile. We explain these items in Chapter 3. This information is useful to the focal firm in formulating an appropriate strategy and in predicting competitors' probable responses. Sources that can be used to gather information about an industry and companies with whom the focal firm competes are listed in the Appendix. Included in this list is a wide range of publications, such as periodicals, newspapers, bibliographies, directories of companies, industry ratios, forecasts, rankings/ratings, and other valuable statistics.

Internal Analysis Assessing a firm's strengths and weaknesses through a value-chain analysis facilitates moving from the external environment to the internal environment. Analyzing the primary and support activities of the value chain will help you understand how external environmental trends affect the specific activities of a firm. Such analysis helps highlight strengths and weaknesses (see Chapter 3 for an explanation and use of the value chain).

For purposes of preparing an oral or a written presentation, it is important to note that strengths are internal resources and capabilities that have the potential to be core competencies. Weaknesses, on the other hand, are internal resources and capabilities that have the potential to place a firm at a competitive disadvantage relative to its rivals. Therefore, some of a firm's resources and capabilities are strengths; others are weaknesses.

When you evaluate the internal characteristics of the firm, your analysis of the functional activities emphasized is critical. For instance, if the strategy of the firm is primarily technology-driven, it is important to evaluate the firm's R&D activities. If the strategy is market-driven, marketing activities are of paramount importance. If a firm has difficulties, performance evaluation would require careful evaluation. In fact, because of the importance of financial health, most cases require financial analyses. Chapter 2 of the Concepts text lists and operationally defines performance measures. Leadership, organizational culture, structure, and control systems are other characteristics of firms you should examine to fully understand the "internal" part of your firm.

Identification of Environmental Opportunities and Threats and Firm Strengths and Weaknesses (SWOT Analysis)

The outcome of the situation analysis is the identification of a firm's strengths and weaknesses and its environmental threats and opportunities. The next step requires that you analyze the strengths and weaknesses and the opportunities and threats for configurations that benefit or do not benefit your firm's efforts to perform well. Case analysts, and organizational strategists as well, seek to match a firm's strengths with its external environmental opportunities. In addition, strengths are chosen to prevent any serious environmental threat from negatively affecting the firm's performance. The key objective of conducting a SWOT analysis is to determine how to position the firm so it can take advantage of opportunities, while simultaneously avoiding or minimizing environmental threats. Results from a SWOT analysis yield valuable insights into the selection of a firm's strategies. The analysis of a case should not be overemphasized relative to the synthesis of results gained from your analytical efforts. You may be tempted to emphasize the results from the analysis in your oral or written case analysis. It is important, however, that you make an equal effort to develop and evaluate alternatives and to design implementation of the chosen strategy.

Strategy Formulation—Strategic Alternatives, Alternative Evaluation, and Alternative Choice

Developing alternatives is often one of the most difficult steps in preparing an oral or written presentation. Development of three to four alternative strategies is common (see Chapter 5 for business-level strategy alternatives and Chapter 7 for corporate-level strategy alternatives). Each alternative should be feasible (it should match the firm's strengths, capabilities, and especially core competencies), and feasibility should be demonstrated. In addition, you should show how each alternative takes advantage of environmental opportunities or protects against environmental threats. Developing carefully thought-out alternatives requires synthesis of your analyses' results and creates greater credibility in oral and written case presentations.

Once you develop strong alternatives, you must evaluate the set to choose the best one. Your choice should be defensible and provide benefits over the other alternatives. Therefore, it is important that both alternative development and evaluation of alternatives are thorough. You should explain and defend your choice of the best alternative.

Strategic Alternative Implementation—Action Items and Action Plan

After selecting the most appropriate strategy (the one most likely to help your firm earn above-average returns), you must turn your attention to implementation-related issues. Effective synthesis is important to ensure that you have considered and evaluated all critical implementation issues. Issues you might consider include the structural changes necessary to implement the new strategy. In addition, leadership changes and new controls or incentives may be necessary to implement strategic actions. The implementation actions you recommend should be explicit and thoroughly explained. Occasionally, careful evaluation of implementation actions may show the strategy to be less favorable than you thought originally. A strategy is only as good as the firm's ability to implement it.

Process Issues

You should ensure that your presentation (either oral or written) is logical and consistent throughout. For example, if your presentation identifies one purpose, but your analysis focuses on issues that differ from the stated purpose, the logical inconsistency will be apparent. Likewise, your alternatives should flow from the configuration of strengths, weaknesses, opportunities, and threats you identified by analyzing your firm's external and internal environments.

Thoroughness and clarity also are critical to an effective presentation. Thoroughness is represented by the comprehensiveness of the analysis and alternative generation. Furthermore, clarity in the results of the analyses, selection of the best alternative strategy, and design of implementation actions are important. For example, your statement of the strengths and weaknesses should flow clearly and logically from your analysis of your firm's internal environment.

Presentations (oral or written) that show logical consistency, thoroughness, clarity of purpose, effective analyses, and feasible recommendations (strategy and implementation) are more effective and are likely to be more positively received by your instructor and peers. Furthermore, developing the skills necessary to make such presentations will enhance your future job performance and career success.

References

1. C. Christensen, 1989, Teaching and the Case Method, Boston: Harvard Business School Publishing Division; C. C. Lundberg, 1993, Introduction to the case method, in C. M. Vance (ed.), *Mastering Management Education*, Newbury Park, Calif.: Sage.
2. C. C. Lundberg and C. Enz, 1993, A framework for student case preparation, *Case Research Journal* 13 (Summer): 133.
3. J. Soltis, 1971, John Dewey, in L. E. Deighton (ed.), *Encyclopedia of Education*, New York: Macmillan and Free Press.

Abstracts and Indexes
Periodicals

ABI/Inform
Business Periodicals Index
Canadian Business & Current Affairs
EBSCO Business Source Premier
InfoTrac Custom Journals
InfoTrac Custom Newspapers
InfoTrac OneFile
Lexis/Nexis Academic
Public Affairs Information Service Bulletin (PAIS)
Readers' Guide to Periodical Literature

Newspapers

National Post
The Globe and Mail
Canadian Business
Financial Times
NewsBank—Foreign Broadcast Information
NewsBank—Global NewsBank
New York Times Index
Wall Street Journal/Barron's Index
Wall Street Journal Index
Washington Post Index

Bibliographies

Encyclopedia of Business Information Sources

Directories
Companies—General

America's Corporate Families and International Affiliates
D&B Million Dollar Database (http://www.dnbmdd.com)
Hoover's Online: The Business Network (http://www.hoovers.
   com/free)
Standard & Poor's Corporation Records
Standard & Poor's Register of Corporations, Directors & Executives
   (http://www.netadvantage.standardandpoors.com)
Ward's Business Directory of Largest U.S. Companies

Companies—International

America's Corporate Families and International Affiliates
Business Asia
Business China
Business Eastern Europe
Business Europe
Business International
Business International Money Report
Business Latin America
Directory of American Firms Operating in Foreign Countries
Directory of Foreign Firms Operating in the United States
Hoover's Handbook of World Business
International Directory of Company Histories
Mergent International Manual
Mergent Online (http://www.fisonline.com)
Who Owns Whom

(continued)

Companies—Manufacturers

Thomas Register of American Manufacturers
U.S. Manufacturer's Directory, Manufacturing & Distribution, USA
U.S. Office of Management and Budget, Executive

Companies—Private

D&B Million Dollar Database (http://www.dnbmdd.com)
Ward's Business Directory of Largest U.S. Companies

Companies—Public

Annual reports and 10-K reports
Disclosure (corporate reports)
Mergent's Manuals:
　　Mergent's Bank and Finance Manual
　　Mergent's Industrial Manual
　　Mergent's International Manual
　　Mergent's Municipal and Government Manual
　　Mergent's OTC Industrial Manual
　　Mergent's OTC Unlisted Manual
　　Mergent's Public Utility Manual
　　Mergent's Transportation Manual
Standard & Poor's Corporation, *Standard Corporation*
　　Descriptions (http://www.netadvantage.standardandpoors.com)
　　　　Standard & Poor's Analyst's Handbook
　　　　Standard & Poor's Industry Surveys
　　　　Standard & Poor's Statistical Service
Q-File

Companies—Subsidiaries and Affiliates

America's Corporate Families and International Affiliates
Standard & Poor's Analyst's Handbook
Standard & Poor's Industry Surveys (2 volumes)
U.S. Department of Commerce, *U.S. Industrial Outlook*
Who Owns Whom

Industry Ratios

Dun & Bradstreet, *Industry Norms and Key Business Ratios*
RMA's Annual Statement Studies
Troy Almanac of Business and Industrial Financial Ratios

Industry Forecasts

International Trade Administration, *U.S. Industry & Trade Outlook*

Rankings and Ratings

Annual Report on American Industry in *Forbes*
Business Rankings Annual
Mergent's Industry Review (http://www.worldcatlibraries.org)
Standard & Poor's Industry Report Service (http://www.
　　netadvantage.standardandpoors.com)
Value Line Investment Survey
Ward's Business Directory of Largest U.S. Companies

(continued)

Statistics

Statistics Canada

Bureau of the Census, U.S. Department of Commerce, American Statistics Index (ASI)

Economic Census publications

Statistical Abstract of the United States

Bureau of Economic Analysis, U.S. Department of Commerce, Survey of Current Business

Internal Revenue Service, U.S. Department of the Treasury, Statistics of Income: Corporation Income Tax Returns

Statistical Reference Index (SRI)

Activplant: The European Opportunity

Stewart Thornhill

Brodie B. Christ

Monday Morning

On Monday January 30, 2006, Dennis Cocco, chief executive officer (CEO), and Chuck Frosst, chief operating officer (COO) of Activplant Corporation, sat debating the European market opportunity. Frosst wondered aloud:

> Can we financially afford to enter Europe? Can we afford to put substantial human resources into developing and implementing that market at all? I mean, we can get the financing, but that doesn't mean it's the best idea.

Of Activplant's current customers, more than 90 per cent were located in North America. Recently, many larger customers had been attempting to pull Activplant into the European market so that the company could provide more extensive support. Cocco responded:

> Listen, we have now proven ourselves in the North American auto manufacturing market. I don't understand what we're waiting for. We know that our product is easily transferable to Europe. We also know that our current "doggy-paddle-to-Europe" strategy isn't going to build us the market. Potential customers are not going to meet us in the middle of the Atlantic. We have to go get them and we have to do it before our competitors do.

Frosst responded:

> I don't know, Dennis. It sounds like a lot of risk for a company our size. Don't forget that it's not just our customers we have to pay attention to. Our investors are watching closely as well.

Background

Activplant Corporation was a London, Ontario-based software firm specializing in manufacturing intelligence (MI). Essentially, MI is the ability to monitor, measure and analyse the performance of factory automation systems. Activplant was founded by a group of technology entrepreneurs in 1998. It was a privately held company supported by significant investments from world-class companies, such as Ford Motor Company, Ventures West Management, the Canadian Science and Technology Growth Fund and the Bank of Montreal Capital Corporation.

Activplant had installations all over the world, the majority within North America. It controlled 80 per cent of the automotive original equipment manufacturer (OEM) plants that had MI software in North America. Much of the North American market was still unexplored,

Richard Ivey School of Business
The University of Western Ontario

as were Europe and Asia. Current customers included Toyota, Gillette, Ford, Honda, Chrysler, Visteon and Magna. Historically, Activplant had acquired customers on a plant-by-plant basis. In the future, they looked forward to gaining sales for installations across an entire enterprise, which had become the focus of the current sales process.

The Activplant Product

Activplant was a web-deployed, fully scalable enterprise manufacturing intelligence solution designed to work across an entire operation from the smallest to the largest plants. Activplant collected data from any source on the factory floor and integrated it with business logic, reporting capabilities, analysis and intelligent discovery via alerts. From the integration of these elements, managers and decision-makers across the enterprise had a tool to identify constraints on the plant floor with the goal of maximizing throughput. The software worked on fundamental manufacturing process principles and had been proven useful for automotive, consumer goods, and food and beverage manufacturers with discrete and hybrid manufacturing processes.

The Product/Service Offering in North America

Licensing

Activplant sold its software on a license basis. The license fee was paid one time and was followed with an annual maintenance fee that included upgrades, bug fixes and access to a support help desk. License fees were the major source of revenue for Activplant, which had placed greater emphasis on the product than on services as a driver for growth. As well, the service revenue was dependent on the license being purchased.

The software license allowed the customer to have the Activplant software suite installed and set up to begin monitoring any manufacturing equipment that the suite was attached to. The larger the installation and the more manufacturing machines that were being monitored, the more license revenue Activplant generated. However, for larger deals, Activplant would lower its per-installation price, making the return-on-investment proposition more attractive for the customer.

Maintenance/Support

Activplant North America currently had staff available by phone for customer service to provide both knowledge

support and assistance with maintenance and upgrades. The web-based platform allowed Activplant staff in London to see precisely what was occurring on the factory floor, assess the situation and offer assistance, all without being physically present.

Training

From its headquarters, Activplant ran a training facility for customers to learn the specifics and details of the software. Activplant offered an extensive array of training programs to ensure customers could maximize their Activplant investment. Courses were designed to train customers in implementing, supporting, administering and effectively using various Activplant solutions. The courses were instructor led and used hands-on labs and examples to reinforce the course material provided. The training options included courses at the London headquarters, customized on-site training and, where required, training in prominent U.S. locations. Training for the software could take a number of weeks to complete.

The Sales Process

The Activplant sales method could be a grueling six- to 12-month process, due to the complexity of clearly illustrating the product's value and the substantial investment required from potential customers. Activplant had sales managers who visited potential clients and provided pitches, as well as inside sales representatives who generated and qualified leads. There was a very technical aspect to selling the product that required a technical expert. While the sales managers targeted the decision makers in an organization (CEOs, COOs, VPs), the technical sales representative needed to convince the internal engineers and technical staff of ease of integration and the aspects of the product that would improve production.

The Services Process

The value proposition of the services process was to provide customers with timely and effective services, such as installation and customization of the product, to best suit the customer's needs. All of Activplant's services in North America were supplied by internal staff at Activplant. The complexity of the product was such that having internal staff providing services ensured the requisite level of quality.

This component of the Activplant solution was complex and required substantial resource commitment for both Activplant and the customer. Services at Activplant could be broken into a number of different categories: installation, training and support. The installation process could be broken down into three further subsections:

Discovery, the survey of the plant by an Activplant consultant to assess specifically how the installation would proceed; Delivery, the installation of the software, including tests to ensure that it was communicating with the line machinery; and Maintenance, Activplant's updates and software "tweaking" to suit the specific needs of the company. The personnel and resources required could fluctuate substantially, depending on the size of the implementation.

The European Opportunity

Activplant currently had some customers in Europe, none of which had been actively pursued by sales. Activplant had either been pulled into Europe by current customers (e.g. Ford and Visteon) or had been pursued by proactive companies (e.g. Gillette and Duracell in the United Kingdom). The offerings had been provided on an ad hoc basis.

A European go-to-market strategy would require a product that supported multiple languages in some fashion. This requirement could be partially satisfied by the pre-installation customization/configuration, by which labels (text on the screen) of the local language were entered into the system. Although this solution might have been adequate as a temporary means to enter the European market, a complete internationalization could be required in order to compete effectively with local and global companies.

Full internationalization of the Activplant Software Suite would likely cost more than $2 million as a one-time cost and approximately $300,000 per language to translate the interface.[1] Internationalization of the software would enhance the product in three ways: it would allow administration of the software in local languages; enable local dependent representation of data (for example, currency, date and time values), and cover all the necessary character sets, including double-byte character sets that would be required for markets in Asia. Among these three objectives, being able to display data in a format consistent with the appropriate locale was the most important.

Operating since 1998 on investments from venture capitalists (VCs), Activplant had just achieved its first year of profitability in fiscal year 2006. A European strategy would be funded entirely by Activplant's cash and operating income currently on hand, since the current investors were not committing any additional funds at this time.

Services

Existing European customers had experienced slow responses when problems were encountered, partly due to the time zone difference between Europe and North America. In addition, reliance on partners in the past to deliver quality services had yielded mixed results, since there had not been a vigorous partnership program to ensure the quality of services. Therefore, being able to provide quality services more consistently and more timely by having a local presence would make Activplant a better vendor for customers' business needs.

To deliver this value proposition, Activplant would need to deploy its own resources, or work with partners. Either option would require active management and execution by Activplant.

Maintenance/Support

For reasons similar to that of installation services, European customers would value local on-going support. Running a support center in Europe from the first year would likely be too expensive for the relatively small volume of sales; however, pager or phone support by local Activplant personnel could satisfy customers' needs for responsiveness. A protocol needed to be developed to standardize the process by which support requests through the support personnel in Europe were handled, so that responsiveness and cost would be well balanced. For example, requests could be classified into multiple levels, but it remained to be determined which issues staff in Europe would be responsible for and which issues staff in North America would need to address.

Training

Activplant could provide training to customers through its certified partners in Europe; alternatively, it could attempt to provide training itself, either locally at the customer's site or in Canada. A partnership training strategy provided an opportunity for the partners to learn about Activplant's products in depth, strengthening the partners' ability to provide services and support in the future. One of the difficulties regarding outsourcing services and support tasks to the partners was their lack of knowledge of the product. By offering European partners the training business, Activplant received a greater benefit of educating the partners themselves, allowing more flexibility in its operations in the future. For example, if the operation needed to be

---

[1] All funds in U.S. dollars unless otherwise specified.

scaled up rapidly due to market demand, Activplant might need to offload some of the tasks to its partners since it may not be able to expand its capacity as drastically.

Competitors Across the Globe

Manufacturing software had yet to be clearly defined as a market, and it was difficult to determine whether a company offered solutions that overlapped or complemented Activplant's solutions in this growing and convoluted solution space.

Some of the competitors to be aware of in Europe included the following:

Wonderware/Invensys

- Performance management solutions with real-time capability. Claimed 30 per cent of the factories in the world used Wonderware software.

Rockwell

- A global provider of manufacturing hardware and software systems. Recently acquired Manufacturing Execution Systems (MES) provider Datasweep.

SAP/Lighthammer

- A German enterprise resource planning (ERP) solution provider driving toward manufacturing solutions. Acquisition of Lighthammer had provided portal capabilities for manufacturing.

OSIsoft

- A manufacturing intelligence company with a joint venture in Germany.

Matrikon

- A provider of manufacturing intelligence solutions for process, hybrid and discrete manufacturing with offices in Ireland and Germany.

UGS

- Broad scope of product lifecycle management solutions, including some MES products. A global company with presence in Europe.

Iconics

- A provider of manufacturing intelligence solutions from the HMI/SCADA end of the space with many locations throughout Europe.

Citect

- An MES provider with strong global approach based in Australia.

In general, the market growth for manufacturing intelligence and performance management solutions was accelerating. As some of the larger brand-name global players, such as Rockwell, GE and SAP, acquired smaller well-developed software platforms, Activplant needed to maintain adequate market share and size or it would risk being pushed out of the market. In addition, as competitive platforms increased their scope, the value proposition in Activplant's discrete manufacturing software solution became less distinctive.

Partners
Solution Partners

Activplant had engaged in two relationships with other firms in order to sell its product in Europe. These relationships were developed based on the desire of these two firms—ATS and Systema—to sell Activplant software. A commission was paid based on the amount of sales that Activplant received from these partners.

These two partners fell into separate areas of expertise. ATS had competencies in the smaller details of the installation and provided additional services to the end customer. ATS's motivation was to either include Activplant products as an add-on to increase revenues or as a selling feature to help ATS secure contracts.

Systema approached the customer in a manufacturing consultant capacity, using the Activplant software data to supplement its own consultancy services. Activplant's relationship with Systema was established recently and had not yet generated any deals, although Systema had indicated that several were in the pipeline.

The solution partners did not have the sales expertise to make the enterprise deals that were Activplant's current focus. These types of solution partners often had a number of different software products that they could offer to their clients. Changes in the levels of commission or preferences of the client could affect a partner's desire to sell one product over another. The Activplant software suite was not a significant portion of either partner's revenue. Partners did not have exclusivity agreements, but ATS has been hinting that such an arrangement would "enable" them to sell more Activplant product.

Integration/Technology Partners

Initially, customer installations, support and other services would not be sufficient to cover the costs of a complete services team in Europe, although many functions would still be required. Some functions could be covered by the North American office. Other functions, such as installation and multi-language support, would need to be provided in Europe. Integration partners had proven capable in the past, and Activplant was wise to continue to utilize them to make up for the lack of infrastructure in Europe. Installation was also not one of Activplant's core competencies. The services components of the Activplant process could be coordinated by staff in Europe, remotely from Canada with frequent flights to Europe or managed by the partners in Europe.

Channel Partners

There were advantages to creating, growing and strengthening relationships with either large players in the business solutions industry who would have interconnected software products, such as Microsoft, Oracle and SAP, or larger consulting firms, such as Accenture or Tata.

There was a potential to leverage Activplant's current relationship with Microsoft by engaging Microsoft to promote Activplant solutions as part of its portfolio for manufacturing clients. However, Microsoft did not participate in direct sales; Microsoft did not even sell its own product directly. Since the outcome of a Microsoft-dependant strategy was questionable, and, outside of Activplant's control, sales needed to be generated by a sales force to ensure that targets were met. A Microsoft partner strategy would likely become a greater source of lead generation in the future, but it was still unproven.

Revenue

According to past sales experience, it was estimated that one Activplant sales representative in Europe could, on average, conclude two deals in one quarter. The average size of one deal was US$100,000 (excluding services and support contract). Since a typical sales cycle was six to eight months, the first deal closed by the European operation, excluding deals currently in the sales process, would likely occur in the third quarter after entry. Partners in Europe pursuing their selling efforts were also assumed to be able to conclude two deals per quarter.

Market Size

The estimated automotive market for Activplant in Europe was $343 million as compared to the estimated $300 million market in North America. Suppliers

outnumbered OE manufacturers by a ratio of 22 to one. The automotive industry comprised nearly 80 per cent of Activplant's current revenues.

	North American Plants	European Plants
OEMs	90[2]	94
Suppliers	1,910	1,986[3]
Total	2,000[4]	2,080

The average deal size for Activplant was $100,000, but the range could range from $30,000 for small single plant deals to $3 million for enterprise-wide installations.

Staffing

The most significant factor affecting profitability in the European market was employee payroll. Salaries for various positions could be assessed first as if the employees were hired in Canada and worked in Canada, then a 30 per cent premium could be added to account for the higher wage level and benefits in Europe. Finally, the premium-added cost was converted to U.S. dollars to be comparable with revenue figures.

Financial assumptions are detailed in Exhibit 4.

Alternatives

There were two main components to the decision to launch Activplant in Europe from personnel and operations perspectives.

The first component involved the method used to sell the product. This selection answered questions such as the following: Will Activplant involve partners in the selling process? Will Activplant have sales staff full-time in Europe? If so, how many? Will enterprise deals be managed from Europe or Canada? This part of the decision is known as the Sales Process.

The second component was the method by which Activplant would deliver the sold services in Europe. It would answer such questions as: Who will deliver support, and from where? How will services be provided? How will Activplant deal with training? This piece was known as Services.

The selected option from the Sales Process with the selected option from Services would combine to form the basis of a European Entrance Strategy.

---

[2] *Automotive News* http://www.autonews.com/assets/PDF/CA31631024.PDF for NA OEM.
[3] http://www.emcc.eurofound.eu.int/automotivemap/
[4] Activplant Market Sizing and Roadmap, October 18, 2005.

Sales Alternatives

Activplant would like to sell both single plant deals and large deals, which would involve multiple plants across an entire enterprise. Given those segments, Activplant could decide who would be responsible for single plant sales (solution partners, full-time staff in Europe or sales staff in Canada) and who would be responsible for enterprise deals.

Using solution partners to pursue enterprise deals would require the development of a partner management strategy to ensure consistent messaging and quality of the sales process. This approach would require a partnership manager. If Activplant had staff directly in Europe, these staff would require a senior account manager and a regular account manager.

Staff Requirements		
Option	Title	Cost (CDN$)
Solution Partners	Partnership Manager	$150,000 × 130% = $195,000
Activplant Staff in Europe	Account Manager, Senior Account Manager	$125,000 × 130% + $150,000 × 130% = $357,500

Services Alternatives

Similarly, the services that Activplant performed after an installation comprised two components: Project Delivery and Solution Consulting. Project delivery referred to lower-end work, such as machine programming and product installation, but also the coordination and management of these tasks. Currently, these tasks were mostly performed by integration partners where they performed the work and managed the project. It was lower margin work that required substantial human resources. Solution Consulting was higher end, knowledge- and expertise-intensive fine-tuning of the product so that the client could glean the most benefit. Occasionally, clients preferred to take on this task themselves, believing that they could do it better than Activplant and/or their partners.

Each services component, Project Delivery and Solutions Consulting, could be performed either by Activplant staff in Europe, remotely by Activplant staff in Canada or by integration partners (for project delivery) and solution partners (for solution consulting). The latter often allowed solution partners to upsell their own consulting services or software add-ons and could add quite substantially to their revenue on an Activplant installation.

The Sales and Services staffing and strategy decisions are exclusive of each other.

Criteria

The principal objectives of a European entrance were to ensure revenue growth (approximately $1.5 million in year one), and achieve profitability by the end of year two. To evaluate the alternatives for sales and services operations, Activplant began to review the options based on the following considerations:

- Quality of Execution
- Risk of Brand Damage
- Feasibility
- Governance and Control

What Now?

Should Activplant develop a partnership strategy and spend resources supporting partners in the selling process in Europe, or should it perform the selling process directly and build a European sales team? A partnership development strategy would require investment in new training and additional incentives for solution partners, but a new European operation could bring with it higher costs and greater risk.

Option	Title	Cost (CDN$)
AP Europe manages project delivery and consulting	Project Manager	$150,000 × 130% = $195,000
AP Europe project manages all service components and performs project delivery	Project Manager, Project Delivery Personnel	$150,000 × 130% + $90,000 × 130% = $312,000
AP Canada manages services remotely	None	Travel, contracting partners to do delivery
Partners manage services	None	$0

As Frosst and Cocco sat discussing the various main issues involved, they knew that each issue could essentially be broken down into three options: going it alone, utilizing partners or temporarily not going. Each option had its benefits and drawbacks. Now all they had to do was decide, keeping in mind that this decision could have major effects on the future of the company.

Exhibit 1   Sales Cycle

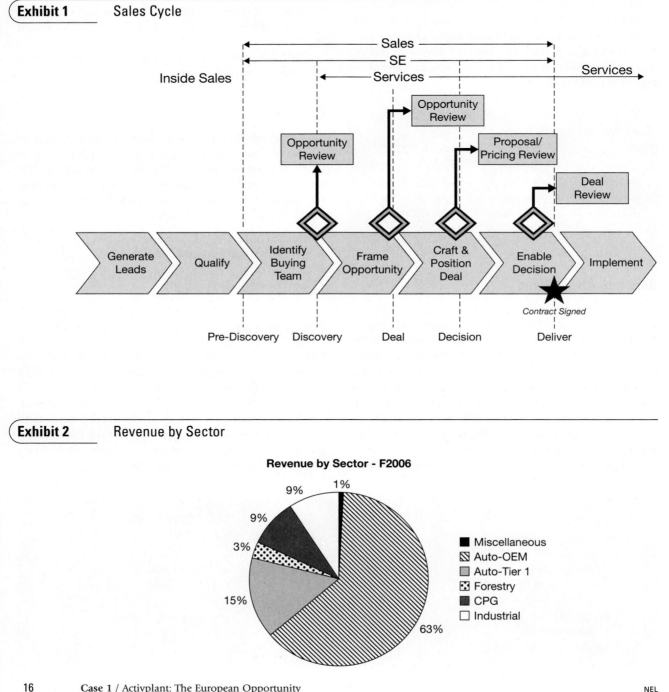

Exhibit 2   Revenue by Sector

Exhibit 3 Competitive Landscape

Software Provider	Operational Scope	Geographic Focus	Manufacturing Focus
Activplant	Data Acquisition/ Performance Analysis	NA/Minimal EU	Discrete
Wonderware	Data Acquisition/ Automation Software	EU/Some NA	Process/Hybrid
Rockwell	Data Acquisition/ Process Mgmt/ Automation software	NA/EU	All
SAP/Lighthammer	Portal/Dashboard/ Middleware/ERP	EU/NA	Discrete
OSIsoft	Data Acquisition/ Performance Analysis	NA/Some EU	Process/Some Hybrid
Citect	MES	AMEA	Process/Some Hybrid and Discrete
Iconics	Dashboard/ Performance Analysis	EU	Discrete
UGS	Product Tracking/ ERP/CRM	Europe	Hybrid/Discrete
Matrikon	Data Acquisition/ Performance Analysis	NA/Some EU	Process/Some Hybrid

Source: Company documents.

Exhibit 4 Financial Assumptions

Average Number of Deals per Account Manager per quarter = 2

This figure is to be discounted for Year 1 because of the effort required to build the infrastructure, time required for training, as well as setting up the operation.

Salary difference between Canadian market and the European Market = + 30%

Office Related Expense = US$500 per month per person

HQ.com rate

Cost for the following positions in Canada:

Director/Senior Account Manager:	Cdn$150,000 + commission (5%) of up to $100,000
Account Manager:	Cdn$125,000 + commission (5%) of up to $100,000
Sales Engineer:	Cdn$150,000
Project Manager:	Cdn$150,000
Service Personnel:	$80,000 — $100,000 (Cdn$90,000)
Partnership Manager:	Cdn$125,000 + bonus

(continued)

| Exhibit 4 | Financial Assumptions (continued) |

Salary difference between Canadian market and the European Market = + 30%

Service Margin: 20%
Potential Service Revenue / License Revenue = 100%

Sales Cycle: Six months to eight months

Average Deal Size — License: US$100,000
Average Deal Size — Support: US$15,000

Exchange Rate Cdn$/US$ = 1.15

2-year range = 1.40 to 1.15

- The value of the U.S. dollar is still under downward pressure, due to the economic conditions of the United States. For example, the United States has been running a current account deficit for many years, which suppresses the value of the U.S. dollar. There is a common belief that the U.S. dollar is due for a downward correction. Thus we expect the U.S. dollar to remain in its low level at Cdn$1.15 per US$1.00.

Exchange Rate Euro/US$ = 0.82

2-year range = 0.74 to 0.86

- We expect the euro to fluctuate between its 2-year range. The current exchange rate is 0.82 euro per US$1.00, which will be used in our projection.

AGF Management Limited

Joe Martin
University of Toronto

Introduction

As Blake looked out the window of the giant 747 he could see clearly the Sea of Okhotsk and the eastern coast of the Russian Federation. Soon the plane would cross the International Date Line and he would have a whole extra day in the week to work. But is that what he wanted?

As he thought back on his visit to Japan he did so with satisfaction. He had just completed a deal with Maruhachi Securities, a Japanese brokerage company, whereby AGF acquired a 5% position in the company. Only last year AGF had become the first Canadian mutual fund company to open a representative office in Japan and in the summer just past they had launched five offshore funds available only to Japanese investors.

As the rest of the Western world was retreating from Japan AGF was advancing. And not just in Japan but also in China and Singapore. All of this was in line with his goal of creating a global company with a Canadian home.

Given the long flight ahead of him he couldn't help thinking further back to the tumultuous mid 90s when AGF had acquired 20/20, another mutual fund company. That acquisition had almost caused him to resign his position as Vice President of Marketing and go elsewhere. But he saw the opportunity, the challenge and stayed with it. In 1997 he had become President and

Chief Operating Officer of AGF and in 2000 he had been appointed CEO as well as President.

The late 90s, right up to and including 2000 had been great years. AGF, which in 1995 had revenue of less than $90 million and mutual fund assets under management (AUM) of less than $4.5 billion, ended 2001 with revenues nearly six times greater—over half a billion dollars—and AUM more than six times larger—close to $30 billion.

Beyond those raw numbers AGF had entered the new millennium as a much more significant player, not just in Canada, but also increasingly on the global scene. Who would have believed it in the mid 1990s? No, in spite of the short-term pain of the 20/20 deal it had provided the springboard for the success of the past five years.

But 2001 was a different year, a much different year. Nothing like this had been seen for a decade. All year the markets had been hurting and there had been significant redemptions of mutual funds in the industry. The competitive scene was fierce with major mutual fund companies merging as well as competition from the big banks and from large US players. New products were appearing which had lower margins and then September 11 had occurred hurting markets further. While there were signs of recovery, the economy was now officially in recession. On top of all that there were increasing signs of public concern in regard to management expense ratios (MER).

As the flight moved towards the International Date Line, Blake's thoughts moved back and forth between the tumult caused by the acquisition of 20/20 and his near decision to quit, to the extraordinary success of the late 1990s and to the storm clouds of the early 2000s.

The Acquisition of 20/20—a Watershed Event

After the Second World War a new financial product entered the consumer field in Canada—the mutual fund. Already available in the United States mutual funds became a popular personal savings alternative to whole life insurance in Canada.

AGF was a pioneer in this new field. Established in 1957, its original purpose—to provide opportunity to the average Canadian to invest in the American economy—had been unique at the time. The original fund offering had been called American Growth Fund, hence the name AGF.

By 2002, the Company had grown to the point where they offered more than 70 funds covering a wide variety of investment opportunities and was regarded as one of the major players in the Canadian industry (see Exhibit 1). While most of the large funds ($1 billion+) were North American—the original American Growth and the Canadian trio of Dividend, Tactical Asset Allocation and Stock—their largest single fund was the giant International Value fund with assets of nearly $7 billion.

And there were other International/Global funds with assets in excess of $1billion as well: Continental Funds—Europe, Asia and Latin America, plus Country Funds—Japan (established as early as 1969), China, India and Germany. Indeed, if you looked at their AUM they were evenly split between Canada and Global with 42% each and the balance in the United States.

That was not the case back in the mid 90s when the decision was made to do the merger with 20/20, a company two-thirds the size of AGF at that time. The first half of the 90s had been good for AGF and its shareholders. Top line had more than doubled to $87.6 million. Bottom line had done even better, increasing by more than 3.5 times to nearly $17 million. Earnings per share were right in line with that growth. And AUM had climbed to $4.5 billion in 1995 from $1.7 billion in 1991.

These were remarkable achievements but Warren Goldring, the founder and controlling shareholder, knew they were not enough to survive into the next century. Warren had been leading AGF since its beginning and he knew that AGF had to be bigger. The industry was over populated and was consolidating. The bigger players (like the Investors Group, based in Winnipeg but owned by Montreal based Power Corp) were much larger than AGF. American firms like Fidelity were entering the market, as were Canadian banks and life insurance companies.

Warren also knew that in order to become more sophisticated in terms of technology, crucial to keeping up to date, it would be necessary to obtain a bigger base.

20/20 was a smaller mutual fund than AGF but not that much smaller, about two-thirds the size ($4.2 billion

---

Exhibit 1	The Canadian Mutual Fund Industry

Twenty-five companies control 94.5% of the nearly $400 billion in Net Assets as of October 2001. Within those 25 companies there are a variety of groupings.

The largest company, with nearly $40 billion of AUM, is Investors Group, a Winnipeg-based, Power Corp controlled company. Investors is the only Mutual Fund Company that sells funds through agents directly tied to the Company. Their sales model is based on the old industrial model of life insurance agents that worked exclusively for one company, e.g., London Life, who would sell their products door to door.

Recently Investors purchased Mackenzie, a large independent Toronto based Mutual Fund Company, with AUM of over $30 billion that sells through the more conventional channels of investment dealers and financial planners. While they are continuing to operate separately the two companies together control 17.5% of the AUM in Canada.

Other than Mackenzie there are 14 independent mutual fund companies in Canada. Three of the largest of these are American—Fidelity, Franklin Templeton and AIM. The largest of the Canadian independents are AGF, CI and AIC.

The big five Canadian banks are all in the business as are National Bank and Hong Kong Shanghai. The Royal is the largest, followed by TD. Much of the bank business is in money market funds as distinct from equities. A number of life insurance companies have tried selling mutual funds but the only one which has had any success is Waterloo based Clarica.

In addition there are what is known as direct "no load" funds that sell directly to consumers. The largest is Vancouver-based Phillips, Hager & North. Altamira is also in this business.

Table 1 lists the ten largest mutual funds in Canada in terms of net assets and regardless of ownership or method of distribution.

Company	Net Assets	Market Share (%) Assets
Investors Group	39,257	9.9
Royal Mutual Funds	34,288	8.6
AIM Funds Management	31,484	7.9
Mackenzie Financial	31,106	7.8
TD Asset Management	30,273	7.6
Fidelity Investments	30,152	7.6
AGF Funds	26,351	6.6
CIBC Securities	24,720	6.2
CI Mutual Funds	20,031	5.0
Franklin Templeton	18,361	4.6

vs. $2.8 billion). Based in Oakville, it was led by a former Olympic medallist who had surrounded himself with a tightly knit team. However 20/20, a public company, was 35% owned by Connor, Clark & Lunn, a pension management firm, 15% owned by the management team and the remainder was in the hands of the investors.

The pension fund, based in Vancouver, wanted out of 20/20 because the business was taking too much of its time and capital. The 20/20 management team led by Wood wanted greater control of management. And AGF wanted to grow. Here was a real confluence of interests and so in December 1995, the $100 million+ deal was done and John Wood, who had been President of 20/20 became the new President of AGF, now a mutual fund with $7 billion of assets under administration.

The 20/20 purchase brought some real strength to AGF. The good news was a greater scale of assets under management, a broader product mix, additional distribution channels including financial planners to complement AGF's strong investment dealer base, and access to quality investment advisors such as San Diego-based Brandes Investment Partners and Chicago-based Driehaus.

The deal permitted AGF to deploy their surplus cash (they had over $60 million in 1995) and to step up their cash flow. As the CFO has noted "cash is real." The economics of the transaction were outstanding, notwithstanding the operational integration issues. The acquisition price was 4 to 5 times cash flow from operations versus the 9 times figures that Investors paid for Mackenzie and AIM paid for Trimark in 2000. And AGF doubled in size (see Exhibit 2).

Yet, like most mergers this one did not go easily. The fundamental issue was a difference in business philos-

ophy. 20/20 was a marketing organization that used outside investment managers for their funds. AGF believed in having a blend of in house and external managers. This was not simply a philosophical issue in Warren's mind, it was an economic issue as well.

The differences were resolved when suddenly a change occurred in April, 1996, the three senior 20/20 people departed. Blake Goldring, who had wondered about his future only months earlier was promoted, along with Clive Coombs, a long time AGF employee, to Senior Vice Presidents: Blake for marketing and sales, Clive for fund management.

Five Years of Success: 1996–2001

As he looked back on the five years after the 20/20 acquisition in 1996, Blake reviewed results that had been so good they were staggering (see Exhibit 3). Top line had grown nearly three fold, from under $200 million to in excess of half a billion dollars. So had mutual fund assets under administration (AUM) growing three fold from $10 billion to close to $30 billion. Bottom line had done even better, due to synergies and expense management and was up nearly four fold, from over $20 million to nearly $90 million. Shareholders had done well too. Earnings per share were up from $0.37 to $1.12 and share price had jumped to $24.00 at calendar year end 2001 from the $5.00 range at the end of 1996.

Those were the numbers. But really, there were four or five reasons that the Company had achieved such results. In any mutual fund company you had to be strong in terms of marketing and sales (creating the demand); in terms of fund management (having a group of funds

Exhibit 2 — AGF Financials

YEARS ENDED NOV. 30	1995	2000	2001
REVENUE			
Mutual fund operations	$79,366,369	$496,107,000	$624,663,000
Trust Company	8,261,990	12,574,000	15,331,000
TOTAL	87,628,359	$508,681,000	$639,994,000
EXPENSES			
Mutual fund operations	$133,227,181	$352,802,000	$477,699,000
Trust Company	8,521,649	10,443,000	13,889,000
TOTAL	141,748,830	363,245,000	191,588,000
INCOME BEFORE TAX	141,748,830	145,436,000	148,406,000
INCOME TAXES	14,840,811	49,541,000	14,867,000
NET INCOME FOR YEAR	$22,403,086	$95,931,000	$163,764,000

Exhibit 3 — Five Year Highlights

Item	1997	1998	1999	2000	2001
Total Rev. or Top Line (000s)	$236,759	$288,822	$356,703	$508,681	$624,663
Net Income or Bottom Line (000s)	$40,489	$48,777	$61,710	$95,931	$163,764
Share Price Per Share $	$9.15	$11.60	$11.65	$24.50	$24.00
AUM ($000,000)	12,429	15,015	18,705	26,979	27,482

with superior returns—a 'supply'—that could be sold); and a strong administrative and client service functions.

At AGF they had all of that in spades. In terms of marketing and sales they had high brand awareness through their innovative "What are you doing after work?" program, which had been honoured by the industry with the "Best Print Advertising" and "Best Overall Campaign" awards.

In addition, a key focus over the past five years had been on a revamped emphasis on sales. They had wide sales and distribution channels, some of it dating back to the merger with 20/20, some of it more recently acquired with the acquisition of another player, Global Strategy, earlier that year.[1] Now they were well placed with multiple distribution channels—brokers and planners, as well as selected and specialized products through banks, discount brokerages and insurance companies. They even had links with Investors Group that used its tied agency channel to sell products 'manufactured' by AGF, amongst others.

In terms of fund management, 77% of their mutual fund assets were in the 1st or 2nd quartile of performance on a three-year time horizon. If you looked out further they did even better with 85% in the top two quartiles over a five-year horizon and 92% over a ten-year time horizon. Yes, it could be safely said that they had excellent fund management.

In terms of administrative excellence he was equally confident. After all one of the things AGF brought to the Global Strategy acquisition was an ability to gain cost synergies and to improve Global's redemption position. He was committed to back office and administrative support for financial advisors and investors. And the proof lay in the high ranking they received in all the independent surveys of industry call centers, client service and response time.

---

[1] Global Strategy had Assets Under Management of $5.6 billion. In addition they brought an exclusive advisory relationship with Rothschild Asset Management.

Overarching all of this were their international initiatives. Rather than resting passively in Canada, Warren had decided more than a decade ago to go international and established a European presence in Dublin. In the mid 90s the firm had decided to replicate their European model by establishing an Asian presence in Singapore. Then they had invested in London by buying a significant ownership stake in NCL, a UK based private client asset management and institutional fund management company. Finally in 2000 they had opened an office in Tokyo as well as a representative office in Beijing for the marketing, promotion and potential distribution of its mutual funds.

Clouds on the Horizon—2002

By the beginning of 2002, this rosy picture had clouded over. There was aggressive merger activity within the industry—most notably the acquisition of Mackenzie by Investors creating a Canadian giant with a combined AUM of close to $70 billion, more than twice that of AGF. There was also the acquisition of Trimark by the British firm, Amvescap.

American players, AIM and Fidelity and Franklin Templeton, now accounted for over a fifth of all Assets Under Management in Canada and represented formidable competition given the economies of scale, which went with their huge size in the giant US market. They also had the ability to pounce on other Canadian players, given the weakness of the Canadian dollar.

Bear market conditions of 2001, exacerbated by September 11, plus the arrival of a plethora of new products all spelled challenge.

The impact of all this on the Canadian mutual fund industry was:

- year to date declines in fund flows other than money market sales;
- a 70+% industry decline in year to date equity sales;
- sub zero market returns, which added to the chill and put a freeze on margin expansion;
- unpredictability of earnings.

Yes, there were bright spots. In spite of competitive pressures from the giant gorilla, Fidelity, and the big five Canadian banks (not to mention a few smaller independents such as AIC Limited and CI Mutual Funds) AGF was doing well. In the first three quarters of the year their net sales were over $2 billion. This not only led the industry but was 22% of total net industry sales. Truly, a remarkable performance in a down market!! A key reason for this performance was that low redemptions of AGF funds helped offset their decrease in gross sales resulting in higher net sales (gross sales − redemptions = net sales).

More worrisome for the medium to longer term was fund performance. While five year returns were outstanding and three year returns were very good, one year returns for all funds was −13%, which may have been average, but not what the distribution channel wanted for their customers.

Surely these were short-term issues caused by the economic slow down and exacerbated by the tragedy of September 11. What were the longer-term issues?

In terms of marketing there was the absolute necessity of continuing to build brand equity in order to continue to have AGF products distributed by third party channels. In terms of sales, distribution would be center stage. The huge proliferation of retail funds—as the Chairman pointed out there were now more funds than there were stocks—would cause the focus to continue to shift from manufacturing to distribution. While firms that generated consistently superior performance could rest assured that customers would seek out their products, most fund companies, including his own, depended increasingly on third party distributors to sell their funds to end customers.

On the fund management side the issue was clearer and that was to sustain superior performance. Strong performance was absolutely essential to long-term success.

On the administrative side there were two issues; meeting rising customer expectations, and controlling risk. Customers today expected regular, personalized information not simply semi annual customer statements which arrived weeks after the half-year period. In addition internal operational risks had to be managed with an enterprise-wide risk management process.

Straddling both sales and marketing and administration was the whole issue of the Internet. The net provided the opportunity to improve customer service and to drive sales. But Blake was not clear in his own mind, just how to do it.

Finally there was the broader longer-term issue of globalization. Did AGF have the right strategy of building an international presence based in Canada? Or was this the time to sell out to one of the giant international players?

What Now?

Finally, Blake dozed off to sleep, only to be wakened as the plane began its descent into the Vancouver airport.

He thought back to the traumatic events of 1996, to the thrill of succeeding his father first as President and then as CEO and to the wonderful legacy his father had left. There were so many high points in the past five years it was impossible to count them.

And then his mood changed as he thought about the challenges of 2002 and beyond.

Maybe it was time to bring in that bright young management consultant Blake had interviewed several times and knew well. This MBA student seemed smart enough and had worked for AGF five years ago, departed on good terms, and had a sound reputation for good analytical work and a strong work ethic.

But what problem would he ask her to solve? Perhaps he should leave it wide open and let her give him an independent outsider's point of view.

The assignment would be simple. Reporting directly to him as CEO, she would be given all the facts as outlined and asked to assess the situation, then do a diagnosis and give him an objective evaluation of the situation. He would expect a set of recommendations on how to move forward, including next steps.

AMD in 2005: Coming Out of Intel's Shadow?

Ravi M

Intel underestimated us and their arrogance didn't allow them to take hold of what they were doing.

—*Benjamin J. Williams, AMD*[1]

In 2004, Hector Ruiz (Ruiz), CEO of Advanced Micro Devices (AMD), was reflecting on how his company was faring in its battle with Intel in the 64-bit microprocessor market. Itanium I, Intel's first 64-bit microprocessor had failed. Itanium II had also elicited a lukewarm response from the market. But Opteron, AMD's 64-bit microprocessor, released in mid-2003 was still receiving strong performance reviews. By 2004, many companies such as Microsoft, IBM and HP, which had been staunch supporters of Intel, had started using Opteron. Even Sun Microsystems (Sun), a company that traditionally used its own SPARC chips, had started using Opteron. These companies saw AMD as a means to increase their market share by offering high-quality but low-priced products. As a result, by 2004, AMD had become a major supplier of microprocessors in the server market.

Historically, AMD had ranked a distant second in PC microprocessors with a market share of about 15%, compared to Intel, which had about 80%. In the past,

AMD had made inroads into Intel's market share only to see Intel strike back with steep price cuts and faster introduction of new models. As 2004 got underway, analysts wondered whether AMD was finally ready to come out of Intel's shadow.

Opteron

Designed to run existing 32-bit applications and offer customers a smooth transition to 64-bit computing, Opteron promised a dramatic improvement in performance. It also reduced the total cost of ownership (TCO).[2] Opteron came in three versions: the 100 series (1-way), the 200 series (1- to 2-way), and the 800 series (up to 8-way).

AMD had positioned Opteron as a microprocessor with a scalable architecture designed to meet current and future business needs. Opteron was designed to scale from one to eight processors. This aided system designers by reducing the cost and complexity of building servers and workstations. It also reduced cost and increased server scalability.

One of the most important features of Opteron was HyperTransport Technology, which aimed at removing

---

[1] Director of AMD's server and workstation business unit, AMD Says Intel Pride Came Before 64-32 Fall, 17th February 2004, *www.theinquirer.net*.

[2] Total cost of ownership (TCO) is a model developed by Gartner Group to analyze the direct and indirect costs of owning and using hardware and software. Managers of enterprise systems use various versions of TCO to lower costs while increasing the benefits of information technology deployments.

I/O bottlenecks,[3] increased bandwidth/speed, and reduced latency.[4] For workstation users, this meant increased graphics throughput (up to 8x AGP), quicker loading of applications and large data sets, better multi-tasking, and smoother transition across applications.

HyperTransport technology was useful for any application where high speed, low latency and scalability were necessary. This technology reduced the number of buses while providing a high-performance link for PCs, workstation and servers, as well as numerous embedded applications and highly scalable multiprocessing systems.

AMD had designed the new microprocessor to allow customers to migrate to 64-bit computing without any significant sacrifice of the existing code base. The technology aimed at providing full speed support for x86 code base, offering high performance levels for existing 32-bit applications. It provided a large memory, which was useful for computationally intensive applications, such as databases, ERP, decision support, scientific and technical modeling, etc. It also helped lower TCO and network management complexity through a unified architecture for desktop, notebook, workstation and server, and platform flexibility.

Opteron's target segments included companies that required faster database transactions, customers needing quick graphics response such as in the CAD[5] industry, which had computationally intensive tasks for modeling and scientific applications.

Though Opteron was designed for high-end servers it could also run like 32-bit (Pentium and Athlon) processors in most PCs. A PC version of Opteron was also expected to be available unlike Intel's Itanium 2. Opteron prices ranged from $283 to $794, compared to Itanium 2's $1,338 to $4,226. Opteron's design made it fully backward compatible with existing 32-bit applications. That differentiated it from Itanium 2, which used a different architecture.

By offering both 64-bit and 32-bit operation with the same chip, AMD believed that Opteron systems would be the perfect upgrades for aging servers that used Intel's Pentium and Xeon processors. AMD also had plans to introduce a 64-bit processor for home computers in 2003. The Athlon 64, due for release in September 2003, would be the first such chip aimed at the consumer market. In early 2003, there were no 64-bit applications for consumers, but AMD believed that once Athlon 64 machines were available, multimedia and game software companies would write programs to take advantage of their power.

David vs. Goliath

For more than 30 years, AMD had been challenging Intel in the semiconductor industry. Intel had been able to control x86 microprocessor and PC system standards and dictate the type of products the market required of competitors. Intel's financial muscle allowed it to market its products aggressively, offer special incentives and to wean away customers who did business with AMD. Intel had longstanding partnerships with both software developers and hardware manufacturers. Intel exerted substantial influence over PC manufacturers and their distribution channels through the *"Intel Inside"* brand and other marketing programs.[6]

Intel spent substantially greater amounts on R&D than AMD did. For instance, Intel was expected to generate revenues of $34 billion in 2004 with projected profits of $7.35 billion. This meant Intel earned in 11 days what AMD made in a year. In January 2005, Intel had a $14 billion cash reserve compared to AMD's reserves of about $1.1 billion.

The microprocessor market was characterized by short product life cycles and migration to ever-higher performance microprocessors. To compete successfully against Intel, AMD realized the need to make the transition to new process technologies at a rapid pace and offer higher-performance microprocessors in significantly greater volumes.

Things had started looking up for AMD since the late 1990s. The Internet boom had increased the appetite of consumers and businesses' for microprocessors. But this time, Intel had finalized plans to make a paradigm shift in its architecture by tying-up with HP to make the Itanium series of microprocessors.

Till then, Intel had relied on what was termed the x-86 architecture. These chips processed data in chunks of 32-bits of information. Itanium would process the data in chunks of 64-bits at a time. Intel believed that

---

[3] According to citeseer.ist.psu.edu, any socket in the back of a computer that you use to connect to another piece of hardware is called an I/O (input/output) port. CPU speeds are improving at a dramatic rate, while disk speeds are not. This technology shift suggests that many engineering and office applications may become so I/O-limited that they cannot benefit from further CPU improvements. This is called an I/O bottleneck.

[4] Webopedia defines latency as the amount of time it takes a packet to travel from source to destination. Together, latency and bandwidth define the speed and capacity of a network.

[5] www.learnthat.com defines CAD (Computer Aided Design) as a general term referring to applications and the method to design things using one's computer. CAD is used to design buildings and items. A popular CAD program is AutoCAD.

[6] AMD Annual Report, 2002.

this new architecture would be a groundbreaking innovation and pave the way for Intel's domination. But Intel's folly, according to many analysts, was to create Itanium in such a way that software that ran using the new chip had to be re-written. While Itanium promised much faster processing prowess than existing chips, the difficulties associated with software-migration put-off many potential customers.

AMD, which won a lengthy legal dispute with Intel in the 1990s to make microprocessors in the x-86 mode, realized that if Intel moved into a new architecture, it would effectively create a new industry and eventually dominate it. AMD moved quickly to create its own 64-bit microprocessor in 1998. AMD realized that the need of the hour was to build a better microprocessor than Intel had (Itanium) and one that did not require software upgradation. Founder Sanders made it clear to his senior managers that AMD's very future depended on Opteron.

New Optimism

AMD believed that Opteron's USP was not requiring any software upgrades when moving from 32-bit to 64-bit architectures. This feature would make Opteron much more user-friendly than its rival Itanium, which required users to re-write existing 32-bit software code during migration.

By 2004, Opteron was receiving favorable reviews from manufacturers. The company grabbed 7% of the low-end server market, up from almost nothing a few years back. It accounted for 50% of the US retail store sales for desktop PCs in August 2004. Even as Intel announced lower than expected sales for 2004 due to decreasing demand, AMD did not see any indication of a slowdown. Many companies seemed to have realized the benefit of not having to re-write their code. Microsoft had committed itself to making a version of its Windows Server and Windows XP desktop software for the new AMD chips, though the software giant had not indicated a release date. Microsoft believed that many of its customers were interested in the AMD implementation. When Microsoft ran applications written for 32-bit chips on an Opteron server loaded with the new Windows 64-bit operating system, the programs performed considerably better than on 32-bit Windows. Microsoft was not willing to place all its bets just on Itanium 2. Besides,

AMD had been much faster in launching the consumer version of Opteron chips than Intel.

The leading Linux software maker, Red Hat offered Linux for Opteron. IBM offered a compatible version of its heavy-duty DB2 database software. Some IBM customers were already using the technology, in beta [test] form, and they were planning the chip for deployment by early 2003.

A handful of specialized server makers, like Angstrom Microsystems had signed on to use Opteron. AMD had also sold Opteron-based evaluation units to customers such as the Hollywood special effects house Pixar Animation Studios (producers of *Toy Story*, *Finding Nemo*, among others) that could use Opteron-based systems to produce its computer-generated movies faster and cheaper. Meanwhile, Sun, which was trying to open up its Solaris products to other architectures, was looking at incorporating Opterons in some of its blade servers.[7] Despite the possibility of affecting sales of its UltraSPARC processors, Sun started endorsing Opteron by 2004.

HP, which had developed the core of the Itanium architecture along with Intel, seemed to be placing all its bets on Itanium 2. But for certain data intensive operations, HP's tests showed that Opteron performed better than Itanium 2. Although HP insisted that it would remain committed to Itanium 2, it was looking seriously at Opteron. In November 2004, HP announced a range of servers featuring Opteron.

Even Dell, the strongest player in the PC market and traditionally a staunch Intel user, had plans to tap this market. Randy Groves, Dell's chief technology officer explained,[8]

> *"What makes this different from past AMD discussions is that until now AMD's value proposition has been Intel compatibility at a lower cost. Now it's not a pricing discussion. This is something Intel doesn't have."*

But Dell had a high degree of loyalty to Intel, largely due to the support it received from Intel. Intel paid Dell for marketing its products, when Dell carried the logo of Intel. Analysts felt that Dell would wait and see if AMD could make Opteron consistently in large volumes.

In 2003, IBM announced it would be sharing technology and manufacturing know-how with AMD, fueling speculation that Opteron and Athlon 64 would be manufactured in IBM's plants. IBM was also critical of

---

[7] A single circuit board populated with components such as processors, memory, and network connections that are usually found on multiple boards. Server blades are designed to slide into existing servers. Server blades are more cost-efficient, smaller and consume less power than traditional box-based servers (Source: http://e-comm.webopedia.com/TERM/S/server_blade.html).

[8] Kirkpatrick, David; Tkaczyk, Christopher. "See This Chip?" *Fortune*, 3rd February 2003, Vol. 147, Issue 3, pp. 52–59.

Intel's scalability[9] claims and seemed to be taking a liking to the combination of Opteron and Linux.

Microsoft ultimately expected to support the Opteron in a manner similar to how it had first supported Itanium, with an interim release product specific to that CPU. AMD expected Opteron would have 32-bit support in Windows Server 2003, with 64-bit support following sometime later. SuSE, a company that made Linux-based products in Nuremberg, Germany and Red Hat, another Linux company, reported that they would provide Linux software written for Opteron.

The bulk of AMD's microprocessor product sales came from the company's seventh-generation x86 Microsoft Windows compatible AMD Athlon and AMD Duron microprocessors. The company designed its AMD Athlon and AMD Duron microprocessors around RISC (reduced instruction set computer architecture). RISC allowed microprocessors to perform fewer types of computer instructions and operate at a higher speed. AMD's Athlon and Duron microprocessors were compatible with operating system software such as Windows XP, Windows 2000, Windows 98 and Windows predecessor operating systems, along with Linux and UNIX.

A New Leader

"We are here to stay. We're not going away."

—*Ruiz.*[10]

Jerry Sanders (Sanders) had been the architect behind AMD's success for over 30 years. He had single-handedly built AMD from scratch and given Intel a run for its money over the years. By the late 90s, Sanders realized the time had come for succession planning. Having crossed 60, he had also come under pressure from the board of AMD to pick an able person to see AMD's plans through in the 64-bit game. Shortly before he announced his retirement, Sanders had handpicked Hector Ruiz (Ruiz) to head AMD.

Sanders had started courting Ruiz when he was running Motorola's semiconductor division. Sanders quickly realized Ruiz was the best person to run AMD,[11]

"I'm an impact guy; Hector's a process guy. I got to know Hector and realized that he was a corporate kind of guy—he knew the details of inventory and supply-chain management, things that were not my thing."

When Ruiz was at Motorola, he and Sanders had spent two years working together on flash memory development and copper technology through their respective companies.

Sanders had tried to buy the semiconductor business of Motorola and merge it with AMD but the plans failed because of resistance from Motorola CEO Chris Galvin. Sanders then invited Ruiz to become the COO of AMD and promised to turn over the mantle by 2002. Despite Motorola's efforts to hold him back, Ruiz accepted the invitation.

Things were not going well for AMD when Ruiz arrived. The dot-com bubble had just burst and AMD was moving into the red. There were many problems with AMD's microprocessors that needed to be addressed immediately. Ruiz laid off about 5000 workers, closed two factories and pursued cost cutting and outsourcing. But he did not cut R&D expenses. In 2002, AMD, despite losing $1.3 billion on revenues of $2.7 billion, spent 30% of its revenues on R&D.

Ruiz also kept hiring key personnel to work on Opteron. He acquired two smaller companies with a lot of technical talent. Ruiz became the CEO in 2002 while Sanders remained chairman. Later that year, Sanders relinquished the post of chairman to Ruiz.

Ruiz, who was simpler, hands-on and democratic was a stark contrast to Sanders, who was known for his flamboyance.

"Under Jerry, frankly, the company was very autocratic and power-centric." CFO Bob River, who worked with both men commented, *"Jerry's style was homerun or strikeout, with nothing in between. Either you had a great year or it was a flaming disaster. Hector's more process-driven. Now we worry more about getting men on base".*

—*Ruiz.*[12]

Sanders was widely perceived to be an outsized personality, who managed strategy single-handedly, and made all the critical decisions by himself. As a result, Wall Street viewed AMD as a company that was prone to high risks. In contrast, Ruiz, who had come up from humble beginnings, was shy and retiring. He was known to listen to people before taking a decision.

"There will certainly be a marked contrast [leadership change] just because Sanders is known as a boisterous personality and has always been very enthusiastic in his

---

[9] Scalability: Measure of how easily a system can be configured (by adding or subtracting processors and memory etc.) to make it more or less powerful to supply the required processing power.

[10] "Suddenly its AMD inside," *BusinessWeek,* 20th September 2004.

[11] Kirkpatrick, David; D. K. "Chipping Away At Intel," *Fortune,* 1st November 2004, Vol. 150, Issue 8, pp. 44–50.

[12] Kirkpatrick, David; D. K. "Chipping Away At Intel," *Fortune,* 1st November 2004, Vol. 150, Issue 8, pp. 44–50.

management style. Hector, as an engineer, is generally more soft-spoken and generally more thoughtful."

—a former Motorola employee[13] who had worked under Ruiz.

Ruiz stressed the need to please customers. He spent a lot of his time in building new alliances like a joint venture with Sun whereby AMD would power Sun's low-cost servers with Opteron. This seemed a remarkable achievement as the vertically integrated Sun had traditionally used its own SPARC chips.

Looking Forward

In 2004, AMD released a series of microprocessors for corporate users. It introduced new manufacturing techniques and pushed aggressively a new technology, which put several microprocessors on a single chip.

AMD also planned to be among the first to introduce dual-core processors for servers and desktops. These chips would have two processors engraved into one chip, for better performance. Although Intel was planning to launch its dual-core processor line by the end of 2005, AMD's engineers were optimistic about getting to the market much before their larger rival did.

Ruiz had created new business divisions within AMD that would focus on incorporating chips in cell phones and consumer electronics. A marketing push with ads in the *Wall Street Journal* and other eminent newspapers had also been kicked off.

In early 2005, AMD announced that its new chip, Turion 64, would be available in notebooks by June 2005, to compete with Intel's Centrino and Transmeta's Astro. AMD believed that Turion would usher in a new era in mobile computing. Turion 64 mobile targeted highly mobile business professionals and consumers who demanded reliable, high-performance notebook PCs with long battery life, outstanding wireless compatibility, rich graphics and enhanced security. One AMD official commented,[14]

"AMD Turion 64 mobile technology represents freedom and mobile performance personified. We expect this new product family will set a precedent for mobile PCs in the same way that AMD Opteron did for servers."

In 2004, AMD gained about one percentage point of the microprocessor market, bringing its share to 15.8%.[15] AMD was expected to book a record $5.1 billion in full-year sales as well. The stock, at $21.73 by December 2004, had doubled in value since September 2004. AMD had laid out ambitious plans for its future, 10% of the low-end server market by the end of 2004, 30% of the corporate PC market and 50% of the consumer PC market by 2009. Not withstanding these ambitious plans, AMD realized Intel could not be underestimated. In 1999, AMD had been at the cutting edge, having unveiled Athlon, which was faster than Intel's comparable processor at the time. Then, Intel had caught up and eventually leapfrogged AMD in processor performance. AMD started losing money.

Intel was not the only threat to AMD. South Korea's Samsung Electronics had been spending heavily on chip-factory equipment and manufacturing capabilities. Texas Instruments, which competed against Intel in cellular phone chips, was at work on a $3 billion advanced factory of its own.

For AMD, 2004 had been a good year. The company had gained market share from Intel and seen its stock price and cash reserves go up. But 2005 had begun on a bad note. On January 10, the company announced that earnings from the fourth quarter of 2004 would be much below Wall Street's expectations. As soon as this announcement came, AMD's stock price tumbled 25% to about $14 from about $25 at the end of 2004 (See Exhibit 3).

AMD had to lower its earning estimate because Intel reduced its flash memory[16] chip prices. Intel earned only about 7% of its total revenues from this segment, whereas AMD earned about 50% of its revenues from flash memory chips. Shortly after AMD announced weak earnings, Intel indicated strong fourth quarter 2004 earnings. This further hurt AMD's stock.

Ruiz believed that his company's flash memory performance was *"freaking dismal."*[17] He also indicated he was strengthening AMD's flash memory business. AMD lost $30 million on sales of $1.26 billion in the last quarter of 2004. This happened despite processor sales rising 26 per cent over the corresponding period in 2003.

"It was an underwhelming end to an otherwise great year."

—Ruiz.[18]

---

[13] "Ruiz's Influence on AMD," *Austin Business Journal*, 19th April 2002.
[14] "Turion is Notebook Opteron," *www.techtree.com*, 10th January 2005.
[15] According to chip consultancy Mercury Research.
[16] Flash memory chips store data in cell phones and other electronic appliances. Apart from Intel and AMD, Samsung is a large player in flash memory chips.
[17] "AMD Profits Disappear in a Flash," *www.theregister.co.uk*, 19th January 2005.
[18] "AMD Might Sell Off Flash Business," *www.theinquirer.net*, 19th January 2005.

Exhibit 1   AMD's Stock (January 2000–January 2005)

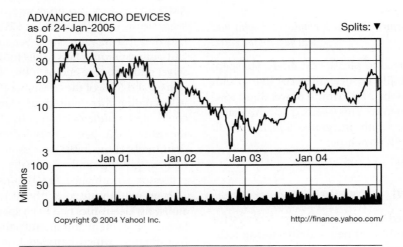

ADVANCED MICRO DEVICES
as of 24-Jan-2005

Splits: ▼

Source: http://finance.yahoo.com/

Exhibit 2 AMD Product Roadmap

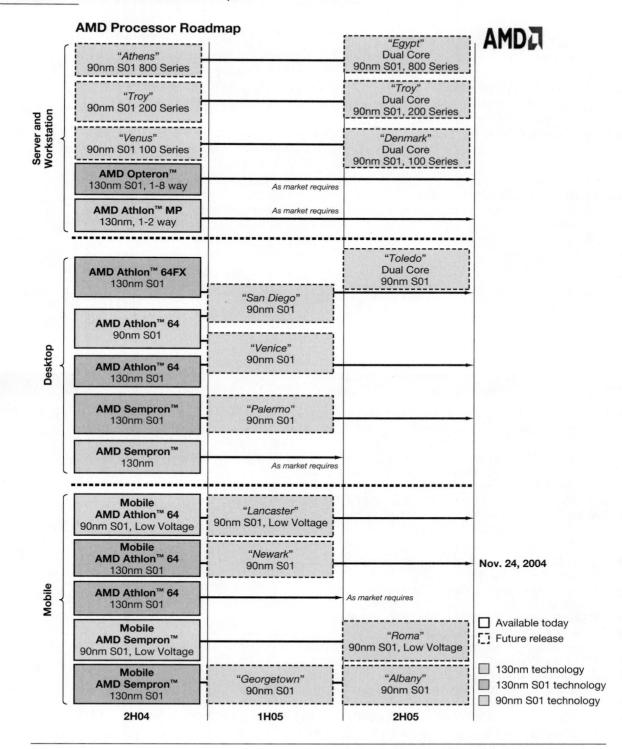

AMD Processor Roadmap

Source: www.amd.com

Exhibit 3 — Opteron Features

Feature	Benefit
Simultaneous 32- and 64-bit computing capabilities	Allows users to run 32-bit and/or 64-bit applications and operating systems as they desire—without sacrificing performance
Support of up to three (3) coherent HyperTransport links, providing up to 19.2GB/s peak bandwidth per processor	Provides substantial I/O bandwidth for your current and future application needs
256 Terabytes of memory address space	Creates a significant performance benefit for applications in which large (or many) datasets are held in memory
Scales from 1-way to 8-way across entire data or compute centers utilizing the same hardware and software infrastructure	Allows for maximum flexibility in IT infrastructure, helping contribute to bottom line success
Integrated memory controller reduces latencies during memory access in a SMP server system	Yields fast computational processing for increased performance and productivity

Source: www.amd.com

Exhibit 4 — AMD—Timeline of Important Events

- May 1, 1969—AMD incorporates with $100,000.
- September 1969—The company moves to new headquarters at 901 Thompson Place, Sunnyvale.
- November 1969—First good die emerges from Fab 1, the Am9300, a 4-bit MSI shift register.
- May 1970—AMD ends its first year with 53 employees and 18 products, but still no sales.
- 1970—First proprietary product introduced, the Am2501.
- November 1972—Producing wafers in newly built 902 Thompson Place.
- September 1972—AMD goes public, issuing 525,000 shares at $15 a share.
- January 1973—First overseas manufacturing base in Penang, Malaysia, in volume production.
- 1973—Profit-sharing is implemented.
- 1974—AMD closes fifth fiscal year with $26.5 million in sales.
- May 1974—To commemorate its fifth anniversary, AMD holds employee street fair and gives away a TV, 10-speed bikes and barbecues.
- 1974—915 DeGuigne Building in Sunnyvale completed.
- 1974-75—Recession causes AMD to implement 44-hour workweek for professional personnel.
- 1975—AMD enters the RAM market with the AM9102.
- 1975—"People first, products and profit will follow."—Jerry Sanders
- 1975—AMD's product line includes the 8080A standard processor and the AM2900 family.
- 1976—AMD's first big Christmas Party held at Rickey's Hyatt House in Palo Alto.
- 1976—AMD and Intel sign patent cross-license agreement.
- 1977—Siemens and AMD established Advanced Micro Computers (AMC).
- 1978—AMD opens an assembly facility in Manila.
- 1978—The company reaches major sales milestone: $100 million annualized run rate.
- 1978—Groundbreaking on manufacturing facility in Austin.
- 1979—Production started in Austin.
- 1979—Company shares listed on New York Stock Exchange.

(continued)

| Exhibit 4 | AMD—Timeline of Important Events (continued) |

- 1980—Josie Lleno wins $1,000 a month for 20 years at "Christmas in May" party at San Jose Convention Center.
- 1981—AMD chips fly aboard Columbia Space Shuttle.
- 1981—San Antonio facility is constructed.
- 1981—AMD and Intel renew and expand their original cross-licensing agreement.
- 1982—First product line (MMP) begins operation in Austin with four employees.
- 1982—AMD and Intel sign technology exchange agreement centering on the iAPX86 family of microprocessors and peripherals.
- 1983—AMD introduces INT.STD.1000, the highest quality standard in the industry.
- 1983—AMD Singapore incorporated.
- 1984—Construction begins on the Bankok facility.
- 1984—Construction begins on Bldg. 2 in Austin.
- 1984—AMD is listed in "The 100 Best Companies to Work for in America" book.
- 1985—AMD makes list of Fortune 500 for first time.
- 1985—Fabs 14 and 15 begin operation in Austin.
- 1985—AMD launches the Liberty Chip campaign.
- 1986—The 29300 family of 32-bit chips is introduced.
- 1986—AMD introduces the industry's first 1-million-bit EPROM.
- October 1986—Weakened by the long-running recession, AMD announces its first workforce restructure in over a decade.
- September 1986—Tony Holbrook named president of the company.
- 1987—AMD establishes a CMOS technology with Sony.
- April 1987—AMD initiates arbitration action against Intel.
- April 1987—AMD and Monolithic Memories Inc. agree to merge.
- October 1988—SDC groundbreaking.
- May 1989—AMD establishes office of the chief executive, consisting of top three company executives.
- May 1990—Rich Previte becomes president and chief operation officer. Tony Holbrook continues as chief technical officer and becomes vice chairman of the board.
- September 1990—Silicon starts through the SDC.
- March 1991—AMD introduces the AM386 microprocessor family, breaking the Intel monopoly.
- October 1991—AMD ships its millionth Am386.
- February 1992—Five-year arbitration with Intel ends, with AMD awarded full rights to make and sell the entire Am386 family of microprocessors.
- April 1993—AMD and Fujitsu establish joint venture to produce flash memories.
- April 1993—First members of the Am486 microprocessor family are introduced.
- July 1993—Groundbreaking of Fab 25 in Austin.
- 1993—Plans for the AMD-K5 project are announced.
- January 1994—Compaq Computer Corp. and AMD form long-term alliance under which Am486 microprocessors will power Compaq computers.
- February 1994—AMDers begin moving into One AMD Place in Sunnyvale.
- February 1994—Digital Equipment Corp. becomes foundry for Am486 microprocessors.
- March 10, 1994—Federal court jury confirms AMD's right to Intel microcode in 287 math coprocessor trial.
- May 1, 1994—AMD celebrates 25th anniversary with Rod Stewart in Sunnyvale and Bruce Hornsby in Austin.

- 1995—Construction begins on the Fujitsu-AMD Semiconductor Limited (FASL) joint venture facility.
- 1995—Fab 25 is completed.
- 1996—AMD acquires NexGen.
- 1996—AMD breaks ground for Fab 30 in Dresden.
- 1997—AMD introduces AMD-K6 processor.
- 1998—AMD unveils AMD Athlon processor (formerly code-named K7) at Microprocessor Forum.
- 1998—AMD and Motorola announce long-term alliance to develop copper interconnect technology.
- 1999—AMD celebrates its 30th anniversary.
- 1999—AMD introduces AMD Athlon processor, the world's first seventh-generation processor for Microsoft Windows® computing.

(continued)

Exhibit 4 | **AMD—Timeline of Important Events** (continued)

- 2000—AMD announces Hector Ruiz is appointed president and COO.
- 2000—AMD Japan celebrates 25-year anniversary.
- 2000—AMD's first quarter sales surpass 1 billion dollars for first time in company history.
- 2000—AMD commences first revenue shipments from Dresden Fab 30.
- 2001—AMD introduces AMD Athlon™ XP processor.
- 2001—AMD introduces AMD Athlon MP dual processor for servers and workstations.
- 2002—AMD and UMC announce a comprehensive alliance to own and operate a 300-mm wafer fabrication facility in Singapore and collaborate on advanced process technology equipment.
- 2002—AMD forms Personal Connectivity Solutions business unit with acquisition of Alchemy Semiconductor.
- 2002—Hector Ruiz succeeds Jerry Sanders as Chief Executive Officer of AMD.
- 2002—AMD introduces first Flash memory device based on MirrorBit™ architecture.

Source: www.amd.com

Exhibit 5 | **AMD—Key Financials**

VALUATION MEASURES

Market Cap (intraday):	7.69B
Enterprise Value (23-Nov-04)[3]:	8.50B
Trailing P/E (ttm, intraday):	47.96
Forward P/E (fye 28-Dec-05)[1]:	29.11
PEG Ratio (5 yr expected)[1]:	2.67
Price/Sales (ttm):	1.55
Price/Book (mrq):	2.88
Enterprise Value/Revenue (ttm)[3]:	1.72
Enterprise Value/EBITDA (ttm)[3]:	5.94

FINANCIAL HIGHLIGHTS

Fiscal Year

Fiscal Year Ends:	28-Dec
Most Recent Quarter (mrq):	30-Sep-04

Profitability

Profit Margin (ttm):	2.89%
Operating Margin (ttm):	5.02%

Management Effectiveness

Return on Assets (ttm):	2.04%
Return on Equity (ttm):	6.70%

Income Statement

Revenue (ttm):	4.94B
Revenue Per Share (ttm):	11.828

(continued)

Exhibit 5   AMD—Key Financials (continued)

Revenue Growth (lfy)[3]:	30.50%
Gross Profit (ttm)[2]:	1.19B
EBITDA (ttm):	1.43B
Net Income Avl to Common (ttm):	164.31M
Diluted EPS (ttm):	0.437
Earnings Growth (lfy)[3]:	N/A

Balance Sheet

Total Cash (mrq):	1.19B
Total Cash Per Share (mrq):	3.23
Total Debt (mrq)[2]:	2.04B
Total Debt/Equity (mrq):	0.795
Current Ratio (mrq):	1.926
Book Value Per Share (mrq):	7.226

Cash Flow Statement

From Operations (ttm)[3]:	1.11B
Free Cashflow (ttm)[3]:	−19.61M

Stock Price History

Beta:	3.101
52-Week Change:	23.87%
52-Week Change (relative to S&P500):	9.57%
52-Week High (17-Nov-04):	22.49
52-Week Low (3-Sep-04):	10.76
50-Day Moving Average:	15.34
200-Day Moving Average:	14.57

Share Statistics

Average Volume (3 month):	11,241,727
Average Volume (10 day):	16,833,000
Shares Outstanding:	367.07M
Float:	356.10M
% Held by Insiders:	2.99%
% Held by Institutions:	65.88%
Shares Short (as of 8-Oct-04):	64.70M
Daily Volume (as of 8-Oct-04):	N/A
Short Ratio (as of 8-Oct-04):	6.725
Short % of Float (as of 8-Oct-04):	18.17%
Shares Short (prior month):	58.64M

Source: Data by Reuters, Yahoo Finance, finance.yahoo.com

Bibliography

1. Fay, Joe. "Dell Hints at Plans for AMD's Opteron," *Unigram.X*, 3rd May 2002.
2. Abbinanti, David. "AMD Support," *VARBusiness*, 22nd July 2002, Vol. 18, Issue 15, p-80.
3. Popovich, Ken. "IBM backs AMD's Opteron processor," *eWeek*, 5th August 2002, Vol. 19, Issue 31, p-20.
4. Popovich, Ken. "Cray supercomputer to tap AMD's Opteron," *eWeek*, 28th October 2002, Vol. 19, Issue 43, p-15.
5. Moltzen, Edward F. "Price Talk Envelops AMD Opteron," *Computer Reseller News*, 23rd December 2002, Issue 1026, p-8.
6. Morgan, Timothy, Prickett. "Newisys Causes A Stir With AMD Opteron Servers," *Computergram Weekly*, 13th January 2003, Issue 1043, p-102.
7. Kirkpatrick, David; Tkaczyk, Christopher. "See This Chip?" *Fortune*, 3rd February 2003, Vol. 147, Issue 3, pp.52–059.
8. Keltcher, Chetana N.; McGrath, Kevin J.; Ahmed, Ardsher and Conway, Pat. "The AMD Opteron processor for multiprocessor servers," *IEEE Micro*, Mar/Apr 2003.
9. "Appro Readies Blade Servers Based on AMD Opterons," *Computergram Weekly*, 9th April 2003.
10. Robertson, Jack. "AMD Opteron woos conservative server market," *EBN*, 21st April 2003, Issue 1359, pp.3–5.
11. Randazzese, Vincent A. "AMD'S Opteron ups Ante vs. Intel's Xeon," *Computer Reseller News*, 28th April 2003.
12. Kovar, Joseph F. "Opportunity rich for 64-bit AMD Opteron," *Computer Reseller News*, 19th May 2003, Issue 1046, p-65.
13. Piven, Joshua. "AMD'sOpteron Aims at Itanium in 64-Bit Battle," *Computer Technology Review*, June 2003.
14. Morgan, Timothy, Prickett. "IBM Debuts Servers Based on AMD Opterons," *Computergram International*, 31st July 2003.
15. "AMD Opterons Power Supercomputer," *Electronic News*, 4th August 2003, Vol. 49, Issue 31.
16. Fay, Joe. "AMD's Opteron Pricing to Track Xeon," *Unigram.X*, 15th August 2003.
17. Moltzen, Edward, F. "AMD Opteron gets lift from distributors," *Computer Reseller News*, 25th August 2003, Issue 1059, p-122.
18. "AMD Powers Down for 2004," *Computergram Weekly*, 19th September 2003.
19. Gomes, Lee. "Intel Turns to a Stunt As Challenger AMD Beats It to the Market," *Wall Street Journal - Eastern Edition*, 29th September 2003, Vol. 0242, Issue 63, p-1–2.
20. "AMD Aims for 45nm in 2007," *Electronic News*, 3rd October 2003.
21. "AMD to Set up Fully Owned Company in China," *Asia Intelligence Wire*, 5th October 2003.
22. Clark, Don. "AMD's Opteron Chip Puts Pressure on Rival Intel," *Wall Street Journal - Eastern Edition*, 13th February 2004, Vol. 243, Issue 31.
23. Wolfe, Alexander. "AMD's 64-Bit Gambit," *VARBusiness*, 23rd August 2004, Vol. 20, Issue 18, pp.40–45.
24. Kirkpatrick, David; D. K. "Chipping Away At Intel," *Fortune*, 1st November 2004, Vol. 150, Issue 8, pp.44–50.
25. Kenedy, Kristen. "AMD Opteron Sets Out To Surf Virtualization Wave," *CRN*, 6th December 2004, Issue 1124, p-55.
26. "Turion is Notebook Opteron," *www.techtree.com*, 10th January 2005.
27. "AMD Profits Disappear in a Flash," *www.theregister.co.uk*, 19th January 2005
28. "AMD Might Sell off Flash Business," *www.theinquirer.net*, 19th January 2005.
29. AMD Annual Report, 2002.
30. http://finance.yahoo.com/

Becoming Competitive: An Industry Note on the Canadian Telecommunications Industry*

Shamsud D. Chowdhury
School of Business
Dalhousie University

Jerry Paul Sheppard
Faculty of Business Administration
Simon Fraser University

If it were a chess game, Michael Sabia had captured Darren Entwistle's most important piece. Sabia, Bell CEO, hired George Cope from Telus in 2005. Cope had been critical to Telus' success as Telus Mobility president. However, the Canadian telecommunications industry was never a chess game, and was increasingly becoming a bench emptying hockey brawl. While George Cope's move may have been a major event for the large national competitors, lesser players were also making moves of their own. After Cope went to Bell Canada, Bell's Consumer Markets President, Pierre Blouin left to head-up MTS Allstream. Other companies were joining the fray: Rogers was already into wireless and Internet, and were poised to develop traditional phone services, as was Shaw. To insure solid fortunes for all their companies, Bell's Sabia, Telus' Entwistle, MTS's Blouin, and Ted Rogers and Jim Shaw at their companies would need to take a careful look at the industry's direction.

Introduction

If it were a chess game, Michael J. Sabia would have just captured Darren Entwistle's most important piece. Sabia, CEO of Montreal based Bell Canada, had just hired George Cope from Burnaby B.C. based Telus Corporation in late 2005. Cope was second in command to Entwistle at Telus and Cope had been critical to the company's growth. Cope, as CEO of Clearnet from 1987 to 2000, had built that firm into a major wireless competitor. When Telus bought Clearnet in 2000, Cope, headed-up the new Telus Mobility group—the area that would drive growth at Telus over the ensuing years.

However, the Canadian Telecommunications Industry (CTI) is no chess game. In many ways the CTI was becoming a bench emptying youth league hockey brawl—complete with parents, fans, and passers-by jumping on to the ice. While George Cope's move may have been a major event for the large national competitors, lesser national players like Toronto's MTS Allstream needed to make their own moves. Thus, after George Cope had gone to Bell Canada, Pierre J. Blouin (Bell's Group President of Consumer Markets) left to head-up MTS Allstream (Canada's number three phone company). Major regional players, like Halifax based Aliant Inc. also needed to carefully look at the industry and plot their own course. Others were joining the fray as well. Toronto's Rogers Communications was already in the wireless and high speed Internet sectors, and they were poised to develop more traditional phone services. The same held for Calgary's Shaw Communications.

To insure solid futures for all their companies, a careful analysis of the industry would be needed by all these players. This meant that Sabia at Bell, Entwistle at Telus, Blouin at MTS, along with Jay Forbes at Aliant, and Ted Rogers and Jim Shaw at their own companies

*The authors are grateful to the Centre for International Business, School of Business Administration, Dalhousie University for financial support for this case. The authors acknowledge the research assistance of Ron Evans, Thomas Rankin, Jason Pandelbury, and Gayle Murdoch at various stages in the development of the case.

would need to be taking a careful look at where the industry was likely to go.

Overview of the Canadian Telecommunications Industry

When we speak of the Canadian telecommunications industry (CTI), little do we realize that at one point in time there was just one telephone company in Canada. In 1880, Bell Canada, a subsidiary of the American Bell Telephone company, was given the exclusive right to sell telephone service across Canada. Ideally, such a monopoly would strive to provide universal service—service to all Canadians. However, such an endeavour is costly and Bell Canada resisted providing service to more rural areas. Parliament then withdrew the monopoly because Bell neglected to institute service to these more rural areas. Later, telecommunications arrangements were instituted in the 1930s that were directed toward achieving more universally accessible service and to prevent monopoly firms from exercising market power over their captive customers. To preserve the perceived efficiencies available to natural monopoly firms, and to ensure that they met social policy objectives (such as universality), regulation was designed to protect the monopoly service providers from competition.[1]

Yet, competition was introduced gradually to the Canadian telecommunications service market over a number of years through policy and regulatory initiatives by the federal government and its regulator, the Canadian Radio-television and Telecommunications Commission (CRTC). The process started in 1979 with the end of the telephone companies' monopoly on private lines interconnected with the public switched telephone network. This was soon followed by similar liberalization in 1980 of the market which provides telephones and other customer premises equipment. In the 1980s, competition was allowed in the resale of certain telecommunications services.[2]

The pace of liberalization accelerated in the 1990s. Economic growth and technical innovations altered the traditional telecommunications landscape in Canada, creating a highly competitive industry structure. In 1992, the market for public long distance voice services was opened to competition. This was consistent with the policy objectives of legislation introduced by the government earlier that year, which passed into law in 1993 as the *Telecommunications Act*. The Act provided the legislative framework for future initiatives to introduce competition in the telecommunications market. Through the licensing of the Personal Communication Service (PCS) spectrum in 1995 under the *Radiocommunication Act*,

more competitors were allowed into the mobile cellular telephone market. In 1997, the CRTC announced the regulatory framework for competition in local telephone services. In 1998, the CRTC liberalized the public pay telephone service market.[3] Appendix A provides a list of major milestones in the evolution of the CTI toward a more competitive market.

Today, the CTI is a highly lucrative one (see Appendix B). Despite a slowdown in revenues, as a result of sustained growth in the wireless segment and cost containment in the wireline segment, operating profits surged in the telecommunications services industry in 2004. In total, the industry generated operating revenues of $34.1 billion in 2004, which marked an increase of 3.7% over the operating revenues of 2003. However, against this 3.7% increase of operating revenues, operating profits rose a robust 16.3% to $7.2 billion.[4]

Since 1998, the majority of the increases in CTI total revenue stemmed from growth in the wireless segment. This segment's revenue growth has increased at an average annual rate of 15 per cent. Conversely, the revenues generated by the wireline incumbents and competitor segments, as well as the resellers, satellite and other market segments, have been relatively stagnant since 1998, and in some cases these segments have witnessed even small declines.[5]

The purpose of this industry note is, first, to evaluate the broader macro-environment in which the CTI operates, second, to outline a boundary for the industry and, finally, to show how the immediate forces commingle to shape the profitability of telephone service providers in the defined boundary.

Macro-environment

The CTI has undergone extensive changes over the last few years. Not only has the environment changed in terms of political/legal issues, but in terms of technological, social, and a range of other dimensions as well.

Political/Legal

The Government of Canada has a vested interest in the infrastructure that provides access to communication on a national and international level. The Government protects this interest through the CRTC and the Telecommunications Act. Historically, the creation and development of telecommunications in Canada was a government initiative. Today, the CRTC recognizes that more liberalization and privatization is necessary to maintain and increase innovation in the telecommunications industry within Canada. As technology is now outpacing regulation, the Government has been able to introduce competition in the long-distance telephone, cable, and satellite infrastructures. A relaxed regulatory telecommunications framework is an inexpensive way to introduce new technology in the CTI and reduce price to the ultimate consumer. In response, companies like Bell Canada and Telus have been able to gain considerable market share by purchasing smaller, regional companies, and fostering a more consolidated industry.

The CTI is facing increasing competition from traditional phone companies, as well as new competitors. In addition, cable companies have started moving into the telecommunications market. Companies like Vonage Canada offer Voice over Internet Protocol (VoIP) that can be run over cable lines. Interestingly, however, the traditional telephone companies are also responding by moving into providing television through their phone lines.[6] In fact, the real competition may well not be among competing phone companies, but among the traditional phone and cable companies—either of which can provide the full range of voice, video, Internet, and wireless products.

Technological

Technological advances are playing a significant part in reshaping the established telecommunications industry. For example, fibre optics are steadily replacing copper wire as an appropriate means of communication signal transmission. Fibre allows for higher bandwidth and capacity. Although voice telephone communications have long been the predominant service offered by established telephone companies, the emergence of the Internet has facilitated the transfer of more data and voice communication. The transmission of such content relies on digital technologies that use telecommunications networks more efficiently than do conventional systems. Telecommunications providers have invested heavily in networks of computerized switching equipment, called packet switched networks, to route vast amounts of digital signals.

An increasingly popular option for businesses and individuals is Voice over Internet Protocol (VoIP). Voice signals can now be bundled together with data using Internet Protocol (IP) technology, reducing the need for a traditional telephone company wired line. Because the VoIP can be run over the Internet or the cable lines, traditional cable companies, such as Rogers Communications, Shaw Communications, and Videotron Ltée, are easily encroaching into the telephone business. The VoIP technology has facilitated the easy entry of cable companies into the telecom industry. VoIP is attracting attention from many, including traditional telephone companies. The Canadian VoIP will be worth approximately one billion by 2008.[7] The situation for the traditional phone companies is somewhat more complex, however. To operate their Internet systems, the traditional phone companies use expensive Asynchronous Digital Subscriber Line (ADSL) connections that can cost hundreds of dollars more per connection than the systems used by traditional cable companies. The difference is that the phone ADSL is a dedicated private line and the cable companies make users share a common connection. This means that traditional phone company lines will always work at a steady, and potentially faster, rate and have better security while traditional cable company lines will bog down during heavy traffic periods and have lower security. However, with sufficient encryption codes security should not be a problem, and the traditional cable companies have been able to run their connections at a higher speed than the traditional phone companies most of the time.

The traditional phone companies can also substantially pare their costs through the use of IP. They can use the IP to combine voice and data into selling a range of cutting-edge services to the customers and strike back at the cable firms. With the IP technology, the telephone companies can offer TV service over their networks. MTS and Aliant have already launched such a service, and Bell and Telus have been working on developing their own versions of the service.[8]

Economic

The broader economic conditions of the country greatly affect the CTI. On the one hand, the economic forces can lead to an increase or decrease in demand for telecom services both domestically and internationally. On the other hand, economic forces can increase or decrease the cost of expansion.

The Canadian economy has enjoyed relative stability and consistent growth over the last decade. This consistency and growth, in turn, left consumers with more discretionary income, relieving some of the competitive pressure within the telecom industry. The low interest rate of the late 1990s allowed a huge expansion of the telecom industry. The low cost of borrowing also allowed the traditionally capital-intensive telecom industry to expand rapidly. Moreover, low interest rates have resulted in a relative easier lower barrier to entry into the CTI. This has allowed several telecommunication companies to operate, succeed, and expand within Canada.

The newest economic threat to the telecommunications industry is the exchange rate. During 2005, the Canadian dollar soared to over 80 cents, making

Canadian exports more expensive for foreign importers. Due to a strong Canadian dollar, Canadian telecom companies do not have the price advantage they previously enjoyed in-so-far as international expansion is concerned. This economic trend has cumulated in the institution of a monetary policy geared toward controlling inflation and increasing interest rates.[9] This slows consumer consumption of telecommunications domestically, thus resulting in the dampening of growth of the industry.

With air travel becoming increasingly expensive due to mounting fees such as NAV CANADA, fuel and insurance surcharges, air travelers security tax and airport fees, it is becoming much more economical to simply communicate via the Internet instead of in person. This is reinforced by the variety of available service providers and communication package deals. The Internet service providers, who have increased their expenditures on high-speed infrastructure for providing subscribers with a wider range of online services, provide a good example.[10]

Socio-cultural

In Canada, communication devices are becoming a social norm. What used to be an indication of success or wealth is now so commonplace that companies are targeting younger and younger demographics. Students of all ages have grown up using the Internet as a common means of communication. This has given rise to the eager acceptance of two-way paging, text messaging, and cell phones specifically targeted to kids. This trend separates aging baby boomers from the tech-savvy younger generation of Canadians.

Given the above, there is a "digital divide", indicating a growing gap between Canadians who have access to the Internet and those who do not.[11] As of 2003, out of a total 12.3 million households in Canada, 6.7 million have access to the Internet at home.[12] Around 65% of the 6.7 million households with the Internet have a high-speed hookup, which is an increase of 56% from 2002.

There are still many households in Canada without access to the Internet; in fact, approximately 3.6 million Canadian households have never used the Internet.[13] With regard to lower income families, 49% of Canadians without the Internet also had below-average household income. The majority of these households consist of few people with no children. Conversely, low income households are experiencing the largest growth rate for connections from work and home. As well, this group of Canadians is utilizing the broadest variety of Internet locations. As VoIP has reduced the need for a traditional telephone wired line, it has turned the nonusers of the Internet into its one of the market's highest potential growth areas. This has important ramifications for the CTI regarding the changing faces of its users.

Demographic

Canada has a well-educated and growing workforce. From the beginning of 2002 through 2004, the Canadian economy added more than one million jobs.[14] Roughly 25% of the workforce has some high-school education, another 20% has trade certificates or non-university diplomas, and about 10% has attended a university. The birth rate in Canada has been slowly declining: immigration from Africa, Asia, Eastern Europe, and Latin America has been largely responsible for the growth of its workforce. High turnover of workers has been a problem in some fast-growing sectors, such as information technology, but it has not been a source of great concern for the telecom industry. Younger consumers, who tend to be the early adopters of new technology, are experiencing growth in both population and income level. Baby boomers (people born in between 1946 and 1964) and seniors (age 55 and up) are experiencing the largest growth in population.

Global

There is a regulated minimum 80% Canadian ownership requirement for most segments of the CTI. However, the World Trade Organization's (WTO) General Agreement for Trade in Services (GATS) has liberalized parts of the global communications industry. Ownership restrictions have been eliminated in the reseller category, enabling foreign competition in that segment only. However, the trade restrictions have been lifted in terms of hard goods, enabling competition from foreign manufacturers of complementary goods, such as telephone sets, wires, and cables. This impacts the CTI on the supplier side and allows for cheaper inputs.

General Competitive Analysis

With rapid technology convergence, the Canadian telecommunications industry boundary lines are becoming blurred. Telecommunications in Canada used to be governed by the CRTC, even though telephone providers were separated from television broadcasters and cable companies. The three industries unfolded very differently and faced unique competitive pressures. Today convergence is the buzzword in the CTI. Consequently, there is increased crossover and duplication of services offered in the CRTC and the North

American Industrial Classification System (NAICS) schemas. Therefore, in terms of defining the industry boundary, there is no discernible delineation between the many areas defined by the CRTC and the NAICS. Most firms competing in one sector are also present in the others. Therefore, the industry can be divided into several segments with several major players in each segment (see Appendix C). Based on Appendix C, it could be argued that the CTI is composed of traditional wireline telephone service providers (local and long distance) and the Internet service providers. Although we will maintain this broad classification in the following analysis, we divide the traditional wireline telephone services into local and long distance because of the volume of revenue each generates. The following section presents a review of the major players in each segment of the telecommunications market in Canada.

Rivalry among the Incumbents

Wireline Local Service Market. The local service segment of the Canadian telecommunications market is made up of revenues generated by providing households and businesses with wireline access to the Public-Switched telephone network.[15] Revenues in the wireline segment fell 4.6% to $23.0 billion in 2003, following a 3.1% decline in 2002. This segment experienced year-over-year declines in its operating revenues in every quarter but one in 2002 and 2003.[16]

Most of the wireline local service market in Canada is controlled by the Incumbent Local Exchange Carriers (ILECs). These companies are NorthwesTel, BellWest, Telus, SaskTel, MTS Communications Inc., Bell Canada and Aliant. Some forty-four independents also operate local exchange services in Canada and are registered with the CRTC as Competitive Local Exchange Carriers (CLECs).

While mostly regional in scope, two ILECs have stepped up the competitive jockeying over the past several years. Bell Canada and Telus Communications have both entered into what can be described as national strategies. Telus moved east and into Bell Canada's territory by acquiring QuebecTel, the Quebec assets of Axxent, as well as Williams Communications and PSINet's Canadian operations and facilities. Bell Canada has, in turn, captured customers in traditional Telus operating territory through Bell Nexia and Bell Intrigna in western Canada.

Telus and Bell Canada dominate the market segment in terms of size and in terms of revenues. Bell controlled 55.6% of market share (of about $7 billion) versus Telus' 24.7% in 2001. Aliant, the third largest ILEC in Canada, controlled 8.4% of market share and operates exclusively in Atlantic Canada. Other ILECs control a total of 9% of market share while the CLECs control 2.3%. Telus' aggressive acquisition strategies have intensified the rivalry with Bell Canada in the market. Telus' acquisition of QuebecTel put the company on more even footing with Bell Canada and the competitive battle has heated up with 'Acquisition Expert' CEO Darren Entwistle leading the Telus charge.

Nationwide, Aliant and the other CLECs have a much lower level of competitive rivalry with the two largest ILECs; Aliant because of its strictly regional focus, and the other CLECs because of size and the financial difficulty of competing in small sections of urban markets versus the regional ILECs.

Wireline Long Distance. Competition in the wireline long distance market has increased since 1992 when the CRTC eliminated the incumbent telecommunications carriers' monopoly in the provision of public inter-exchange voice services. There are now many independent long distance service suppliers that compete with the ILECs. Rivalry in this segment is strong because the substitutability of the products is increasing (email, wireless long distance) and the switching costs for consumers are very low. Demand for the product is also slowing—long distance service revenues dropped 17.6% in 2001[17] which has added to the intensity of the competitive rivalry. Bell Canada saw smaller drops in long distance revenues (5.9%) than did the other ILECs (25%) or the wireline competitive long distance service providers (22%).[18]

Wireless Service Market.[19] The cellular or personal communications service (PCS) market is the most highly competitive telecommunications market in Canada. A flood of new competitors have fueled product and service innovation and the segment has continued to grow consistently. For example, according to the Canadian Wireless Telecommunications Association, its total membership in 2005 reached a staggering 175.[20] Revenues in the wireless segment increased 13.6% to $8.2 billion, fuelled by an 11.5% gain in subscribers and a 3.0% increase in revenue per subscriber. The industry also improved its operating margin to 17.3% from 14.0% in 2002.[21]

In October of 2001, an "enhanced reciprocal agreement"[22] was signed by the wireless divisions of Bell, Telus and Aliant which expanded access to each other's wireless networks. This agreement brought competition to rural regions not previously serviced by multiple providers and built upon previous agreements concerning reselling and roaming. This agreement seems to be a strategic move by the ILECs to stymie competition from wireless competitive service providers.

The large number of competitors and the relative parity of the top three providers in terms of wireless service revenue market share—Bell 25%, Telus 30.4%, and Rogers AT&T 27.6%—has meant that rivalry is intense in this market. The customer's cost to switch brands is also quite low although many strategies—including locking customers into contracts—have been attempted to maximize these costs. (*Note: Wireless Long Distance Services are a minimal revenue generator in the wireless/PCS market and so are exempted from this discussion.*)

Suppliers

Suppliers to the telecommunications industry are varied in their scope and level of involvement with service providing firms such as Telus. For the purpose of simplifying the discussion of supplier/seller forces, suppliers will be divided into two groupings. The first grouping contains those suppliers which provide technology to the competing firms. This technology ranges from satellite and transmission technology, to fiber optics, to the cell phones provided by the competing firms to their customers. The second grouping contains those suppliers which provide service, such as access to wireless and wireline bandwidth, to resellers in the industry. The following two sections will more closely examine the competitive pressures stemming from supplier-seller collaboration and bargaining within each of these two groupings.

Technology Supplier. The continued liberalization of the telecommunications industry in Canada has forced competing firms to be proactive in their acquisitions of new technology. Competition has sparked innovation of old products and the introduction of new technologies and services. Consumer demand for these services has meant that for a major carrier to be competitive, it has to be on the forefront of new technology. As such, the involvement of technology suppliers in the competitive environment has increased. Providers of high bandwidth fiber optic cables are an example of this. The voracious appetite of consumers for faster, high quality transmissions—for Internet and cable television—has increased the power of suppliers of these technologies vis-à-vis the competing firms. Northern Telecom is a prime example of a firm that has staked a solid position as a supplier of transmission materials to the telecommunications market.

On the wireless side, manufacturers of cell phones and personal communications devices have also seen their relative positions grow. The wireless segment is the fastest growing in the Canadian telecommunications industry and the demand for wireless devices has grown accordingly.

Wire Time Suppliers. The resellers segment is the smallest segment in the Canadian telecommunications market. The total sales in this segment amounted to $1.3 billion in 2003.[23] Resellers are companies which purchase bandwidth or wire time from an incumbent and resell the product to the end user at what are usually discounted prices. The arrangement is beneficial to all parties involved. The incumbent—the supplier of bandwidth or wire time—generates revenue from otherwise unused resources; the reseller receives a healthy margin by buying the wire time at a discounted price and reselling at a discounted price, and the end user is able to purchase cheap long distance and local calling.

Buyers

The buyers in the Canadian telecommunications industry are, once again, varied in their scope of involvement within the overall process. There are many products/services offered by the competitive rivals and likewise many different kinds of buyers for these services. For the purpose of simplification, the buyers in the industry have been divided into two groupings. The first group involves those buyers that purchase communications services from the competitive rivals. These services can be wire or wireless telephone service and various other types of data transmission (i.e. Internet service, wireless Internet service, long distance). Buyers of these services can be individuals, businesses or government agencies. The second group of buyers (which was already partially discussed in the suppliers section) is those firms which purchase wire or wireless time and are the resellers.

There are many different communications services that are purchased by buyers from the competitive rivals. These will be grouped into three sub-categories—basic wireline services, wireless services, and other services.

Wireline Local Services. Basic wireline services are provided for the most part by the regional incumbents. The regional incumbents are at a significant advantage over the smaller wireline competitive service providers as they are often proprietary owners of the wireline infrastructure. While regulations have been loosened to allow for competition for basic wireline services, the wireline competitive service providers have not met up to the challenge. As such, the power of buyers of basic wireline services has remained very low. The Canadian affinity for wireline service as the staple mode of communication, coupled with the lack of wireline substitutes in most markets means that substitutability, and therefore buyer power, is low.

Wireline Long Distance Services. Competition in wireline long distance services has continued to increase since

1992 when the CRTC eliminated the incumbent carriers' monopoly in the provision of publicly inter-exchange voice transmissions. As of December 2003, 632 long distance providers were active in Canadian markets.[24] Coupled with a decline in revenues for major long distance operators and minor consolidations and exits of the market, buyers of long distance services have seen their power dramatically increase in the last decade. The numerous choices available have made the sub-segment very competitive and buyer power is high owing to the numerous substitutes. Also, switching costs for long distance services are relatively low and are not often linked intrinsically to service bundles provided by the competitive rivals.

Wireless Services. Wireless service providers operate within a very competitive environment. In all markets from coast to coast there are many available options for a potential buyer of wireless services. The cost of service (wireless coverage) is normally fixed and therefore similar from company to company so providers compete on hardware and service bundles instead. Owing to the large number of competitors and extremely competitive pricing, the power of the buyers of wireless services is high.

Other Services. Providers of other services also operate in a very competitive environment. Internet service provision is an especially competitive sub-segment of the Canadian telecommunications industry. Internet service providers (ISPs) are numerous in major markets and pricing is competitive. As such, buyers of Internet services have a relatively high degree of power.

Resellers as Buyers. The largest segment of resellers are those companies which provide wireline long distance services. Their buying power is relatively low and they often operate in markets which are largely dominated by the incumbents, who are in turn their suppliers. Substitutability of the supply remains low which has kept buyer power low. However, recent years have seen the consolidation of long distance resellers—in 1998 TigerTel Services purchased several resellers: Whistler Telecom Inc., Long Distance Atlantic, Argos Alliance and TelNet Communications. A nationwide long distance reseller with financial clout could be able to increase the power of the reseller as buyer in the future.

New Entrants

When considered as a whole, there are very few likely new entrants. Entry cost is very high. For example, after spending billions to become a solid competitor in the wireless market, Microcell—doing business as Fido— was still losing money and was eventually taken over by Rogers Communications. The most likely entry moves

are likely to be those by the traditional cable companies into traditional wireline markets. Thus, Rogers Communications and Shaw Communications are of particular interest.

Rogers Communications, of Toronto, is a Canadian based communications company with business in cable television, high-speed Internet access, video retailing, wireless voice and data communications services, radio, television broadcasting, televised shopping and publishing. Although in 2004, Rogers experienced revenues of CAD$5.6 billion, an increase from CAD$4.8 billion in 2003, the company did have a net loss of CAD$13.2 million in 2004 compared to a CAD$100.3 million net income in 2003.

Shaw Communications, based in Calgary, is a Canadian communications company focusing on broadband cable television, Internet, digital phone and satellite direct-to-home service. In 2004, Shaw increased revenues by 4.1% to CAD$2 billion with a net income of over CAD$90 million. The 2004 net income was a significant achievement as compared to the CAD$46.9 million loss in 2003.

For the further discussion of the threat of potential new entrants into the CTI, it will again be important to divide the industry into its segments and discuss each individually. Accordingly, we will focus on three different segments: wireline local service, wireline long distance, and wireless service.

Wireline Local Service Market. The threat of new entrants to the wireline local service market is likely to increase. Although there are currently thirty-six independent competitive wireline service providers registered as CLECs nationally, they tend to compete for high traffic business in dense urban areas. It is likely that this segment will soon be saturated and new entrants to the wireline local service market from these types of providers will cease. Traditionally entrance to the market is also financially risky because the capital requirements that must be met to compete with ILECs that enjoy great regional economies of scale. However, true entry into the market will occur with the advent of VoIP (Voice over Internet Protocol) carried over cable providers.[25] There are a wide range of providers and none of their services need to run on telephone lines. These providers can range from cable providers themselves (like Vidéotron Télécom) or carriers that use others' broadband services (like Vonage or Primus). If there is a hot area in this market segment it is the provision of wireline-like services via VoIP.

Wireline Long Distance Market. The threat of new entrants to the wireline long distance market is significantly higher than for local service. Because of the regulatory changes of the early 1990s, it is relatively inexpensive for a firm wishing to enter the wireline long distance market as a reseller. Brand preference and customer loyalty also appear to be lower in the long distance segment which is supportive of the low-switching costs and high substitutability that exist. Although the number of long distance providers increased substantially over the past 10 years, the number of new entrants has slowed as resellers have begun to consolidate and as smaller firms have been forced to exit the market. Again, the advent of VoIP means that competitors providing VoIP service can offer long distance service. VoIP long distance is usually a flat fee per month rather than per minute charge. In many cases the flat fee can be far less expensive for the consumer.

Wireless/Personal Communications Services. The entry barriers to the wireless/personal communications services (PCs) segment of the Canadian telecommunications industry are high. Capital requirements for the infrastructure necessary to run a wireless network cost substantial amounts of money. Another entry barrier to the wireless/PCS segment is the scarcity of spectrum. Companies wishing to be wireless providers must apply to the CRTC for spectrum space which is often not available.

The large number of competitors as well as the economies of scale enjoyed by Bell, Telus, Rogers and AT&T means that the threat of new entry into the wireless/PCS market is very low. The agreement between Bell, Aliant and Telus to share their network capabilities has only increased the barriers to entry.

Substitutes

Considering most of the major players participate in all of these segments, substitutability does not exist outside of the industry as it has been defined. In essence, each segment in the industry can be seen as a substitute for every other in that they are all modes of communication. In this situation, each domain of the larger CTI has to be considered as an industry. However, because most of the large rivals in the industry are entrenched in multiple forms of telephone services, there are no real substitutes to the offerings of the CTI. Within the CTI, specific technologies are interchangeable, creating internal substitutes for individual products. For example, the VoIP is a substitute for wirelines and wireless services. But most large telephone companies offer three of them. This interchangeability effect creates a cannibalistic effect by which one sector of the industry is growing to the detriment of the other segments. This loss should not be that insidious because losses on some services are likely to be offset by the gains from other services.

Conclusion

Overall, there is no gainsaying the fact that competition in the telecommunications industry is very intense. Two major factors in the external environment—deregulation and technological advances—have drastically changed the nature of competition in the industry during the last two decades. Deregulation has freed companies from some government-mandated pricing controls on the one hand, and has opened up a once protected industry to competition in all segments. Deregulation has allowed for large non-industry participants and small upstarts to compete head on head with large telecommunications companies. Technological innovation has created new opportunities in the industry, especially in the wireless and Internet sectors. New technologies have also opened-up the opportunity for old line telecom companies to move into markets previously occupied solely by cable providers. The wireline business, though declining, is effectively attracting entrants through advances in VoIP technology. Therefore, the next decade will witness fierce battles in all segments of the industry and some new ones!

Endnotes

1. Government of Canada Competition Bureau. "*The State of Telecommunications Competition in Canada.*" Retrieved from http://competition.ic.gc.ca/epic/internet/incb-bc.nsf/en/ct01457e.html
2. Industry Canada. "*The Evolution of Competition in the Canadian Telecommunications Service Market.*" Retrieved from http://strategis.ic.gc.ca/epic/internet/insmt-gst.nsf/en/sf06283e.html
3. Ibid.
4. Statistics Canada. http://www.statcan.ca/Daily/English/040413/d040413c.htm
5. "*Telecommunications Service in Canada: An Industry Overview,*" op cit.
6. Shaw, G. 2005. Telus markets digital television aimed at luring cable viewers from Shaw. *The Vancouver Sun*, Dec 14: D.3 (Final Edition); McLean, C., & Brethour, P. 2006. Telecoms. *The Globe and Mail*, Report on Business, October 8, p. B4.
7. Ibid. and SeaBoard Group, *The Globe and Mail*, Saturday, October 8, 2005, p. B4.
8. Ibid.
9. Bank of Canada, 2005, http://www.bankofcanada.ca/en, accessed December 28, 2005.
10. Statistics Canada, July 2004. *The Daily: Household Internet Use Survey.* Retrieved from http://www. statcan.ca/Daily/English/040708/d040708a.htm in November, 2005.
11. Birdsall, W. F. 2000. The digital divide in the liberal state: A Canadian perspective. October 20. Retrieved from www.firstmonday.org/issues/issue5_12/birdsall/#b5 November 30, 2005; Sciadas, G. 2002. The digital divide in Canada. *Canadian Economic Observer*, 15 (11): 22–28.
12. Statistics Canada, July 2004. *The Daily: Household Internet Use Survey.* Op Cit.
13. Ibid.
14. Economist Intelligence Unit, 2005. http://www.eiu.com.ezproxy.library.dal.ca/index.asp. Retrieved on October 14, 2005.
15. Government of Canada Industry Report, 2002. http://strategis.ic.gc.ca/epic/internet/insmt-gst.nsf/en/ sf05637e.html. Retrieved Nov 30, 2005.

16. Statistics Canada. http://www.statcan.ca/Daily/English/040413/d040413c.htm. Retrieved Nov 30, 2005.
17. Canadian Government. 2002. *Industry Report 2002*, Retrieved from http://strategis.ic.gc.ca/epic/internet/insmt-gst.nsf/en/sf05637e.html. Retrieved Nov 15, 2005: 2–15.
18. Ibid.
19. Wireless Long Distance Services are a minimal revenue generator in the wireless/PCS market and so are exempted from this discussion.
20. Canadian Wireless Telecommunications Association, 2005. http://www.gdsourcing.com/statslink canada/Sample/SearchCommunications.asp. Retrieved November 10, 2005.
21. Statistics Canada. http://www.statcan.ca/Daily/English/040413/d040413c.htm. Retrieved November 9, 2005.
22. Canadian Government Industry Report 2002, pp. 2–19. Retrieved from http://strategis.ic.gc.ca/epic/internet/insmt-gst.nsf/en/sf05637e.html. Retrieved November 22, 2005.
23. Statistics Canada, 2004. *Survey of telecommunications service providers: April 2004*. http://strategis.ic.gc.ca/epic/internet/insmt-gst.nsf/en/sf06004e.html.
24. Government of Canada. 2002. *Telecommunications Industry Report*. http://strategis.ic.gc.ca/epic/internet/insmt-gst.nsf/en/sf05637e.html. Retrieved November 7, 2005.
25. Heinrich, E. 2005. Competition Calling. *Canadian Business*, 78 (10): 26–29.

Appendix A   Competitive Canadian Telecommunications Market Milestones

1979 • Telecom Decision CRTC 79-11—*CNCP Telecommunications: Interconnection with Bell Canada*, (17 May).

1982 • Telecom Decision CRTC 82-14—*Attachment of Subscriber-Provided Terminal Equipment* (23 Nov.).

1984 • Licensing of competitive cellular telephone service providers.

1987 • Privatization of Teleglobe.

1989 • Supreme Court confirms federal jurisdiction over "Stentor" telephone companies.
     • *Radiocommunication Act* updated.
     • *Canada–U.S Free Trade Agreement:* provided for Canada-U.S. competition in the provision of enhanced telecommunication services (1 Jan.).

1992 • Telecom Decision CRTC 92-12—*Competition in the Provision of Public Long Distance Voice Telephone Services and Related Resale and Sharing Issues* (12 June).
     • Privatization of Telesat Canada.

1993 • New pro-competitive *Telecommunications Act* comes into force.

1994 • *North American Free Trade Agreement (NAFTA):* provided for North American-wide competition in the provision of enhanced telecommunication services (1 Jan.).
     • Supreme Court confirms federal jurisdiction over "independent" telephone companies.
     • Federal government commitment to Canadian Information Highway Strategy. Information Highway Advisory Council (IHAC) established.
     • Global and regional mobile satellite policy announced.
     • Telecom Decision CRTC 94-19—*Review of Regulatory Framework* (16 Sept.).

1995 • Licensing of competitive wireless Personal Communications Services (PCS).
     • Licensing of Local Multipoint Communications Systems (LMCS).

1996 • Government's Convergence Policy (1 Aug.).
     • Federal government releases, *Building the Information Society: Moving Canada into the 21st Century—* Provides an information highway plan of action.
     • Mobile satellite launch (MSAT).

1997 • Telecom Decision CRTC 97-8—*Local Competition* (1 May).
     • Telecom Decision CRTC 97-9—*Price Cap Regulation and Related Issues* (1 May).
     • Telecom Decision CRTC 97-15—*Co-location* (16 June).
     • Telecom Decision CRTC 97-18—*Implementation of Price Cap Regulation—Decision Regarding Interim Local Rate Increases and Other Matters* (18 Dec.).
     • 69 countries reach agreement on basic telecommunications under the WTO (15 Feb.).

1998 • Telecom Decision CRTC 98-2—*Implementation of Price Cap Regulation and Related Issues* (5 March).
     • Telecom Decision CRTC 98-8—*Local Pay Telephone Competition* (30 June).
     • Telecom Decision CRTC 98-17—*Regulatory Regime for the Provision of International Telecommunications Service* (1 Oct.).

(continued)

- Telecom Decision CRTC 98-22—*Final Rates for Unbundled Local Network Components* (30 Nov.).
- End of Teleglobe monopoly (1 Oct.).

1999
- Telecom Decision CRTC 99-16—*Telephone Service to High-Cost Serving Areas* (19 October 1999).

2000
- End of Telesat's monopoly (1 March).
- Order in Council P.C. 2000-1053—Requires the CRTC to submit a report to the Governor in Council annually, for the next five years, on the status of competition in the Canadian telecommunications market and on the availability of advanced telecommunication services in all regions (26 June).
- Decision CRTC 2000-745—*Changes to the Contribution Regime* (30 November 2000).
- Decision CRTC 2000-746—*Long-Distance Competition & Improved Service for Northwestel Customers* (30 Nov.).

2001
- Decision CRTC 2001-238—*Restructured Rate Bands, Revised Loop Rates and Related Issues* (27 April).
- CRTC releases inaugural report on the status of competition in the Canadian telecommunications industry (28 Sept.).
- Decision CRTC 2001-756—*Regulatory Framework for the Small Incumbent Telephone Companies* (14 Dec.).

2002
- Telecom Decision CRTC 2002-34—*Regulatory Framework for the Second Price Cap Period* (30 May).
- Telecom Decision CRTC 2002-43—*Implementation of Price Regulation for Télébec and Telus Québec* (31 July).
- Industry Minister Allan Rock asks the House of Commons Standing Committee on Industry, Science & Technology to undertake a review on the foreign investment restrictions in the telecom industry (19 Nov.).
- CRTC releases 2nd annual report on the status of competition in the Canadian telecom. industry (20 Dec.).

2003
- Government partners with Wi-LAN Inc. to bring affordable broadband to remote and rural areas (2 April).
- Government partners with Vistar Telecom. to enhance wireless communications technology (26 April).
- Industry Minister Allan Rock announces recipients of second-round funding of $1.7 million funding for broadband business development for first nations communities (7 July).
- Decision CRTC 2003-52—*Procedural determination in the Competitor Digital Network Access service proceeding re application made by the CDN Cable TV Assoc.* Cable carriers come under the telecom umbrella (1 Aug.).
- Industry Minister Allan Rock announces a new Satellite Coordination Agreement with Mexico that will reduce interference, provide stable, cooperative environment and ensure room for expansion (25 Sept.).

2004
- Industry Canada auctions the 2300 MHz and 3500 MHz Band: 22 companies participate in buying 392 licences with bids totalling over $11.2 million (19 Feb.)
- Telecom Decision CRTC 2004-34—*FCI Broadband—Request to lift restrictions on the provision of retail digital subscriber line Internet services to business customers.* Allows CLECs DSL connections (21 May)
- Industry Canada announced selection of Ciel Satellite Communications to develop a commercial broadcasting satellite at Canada's orbital position to provide services to the Canadian market by 2009 (24 Sept.).
- Industry Minister David Emerson announces that the Government is introducing legislation that would create a 'do not call list' to reduce the volume of telemarketing calls received at home (13 Dec.)

2005
- Industry Canada announces 306 licences sold to 12 companies in an auction of wireless frequencies generating $56.6 million to enable carriers to extend wireless broadband access in rural and urban areas (3 Feb.).
- Telecom Decision CRTC 2005-28—*Regulatory framework for VoIP* (12 May).
- Industry Minister David Emerson announces legislation to amend the *Telecommunications Act* to give the CRTC the power to levy substantial penalties against carriers that violate its decisions or provisions of the Act (14 Nov.).

Source: Industry Canada (2005)

The following table provides a financial overview of the telecommunications services and describes the contribution the telecommunications service industry makes to the overall Canadian economy. The focus is on gross domestic product (GDP), employment, salaries, capital investment and price trends.

GDP (Value Added) (millions of 1997 dollars)

	2000	2001	2002	2003	2004
Telecommunications Services	24,357	26,214	28,400	29,256	30,277
Overall Economy	943,738	957,257	986,070	1,008,945	1,040,779

Employees (thousands)

	2000	2001	2002	2003	2004
Telecommunications Services	103.7	104.9	105.1	110.8	114.3
Overall Economy	14,788.6	14,946.7	15,307.9	15,665.1	15,949.7

Average Salary

	2000	2001	2002	2003	2004
Telecommunications Services	44,272	45,079	45,845	46,639	47,588
Overall Economy	34,090	34,705	35,417	36,915	38,414

Financial Data Telecommunications Services (millions of current dollars)

	2000	2001	2002	2003	2004
Operating Revenues	30,331	32,358	33,223	32,879	34,092
Operating Profit	4,268	4,154	4,548	6,230	7,243

Prices (CPI 1992=100)

	2000	2001	2002	2003	2004
Telecommunications Services	112.4	116.4	117.4	118.5	119.4
All Items	113.5	116.4	119.0	122.3	124.6

Analytical Table—Telecommunications Services (% of Canadian Total)

	2000	2001	2002	2003	2004
GDP	2.3%	2.5%	2.7%	2.9%	2.9%
Employees	0.7%	0.7%	0.7%	0.7%	0.7%
Average Salary	130%	130%	129%	126%	124%

Analytical Table—Telecommunications Services (% change from last year)

	2000	2001	2002	2003	2004
GDP	16.6%	12.6%	8.8%	3.0%	3.5%
Employees	2.1%	2.2%	0.1%	5.4%	3.2%
Average Salary	0.2%	1.8%	1.7%	3.5%	2.0%
Prices	1.8%	3.9%	1.6%	0.2%	0.8%

Numbers may not add up due to rounding.

Source: Statistics Canada, CANSIM database, as of March 2003.

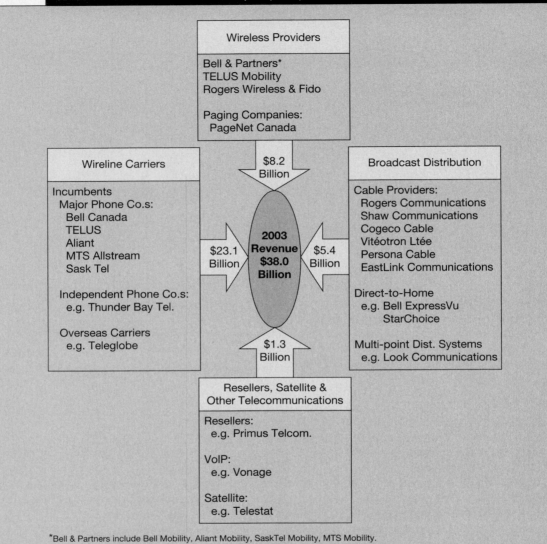

Wireless Providers

Bell & Partners*
TELUS Mobility
Rogers Wireless & Fido

Paging Companies:
  PageNet Canada

$8.2 Billion

Wireline Carriers

Incumbents
  Major Phone Co.s:
    Bell Canada
    TELUS
    Aliant
    MTS Allstream
    Sask Tel

Independent Phone Co.s:
  e.g. Thunder Bay Tel.

Overseas Carriers
  e.g. Teleglobe

$23.1 Billion

2003 Revenue $38.0 Billion

$5.4 Billion

Broadcast Distribution

Cable Providers:
  Rogers Communications
  Shaw Communications
  Cogeco Cable
  Vitéotron Ltée
  Persona Cable
  EastLink Communications

Direct-to-Home
  e.g. Bell ExpressVu
       StarChoice

Multi-point Dist. Systems
  e.g. Look Communications

$1.3 Billion

Resellers, Satellite & Other Telecommunications

Resellers:
  e.g. Primus Telcom.

VoIP:
  e.g. Vonage

Satellite:
  e.g. Telestat

*Bell & Partners include Bell Mobility, Aliant Mobility, SaskTel Mobility, MTS Mobility.

Source: Industry Canada. 2004. Telecommunications Services in Canada. Ottawa: Industry Canada. Figure 21.2.

Bell Canada: The VoIP Challenge

Rod White

Michael Raynor

Daniel Day

In December 2004, Ron Close was deep in thought as he headed home from his meetings with Michael Sabia, the president and chief executive officer, and Pierre Blouin, Bell Canada Enterprises' group president—consumer markets. It was December 2004 and Close had just been offered the position of president, consumer VoIP for Bell Canada, Canada's largest telecommunications company.

VoIP, or voice over Internet protocol (a telephone-like service operating over the Internet), seemed poised to sweep away the foundations of the traditional fixed-line telephone companies. The legacy telephone services ran on billions of dollars worth of switched-circuit infrastructure. Unregulated VoIP market entrants were starting up with a few million dollars investment. VoIP providers were now able to provide comparable quality voice communication to anyone with a high speed Internet connection (HSI), largely bypassing the public switched telephone network (PSTN). From their low-cost base, they were offering a "second-line" telephony product with sophisticated features at lower prices. Canadian cable TV companies, already the market leaders in high speed Internet access, were announcing imminent launches of VoIP-based telephone service.

After an undergraduate degree from the Ivey Business School, Close began his career at Andersen Consulting, followed by a stint at Motorola. By the 1990s, he had made the transition to an entrepreneurial startup. He was the co-founder and president of Netcom Canada, a successful Internet company. He sold this firm in 1999 as valuations were soaring. His subsequent roles included president at AT&T Canada's Internet division, and after a much-needed world tour with his family, he invested in, and as chief executive officer (CEO) ran Nextair, a troubled wireless software company. While Close's personal finances were comfortable, managing Nextair's day-to-day cash flow problems and its impact on his personal resources created considerable stress. When, earlier in December, a headhunter had approached him to discuss the Bell VoIP opportunity, Close was in a receptive mood.

In their meetings, Sabia and Blouin had both given Close the same message: Bell needed VoIP, but a disruptive VoIP service would not succeed within the established Bell organization. Sabia was adamant that forces within Bell would hamper VoIP start-up efforts. In essence, Close was offered the opportunity to establish a new, autonomous division separate from the existing Bell organization. He was told his new business unit could set features and pricing to ensure market and competitive viability of the new VoIP service. Blouin had also speculated about Bell's reaction to independent VoIP pricing policy and consequent margin erosion.

The possibility of building a nimble and independent organization, unshackled by Bell's legacy systems, certainly didn't lack challenge and excitement. Yet Close wondered, was this really the disruptive challenge it

seemed? What were the implications of an enterprise that cannibalized the legacy service revenues at lower margins? Was this one he wanted to take on?

Voice over Internet Protocol

By 2004, VoIP functionality could be delivered in any of three ways. First, it could operate PC-to-PC (also called P2P) using readily available software and a headset; second, PC-to-phone, where a computer user was able to connect to the public network (PSTN) from a software VoIP application; and third, phone-to-phone using a special modem called an analogue telephone adaptor (ATA) to connect the phones to the Internet.

In the first mode, the user installed VoIP application software on their PC that provided entirely free voice communication over the Internet. Early P2P VoIP applications first appeared in the mid-1990s. But because of the limited bandwidth of dialup internet connections and software limitations, they did not work well and appealed primarily to technophiles. More recently, computer voice applications such as Microsoft's Messenger were exploiting the growing adoption of broadband Internet service, and the higher data rates possible, to incorporate PC-to-PC voice capabilities. In 2002, the inventors of the KaZaa file-sharing software started up Skype, a free voice application with quality equivalent to PSTN. Skype was simple to install, and permitted simultaneous voice, text messaging and file transfers.

Skype was a leader in providing the second mode of VoIP communications, PC to PSTN. SkypeOut was introduced in mid-2004, and for a small fee allowed a PC user to call a telephone anywhere in the world. There were many providers of this type of service and their offerings were evolving rapidly. Recently PC users could acquire a telephone number and be called by anyone connected to the PSTN (the recently announced SkypeIn was an example of this service). Additional features like voicemail and conference calling were becoming part of these VoIP applications.

The third mode, phone-to-phone or modem-based residential VoIP offerings had achieved voice quality equal to PSTN. This service was often called over-the-top (OTT) VoIP because the user purchased and self-installed an ATA modem, connecting it to, and usually placing it on top of their HSI modem. Because of the high data rates required, higher quality voice VoIP was achieved only over broadband Internet connections. The ATA modem connected to the VoIP provider's network automatically. Once a phone handset was plugged into the other port on the ATA it mimicked PSTN service. Calls were made simply by dialing the destination number.

The VoIP service provider typically levied a monthly fee that varied with the free calling area and service options selected by the consumer. Calls outside this area were billed per-minute, or were included in a flat-rate "long-distance" fee. The chief advantage was that a long-distance VoIP-initiated call to the PSTN could be routed over the Internet, and switched to the PSTN as a local call at the destination, requiring the provider to pay a fee only for the local interconnection, and avoiding long-distance telephony costs altogether. An existing telephone number could often be retained (depending on local regulations). The customer configured the features through a web-based interface on a computer connected to the Internet. Vonage, a US-based VoIP service provider, was a typical example.

Since VoIP was a software service, these vendors were able to implement and bundle in a wide range of features without significant additional cost. In contrast, these had typically been provided for additional fees, or were previously unavailable to PSTN customers. Available features included: a choice of area codes; multiple numbers from different area codes so that frequent PSTN callers could reach the subscriber with local calls; call forwarding simultaneously to several numbers; voicemail retrieval anywhere by Internet/computer or forwarded by email; instantaneous viewing and management of calls, charges and service features via a web-based interface; directories of contacts; and all the regular PSTN telephone features. Because VoIP was location-independent, regardless of the area code assigned, the user could travel or move house, plug in the portable modem (often pocket-sized) into any HSI connection, and continue as before. The modem worked worldwide (see Exhibit 1).

Despite these advantages, VoIP telephony was not a perfect substitute for conventional PSTN service; there were several significant drawbacks. First, a power interruption at the subscriber's premises could cause loss of service. Traditional PSTN phones were powered independently through the telephone line. Central offices or exchanges had emergency power generators to guarantee there was always a dial tone. To ensure near-equivalent reliability, the VoIP router, modem and phone had to be provided with a hefty and expensive backup power supply, with attendant maintenance issues and cost. Portable modems (such as those used by Vonage) were unable to incorporate backup power. Second, since the connection was not tied to a specific location, it was difficult to provide 911 services, even if the VoIP provider was able to connect the call to an appropriate emergency centre. Third, VoIP was not yet practically feasible for wireless customers; but in many markets wireless telephone users had surpassed the number of fixed-line

Exhibit 1 | Representative VoIP Services

Mode	Service Provider	Model	Cost/ month	Estimated Subscribers 12/04
PC-to-PC	Windows/MSN Messenger	P2P; voice chat.	Free	All MS OS users
	Freeworld Dialup	P2P; public Internet; SIP-phoneset enabled (no computer needed to talk); interconnects (peering) with many other services. No direct PSTN interconnect but can peer with per-minute services.	Free	500,000
PC-to-PSTN	Skype	P2P; public Internet, proprietary protocol, not compatible with other providers. Encrypted, firewall traversal, no service charge but PSTN interconnect at per minute rates (approx. $0.03 per minute).	Free	21 million
Phone-to-Phone	Vonage (worldwide)	Boxed VoIP/public Internet service.	$20–$45	360,000
	Primus Canada	Local Telephone/HSI/VoIP. Dedicated fiber network/gateways.	$12–$34	< 30,000
	Sprint Canada	Local Telephone/HSI/VoIP. Dedicated fiber network/gateways.	$20–$54	< 30,000

users. Fourth, VoIP had difficulty handling calls from interactive TV systems, alarm systems, faxes, etc. Fifth, as a software application, VoIP might prove to have unanticipated security vulnerabilities rendering the network prone to catastrophic attacks. And finally, VoIP quality of service deteriorated if any part of the transmission link, even momentarily, was overloaded. A service provider with a network of dedicated capacity spanning the calling area could provide a quality advantage by giving priority to their VoIP calls over other Internet traffic.

Bell Canada

Founded in 1880, Bell was the legacy telephone company in Canada. Originally a monopoly holding Canadian rights to the Bell telephone patent, it had sold assets early in its history to concentrate on its core territories of Ontario and Quebec. By 2004, the telephone industry in Canada was dominated by three regional,

regulated, near-monopolies. Telus operated service in British Columbia and Alberta, SaskTel in Saskatchewan, and Bell Canada in Ontario and Quebec, and also through Bell's majority stake in Aliant, the Eastern provinces. More than 50 small local telephone companies, relics of early competition in the industry, remained in business in Bell Canada's territory.

In 2004, BCE (Bell Canada's parent) was ranked Canada's 14th largest company, with revenues of US$19.2 billion and net earnings of US$1.52 billion. The regulated Bell Canada division provided all BCE's profit. At year-end 2004, Bell claimed 27 million customer connections through its telecommunications networks. Bell Canada provided fixed-line telephone and Internet services across 12.9 million residential and commercial local lines in its core territory of Ontario and Quebec. It served approximately 1.5 million residential customers in the Atlantic region through its majority stake in Aliant, and the sparser population across the north through Northwestel and others. Its Bell West subsidiary provided competitive local telephone service in Western Canada. Through a recent acquisition Bell had extended its Canadian high-capacity fibre network across Western Canada and into the United States. Bell also offered nationwide mobile telephony, satellite television and numerous other communications and information technology-related services (see Exhibit 2). While mobile telephone, high-speed Internet and video segments were showing strong growth, the fixed-line and long-distance segments were in decline (see Exhibits 3 and 4).

Throughout the 1990s, a massive wave of mergers swept through the communications and media industries globally, with giants such as Time-Warner-AOL extending their reach across film and television programming, music, print media, communications, Internet services and cable TV delivery. BCE similarly formed alliances with various media interests and acquired print and television assets. It diversified into IT services technologies, various fixed and wireless communications and acquired a newly privatized satellite operator, Teleglobe. The widespread expectation was that superior performance would be driven by the convergence of newly emerging communications technologies and media content production. The emergence of HSI connections to the consumer at the close of the 20th century seemed to confirm these predictions, as ever more consumer media delivery migrated onto the Internet protocol (IP) platform and became accessible through online sources. Bell Canada's modern national telecommunications networks, its respected household name and its reputation for reliable service, seemed to position it well to exploit media and communications convergence. With its full suite of services, Bell was well positioned to become the major integrated provider of digital content to the home.

Regulation

Canadian telephone services were regulated and supervised by the Canadian Radio-television and Telecommunications Commission (CRTC). The CRTC had been actively promoting competition in, first, long distance and then in local telephone service provision. At the end of 2004, competitive local telephone services had captured only a six per cent share;[1] however this was before the appearance of new independent VoIP services.

Telephone and cable TV companies had long competed in Internet access, and new technologies were rapidly erasing the barriers to competing in each others' regulated services as well; each industry possessed a network of installed connections to the majority of Canadian homes. The stance of the CRTC on VoIP regulation would determine the future competitive environment. Paradoxically, the incumbent phone operators had argued that the new VoIP services were software ("retail Internet applications") rather than telephony, and thus, according to a 1998 CRTC Internet ruling, were exempt from regulation. This would permit free competitive entry but also give Bell latitude to set its own pricing.[2] The cable operators, poised to enter the VoIP market, took the view that any VoIP service offered by the telcos should be price regulated.

In April 2004, the CRTC published preliminary findings that VoIP would be regulated in the same manner as PSTN service. Up to this point, the incumbent telecommunications firms faced regulated pricing in their home territories (defined by area code) but not elsewhere, whereas the competitive entrants faced no such regulatory controls. The CRTC had stated in its preliminary findings that any VoIP services offered by the incumbent telcos which supplied a regular phone number and functionally mimicked fixed-line services were to be similarly regulated. However, PC-to-PC voice services would not be regulated. In short, local service provision continued to be regulated for incumbents, while new entrants were free of price controls, whether they provided fixed-line or VoIP service. All were required to provide 911 service and support the national contribution mechanism that subsidized rural service provision.

The CRTC's intention was to foster a greater level of local service competition. However, it may simply have misread the competitive situation. The Canadian HSI market was relatively undifferentiated and uncompetitive; the dominant telephone and cable companies offered similar products at similar pricing. One industry observer stated: "Unlike traditional local phone service, VoIP dominance is not dependent upon local phone service control. Rather, the real danger lies with insufficient competition in the provision of high-speed Internet access, which serves as the prerequisite to effective VoIP services."[3] Indeed, industry luminaries were promoting 'universal broadband service' in place of universal telephone service subsidies. In Alberta, Canada, Bell was building a province-wide network of high-capacity optical fibre to provide such universal HSI service under contract to the provincial government.

[1] "Status of Competition in Canadian Telecommunications Markets," *CRTC*, November 2004.
[2] The CRTC set both the maximum and minimum amount the telcos could charge for voice services.
[3] "CRTC Picks Wrong Analogy in Net Telephony Ruling," *Toronto Star*, May 16, 2005.

Exhibit 2   BCE Corporate Structure

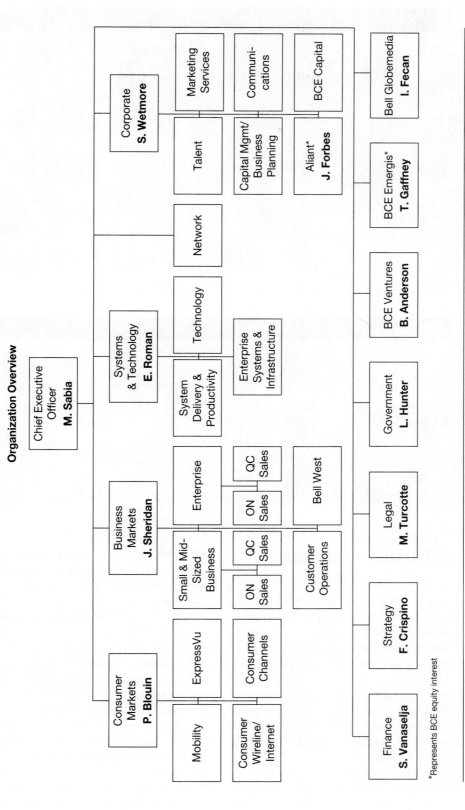

Organization Overview

Source: Bell Canada Enterprises Inc.

*Represents BCE equity interest

Exhibit 3   BCE Performance by Segment, 2004

	Revenue	% Revenue Growth on Prior Year	EBITDA
BCE Inc.	19,193	2.4	7,564
Bell Canada	16,787	1.6	7,111
Local & Access	5,572	(0.5)	
Long Distance	2,327	(8.5)	
Wireless	2,818	14.5	
Data/HSI	3,640	(2.1)	
Video	850	12.0	
Other	1,580	3.1	

Source: Company Annual Report, 2004.

Exhibit 4   Bell Canada Subscriber Base, 2004

	Subscription Base (thousands)	% Subscriber Growth on Prior Year	Subscriber Acquisition Cost, Cdn$
Fixed-line Telephone	8,332	(1.7)	N/A
High-Speed Internet	1,808	24	N/A
Video	1,503	7.7	571
Wireless Telephone	4,925	10.4	411

Bell Canada's Consumer Products Strategy

Bell operated seven networks, each configured to provide a different service. Under accelerating pressure from alternate long-distance service providers, competitive local service entrants and VoIP providers, Bell planned to simplify its structure to three interrelated networks, all functioning on IP platforms. In the process, it would eliminate a number of obsolete data services, migrating customers to IP. With associated simplifications to Bell's commercial and residential service delivery model, this was expected to reduce its annual operating costs by $1 billion to $1.5 billion by year-end 2006.

In October 2003, Bell announced trials of Internet-protocol TV (IPTV) service. Bell had recently deployed new technology on its nationwide fiber network, allowing it to efficiently carry VoIP telephony and IPTV alongside circuit-switched traffic. It was starting to deploy new technologies on its local networks that permitted residential service at 26 megabits per second (Mbps)—compared to three or four Mbps for regular HSI service—sufficient capacity to permit simultaneous high-definition IPTV, Internet access and VoIP service over the "last mile" connection to the home.

To reduce customer churn and increase service cross-selling opportunities in the residential market, Bell continued to aggressively market discounted bundling of multiple products, granting a $5 per month discount on each bundled service, in exchange for two-year contracts; in 2004, it sold 370,000 such bundles. Meeting competition from competitive local service providers head-on, it had included with its bundles a $5 per month long distance plan, giving customers 1,000 minutes calling time anywhere in North America. These strategies appeared to be paying off: in 2004, Bell increased its HSI subscriber base by 24 per cent to 1.8 million. More than 86 per cent of Canadian households had access to high speed Internet; however, only 36 per cent of all households subscribed. Clearly, strong growth was possible for some time yet. In contrast, the number of local phone lines decreased by approximately 1.1 per cent, due both to new competition and new HSI subscribers discontinuing second lines previously used for dialup modems. Long-distance revenues continued their steady decline, decreasing by 11 per cent in 2004.

Underlying all of Bell's consumer offerings was an implicit guarantee of the high service reliability and maintenance standards that had characterized fixed-line telephony for a century.

The Cable Competitors

Increasingly the cable companies offered services competing with those of Bell. Their regulated television service was offered in exclusive but limited territories overlapping Bell's telephone service area. Rogers had the largest cable network in Ontario but Cogeco and Shaw were also significant players. Vidéotron and Cogeco were the large players in Quebec (see Exhibit 5). In 1985, Rogers introduced a national wireless telephone service and purchased an interest in a competitive long-distance provider, Unitel, in 1992. Bell Canada launched its Canada-wide direct-to-home satellite TV service in 1997 to compete with cable television. While Bell introduced

Exhibit 5	Cable Competitors within Bell Canada Service Area				
	BCE	Rogers	Shaw	Cogeco	Videotron/ Quebecor
Corporate Results					
Revenue, $M	19,193	5,608	2,080	648	10,982
EBITDA, $M	7,564	1,734	926	215	1,759
ROE%	12.0	−2.9	2.8	−3.2	7.9
Assets, $M	39,143	13,272	7,557	1,929	14,404
Debt/Equity	0.9	2.8	1.1	2.4	2.4
Telecom/TV					
Revenue, $M	16,787	4,730	2,080	527	879
EBITDA, $M	7,111	1,659	926	203	364
Subscribers, k					
Wireline	12,905	—	—	—	—
Wireless	4,925	5,518	—	—	—
HSI	1,808	937	1,021	245	1,064
Cable/DTH TV	1,503	2,930	3,491	503	1,450
Core network area (cable/fibre)	Ontario & Quebec	Ontario, New Brunswick, Newfoundland	British Columbia, Alberta, Manitoba, N.W. Ontario	Ontario & Quebec (scattered territories)	Quebec
Core services	PSTN, HSI	Cable TV, HSI	Cable TV, HSI	Cable TV, HSI	Cable TV, HSI
Other services	Nationwide wireless, satellite TV and long distance telephony network	Nationwide wireless	Nationwide satellite TV		
VoIP launch date	2005	2005	2005*	2005	2005

*Service to be launched across Western Canada with Bell Canada providing wholesale telecoms and PSTN interconnect services.

dialup Internet access in 1995, the cable companies were the first to market with high speed Internet service in the late 1990s and still held a 55 per cent share in this market. In 2004, Bell was conducting trials of an IP-based TV service over its wire network. While competition had emerged across the spectrum of services, the cable companies did not have the scale or geographical reach of Bell and most were highly leveraged.

In 2004, the major Canadian cable TV providers announced "quadruple-play" bundled offerings of digital TV, HSI, wireless telephones (offered directly or through partners) and now VoIP, starting early in 2005. Their VoIP service would be configured to use a multi-purpose modem in place of the existing Internet modems. Although the details were not public, it was expected they would include battery backup (unlike OTT VoIP offerings such as Vonage's using portable modems). And importantly, they need not require purchase of HSI service. Unlike OTT VoIP offerings, features additional to the basic telephone package could be ordered on an individual basis or in packages, much like regular Bell PSTN service, making these services accessible to users without computers or Internet.

Installation required a service call and an expense of several hundred dollars. In order to wire its VoIP modem into the residential telephone wiring to "light up" all the jacks, the cable TV company installer must first enter the premises to install the modem, and then disconnect the telephone company service lines. Doing so would impede Bell's ability to win such customers back.

With battery backup and fixed location the cableco VoIP services would not have the 911 or power interruption problems of OTT VoIP. However, historical reliability rates for cable service were low compared to the telephone system, creating a potential barrier to consumer acceptance for their proposed primary-line service.

While their pricing had not yet been announced, the cablecos were expected to enter at a level highly competitive with Bell, the regulated incumbent. The cablecos were preparing to mount an assault on Bell's share of customer connections, offering the convenience of a single billing for all communications and TV services. Moreover, with 56 per cent of the 4.5 million Canadian residential subscribers to HSI service,[4] cable firms were expecting to convert 30 per cent to VoIP within four years of introducing the service.[5]

VoIP: A Disruptive Innovation?

Vocaltec of Israel marketed the first consumer software for computer-to-computer VoIP in 1995. While "calls" were free, the call quality was poor, and user features rudimentary. The low transmission rates possible over dialup consumer Internet connections resulted in static, echo, and latency (missed packets and gaps), making conversation, or even maintaining connections difficult. At this early stage VoIP was ignored by most telephone customers.

By 2004, VoIP had progressed from its start as a quirky product of interest only to technology hobbyists, and had become a competitive telecommunications delivery medium. As the base of HSI subscribers increased, VoIP P2P computer software for individual users had been redesigned to exploit HSI's higher data capacity and provided near-PSTN quality. Third-party networks permitted these services to interconnect to the PSTN to call regular telephones, increasing their functionality. Several entrants including Vonage, a leading U.S. VoIP provider, had launched residential modem-based VoIP service in Canada during 2004 (see Exhibit 1). Every major cable television operator in Bell's service areas had announced plans to offer telephone service using VoIP during 2005.

Estimates for the rate of uptake at the end of 2004 were tiny, and varied from 10,000[6] to 32,800;[7] analysts cited the lack of "dry loops" (Bell did not sell HSI service without underlying voice service), lack of consumer awareness and the small size and lack of credibility of VoIP providers as factors. However Vonage, claimed to be adding 30,000 new subscribers per month in the United States. Skype claimed to have added more than two million subscribers in the United States and 21 million worldwide in the last year. Due to its peer-based structure, Skype was able to add 150,000 users per day without any equipment or marketing costs. Pundits estimated that the Canadian VoIP subscriber base would expand to 250,000 by the end of 2005,[8] and over two million by 2008,[9] with incumbent telecom firms retaining only 25 per cent of this market segment. In the words of Michael Sabia, head of BCE:

> There will also be a constellation of smaller players attracted by the much lower barriers to entry in an IP world. Primus and Vonage, for example, are offering national and even continent-wide Internet telephony with an investment of just $20 million or $30 million. That's a world—truly—a world of no barriers when compared to

---

[4] "Status of Competition in Canadian Telecommunications Markets," *CRTC*, November 2004.

[5] Goldman Sachs, quoted in "Hanging Up the (Old) Phone: IP Communication in 2004," *Stanford Graduate School Business Press*, p. 13, SM-127.

[6] Ian Angus, *Edmonton Journal*, March 7, 2005.

[7] Seabord Research, *National Post*.

[8] Michael Sone Associates, *Winnipeg Free Press*.

[9] Seabord Research, *National Post*.

the billions of dollars telecom companies spend to build and maintain their networks.[10]

VoIP telephony was a software service that operated independently of the technology used to deliver the HSI connection. Due to VoIP's minimal requirements for dedicated infrastructure, third-party VoIP providers were able to provide telephone service to any HSI subscriber at low prices, albeit without the reliability and 911 functionality of fixed-line service. A VoIP service often included all the optional features offered by fixed-line operators, voicemail, forwarding of voicemail to e-mail, multiple simultaneous forwarding of incoming calls, multiple area codes, and unlimited North American long-distance calling, for $35 to $45 a month, assuming the subscriber already had HSI. Comparable telephone service from Bell cost approximately $64. Basic VoIP service, with most of the software features but charges for long-distance usage, was on offer for $20 or less a month.

New VoIP entrants still had to convince customers to switch. After signing up the "early adopters," further customer acquisition could be expensive. Vonage's advertising costs alone had been estimated at US$400 per new customer. The telephone incumbents appeared to hold the high ground, with established voice customer relationships covering the majority of the market.

Close's Decision

From his discussions with Blouin and Sabia, Close understood that Bell was willing to pursue a disruptive route to residential VoIP service and to cannibalize existing voice revenues if necessary. Bell had already developed an OTT VoIP product comparable to Vonage's offering and had conducted limited trials. It too used a pocket-sized modem that could plug into any HSI connection, and lacked backup power. However, as Close summarized the situation:

> *Bell already has $25 million to $40 million invested in a VoIP product; it has a fantastic GUI, great demos and product. But there are problems with the billing system. There are significant concerns with quality of service and competitive differentiation. There appears to be no unique and compelling value proposition. The launch has been delayed because senior management does not have a clear picture of the overall strategy. Basically, VoIP implementation is quite dispersed. No one is really in charge; there are VoIP people, but for the most part, they are matrixed into other parts of Bell. It is an organizational as well as economic issue.*

Despite the apparent lack of momentum, BCE's 2004 annual report targeted 100,000 residential VoIP customers by December 2005.

It was apparent to Ron Close from his discussions at Bell that there was considerable uncertainty as to the possible implications of introducing VoIP. If Bell promoted a VoIP service, it could raise consumer awareness and the perceived legitimacy of the technology, paradoxically accelerating migration to competitive offerings by other entrants. In addition, Bell had been able to protect its customer base in recent years by bundling HSI with the underlying basic telephone service. Yet, to offer the OTT residential VoIP product, Bell would have to first unbundle HSI from voice, leaving its customers free to consider competitive services. And approximately $6 billion of Bell Canada's $7.1 billion EBITDA in 2004 was derived from fixed-line telephone and Internet service revenues. On the positive side, opportunities to rebundle HSI with new services such as VoIP and IPTV might be expected to expand Bell's profitable HSI customer base and value-added product revenue.

At first blush, the VoIP initiative, under the conditions Sabia had offered, looked like an ideal situation for an executive with Close's background. In developing new services for the 'digitally wired household,' Close felt Bell Canada could contribute technical expertise and resources second to none. Given Bell's 97 per cent market share, its customer database and its ability to put inserts in the seven million bills going out each month to consumers, the new enterprise would have marketing leverage he could only dream of in previous technology startups. Also, the VoIP opportunity was just the first of many possibilities in servicing the digital home.

Yet Close was grappling with a number of concerns. How significant was the disruptive potential of this emerging technology? If it were positioned as an independent value-added service, what would be its effects on Bell's core business? How could it be differentiated from the offerings of other providers like Vonage, Primus or the cablecos? How should it be structured within the organization? What would the decision mean for Close's future within Bell?

Bell faced mounting competition. Low-cost entrants were already in the market, the cable companies' entrance was imminent and Bell was only now readying VoIP for commercial launch. The regulator's response to VoIP was uncertain, but the CRTC had favored new entrants over incumbents in its preliminary ruling. Would Bell have to fight with its hands tied? Moreover, Bell had limited success with its previous forays into faster paced, unregulated ventures. Was this a challenge Close wanted to take on? He had some thinking to do before his next meeting with Sabia early in the new year.

---

[10] Michael Sabia, president and chief executive officer of BCE Inc., address to the Canadian Chamber of Commerce, February 25, 2004.

Blu–ray and HD DVD: Betamax–VHS 'Format Wars' Redux?

S. S. George

V. N. Prasad

S. Govind

"...obsessed with owning proprietary formats, Sony keeps picking fights. It keeps losing. And yet it keeps coming back for more, convinced that all it needs to do is push a bigger stack of chips to the center of the table."[1]

—*Jonathan Last in the* Philadelphia Inquirer, *in June 2006.*

"I don't think Toshiba will back down. Sony is unlikely to give up either. Inevitably there is going to be some confusion in the market and there's going to be another standard war."[2]

—*Analyst Carlos Dimas, in 2004.*

"Those who cannot remember the past are condemned to repeat it."

—*George Santayana, US philosopher, in* The Life of Reason, *1905.*

Introduction

In June 2006, Sony Corp. (Sony), one of the world's largest media corporations, released seven movie titles[3] (including *The Terminator, Black Hawk Down,* and *XXX*) on

Blu-ray[4]—a next generation DVD[5] format. The releases came a couple of months after the introduction of HD DVD players, and the release of several movies on HD DVD, a rival format developed by Toshiba Corp.[6] (Toshiba), a multinational electronics company. Blu-ray and HD DVD were at the center of a format war, which would decide the successor to the existing DVD format. Though both formats used similar technology, larger data storage capacity and better security features seemed to have given Blu-ray a slight edge over the HD DVD format.

This was not the first time that Sony was involved in a format war. In 1975, it had launched a video system targeted at the home market called 'Betamax'. Though it was quite popular initially, Betamax later had to compete with the Video Home System (VHS), a rival video format launched by JVC[7] in 1976. Through the 1980s, VHS sales far surpassed that of Betamax. Sony's failure to establish Betamax as the standard format was attributed largely to its sluggishness in forming alliances with others in the industry. Sony's marketing communication and promotion strategies were also blamed for the failure of Betamax.

Not wanting the Blu-ray to meet with the same fate as some of its earlier proprietary formats,[8] Sony made quick moves to form alliances with other electronics firms, PC

---

[1] "One last thing/Setting the stage for another flop?" www.philly.com, June 04, 2006.

[2] "DVD developers set for format war," www.macmoviemaker.com, November 12, 2004.

[3] By July 14, 2006, Sony Pictures had 26 movie titles on Blu-ray.

[4] The Blu-ray is named after the core technology used—a blue violet laser to read and write data on an optical disc. It is a combination of 'blue' (blue violet laser) and 'ray' (optical disc). The character 'e' was intentionally dropped so that the name could be registered as a trademark.

[5] DVD (sometimes known as the Digital Video Disc or the Digital Versatile Disc) is an optical disc storage media format. It is used for the purpose of data storage, especially movies. The optical disc used in computing, sound and video reproduction, is a flat circular, usually polycarbonate disc upon which data is stored in the form of pits inside a flat surface. The data is accessed by using a laser to illuminate the special material on the disc, which is usually aluminum.

[6] Toshiba is a Tokyo, Japan-based electronics manufacturing firm. It is the seventh largest integrated manufacturer of electric and electronic equipment in the world. Toshiba has a presence in diversified businesses like digital products, semiconductors, social infrastructure, home appliances, etc.

[7] Victor Company of Japan was referred to as JVC. It was established in Japan in 1927. In 1953, it became a subsidiary of Matsushita—a leading Japanese Electronics manufacturer which sold electronic goods under the brands Panasonic, National, Quasar, Technics, and Ramsa.

[8] Apart from the Betamax, Sony suffered reversals on its Minidisc, Universal media disc (UMD) for the Playstation Portable, Sony Connect, a competitor to Apple's iTunes, Super Audio CD which competed with DVD-audio, etc.

makers, and Hollywood studios. It formed the Blu-ray Development Association (BDA) in order to ensure support for the format. It also carried out an extensive promotion and PR campaign. Though HD DVD had certain advantages in cost because of a cheaper manufacturing process, Sony was confident that Blu-ray's greater storage capacity, superior video quality, and better copyright protection features along with the fact that it had wider support would help it win the latest format war. This was all the more crucial because much of Sony's future profitability depended on the success of Blu-ray.

Background Note

Masaru Ibuka (Ibuka), an engineer, and Akio Morita (Morita), a physicist, established a company called Tokyo Tsushin Kogyo K.K in Tokyo in 1946. The company started with an investment of ¥ 190,000 and initially employed 20 employees. It undertook repairs of electrical equipment and also attempted to build new products. In the early 1950s, Ibuka convinced Bell Labs[9] to license their transistor technology to his company. Subsequently, in May 1954, Japan's first transistor was launched. In 1958, the company was renamed as Sony.

The company later went on to introduce several breakthrough products in consumer electronics. Some of them were the Trinitron Color Television in 1968, the color video cassette in 1971, the Betamax VCR (video cassette recorder), the world's first home video system, in 1975, the Walkman in 1979, the electronic camera in 1981, the world's first CD Player in 1982, the first consumer camcorder in 1983, the 3.5 inch micro floppy disk in 1983, 8mm video in 1988, the first digital VTR (video tape recorder) in 1985, and the Memory Stick in 1988.

Apart from the technological breakthroughs, Sony also expanded globally. In 1960, Sony Corporation of America was formed. In 1968, Sony UK Limited was established. Sony even established manufacturing facilities in the two countries. It set up a factory in San Diego, USA, in 1972 and another in Bridgend, UK, to cater to the UK and other European markets, in 1974.

Sony also made several acquisitions over the years. In 1988, it purchased CBS Records Group, a music label from CBS, which became Sony Music Entertainment. In 1989, it acquired Columbia Pictures Entertainment, a film and television production company, to form Sony Pictures Entertainment. In 2002, Sony acquired Aiwa Corp., a consumer electronics company. In 2004, it merged Sony Music Entertainment with BMG to form Sony BMG Music Entertainment.

Sony's First Format War

In 1963, Sony introduced the first VTR for use in business and the airline, educational, and medical fields. In 1964, it introduced a new VTR called CV-2000 for home use. In 1971, it launched the 'U-Matic' system, the world's first commercial color video cassette format. In this format, the videotape was housed in a cassette as opposed to the open-reel format prevalent at that time. It had cartridges that used a ¾ inch tape and had a playing time of 90 minutes. Later, Sony developed two players—the VP-1100 video cassette player and the VO-1700 VCR—to play and record on the new tapes respectively. The 'U-Matic' system was quite popular in North America and Japan and was widely used in television stations, schools, and businesses.

In 1975, Sony introduced the Betamax home video system, derived from the 'U-Matic' system, in Japan and USA. Betamax had a ½ inch video cassette recording format that recorded for 60 minutes. Sony signed up several large retailers to market its Betamax VCRs. Sony Betamax SL-6300 VCR was launched in the US market in 1975, priced at US$ 1300.

Betamax vs. VHS

Earlier, in 1974, in order to establish the Betamax format as the standard, Sony had demonstrated the prototype to several electronic manufacturing firms and sought to license the Betamax technology. Initially, companies like Toshiba, Pioneer Corp.,[10] Aiwa,[11] Zenith,[12] and Wega Corp.,[13] signed up. However, several other companies like Matsushita, JVC, and RCA[14] declined. Sony was to learn very soon why JVC did not show any interest in licensing its technology.

---

[9] Bell Labs was the main research and development division of US Telecommunications Company American Telephone and Telegraph Company (AT&T).

[10] Pioneer is a leading Japanese multinational corporation. It is credited with the introduction of several innovative products in the consumer electronics industry like the interactive cable TV, plasma display, organic LED display, DVD Recording, etc.

[11] Aiwa is a Japanese consumer electronics company established in 1951. It introduced several new products like digital audio tape, headphone stereo, etc. In the late 1990s, it slipped into bankruptcy and was acquired by Sony in 2002.

[12] Zenith was an American television and radio manufacturer. It was the inventor of the remote control and introduced HDTV in America. In 1999, after it filed for bankruptcy it was taken over by the South Korean LG Group.

[13] Wega was a leading German audio/video manufacturer. It was acquired by Sony in 1975. In the early 1990s, the brand was phased out by Sony. Later in 1996, Sony launched new televisions using the *Wega* brand.

[14] RCA or Radio Corporation of America was established in 1919. It was a leading radio and television manufacturer. In 1986, it was sold to GE, which later sold its records division to BMG and its electronics division to Thomson SA.

In 1976, JVC introduced VHS, a rival video format that was not compatible with Betamax. By then, Betamax had sold over 100,000 units and had virtual monopoly in the market. JVC's VHS system attracted the attention of consumers primarily because the VHS tapes were capable of longer recording times (two to three hours) in comparison to the Betamax tapes then available, which had a recording time of only one hour. Consumers preferred the VHS format because they could record entire movies or TV programs on it leaving the recorder unattended, unlike the Betamax tapes, which required that the user be around to replace tapes, often mid-way through the program or movie. Therefore, despite enjoying considerable first mover advantage, Sony's Betamax had to cede 30 percent of the market to the VHS format within the first three months of the latter's launch.

JVC chose a strategy of licensing its VHS technology 'cheaply and widely'. Although this resulted in JVC losing substantial potential earnings, it nevertheless led to the wide-scale adoption of the VHS format by other consumer electronics firms. Sony, on the other hand, kept the Betamax standard proprietary and charged heavily to license it. As a result, several electronic manufacturing companies chose to go with VHS over Betamax. Even those companies which had initially signed up with Sony crossed over to VHS later.

Licensing was seen by many analysts as one of the important factors that tipped the scales in favor of VHS. With several electronics companies backing the VHS format, customers, too, felt that it was safe to buy a VHS machine. The fact that there was a variety of VHS models from different manufacturers available in the market meant that they were spoilt for choice. Analyzing the failure of Betamax, Morita later said, "We didn't put enough effort into making a family. … The other side, coming later, made a family."[15] The larger support also helped VHS players achieve scale which, in turn, helped reduce manufacturing costs. Consumers naturally preferred the VHS video recorders, which were priced around US$ 1,000, to the Betamax players, which were about US$ 200 costlier. VHS tapes were also priced lower than the Betamax ones.

The Betamax format, at least initially, was technically superior to the VHS format, offering better resolution and therefore superior picture quality, and lower video noise. However, over time, the VHS group caught up with Betamax. This was possible because several manufacturers were working on improving the VHS format and kept launching new models and features on a continuous basis. Some of the features like remote pause and built-in timers (Betamax recorders had external timers[16]) were unique to VHS recorders.

Initially, Sony marketed its Betamax on the machine's ability to "time shift" programming—to record a television program off the air even as the person was watching another show on a different channel. However, the VHS group countered this by offering the customers the ability to record four different programs over a one-week period, using the in-built timers in the VHS machines. This was not possible using the external timer in the Betamax machines.

Sony's promotion of the Betamax format was also considered by many to be far from satisfactory. In contrast, the VHS group advertised and promoted the VHS products in every possible way. Also, Sony reduced marketing and promotion efforts for the Betamax products once they became a little popular. It also failed to adequately promote the distinct technological features of Betamax.

Analysts argued that Sony had failed to recognize that items like video recorders were often bought on impulse. The VHS manufacturers realized this and ensured that their products were sold in different types of stores—in some cases, even in supermarkets. Sony persisted on selling its Betamax products only at high-end stores and as a result, failed to reach out to the mass market.

Several analysts also cited Sony's legal problems as one of the reasons behind the company losing the format war. Soon after Sony had launched its Betamax VCRs, Universal Studios had filed a case[17] (the Betamax case) against Sony. In this instance, the company faced what was essentially a first-mover disadvantage—it was the only one named in the case. Analysts felt that the long-drawn case might have caused a loss of focus at Sony.

Other reasons have been put forward for the eventual victory of the VHS format. According to some sources, Sony did not try to keep the Betamax technology all to itself. Therefore, more than restricted licensing, the price advantage enjoyed by VHS VCRs, the longer recording time of the tapes, and lack of adequate manufacturing capacity at Sony, which caused shortages in the availability of Betamax VCRs, could have been significant reasons for the demise of the Betamax format.

---

[15] "Betamax and VHS," Firms and Markets, A mini case, www.stern.nyu.edu.

[16] The external timer in the Betamax came about at the insistence of Morita. He felt that in the event of a clock malfunction, it could more easily be repaired without bringing the whole VCR to the repair shop.

[17] The studio demanded the withdrawal of the Betamax video recording machine, saying that it would allow customers to record programming off air—which they felt was an infringement of copyright. The lower court gave a judgment in favor of Sony. The studio appealed the decision. Later, the US court of appeals reversed the lower court's decision. Finally, the case was heard in the Supreme Court. In January 1984, the apex court, in a historical verdict, reversed the appeals court's decision and pronounced the VCRs as legal.

By 1984, while the Betamax group consisted of a handful of firms, the VHS group included almost 40 companies like Grundig, Hitachi, Matsushita, Mitsubishi, Philips, RCA, and Sharp—some of the biggest consumer electronics firms in Japan, Europe, and the US.

VHS Wins…

By the mid-1980s, sales of VHS machines were far ahead of Betamax. With the availability of video cassette players, more people were keen on watching movies in the comfort of their homes. Sensing a demand, JVC licensed the VHS technology to movie studios so that they could release their movies on VHS. Thus, for a time, video cassettes of just-released movies were available only on VHS. By the time movies came to be released in the Betamax format, Betamax was already on its way out. Also, when video cassettes were released, the studios expected that people would buy them the same way that they bought audio cassettes. However, a majority of the people in the US opted to rent the tapes rather than buy them. This led to the rapid emergence of video rental firms in the US, which went on to play a significant role in deciding the *de facto* home video standard.

The video rentals preferred the VHS format because in this format each movie required only one tape, which meant that it occupied less shelf space compared to a title in the Betamax format, which came as a two-tape set. VHS tapes also cost less than Betamax tapes. In addition,

if a customer lost or damaged one tape of a two-tape movie in the Betamax format, it meant that both tapes had to be replaced—a problem that did not occur with movies in the VHS format.

However, it was not certain whether the video rentals were the deciding factor in the eventual decline of the Betamax format, and the decline in the sales of Betamax machines. Some analysts argued that it was the decline in the sales of Betamax VCRs and consequent fall in the demand for Betamax tapes that prompted video rentals to either limit or completely stop their purchase of movie titles on Betamax. Others were of the view that with rentals choosing to stock more VHS tapes in preference to Betamax, the demand for Betamax machines saw a fall. Either way, the net effect was that the VHS format thrived, while Betamax withered away.

By 1988, the VHS format completely dominated the market, leading to the almost total disappearance of the Betamax format. Sony did spend millions trying to revive Betamax but by that time it was too late for it to make a comeback (*See Exhibit 1 for market shares of Betamax and VHS between 1975 and 1988*).

Sony gradually phased out the Betamax line. The final climbdown came in 1988 when the company adopted the rival standard, and began selling VHS VCRs. Sony's experience with its Betamax format became a part of the curriculum of many a business school the world over. Betamax also found its way into slang with the word being used as a verb ('Betamaxed') to mean a superior technology losing out to a popular technology. The

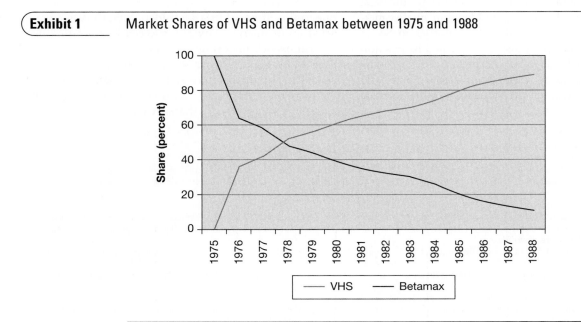

Exhibit 1   Market Shares of VHS and Betamax between 1975 and 1988

Source: Betamax and VHS, Firms and Markets, Mini-case, www.nyu.edu.

success of VHS and the failure of Betamax underlined the importance of alliances and marketing in the wars between competing standards. The fact that VHS won the war indicated that superior proprietary technology was not necessarily a guarantee for success in the marketplace.

...But Does Sony Lose?

Although the VHS format was the clear winner in the Betamax-VHS format war, it was a debatable issue whether Sony was the 'loser'. The competition between the two standards lasted a little over a decade and during that period Sony had sold several million Betamax VCRs. When the company finally started producing VHS video recorders in 1988, these sold well in Japan as well as in other countries. Masaaki Morita (Masaaki), then deputy president, Sony, said, "Speaking frankly, we didn't want to manufacture VHS. However, you don't conduct business according to your feelings. Let's look at reality. The demand is getting stronger in the marketplace for Sony-made VHS products."[18]

Though VHS went on to become the standard, it did not bring in much profit to the original backers of the standard. JVC, the developer of the technology, reportedly made little money because it had opted to license its technology at a nominal rate. The other players in the VHS group had to fight among themselves for market share and this led to price cuts and shrinking margins. The intense competition also led to higher marketing costs, which further affected their profitability.

Though VHS came to rule the US and Europe, the most important markets, Betamax found favor in smaller markets like the Philippines and some countries in South America. Meanwhile, Sony also consolidated its position in the professional video market. The Betacam,[19] a derivative of Betamax, was a major hit with professionals and broadcasters. Matsushita did launch the MII,[20] derived from the VHS, to compete with the Betacam; however,

this failed to catch on among professional users. Sony completely dominated[21] the professional video recording market from the 1980s till the late 1990s with products like the Betacam, the Betacam SP, and the Betacam Digital series. The fact that the professional market provided higher margins helped Sony's balance sheet. Even in the home-use segment, Sony's VHS VCRs were sold in large numbers. "In any event, Sony aims to posture itself as the number one comprehensive VCR manufacturer, with Betamax for high quality picture and recording, 8mm formats for optimal compact personal use, and VHS for home video rental,"[22] said Masaaki.

The Intervening Years

In the late 1980s, Sony along with Philips, Matsushita, and JVC developed and released a compact disc (CD) that could store video—both still and motion—in addition to audio. These discs were called Video CDs (VCD). Although VCDs were not popular in the more sophisticated western markets due to poor video quality and lack of support from the entertainment industry, they became popular in Asia because of their low prices.

The VCD was, in a way, a precursor to the DVD. In the early 1990s, two separate groups started work on developing a new high-density optical storage standard. While Sony and Philips developed the MultiMedia Compact Disc (MMCD),[23] the Super Density Disc (SDD)[24] was developed by Toshiba and Time-Warner Inc.[25] The SDD was also supported by Matsushita Electric, Hitachi Ltd.,[26] Mitsubishi Electric Corp.,[27] Pioneer, Thomson, and JVC. This time, a possible format war was averted due to the efforts of IBM's president, Lou Gerstner, who acted as an intermediary and succeeded in uniting the two camps behind a single standard.

Philips and Sony gave up their MMCD format and agreed to accept Toshiba's SDD as the standard format with two modifications.[28] Sony agreed to this arrangement in exchange for a share in the royalties that the

---

[18] "Becoming a comprehensive video manufacturer," www.sony.net/Fun.

[19] Betacam was different from Betamax in the sense that it recorded everything in the form of components at a high linear speed that helped it have better video and audio quality.

[20] MII, derived from VHS, was manufactured by Panasonic in 1986 as a competitor to Sony's Betacam. It was a failure because of insufficient marketing and the unreliability of the product.

[21] <http://www.terraguide.com/formats.html.>

[22] "Becoming a comprehensive video manufacturer," www.sony.net/Fun.

[23] MMCD was a single-sided compact disc that provided up to 7.4 GB of data capacity in a dual-layer configuration, or 3.7 GB on a single-layer disc. It was fully backward compatible with CD audio and CD-ROM discs. It was used for video applications, for which it offered a playback of up to 270 minutes of MPEG-2-quality video. It was also used for computer application as a high-density CD-ROM. (Source: www.nokia.com)

[24] SDD was a double-sided compact disc that provided 9 GB of data capacity. A later version SDD was single sided but had dual layers. It was also backward compatible with CD audio and CD-ROM discs.

[25] Time Warner, based in New York, is the world's largest media company with divisions in Internet, publishing, film, telecommunications and television divisions. It was formed after the merger of Warner Communications and Time Inc in 1987.

[26] Hitachi founded in 1910 in Tokyo, Japan is a consumer electronics manufacturing company.

[27] Mitsubishi Electric established in 1921 is one of the core companies of the Mitsubishi group—a large group of independently operated Japanese companies, which share the same brand name.

[28] The first modification was the adoption of a pit geometry that allowed "push-pull" tracking, a proprietary Philips/Sony technology. The second modification was the adoption of Philips' EFMPlus. The advantage of EFMPlus was its high resilience against disc damage such as scratches and fingerprints. (Source: cs-exhibitions.uni-klu.ac.at)

makers of DVD players paid to the companies that developed the technology and the standard format.

In 1995, the 'DVD Consortium'—an independent body consisting of the creators of the technology—was formed. In May 1997, the DVD Consortium was replaced by the DVD Forum, which was open to all electronics manufacturing/marketing companies. The first DVD players and discs became available in November 1996 in Japan, in March 1997 in the US, in 1998 in Europe, and in 1999 in Australia. In the late 1990s and early 2000s, DVD gradually overtook VHS as the most popular format for video and DVD players went on to become the fastest selling consumer electronics device of all time.

Sony and the Blu-ray

The non-adoption of its MMCD format was a significant blow for Sony. "It was an enormous loss of face and had very significant commercial consequences for Sony,"[29] said Warren Lieberfarb, former Warner Home Video president often called the father of the DVD, who was a consultant to Toshiba and a leading advocate of HD DVD.

The rapid acceptance of the DVD technology benefited Toshiba and the supporters of SDD more than Sony. Even though Sony received a share in the royalties that DVD manufacturers paid, it was relatively insignificant compared to Toshiba's earnings from the technology.

To change this situation, Sony had to become the first company to develop the next generation in video technology. At that time, the company was already developing the Professional Disc for DATA[30] (PDD) based on an optical disc system. PDD was very expensive; therefore, some modifications were made to the format to make it affordable to the average consumer. This led to the development of the Blu-ray Disc in the early 2000s. Around the same time, Toshiba and NEC Corp.,[31] were working on the 'Advanced Optical Disc' (AOD), their precursor to the HD DVD.

To achieve broad acceptance of the "Blu-ray Disc" format, Sony was quick to form an association called the Blu-ray Disc Founders (BDF) in May 2002. The association included Hitachi, LG Electronics Inc., Matsushita, Pioneer, Mitsubishi, Philips, TDK, Samsung Electronics Co. Ltd., Sharp Corporation, and Thomson Multimedia.

Prototypes of both discs were unveiled for the first time at CEATEC[32] 2002. In August 2003, Toshiba and NEC proposed to the DVD Forum that AOD be adopted as the next generation DVD. The developers of Blu-ray did not approach the forum as they felt that the Blu-ray was a new generation system that did not require the patronage of the DVD Forum. Moreover, the fact that it already enjoyed the support of most of the major member companies in the DVD Forum added to Sony's confidence. In November 2003, the DVD Forum adopted AOD and drafted the HD DVD format specifications.

In January 2004, HP and Dell, the world's two largest PC manufacturers (together, they accounted for around 30 percent of the global PC market) joined BDF. In May 2004, the BDF was renamed BDA or the Blu-ray Disc Association. This was done to seek new members to support the Blu-ray format, in addition to the founder members (*Refer to Exhibit 2 for a list of prominent members of BDA*).

In September 2004, Toshiba, Memory-Tech Corporation, Sanyo Electric Co., Ltd., and NEC, who were the main backers of HD DVD, formed the HD DVD Promotion Group. This association was formed to promote the development of HD DVD hardware and content (*See Exhibit 3 for a list of prominent members of HD DVD Group*).

Despite the emergence of a rival format, the members of the BDA, including Sony, were confident that the superiority of the Blu-ray technology would see the format through as the standard. According to the BDA, the Blu-ray format had several superior features compared to HD DVD. Apart from the higher storage capacity, Blu-ray supposedly had better copyright protection mechanisms, online capabilities, higher resolution (1080p), and advanced interactivity features. "In terms of technology, we have no weak points. Our format is superior on all counts,"[33] said Sony executive officer Kiyoshi Nishitani (*Refer to Exhibit 4 for features of Blu-ray and Exhibit 5 for a comparison of Blu-ray, HD DVD, and DVD*).

Forming Alliances

Learning from its Betamax experience, Sony set out to secure wider support, from companies ranging from content providers to computer makers, for the Blu-ray format.

---

[29] "Format wars, episode II: The DVD," www.hometheaterdiscussion.com, June 27, 2005.

[30] Professional Disc for DATA (PDD or ProDATA) is a recordable optical disc format, which was introduced by Sony in 2003. It utilized blue-violet lasers for reading and writing, which allowed for much higher density data to be stored on optical media. PDD had a storage capacity of 23 GB, a data transfer rate of 11MB/s for reading and 9MB/s for writing. PDD drives and media were available in the market in 2004. (Source: www.wikipedia.com)

[31] NEC (Nippon Electric Company Ltd.) headquartered in Tokyo, Japan is a leading global information technology company.

[32] CEATEC JAPAN (Combined Exhibition of Advanced Technologies) is the largest annual international exhibition in Asia for the technology and electronics industry, including the fields of imaging, information, and communications.

[33] "DVD developers set for format war," www.macmoviemaker.com, November 12, 2004.

Exhibit 2 | Prominent Members of BDA

Board of Directors	Apple, Dell, HP, Hitachi, LG, Mitsubishi Electric, Panasonic, Pioneer, Philips, Samsung, Sharp, Sony, TDK, Thomson, Twentieth Century Fox, Walt Disney, Warner Bros.
Contributors	Adobe Systems, Canon Inc, Dolby Laboratories Inc, Electronic Arts Inc., Kenwood Corporation, Lionsgate Entertainment, Nero, Paramount Pictures Corporation, Sony BMG Music Entertainment, Sun Microsystems, Inc., Universal Music Group, Victor Company of Japan Ltd., Fuji Photo Film Co. Ltd, DTS Inc, etc.
Members	BenQ Corp, Daewoo Electronics Corp, Daikin Industries Ltd., Lenovo, Sanyo Electric Co. Ltd, Toppan Printing Co. Ltd, Vivendi Universal Games, Yamaha Corporation, Pinnacle Systems, etc.

Source: www.blu-raydisc.com.

Exhibit 3 | Prominent Members of the HD DVD Promotion Group

Chair Company, Secretary	Toshiba Corporation
Vice-Chair Company	Memory-Tech Corp, NEC Corp.
Auditor	Sanyo Electric Co., Ltd.
General members	Canon Inc, Hewlett-Packard Company, Fuji Photo Film Co. Ltd., Hitachi Maxell Ltd., Kenwood Corp., Microsoft Corp., Lenovo Japan, Universal Pictures, Warner Home Video, Paramount Home Entertainment, etc.

Source: www.hddvdprg.com.

Recognizing the critical role that Hollywood studios played in the success of the VHS format, Sony went all out to woo these studios to adopt the Blu-ray system. It also tried to garner support for Blu-ray among electronics firms, technology firms, and game development companies. Sony even sought support from Matsushita, its major rival.

Sony's efforts began bearing fruit when some major Hollywood studios announced their support for Blu-ray. In October 2004, 20th Century Fox announced that it was joining the BDA. In December 2004, the Walt Disney Company and its home video division, Buena Vista Home Entertainment, announced their support for Blu-ray. However, the support was non-exclusive.

In March 2005, Apple Computer announced its support for Blu-ray and joined the BDA. In April 2005, Sony purchased Metro-Goldwyn-Mayer (MGM), a movie studio, for US$ 5 billion—a move that was expected to allow Sony to provide a huge library of classic movies in the Blu-ray format. This, in addition to the catalog of Columbia Tri-Star[34] (owned by Sony), gave Sony a good supply of high-definition content for Blu-ray players. In August 2005, Lions Gate Home Entertainment[35] announced it would release its content in the Blu-ray disc format. At the end of 2005, Warner Brothers and Paramount Pictures, major studios, announced that they would release movie titles on Blu-ray as well. This was a major victory for Sony because the two studios had initially declared exclusive support for HD DVD (*See Exhibit 6 for a list of movie titles on Blu-ray*). As of early 2006, out of the six large Hollywood studios, only Universal Studios supported HD DVD exclusively. (*See Exhibit 7 for a list of movie titles on HD DVD*).

Sony also succeeded in winning support from several game development companies. In January 2005, leading game developers Electronic Arts and Vivendi Universal

[34] Columbia TriStar Motion Picture Group, with Columbia Pictures (CP) as its subsidiary, and TriStar Pictures, Inc., as the subsidiary of CP, was acquired by Sony Pictures from Coca-Cola in the late 1980s.

[35] The home video and DVD distribution arm of Lions Gate Entertainment. It is mostly concerned with the distribution of Lions Gate Film Library containing 8,000 films obtained mostly through output deals from other studios.

| Exhibit 4 | More about the Features of Blu-ray |

The quest for a new and advanced video format is never-ending. Though the DVD was hailed as a remarkable improvement over the VCD, both in terms of picture quality and other features, it soon lagged behind in the developments made in video technology.

Studios began offering a large amount of bonus material for which a DVD was proving to be insufficient. Also, when DVDs became vulnerable to piracy (The copy protection method on DVD is called Content Scrambling System[36] (CSS). In 1999, with the release of a DeCSS system, achieved through reverse engineering, the CSS system on DVD was broken) the need for a new copy protection method was felt. The most important reason for the need of new technology, however, was the introduction of High Definition TV (HDTV). Standard Definition TV (SDTV) had a resolution of 480p (progressive format[37]) while HDTV had a resolution of 720p or 1080i (interlaced format[38]). SDTV and HDTV were the two categories of display formats for digital television (DTV) transmissions. The problem with DVDs was that they supported only SDTV and didn't have the necessary storage capacity for HDTV.

Blu-ray is capable of recording over two hours of digital HD video and more than thirteen hours of SD video on a single disc. This is possible because Blu-ray utilizes a lens with a greater numerical aperture (NA) than HD-DVD. The laser spot can be focused with greater precision to fit in 67 percent more data than on an HD DVD disc of the same size.

Another important part of the Blu-ray standard was its online capabilities. Consumers could download extras, update content via the web, and watch the live broadcast of special events. Moreover some features on the disc could be kept locked. To access the locked material, purchasers simply had to contact the media owner. The purchaser could pay online and the locked material could be instantly activated. In this way, media companies expected to reduce distribution costs and keep the percentage paid to the retailer to a minimum.

The high data storage capacity made the Blu-ray suitable not only for movies but also for other applications like PC data storage and consumer electronic devices such as videogame consoles. The technology also gave the studios and game makers room to develop new and interactive features.

> *BD-ROM—read-only format for distribution of HD movies, games,*
> *software, etc.*
> *BD-R—recordable format for HD video recording and PC data storage.*
> *BD-RE—rewritable format for HD video recording and PC data storage.*
> *BD/DVD hybrid format, which combines Blu-ray and DVD on the same*
> *disc so that it can be played on both Blu-ray players and DVD players.*
> *Source: www.blu-ray.com.*

Blu-ray supports the AACS (Advanced Access Content System) standard, which calls for scaling down HD content to a low resolution if the player is not connected to a HDCP (High-bandwidth Digital Content Protection)-compliant connection.

Apart from the AACS, two other copyright protection mechanisms—the 'ROM Mark' and BD+—are installed on Blu-ray machines. The ROM mark is a cryptographic element overlaid on a "legitimate" disc. If a disc player fails to detect the mark, the disc will not play. This is adopted to deal with video-camera-in-the-theater copies and mass counterfeiting of content. The BD+ deals with a situation when the AACS system is cracked. The BD+ allows updation of the encryption scheme (via the Internet). All affected players can also be shut down remotely.

Mandatory managed copy (MMC) is another feature of the Blu-ray format. This enables consumers to make limited legal copies (authorized by the media owners through the Internet) of their Blu-ray movies for personal use. These features were adopted in order to attract US movie studios for whom DVD sales and rentals accounted for about 55 percent of the revenue from feature films (as of 2004).

Compiled from various sources.

---

[36] CSS is an encryption system that is incorporated into DVD products to prevent unauthorized copy.

[37] Progressive formats convey all of the lines of resolution sequentially in a single flash, which makes for a smoother, cleaner image, especially with sports and other motion-intensive content.

[38] In interlaced format the odd-numbered lines of resolution appear on the screen first, followed by the even-numbered lines—all within 1/30 of a second. This is more popular and less expensive than the progressive format.

Exhibit 5

Exhibit 5 | **A Comparison of the Features of Blu-ray, HD DVD, DVD**

S.No.	Parameters	Blu-ray	HD DVD	DVD
1	Storage capacity			
	single layer	25GB	15GB	4.7GB
	dual layer	50GB	30GB	8.5GB
2	Laser wavelength	405nm (blue laser)	405nm (blue laser)	650nm (red laser)
3	Numerical aperture (NA)	0.85	0.65	0.60
4	Disc diameter	120 mm	120 mm	120 mm
5	Disc thickness	1.2 mm	1.2 mm	1.2 mm
6	Protection layer	0.1 mm	0.6 mm	0.6 mm
7	Hard coating	Yes	No	No
8	Track pitch	0.32 μm	0.40 μm	0.74 μm
9	Data transfer rate (data)	36.0Mbps (1x)	36.55Mbps (1x)	11.08Mbps (1x)
	Data transfer rate (a/v)	54.0Mbps (1.5x)	36.55Mbps (1x)	10.08Mbps(<1x)
10	Video resolution (max)	1920 × 1080 (1080p)	1920 × 1080 (1080i)	720 × 480/720 × 576 (480i/576i)
11	Video bit rate (max)	40.0Mbps	28.0Mbps	9.8Mbps
12	Video codecs	MPEG-2 MPEG-4 AVC SMPTE VC-1	MPEG-2 MPEG-4 AVC SMPTE VC-1	MPEG-2
13	Audio codecs	Linear PCM Dolby (Digital, Digital Plus & TrueHD) DTS Digital Surround DTS-HD	Linear PCM Dolby (Digital, Digital Plus, & TrueHD) DTS Digital Surround DTS-HD	Linear PCM Dolby Digital DTS Digital Surround
14	Interactivity	BD-J	iHD	DVD-Video

Source: www.blu-ray.com.

Exhibit 6 | **Some Movie Titles Available on Blu-ray**

Terminator 2: Judgment Day	Basic Instinct: Risk Addiction	Black Hawk Down
The Terminator	S.W.A.T.	RoboCop
XXX	Species	Sense and Sensibility
The Fifth Element	Resident Evil: Apocalypse	Memento
Crash	Kung Fu Hustle	The Big Hit

Source: www.dvdtown.com.

Exhibit 7 | Some Movie Titles Available on HD DVD

The Bourne Supremacy	Rumor has it...	Million Dollar Baby
Constantine	The Perfect Storm	Last Samurai
Apollo 13	The Fugitive	Lara Croft: Tomb Raider
U-571	Assault on Precinct 13	Lethal Weapon
The Bone Collector*	The Interpreter*	Spy Game*

*to be released in the second half of 2006.
Source: www.dvdtown.com.

Exhibit 8 Revenue Share of Sony's Divisions for FY 2005

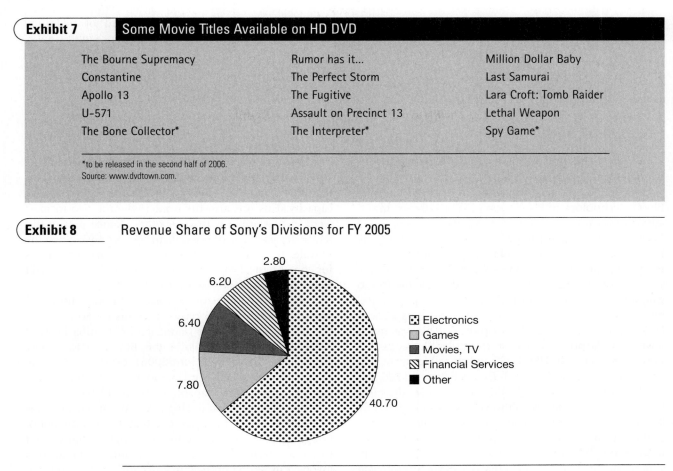

- Electronics
- Games
- Movies, TV
- Financial Services
- Other

2.80
6.20
6.40
7.80
40.70

Source: Marc Gunther, The Welshman, the Walkman, and the Salarymen, *Fortune Magazine*, June 19, 2006, pg 38–46.

announced their support for the Blu-ray format. This was a big boost to Blu-ray in the battle for supremacy as gaming was a US$ 20 billion industry worldwide and was as important as the film industry, in terms of size.

Promoting Blu-ray

Realizing the importance of promotion and consumer communication in securing acceptance for the Blu-ray format, Sony made efforts to get its message across to the end-users. It also hoped to use the strength of its movie, music, electronics, and games divisions to promote Blu-ray. The different divisions of Sony aimed to present a united front, promoting all products related to high-definition in order to give greater exposure to Blu-ray. "This crosses every part of our company. Blu-ray is (a) technology that will drive PC sales, consumer electronic sales, movie sales,"[39] said Ben Feingold (Feingold),

Worldwide President, Sony Pictures Home Entertainment (*See Exhibit 8 for the revenue shares of Sony's divisions in 2005–06*).

Since Blu-ray players would play DVDs as well, Sony decided on a communication strategy wherein it would indicate that movie titles were available on both DVD and Blu-ray. "We're saying it's available on DVD and on Blu-ray. That will be the strategy,"[40] said Feingold. When Sony released movie titles such as *Underworld* and *Underworld: Evolution* on DVDs, it promoted them through TV commercials. These commercials informed the customers that the titles were 'available also on Blu-ray.'

Sony organized Blu-ray product demos in Sony Styles, its company-owned stores. The company also organized several promotional events aimed at the media. It invited people from the media to view clips on Blu-ray and on HD DVD and experience the 'difference'.

---

[39] "Sony cross-promotes for Blu-ray," www.videobusiness.com, June 05, 2006.
[40] "Sony to launch Blu-ray marketing blitz," www.highdefdigest.com, June 06, 2006.

To further expand the variety of Blu-ray Disc offerings, Sony announced the release of two music video titles in the format—'*Rod Stewart: Live at the Royal Albert Hall*' and '*John Legend: Live at the House of Blues*', both shot in high definition format. "These dynamic concerts from John Legend and Rod Stewart have all of the immediacy and excitement of a live performance, giving fans high-definition video and uncompressed sound for an extraordinary entertainment experience,"[41] said Thomas Hesse, president of Sony BMG Music Entertainment's Global Digital Business unit.

Sony had announced in 2004 that it would be using Blu-ray technology in Playstation3 (PS3)—its next generation video game console.[42] The PS3, the successor to the PlayStation2 (PS2), was to be launched in June 2006. The much-anticipated PS3 was to be the last word in gaming technology and Sony expected the PS3 to replicate the success[43] of the PS2. Sony also planned to use the PS3 to gain a back-door entry for the Blu-ray into more households. Therefore, Sony was expected to price its PS3s at US$ 499 (20GB) and US$ 599 (60GB). This was much lower than the price point at which regular Blu-ray players were expected to sell (US$ 1,000 and above) (Sony reportedly was to incur manufacturing costs between $725 and $905 on each unit of PS3). "Without a doubt, the most important product for them this year is the PS3. Not only has it been a huge revenue and profit generator for them in the past, it is a Trojan horse for Blu-ray, which has big implications,"[44] said Ross Rubin, an electronics industry analyst for the NPD Group, a market research firm. Even if PS3s-with-a-Blu-ray-player were to be priced lower than regular Blu-ray players, the price was expected to be perceived as high because Microsoft's Xbox 360, the main competitor to the PS3, was priced lower at US$ 399[45] (at the time of its launch in November 2005 in the US).

Format Wars—Act II?

While Sony was busy preparing for the launch of the PS3 and other Blu-ray products, the rival camp was also launching new products, an indication that the new format war was picking up momentum. The two sides had briefly tried for a compromise in 2005, but their inability to reach an agreement only added fuel to the conflict. One of the main reasons quoted for the failure of the compromise move was the difference in the make-up of the disc—while the HD DVD disc required a 0.6 millimeter coating, a Blu-ray disc required 0.1 millimeter. This difference would cause a significant escalation in manufacturing costs for Blu-ray products.

HD DVD's thick coating was the same as the coating used in older DVDs, and required no major changes in manufacturing equipment. On the other hand, the thin coating on a Blu-ray disc required all-new manufacturing equipment. This feature could not be altered, as this was the main reason why Blu-ray discs had a greater storage capacity. This was also the reason why the two formats were incompatible with each other. "Since they're different designs, it's not possible to compromise down the middle. To come up with a mix of the two approaches for that physical layer would not be practical,"[46] said Brian Zucker, technology strategist at Dell.

The high manufacturing cost of Blu-ray discs and players was expected to cause problems for Sony. In the US, the HD DVD player (launched by Toshiba in April 2006) cost US$ 499 while the Blu-ray Disc player (launched by Samsung in June 2006) cost US$ 999. While Blu-ray discs cost between US$ 30 and US$ 40 each, the HD DVD discs were available for around US$ 30. However, Sony claimed that the high costs of Blu-ray products were not a matter of concern and that it was confident of bringing down costs in the future. It argued that since it was a new technology, there were significant initial costs involved in setting up new manufacturing lines and that once the format became widely accepted, there would be a reduction in manufacturing costs. "If we had made the determination solely based on cost, we would never have launched DVD. And that's absurd,"[47] said Adrian Alperovich, executive vice president, Sony Pictures.

Though several companies were backing the Blu-ray format, Sony could not bank on their continuing support if the situation were to evolve in favor of HD DVD, and against Blu-ray. Initially, companies in the PC industry (HP, Dell, and IBM) had strongly backed Blu-ray, but later changed their stance and stated that they would support both formats. Most movie studios were also covering their bets and had announced plans to release titles in both formats with price being the differentiator. Moreover, the

---

[41] "Sony readies first two music titles for Blu-ray," www.highdefdigest.com, June 05, 2006.

[42] The Playstation and Playstation2 (PS2) were very successful game consoles launched by Sony in 1995 and 2000 respectively. Despite its limited previous experience in the gaming industry and intense competition from Sega and Nintendo, Sony was able to become the market leader because of the depth and quality of its range of games.

[43] Sony had installed a DVD player in the PS2 in order to guarantee a presence in electronic stores that did not usually sell games consoles. This resulted in Sony selling PS2s to consumers who otherwise might not have purchased a games console. This proved to be a very successful strategy and as of November 2005, Sony had sold 100 million PS2 units—far outselling its closest competitor, Microsoft's Xbox.

[44] "The Welshman, the Walkman, and the salarymen," money.cnn.com, June 01, 2006.

[45] The 'basic' Xbox 360 with a wired controller was priced at US$ 299, while a 'premium' model with external hard drive and other extras sold for US$ 399.

[46] "Format wars, episode II: The DVD," www.avsforum.com, June 26, 2005.

[47] "Cost questions dog Blu-ray DVD's lead," www.zdnet.com, November 29, 2005.

HD DVD format was supported by Microsoft and Intel.[48] Microsoft had also announced plans to introduce HD DVD drives in its new Xbox 360, which would help the HD DVD format achieve deeper penetration.

Analysts were of the opinion that the need for High Definition products like Blu-ray and HD DVD would be felt only when High Definition Television (HDTV) broadcasts became popular in the US. They reasoned that since DVD recorders would not be able to record HDTV content, HD recorders (Blu-ray/HD DVD recorders) would find many takers. Also, if the viewer wanted a superior viewing experience, an HDTV was required to view an HD disc. However, in the US, as in several other countries, most households did not have HD receiving capabilities (HDTV sets or the requisite set-top boxes), despite the country framing rules[49] requiring all broadcasters to shift to HD by 2006 (as of 2006, only 26 percent of US households had HDTVs). The delay in the adoption of HDTV was expected to become a major obstacle in the adoption of Blu-ray/HD DVD technology.

Toshiba had launched its HD DVD players and released several movies in the HD DVD format in April 2006, while Sony had to postpone the launch of its products, which included players, recorders, drives, writers, etc., due to various unspecified reasons. Analysts speculated that this was probably due to the complicated design of Blu-ray. However, Samsung was able to launch a Blu-ray player to coincide with the release of the Blu-ray movie titles in June 2006. Sony also launched its *VAIO* notebook computers with an in-built Blu-ray player around the same time. Yet, most other companies like Pioneer had postponed the launches of their Blu-ray products (*Refer to Exhibit 9 for Blu-ray products to be launched by various players*).

After the launch of its HD DVD products in April 2006, Toshiba intensified its marketing efforts. The company organized live demonstrations of the technology in 40 cities across the US. This was done to train and educate retail salespeople on the benefits of the technology. It arranged to have displays of the HD DVD technology at stores to attract customers. Toshiba also had plans to step up the supply of HD DVD players.

While Sony and Toshiba were slugging it out, newer, and supposedly better, technologies were under development at other companies. These included the Digital Multilayer Disk (DMD),[50] the Forward Versatile Disc

Exhibit 9	Companies Planning to Offer Blu-ray Products		
Blu-ray Players	**Blu-ray Recorders**	**Blu-ray Drives**	**Blu-ray Media**
LG	LG	LG	LG
Mitsubishi	Mitsubishi	Panasonic	Panasonic
Panasonic	Panasonic	Philips	Philips
Philips	Philips	Pioneer	JVC
Pioneer	Pioneer	Samsung	Maxwell
Samsung*	Samsung	BenQ	Memorex
Sharp	Sharp	HP	Optodisc
Sony	Hitachi	Sony	Fujifilm
	JVC		Ricoh
	Yamaha		Ritek
	Zenith		TDK
	Sony		Verbatim
			Sony

*-launched in June 2006.
Source: www.blu-ray.com.

---

[48] Intel, short for Integrated Electronics, was founded in 1968. It has grown to become one of the world's largest semiconductor manufacturing companies. It also manufactures motherboard chipsets, networking ICs, etc.

[49] In the USA, the federal government framed a 15-year industrial policy in the early 1990s to ensure that there is a complete transition to DTV (Digital TV) by 2006. In 1997, the rule was amended to allow broadcasters to continue analog broadcasts until 85 percent of Americans had HDTV-receiving capabilities. The digital transition rules were codified in the Balanced Budget Act of 1997.

[50] DMD is an optical disc format created by D Data Inc., and had a storage capacity of 21 GB.

Case 6 / Blu-ray and HD DVD: Betamax–VHS 'Format Wars' Redux?

(FVD),[51] the Versatile Multilayer Disc (VMD)[52] and the most advanced of all—the Holographic Versatile Disc (HVD). The HVD[53] would have features far superior to both Blu-ray and HD DVD.

The rival new generation DVD formats also had to consider the threat from the growing size of hard discs on multimedia computers and the increasing number of websites that provided high definition content for downloading. The websites operated by Yahoo!, Google, Cinemanow, etc., offered consumers the facility to download movies over the Internet. "The longer the format war goes on, the more opportunity smart players in the cable and IPTV[54] and online spaces have to build market share,"[55] said Laura Behrens, an analyst at Gartner Industry Advisory Services.

Outlook

According to analysts, the format with the greater selection of movies had a better chance of ending up as the new standard. Hence, Sony was ensuring the release of a larger number of movie titles on Blu-ray. At least some industry analysts expected Blu-ray to overcome HD DVD. "Blu-ray is not only technically superior to HD DVD, it has a far stronger corporate backing, and has demonstrated the ability to have more content available to push the format,"[56] said gadgets blog Gizmodo in a feature. According to Ted Schadler, analyst at Forrester Research, "After a long and tedious run-up to the launch, it is now clear to Forrester that the Sony-led Blu-ray format will win. But unless HD DVD abandons the field, it will be another two years before consumers are confident enough of the winner to think about buying a new-format DVD player."[57] The two formats (Blu-ray and DVD) were most likely to co-exist for some time until HDTV became more widespread.

In February 2006, Sony had announced that it would postpone the launch of the PS3 with the Blu-ray player. Reports suggested that it was improving its console's Blu-ray disc player's copyright protection capabilities. The company announced that it would launch the PS3 in time for the main shopping season in the US—November 2006. The repeated postponement of the launch of the PS3 was set to cause a fall in the group net income of Sony by more than half for the fiscal year ending March 31, 2006, to US$ 592 million from US$ 1.4 billion for the previous fiscal year.

This postponement also dealt a blow to Sony's bid to improve profitability through Blu-ray products. Sony incurred losses in its electronic business segment in 2004 and 2005 and was banking heavily on the new format to improve profitability (*See Exhibit 10 for the operating income of various Sony divisions and Sony's financial highlights*). Sony had already spent several hundred millions on research and development for the Blu-ray format. The fate of Blu-ray was expected to have a far-reaching effect on the company's future.

From the customer's point of view, the Blu-ray vs. HD DVD format war seemed premature. Considering that it had been only a few years since the DVD format was launched, customers, in general, were not too keen on buying new hardware/software. "My suspicion is that most consumers will—and frankly, should—wait for prices to fall, and more movie titles to become available. Regular DVD gear is still cheap and good quality, with a broad choice of titles,"[58] said Edward C Baig of *USA Today*. Even if a few customers were willing to buy the new machines, they would be nervous about investing in a format that could quickly become obsolete. James Penhune, media analyst, Strategy Analytics[59] said, "When you introduce an element of confusion, you're encouraging the consumer to put off the purchase. That's been the case with previous format wars."[60]

There were also indications that this format war could turn out to be quite different from the first one. Although previously it had been believed that licensing issues would make such a move impossible, there were reports that LG, Samsung, and Toshiba were planning to launch dual format Blu-ray and HD DVD players—devices that could play discs in both the competing formats.

---

[51] FVD, developed by a Taiwanese consortium and introduced in China, is an optical disc format using the red laser. It has a storage capacity of 11 GB and uses the Windows Media Video 9 technology to store two hours of high definition content on a disc.

[52] VMD is an optical disc technology developed by New Medium Enterprises Inc., London. It uses the red laser to store 20 GB to 40 GB per disc. The company intended to market its format mostly in China and India with a possible expansion into Eastern Europe, Russia, and South America.

[53] The HVD is being developed by Optware (a Japanese company) in association with Fuji Photo and CMC Magnetics. It involves the combination of the red and blue lasers to form a single ray. This was expected to increase data storage capacity on a DVD to 1 TB (1000 GB or 20 times as that of Blu-ray). In February 2005, the three developer companies allied with Nippon Paint, Pulstec Industrial, and Toagosei to form the "HVD Alliance". As of 2006, the format was still under development.

[54] IPTV is a system where a digital television service is delivered using the Internet Protocol over a network infrastructure, which could include delivery by a broadband connection.

[55] "DVD format battle rages at gadget show," www.taipeitimes.com, January 08, 2006.

[56] "Blu-ray has already won," www.gizmodo.com, October 22, 2004.

[57] "Blu-ray to win format war?" www.businessweek.com, October 21, 2005.

[58] Edward C Baig, "Samsung's new Blu-ray DVD player is pretty nifty—and pretty pricey," www.usatoday.com, June 21, 2006.

[59] Strategy Analytics was founded in 1968 in Boston, USA. It is an international research and consulting firm that studies the opportunities and changing dynamics in the fields of Information, Communication and Entertainment.

[60] "Format wars, episode II: The DVD," forums.dvdfile.com, June 26, 2005.

Exhibit 10

A. Share of Sony's Divisions in the Company's Operating Income 2005–06

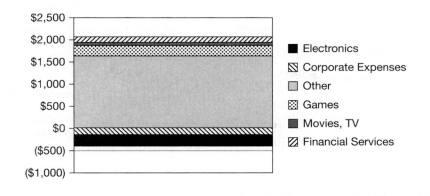

■ Electronics
◩ Corporate Expenses
▢ Other
▩ Games
▨ Movies, TV
▨ Financial Services

Source: Marc Gunther, The Welshman, the Walkman, and the Salarymen, *Fortune Magazine,* June 19, 2006, pg 38–46.

B. Sony's Financial Highlights by Business Segment

	2003	2004	(in Billion ¥) 2005
Electronics			
Sales	5096.0	5042.3	5021.5
Sales and Operating Revenue	4624.2	4828.3	4786.2
Operating (Loss) Income	659.0	(6.8)	(34.3)
Games			
Sales	955.0	780.2	729.2
Sales and Operating Revenue	936.3	753.7	702.5
Operating (Loss) Income	112.7	67.6	43.2
Music			
Sales	466.3	440.3	249.1
Sales and Operating Revenue	433.1	409.5	216.8
Operating (Loss) Income	(28.3)	(6.0)	8.8
Pictures			
Sales	802.8	756.4	733.7
Sales and Operating Revenue	802.8	756.4	733.7
Operating (Loss) Income	59.0	35.2	63.9
Financial Services			
Sales	537.3	593.5	560.6
Sales and Operating Revenue	509.4	565.7	537.7
Operating (Loss) Income	22.8	55.2	55.5
Others			
Sales	261.1	266.3	254.4
Sales and Operating Revenue	167.9	172.8	182.7
Operating (Loss) Income	(28.3)	(12.1)	(4.1)

Source: Sony Annual Report, 2005.

References & Suggested Reading

1. **Toshiba taking loss on initial HD DVD player shipments, iSuppli says,** June 26, 2006, www.digitimes.com.
2. Clint DeBoer, **10 reasons why High Definition DVD formats have already failed,** June 21, 2006, www.audioholics.com.
3. Greg Sandoval, **Hi-def DVD format war just got hot,** April 19, 2006, www.cnet.co.uk.
4. Leo Lewis, **Toshiba is first to the draw in war for the next generation of DVDs,** March 22, 2006, www.business.timesonline.co.uk.
5. Jennifer Netherby, **High-def to get limited launch. Sony, Warner movies headed only to stores with players,** February 02, 2006, www.videobusiness.com.
6. Carl Howe, **The Wall St. Journal's faulty conclusion from the VHS-Betamax war (SNE),** January 26, 2006, www.ce.seekingaplha.com.
7. Aaron Dobbins, **HD DVD: Blu-ray has problems,** www.betanews.com, January 07, 2006.
8. Jacqueline Oud, **DVD marketing war: Sony's Blu-ray against Toshiba's HD-DVD,** December 22, 2005, www.marketing-planet.com.
9. **Analyst backs Blu-ray,** October 24, 2005, www.pcpro.co.uk.
10. Simon Perry, **Unified DVD format trouble confirmed,** August 24, 2005, www.digital-lifestyles.info.com.
11. Andy Patrizio, **What's next for DVD? Blu-ray and HD-DVD battle for your home theater,** June 16, 2005. www.tgdaily.com.
12. **The chronicles of a futile battle: Blu-ray vs. HD-DVD: Is DVD fading away?** March 13, 2005, www.softpedia.com.
13. Steve Busfield, **Titanic battle over new DVD format,** www.money.guardian.co.uk, November 23, 2004.
14. Faultline, **Microsoft supporting Blue Laser? What about Blu-ray? Err, maybe,** July 31, 2004, www.theregister.co.uk.
15. Wally Bock, **Postcards from the digital age lessons from Betamax and the Macintosh Computer,** March 08, 2004, www.bockinfo.com.
16. **DVD future hits fork,** November 14, 2003, www.dvd-recordable.org.
17. **Betamax and VHS,** Firms and Markets, Mini-case, August 28, 2002, www.nyu.edu.
18. **Recordable DVD's - Betamax/VHS all over again,** February 25, 2001, www.d-silence.com.
19. **A closer look at Blu-ray vs. HD DVD burning,** www.burnworld.com.
20. Al Fasoldt, **How Sony killed Betamax,** 1988, www.aroundcny.com.
21. www.blu-raydisc.com.
22. www.wikipedia.com.
23. www.hddvdprg.com.
24. www.techspot.com.
25. www.blu-ray-technology.com.
26. www.macworld.com.
27. www.videohelp.com.
28. www.engadget.com.
29. www.betainfoguide.com.
30. www.gizmodo.com.

CCL Industries Inc.: Divesting the Custom Division

Larry Tapp

Trevor Hunter

Introduction

In 2004, Donald Lang, vice chairman and chief executive officer (CEO) of CCL Industries Inc. (CCL), faced an important strategic decision. The firm was contemplating selling its Custom Manufacturing Division. This division had been the basis for CCL's founding and still contributed approximately 34 per cent of overall earnings. Although the firm had acquired and divested many business units throughout its history, this divestment was perhaps the most significant in terms of its historical importance. Since Lang's father had founded CCL 54 years earlier as a custom manufacturer of aerosols and other consumer products for other firms, the divestment of this division represented a major change to the essence and strategy of the firm. Lang knew that he would need all his knowledge and experience, as well as that of the board of directors, to decide if such a transaction made strategic and economic sense.

CCL Industries Inc.[1]

CCL Industries Inc. was originally known as Connecticut Chemicals Limited (CCL), one of the first fillers of aerosol products in North America. Through a series of acquisitions over the decades, the firm became a leading producer of value-added outsourcing custom products and packages for numerous large consumer packaged goods companies. The firm evolved into three lines of business: Container, Label and Custom Manufacturing. In 2003,

CCL employed approximately 6,100 people at 42 production facilities around the world. Throughout most of CCL's history, the Custom Manufacturing Division was the largest business unit of CCL, and, as a result, CCL was mostly identified as an outsourcing company.

CCL's customers included some of the largest packaged goods retailers and manufacturers in the world. As such, their clients were located in multiple locations and required container, label and manufacturing solutions for hundreds of specific products.

The Container Division produced specialty containers, such as recyclable aluminum cans, bottles and plastic tubes. These containers were manufactured for the consumer products industry from five plants located in the United States, Canada and Mexico. The Label Division produced labels and other promotional products, such as pressure-sensitive, in-mold and expanded content labels, packaging inserts and shrink sleeves. These products were purchased by customers in the personal care, food, beverage, healthcare, battery and chemical industries from 32 locations around the world. The Custom Manufacturing Division produced personal care, over-the-counter medication and specialty food products in aerosol and liquid format. These products were shipped to global customers from four wholly owned operations in North America and six jointly owned facilities in Europe. Exhibit 1 presents selected divisional financial information.

---

[1] Much of the information in this section was found in the 2004 CCL Annual Report.

Richard Ivey School of Business
The University of Western Ontario

RESULTS OF OPERATIONS

	2004	2003	2002
Divisional sales			
Custom Manufacturing	$800.3	$801.0	$908.9
Container	212.7	217.0	231.8
Label	500.9	412.1	403.8
Sales of continuing operations	1,513.9	1,430.1	1,544.5
Sales of disposed operations	4.6	88.3	140.4
Sales as reported by the Company	$1,518.5	$1,518.4	$1,684.9
Income from operations			
Custom Manufacturing	$37.2	$44.1	$54.8
Container	17.2	21.7	18.4
Label	54.4	33.6	31.3
Contribution from continuing operations	108.8	99.4	104.5
Income from disposed operations	0.6	11.1	12.3
Divisional operating income	$109.4	$110.5	$116.8
Identifiable Assets			
Custom Manufacturing	$411.9	$314.4	$378.7
Container	261.7	249.6	404.7
Label	512.5	520.9	404.0
Corporate	87.9	107.0	155.5
Total	$1,274.0	$1,191.9	$1,342.7
Goodwill			
Custom Manufacturing	$65.9	$35.6	$40.5
Container	51.5	54.6	63.8
Label	198.1	207.8	170.7
Corporate	–	–	–
Total	$315.5	$298.0	$275.1
Depreciation & Amortization			
Custom Manufacturing	$21.0	$19.2	$20.2
Container	17.7	22.2	30.2
Label	28.6	24.9	24.2
Corporate	1.1	1.1	1.0
Total	$68.4	$67.4	$75.8
Capital Expenditures			
Custom Manufacturing	$19.8	$29.1	$22.3
Container	44.9	34.2	14.8
Label	46.8	48.8	33.7
Corporate	.3	.1	.6
Total	$111.7	$112.2	$71.4

Note: All figures are in millions. Numbers have been rounded and may not total exactly.

Donald Lang and the CCL Board

After graduation from the Richard Ivey School of Business, in London, Ontario, Lang worked at Nabisco Canada for two years prior to joining CCL in 1982. Over the years, Lang spent most of his years in operating roles in CCL's first and largest business unit, CCL Custom Manufacturing, and eventually rose to the position of president of CCL's Custom Manufacturing Division in 1992; president and chief operating officer (COO) of CCL in 1998; president and CEO in 1999; and finally vice chairman and CEO in 2005.

Donald Lang had a very strong ethic towards good governance. Despite the firm's dual-class share structure in which the Lang family owned a majority of the voting stock, the CCL board was made up of a majority of outside and independent directors, including a non-executive chair. Neither Lang nor his brother Stuart (president of CCL Label International) sat on any of the committees of the board of directors, resulting in a fully independent board. Exhibit 2 presents profiles on CCL's directors in 2005. Exhibit 3 presents a brief description of CCL's corporate governance structure.

Although many of the directors served on other boards, most agreed that the CCL board was one of the most effective. Director Tom Peddie commented on the board's effectiveness:

> The board was made up of individuals who had high personal integrity, who were committed to the board, and therefore committed in their time and would not "just show up," and believed in the potential value of the company. They were successful individuals with a variety of experience and the ability to express an opinion.

Exhibit 2 CCL Industries Inc. Board Profile

Directors

Jon K. Grant, O.C., B.A. (Hon.), LL.D. Chairman

Jon K. Grant is chairman of the board of CCL Industries, chairman of the board of Atlas Cold Storage and vice chair of Agricore United and a director of AXA (Canada) Insurance. He is also retired chairman and CEO of Quaker Oats Company of Canada Limited, retired chairman of Laurentian Bank, and past chair of the board of governors of Trent University. He is a former chairman of Scott Paper Limited and Canada Lands Company and is currently chair of the Nature Conservancy of Canada. Mr. Grant has served as a director of CCL since 1994.

Paul J. Block

Paul J. Block is chairman and CEO of Proteus Capital Associates, LLC, an investment banking firm, operating partner of Behrman Capital, a private equity group, principal of Sea Change Group, a private equity group, and president of Versadial, a wholly owned division of Sea Change. Previously, Mr. Block was a senior consultant to Lehman Brothers, senior advisor to American International Group (AIG) and chairman and president of Revlon International. Mr. Block is a board member of the China Retail Fund and the Shanghai-Syracuse University International School of Business and is a member of the Advisory Board of the Syracuse University School of Management. Mr. Block has served as a director of CCL since 1997.

Susan J. Cook, M.B.A., B.A.

Susan J. Cook is the vice-president, Human Resources, of Eaton Corporation, in Cleveland, Ohio. Previously, Ms. Cook held the position of vice-president, Human Resources, at Tandem Computers Inc., after a 17-year career in human resources at IBM Corporation in Boca Raton, Florida. Ms. Cook joined the CCL board in 2004 and also serves on the boards of the HR Policy Association in Washington, D.C., and the Center for Advanced Human Resources Studies at Cornell University. She is also on the board of the Achievement Center for Children in Cleveland, Ohio.

(continued)

Exhibit 2 | CCL Industries Inc. Board Profile (continued)

Dermot G. Coughlan, F.C.C.A.—U.K.

Dermot G. Coughlan is chairman and CEO of Derland Holdings Inc., a private investment holding company. He is also the former founder, chairman and CEO of Derland Industries Limited. Mr. Coughlan has served as a director of CCL since 1991. He is a member of, and has served on, the board of the Chief Executives Organization in addition to a number of community and private boards. He currently provides international consulting services to a variety of major industrial concerns worldwide.

Jean-René Halde, M.B.A., M.A.

Jean-René Halde has been CEO of Experlead Corporation, an advisory service firm to senior management and boards since September 2003. He has extensive experience as a CEO having assumed that role for the past 25 years at: Metro-Richelieu Inc., Atlantique Image & Son Inc., Culinar Inc., Livingston Group Inc. and Irwin Toy Limited. Mr. Halde is chairman of OMERS Capital Partners and a member of the World Presidents Organization and the Institute of Corporate Directors. He has served as a director of CCL since 2001.

Donald G. Lang, B.A. (Hon.) President and CEO

Donald G. Lang became president and CEO of CCL in 1999. Previously, he was CCL's president and COO, after leading the CCL Custom Manufacturing Division in Chicago, Illinois for five years. A twenty-three year veteran of CCL, Mr. Lang has been a company director since 1991, is on the boards of ColepCCL and AGF Management, a mutual fund company, and on the Board of Governors for Junior Achievement of Central Ontario. Mr. Lang holds an Honours Bachelor of Arts degree from the Richard Ivey School of Business, University of Western Ontario.

Stuart W. Lang, B.Sc. (Eng.) President, CCL Label International

Stuart W. Lang became president, CCL Label International, in February 2002. Previously, he was president of CCL Label Canada/Mexico and has been a director since 1991. He has held senior positions throughout the Custom Manufacturing and Label Divisions since joining the Company in 1982. Prior to this, Mr. Lang played for the CFL's Edmonton Eskimos for eight years following his graduation from Queen's University in Chemical Engineering in 1974.

Thomas C. Peddie, FCA

Tom Peddie is senior vice-president and CFO of Corus Entertainment. Mr. Peddie also has extensive media experience both in broadcast and print, as president of WIC Western International Communication. He held the CFO position at CTV Television Network and the Toronto Sun Publishing Corporation. Mr. Peddie previously held the position of CFO for Campbell Soup's international operation in the U.S. Mr. Peddie is a chartered accountant and holds an Honours Bachelor of Commerce degree from the University of Windsor. Mr. Peddie has served as a director of CCL since 2003.

Lawrence G. Tapp, LL.D.

Lawrence G. Tapp retired as dean of the Richard Ivey School of Business in June 2003. He is an international chief executive officer as well as an innovative educator. Mr. Tapp is the chairman and director of ATS Automation and Call-Net Sprint, lead director of Wescast Industries and a director of Talisman Energy. A CCL director since 1994, Mr. Tapp was vice chairman, president and CEO of Lawson Mardon Group Ltd. from 1985 to 1992.

Source: CCL Industries Inc. 2004 Annual Report.

Exhibit 3   CCL Industries Inc. Corporate Governance Structure

CCL has adopted formal governance practices in accordance with the guidelines published by the Toronto Stock Exchange (TSX) and the Ontario Securities Commission (OSC). The guidelines set out recommendations concerning the responsibilities, composition, and practices of boards of directors and their committees.

Mandate of the Board

CCL's board has a written mandate which includes among the duties and objectives of the board; the approval and monitoring of the strategic, business and capital plans of the corporation; succession planning for senior management; assessment of risk factors affecting the corporation; and ensuring the integrity of the reporting and information controls that enable the board to function effectively.

Composition of the Board

Best practices in corporate governance recommend that the majority of directors on the board be independent directors. At present, seven of the company's nine directors are independent.

Board Committees

The TSX recommends that committees of the board generally be composed of outside directors (meaning directors who are not employees of the corporation), a majority of whom are also unrelated directors, which denotes directors who have no material interests or relationships with the corporation other than as shareholders. A full description of the committees' mandates is available in CCL's Management Proxy Circular.

Director	Audit	Human Resources	Nominating and Governance	Environment and Health & Safety	Outside	Unrelated
Paul J. Block	✓	✓Chair			✓	✓
Susan J. Cook		✓			✓	✓
Dermot G. Coughlan	✓	✓			✓	✓
Jon K. Grant		✓	✓	✓Chair	✓	✓
Jean-René Halde			✓Chair	✓	✓	✓
Thomas C. Peddie	✓Chair				✓	✓
Lawrence G. Tapp	✓		✓		✓	✓

Note: As inside directors, Donald Lang and Stuart Lang are not members of any board committees.
Source: CCL Industries Inc. 2004 Annual Report.

Director Dermot Coughlan echoed this sentiment:

As boards go, this is a pretty strong board. It has most of the disciplines represented, in fact, I think all of them. There is good communication and openness between management and the board. The board has "in camera" or private sessions before meetings, exclusive of management and controlling shareholders, so there is open discourse and an excellent level of trust. This makes for a satisfactory situation, with mutual respect among the directors, *which also helps to improve corporate governance and effectiveness.*

Over the years, CCL had grown both organically but also through acquisitions. Further, under Donald Lang, the firm had not shied away from divesting businesses when there was an opportunity. However, prior to the appointment of Lang as CEO, there had been a feeling at the board level that acquisitions and divestments lacked a strategic focus. With the arrival of Lang, the board began to focus more on obtaining justification for these actions. As Director Tom Peddie noted:

> You do not want to be in a situation where management comes to the board and it's a surprise that they want to do a particular acquisition or divestiture.
>
> As the board was transitioning to the new management team, there was a degree of paranoia over past costly acquisitions that did not meet financial expectations or deliver the promised synergies.
>
> What happened was the board continued to challenge the strategy and say, "I'm sorry guys, we don't quite understand the strategy. It doesn't matter what the price is if it's not a strategic fit."
>
> One of the other things we did was to push for a post mortem. . . "Show us how you did relative to what you said you were going to do." The board focused on getting management to talk about its strategy—we don't need to, or should not execute acquisitions or divestitures unless we have a clearly articulated and acceptable strategy.

With a board that would challenge his actions, Lang had to make sure he was prepared before any strategy was presented.

The CCL Custom Manufacturing Opportunity

> We were always faced with the fact that the Custom Manufacturing Division, which was quite wide-ranging within itself, probably clouded CCL's market valuation.

Although Custom was a very good and profitable business, it was something that I think the investment community found hard to understand. It was a developing concept, driven by Don Lang, that the divesting of Custom should be considered.

—*Dermot Coughlan, CCL board member*

While there was some similarity among the firm's divisions, CCL essentially ran three different types of business servicing the same customers. It was felt, however, that this diversity of product had created a lack of understanding of the firm's value and confusion among investors leading to what management had felt was an undervalued stock price for a company that had consistent sales growth and profitability. Exhibit 4 presents the stock price for the years 2000 to 2004. William Chisholm, an investment analyst who had followed CCL since the 1970s, described the market's view toward CCL:

> The Custom Manufacturing business and some of the Label and Container businesses weren't highly interrelated to each other. You could basically sell any one of them and not affect the other divisions.

Director Dermot Coughlan notes that this situation did not go unnoticed by the board:

> We cut back our scope of acquisitions so that essentially the focus was on the existing label business that the market could understand and appreciate the strategic advantages. The previous management had made a number of acquisitions for which they overpaid. These acquisitions underperformed to expectations then management tried to make up

---

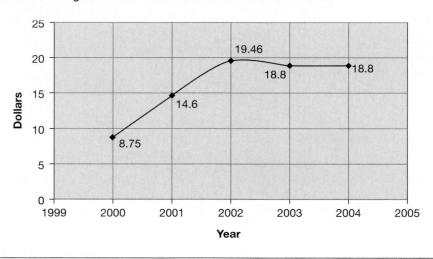

Source: Compustat.

for this by a flurry of more acquisitions. There were write-offs, followed by reorganizations etc. etc. and I think the Street [investment community] got a little fed up with that.

Aside from an undervalued share price, Lang had market considerations, which suggested divesting the Custom Manufacturing Division. Each of the three divisions competed in industries that were highly fragmented in terms of size and location of competitors. In recent years, the areas of sales and profit growth for the CCL had shifted from the Custom Manufacturing Division to the Container and Label divisions. This shift was partly due to a strategic effort on the part of management, but also due, to a greater extent, to changes in the industries.

In the Custom Manufacturing Division, there were fewer opportunities to differentiate and add value, and the Division was forced to compete on price and service, which could be easily undercut. CCL's other two divisions had much greater potential to provide value that was not tied to price, which meant they had a more competitive and defensible position in the industries in which they operated. Director Tom Peddie outlined the board's perspective on CCL's businesses and their markets:

CCL's principal customers were international marketers of consumer products who wanted supply chain partners to support them as they expanded globally.

One area where we felt CCL could be a strong global competitor was in the Label area where we had expertise and an operating style that we could duplicate globally, quite effectively. In the case of the Custom Division, it was really only satisfying a particular need and was more difficult and costly for us to replicate around the world. The feeling was that it was not replicable, capital intensive, and a little too commodity based, so why don't we consider exiting it?

As CEO, Lang tried to balance the needs of his employees with the need to maximize shareholder value and the market realities. Around 2002, there had been some investigation into selling the Custom Manufacturing Division to an income trust structure, and discussions had progressed a fair bit. The decision to sell was based on the same market rationale, but CCL faced the same challenge of getting the market to properly and fully value the initial public offering (IPO). As such, the deal was halted.

Approaching the CCL Board

Although Lang had been considering the sale of the Custom Manufacturing Division for some time and had pursued an IPO by means of an income trust structure, he knew there was still considerable discomfort with the board. The board's concern related to the materiality of the Custom Manufacturing Division business and the concerns that the market would have in CCL's ability to wisely and promptly reinvest the sale proceeds. From Lang's perspective, he knew that to be successful, he needed the board's total support before the Custom Manufacturing Division could be divested. Although it seemed that informally, there was agreement, the question now was how to proceed formally.

Lang had to articulate how this move would affect the investment community and what CCL could expect of its share price. What would the investment community want to see happen? How best should CCL use the proceeds of the sale to improve the business? Would the investment community understand the strategy and how it would benefit the firm? Lang had an excellent board at his disposal to investigate these concerns; the task now was to use it.

Coach Inc.: From Staid to Stylish

Shirisha Regani

S.S. George

Smitha Moganty

"We've been enjoying a sweet spot. We created a lane called accessible luxury and it feels like a superhighway."[1]

—**Lew Frankfort, CEO of Coach Inc., commenting on the positioning of the Coach brand, in December 2005.**

"The Coach brand represents a unique synthesis of magic and logic that stands for quality, authenticity, value and a truly aspirational, distinctive American style."[2]

—**Reed Krakoff, president and creative director of Coach Inc., in May 2004.**

"I don't know how you find a story that's accelerating sales growth on the top line at the same time as expanding margins as much as these guys."[3]

—**Michelle J. Picard, investment analyst, Geneva Capital Management Ltd.,**[4] **in July 2003.**

Introduction

In April 2006, Coach Inc. (Coach), a New York-based designer and marketer of superior quality, 'modern American classic' accessories, featured among the 21 top luxury fashion brands in the US in the '2006 Luxury Brand Status Index Survey of Luxury Fashion Designers' (LBSI) conducted by the Luxury Institute.[5] The survey rated the top luxury fashion brands in the US, which included popular fashion houses like the Gucci Group (Gucci), the Hermès Group (Hermès), Giorgio Armani S.p.A. (Armani), LVMH Moët Hennessy Louis Vuitton S.A. (LVMH), The House of Chanel (Chanel), and Prada S.p.A. (Prada) (*Refer to Exhibit 1 for details of some of the popular fashion labels in the US*).

Coach was one of the few 'American' brands to have featured on the index, as the luxury products market in the US was largely dominated by European fashion labels. However, although Coach was recognized as a luxury brand, it had a unique positioning in that the prices of its products were significantly lower than other high-end fashion labels. According to the Luxury Institute, Coach was "the strongest fashion brand among the more mass-oriented luxury brands purchased by wealthy consumers"[6] in the US.

Coach, which was started in 1941, was one of the oldest handbags and accessories brands in the US. Over the years, the company became well known for its sturdy and high-quality leather handbags and accessories.

---

[1] "Coach still has room in the bag to grow," http://news.findlaw.com, December 14, 2005.

[2] Kitty Go, "Coach class," www.inq7.net, May 18, 2004.

[3] Kathleen Gallagher, "Coach's new styles a hit, analyst says," http://www.jsonline.com, July 6, 2003.

[4] An investment management firm based in Milwaukee, USA. It offers services in the areas of individual and institutional asset management.

[5] It is an independent research institution that focuses solely on the top 10 percent of the USA's wealthy. For the 2006 LBSI, the institute surveyed more than 500 American households with a minimum of $200,000 in gross annual income and a minimum net worth of $750,000 (including home equity). (Source: www.luxuryinstitute.com)

[6] www.luxuryinstitute.com.

Company	Brands*	Products	Revenues for 2004
Gucci Group N.V. (As of early 2006, the company was a subsidiary of PPR S.A., a French conglomerate)	Yves Saint Laurent, Bottega Veneta, Boucheron, YSL Beauté, Sergio Rossi, Alexander McQueen, Bédat & Co., Stella McCartney, Roger & Gallet, Balenciaga, and Gucci	Handbags, ready-to-wear, luggage, shoes, small leather goods, jewelry, timepieces, perfumes, cosmetics, eyewear, and skincare products	–
The Hermès Group (a Paris-based luxury goods company)	Hermès	Ready-to-wear, perfumes, scarf rings, baby products, home décor, jewelry, handbags, and luggage	–
Giorgio Armani S.p.A (an Italian designer goods company)	Armani Collezioni, AJ Armani Jeans, Armani Junior, Emporio Armani, A/X Armani Exchange, Armani Casa, and Giorgio Armani	Ready-to-wear, perfumes, watches, and other accessories	£919.6 million
LVMH Moët Hennessy Louis Vuitton S.A. (As of early 2006, Christian Dior S.A., a popular French fashion house, had a 42 percent stake in LVMH)	It is the parent company of close to 50 companies with each operating a few sub-brands	Ready-to-wear, wines and spirits, leather goods, perfumes, watches, jewelry, accessories, handbags, and retailing	£8,936.0 million
The House of Chanel (a Paris-based designer goods company)	Chanel	Ready-to-wear, perfumes, cosmetics, jewelry, handbags, and accessories	–
Prada S.p.A. (an Italian fashion goods company)	Prada and Miu Miu (the brand was used to sell low-priced products)	Ready-to-wear, perfumes, handbags, shoes, and accessories	$1,991.40 million

The list is not exhaustive.

Source: Compiled from various sources.

By the time Sara Lee Corp. (Sara Lee)[7] bought the company in 1985, Coach had become a premium leather accessories brand in the US. Under Sara Lee, Coach underwent a major expansion and entered the overseas market.

However, by the early 1990s, Coach had lost some of its cachet, as other premium brands offered customers products that were 'hip and trendy'. In contrast, Coach was mainly known for its classic and staid designs.

In the late 1990s, Coach underwent a transformation under the management of its then CEO, Lew Frankfort[8] (Frankfort), who, along with the company's president and creative director, Reed Krakoff (Krakoff), undertook certain measures that helped the company revive its

---

[7] Founded in 1939, Sara Lee was a consumer goods company based in Illinois, USA. As of 2006, its main businesses included food and beverages, branded apparel, and foodservice. For fiscal 2006, Sara Lee's revenue amounted to $15.9 billion.

[8] Frankfort joined Coach in 1979 as vice president of business development. He became the president of the company in 1985, when Sara Lee purchased Coach from Miles Cahn, the owner of Coach at that time. Frankfort was named the CEO of Coach in 1996.

Case 8 / Coach Inc.: From Staid to Stylish

image in the market. By the end of 2005, the company was in a strong financial position, and its revenues in 2005 were more than three time its revenues in 2000.

Background

Coach was established in 1941, as a small leather goods manufacturing unit operated by Miles Cahn (Cahn) and six leather artisans, in a loft in Manhattan, New York. The unit produced high quality leather handbags, and was run as a family business by the Cahn family.

Over a period of time, Cahn brought in some significant improvements to the leather manufacturing process at the company. He developed a new method of leather processing, which made the leather strong, yet soft and flexible, and gave it the ability to absorb dye well, allowing it to acquire a deep color tone. (He developed this new way of treating leather to improve its quality after he observed how the leather of baseball gloves became soft and supple over a period of time as a result of abrasion and wear.)

After adopting the new processing technology, Cahn began producing women's handbags made out of thick cow skins. This was an innovative idea as, at that time, handbags were usually made out of thin leather pasted on cardboard. Cahn sold the cowhide handbags under the Coach brand name. Gradually, the Coach brand became popular in the US and the company became well known as a maker of high-quality leather handbags. Over time, Coach came to be recognized as a premium brand that offered superior quality leather goods in classic styles.

In the late 1970s, Cahn introduced a catalog, through which he started selling Coach products. In 1981, he opened the first exclusive Coach retail store. During the early 1980s, Cahn opened more specialty stores in the US that exclusively sold Coach products. By this time, the demand for Coach products had outgrown their supply. As a result, Cahn began rationing the products to select vendors.

In the mid-1980s, Cahn decided to retire from business, and sold the company to Sara Lee in 1985. At that time, Coach owned a flagship store on Madison Avenue, New York, and six other boutiques at various locations in the US.

Coach underwent rapid expansion under Sara Lee. Sara Lee expanded Coach's product portfolio over the years, and accessories such as briefcases, luggage, etc.

were introduced under the Coach brand. Further, the company opened more stores, and increased the brand's presence in various departmental stores in the country through the store-in-store format. By the late 1980s, Sara Lee was operating 12 exclusive Coach retail stores and nearly 50 boutiques selling Coach products within larger departmental stores.

During the late 1980s, Sara Lee was unable to meet the increased demand for Coach products, as it did not have sufficient production facilities. The company was reported to have even cut down the number of retail outlets as it was unable to meet the demand. Eventually, in 1988, Sara Lee opened a new factory in Florida. This was the first time that Coach had moved production outside New York. The production from the new plant was supplied to 22 freestanding stores and 300 different retailers. Over the years, Sara Lee opened more manufacturing facilities for Coach products within and outside the US.

Sara Lee opened Coach's first overseas store in London in 1989. By the early 1990s, Sara Lee had exclusive Coach stores in Germany, Italy, and some Asian countries like Japan and Singapore. Japan was a key overseas market for Coach because the country was one of the largest markets for luxury goods in the world.[9] By the early 1990s, the overseas market accounted for close to 10 percent of the total Coach sales.[10]

In October 2000, Coach was spun off as a publicly traded company, under the name Coach Inc. By 2005, Coach's revenues were more than three times what they had been in 2000, and the share price had increased by almost 900 percent since its IPO (*Refer to Exhibit 2 for Coach's consolidated statement of income from 1999 to 2005, and Exhibit 3 for Coach's share price between 2001 and 2006*).

As of early 2006, Coach sold a range of accessories like bags, watches, footwear, sunglasses, and outerwear for both men and women in 19 countries worldwide. For fiscal 2006, Coach's total revenues stood at $2,111.50 million.[11]

Creating a New Coach

Despite earning a good reputation for the quality of its products, over the years Coach had lagged behind its competitors on the 'trendiness' dimension. The company had built its reputation on classic designs in elegant styles, because of which its main customers were older women who gave precedence to quality over

---

[9] "Coach's driver picks up the pace," www.businessweek.com, March 29, 2004.
[10] www.fundinguniverse.com.
[11] $ (Dollars) refer to US Dollars in this case study.

(In Millions of $)

Particulars	July 3, 1999	July 1, 2000	June 30, 2001	June 29, 2002	June 28, 2003	July 3, 2004	July 2, 2005
Net sales	507.00	547.10	613.90	716.50	949.40	1,316.30	1,704.10
Licensing revenue	0.80	1.80	2.20	2.90	3.80	4.80	6.30
Total net sales	507.80	548.90	616.10	719.40	953.20	1,321.10	1710.40
Cost of sales	226.20	220.10	218.50	236.00	275.80	331.00	399.60
Gross profit	281.60	328.80	397.60	483.40	677.40	990.10	1310.80
Selling, general and administrative expenses	255.00	272.80	291.30	346.40	433.70	545.60	689.00
Operating income before reorganization costs	26.60	56.00	106.30	–	–	–	–
Reorganization costs	7.10	–	4.60	3.40	–	–	–
Operating income	19.50	56.00	101.70	133.60	243.70	444.50	621.80
Net interest expense	0.40	0.40	2.40	0.30	−1.10	−3.20	15.28
Income before provision for income taxes	19.10	55.60	99.40	133.30	244.80	447.70	637.60
Provision for income taxes	2.40	17.00	35.40	47.30	90.60	168.00	235.30
Minority interest, net tax	–	–	–	0.20	7.50	18.00	13.60
Net income	16.70	38.60	64.00	85.80	146.60	261.70	388.70

Coach's year ended on the Saturday closest to June 30.

Source: www.coach.com.

fashion. By the mid 1990s however, it was clear that although Coach's products were still highly valued for their quality, the brand was losing its shine as trend conscious people preferred to be seen with stylish European brands like LVMH, Prada and Gucci.

After Frankfort became the CEO of Coach in 1996, he set about reviving the Coach brand. He, along with Krakoff (who was previously a designer for Tommy Hilfiger Inc., a US-based designer apparel and accessories company), brought about several changes aimed at upgrading Coach's style quotient.

Coach's Product Strategy

From its inception, Coach's product strategy was to produce timeless, classic pieces which would not be subject to the vagaries of fashion. In keeping with this strategy, Coach generally did not change its designs to suit the trend of the moment.

Because of this, Coach's leather goods were identified with classic and elegant designs, rather than being known as fashionable. However, despite staying away from fashion trends, what set Coach apart from its competitors was that it offered durable and functional handbags in superior quality leather. It was said that the average life of Coach handbags was around 15 years, and when maintained well, they could last well up to 40 years. Coach also offered lifetime service to its customers. The company offered repair services and also replaced some parts of Coach products for free, with the customer bearing only the shipping cost.

During the mid-1960s, Coach started producing new designs of handbags under the direction of the company's first designer, Bonnie Cashin (Cashin). Cashin introduced innovative designs, which included the removable shoulder strap, built-in change purses, and brass toggle closures (a type of lock for handbags). The brass toggle closure was hugely popular, and reportedly revolutionized the handbag industry at that time.

Exhibit 3   Coach: Share Prices from 2001 to 2006

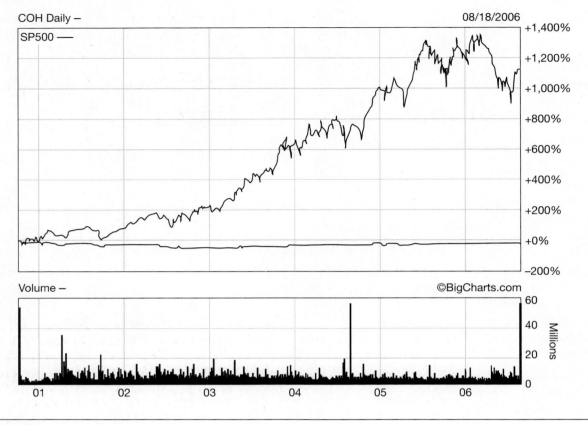

COH Daily –   08/18/2006

SP500 —

©BigCharts.com

Volume –

Source: http://bigcharts.marketwatch.com/

Some of Coach's popular designs during the late 1960s and 1970s included the bucket bag, the fringe 'shimmy' bag, etc. Gradually, Coach acquired a 'country club' image in the US, which strengthened its position as a maker of high-end leather goods.

During the 1980s, after Sara Lee bought the company, it extended the Coach brand to products other than bags, such as travel goods, coats, etc. After the acquisition, Coach's sales increased from $20 million in 1985 (when the product range consisted mainly of handbags and accessories like belts) to more than $500 million in 1997 (when the products range consisted of items like handbags, luggage, wallets, etc.).

By the mid-1990s, Coach leather goods were available at high-end retail stores in the US like Bloomingdale's and Saks Fifth Avenue (apart from company-owned retail outlets, factory stores, and through the Coach catalog).

Coach's portfolio mainly consisted of handbags, travel goods, and other accessories. However, even at this time, Coach's leather goods were known more for their durability and functionality than for their trendy designs.

It was also during the mid-1990s that the US fashion industry was hit by 'business casual,'[12] and more and more women were becoming trend-conscious. Trendy designer bags made of non-traditional materials such as fabric, nylon, etc., were gaining popularity among women. Coach however, continued to offer 'sturdy' leather goods. The result—it lost customers to other designer brands like Kate Spade, Prada, and the like, which had kept up with fashion trends. Changes in customer preferences started having an adverse impact on the company as Coach experienced declining sales from the mid 1990s.

---

[12] It was originally defined as no tie, button-down shirt and slacks for men, and a skirt or slacks and blouse or shirt for women. However, business casual can also be a more casual denim shirt for men with a casual tie (madras plaid), and perhaps a blazer or a vest or sweater over a shirt, depending on what is accepted in the particular industry. In many instances, business casual has become even more informal, allowing for a polo shirt or corporate logo shirt and a skirt or slacks. (Source: http://content.monstertrak.monster.com)

In second half of the 1990s, Frankfort began his efforts to reposition the Coach brand. He believed that Coach still held some significance for customers. He was of the firm view that customers still liked Coach, and that "women were walking around with Coach wallets in their Prada handbags."[13] However, what was holding Coach back was the fact that it was not perceived as a trendy product by customers. Frankfort started looking out for a designer who 'believed' in Coach, and who was ready to revive it without taking away its classic traits.

Enter Krakoff

Krakoff joined Coach in 1996, and eventually became instrumental in transforming Coach from a 'stodgy' brand into a hip one. He joined Frankfort in taking measures to revive Coach's fortunes and transforming it into a 'lifestyle brand.'

Krakoff was reportedly a huge fan of Coach. On one occasion, he said, "I grew up with Coach. . . . They were even made near where I lived. It was almost in my blood."[14] It was this conviction Krakoff had in the Coach brand that made Frankfort choose him as the company's creative director. Reportedly, Frankfort also revamped the executive ranks at the company, firing many of the top managers, around the time Krakoff was hired.

Frankfort believed that Krakoff 'understood' the strengths and weaknesses of the Coach brand well, and so was the right person for the job. Further, he had also worked at well-known fashion houses like Polo Ralph Lauren and Tommy Hilfiger, which were known for being trendy. "I felt he'd be able to balance magic with logic, keeping the best of Coach and infusing the edge it needed," said Frankfort.[15]

Krakoff realized that Coach was a well-recognized and respected brand in the US. According to him, Coach had a nostalgia factor among American customers as they had known the brand for almost 60 years. He said, "Everyone has a link to a Coach product. When I got here I realized that's the foundation. But I had to update the image."[16]

Krakoff thought that Coach's declining popularity was mainly because the brand was no longer considered fashionable. Coach's designs were not innovative and the products largely catered to female customers aged 40 and above. Krakoff decided that Coach needed an image makeover to make the brand relevant to young people.

At the same time, Krakoff also believed that Coach needed to maintain its 'classic image' in order to retain the company's loyal customers. Accordingly, the theme for Coach products remained classic; however, the designs and styles were modified to appeal to younger customers. According to Krakoff, Coach's designs represented 'modern classic' or classic American designs and styles with a modern twist. "We seek to be the leading brand of quality lifestyle accessories offering classic, modern American styling," he said in 2004.[17]

Also, as of the mid-1990s, Coach was mainly known for its leather goods, while other designer brands offered a variety of products such as eyewear, apparel, and even furniture. After Krakoff took over, he extended the Coach brand to products like home furnishings, clothing, watches, etc. In 1999, Coach launched a 28-piece furniture line of high-end leather couches, chairs, and ottomans, which were priced in the range of $650 to $6,300.

Commenting on the product line expansion, Frankfort said in 1999, "We're in the midst of a transition from a leather goods brand to a lifestyle accessories brand."[18] Expanding the Coach product portfolio was also expected to reinvigorate the declining sales of the company.

The New Collections

Krakoff's main task at Coach, however, was to burnish Coach's image and transform it into a fashion label. To achieve this, he designed new Coach bags and accessories keeping the young customer in mind. Under his direction, Coach began offering products that were made with materials other than pure leather. Krakoff experimented with materials like nylon, fabric, and variants of light-weight leathers in his new collections.

In the late 1990s Coach started introducing new collections that were designed to appeal to the younger customer. In late 1997, the company launched the Ergo Collection, in which it introduced a new rounded shape for bags. In 1998, it introduced the Neo handbags, made of a combination of leather and other materials like nylon.

In 2000, Coach introduced the Coach Hamptons Collection. This line included a collection of handbags

[13] Joanne Gordon, "Serial tinkerer," www.forbes.com, September 3, 2001.

[14] Michael Hainey, "In the bag," www.departures.com, July–August 2003.

[15] Catherine Curan, "Reed Krakoff," www.newyorkbusiness-risingstars.com, 2002.

[16] Michael Hainey, "In the bag," www.departures.com, July–August 2003.

[17] Kitty Go, "Coach class," www.inq7.net, May 18, 2004.

[18] C. J. Rewick, "Trying new accessories," *Crain's New York Business*, June 21, 1999, Issue 25.

and accessories in a variety of shapes and fabrics. The Hamptons Collection was successful as it had trendy designs and styles (in contrast to the pure classic styles traditionally offered by Coach), which appealed to fashion-conscious customers.

Coach also gained more visibility after expanding its portfolio to include other products like eyewear, apparel, etc. By 2000, Coach was selling handbags, business cases, time management products (include planners, folios, etc.), luggage and travel accessories, watches, outerwear, gloves and scarves, furniture and home furnishings, footwear, and eyewear.

In 2001, Coach unveiled a new line of handbags and accessories under the name, the Signature Collection. In this collection, Krakoff introduced a unique 'interlocking 'C' pattern' on the bags and accessories. The Signature Collection was a runaway success and the 'C' pattern became synonymous with the Coach brand. Commenting on the new pattern, Krakoff said, "The idea was to make a pattern that wasn't a logo, because Coach is an understated brand. We decided to do something understated and a little different, so that when you look at this abstract 'C,' it's just a design, really."[19]

The Signature Collection went on to become the best seller among all of Coach's collections. In 2001, the Signature Collection line generated 68 percent of Coach sales.[20] Coach's sales grew at a rate of 20 percent in 2002 (it was 12 percent in 2001). According to analysts, the main reason for the success of the Signature Collection was the newly introduced 'C' print on the merchandise, which created a feeling and look of exclusivity, similar to high-end prints from Chanel or LVMH (for instance, Chanel's products could be identified by their 'CC' logo and Louis Vuitton's products by their unique 'LV' monogram. According to analysts, the success of the Signature Collection put Coach in the league of high-end fashion labels. After the success of the Signature Collection, Coach became a favorite with the 'fashion elite' in the US, and started being featured in fashion magazines like *Vogue*.

The popularity of the Signature Collection's 'C' pattern was such that Coach went on to introduce several variations in its design. Over the years, Krakoff introduced a small 'C' print, a large 'C' print, and a scribble 'C' print, among others. Krakoff also regularly updated the Signature Collection, using new colors, styles, and fabrics.

However, Coach did not rely on only the Signature Collection, but kept launching new collections. Coach's collections in this period included the Soho Collection and the Chelsea Collection. Under Krakoff's direction,

Exhibit 4	Coach's Product Portfolio in 2005

Category	% of Sales
Handbags	64
Women's accessories (include wallets, wristlets, cosmetic cases, keyfobs, and belts)	20
Business cases	4
Outerwear, gloves, hats, and scarves	3
Weekend travel (cabin bags, duffles, suitcases, garment bags, and accessories)	1
Footwear, sunwear, watches, and other small categories	1

Source: www.coach.com.

Coach's designs and styles had expanded from around 80 all-leather designs in muted colors in the late 1990s, to around 130 designs in seasonal palettes, and a variety of materials like exotic skins, plastic, cloth, etc. by 2005–2006 (*Refer to Exhibit 4 for Coach's product portfolio in 2005 and Exhibit 5 for Coach's product mix as of August 2006*).

Coach was one of the few high-end brands that brought out new designs and styles every month instead of twice a year. By updating its designs and styles frequently, the company maintained the freshness of the brand. The frequent launch of new collections was also meant to encourage multiple purchases by trend-conscious customers who liked to be seen with the latest in everything.

By the early 2000s, Coach had also begun to target men in addition to its core market which was constituted by women. In early 2002, Coach unveiled a new men's line with products like shoes, business cases, bags, and belts, among others.

Part of Coach's success in the early 2000s was also attributed to the novelty of the products it offered. For instance, in 2005, Krakoff designed iPod cases to match Coach handbags and other accessories. This product was a hit with trend conscious young people. Coach's unique wristlet (a small purse that could be worn around the wrist), which was available in several designs was also a popular product.

Krakoff also paid special attention to the design of cases for Coach's eyewear. "Since we are known for our

---

[19] Sandra Dolbow, "Substance and style in the bag," *Brandweek*, October 14, 2002.
[20] www.coach.com.

| Exhibit 5 | Coach's Product Mix as of August 2006 |

Handbags	Women's Accessories	Travel and Business	Men's Accessories	Others
• Chelsea Collection • Soho Collection • Signature Stripe Collection • Hamptons Weekend Collection • Soft duffles • Shoulder totes • Classic Signature Collection • Legacy Collection • Special Occasion Collection	• Wallets/Card cases (Signature/ Leather wallets) • Wristlets • Cosmetic cases • Shoes • Sunglasses • Key rings • Charms • Watches • iPod cases • Cell Phone Accessories • Silk scarves • Hats/Outerwear • Personal accessories • Belts • Leather care	• Men's: Briefcases Messenger bags Totes Business accessories Planner/Organizer refills Travel • Women's: Totes Briefcases Business accessories Planner/Organizer refills Travel	• Wallets and Card cases • Shoes • Belts • Key rings • iPod/Electronic accessories • Cases • Watches • Sunglasses • Hats/Outerwear • Leather care	• Baby: Bags Hats Socks and shoes Blankets Key rings, Picture frames, etc. • Pet: Pet dog collars Dog leashes

Source: www.coach.com.

bags, it's important our eyeglass cases are seen as distinctive in their own right—not just something free that comes with the eyewear... We want the cases to go above and beyond their functionality and be an object the wearer wants to carry as an accessory," he said.[21]

By the early 2000s, Coach's extended portfolio allowed the company to reduce its dependence on Christmas holiday sales. (Holiday sales had accounted for almost half of the company's sales before the early 2000s.) Coach also introduced special products during the holiday season to be sold as gift items. For instance, during the Christmas holiday season of 2005, Coach introduced a 'wristlet Lipstick Case' and a Signature Collection 'baby bag' (for style conscious mothers).

Partnerships

Traditionally, Coach's main business consisted of designing, manufacturing, and marketing leather goods; this remained so even in the early 2000s. The company carried out most of its product extensions through licensing. For instance, it entered into a licensing agreement with the Movado Group,[22] to offer Coach-branded watches (*Refer to Table 1 for Coach's licensing agreements as of 2000*).

Apart from licensing, Coach also brought out co-branded products into the market. For instance, in 1996, the Toyota Motor Corporation USA (Toyota), and Coach entered into an agreement whereby Toyota launched an exclusive range of Lexus cars called the 'Lexus Coach Edition' that came with Coach's leather interiors.[23]

The Role of Marketing Research

In the late 1990s, Coach increased its focus on market research. Frankfort thought that new styles and designs alone would not be sufficient to revive the Coach brand. The company had to ensure that it produced products that customers wanted, all the while retaining the brand's classic traits.

[21] Gloria Nicola, "Head Coach," www.2020mag.com, September 2, 2003.
[22] The Movado Group is a leading Swiss watch company.
[23] Toyota and Coach came out with three Lexus Coach Editions in 1996, 1997, 1998. The companies renewed their partnership in 2001 and came up with a limited edition Lexus Coach Edition.

Table 1	Coach's Licensing Partners as of 2000			
Category	Licensing Partner	Introduction Date	Territory	License Expiration Year
Watches	Movado Group Inc.	Spring 1998	US and Japan	2006
Footwear	Jimlar Corporation	Spring 1999	US	2008
Furniture	Baker Furniture Company	Spring 1999	US and Canada	2008
Eyewear	Signature Eyewear Inc.	Spring 2000	US and Canada	2009

Source: www.secinfo.com.

With this in mind, Frankfort asked Krakoff to design products that had the right balance of 'logic and magic.' Coach's new products were meant to be stylish and trendy, yet durable and functional. They were intended to meet the needs and requirements of the customers, and not just be 'fashionable.' Extensive market research was conducted to help the company understand the needs of customers and to design products accordingly.

This focus on customer needs was one of the factors that set Coach apart from other high-end fashion labels. At other fashion houses like Gucci, LVMH, and others, the styles were often dictated by the chief designer's tastes and expectations from the market. At Coach, however, the design process was customer-centric, and depended on customer surveys and market research reports to provide inputs for designing new products.

In the early 2000s, Coach began spending millions of dollars on customer surveys (in 2001, it spent around $2.5 million, considered a large amount for a relatively small company like Coach) in order to understand customers' needs and preferences better.

Typically, market research was conducted for up to a year before a new product was launched. As part of this research, company representatives spoke to hundreds of customers. Coach interviewed about 15,000 customers a year in its own stores. The questions could include anything from the right length of a handbag strap, to customers' perception of fashion, to their shopping habits.

After conducting the initial survey, Coach tested the new products in a cross-section of stores across the country six months before a collection was launched. Coach even asked customers to grade the proposed new products against the existing or older products. According to Krakoff, one of the popular methods to

ensure the success of his designs was to test them using focus groups.

However, Krakoff also knew that market research did not always help in identifying the best designs. He said, "We test every single bag and product before we send it to the store. But we know how to use the information. It can tell you whether a bag is too heavy or uncomfortable, but it can't tell you whether it's right for the future. It's my job to be on top of that."[24]

In fact, market research at Coach was used for a variety of purposes and not just to find out customer opinions about a new product. For instance, Coach conducted telephone surveys of close to 500 people at a time in order to measure brand awareness and to track customer tastes. Reportedly, the popular "C" print of the Signature Collection was also conceived after a telephone survey revealed that Coach was not paying sufficient attention to styling its handbags and making them trendier.

In 2001, Coach conducted a poll in Japan to gauge customer reactions after the launch of the Signature Collection. The poll was conducted among 400 Japanese women who bought items from the Signature Collection. The poll revealed that 37 percent of these women were first-time buyers. Of them, 30 percent were below 26 years of age, which proved that Coach's designs had finally begun attracting younger customers.[25]

Reportedly, Frankfort periodically visited Coach stores and talked to the customers in order to get customers' views first-hand. According to him, this helped him gain valuable insights into customers' shopping behavior. For instance, because of his direct interaction with customers, he realized that the Internet might not be an effective medium to make actual sales. Frankfort

[24] Sandra Dolbow, "Substance and style in the bag," *Brandweek*, October 14, 2002.
[25] Joanne Gordon, "Serial Tinkerer," www.forbes.com, September 3, 2001.

observed that women were "tactile shoppers" and therefore had the desire to try bags on, feel the material, and consult their friends before making the actual purchase. Therefore, Frankfort believed that the Internet could be used to push women into stores, and not just to make actual sales online. Said Peter Daboll, president and CEO of comScore Media Metrix (Metrix),[26] "While sales on luxury goods sites are significant, most visitors use these sites to research a potential offline purchase."[27]

In keeping with this idea, Frankfort made a serious effort to enhance the visitor experience at the company's website, www.coach.com.[28] According to research conducted by Metrix, www.coach.com had 2.71 million unique visitors[29] in 2005, and ranked first in the Jewelry/Luxury Goods/Accessories category. According to analyst estimates, if Coach managed to convert even one percent of that site traffic into actual sales (of an average of $198, as this was the price of a low-end Coach bag at that time), then Coach would be making sales of around $5.4 million.

Frankfort also insisted that all the top executives chart sales for every store and every type of merchandise every day (during the holiday period, they would get three updates daily). This was another practice that helped Coach in understanding the needs and buying behavior of its customers. Every month Coach's CEO, COO, and CFO met to review and revise the annual sales estimates for each Coach store. As a result of one such revision, Coach found out that the demand for the Ergo bags was exceeding their supply. Within a few days, Coach had ramped up the production of the bags to meet the demand.

Frankfort made it a point to see to it that all Coach stores restocked based on the regional sales reports. For example, regional sales reports revealed that customers in suburban Chicago still preferred classic-looking Coach bags to the new trendier styles. Said Bob Drbul, analyst, Lehman Brothers, "Their execution and business planning is in the league of a Wal-Mart or a Target."[30]

The 'Accessible' Luxury Brand

In addition to product innovation, one of the major factors that contributed to Coach's success was its unique positioning in the high-end luxury market. Coach's products were known for their high quality, but were priced lower than other designer products. In other words, Coach positioned itself as an 'accessible luxury brand.' Frankfort and Krakoff understood that price was a source of competitive advantage for the brand, and maintained the same positioning even in the early 2000s.

In the early 2000s, the prices of Coach bags started from around $200. In contrast, bags from Yves Saint Laurent[31] and LVMH started at around $1000. Analysts noted that due to Coach's unique pricing, its products appealed to buyers of premium products as well as to those customers who did not regularly buy luxury products, but who were willing to spend a little extra to buy them occasionally. This ensured that the market for Coach's products was larger than that for other high-end products.

However, Coach was also careful to ensure that the low prices did not dilute the value of its brand or its luxury image in the market. It never marked down the prices of its products in its regular stores or on the Coach website, as it thought that this might dilute the brand's value. The company also did not permit department stores selling Coach products to cut prices. And unlike many other designer brands, Coach never held a sale during holiday seasons and always sold its products at full price.

However, Coach did sell its products at discounts through a different channel—the factory outlets, which were generally situated at a considerable distance from the full-price stores. At the factory outlets, Coach sold only older styles or collections, irregular products, discontinued models, etc., never the latest products.

According to research conducted by Coach, the average full-price shopper at its outlets was aged 35, educated, and a single or newly married working woman. An average factory-outlet shopper was older at 45, educated, married, and likely to look for bargains. Therefore, there was little overlap in the profiles of the shoppers at factory outlets and full price stores.

Factory outlets, according to the company, were as lucrative as its full-price stores. According to Frankfort, an average customer spent close to $770 per year in a factory outlet, compared to the $1,100 spent by a customer in a full price store. He said, "They're (factory outlet shoppers) as brand loyal as our full-price shoppers. These are professional moms who want beautiful, well-made brands at low prices."[32]

---

[26] A global market research provider and consultant for Internet usage, audience measurement and e-commerce tracking data. (Source: www.comscore.com)

[27] Traci Purdum, "Coach Inc.: Alligators, pythons and iPods—Oh my," www.industryweek.com, January 5, 2006.

[28] Coach launched its website, www.coach.com, in 1999.

[29] The total number of visitors from unique IP addresses.

[30] Julia Boorstin, "How Coach got hot," *Fortune*, October 28, 2002, Issue 8.

[31] A popular fashion brand owned by the Gucci Group.

[32] "BW 50: Coach's split personality," www.businessweek.com, November 7, 2005.

Affordable prices at the mainstream stores as well as the factory outlets meant customers could make multiple purchases of Coach products. For instance, the company's promotions conveyed the idea that its bags offered more than just utility, and that they could even be used as accessories to match outfits. Said Robert Ohmes, a retail analyst at Morgan Stanley, "Coach has not just gained market share from those trading up and trading down. It may be stimulating incremental business [by inducing people to buy more products]. It changed the way its particular market worked."[33] Analysts noted that credit should also be given to the company's strategy of adding to its product line on a regular basis.

Reportedly, Coach products were also a favorite choice among customers as gift items during holiday seasons. Said a Coach customer, "Coach is always a nice thing to give because you get a lot of value for money, and the name itself makes a statement."[34] Coach even offered 'pre-wrapped' Coach products in the mid-2000s, to cash in on the popularity of its products during the holiday seasons.

According to analysts, customers did not mind purchasing multiple Coach products because they were affordable, trendy, durable, and more importantly, were considered 'high-end products.' Said Andrea Martin, a Coach customer, "It's not such a splurge for something you can use a few times a week. The quality of their stuff is amazing."[35]

BusinessWeek, a prominent business magazine, wrote: "Coach bags typically cost around $200 to $400. Yet a lot of buyers put it alongside names such as Gucci, Versace, and Dior. What makes Coach shoppers feel like they are in the same league as those tony names are the goods' quality and eye-pleasing designs, as well as the luxurious stores where they are sold."[36]

In fact, many believed that Coach brand's value was enhanced by the fact that despite lower prices, Coach products were of a quality that matched or even surpassed luxury brands. Frankfort insisted that Coach maintain its reputation for quality and customer service, as these were the features that continued to attract customers to the brand. He ensured that these qualities were not lost when the company went in for an image overhaul.

According to Frankfort, "One of our challenges is to offer understandable fashion and to not alienate our core. Some of our customers are looking for classic, enduring styles that complement their wardrobe. Some are status-oriented; others are more utilitarian and want a functional bag. We don't want to alienate them while we bring in new consumers."[37]

Coach kept several 'classic traits' intact to avoid making the brand too unfamiliar to customers after its makeover. Traditionally, Coach handbags were provided with a unique tagged number. Over the years, the tags became a sort of style statement and, in a way, provided authentication for Coach handbags (*Refer to Exhibit 6 for*

Exhibit 6   Ways to Identify Authentic Coach Products

- Dust bag: Coach products that came with a dust bag were brown in color and had the Coach logo in front of the bag.
- Tags: Most of the Coach products came with a signature Coach Swing Tag.
- Serial Numbers: All Coach products came with a Coach logo, serial number and/or Coach creed.
- Stitching: The stitching on Coach products was always even and generally, the stitching was in the same color as that of the leather.
- Hardware: Coach products used only high-quality and light-weight metals like brass, nickel, or gunmetal. In addition, Coach only used coated metal which implied that the hardware would never peel or chip.
- Design: The "C's" were always paired on the outside of the bag. When in a row, the "C's" were always in even number. Also, a "C" was never cut off by the seaming. The end of a "CC" always touched the side of the other "CC" in the pattern.

Source: Adapted from http://en.wikipedia.org/wiki/Coach_ (company).

---

[33] Julia Boorstin, "How Coach got hot," *Fortune,* October 28, 2002.
[34] Samantha Jonas-Hain, "Crystal to cashmere: Holiday gifts for women," www.foxnews.com, December 12, 2005.
[35] "BW 50: Coach's split personality," www.businessweek.com, November 7, 2005.
[36] "BW 50: Coach's split personality," www.businessweek.com, November 7, 2005.
[37] Sandra Dolbow, "Substance and style in the bag," *Brandweek,* October 14, 2002.

ways to identify an authentic Coach product). Even as of 2006, Coach handbags came with logo-embossed tags that dangled from the bags.

Functionality was another important feature of Coach's handbags. This element was stressed in the design of the new Coach bags also. What was noteworthy was that every part of a Coach bag had a function, and nothing was added for a purely cosmetic purpose. "All of our products, whether they be bags, belts or eyewear, must embody functionality, an innovative use of materials, distinctive style and sensibility," said Krakoff.[38] Coach bags did not have any superfluous buckles, zippers, or chains. All of them had straight double-stitching and reinforced edges to help them keep their shape, and there were no loose threads.

On the customer service front, Coach launched a program called 'Coach by Special Request' in 2005, which allowed customers to order classic and special edition Coach products, with the products being directly shipped from the factory to the customers' home.

Commenting on Coach's unique positioning, Frankfort said in 2005, "We see unlimited longevity in being a model brand offering accessible luxury accessories."[39]

Image Makeover

In the late 1990s, Frankfort and Krakoff undertook an extensive image building exercise for the Coach brand. As the creative director of Coach, Krakoff was responsible for overseeing the 'creative side' of activities like advertising, catalogs, direct mail, store design, visual, and public relations.

Store Redesign

Under Krakoff's direction, Coach's stores were done up keeping the brand's new image in mind. Until the late 1990s, Coach's retail outlets looked rather dull and tacky, and people thought the store looked more like a library than a retail outlet. The earlier outlets had had an old-fashioned design with a reception area, mahogany walls, and marble floors, with a full range of Coach's products stacked on shelves.

In the late 1990s, Krakoff redesigned the stores around a white theme. The new stores had white walls and furniture, and the products were displayed in sleek white showcases. The new stores were spacious and had high ceilings. The lights also were arranged high up in the ceiling and created a pleasing ambience, while displaying the merchandise to the best advantage. It was thought that the new store design gave an upscale image to Coach. In addition to revamping the exclusive retail outlets, Coach also redecorated its factory-stores. This was because the factory-stores were not just a channel to dispose of Coach's irregular or out-of-date products, but an important venue where the company could discover customer tastes and preferences. A significant portion of the company's sales also came from the factory outlets.

Advertising

Advertising also played a crucial role in repositioning the Coach brand in the late 1990s. During this time, the company launched a new advertising campaign that was created in-house. The new ads were a continuation of the "Living Legends" ads used during the early and mid-1990s. The "Living Legends" ads showed Coach as an 'American Legacy'. In keeping with this theme, the ads featured the basic product on a white background, and against portraits of descendants of legendary American personalities (like Maria Cooper Janis, the daughter of Gary Cooper, an American movie star) toting Coach bags. It was felt that these ads created snob appeal for the brand. Said Kurt Barnard, a retail consultant, "They seemed more standoffish and arrogant; more the exclusive domain of the rich."[40] More importantly, these ads failed to attract young customers.

However, the new "Legends" ads used more contemporary models. They featured Candice Bergen, a television actress and model, John Irving, a well-known novelist and a screenplay writer, and others who were popular with the younger generation. Later on, Krakoff used younger actresses and models like Marisa Tomei, Mandy Moore, etc. as he thought these celebrities were more capable of influencing the fashion preferences of younger customers.

Coach's new ads looked brighter and more colorful, with images that focused sharply on the product. For this, Krakoff hired reputed photographers like Mario Testino (Testino) who shot attractive pictures. These ads were released in the media and displayed prominently at Coach stores.

The new ads helped create a more youthful image for Coach. Said Mandy Moore, a popular actress and singer in the US, who modeled for the Coach brand in 2005, "I used to think that Coach was a classic, grownup brand.

38 Gloria Nicola, "Head Coach," www.2020mag.com, September 2, 2003.
39 Justin Schack, "The Best CEOs in America," www.globalpaymentsinc.com, January 2005.
40 "Teaching an old bag some new tricks," www.businessweek.com, June 9, 2003.

Now I see it's very iconic to America. . . . I don't think it takes itself too seriously. The ad campaign breathes a youthful vibe . . . energetic, colorful and cheerful."[41]

Production

Coach had maintained high standards of manufacturing right from its inception. Even as a small leather goods company back in the early 1940s, Coach selected only the top 10 percent quality of leather for its products (the company maintained this policy even in the early 2000s).

Not only did Coach use the best quality leather, but it also paid special attention to how the leather was treated and processed. The company's manufacturing process was designed to give the 'glove tanned' look, feel, and quality to its products. The leather was slow cured by rotating it in large drums for several days, after which it was treated using extracts from plants and aniline dyes[42] to produce a softening effect and to bring out the individual grains in each piece of leather.

So concerned was Cahn about the quality of the production process that he refused to move the factory out of Manhattan, despite rising rents and taxes over the years. He believed that if the factory was moved to a different place with a new set of workers, it might affect Coach's production methods, and ultimately the quality of its products.

When Coach was taken over by Sara Lee in 1985, the company reportedly promised Cahn that there would be no change in the way the business was run. This meant that Sara Lee also had to adopt the same production standards followed by Cahn. Under Sara Lee, Coach underwent a major expansion, which meant that the company also had to expand production. Even so, it continued to maintain the same quality standards.

After going public in 2000, Coach started outsourcing manufacturing to low wage countries. In 2000, Coach's net income increased by 131% to reach $38.6 million. Part of these gains came about as a result of a major cost-cutting effort in which the company closed factories in Europe and shifted production to low-wage countries like China and the Dominican Republic. By 2002, Coach had closed all its manufacturing facilities and outsourced the function to 40 plants located in 15 countries worldwide. This helped the company in lowering costs and also in getting the designs to the market faster. Because of these cost savings, the gross margin of Coach rose by 24 percent over the five years beginning 1997.[43]

However, even though Coach outsourced all its manufacturing, the company continued to maintain high production standards. It was observed that Coach rejected five potential manufacturers for every one it finally selected, and regularly sent Coach officials on spot inspection visits to the off-shore factories.

The company also had strict quality standards, and ensured that all the off-shore factories adhered to them. In 2001, Coach developed a book of production standards that outlined the company's stringent quality requirements with regard to the production methods. It listed among other things, instructions on how to inspect raw materials (for instance, leather could not be too soft), and how to align the edges of purses.

Frankfort was known to be a hands-on manager. He was reported to even take part in the design decisions of the company. Said Frankfort, "No color in a window, no color in a bag unless I understand it. Everything has to make sense."[44]

Coach's Expansion Strategy

In the early 1990s, Sara Lee sold Coach products mainly through Coach retail stores, the catalog, and through Sara Lee-owned retail outlets. As of 1996, Coach products were sold through 141 company-owned retail stores in the US and 147 stores located outside the country. By 1999, this number had increased to 165 retail outlets in the US and 150 stores outside the US (mainly in Europe and Asia).

In the late 1990s, Frankfort embarked on a massive expansion spree. Coach followed a 'multi-channel international distribution model' to reach a larger number of customers. Frankfort believed that increasing Coach's distribution was one of the primary growth drivers for the company. Under Frankfort's management, Coach increased its presence nationally and internationally by opening new stores in new as well as existing markets, and expanding the company's most productive stores.

By the early 2000s, Coach sold its products through different channels such as Coach stores, Coach catalogs, Coach factory stores, limited duty-free locations, authorized department stores, and the company's website.

As of 2005, Coach's direct-to-customer sales came from its catalogs, its online stores, its 193 company-owned North American retail stores, and its 82 North American factory stores. The company's indirect sales came from 94 international department stores, and around 1,000 department stores in the US. Coach Japan

---

[41] www.mandymoorenet.com.
[42] Aniline is an organic chemical compound, which is mainly used in the manufacture of dyes and drugs.
[43] Julia Boorstin, "How Coach got hot," *Fortune*, October 28, 2002, Issue 8.
[44] Sandra Dolbow, "Substance and style in the bag," *Brandweek*, October 14, 2002.

Exhibit 7 | Coach's Net Sales by Business Segment from 1999 to 2005

(In Millions of $)

Particulars	July 3, 1999	July 1, 2000	June 30, 2001	June 29, 2002	June 28, 2003	July 3, 2004	July 2, 2005
Direct sales	336.5	352	391.8	447.1	559.5	726.5	935.5
Indirect sales	171.3	196.9	224.3	272.3	393.7	594.6	774.9

Coach's year ended on the Saturday closest to June 30.

Source: www.coach.com.

Inc. (Coach Japan), the company's Japanese subsidiary, also operated 103 retail stores, department store shop-in-shops, and factory stores. (*Refer to Exhibit 7 for Coach's net sales by segment from 1999 to 2005*). Apart from this, it also generated revenues from wholesale through business-to-business programs (such as corporate gifts).

In 2005, Coach announced that over the next four years, it would open 100 new Coach full-price stores across the US and Canada, to bring the total number of full-price stores in the North American region to nearly 300.

Although Coach had a presence in 19 countries worldwide, Japan was its key international market. Coach realized that Japan could be a lucrative market, after it saw that its Signature Collection handbags sold extremely well in the country in 2001. Reportedly, around 20 percent of Coach's total annual sales in 2001 came from Japanese shoppers.[45] This, despite the fact that Japan was already crowded with luxury brand names like LVMH and Gucci (the top selling luxury brands in Japan at that time).

Since 2001, Coach had been making serious efforts to improve its Japanese operations. The company released its latest designs and styles in the country and sometimes even modified its designs to suits the tastes and preferences of its Japanese customers. Over the years, Coach also opened several exclusive retail stores, in addition to specialty stores and factory stores in Japan.

In 2001, Coach set up Coach Japan Inc. (Coach Japan), a joint venture with Sumitomo Corp. (Sumitomo).[46] By 2002, Coach Japan had almost three percent of the luxury handbag and accessories market in Japan.

Analysts noted that by 2004, Coach's Japan sales were growing four times faster than its rival and the top selling luxury handbags and accessories brand in Japan, LVMH. In the same year, Coach replaced Gucci as the second largest luxury handbag and accessories brand in Japan. By early 2005, Coach Japan was contributing close to 22 percent of Coach's total sales.[47]

Coach Japan adopted a two-pronged strategy for growth. The company planned to improve its distribution through expansion, and to stimulate demand for Coach products to gain a larger share of the accessories market in Japan. In 2005, Coach announced that it would open as many as 140 stores in Japan (including a minimum of 15 company owned stores) over the next four years.

In July 2005, Coach acquired Coach Japan by purchasing Sumitomo's stake in the venture for $120 million.[48]

Outlook

As of early 2006, the US contributed around 70 percent of the total sales of Coach, while Japan contributed around 22 percent of the sales (the US and Japan together accounted for close to 70 percent of worldwide spending on luxury handbags). Therefore, Frankfort decided to increase the company's retail presence in these two markets. However, he also believed that Coach could have better opportunities by creating (or targeting the existing) demand for its products in emerging markets.

In early 2006, Coach announced the next phase of its international expansion strategy. The company said that it would focus on Asia and other emerging markets to

[45] http://www.corporate-ir.net

[46] Sumitomo is a Japanese conglomerate with interests in areas such as machinery and electricity, transportation and construction systems, metals, electronics and network, consumer goods and services, mineral resources and energy, finance and logistics, materials and real estate, and media.

[47] Parija Bhatnagar, "Coach: Money in the bag," http://money.cnn.com, January 24, 2005.

[48] Indirect sales no longer included the sales from Coach Japan, after Coach acquired the complete ownership of the joint venture.

take advantage of the immense growth opportunities these markets offered.

In May 2006, Frankfort promoted Ian Bickley, president and CEO of Coach Japan, as president, Coach International, a division that oversaw Coach's international operations. Also in the same month, Victor Luis was appointed president and CEO of Coach Japan. "These organizational changes demonstrate Coach's deep commitment to growing our international business," said Frankfort.[49]

Apart from this, Coach also took several measures to increase its presence in the US. The company entered into an agreement with General Growth Properties Inc. (General Growth), a Chicago-based company that operated a chain of malls in the US, to enable Coach to open 25 new stores and expand the 10 existing ones in General Growth malls by 2008.

Further, in the first half of 2006, Coach extended its presence to smaller towns and mid-sized cities in the US like Evansville, Columbus, and Overland Park. Not only that, it also planned to open new stores in cities like Oklahoma City and Omaha, which were not really known as fashion centers.

While growth was good for the brand, some analysts were critical about the advisability of an upscale brand becoming so ubiquitous. Said Milton Pedraza of the Luxury Institute, "To be unique and exclusive you can't be ubiquitous. There's a fine line, and if you go into these smaller cities, I think you can cross that line."[50]

Another point of concern was the success of Coach's factory outlets. For instance, in fiscal 2005, a factory outlet at Woodbury Common, New York, the company's best selling factory store, generated close to $20 million in sales which was almost on par with Coach's flagship store in Madison Avenue, New York. According to analysts, the popularity of Coach's factory outlets could cheapen the brand's image. However, Frankfort maintained that the customers who visited the two stores were very different. Said Lori Wachs, a portfolio manager and retail analyst at Delaware Investments, "There is no question it is a very different mindset. The one wants fashion first and the other is a discount shopper."[51]

In early 2006, Krakoff unveiled a new line called the Legacy Collection. The line was launched to mark Coach's 65th anniversary, and was an updated version of Coach's traditional designs. Coach also launched a new Monogram Collection under its popular Signature Collection. In the new line, customers could customize their Coach products by embossing up to three initials of their choice on the products they bought. In early 2006, Coach was also named the most 'splurgeworthy luxury brand' in retail in the US by the *Women's Wear Daily*,[52] putting it ahead of popular labels like Ralph Lauren, Donna Karan, Hermès, Prada, and Fendi.

However, analysts pointed out that the brand's future success depended on whether Coach would be able to come up with new and innovative designs. Now that Coach had been established as a trendy brand, customers would no longer be satisfied with just the quality of the company's products.

Additional References & Readings

1. C. J. Rewick, **Trying new accessories,** *Crain's New York Business,* June 21, 1999, Issue 25.
2. Robert Barker, **Coach may carry too much baggage,** *BusinessWeek,* November 9, 2000.
3. **Coach Lexus renew partnership to produce Coach Edition ES 300,** www.theautochannel.com, January 5, 2001.
4. Joanne Gordon, **Serial tinkerer,** www.forbes.com, September 3, 2001.
5. Courtney McGrath and Erin Burt, **Coach connects,** *Kiplinger's Personal Finance,* April 2002, Volume 56, Issue 4.
6. Sandra Dolbow, **Substance and style in the bag,** *Brandweek,* October 14, 2002.
7. Julia Boorstin, **How Coach got hot,** *Fortune,* October 28, 2002, Issue 8.
8. Catherine Curan, **Reed Krakoff,** www.newyorkbusiness-risingstars.com, 2002.
9. **Teaching an old bag some new tricks,** www.businessweek.com, June 9, 2003.
10. LouAnn Lofton, **Coach's success story,** www.fool.com, June 12, 2003.
11. LouAnn Lofton, **Coach keeps it up,** www.fool.com, June 26, 2003.
12. Kathleen Gallagher, **Coach's new styles a hit, analyst says,** http://www.jsonline.com, July 6, 2003.
13. Michael Hainey, **In the bag,** www.departures.com, July–August 2003.
14. Gloria Nicola, **Head Coach,** www.2020mag.com, September 2, 2003.
15. Erika Engle, **Coach brings bags, boots and baubles to its new store,** http://starbulletin.com, November 14, 2003.
16. Robert Berner, **Coach's driver picks up the pace,** www.businesweek.com, March 29, 2004.
17. Kitty Go, **Coach class,** www.inq7.net, May 18, 2004.
18. Justin Schack, **The Best CEOs in America,** www.globalpaymentsinc.com, January 2005.
19. Barbara Woller, **Coach Inc. is having a smooth ride,** www.thejournal-news.com, May 23, 2005.
20. **BW 50: Coach's split personality,** www.businessweek.com, November 7, 2005.
21. Samantha Jonas-Hain, **Crystal to cashmere: Holiday gifts for women,** www.foxnews.com, December 12, 2005.
22. **Coach still has room in the bag to grow,** http://news.findlaw.com, December 14, 2005.
23. **It's in the bag,** www.nyse.com, December 2005.
24. Traci Purdum, **Coach Inc.: Alligators, pythons and iPods - Oh my,** www.industryweek.com, January 5, 2006.

---

[49] "Coach announces strengthening of international operations," http://news.morningstar.com, May 1, 2006.

[50] Jonathan Birchall, "Coach puts Midwest destinations on the timetable," http://us.ft.com, July 7, 2006.

[51] Lauren Foster, "Coach sales strategy is in the bag," http://us.ft.com, April 17, 2006.

[52] www.courant.com.

25. Kate Betts, **It's all in the bag,** www.time.com, March 20, 2006.
26. Lauren Foster, **Coach sales strategy is in the bag,** http://us.ft.com, April 17, 2006.
27. Lauren Foster, **Coach sales strategy is in the bag,** http://us.ft.com, April 17, 2006.
28. **Coach announces strengthening of international organization,** http://news.morningstar.com, May 1, 2006.
29. Lorene Yue, **General Growth to add more Coach stores to its malls,** www.chicagobusiness.com, May 18, 2006.
30. Tom Gardner, **Is it time to buy Coach?** www.fool.com, June 27, 2006.
31. Jonathan Birchall, **Coach puts Midwest destinations on the timetable,** http://us.ft.com, July 7, 2006.
32. Nicole Weston, **Get your Coach bag monogrammed,** www.luxist.com, July 20, 2006.
33. Greg Morago, **Put me in Coach,** www.courant.com, July 30, 2006.
34. www.stateoftheindustry.com.
35. www.coololdstuff.com.
36. http://searchwarp.com.
37. http://www.library.ucla.edu.
38. www.ftbusinessofluxury.com.
39. http://news.moneycentral.msn.com.
40. http://www.industryweek.com.
41. http://knowledge.wharton.upenn.edu.
42. www.iht.com.
43. www.fastcompany.com.
44. www.saralee.com.
45. www.coach.com.

Compassion Canada

W. Glenn Rowe

Hari Bapuji

Barry Slauenwhite, chief executive officer (CEO) of Compassion Canada, had reason to be happy when he reviewed the figures of sponsorship growth in 2002. Compassion Canada had grown from 18,684 sponsorships in 2001 to over 21,886 in 2002, a growth of 17 per cent against the 11 per cent projected for the year. However, Slauenwhite needed to turn his attention to the target of reaching 100,000 sponsorships by 2013. In the last 10 years, Compassion Canada had only doubled its sponsorships. Now, the goal was to achieve a five fold growth in the same amount of time. He needed a strategic plan that was based on a comprehensive analysis of the competitive landscape and resources and capabilities of Compassion Canada.

Compassion International Incorporated

Compassion Canada was associated with Compassion International Incorporated, a Christian non-profit ministry dedicated to the long-term holistic development of poor children, particularly those in developing nations. Everett Swanson, an American evangelist, established the ministry in 1952 in the basement of his house in Chicago. During the early 1950s, Swanson went to South Korea to preach to soldiers. In Korea, he witnessed the conditions in which many orphaned and abandoned children lived. He was moved by their condition and established the Everett Swanson Evangelist Association (ESEA). He appealed to American sponsors to help the needy Korean children with their schooling, clothing, food and health care. In his words:

> Christians have a responsibility to share with those in need. Surely our homes are the finest in the world, and our children are well clothed and happy. Our tables are spread with good things, and we enjoy many luxuries. Our babies do not need to cry for food or milk. We ought to thank God for His great goodness to America. But while God is good to us, in Korea there are thousands of boys who walk the street carrying a little tin can or pail, begging for a little morsel of bread. More Americans put more in their garbage can everyday than Koreans have to eat.

Soon ESEA grew and attracted a large number of supporters who were willing to sponsor the costs of providing food, education and health care to the needy children. In 1963, ESEA changed its name to Compassion International Incorporated. It worked solely in South Korea until it expanded its operations to Indonesia and India in 1968. As of June 2002, its operations spanned over 22 countries in Africa, Asia, the Caribbean, Central America and South America, helping a total of 350,484 children in these countries with food, shelter, health care and education. ESEA consisted of eight entities: Compassion International Incorporated, the founding entity in the Compassion International

Hari Bapuji prepared this case under the supervision of Professor Glenn Rowe solely to provide material for class discussion. The authors do not intend to illustrate either effective or ineffective handling of a managerial situation. The authors may have disguised certain names and other identifying information to protect confidentiality.

Richard Ivey School of Business
The University of Western Ontario

Incorporated (United States); Compassion Canada; TEAR Fund Great Britain (Compassion United Kingdom); Compassion Australia; TEAR Fund New Zealand; SEL France; Compassion Netherlands; and Compassion Italia. A brief sketch of Compassion organization is presented in Exhibit 1.

Compassion Canada

Compassion Canada was established in 1963. It began its operations in the basement of a home in Blenheim, Ontario, and moved to its own office suite in London, Ontario, in 1972, shifting to a bigger office space in 1986. Compassion Canada's activities, as reflected in its mission and purpose, revolved around helping needy children in developing countries in the areas of education, food, health care and overall development.

Mission

> In response to the Great Commission, Compassion Canada exists as an advocate for children, to release them from their spiritual, economic, social and physical poverty and enable them to become responsible and fulfilled Christian adults.

Purpose

> Assisting children to be:
> - Christian in faith and deed
> - Responsible members of their family, church and community
> - Self-supporting
> - Able to maintain their health

In pursuit of its mission and purpose, Compassion Canada found individuals who were willing to sponsor the expenses for children, linked individual sponsors with individual children and helped them maintain that link. Compassion Canada believed that most people cared enough to help needy children, if they could find a dependable and reliable mechanism through which to do so. Compassion Canada aimed to provide that mechanism in an efficient manner so that most of the money collected from the sponsors was spent on the children. In addition, it implemented projects aimed at child development through partnerships with local churches and community members who approached Compassion Canada and were approved through a stringent screening process.

"The child is the absolute key to whatever we do," said Slauenwhite. The activities of Compassion Canada aptly reflected that. As mentioned, it found sponsors who would support one or more children by giving Cdn$31 per child per month as a tax-deductible donation. In addition, Compassion Canada found donors who would support larger projects aimed at developing the communities in which the sponsored children lived. A list of current community projects of Compassion Canada is presented in Exhibit 2.

Child Sponsorship

An individual willing to sponsor a child was required to make a tax-deductible donation of Cdn$31 per month to Compassion Canada. Sponsors could choose the child of their choice or request Compassion Canada to randomly select one. The child so sponsored would be enrolled in the project of Compassion Canada and provided education, food and health care. When Compassion Canada enrolled a child in any of its projects, the funds were committed to help the child through to graduation from school (usually until attaining the age of about 16 or 17 years, depending on the education system of the country in which the child lived). However, it was not binding on the sponsor to continue to sponsor a child until this age. Sponsorship could be discontinued anytime.

Compassion Canada facilitated the interaction between sponsor and child. The sponsor was encouraged to write to the child regularly and was allowed to send monetary gifts two times in a year. Compassion Canada suggested that such gifts be in the range of $15 to $40. Implementation agencies helped the child in writing to his/her sponsor three times in a year. Compassion Canada sent the sponsor periodic updates on the progress of the child. In addition, it sent a biannual publication (Compassion Today) that featured Compassion Canada's work worldwide and a newsletter about Compassion Canada's work in the country where the child lived. If a sponsor decided to visit his/her child, Compassion Canada provided translators and gave out necessary information to the sponsor. The customer service centre of Compassion Canada handled the interaction with all sponsors.

Compassion Canada was very particular about emphasizing its belief in Christianity and its philosophy of using the Christian message to help develop each child and that child's family. It believed that church was a reliable and dependable infrastructure in most parts of the world. Therefore, it partnered only with churches and Christian agencies to support each child and to implement community projects. It focused on obtaining sponsorships from Christians, particularly the Evangelical Christians because Christians have a 'biblical obligation' to help the poor. Of Compassion Canada's over 20,000 sponsor-base, 60 per cent were Evangelical Christians while 37 per cent were other Christians. The remaining three per cent were non-Christians who shared the philosophy of Compassion Canada in its entirety.

It is not simply child sponsorship that we are interested in but child development in a Christian way. If we have a large number of non-Christian sponsors, it would be difficult for them as well as for us. There were occasions when we turned down offers of huge money from some donors because they did not share our philosophy. They would either ask us to work on areas that we were not interested in or ask us to be secular. In fact, we even stopped actively approaching the Canadian government for financial support because it expected agencies that received government aid to maintain a secular nature in their activities. In addition, government aid had the potential of diverting a large part of our energies towards interfacing with them.

Barry Slauenwhite, CEO

In the past, Compassion Canada targeted all segments of the population, including young and high school-age sponsors who were more ready to lend a helping hand. However, over time, the focus has been refined to target young married couples and post high school sponsors who tended to remain sponsors for a longer time. Compassion Canada enlisted the support of sponsors largely through promotion and advertising. It adopted a multipronged approach to promotional campaigning. First, it deployed Christian speakers and artists who supported Compassion Canada and were willing to promote its cause as part of their speaking or singing engagement. These artists became the ambassadors of Compassion Canada's cause. Second, it advertised on a growing network of 15 Christian radio stations throughout Canada. Third, it requested sponsors to promote its cause, in what was termed 'Awareness to Advocacy'. Sponsors were encouraged to approach pastors to promote Compassion Canada one Sunday each year; the Sunday selected was the last Sunday in May. Further, sponsors were encouraged to enrol new sponsors and volunteer their own time and effort to promote the cause of Compassion Canada.

Compassion Canada acquired sponsors through many ways. It participated in Christian events such as Kingdom Bound, Creation West, Teen Mania, Missions Fest Edmonton, and YC Edmonton. It helped sponsor these events and used them to promote the concept of child sponsorship and enrol new sponsors. It received sponsorships as a result of the Compassion Sunday that was held in churches. Speakers and artists who promoted the cause of Compassion Canada often persuaded their audience members to sponsor children. Compassion Canada's own staff, volunteers, existing sponsors, Internet and the Compassion Today magazine were other sources through which new sponsors were acquired. Acquisition of sponsorships through each of these sources is presented in Exhibit 3.

Acquiring sponsors was not an easy task and required investment of resources in advertising and marketing. Compassion Canada believed that it was important to be cost-effective, not only in sponsor management but in the sponsor acquisition as well. Accordingly, the ministry strived to bring down these costs continuously each year. In 2001, Compassion Canada spent an average of $103 to acquire a sponsor, whereas in the years 1999 and 2000, the costs were $121 and $130, respectively.

Compassion Canada strived to ensure that overhead costs (cost of raising funds and administration costs) were less than 20 per cent and program costs (costs towards child support, grants and services, field services, sponsor ministry and gifts in kind) were over 80 per cent. A breakdown of the costs over the last five years is presented along with a pictorial representation of how sponsorship money was spent in Exhibit 4.

Compassion Canada consisted of 27 full-time employees. Besides the full-time employees, many individuals who shared its cause volunteered their services. These volunteers attended the office as per a prearranged work schedule and performed activities such as mailing, reading letters, sending letters, etc. About 40 volunteers performed the work of three full-time staff members in 2002. Availability of staff was reviewed every quarter to ensure that an appropriate number of employees were available to smoothly manage the operations. An additional employee was hired for every 1,000 new sponsorships expected. When a new employee was hired, besides the qualifications, their sense of commitment to Compassion Canada's cause and philosophy was evaluated. Typically, Compassion Canada employees were over-qualified for their jobs but joined because they had *'a sense of calling'* and decided to do something that was intrinsically satisfying. Each employee was trained in Compassion Canada's systems department for a period of six months before being given a formal responsibility. Compassion Canada had not laid off any employee in its 40-year history although some were asked to leave for reasons of under-performance.

When an employee had served Compassion Canada for a period of five years, that person was sent to visit one of the overseas projects to meet with sponsored children and to witness in person the real impact of their work. Major events and achievements were celebrated within Compassion Canada. For example, when Compassion Canada crossed the 20,000 sponsorships mark,

Slauenwhite organized a huge dinner for the employees because crossing that mark meant that Compassion Canada had *changed the lives of 20,000 children.*

Compassion International Incorporated, with which Compassion Canada was associated, relied heavily on planning and co-ordination. Consequently, Compassion Canada was required to send monthly projections of its growth to Compassion International Incorporated. These projections were made one year in advance and were based on sound planning. Each of the projections was supported by the campaign events planned, number of people expected to attend and the number of people likely to become sponsors. When an individual became a sponsor, their profile was prepared and added to the sponsor database. These profiles were periodically analysed to understand the characteristics so that persons with similar profiles could be targeted in the future for child sponsorships. Although the growth in Compassion Canada was high, it was controlled growth.

Child Development Strategy

Compassion Canada's approach to child development was different than the approach of other similar organizations. The organization believed that to develop a child, one must help the child directly by providing food, education, health care, shelter and spiritual development in a Christian way. Accordingly, Compassion Canada focused most of its energies on child sponsorship. Other agencies followed a somewhat different strategy. They focused their energies on helping the communities and families to become self-sufficient. Focus on children was, therefore, not as visible in their projects and activities, although their mission was 'child development.'

Most of the child sponsorship agencies followed a community-based approach to child development, while Compassion Canada employed a direct approach in which the child sponsorship money was spent exclusively on child development by linking the sponsor and the child on a one-to-one basis. Compassion Canada's other programs ran parallel to child sponsorship and supported child development in an indirect manner. The organization raised money for community projects through a separate stream, and utilized them and accounted for them under a separate heading. On the other hand, the money raised by the organizations that followed the community-based approach was pooled together and centrally allocated for various projects aimed at child development, including direct benefits to children in the form of education, food and health care. Among the child sponsorship agencies in Canada, World Vision Canada, Foster Parents Plan and Christian

Children's Fund of Canada were prominent competitors for the sponsorship revenue that Compassion Canada needed to fulfil its mission. Financial and other details of these organizations and Compassion Canada are presented in Exhibit 5.

World Vision Canada

World Vision Canada (WVC) was 'a Christian humanitarian organization that reached out to the World's poor.' It was established in 1950 to care for orphans in Asia. WVC worked to 'create a positive and permanent change in the lives of people suffering under the oppression of poverty and justice through long-term sustainable development.' WVC's approach to child development was based on its community-based strategy, i.e., to initiate projects that were aimed at community development so that the community itself became self-sufficient over time and took care of its children. It developed an area development program (ADP) model to help communities achieve sustainable development. Activities included emergency relief (in cases of natural calamities such as drought, floods, earthquake, etc.), health related projects (such as tuberculosis, AIDS and nutritional health projects), and long-term development projects (such as sanitation, irrigation, vocational training and farming).

Almost 80 per cent of WVC's funding came from private sources, including individuals, corporations and foundations. The remainder came from governments and multilateral agencies. Besides the cash contributions, WVC accepted 'gifts in kind,' typically food commodities, medicine and clothing donated through corporations or government agencies.

Approximately half of WVC's programs were funded through child sponsorship. In 2001, more than 207,000 Canadians supported its child sponsorship program. The money so received from Canada and other countries across the world was pooled together and centrally allocated to projects that were designed to support 1.6 million children in 40 countries.

Foster Parents Plan

Foster Parents Plan (FPP) of Canada was a member of Plan International, which was founded in 1937, as "Foster Parents Plan for Children in Spain" to help children whose lives were disrupted by the Spanish Civil War. With the outbreak of the Second World War, Plan International extended its work to include displaced children within war-torn Europe in the 1940s. Gradually, its operations expanded to other countries and as of 2001, it was organized into 16 national organizations, of which Canada was one (also known as donor countries), an international headquarters and over 40 program countries.

FPP implemented projects in health, education, water, sanitation, income-generation and cross-cultural communication. Most of the funds for its community projects came from individual sponsors. FPP actively involved local communities in setting up and implementing projects, including families and children. Its motto was 'sustainable development: a better world for children now and in the long-term future.' FPP believed that to help a child in a lasting way, the organization must also help that child's family and the local community to become self-sufficient.

FFP identified the countries in need of development work with the help of a number of criteria, such as infant mortality rates (more than 25 deaths per 1,000 live births), per capita gross national product (less than US$1,700), and physical quality of life index (less than 80). As of 2001, about 111,000 children were sponsored by Canadians, and more than 1.3 million children were sponsored throughout Plan International worldwide.

After identifying the need, FPP worked in partnership with local non-government organizations and communities to effectively reach its goals. It aimed to work with them as long as was necessary to strengthen their capacity to provide their children with stability, protection and security in a sustainable way. Each community project took at least 10 to 12 years to achieve sustainable development.

In 2001, when Canadian contributions were combined with those of other supporters around the world, over $365 million went to program implementation. Of this amount, over 24 per cent was spent on habitat projects, roughly 20 per cent on education, over 11 per cent on health, 12 per cent on building relationships and six per cent on livelihood.

Christian Children's Fund of Canada

Christian Children's Fund was founded in 1938 by Dr. J. Calvitt Clarke, a Virginia missionary, to care for Chinese-Japanese war orphans. He called it the China Children's Fund. It expanded into Europe during the Second World War and became Christian Children's Fund. CCF Canada (CCFC) was formed in 1960. As of 2001, more than 600,000 children were supported by CCFC and its International Co-operative of Christian Children's Fund around the world.

CCFC believed in making the communities self-sufficient so that children were taken care of by the community in the long run. The sponsorship amount received each month was spent on 'providing food, clothing, shelter, medical care, education, school supplies and love to the sponsored' child. It was also spent to provide food, health care, vocational training, and agricultural expertise to the sponsored child's family and to the child's community. CCFC's projects included clean water wells, immunization programs and micro-enterprise training.

The organization derived its revenue mainly from monthly sponsorship support for children, families and communities. Other sources of support were: donated goods and contributions, general contributions and bequests from public, and restricted or specific contributions that were donated for a particular purpose or project.

Compassion Canada's Target of 100,000 by 2013

Barry Slauenwhite, the chief executive officer of Compassion Canada, believed in taking a professional approach to the management of non-profit organizations. With experience in industry and pastoral service and the sense of God's calling in his heart, he was in a perfect position to professionalize and grow the activities of Compassion Canada.

Compassion Canada had set itself a target of 100,000 child sponsorships by 2013. To achieve that target, the organization needed to reach its projected figure of 26,150 for 2003 and then grow at the rate of 15 per cent per year. Projections and growth in child sponsorships over the past few years are presented in Exhibit 6. Reaching the figure of 100,000 in 2013 would be a great achievement for Compassion Canada for it would mark two milestones: 50 years of operations and 100,000 children.

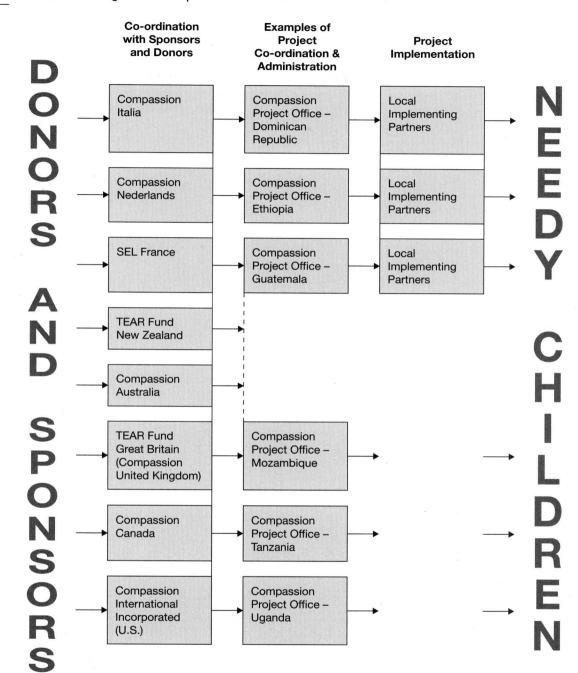

| Exhibit 2 | Community Project Types |

Education
Vocational and Primary Education

These projects focus on skills development for young people. Compassion Canada's primary education efforts are presently related to programs with children that fall outside of standard child development work (e.g., street children). Vocational training involves essential life trade skills for teens in areas such as carpentry, metal-work, hairdressing, tailoring and other clothing pattern work.

Current Projects
- Bujora Children's Home Vocational Training Centre — Tanzania
- Casa de Plastilina Children's Education — Mexico
- Community Leaders Educated AIDS Response (CLEAR) Phase II — Kenya
- Kumi Staff Training — Uganda
- Meals for Children Program: Day Love Children's Project 2001-2002 — Kenya
- Meals for Children Program: Mathare Street Children Rescue Centre 2001-2002 — Kenya
- Mukura Technical School Expansion — Uganda
- Ukuru Community Development — Uganda

Health
Primary Health Care

Compassion Canada's primary health-care partnerships focus on important preventative measures—like immunization, personal hygiene, nutrition, and health training for mothers with children under five years of age.

Current Projects
- Children's Medical Program: House of Hope — Haiti
- Children's Medical Program: Kiwoko Hospital Community Health Care — Uganda
- Community Leaders Educated AIDS Response (CLEAR) Phase II — Kenya
- Dessalines Community Health Program — Haiti
- Rubirizi Gravity Flow Water Project — Uganda
- Ukuru Community Development — Uganda

Clean Water
Clean-Water Supply

Compassion Canada supports initiatives aimed at supplying clean water to families. This may take the form of gravity-fed water systems in mountainous areas, well drilling or spring capping. Often the projects also include a sanitation component, such as the building of pit latrines, as uncontaminated water and effective waste management measures need to be in harmony.

Current Projects
- Agwata Water and Sanitation — Uganda
- Rubirizi Gravity Flow Water Project — Uganda

(continued)

Exhibit 2 Community Project Types (continued)

Micro-Finance
Small-Business Microenterprise Development (MED)

MED helps poor people by giving them access to capital and training so they can launch and grow small businesses. It is highly effective in lifting people from the lowest ranks of poverty and does so in a way that provides dignity and a sense of self-respect. Compassion Canada supports microcredit loan projects, including programming that can involve the parents and guardians of Compassion-sponsored children.

Current Projects
- Dominican Trust Bank — Dominican Republic
- Faulu Microfinance Expansion — Uganda
- Ukuru Community Development — Uganda

Agriculture
Agriculture

Compassion Canada supports community-based efforts that concentrate on objectives such as experimental crops, reforestation activities to conserve water and prevent soil erosion, vaccinations for livestock, the use of organic fertilizers and the developing of small farmers' co-operatives. The co-operatives help farmers to bring their produce to larger markets, while avoiding stiff profit charges from market middle-men.

Current Projects
- Bujora Children's Home Vocational Training Centre — Tanzania
- Casa de Plastilina Children's Education — Mexico
- Comitancillo Fruit Growers Association — Guatemala
- Ukuru Community Development — Uganda

Source: http://www.compassioncanada.ca/ca_communityprojects/project_types.html.

Exhibit 3 Sponsorships by Source (July 2000 to June 2001)

Source	Number
Christian Events	766
Canadian Office (from another sponsor/donor, Web, etc.)	749
Campaigns (such as Compassion Sunday)	529
Speakers	310
Staff	302
Volunteers	213
U.S. Office (from other sponsors, Web, etc.)	116
Artists	46
Advertising (Compassion Today magazine)	31
Other	303

Source: Company files.

Exhibit 4 Usage of Sponsorship Income (1997 to 2002)

Activity	2002	2001	2000	1999	1998	1997
Raising funds	838,367	722,639	676,558	660,881	646,761	601,032
Administration	522,267	495,512	430,420	438,813	335,638	328,519
Child support	6,311,438	5,407,600	4,842,005	4,498,724	3,482,028	3,215,897
Sponsor ministry	431,236	442,808	315,630	266,564	294,198	273,411

Notes:
Child support component reflects the money used to provide learning opportunities for registered and sponsored children.
Sponsor ministry supports letter translation, pays cost of child photographs and other incidental expenses related to strengthening the relationship of child and sponsor

Typical Distribution of Sponsorship Income

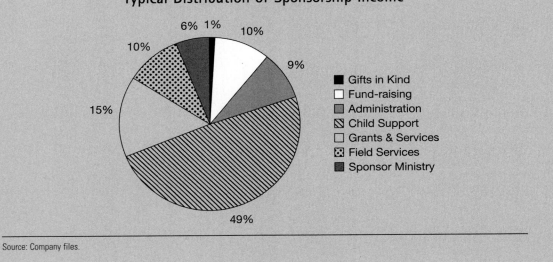

Legend:
- ■ Gifts in Kind
- ☐ Fund-raising
- ▨ Administration
- ▧ Child Support
- ☐ Grants & Services
- ▦ Field Services
- ▨ Sponsor Ministry

Source: Company files.

Exhibit 5

Financial and Operational Details of Compassion Canada and Other Organizations (as of 2001)

Item	Compassion Canada	Foster Parents Plan	World Vision Canada	Christian Children's Fund of Canada
Revenue				
Child Sponsorship Income	7,065,231	36,892,048	131,082,000	9,960,794
Government Grants	185,391	2,507,319	21,292,000	317,568
Investment Income	161,160	577,698	274,000	n.a.
Other Income[1]	890,045	2,294,478	43,074,000	16,962,304
Total Income	8,301,827	42,271,543	195,722,000	27,240,666
Expenses				
Program Expenses[2]	6,690,790	33,575,328	157,002,000	22,633,973
Fundraising[3]	1,026,443	5,233,845	27,675,000	2,296,944
Administration	559,143	3,463,798	8,463,000	1,610,020
Total Expenses	8,276,376	42,272,971	193,240,000	26,540,937
Surplus	25,451	(1,428)	2,482,000	699,729
Number of Children sponsored[4]	18,684	110,000	272,186	n.a.
Number of sponsors	15,945	n.a.	223,995	n.a.
Sponsorship cost in Cdn$ (per month per child)	31	31	31	29

Notes:
1. Other income includes income in the form of bequeaths, value of goods donated, and grants and donations for one or more specified or non-specified causes.
2. Expenses on all programs except in the case of Compassion Canada (where they pertain only to the expenses on child sponsorship).
3. Compassion Canada costs mentioned under two heads: marketing and community development
4. Foster Parents Plan figure based on the information on the Web whereas figures of other agencies are taken from their annual reports.
Source: Company files.

Exhibit 6

Growth in Compassion Canada—Projected versus Actual

Number of children sponsored	2002	2001	2000	1999	1998	1997	1996	1995
Projected	20,775	17,800	16,473	15,732	14,898	14,196	13,330	12,310
Actual	21,886	18,684	16,659	15,377	14,505	13,556	12,818	12,088

Source: Company files.

Cott Corporation, World's Biggest Maker of Retailer-Brand Carbonated Soft Drinks: The Growth Strategies

Srinath Manda

Punam Bihani

"Cott is seizing the future..... As we look ahead we see even more opportunities: to win new customers, to develop new products and to make new acquisitions."[1]

—*Frank Weise, Former CEO, Cott Corporation.*

"Private label has been around for many years, and we respect and aggressively compete with all of our competitors."[2]

—*Ben Deutsch, spokesman, Coca-Cola.*

"The majority of consumers are now looking at retailer brands in a different way. I don't see anything to stop retailer brands from growing."[3]

—*John Sheppard, CEO, Cott Corporation.*

Cott Corporation (Cott), headquartered in Toronto, Canada, is the biggest maker of retailer-brand soft drinks and the fourth largest soft drink company after Coca-Cola, Pepsi and Cadbury Schweppes in the world [Exhibit 1]. The company also makes juices and juice-based products, bottled water, ice tea, energy drinks and flavored beverages. The majority of Cott's products are sold under the brand names of its retailer customers. However, it also produces beverages under its own brand names. Under the leadership of Gerry Pencer, Cott increased the competitiveness of private label soft drinks by lowering the production costs, raising quality, and improving its packaging. Cott made a mark for itself in the Canadian market and then ventured into the US, the UK and Mexico. With rapid growth of private labels due to their increasing acceptance by customers and consolidation of the retail industry, Cott is expected to do well in the future. Further, Cott also has Wal-Mart as its top customer. This is likely to boost Cott's growth in future. However, Cott also faces some challenges. Firstly, private labels are considered inferior to branded products. In addition, the soft drinks industry is witnessing recession. The company also faces stiff competition from Coca-Cola, Pepsi and Cadbury Schweppes. These factors are expected to pose hurdles to Cott's growth in the future.

---

[1] "Cott Corporation reports record breaking results for 2003," http://www.newswire.ca
[2] Leith Scott "Private-label soft drinks bubble up," www.ajc.com, 14th November 2003
[3] Ibid.

Top-10 CSD Companies and Brands

2004 Rank	Company	2004 Market Share	Share Change	2004 Cases (millions)	Volume %Change
1	Coca-Cola Co.	43.1	−0.9	4414.8	−1.0%
2	Pepsi-Cola Co.	31.7	−0.1	3241.7	+0.4%
3	Cadbury Schweppes	14.5	+0.2	1485.9	+2.3%
4	Cott Corp.	5.5	+0.8	564.9	+18.2%
5	National Beverages	2.4	flat	249.4	+2.2%
6	Big Red	0.4	flat	41.5	−0.5%
7	Red Bull	0.3	+0.1	30.0	+45.0%
8	Hansen Natural	0.2	+0.1	20.2	+56.6%
9	Monarch Co.	0.1	flat	9.8	+7.6%
10	Rockstar	0.1	+0.1	9.7	+154.5%
	Private label/other	1.7	−0.3	171.5	−11.2%
	Total Industry	100.0		10239.4	+1.0%

Source: "2005 Press Release top-10 CSD", www.beverage-digest.com

Growth of Retailer-Brand Soft Drinks

Retailer brand products, also known as private labels, started in the Philippines in the 19th century, and the pioneer in retailing private label products was Supervalue Inc., operator of the SM Supermarket chain. Private label carbonated soft drinks (CSDs) were introduced in the early 20th century. Their popularity, however, diminished when branded CSDs extensively advertised to promote their products. During the early 1970s, sales of private label soft drinks picked up as consumers began to prefer cheaper products to branded, costly products. During that time, 'Private Labels' were known as "generics," i.e., low quality products packaged in minimal wrappings. In the 1980s there was a renewed interest in branded soft drink. But this time, private label CSDs retailers responded by improving quality. By the 1990s, popularity of private label soft drinks grew to the extent that supermarket chains showed private label soft drinks alongside well-known soft drink brands. There was a high consumer acceptance of private label soft drinks. The Atlanta Journal-Constitution, a leading daily in Atlanta, US, reported that for the period 1997 to 2002, sales growth of private label CSDs was twice as fast as that of the total soft drinks market. This was helped by sluggish economic growth and growing acceptance of private label products. An Information Resources Inc. report in November 2003 depicted the total market penetration of private label soft drinks across different distribution channels [Exhibit 2]. According to the report,

% of Private Label Penetration

Beverage	Wal-Mart	Supermarkets	Food, Drug & Mass
CSDs	15.0	7.0	6.0
Bottled Water	49.0	22.0	21.0
Milk	66.0	60.0	58.0

Source: "Fall 2004 Closure Report," http://cmadc.firstcontactsuite.com

Wal-Mart, world's biggest retailer, alone accounted for 15% of total penetration of private labels in CSDs. Market estimates until 2008 illustrate a promising future for private label soft drinks.[4] Success of Wal-Mart is expected to create lucrative conditions for additional private label CSD growth. Canada-based Cott Corporation is the biggest player in the private label CSD market.

Cott Corporation: The Growth Strategies

Cott was founded by a Montreal clothier, Harry Pencer, in 1955 to import bottled and canned soft drinks into Quebec from the US. Between 1955 and 1982, Cott was an importer of soft drinks under Harry Pencer. After Harry Pencer's death in 1983, his three sons—Samuel, Gerry, and Bill—inherited Cott. Samuel joined the company in 1983 and was in charge of Cott till 1987. During these years, Cott continued in the same line of business of importing soft drinks. It was under Gerry, who became CEO of Cott in 1988, that the $15-million-a-year[5] regional bottler was transformed into the largest supplier of private label soft drinks in the world.

In early 1990, Gerry discovered that Canadian supermarket chain Loblaws required a new supplier for its 'President's Choice cola'. Gerry met Dave Nichol, Director of new product development for Loblaws, who expressed the requirement for a cola product as good as Coke or Pepsi but of a lower price. Within a few weeks, Gerry returned to Nichol's office with the rights to use the cola company, Royal Crown Cola Inc's (RC) recipe. Nichol helped Cott modify RC's cola recipe and relaunch President's Choice cola in March 1990. It was an instant hit, and accounted for majority of Loblaw's sales. Gerry said, "The whole side of the business where Cott competed had been in decline for the last 25 years, and that was because if you bought private label you'd expect to pay less, but you would also expect to buy quality that was not as good as the national brand." He added, "So, we saw that there was an opportunity—that if you put a superior product in a package, and if you made that package comparable to the national brand, and if you priced it right, if the only real difference was cost, then the consumer was going to opt for it."[6]

Gerry drew his inspiration for this concept from his experience as a founding shareholder on the board of Onex Corp. Onex was a global company that operated in a variety of industries including electronics, automotives,

entertainment, healthcare and food. Onex owned the baking and dairy business, Beatrice, in Canada, which in turn owned the cookie business, Colonial, and Colonial manufactured 'Decadent' cookie. The Loblaws supplied 'Decadent' cookie under their brand name, which became a private label success story in the market. Gerry said, "The first people to really take hold of that concept were the President's Choice people, Loblaws, and what they've done in creating a value-added program. That gave us the opportunity to have someone go out and make the statement that our product, in an independently-run blind test, does every bit as well as either of the great national brands. So why pay $2 more for it? That's really what our success is all about."[7]

Cott was able to make a mark in the Canadian drinks manufacturing market by lowering production costs, maintaining quality and improving its packaging. Following this, Cott expanded into the US and UK markets largely via acquisitions. In May 1994, Cott entered the US market by acquiring the assets of beverage companies, Vess Beverages, Inc. and Vess Specialty Packaging Company including their manufacturing facilities in St. Louis, Missouri and Sikeston. In the same year, Cott entered the UK market by acquiring Benjamin Shaw, a British soft drinks company.

By the mid-1990s, Cott had grown into a multi-million dollar business [Exhibit 3]. Competitors Coca-Cola and PepsiCo began to initiate measures to deal with the new competition. Roberto Goizueta, former CEO of Coca-Cola, who had in 1992 dismissed private label as a "passing fancy", invited analysts to discuss 'the retailer brand strategy as advocated by Cott.' Ron McEachern, Pepsi-Cola Canada Ltd's former president, said, "Certainly, the threat of private label is real enough. In Canada, Coca-Cola Beverages lost $143 million in 1993 and closed eight plants—in part because it lost share to private label brands. Pepsi's new Pepsi Max cola and Nabisco's Chunks Ahoy! cookie probably owe their existence to the private label threat." He further added, "Innovation hadn't been there from the national brands. The growth of premium private label is a wake-up call."[8] Pepsi and Coca-Cola responded to the competition posed by Cott by reinforcing their own brands and cutting prices.

In January 1997, Cott acquired Premium Beverage Packers, Inc (Premium). Premium was Cott's largest carbonated soft drinks co-packer in the US, with bottling facilities located in Wyomissing, Pennsylvania. In March 1997, Cott acquired Texas Beverage Packers, Inc., a CSDs

[4] "The World Market for Private Label," www.mindbranch.com
[5] "Personality Profiles by Allen Jones," http://home.golden.net
[6] Ibid.
[7] Ibid.
[8] "Chapter 12—Brand STRATEGY ARCHITECT", http://www.knowledgeboard.com

Exhibit 3	Cott Corporation, Financial Information, 1996–2004

Income Statement

Year	Revenue ($ mil.)	Net Income ($ mil.)	Net Profit Margin
Dec 04	1,646.3	78.3	4.8%
Dec 03	1,417.8	77.4	5.5%
Dec 02	1,198.6	3.9	0.3%
Dec 01	1,090.1	39.9	3.7%
Dec 00	990.6	25.4	2.6%
Dec 99	990.8	18.5	1.9%
Dec 98+	958.5	(109.5)	–
Jan 98	1,017.0	(5.3)	–
Jan 97	1,002.	25.3	2.5%
Jan 96	929.4	(21.4)	–

Source: "Cott Corporation-Historical Financials and Employees," http://premium.hoovers.com

manufacturer. In the same year, Cott acquired UK-based manufacturer and distributor of consumer foods, Hero Drinks Group Limited (Hero). This acquisition gave the company access to Hero's state-of-the-art manufacturing facilities, including the production of polyethylene terephthalate for plastic bottles (PET). These acquisitions transformed Cott from a company that depended on third parties for much of its production to one that produced most of its beverages.

In 1998, the Pencer family sold a 30%[9] stake in Cott to leveraged-buyout firm Thomas H. Lee. In the same year Gerry Pencer died and Frank Weise was named CEO. To gain full control over its concentrate supply, Cott purchased the Cola company, Royal Crown (RC) Cola's beverage concentrate business as well as proprietary technology and a manufacturing facility from Cadbury Schweppes for $94 million[10] in July 2001. With the acquisition, Cott secured control of concentrate formulas, a key ingredient of its core products. In the year 2002, Cott entered Mexico through a joint venture with bottler, Embotelladora de Puebla, to form Cott Embotelladores de Mexico S.A. de C.V. (CEMSA). Cott Corporation executive vice-president and chief financial officer, Raymond P. Silcock, said, "We expect this new venture to break even this year and to be accretive to earnings in its first full year of ownership."[11] Cott purchased the retailer

brand beverage of North Carolina's Quality Beverage Brands, L.L.C. in December 2003.

In the period since its inception, Cott developed core markets in the US, Canada and the UK. The US became the biggest market for Cott's soft drinks. In the US, sales of retailer-brands (private label brands) commanded 11 per cent of the $24 billion soft drinks market. Cott was responsible for 66%[12] of those sales. The country accounted for 74% of Cott's sales for the year 2004 [Exhibit 4]. Cott supplied to more than 50[13] retail chains

Exhibit 4	Region Wise Sales of Cott Corporation for the Year 2004

2004 Sales		(in $ Million)
Area	$ mil.	% of total
US	1,221.8	74
Canada	189.5	12
UK & Europe	186.9	11
International	48.1	3
Total	1,646.3	100

Source: "Cott Corporation-Products/Operations," http://premium.hoovers.com

[9] "COTT CORP /CN/- 10-K Annual Report - 01-01-2000," www.getfillings.com
[10] "Headlines:1982 through 2004," beverage-digest.com
[11] "Cott, soft drink supplier enters Mexican market," www.ift.org, June 21st 2002
[12] Ward Andrew "Cott's drinks sales continue to fizz," *Financial Times*, June 22nd 2005
[13] "Chapter 12—Brand STRATEGY ARCHITECT," op.cit.

in the US, including giants such as Wal-Mart, and Safeway, the second-largest supermarket in the US. Cott manufactured "Sam's American Choice" cola for Wal-Mart and "Safeway Select" cola for Safeway. In the US, Cott operated through an indirect wholly owned subsidiary, Cott Beverages Inc. The company had a concentrate production plant and a research and development center in Georgia, employing over 1400[14] people and operating eight bottling facilities.

Canada was the second biggest market for Cott's products. Cott manufactured 85%[15] of the private label soft drinks sold in Canada. The country accounted for 12% of Cott's sales for the year 2004. Cott manufactured 'Great Value' cola for Wal-Mart, 'President's Choice' cola for Loblaw's, 'Master Choice' cola for the food retailer, A&P's, and 'Our Compliments' cola for the food retailer, Oshawa Group Ltd., among others in Canada. There the company operated through Cott Beverages Canada division. The company employed nearly 700 people[16] and operated seven bottling facilities.

In the UK, retailer branded soft drinks accounted for almost one-third of the market and Cott had about a 40%[17] share of retailer branded soft drinks. Cott supplied its products through Wal-Mart-owned Asda, the UK's second-largest food retailer, and J Sainsbury, UK's third-largest grocery retailer. It manufactured 'Sainsbury Classic' cola for J Sainsbury. There the company operated through an indirect wholly owned subsidiary, Cott Beverages Ltd.

The majority of Cott's products are sold under the brand names of its retailer customers. However, it also produces beverages under its own brand names such as Cott, Stars & Stripes, Vess and Vintage. Cott has also diversified into manufacturing juices and juice-based products, bottled water, ice teas, organic drinks, energy drinks and flavored beverages but majority of sales come from soft drinks. John Sheppard succeeded Weise as CEO in 2004. For the financial year ended December 2004, the company generated sales of $1,646.3 million, up 16.1% compared to the previous year, and earned a net income of $78.3 million.[18] In 2005, Cott Beverages Ltd. acquired 100% of the shares of Macaw Holdings Limited, the largest privately owned manufacturer of retailer brand CSDs in the UK. The acquisition significantly expanded Cott's UK business and is expected to add approximately $100 million in annual sales. According to Andy Murfin, senior vice president of Cott Corporation, "The acquisition of Macaw gives Cott U.K. the scale and efficiency to continue its growth strategy."[19]

The Future

As of 2004, in the entire developed world, sales of soft drinks experienced low growth as calorie-conscious consumers switched to other alternatives, such as bottled water. But Cott's sales did not follow that trend. Its growth was four times greater than Coca-Cola's growth. According to John Sheppard, "Even if the overall carbonated soft-drinks category declines we will continue to grow our [Cott] share."[20]

Analysts believe that there are significant opportunities for Cott's further growth. Cott is expected to gain from the rapid growth of private labels. *Financial Times* writes, "There has been an expansion in private label consumer goods, with retailers offering their own brands of everything from pasta to pet food." As of 2004, retailer brands account for one in five items sold in the US. In Europe the proportion is greater.[21] Statistics released from Information Resources Inc. (IRI), the market research firm that compiles information for the Private Label Manufacturers Association's (PLMA) Industry Yearbook, revealed that many large national brand companies are losing market share to private labels. Improved quality and marketing is believed to have increased the acceptance of private labels by customers. Research shows that seven out of ten consumers rate the quality of private label products as equal or superior to national brands, yet prices of private labels, on an average, remain 31% lower.[22] According to Brian Wansink, a professor of Marketing and Nutritional Science at the University of Illinois, most of today's private label products taste good and are packaged nicely. Another reason for growth in private label products as observed by *Financial Times* is that retail industry consolidation has shifted power from manufacturers to retailers. According to Wendy Nicholson, analyst at Citigroup, private labels help retailers to build brand equity, widen consumer choice,

[14] "Cott Corporation-Company Profile-Computer Business Review," http://cbronline.com
[15] "Chapter 12—Brand STRATEGY ARCHITECT," op.cit.
[16] "Cott Corporation-Company Profile-Computer Business Review," http://cbronline.com
[17] "Market Reports-View Sample data," www.beveragemarketing.com
[18] Cott Corporation-Company Profile-Computer Business Review," op.cit.
[19] "Cott Corporation announces acquisition of Macaw Soft Drinks in the U.K.," www.quote.com, August 10th 2005
[20] "Cott's drinks sales continue to fizz," op.cit.
[21] Ibid.
[22] Ibid.

improve profit margins and increase negotiation power over branded manufacturers.

The *Financial Times* opined that in the UK, retail consolidation is advanced. The top five retailers in the UK represent 75% of the market and the market share of private label soft drinks is 28%. Cott is expected to gain from this advanced retail consolidation in the country. In the US, soft drinks are central to any private label because they represent 5% of US grocery store sales. Cott is expected to gain from this as nearly three-quarters of Cott's revenues come from the US.[23] Further, according to Sheppard, the company has fulfilled only a fraction of its potential in the country and has, therefore, tremendous scope for future growth. Sheppard said that he is hopeful that as US retail-consolidation continues, the market share of private label soft drinks in the US is likely to come closer to the share they command in the UK.

Cott is also likely to benefit from the growth of Wal-Mart, its top customer, which accounts for more than 40%[24] of the company's total sales. As the consolidation of the retail industry continues, Wal-Mart is expected to do well in the future. According to a *Forbes* article, Wal-Mart plans to add 310 new stores and 30 new Sam's Clubs[25] to its stable of 3,625 locations in 2005.[26] One retail analyst expects that by 2010, Wal-Mart will have 3,000 "Supercenters,"[27] up from 1,600 as of 2004.[28] Such growth is likely to increase Wal-Mart's share of the retail market, thereby benefiting Cott also.

In addition, as opined by Euromonitor International, world's leading provider of global business intelligence and strategic market analysis, competition being fierce in the soft drink business, new products are constantly demanded to continually regenerate consumer interest. Here, Cott is likely to have an edge over its competitors, Coca-Cola, Pepsi and Cadbury Schweppes, as it has the advantage of producing brands for several different clients and is, therefore, not burdened by the extensive advertising and promotional expenses that Coke or Pepsi must bear. According to Sheppard, "I see continued growth opportunities for retailer brands. Initiatives we have in place are packaging innovation, new

flavours and diet products are receiving strong, positive responses from our customers." He further added, "The earnings from energy drinks and alternative channels in Canada, the new-product successes from our non-carbonated line in the U.K. and the continued focus on efficiencies in our U.S. system will help to position Cott well for top-and bottom-line growth through the balance of 2005."[29] Credit Suisse First Boston expects Cott to increase sales by 10% to $1.8 billion and operating profits by 7% to $220 million for the financial year ending December 2005.[30]

Cott expects Macaw's acquisition to enhance its sales growth. According to Sheppard, "The purchase of Macaw represents a significant strategic investment in our U.K. business. The additional production capacity and Macaw's manufacturing capability in the fast-growing aseptic beverage segment will allow us to expand the variety of products and packages we offer and enhance the service we provide to our customers."[31]

But along with the attractive growth opportunities, Cott is expected to face several challenges. *Financial Times* observed that, as of 2004, the soft drinks industry was witnessing stagnant sales and sluggish growth, partly because of the increasing popularity of bottled water. This recession in the CSD market is likely to impact the growth of Cott in the future. Cott estimates sales growth for the year 2005 to be between 6% and 8% down from previous estimation of 8% to 10%. Earnings per share are now expected to be between $1.06 and $1.11, down from the earlier expectation of $1.14 to $1.18.[32] According to Sheppard, ". . . Due to the slowing growth for carbonated soft drinks, the recovery will be slightly slower than previously anticipated."[33]

Financial Times reported that though the fastest growth of Cott's products is among higher-income families who judge products by value, retail brands are still bought more often by low-income consumers. This implies that the perception that private labels are inferior to branded products is still prevalent. Former Coca-Cola chairman and chief executive officer, Douglas Ivester, dismissed private label manufacturers as "parasites."[34] Wansink, who studied branding at the University of Illinois, conducted

[23] Ibid.

[24] Ibid.

[25] Sam's Clubs are Wal-Mart's warehouse stores.

[26] "Wal-Mart's Growth and Vulnerable Retail Sectors," http://www.uwex.edu, November 2004

[27] Supercenters are Wal-Mart's stores in the US.

[28] "Wal-Mart's Growth and Vulnerable Retail Sectors," op.cit.

[29] "Beverage firm Cott cuts growth forecast as Q2 profit dips," www.beverageworld.com

[30] "Cott's drinks sales continue to fizz," op.cit.

[31] "Cott Corporation announces acquisition of Macaw Soft Drinks in the U.K.," www.quote.com, August 10th 2005

[32] "Beverage firm Cott cuts growth forecast as Q2 profit dips," op.cit.

[33] Trichur Rita "Beverage firm Cott cuts growth forecast as Q2 profit dips to US$25M," http://money.canoe.ca, July 20th 2005

[34] Leith Scott "Private-label soft drinks bubble up," www.ajc.com, November 14th 2003

a test to find out how brand-conscious consumers were regarding the soft drinks. He pitted Coke against Sam's Choice in an annual event he called "Battle of the Brands." As part of the test, Wansink attempted to play a trick on students who took the test. He put Sam's Choice cola in a package labeled for Coke. Many people liked the choice displayed as Coca-Cola better, even though it was Sam's. Thus it would be a challenge for Cott to change the perception surrounding private label brands.

Analysts were apprehensive that a major threat to Cott is its overdependence on one big customer, Wal-Mart, which generates bulk of Cott's total sales. Analysts warn that such heavy exposure to one customer is risky and could pose problems for Cott.

Further, it is expected to be a big challenge for Cott to compete with highly promoted, global, branded players like Pepsi and Coca-Cola in the highly competitive soft drinks market. For 2005, Coke and Pepsi have already announced a slew of new drinks aimed at winning back consumers. "Coke with Lime" hit the stores in early 2005, following up on the success of "Diet Coke with Lime." Pepsi followed with lime-flavored versions of Pepsi and Diet Pepsi. Both companies also tried to seize

on the popularity of the Splenda artificial sweetener.[35] A reformulated version of "Pepsi One" and "Diet Coke" sweetened with Splenda were released in early 2005. In addition, analysts felt that Cott does not build brand equity the way its competitors do. A majority of consumers drink Cott beverages without knowing about Cott's role as a manufacturer. This is considered to be a disadvantage for Cott viz-a-viz its competitors. Kenneth L. Wolfe, former CEO of Hershey Company, world's largest chocolate company, remarked, "We believe that manufacturers which sell strong brands, constantly nurturing their brands' equity by maintaining excellent quality and value, as well as providing the required, innovative merchandising and advertising programs, will prevail over the longer term." He added "The consumer will demand these products, and private label will find it difficult to establish a beachhead if we are able to maintain a disciplined approach to pricing, that is, keep our costs low and price accordingly."[36] Mr Rober Flaherty, president of Cott USA, however, said, "I am confident that we will address head-on the challenges that we have been facing."[37]

---

[35] Artificial Sweeteners are substances which are not carbohydrates but give a sweet flavor.

[36] Martin Kathryn "The World's TOP 100 Food & Beverage Companies," www.foodengineeringmag.com, January 10th 1999

[37] "Beverage firm Cott cuts growth forecast as Q2 profit dips," www.beverageworld.com

C-11

DHL Bangladesh: Managing HQ–Subsidiary Relations

Hemant Merchant
Florida Atlantic University

Masud Chand
Simon Fraser University

Late in October 2001, Nurul Rahman, special assistant to vice president–human resources (VP-HR) at DHL Bangladesh (DHLB), contemplated his options regarding adoption of a Human Resource Information System (HRIS) that the firm's regional headquarters (HQ) in Singapore had proposed. The HRIS would computerize various human resource management (HRM) routines and provide much needed infrastructure to DHLB's HR department, which had difficulty coping with the organization's rapid growth. Yet, the proposed HRIS was an expensive initiative that DHLB seemed reluctant to adopt not only due to its uncertain payoffs but also because its implementation would solely be DHLB's responsibility. The charge of making an initial recommendation fell on Nurul, who knew his counsel would be heeded by his boss, Mr. Jahar Saha, VP-HR and a DHLB veteran. Mr Saha would almost certainly endorse Nurul's recommendation to the board. Nurul was also aware of the likely political fallout of a wrong choice.

In reaching a decision, Nurul had to balance the claims of various stakeholders, particularly DHLB and its regional HQ (in Singapore) that had often expressed a strong preference for streamlining HR systems across its Asian subsidiaries. Was the HRIS recommended by Singapore appropriate for DHLB? If so, where could DHLB find resources for the initiative's adoption? If not, what modifications would be needed to augment HRIS's suitability for DHLB? Nurul had less than a week to make a recommendation.

DHL Bangladesh

A subsidiary of the privately held DHL Worldwide Express, DHLB was a pioneer and the acknowledged market leader in the air express industry in Bangladesh. DHLB's principal business consisted of delivering time-sensitive documents and parcels worldwide to and from Bangladesh. Created in 1979, DHLB had grown into a US$10 million business by 2002. During this period, DHLB's employee base had increased from five to almost 300. Most of them were based in Dhaka, Bangladesh's capital, where the bulk of DHLB's clientele had their offices.

The rapid economic growth in Bangladesh created opportunities as well as challenges for DHLB. On the one hand, it allowed DHLB to increase its revenues and profitability and to achieve greater visibility within the DHL Worldwide network. On the other hand, this growth significantly increased workload for DHLB employees, who were overworked and stressed.

Although DHLB's organizational structure enabled the firm to grow with Bangladesh's anticipated expansion, the company's various departments had not grown evenly. Nurul recalled:

> In 2000, DHL Asia had implemented a regionwide cost management program. An important aspect of that program was to reduce back-line costs. Consequently, recruitment for back-line departments [such as HR] was frozen, and any new hiring for these departments had to be approved by the regional HQ. In fact, the cost-reduction

initiative was so vital that DHL subsidiaries needed regional approval even if they wanted to fill vacancies created by retirements or turnover. There had been instances where such replacement hiring had not been approved by the regional HQ.

The lopsided growth in DHLB's organizational structure created a bottleneck. Nowhere was this bottleneck more evident than in the HR department, which had been operating with just three employees since 1994, when DHLB had 150 employees. This situation presented a major constraint because DHLB considered people to be its principal resource. This made it imperative that all DHLB employees were well trained and highly motivated. Thus—despite being widely viewed as a "support" function—HR, in fact, played a vital role in DHLB's growth.

HR Department in DHLB

Despite its small size, the HR department in DHLB performed multiple functions whose discharge strained the two executives who were involved in its day-to-day functioning. A key priority for DHLB was employee recruitment at various levels. The bulk of this hiring was at the entry level, where demands upon the HR department were the greatest.

Over the past three years, these HR responsibilities not only had increased greatly because of employee hiring in various departments but also focused on development of generalist skills in the long term. There was also a sharp increase in the training and development of senior executives who were sent abroad for skills-enhancement workshops. Keeping track of these activities and ensuring a structure in which employees could perform multiple tasks increased the demands on the HR department significantly more than it had done at any other period in DHLB's history.

Perhaps the fastest growing HR function was the administration of compensation and benefits. Until 1998, employee benefits were decided on a company-wide basis, and salary increments were based on recommendations of individual department managers. Over the last four years, this policy had changed drastically. Now, all nonsalary benefits were being streamlined to DHL's standards for its Asia-Pacific region.

Likewise, salary increments were now being modeled on the latest techniques, and merit matrices were being implemented across all levels of DHLB. The "new" protocols for administering benefits and compensation created significant pressure on the two HR executives, who were already struggling with keeping up with their other HR obligations.

HRIS Requirements at DHLB

Currently, the core HR functions were managed with nonspecialized software, usually Microsoft's Excel spreadsheet. This software solution had served DHLB well even though it limited ways in which HR data could be manipulated or viewed. With the recent growth in DHLB staff, the HR department found it increasingly difficult to rely on a system that now seemed both "primitive and increasingly unwieldy" to manage. Sensing the imperative for better computerization within the HR department, DHLB management had (in November 2000) approved the acquisition of an HRIS that met the growing company's needs.

After consulting various DHLB stakeholders, the HR department had identified five criteria for selecting an HRIS: (1) ability to automate multiple HR functions, (2) ability to link various HR databases, (3) user friendliness, (4) adaptability to current and anticipated needs, and (5) initial purchase price and operating costs. By December 2000, HR had begun evaluating systems that were offered by local vendors. Although none of the vendors had an existing software application that exactly matched DHLB's needs, most vendors assured DHLB they would be able to develop a satisfactory solution within a reasonable period. All vendors offered DHLB free long-term technical support. Once DHLB decided on a vendor, it would take the vendor about two or three months to customize the solution to the subsidiary's requirements. If all went well, DHLB was expected to have an HRIS operating in approximately six months from the time DHLB placed its order. The system would adequately meet DHLB's needs for the foreseeable future.

Despite their merits, a major limitation of HRIS vendors was that their proposed software solutions would not be compatible with their counterparts in other DHL subsidiaries in the region. This did not seem to matter to some DHLB executives, who simply viewed HRIS as an instrument to ease the increasing HR burden on their subsidiary. Such sentiments were not endemic to DHLB. Other DHL subsidiaries in the region, including those in Pakistan, Nepal, and Sri Lanka, were also considering solutions that suited their unique needs. On various occasions, these subsidiaries had informed regional HQ of their desire to develop customized systems. Indeed, in 2000, DHL's Pakistan subsidiary had already developed an HRIS that it had customized to its own needs. Eager to assist other DHL subsidiaries, and perhaps to share some of its developmental costs, Pakistan had been keen to recommend its own system to other DHL units.

Regional HQ and HRIS

The fungibility of Pakistan HRIS appealed to regional HQ that seriously considered it for the entire region. The regional HQs played multiple roles within the DHL Worldwide network. Regional HQ was also responsible for the overall well-being of DHL's regional operations.

In the latter role, one of the main functions of regional HQ was to take data from its individual Asian subsidiaries and combine them into regionwide reports to facilitate subsidiary management and control. The HR function did not lend itself well to such regionwide analysis. Due to country-specific differences in HR practices, subsidiaries in each country where DHL operated used different types of information and reporting systems. This diversity had strained the regional HQ's personnel in their efforts to consolidate and analyze HR data from DHL Asian subsidiaries. As such, regional HQ always had an interest in standardizing the HR reporting practices across countries. Pakistan's proposal seemed to be just the tool regional HQ was looking for to reduce differences in the functional and reporting styles of DHL subsidiaries across Asia. Nurul recalled:

> From the regional HQ's viewpoint, a single HRIS that worked across different countries made perfect sense. It would considerably reduce the work of regional HR staff as they would no longer need to spend time consolidating and analyzing data from different countries. Besides, standardizing processes across the region was one of regional HQ's main functions. However, differences in reporting styles across countries were not merely cosmetic; they were the products of inherently different HR systems which reflected distinct corporate and legal environments of each country.

In December 2000, the regional HQ asked DHLB to suspend evaluating local vendors and consider DHL Pakistan's offer. In response, the HR manager at DHLB asked for an opportunity to acquaint himself with the Pakistan HRIS system. As he would later learn, the HR managers in DHL Nepal and DHL Sri Lanka had also made similar requests, to which the regional HQ had replied favorably. The meeting to evaluate Pakistan HRIS was scheduled in late February 2001 in Karachi, Pakistan, where DHL Pakistan was headquartered. It was expected that the meeting would be attended by senior HR managers of DHL Bangladesh and DHL Sri Lanka, the country manager of DHL Nepal, and Bruce Newton, the regional VP-HR. The responsibility of representing DHLB at the Karachi meeting had fallen on Nurul because of a scheduling conflict involving Mr. Saha, the VP-HR at DHLB, who would normally have represented his country.

HRIS Search at DHLB

Nurul had joined DHLB relatively recently and was one of the newest and youngest members of the DHLB team. He had graduated from the country's premier business school, which was affiliated with the University of Dhaka. Nurul's ability to deliver "quality" on special HR projects had earned him the respect of his colleagues and brought him to the attention of DHLB's senior management. Nurul had moved up through DHLB's ranks quickly and had earned the trust of Mr. Saha, who had often assigned him to work on key HR projects under his personal supervision. One such project was the search for a suitable HRIS vendor—that is, until the regional HQ put a stop to that search with its own suggestion.

After an extensive analysis, Nurul had shortlisted two local vendors that could easily demonstrate their solutions within a week of being told to do so. Now Nurul had to consider a third option that regional HQ had proposed: the Pakistan HRIS. Doing so would not only significantly delay DHLB's decision about adopting a customized HRIS but also require a very careful scrutiny of the broader context in which the HRIS acquisition decision was situated. Mr. Saha had been informed that regional HQ had now set a date for the HRIS project meeting during which DHL Pakistan would demonstrate its HRIS to the regional HQ and other subsidiary managers. DHL Pakistan hoped to persuade other subsidiaries that its own HRIS was the right software solution to their individual needs.

The Karachi Meeting

The Karachi meeting was as "interesting" as Nurul had expected. During the three-day meeting, DHL Pakistan managers briefed other DHL participants on the HRIS system currently used in Pakistan and acquainted them with the system. The hosts also gave the visitors short user training related to different functionalities of the Pakistan HRIS. Nurul recalled:

> The Pakistan HRIS was complicated software solution that required lot of familiarization to become comfortable with. Although the HR employees at DHL Pakistan appeared to be comfortable with its use, it was clear that this software required a lot of first hand involvement to attain proficiency using it. Despite this, I was surprised that Pakistan had not yet developed any user- or technical-training manuals. While the Pakistan system brought all HR functions together under a comprehensive database, it would require a great deal of customization to be brought up to DHL Bangladesh's requirements. DHL

Bangladesh and DHL Pakistan were very different in terms of their operations and size, and the two countries' HRIS requirements reflected that divergence.

DHL Pakistan was roughly twice the size of DHL Bangladesh, both in terms of revenue and personnel. The Pakistan subsidiary's operations were also much more geographically widespread. Moreover, the roles of HR departments in the two countries were generally different. Indeed, the demonstrated HRIS was primarily designed to meet the Pakistan subsidiary's needs—many of them quite different from those of the Bangladesh subsidiary.

The differences in HR practices manifested themselves in the expectations of the HRIS in each DHL subsidiary. For example, there were variances in the process of calculating gross salary for personnel. Although the calculation algorithm itself was easy to amend, the routine was hardwired into the system so that users could not change the settings from their side. To convert the system to do things in the DHLB style would require changes from the technical side—that is, from the original designers of the system. The DHL Pakistan staff could make these changes before the system was operational in Bangladesh. However, if there were any further changes—even minor ones—based on DHL Bangladesh's methods, or if there were any changes in industrial laws brought about by the government of Bangladesh, the system would have to be reconfigured from the technical side by its designers.

Another major difference was that DHLB often recruited temporary employees who were not eligible for many company benefits, whereas Pakistan regulations required DHL there to treat all employees as regular employees. Such adjustments would further complicate the Pakistan HRIS.

Yet another difference pertained to training records. DHLB maintained a database on training imparted to all employees. In contrast, DHL Pakistan maintained training records only for the last three years. Because these recordkeeping protocols were hardwired into the Pakistan HRIS, they could be not be modified by the user. This meant the existing HRIS software would have to be rewritten by engineers before it could become useful to DHLB. All this suggested DHLB not only would incur significant financial and nonfinancial costs if it adopted the Pakistani HRIS, but it ran the additional risk of downtime and operational dependence on another subsidiary.

Such concerns were downplayed by DHL Pakistan managers. In fact, they assured the visiting executives that their technical team could make country-specific customizations relatively quickly and at a reasonable price. Nurul believed if an application designed by Pakistan were adopted by DHL subsidiaries in the region, it would provide a major boost to DHL Pakistan's standing and influence. It would also raise the odds for Pakistan staff (especially from HR) to move upward to the regional level. Bruce Newton, the regional VP-HR, was highly impressed with the software and was confident of Pakistan HRIS's ability to be the platform for standardizing DHL's HR systems in the region. He let the executives know where he stood. Bruce said at the meeting:

> The Pakistan team has done a fine job of designing this software and I thank them for it. I can see they have put a great deal of thought and effort in designing it. Based on the demonstration we have viewed today, I am confident the Pakistan HRIS can be modified to meet the purposes of all DHL subsidiaries in the region. The only question I have is whether Pakistan can provide the level of technical support that might be needed by DHL's Asian subsidiaries.

The regional HQ's apparent liking for the Pakistan HRIS appeared to be driven by a variety of factors. First, the Pakistan HRIS not only was fully functional but also worked well in Pakistan. Second, the Pakistan HRIS was the quickest way for HQ to achieve its goal to standardize HR reporting systems across Asia. Third, the Pakistan team had assured Bruce that it could easily customize its HRIS to suit other DHL subsidiaries' requirements and that it also had the ability and willingness to provide technical assistance whenever needed. Given Pakistan's continued assurances of support, and perhaps because of Bruce's enthusiasm, the visiting DHL delegates also expressed confidence in the Pakistan HRIS.

Nurul, however, had reservations about the system he had just seen. Although he did not share his thoughts in Karachi, Nurul let his boss know about them when he returned to Dhaka. First, the financial burden of buying into the Pakistan HRIS would be five times that of finding a local solution. A locally developed solution would cost DHLB less than $5,000, whereas the Pakistan system (inclusive of ancillary expenses) would cost approximately $100,000, which would be split four ways among the three countries and the regional HQ. While DHLB management would probably approve this $25,000 expense, the monies would represent the HR department's biggest outlay for the year. Indeed, the outlay would constitute the largest HRIS investment in Bangladesh's "air express" industry.

Nurul's second reservation pertained to the variety of customized modules needed to make the demonstrated HRIS suitable for DHLB's needs. Nurul was particularly concerned about the range of these changes because they would have to be developed around the Pakistan HRIS architecture. Doing so was expected to needlessly complicate DHLB's system:

> *The problems with the Pakistan HRIS suitability for DHLB were both short- and long-term. In the short-term, DHLB would inherit a system that was expensive (probably the single largest line item after salaries on our budget) and complicated. In the long-run, DHLB would have a system that not only was extremely inflexible from the user front, but also dependent on another DHL subsidiary on the technical front.*

Nurul was also concerned about DHLB's technical dependence on the Pakistan subsidiary. He had noticed that DHL Pakistan had an IT specialist whose sole responsibility was to maintain the subsidiary's HRIS. This reinforced Nurul's suspicion that the demonstrated HRIS needed regular technical upkeep. Although DHLB also had IT specialists on its staff, there were fewer of them. In that all software changes would be designed in Pakistan—over which Bangladesh had no authority—DHLB would be at the Pakistan subsidiary's mercy vis-à-vis any and all technical assistance. Seeking the regional HQ's intervention was not a sustainable solution and, moreover, would make DHLB staff "look bad" to the regional office. Additionally, software documentation on user as well as technical platforms was either inadequate or nonexistent. DHL Pakistan would have to provide this

documentation before its reconfigured HRIS system could be implemented in Bangladesh.

DHLB and Its Regional HQ

Mr. Saha relayed these concerns to regional HQ, which had psychologically bought into what DHL Pakistan had to offer other DHL subsidiaries in the region. This was an important point that DLHB could not afford to ignore. DHLB reported directly to the Singapore-based regional HQ, which played an important strategic role in the DHL system.

The responsibility for fulfilling this role fell on the regional management team, which consisted of Asia-region VPs and some other top-level executives. This group had line authority over country-level top management and was ultimately responsible for the overall success of DHL in Asia. The regional VPs were important members of the group and served as principal advisers to the functional area VPs in individual countries: It was very rare that their "advice" was not heeded by subsidiary VPs. Although regional VPs did not have direct control over subsidiary VPs, the regional VPs had "very real power" and could significantly enhance or diminish the career prospects of subsidiary-level managers.

At the country level, all functional area VPs were in a quasi-matrix reporting structure (see Exhibit 1). A functional area VP reported directly to his country manager

Exhibit 1   DHL Bangladesh Matrix Structure

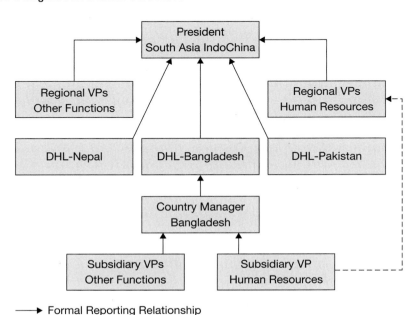

→ Formal Reporting Relationship
--→ Informal Reporting Relationship

and also, indirectly, to the regional VP holding that particular functional portfolio. Thus, Mr. Saha also reported to Bruce Newton, the regional VP-HR. The regional VPs did not have line authority over their country-level counterparts and could not issue direct orders to subsidiary VPs. Rather, the regional VPs' role was to coach, guide, provide expert knowledge, and lead cross-national projects. At least on paper, the regional HQ played a paternal role.

In reality, however, the regional VPs often wielded significant influence over country-level VPs, as most major country-level decisions required regional approval. Subsidiary-initiated projects not supported by a regional VP were rarely approved at the country level. Thus, regional VPs were crucial individuals to get on board whenever any major country-level program was initiated. Their influence was further magnified by their role as functional advisers to the regional president, who had direct authority over country management teams.

DHL also followed a 360-degree feedback model for evaluating the performance of its senior managers worldwide. This process involved seeking feedback from an individual's immediate supervisor, peers, subordinates, and customers as well as the regional management team. Thus, a regional VP's feedback played a crucial role in the career progression of an individual senior manager—especially if a country-level VP had any regional-level aspirations. The regional VP's strong endorsement was absolutely essential for any move to the regional office. An ambitious and upwardly mobile VP at the country level would think long and hard before turning down any advice from the regional VP. One written negative comment by a regional VP in a performance appraisal could easily be a career killer for the concerned country-level VP.

The HRIS Decision

Given the competing interests of various stakeholders, Nurul knew he had a tough recommendation to make. On the one hand, dropping the Pakistan HRIS customization idea was worth consideration. The modification might not live up to its potential in DHLB, and there still were Bangladeshi vendors willing to do the job for a fraction of the cost. On the other hand, DHLB had already spent considerable time and money on this project and could not afford further delays. The subsidiary's discussions with regional HQ and the Pakistan subsidiary managers had exhausted the HR department and, ironically, set it further behind in its day-to-day task completion. In any case, the regional HQ had constantly assured DHLB about Pakistan's commitment and technical support vis-à-vis the HRIS project. Would it not be better to continue with the Pakistan offer and solve potential problems when they arose? After all, the project had backing from the regional HQ.

Whatever Nurul recommended would have major ramifications at all levels. For DHLB, it was foremost a question about possessing the HRIS. Without it, there was no way the HR staff could stretch itself for much longer. It was also imperative to consider relations between the regional HQ and DHLB and between DHLB and other DHL subsidiaries in Asia. How might regional HQ view a deviation—even a "justified" one—from its position? Would it invite greater scrutiny in the future? Would it curtail the subsidiary's operational and strategic freedom? Would it be prudent for DHLB to accede to regional HQ's choice and save organizational energies for a "bigger battle" that might arise in the future? At an individual level, Nurul had to consider potential reprisals from a very powerful stakeholder. Indeed, how would his recommendation affect his own career at DHL? How might other HR staffers be affected? What about Mr. Saha himself? How would Saha view Nurul's integrity? These questions occupied Nurul's thoughts as he looked out of his office window: "What do I tell my boss three days from now? How—and how much—do I justify my recommendation?"

Case Discussion Questions

1. What advantages and disadvantages associated with a matrix structure does this case reveal?
2. For Nurul, identify the advantages and disadvantages for the three options: (1) proceeding with DHL Pakistan's HRIS, (2) proceeding with a local Bangladesh vendor, and (3) negotiating with regional HQ.
3. Rank order the factors in question 2 in terms of their (1) potential for solving DNLB's problems and (2) political importance from the viewpoint of DHLB and regional HQ. For a more detailed analysis, include the following stakeholders: (1) Nurul Rahman, (2) DHLB's HR department, (3) Saha, and (4) DHL Pakistan.
4. If you were Nurul Rahman, what would you recommend?

East Coast Trail Association

W. Glenn Rowe

Natalie Slawinski

On September 12, 2005, Randy Murphy, the president of the East Coast Trail Association (the Association, or ECTA), a non-profit organization located in St. John's, Newfoundland and Labrador,[1] was getting ready to meet with the Land Committee (the Committee). At stake was the future of the East Coast Trail (the Trail), a 540-kilometer coastal and wilderness hiking trail on the island of Newfoundland's Avalon Peninsula. The Committee's efforts to secure access agreements with landowners and to obtain formal recognition and protection from towns located along the Trail was a time-consuming process, requiring considerable effort, while achieving limited results. Meanwhile, the speed at which the coastline was being acquired for residential and commercial development was increasing rapidly. The Committee members knew that the Trail was at risk, and they were running out of time to secure the land access required to continue building the Trail. In fact, without public access to the land, the Association's dream of a 540-km trail would end.

Many changes had occurred within the Association during the summer. A new board of directors had been elected at the annual general meeting in June. The new board members would need to become familiar with the workings of the Association. In addition, several vice president positions on the board had become vacant. Of particular concern, the vice president of Legal and Lands, a well-known St. John's lawyer who had been instrumental in negotiating many of the Association's current land agreements, had decided to step down. The new vice-president of Legal and Lands had been a member of the committee for one year but still had a lot to learn about the position. Murphy had been heavily involved in land issues since he had become president of the Association back in 1996. In addition to his other responsibilities within the Association, he knew that he had to continue his involvement with the Land Committee until the new vice president was ready to stand on his own.

Murphy knew that securing land agreements was a huge job and that the Association lacked the resources and time to continue with that strategy alone. In the past several months, Murphy along with the Association's operations manager, had been involved in negotiating land agreements with five landowners located on the section of trail that was scheduled to be built in 2006 (see Exhibit 1). Without these agreements in place, the ECTA would not receive the funding it required from the federal government's Atlantic Canadian Opportunities Agency (ACOA) to build this section of trail. The results thus far had been

---

[1] The legal name of the province is Newfoundland and Labrador. Newfoundland is the island portion of the province, whereas Labrador is on the mainland of Canada, adjacent to the province of Quebec.

Natalia Slawinski wrote this case under the supervision of Professor W. Glenn Rowe solely to provide material for class discussion. The authors do not intend to illustrate either effective or ineffective handling of a managerial situation. The authors may have disguised certain names and other identifying information to protect confidentiality.

Exhibit 1   Trail Development Schedule

Trail Development Schedule

Development by Path	2006	2007	2008	2009	2010	2011	2012	2013	2014	2015
Long Bay - Quid Vidi	North Start									
Pouch Cove - Flatrock										
Flatrock - Logy Bay										
Topsail - Portugal Cove										
Portugal Cove - Bauline										
Bauline - Pouch Cove					North Complete					
Cappahayden - Chance Cove Park			South Start							
Trepassey - Portugal Cove South										
Portugal Cove South - Cape Race										
Cape Race - Chance Cove Park						South Completed				
Placentia - Colinet							Inland Start			
Colinet - Avalon Wilderness Area										
Avalon Wilderness Area - Ferryland										
Masterless Men									Inland Complete	

Source: Company files.

disappointing. It was taking far longer than anticipated to reach agreements. After six months of negotiating, the Association had obtained two signed agreements, and three agreements were pending further review and discussion with the landowners and their legal counsel.

Murphy thought about the long-term plan for trail development and the need to maintain and secure public access and rights-of-way. Only 220 of the 540 kilometers were complete (see Exhibit 2). Fourteen trail sections remained to be built, six of which were part of

Exhibit 2 Map of East Coast Trail on Newfoundland's Avalon Peninsula

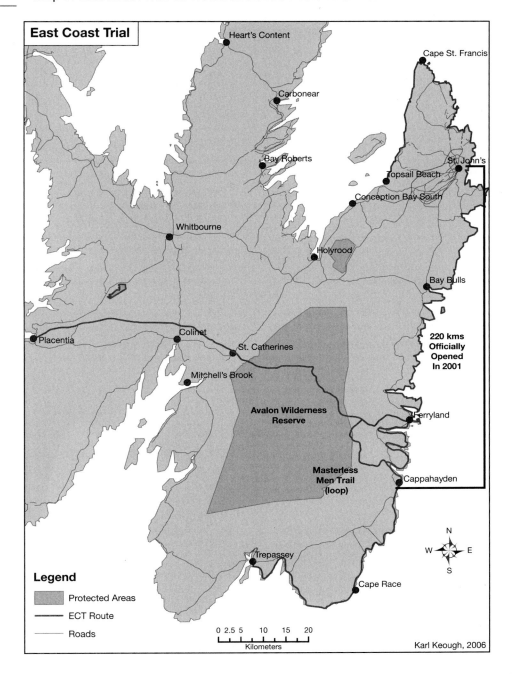

Source: Company files.

the northern trail, the most heavily populated and highest risk area for land development. The threat and probability of losing a significant section of the northern trail was very real, given the complexities of the land issues, the rate of change within the towns, the frequency of the land transactions, the lack of meaningful progress regarding trail protection, and the limited and volunteer resource base of the Association. This threat was the driving force behind the Association's decision to prioritize and raise the urgency to develop the northern section of the Trail. Murphy realized that the success of this decision would have to be supported by more effective short- and long-term strategies to secure the public access and right-of-way protection required to build the remainder of the Trail before the coastline was acquired by commercial and residential developers.

As president of the ECTA for nine years, Murphy realized that his worst fears were beginning to take shape—the coastline was being bought up quickly. Property on the coast of Newfoundland was relatively inexpensive, and the view of the cliffs and the ocean was spectacular. As a result, both residents of the province and visitors from outside the province were increasingly buying property along the ocean. Developers were building homes on prime coastal land, while visitors were buying ocean-front property so that they could spend their summers in the province. In addition, town councils were increasingly being pressured to free up more coastal property for development. The same situation had occurred in a neighboring Atlantic province, Nova Scotia. The result was that very little of that coastline remained accessible to the public. Murphy was concerned that, at the current rate of development, Newfoundland would suffer the same fate as Nova Scotia. He knew that this meeting with the new Land Committee would be critical for developing a new strategy for trail development, given the limited resources of the Association.

Hiking Industry Overview

Hiking had become one of the fastest growing recreational activities in North America, and industry experts were predicting that it would continue to increase rapidly over the next 50 years. Hiking had traditionally been associated with backcountry trekking, but its popularity was growing among day hikers as more and more trails were being developed near population centers. This increase in popularity was due mainly to the recognition of the economic, social and health benefits of hiking.

Given the increased popularity of hiking and the unique landscape to be found in Newfoundland, hiking had become a major attraction for tourists to the province over the past decade. The East Coast Trail, thanks to its marketing efforts and the media coverage it received around the world, had become an important tourist attraction. Given this trend, many regions within the province had begun to build their own trails hoping to lure tourists away from St. John's to more remote, off-the-beaten-path areas of the province. Some of these trail associations and communities had approached ECTA for advice on trail building.

As the only trail system of its kind in Newfoundland, the ECTA had to look to other volunteer-run trail associations in North America for best practices. The Bruce Trail, an 800-km trail system through Ontario's Niagara Escarpment, received approximately 400,000 visits per year and had a large economic impact on the region. The volunteer-based Bruce Trail Association, which had been in existence for 38 years, managed the Trail through nine locally based trail clubs responsible for the maintenance of their respective trail sections. The Appalachian Trail, stretching 3,520 kilometers from Maine to Georgia in the United States, is also managed by volunteers. The Appalachian Trail was run by the Appalachian Trail Conference, made up of 30 trail-maintaining clubs, and relied on partnerships with organizations such as the U.S. National Park Service, for maintenance funding. The conference also solicited donations and operated a trail gift shop. The Appalachian Trail attracted three million to four million people yearly. Although these associations provided some good examples for ECTA to follow, ECTA faced a unique set of challenges that it had to incorporate into its strategic planning.

East Coast Trail Association Background

The East Coast Trail had its beginnings in 1994, when a group of hiking enthusiasts started the construction of a coastal hiking trail to follow the traditional walking paths that had historically linked dozens of communities along the coast of Newfoundland's Avalon Peninsula. In 1995, the East Coast Trail Association was incorporated; its goal was to build and maintain the East Coast Trail from Topsail to Trepassey. This volunteer-run, non-profit, registered charity had 230 volunteer trail-clearers by 1996 and hundreds of fee-paying members. The following year, the Association obtained federal government funds through ACOA to develop a 220-km portion of the East Coast Trail from St. John's to Cappahayden, on what is known as "the Southern Shore." This region of the province, like many others, had been hit hard by the cod moratorium of the early 1990s, during which those employed in the cod fishery lost their jobs. Consequently, the federal government (through ACOA) was eager to bring new sources of economic development to the region. Building a hiking trail through these communities would create jobs in the short term, and in the long run would bring hikers and tourism to the region, thus allowing for the development of small businesses that could benefit from increased tourism, such as bed and breakfasts (B&Bs).

In 2001, the 220-km section of the Trail, built to world-class hiking standards, was officially opened to the public. Hikers could now enjoy a hardened trail that wound along the edge of the ocean, passing through historic fishing villages and along forts, lighthouses and other interesting historical sights. Word began to spread of this unique hiking experience, and the Trail began to draw hikers from around the world eager to experience the unspoiled wilderness, ocean vistas, seabirds, whales and icebergs.

What began as a small hiking club had grown into a large non-profit organization with paid staff, dedicated volunteers and aggressive goals. The end goal was a trail system totaling some 540 km of continuous coastal and inland trails, each path unique and varying in degree of difficulty. Of course, one of the challenges of many non-profits is financial survival. ECTA was no different. Its challenge was to find funding and support to fulfill its mission to develop, maintain and preserve the East Coast Trail while respecting the integrity of the natural environment and the needs of the communities, and delivering a high-quality wilderness hiking experience. The Association also had a vision to be recognized across the country as the premier hiking trail on the east coast of Canada and to be firmly established and sustainable.

Both the mission statement and the vision revealed the values that ECTA engendered: protecting the environment, promoting healthy lifestyles, creating a safe hiking environment, encouraging communities to become involved, sharing the spectacular scenery with people from all over the world and promoting Newfoundland as a premier hiking destination. ECTA needed resources to accomplish its goal of becoming sustainable.

Funding Overview

In the past, the federal government had been a major source of funding for ECTA. In 1997, both ACOA and Human Resources Development Canada (HRDC) had granted funds to develop 220 km of trail. This funding amounted to \$4.5 million[2] over five years. Other funding came from private donations, fundraising, memberships and product sales (see Exhibit 3). As a non-profit organization that did not charge a fee for trail usage, ECTA relied mostly on grants for its income, but the grant-application process was arduous and took up much staff and volunteer time. Not all grant applications were successful, and many grants required specific criteria to be met by the applicants.

Although federal government agencies had financially supported the construction of the first section of the Trail, they had not provided funds for the maintenance of the Trail. ECTA, therefore, relied on donations and volunteer maintenance groups for the upkeep of the Trail. ECTA estimated that between 1997 and 2001, it received \$1.5 million of "in-kind" contributions, which included the cost of volunteer time as well as corporate donations. The Association relied heavily on these two sources of "revenue." Because government funding was becoming harder to obtain, the organization needed to find alternative ways of becoming self-sustainable through its earned revenue.

Since the completion of the first section of the Trail in 2001, ECTA had not received another large grant as it had in 1997. As such, trail building had been put on hold. In order to continue building the Trail, ECTA had to change its strategy. It had divided the remaining Trail into smaller sections, thus requiring less funding for each section. ACOA had also changed its requirements for funding, now requiring that land agreements be in place for a minimum of five years before the agency would grant trail-building funds to the Association.

Competition

As a non-profit, ECTA competed for grants and donations with other trail systems and non-profits. Other communities and trail associations in the province were looking for government grants to build their own trails. Communities located outside the capital region relied more heavily on tourism and were better positioned to attract government funding because of the greater need for funding in rural areas.

In addition, there were many other worthy causes that competed for private donations, corporate sponsorships and members. Many hiking enthusiasts were interested in cultural activities and environmental

---

[2] All dollar references are in Canadian currency.

Case 12 / East Coast Trail Association

Exhibit 3   ECTA Financial Statements—Balance Sheet

(as of March 31, 2005)

Assets	2005	2004	2003
Current			
Cash	$26,089	$28,942	$54,388
Investment Account	$100,352	$66,552	$104,389
Receivables	$54,760	$83,286	$12,837
Inventory	$10,949	$6,104	$5,155
Prepaids	$3,538	$1,009	$1,012
	$195,688	$185,893	$177,781
Capital Assets	$3,557,496	$3,767,447	$3,977,054
Total Assets	$3,753,184	$3,953,340	$4,154,835
Liabilities			
Current			
Payables and accruals	$22,601	$14,270	$15,538
Deferred Revenue	$23,836	$24,231	$22,666
	$46,437	$38,501	$38,204
Deferred contributions	$3,566,117	$3,775,889	$3,985,661
Fund Balance			
Unrestricted	$140,629	$138,950	$130,970
Total Liabilities and Fund Balance	$3,753,183	$3,953,340	$4,154,835

Source: Company files.

ECTA Financial Statements—Income Statement

(year ended March 31)

Revenues	2005	2004	2003
Sale of Merchandise	18,705	33,779	28,484
Cost of Sales	12,328	7,405	2,000
Gross Profit	6,377	26,374	26,484
Memberships	7,580	10,565	14,325
Donations	26,343	29,338	48,752
Corporate Donations	11,000	11,000	11,000
Funding	125,796	143,770	134,775
Amortization of deferred capital contributions	209,772	209,772	209,772
Misc	22,230	12,435	6,173
Total Revenue	409,098	443,254	451,281

(continued)

Expenses

Advertising	12,117	6,036	8,758
Amortization	209,951	209,607	210,088
Conferences	27	1,140	887
Equipment	1,892	423	2,941
IT	1,210	1,675	0
Insurance	5,834	4,494	3,937
Interest and Bank Charges	93	62	770
Licenses and Fees	1,105	1,191	359
Meeting Expenses	251	1,550	0
Travel	1,436	3,161	0
Misc	16	589	1,682
Office	12,432	19,493	14,316
Professional Fees	60,752	0	2,875
Rent	6,400	6,285	6,000
Repairs and Maintenance	1,217	859	237
Telecomunication	3,295	3,754	4,595
Utilities	1,700	1,530	314
Wages	87,691	173,425	126,986
Audit Expense			2,043
Total Expenses	407,419	435,274	386,788
Excess of Revenue over expenses	1,679	7,980	64,493
Fund balances, Beginning	138,950	130,970	66,477
Excess of Revenues over expenses	1,679	7,980	64,493
	140,629	138,950	130,970

Source: Company files.

causes. ECTA had to both maintain its supporters and attract new supporters by emphasizing that it was not only a hiking trail, but an environmental and cultural cause, working to preserve coastal lands from erosion and from development, for future generations to enjoy. Many hikers assumed the Trail was publicly funded and therefore not in need of members, donations or volunteers.

Organizational Structure and Culture

By the time the first 220-km section of the Trail was launched in 2001, the Association was made up of a 15-member volunteer board of directors and three paid staff: an executive director, a fundraising coordinator and a project-based operations manager. The executive committee consisted of a president, vice president Marketing and Communications, vice-president Revenue and Membership Services, vice-president Finance and Support Services, vice-president Trails and, finally, vice-president Legal and Lands. Each vice-president, in turn, coordinated a number of committees whose members comprised board members and a stream of volunteers who gave countless hours each year helping with trail maintenance, administration, marketing, membership, organized hikes and numerous other tasks. All volunteer efforts were supported by the three paid staff positions. The organizational chart for ECTA is shown in Exhibit 4.

Exhibit 4

Organizational Chart
East Coast Trail Association—2005

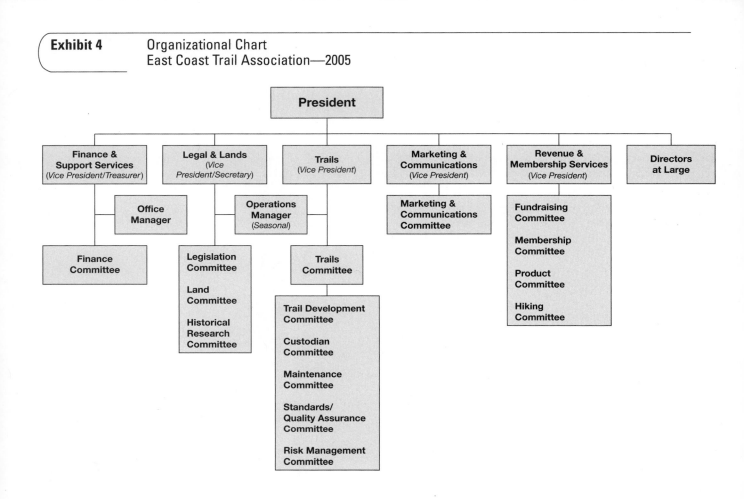

The President

The position of president was a volunteer position. The president chaired the board of directors and the executive committee and coordinated the overall activities of the organization. Murphy had held that position since 1996. In addition to his responsibilities as president, Murphy had been involved with many committees and projects, including the Land Committee, based on the ECTA's needs and priorities, which were driven by the availability of volunteers to support the essential work of the Association. Murphy also volunteered his time to lead hikes along the Trail and was an active trail custodian supporting trail maintenance. Although Murphy had a busy career with Newfoundland and Labrador Hydro (the provincial power generation company), he volunteered a considerable amount of his time to the Association. His passion for the Trail and his service to the Association over many years clearly showed in his focus, drive and commitment to fulfilling the 540-km dream of the East Coast Trail.

The Board of Directors

The board was made up mainly of educated professionals (accountants, lawyers, bankers, business people, university professors, government officials, etc.) who were active in the pursuit of ECTA's goals, giving many hours of free service to the Association. Some, like the vice-president Trails, a professional appraiser, had been on the board for many years. He led the Trail Maintenance Committee, and his experience and expertise were invaluable to the Association. Others, like a retired teacher from Witless Bay, a small community 40 kilometers south of St. John's, were new to the board, bringing new ideas and a fresh perspective. He was also the president of the Irish Loop Tourism Association; since the East Coast Trail passed through this region on the Southern Shore, he was well aware of the economic benefits of the East Coast Trail to the local communities. This active board member was also aware of the need to upkeep and promote the Trail to continue to attract tourists to the area.

In addition to providing the Association with a diversity of experience and expertise, the board members represented a range of interests, from protecting the environment to economic development. Regardless of their interests in the Trail, the board members believed that the Trail was a great asset to the province and to the Avalon Peninsula in particular. There was some turnover every year, representing a loss of continuity; anytime an active board member left, it represented a great loss for the Association. In the summer of 2005, despite the loss of several board members, Murphy had recruited a new group of competent board members and was eager to have the new board tackle the challenges facing the Association.

The Staff

In 2004, after suffering financial setbacks, the board had decided to downsize to a staff of two. The operations manager continued to oversee trail planning, building and maintenance. This job was a seasonal position, which was critical for the future development of the Trail. The position of office manager was created to replace both the fundraising coordinator and the executive director. The office manager would now oversee the administration of the Association. Community relations and fundraising activities, including grant applications, would now be in the hands of board members and other volunteers. These added responsibilities would be a challenge, given the volunteer turnover and the amount of work these efforts required of volunteers. The office manager acted as a coordinator of these efforts. In addition, paid work crews were hired on a project basis, conditional on funding, to support trail development only.

Committees and Volunteers

Given the limited financial resources and staff, several volunteer committees had been created over the years to accomplish the many goals of ECTA. These committees were led, for the most part, by board members who reported their activities back to the board. ECTA had numerous volunteers, many of whom had been with ECTA for several years. The dedication of these volunteers was evidenced by the successes of the Association despite its limited resources.

On the other hand, it was difficult to train and coordinate such a large number of volunteers. Because they were volunteers, they could not always be counted on to deliver what they promised. They gave what time they could but when they were unable to participate or contribute, the activities of a committee might come to a standstill. A problem for many volunteer-based organizations is turnover. ECTA was no different. Given that the Association was very much dependent on the work of volunteers, ECTA needed volunteers who were committed and prepared to invest many hours. Volunteers sometimes left because they felt they could not commit the time or effort required. In addition, the effectiveness of committees in many cases depended on the leadership of committee chairs; however, these committee chairs were also volunteers with busy professional careers, who could not always put in the required time.

The Members

ECTA members were critical to the organization. They paid a yearly membership fee to the Association, and some gave donations in addition to their membership fees. Members were also the most active volunteers. A typical progression was that a hiker would learn about the Association and become a member. Members would then learn about the volunteer opportunities through the quarterly newsletter or by word of mouth. The member would then join a committee and eventually might become interested in serving at the board level. Current members were also important for generating new members through referrals. Another source of membership was the volunteer-led organized hikes, which introduced people to the Trail and provided existing members with a chance to meet other hikers. The hope was that once a person had hiked the Trail, that person would then buy a membership. In reality, this strategy had not worked that well. There was no cost to joining the organized hikes, and many participants did not buy memberships.

One of the membership problems was retention. The number of members had declined in recent years. Some members did not renew their memberships yearly. The other problem was that the Trail was free, and many users did not feel the need to buy a membership. There was also a perception among some users that the Trail and the Association were government-funded and not in need of extra support.

The Struggle for Land Access

The struggle for land access had been ongoing since the East Coast Trail's beginnings. Although the vast majority of the land on which the Trail was located was Crown Land (land owned by the provincial government of Newfoundland and Labrador), 15 per cent was privately owned, and had posed numerous problems for the Association over the years. In the last five years alone, several developments had been built on coastal lands.

One notable development was a large castle that had appeared on a cliff by the edge of the ocean in a community just 15 kilometers outside of St. John's. The castle was owned by a millionaire from California who thought the dramatic scenery a perfect setting for his summer home. The owner had caught ECTA off-guard by building the castle on land along the East Coast Trail. The Trail followed a traditional right-of-way established by the local community through many years of active use. ECTA had not even been aware of the purchase of land or of plans to build the castle when the land was sold in 1999. By 2005, the castle was being completed and the No Trespassing signs were already up. The landowner denied access to the traditional right-of-way and blocked any further development by ECTA, effectively removing 500 meters of coastal trail.

This action had signaled to the Association that it was beginning to lose access to the coastline at a much faster rate than previously thought. For the most part, the Association had managed to negotiate privately and successfully with a number of landowners located along the Trail. Many of them were happy to cooperate and enjoyed having access to the Trail. Others were very concerned about the potential risk and liability associated with hikers crossing their property. Negotiating with private landowners was placing a strain on the Association's limited resources, and the number, frequency and urgency of land cases was growing rapidly. The Association had also been working with the communities to include the Trail in their town plans, but the results had been mixed. Some towns were cooperative, others not. Some notified ECTA when they revised their town plans while others did not. The other issue was that many communities along the Trail were not incorporated and did not have town plans. As a result, it was much harder to ensure that developers and property owners recognized the Trail passing through the property they had purchased.

There had also been some success stories. In 2004, the town of Bay Bulls, 30 km south of St. John's and located along the completed section of trail, had changed the zoning of a piece of property purchased by a developer so that the developer had to recognize the right of way of the Trail. This situation occurred because ECTA had reached an agreement with the town council to recognize the Trail on rezoning applications. This agreement had taken the Association a year to negotiate. Although in recent years ECTA had developed more cooperative relations with towns, the rate of development of coastal property by commercial and real estate developers was increasing, while the Association's resources were decreasing, and volunteers were, for the most part, only available to respond to these matters after hours and on weekends.

A New Strategy

In the previous year, the operations manager and members of the Land Committee had worked countless hours to secure land agreements with the five property owners located along the section of the Trail that was scheduled to be built in 2006. The Association could not get the funding from ACOA without these agreements, and without funding, they could not hire workers to begin building the Trail. Murphy and his team had been working on the agreements for several months, and some were not yet in place. Murphy knew that with 14 sections left to complete over the next nine years, a different strategy for securing land access and obtaining resources needed to be put in place. There were other issues to consider as well if the Association was going to be successful in completing the Trail and maintaining its current 220 km of trail.

Fundraising

The Association's income from product sales, fundraising, memberships and donations had declined in recent years. Attracting donations, organizing fundraisers, distributing the Association's products (mostly clothing and maps), and retaining and attracting new members was time-consuming and challenging. Without a full-time fundraiser, and relying mostly on volunteers, it was difficult to coordinate all of the fundraising efforts. This situation was a cause for concern since the Association had staffing and operational costs it needed to meet. It also needed funds to repair sections of the existing trail and to build future sections of the Trail. In addition, funding from government sources was increasingly difficult to obtain and required numerous volunteer and staff hours. The outcome of such funding applications was uncertain.

The funding for the next section of trail, which was scheduled to commence in 2006, had taken a couple of years to secure. The funding sources included the city of St. John's and ACOA, which would release the funds only once the land agreements were in place. The city of St. John's had contributed because the next section of trail was to start in St. John's and was important for the city's tourism. Where would the Association find funding for the following section and how long would it take to obtain such funding? The following section was scheduled to be built in 2007. With such aggressive timelines, the Association needed to find funds quickly.

Human Resources

The staff, volunteers and members were critical to the functioning of this non-profit organization. The Association was already short-staffed, resulting in an overload of work for both the office manager and the operations manager. The office manager did not have enough time to coordinate volunteer activities. In addition, the availability of the volunteer committee chairs to plan, manage and control the assignments of their committees was less than desirable to meet the day-to-day demands of the Association's workload. The result was that it was not always clear what the committees should be doing and when. Volunteer retention was another problem. There was turnover of board and committee members, and insufficient attention was given to recruiting new volunteers. It was a challenge to retain experienced volunteers as well as to identify and train incoming volunteers. The miscommunications and frustration resulting from the lack of coordination sometimes caused volunteers to leave the Association.

The Consultant's Report

In 2003, the Association requested and received funding from ACOA to hire a consultant to conduct an economic benefits and market analysis. Murphy knew that the Association had to quantify the return on the millions of dollars invested by the federal government in order to leverage new monies for trail development. In addition, he wanted to benchmark the current economic value of the Trail and to forecast its future value. The study, which was completed in June 2005, concluded that the market and media were responding extremely well to the Trail locally, nationally and internationally, and the Trail was having a significant and positive impact on the provincial economy. The report estimated that total annual hiker expenditures in 2004, based on 26,500 hiker trips, were more than $2.3 million, and the forecasted value by 2011 would be $6.1 million and 56,992 hiker trips. Beyond the economic benefits, the report had also highlighted the Trail as an invaluable public recreational resource. In addition, the Association was helping to preserve local heritage and the environment, and was building community pride. The study concluded that the Association should be commended for its success to date and should be given the support and encouragement required to grow this tourism asset to its full potential. Murphy knew that the Trail was having a positive impact on the communities and the province, but now there were numbers to support his belief. The report could now be leveraged to help fund trail development as well as to support the Association's goal to protect and preserve public access to the coastline.

Land Issues

Although land access was becoming more difficult to secure, especially along the more populated northern section of the Trail that was scheduled to be built in the next few years, Murphy knew that the communities had become more supportive in recent years. Several town councils were made up of individuals who understood the tourism potential of the Trail and who were eager to work with ECTA to complete the section of the Trail going through their community. Some communities were also planning to build their own small trails that would loop around and complement the linear East Coast Trail. Some towns were prepared to incorporate the Trail into their town plans to prevent developers from denying hikers access to trail heads. Murphy recalled a time when trying to get community support for the Trail was challenging. Now, it seemed, the communities understood the benefits the Trail brought them, in the form of hiker spending. So much had changed in the last five years. Many were also proud to have the Trail passing through their communities, since hiking was becoming increasingly popular.

Murphy felt that the land issues were too difficult for the Association to handle on its own. Individual agreements with landowners and towns were too time-consuming and uncertain. He thought about approaching the provincial government in the hope of obtaining legislation that would guaranteed public access to the Trail and create a trail corridor. Current legislation was not sufficient. Without legal protection, Murphy feared that the Association might lose the access required to build and operate the 540-km trail.

Murphy was optimistic that the provincial government would pay attention to the Trail. ECTA was well-known locally and was becoming known nationally and internationally among hiking enthusiasts. Articles about the East Coast Trail had appeared in the *Globe & Mail*, *Explore* magazine, a Spanish publication and in the *Los Angeles Times*. The Association had also won numerous awards for its stewardship of the Trail. Murphy felt that the Association had the visibility it needed to garner support for its cause. The Association now also had a consultant's report that quantitatively showed the value of the Trail to the province. The Trail was a unique natural, cultural and historic attraction that not only attracted tourists but was preserving part of the province's natural resources and cultural heritage. Murphy's biggest concern was the willingness of the provincial government to work with the Association and the time it would take to change the legislation. Was this a viable option? In some ways, Murphy felt it was the only option if the Association was going to complete the Trail.

The Time for Action

Murphy knew that it was time to act. He had already seen how quickly public land could disappear. In the blink of an eye, a castle had appeared at the edge of a cliff, blocking the Trail. What was once a path hiked by many eager to view the spectacular scenery was now fenced in and dotted with signs that read "Keep Out," "No Trespassing." Murphy sighed as he thought about the coastline in Nova Scotia, and how quickly that same scenario could occur in Newfoundland. The Association had come so far in 10 years. Hundreds of volunteers had contributed to the dream of the East Coast Trail. What could Murphy and the executive do to protect the Trail? Murphy walked into the Land Committee meeting ready to discuss strategic alternatives and to develop an action plan. The time was now or never.

Embraer: The Brazilian Aircraft Manufacturer's Turnaround and Growth

S.S. George
Shirisha Regani

"Embraer is one of the hottest manufacturers in the industry today. They're willing to push into areas that others haven't explored."

—**Donald Burr, the founder of People Express Airlines,**[1] **in 2004.**[2]

"A lot of people have tried and failed. But since 1960 only one new company and one new country have successfully entered the commercial aircraft market."

—**Richard Aboulafia, an analyst at the Teal Group Corporation,**[3] **in 2005.**[4]

"Years ago our competitors said: 'How dare those ugly ducklings from South America try to sell a jet in the Northern Hemisphere.' Fortunately, they underestimated us."

—**Satoshi Yokota, Embraer's Executive Vice-President for Engineering and Development, in 2006.**[5]

Embraer Launches New Business Jet

In May 2006, Empresa Brasileira de Aeronáutica S.A. (Embraer) announced the launch of its new business jet, the Lineage 1000 (Lineage). The Lineage's design was based on Embraer's successful E-190 regional passenger jet[6] platform, and the aircraft had the capacity to seat between 13 and 19 passengers, depending on the cabin design. The cabin could be split into five zones, and customers could choose from a variety of interior design options, which included putting in a standup shower and a full-size bed. The Lineage was a long haul plane, with a range of 4,200 nautical miles.

Embraer called the Lineage an 'ultra-large' business jet, and was expected to position it against the Boeing Business Jet.[7] The first Lineage aircraft, which was priced around $41 million,[8] was scheduled to enter service in late 2006. The Lineage was the newest addition to Embraer's range of business jets, which included the Legacy 600, the Phenom 100, and the Phenom 300.

---

[1] People Express Airlines was a low cost airline that operated in the US between 1981 and 1987.

[2] Jonathan Wheatley, Diane Brady and Wendy Zellner, "Brazil's Embraer Hits the Stratosphere," *BusinessWeek,* April 19, 2004.

[3] An aerospace and defense consulting firm based in the US.

[4] Russ Mitchell, "The Little Aircraft Company That Could," *Fortune,* November 14, 2005.

[5] Geri Smith, "Embraer: An Ugly Duckling Finds Its Wings," *BusinessWeek,* July 31, 2006.

[6] Regional passenger jets are small aircraft usually seating between 70 and 110 people, and generally used by airlines on short haul flights or on low traffic routes.

[7] The Boeing Business Jet family, introduced in the late 1990s, consisted of a series of aircraft based on the Boeing 737 design platform. The jets could seat between 25 and 50 passengers depending on the cabin configuration.

[8] Dollars ($) refers to US dollars in this case study.

As of mid-2006, Embraer was the fourth largest aviation company in the world (in terms of aircraft deliveries), behind Airbus SAS (Airbus), The Boeing Company (Boeing), and Bombardier Aerospace (Bombardier) (*Refer to Exhibit 1 for a note on the aviation industry and the profiles of major aircraft manufacturers*). In addition to business jets, Embraer also manufactured commercial, military and agricultural aircraft (*Refer to Exhibits 2a and 2b*).

Exhibit 1	The Aviation Industry and Profiles of Major Aircraft Manufacturers

The aviation sector includes all the industries, activities and regulatory bodies that are involved with the production and operation of aircraft and all their components. It includes civil aviation, military aviation, air transport services (passenger and cargo) and air traffic control. Some of the major aircraft manufacturers in the world are The Boeing Company, Airbus SAS, Bombardier Aerospace and Embraer, and smaller players like the Italian-French consortium Aerei da Trasporto Regionale or Avions de Transport Régional (ATR), which manufacture short-haul turboprops.

Traditionally, the US has been a dominant force in the aviation industry, with many of the major civil and military aircraft manufacturers (Boeing, Lockheed Martin and McDonnell Douglas) being based there. But with the setting up of Airbus in 1970, Europe also emerged as a major force.

In the early 2000s, the fastest growing market for aviation was in Asia, with China recording the highest growth. In late 2005, Airbus forecast that China's air travel sector would grow by eight percent a year for the next two decades while Rolls-Royce, which supplies aircraft engines, estimated that growth would be nine percent. Boeing estimated a 7.3 percent growth.[9]

The demand in the civil aviation sector has also been positively influenced by the increasing number of low cost airlines in the USA, Europe and Southeast Asia in the early 2000s. The low cost airline boom primarily increased the demand for medium-range, mid-sized single aisle aircraft.

A brief profile of some of the major aircraft manufacturers:

The Boeing Company: Boeing, founded in 1916 and headquartered in Chicago in the US, is one of the major aviation and aerospace companies in the world. In 2005, the company was the world's largest civil aircraft manufacturer in terms of *value* (with 49 percent of orders and 45 percent of deliveries), overtaking competitor Airbus for the first time since 2000 (although in terms of *number* of orders, Airbus was still the leader with 1,111 orders to Boeing's 1,029 in 2005).[10] Boeing was also the second largest defense contractor behind Lockheed Martin.

As of 2005, Boeing was the largest exporter in the US, serving customers in 145 countries across the world. Boeing's major commercial jets were the Boeing-737, the Boeing-747, Boeing-767, and Boeing-777. The Boeing-787 Dreamliner was due to enter service in 2008. As of mid 2006, Boeing employed more than 155,000 people in 67 countries. In the financial year ended December 2005, Boeing had a net income of $2.5 billion on revenues of $54.8 billion.

Airbus SAS: Airbus initially started out as a consortium of European aviation firms that came together to compete with American companies like Boeing and McDonnell Douglas. What was first known as Airbus Industrie, was set up in 1970 following an agreement between Sud-Aviation (France) and Deutsche Airbus, a German aerospace consortium. The group was joined by CASA of Spain in 1971. Airbus Industrie was based in Toulouse in France. In 2000, DaimlerChrysler Aerospace (the successor to Deutsche Airbus), Aérospatiale (the successor to Sud-Aviation) and CASA merged to form European Aeronautic Defence and Space Company EADS NV (EADS). In 2001, BAE Systems (formerly British Aerospace) and EADS formed Airbus Société par actions simplifiée (Simplified Joint Stock Company) or Airbus SAS, in a 20:80 joint venture.

Some of Airbus's major commercial aircraft include the single-aisle A318, A319, A320, A321 and the wide-body A300, A310, A330, A340 models with capacities ranging from about 110 to 400 passengers. The Airbus A380, the largest aircraft in the world, with a capacity to seat 555 passengers, was expected to enter service in the second half of 2007, two years behind its original schedule. In financial year 2005, Airbus had revenues of €22.3 billion (approximately $28.3 billion). The company employed 55,000 people in mid 2006.

---

[9] "China's Aviation Boom Drives World Market," www.spacemart.com, September 21, 2005. (accessed on October 3, 2006).

[10] From company annual reports. Boeing was expected to overtake Airbus in orders in 2006, after it recorded 487 orders for the first six months of 2006, as against Airbus's 117 orders.

(continued)

Bombardier Aerospace: Bombardier Aerospace was a division of the Bombardier Inc. which also had interests in railways. Bombardier Aerospace was formed in 1986, after Bombardier took over the government-owned Canadair aircraft manufacturing company after it had recorded the largest corporate loss in Canadian business history. Over the years, Bombardier Aerospace acquired several other ailing aircraft manufacturers including the Kansas, USA-based Learjet Company, which built the popular Learjet business aircraft.

In the early 2000s, Bombardier Aerospace manufactured regional commercial jets, business aircraft, defense-related services and fire fighting aircraft. Some of the company's aircraft included the Canadian Regional Jet (CRJ) family of aircraft, the Challenger family of extended range jets, the Global series of aircraft, the Dash-8 Q regional turboprops and the Learjet business jets. In fiscal year end January 2006, Bombardier Aerospace contributed $8.08 billion of Bombardier Inc.'s $14.7 billion revenue.

The following table shows the aircraft deliveries by the major manufacturers in 2004 and 2005:

	Total Units as of December 2005	Deliveries Units 2005	Units 2004	Seats 2005*	Seats 2004*
A318	28	9	10	963	1,070
A319	793	142	87	17,112	10,664
A320	1,469	121	101	18,150	15,150
A321	341	17	35	3,145	6,475
A300/A310	801	9	12	0	0
A330	385	56	47	17,542	12,815
A340	313	24	28	9,420	9,612
A350	0	0	0	0	0
A380	0	0	0	0	0
Airbus	4,130	378	320	66,332	55,786
ATR**	689	15	13	930	786
717-200	150	13	12	1,378	1,272
737-600	59	3	5	330	550
737-700	709	94	109	11,844	13,734
737-800	928	104	79	16,848	12,798
737-900/900ER	52	6	6	1,062	1,062
BBJ/BBJ2	86	5	3	0	0
757	1,049	2	11	400	2,415
767	935	10	9	1,452	2,421
777	539	40	36	13,596	14,152
747-400	642	13	15	832	4,192
747-8	0	0	0	0	0
787	0	0	0	0	0
Boeing	5,149	290	285	47,742	52,596
Bombardier**	2,042	158	195	9,803	11,292
Embraer**	967	141[†]	148[†]	7,914	7,607
Total–Props	1,410	43	32	2,640	1,886
Total–Jets	11,567	939	929	130,081	126,181
Total	12,977	982	961	132,721	128,067

*Estimate; excludes freighter/corporate variants
[†]Includes delivery of 21 Legacy/Military Derivatives in 2005 and 14 in 2004.
**The breakup of the deliveries of ATR, Bombardier and Embraer is provided in Exhibit 4.

Source: Commercial Aircraft (>30-Pax) Orders and Deliveries – December 31, 2005 Aircraft Currently In Production/Development. www.speednews.com, (accessed on September 29, 2006).

(continued)

The following table shows the indicative prices of some aircraft (in millions of US dollars):

Manufacturer/Model	2001	2002	2003	2004	2005
Airbus					
A300B4-600	106.9	109.3	111.8	114.4	117.0
A310-300	84.4	86.3	88.3	90.3	92.3
A318	40.9	41.8	42.8	43.8	44.8
A319	47.0	48.1	49.2	50.3	51.5
A320	52.2	53.4	54.6	55.8	57.1
A330	131.9	134.9	138.0	141.2	144.4
A340	126.3	129.2	132.1	135.2	138.2
A340-600	161.1	164.8	168.5	172.4	176.3
A380	257.7	263.6	269.6	275.8	282.1
Boeing					
737-600	45.2	46.2	47.3	48.4	49.5
737-900	67.0	68.5	70.1	71.7	73.3
747-400	197.4	201.9	206.5	211.2	216.0
767-200ER	108.1	110.6	113.1	115.7	118.3
767-400ER	134.0	137.0	140.2	143.4	146.6
777-200	164.5	168.2	172.1	176.0	180.0
777-300ER	218.9	223.9	229.0	234.2	239.5
787-3	118.7	121.5	124.2	127.1	130.0
Bombardier					
CL-600	26.6	27.2	27.8	28.5	29.1
CL-600 BD-700	42.3	43.3	44.3	45.3	46.3
CRJ900	29.7	30.3	31.0	31.7	32.5
Embraer					
ERJ-135	19.4	19.9	20.3	20.8	21.3
ERJ-140	21.5	22.0	22.5	23.0	23.5
ERJ-145	23.5	24.1	24.6	25.2	25.7

Note: Average prices based on the high and low list prices published by the manufacturers. Prices vary with the configuration, engines, avionics, special features, options included in the final airplane and the quantity ordered. Typical discounts on these list prices are from 5 to 15%.
Source: From "Aircraft Prices and Values," AirGuideOnline.com. http://www.airguideonline.com/airc_ prices.htm (Accessed on October 4, 2006)

Source: This information in this exhibit was compiled from several sources, including http://biz.yahoo.com, www.hoovers.com, www.boeing.com, www.airbus.com, www.bombardier.com and www.wikipedia.com.

Embraer was set up in the late 1960s, as a public sector enterprise by the Brazilian government. After some initial successes, the company ran into trouble in the late 1980s, and was privatized in 1994. Under private management, Embraer concentrated on developing regional jets, which pitted it directly against Canada-based Bombardier (the first company to introduce regional jets) in the aviation market. Embraer made a major foray into business jets with the successful launch of its Legacy 600 in 2000. After this, analysts said that the company was well positioned to take advantage of the rapidly growing market for small- and mid-sized aircraft and business jets in the early 2000s. In 2005, Embraer had a net income of

Embraer's Products

Category	Product
Commercial Aviation Market	• Embraer-170
	• Embraer-175
	• Embraer-190
	• Embraer-195
	• ERJ-135
	• ERJ-140
	• ERJ-145
	• ERJ-145 XR
Defense and Government Market	• Super Tucano
	• AMX
	• EMB 145 AEW&C
	• EMB 145 RS/AGS
	• P-99
Executive Aviation Market	• Legacy 600
	• Legacy Shuttle
	• Phenom 100
	• Phenom 300
Agricultural Aviation Market	• EMB 202 Ipanema

Note: The Phenom 100 and the Phenom 300 were scheduled to enter service in mid 2008 and mid 2009 respectively.
Source: Annual Report 2005, www.embraer.com

Exhibit 2b **Bombardier's Products**

Category	Product
Narrow-Body	• Learjet 40/40 XR
Business Jets	• Learjet 45/45 XR
	• Learjet 60/60 XR
Wide-Body	• Challenger 300
Business Jets	• Challenger 604
	• Challenger 605
	• Challenger 800 Series1
	• Bombardier Global 5000
	• Global Express/Global Express XRS
Regional	• CRJ200
Jets	• CRJ700
	• CRJ705
	• CRJ900
Turboprops	• Q200
	• Q300
	• Q400

Source: Annual Report 2005, www.bombardier.com

$446 million from revenues of $3.8 billion, and employed nearly 17,000 people (*Refer to Exhibit 3 for Embraer's key performance indicators*).

Background Note

Embraer was set up on July 29, 1969 by Brazil's Ministry of Aeronautics. It was the culmination of the country's aviation ambitions,[11] which began to take shape in the 1940s when the Brazilian government formed the General Command for Aviation Technology (CTA – Centro Técnico Aeroespacial) in 1946, and the Aeronautics Technological Institute (ITA – Instituto Tecnológico de Aeronáutica) in 1950.

The CTA was a unit of the Brazilian Air Force, and was the national military research center for aviation and aerospace. It coordinated all technical and scientific activities related to aerospace on behalf of the Brazilian Ministry of Defense. The ITA was a government-sponsored engineering institution and one of the most prestigious colleges in Brazil. It was set up by the Brazilian government to nurture and develop engineering talent in the country. It was a part of the CTA, and its facilities, including its laboratories and R&D centers, were located on the CTA campus. Both the CTA and the ITA played an important role in the 1950s with respect to aeronautical training and development in Brazil.

Over the years, CTA's Research and Development wing, the IPD,[12] worked on several aircraft projects for the Brazilian government. Most of these projects were commissioned by the Brazilian Air Force and were not for commercial use, but through them IPD acquired considerable expertise in aircraft technology.

Exhibit 3   Embraer: Key Performance Indicators

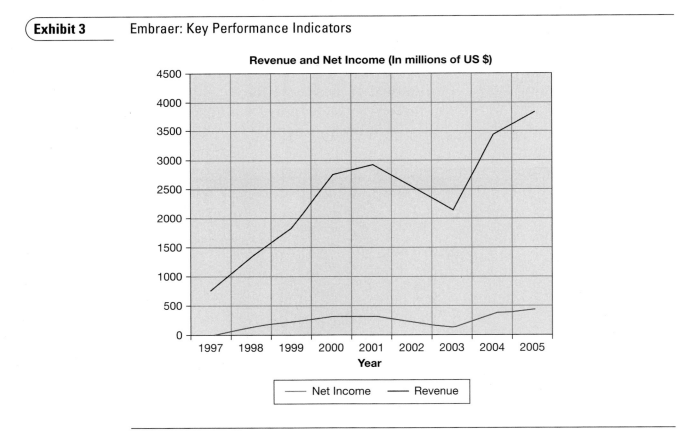

Source: Adapted from "Building a Globally Competitive Company," www.embraer.com, July 2006.

(continued)

---

[11] Since the early 1900s, the Brazilian government had made several unsuccessful attempts at building aircraft. However, it was only after the end of the Second World War (1939–1945) that the government started systematically investing in the necessary infrastructure to develop the capital-intensive aviation industry. Several government supported programs were launched after the War, which resulted in the creation of the CTA and ITA.

[12] IPD stood for Instituto de Pesquisas e Desenvolvimento, or the Research and Development Institute. The IPD was later known as the IAE (Instituto de Aeronáutica e Espaço or the Aeronautics and Space Institute). IPD was set up in 1954.

Exhibit 3   Embraer: Key Performance Indicators (continued)

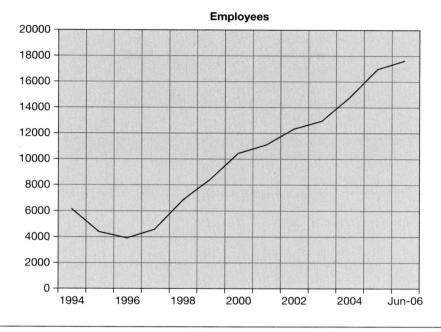

Employees

Source: Adapted from "Building a Globally Competitive Company," www.embraer.com, July 2006.

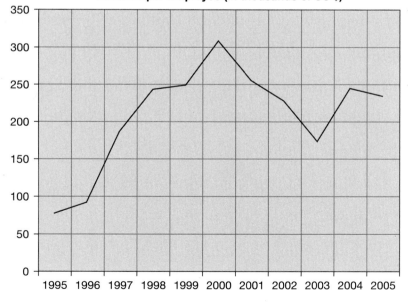

Revenue per Employee (In thousands of US $)

Source: Adapted from "Building a Globally Competitive Company," www.embraer.com, July 2006.

In 1965, IPD was commissioned by the Brazilian Air Force to design and manufacture a turboprop biplane[13] to replace its aging fleet of medium range aircraft. The project, which was known internally as the IPD-6504, was led by French engineer Max Holste, who helped design the aircraft. The aircraft was later named Bandeirante.[14] A prototype of the Bandeirante flew for the first time in 1968.

The following year, the Brazilian government decided to put the Bandeirante into commercial production, and established a state-owned company, Embraer, based in Sao Jose dos Campos in the Sao Paulo state of Brazil, for the purpose (*Refer to Exhibit 4 for a note on Brazil and its economy*). When Embraer was set up, it had 500 employees (many of whom were from the CTA and the ITA), and was headed by Ozires Silva (who had played an important role in developing the Bandeirante prototype). The company's initial target was to build two Bandeirante aircraft a month.

Exhibit 4	Brazil and Its Economy

The Federated Republic of Brazil is the largest country in South America and the fifth largest in the world, in both area and population. The country is considered to be a regional leader and economic power in South America. Brazil was formerly a colony of Portugal, and Portuguese is the official language. Brazil's capital is Brasilia, located in the central western region of the country, and the largest city is Sao Paulo (the capital of the state of Sao Paulo) located in the southeast (the most developed region in the country).

Brazil has vast natural resources and agricultural lands, and a substantial pool of labor. In 2005 the country's Gross Domestic Product (GDP) at Purchasing Power Parity (PPP) was an estimated $1.568 trillion. Brazil has a well developed service sector, which contributed more than 50 percent of the GDP in 2005. In the same year, agriculture contributed approximately 10 percent of the GDP and 40 percent came from industry. According to the estimates of the International Monetary Fund and the World Bank, Brazil ranks ninth in the world in terms of GDP (PPP). The per capita income of Brazil in 2005 was estimated to be $8,584 (which put it in the sixty-eight position in the world rankings), and the GDP growth rate over the previous year was 2.3 percent.

Brazil's main industries are automobiles, steel, aircraft, petrochemicals, consumer durables and computers. The country has considerable mineral resources, making mining an important occupation. The major export products of Brazil are aircraft, iron ore, coffee, steel, vehicles, soybean, orange juice, footwear, textiles, and electrical equipment. As of 2005, the US was Brazil's biggest export destination, with more than 20 percent of the country's exports directed there. Brazil also imported machinery, transport equipment, oil and chemicals from the US and other countries.

Before the early 1990s, Brazil had a government-dominated economy. But in the early 1990s, the government introduced the 'Plano Real',[15] which was a set of measures taken to correct and improve Brazil's economy. The government embarked on a massive privatization drive in 1993–1994, after which several companies were divested. The Brazilian legislature also passed several amendments which facilitated the greater participation of private and foreign investors in the country's economy.

In 1999, the Brazilian Central Bank delinked the country's currency Real from the US dollar, which resulted in a major devaluation of the Real. The Real continued depreciating until late 2002, after which it recovered steadily. In Brazil, the symbol R$ is used before the number and the decimal separator is a comma (,).

As on October 4, 2005, 1US Dollar was equal to 2.17 Brazilian Real.

Refer to Chart 1 for the trends in the exchange rate between the Real and the US dollar. Chart 2 gives the exchange rates of the Canadian Dollar against the US dollar. As on October 4, 2006, 1US Dollar was equal to 1.12 Canadian Dollars.

(continued)

---

[13] A turboprop engine is a type of gas turbine engine, which uses most of its power to drive a propeller. Turboprop engines are generally used on small or slow subsonic aircraft, although there may be exceptions. A biplane is a fixed-wing aircraft with two main wings of similar spans; normally one set of wings is mounted on the top part of the aircraft's fuselage, and the other is on level with the underside of the fuselage.

[14] Bandeirante means 'pioneer' in Portuguese.

[15] Portuguese for 'Real Plan'.

Exhibit 4   Brazil and Its Economy (continued)

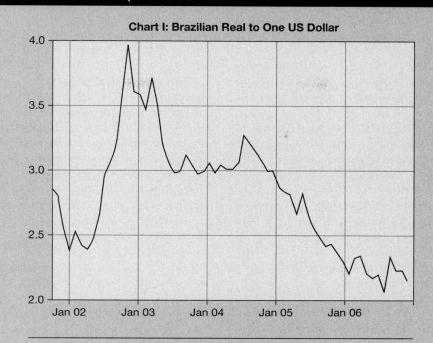

Chart I: Brazilian Real to One US Dollar

Source: Currency Converter, http://finance.yahoo.com

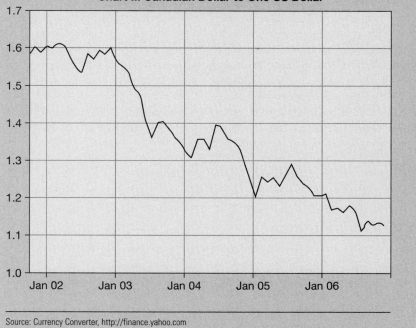

Chart II: Canadian Dollar to One US Dollar

Source: Currency Converter, http://finance.yahoo.com

Source: The information in this exhibit was compiled from several sources including www.wikipedia.com, "2006 CIA World Fact Book," (accessed on October 4, 2006 from www.theodora.com) and www.britannica.com

The first few Bandeirante were delivered to the Brazilian Air Force in 1973. In the same year, the company also recorded its first commercial sale of the aircraft when TransBrasil[16] bought one Bandeirante. In 1975, Embraer started exporting the Bandeirante, and eventually sold 500 aircraft in over 35 countries before its production was halted in the early 1990s. The success of the Bandeirante served to enhance the company's reputation in the global aviation industry.

In the early 1970s, Embraer also began manufacturing agricultural planes for the Brazilian government. Through the 1970s, Embraer developed several models of aircraft for the government as well as commercial clients. Embraer's noteworthy products in the 1970s were the Xingu (which was the company's first pressurized aircraft[17]) and the Tucano (which was its first combat aircraft). The Tucano was considered to be one of the most advanced military training aircraft at that time, and was later used by the defense forces of 14 countries including the UK and France.

In the late 1970s, Embraer started developing a new aircraft, the Brasilia, which was a turboprop regional plane with a capacity of 30 to 40 passengers.[18] The Brasilia was certified in May 1985, and the first aircraft was sold to the US-based Atlantic Southeast Airlines (ASA)[19] in the same year. At the time of its launch, the Brasilia was the fastest and lightest aircraft in the 30 to 40 seat range.

In the early 1980s, Embraer collaborated with Aeritalia (later known as Alenia Aeronautica) and Aermacchi (both Italian aircraft manufacturing companies) to develop a subsonic fighter plane. This project, known as the AMX Program, gave Embraer access to new technologies, which were to play an important role in its future.

The second half of the 1980s however, turned out to be a dark period for Embraer. In the late 1980s, Embraer had partnered with FMA (later known as Lockheed Martin Aircraft Argentina),[20] to manufacture the CBA 123 Vector plane (Vector), which was supposed to be the most advanced turboprop aircraft at that time. True to expectations, the Vector prototype included some of the best technologies of the time. But the aircraft's prohibitive price led to its commercial failure. The project, which had cost $300 million, was eventually cancelled without even a single plane being sold.

The failure of the Vector, combined with the new Constitution of 1988 (which reduced the government's support to the aviation industry),[21] and the end of the Cold War[22] (which led to reduced interest in defense matters), resulted in serious financial trouble for Embraer.

Being a government company, Embraer had lacked a business orientation, and failed to stay in touch with the changes in the business environment over the years. Its products, though technologically advanced, no longer matched the market's needs. In the early 1990s, Embraer drastically cut costs and laid-off more than 50 percent of its employees (from nearly 13,000 employees in 1990, only around 6,100 remained in 1994). In fiscal 1994 Embraer posted $250 million in revenue and $330 million in loss.[23]

Privatization and Turnaround

In December 1994, Embraer was privatized by the Brazilian government. Even after the privatization, the government retained a golden share with veto power which gave it control over strategic issues like sale of shares to foreign investors, employee relationships, and the terms of sale of aircraft to the military. Control over the company was acquired by a syndicate of Brazilian investors, consisting of the Bonazo Group (a holding company with interests in industrial and financial ventures) and two of Brazil's largest government-owned pension funds, Previ[24] and Sistel.[25] Each of these investors held 20 percent of the voting capital of the company.

---

[16] TransBrasil was a Brazilian International Airline. The airline stopped operating in December 2001.

[17] In pressurized aircraft the cabin pressure is maintained at levels close to the ambient atmospheric pressure at around 8000 feet or less, even when the aircraft is flying at much higher altitudes.

[18] The production of Brasilia officially ended in 2002, with 350 units sold.

[19] Atlantic Southeast Airlines is an airline based in Atlanta, Georgia.

[20] The Fábrica Militar de Aviones (FMA, or Military Aircraft Factory) was Argentina's main manufacturer of military aircraft. Formed on October 10, 1927, it was owned by the Argentinean government until 1995, when it was bought by Lockheed Martin. Lockheed Martin is a leading aerospace manufacturer and advanced technology company formed in 1995 by the merger of Lockheed Corporation with Martin Marietta. It is headquartered in Maryland, USA.

[21] Brazil has had a number of constitutions over the years. As of 2006, the constitution in effect was the one ratified in October 1988. The Constitution of 1988 was promulgated under the presidency of José Sarney, and was the seventh constitution of Brazil.

[22] The Cold War was the protracted geopolitical, ideological, and economic struggle between capitalism and communism that emerged after World War II, centering around the global superpowers of the United States and the Soviet Union, and their military alliance partners. It lasted from about 1947 to the period leading to the collapse of the Soviet Union on December 25, 1991. Between 1985 and 1991 Cold War rivalries first eased and then ended. (www.wikipedia.com)

[23] Sandra Arnoult, "Interview: Embraer's President and CEO Mauricio Botelho," *Air Transport World*, August 2006.

[24] Previ was the Bank of Brazil employees' pension fund. It was the largest pension fund in Brazil.

[25] The pension fund of Brazilian telecom major Telebrás. Telebrás was the Brazilian state-owned monopoly telephone system, which was broken up in July 1998 into twelve separate companies and privatized.

Mauricio Botelho (Botelho), the former Executive Director of the Bozano Group, became the new President and CEO of Embraer. Botelho was a mechanical engineer, who had previously worked in the construction and telecommunications sectors in Brazil. He had had no experience in the aviation industry, but Embraer's board apparently had confidence in his ability to revive the company.

Within two months of joining Embraer, Botelho unveiled a strategic turnaround plan to the board. The plan for the first two years of the turnaround period was to concentrate on improving productivity and regaining solvency. Although Embraer had already laid off a large part of its workforce over the early 1990s, Botelho believed that more job cuts were needed in the interests of productivity. Against the advice of many of his associates, he approached Embraer's union leaders to negotiate further layoffs.

At this time, relations between Embraer's management and the trade unions were tenuous, and verged on open conflict. Therefore it was not easy to push for more layoffs. But Botelho reportedly approached the union leaders and offered to share his business plan with them. The union leaders agreed to talk, and Botelho opened Embraer's books to them, and explained his turnaround strategy. He proposed laying off 600 workers and imposing a 10 percent cut in wages for the rest, with overtime hours reduced by half. He promised the union that he would build up the workforce after Embraer achieved a turnaround.

The union leaders analyzed Botelho's plan with the help of an outside consultant. After two weeks of deliberation, the union agreed to cooperate on the condition that, like the rest of the workers, Botelho and the rest of the top management also take a 10 percent pay cut. Botelho agreed and the union finally assented to the layoffs and wage cuts.

Botelho said later that this was the turning point in the revival of Embraer. The management had proved that it was committed to the company and its workers, and the workers had in turn embraced the turnaround efforts.[26]

Creating a Customer-centric Organization

After securing the union's support, Botelho started implementing his turnaround strategy. He realized that while the company faced no dearth of technical talent (Sao Jose dos Campos, where the headquarters of Embraer was situated, was one of the most technically advanced cities in Brazil, and was home to several institutions from where Embraer recruited qualified engineers), Embraer's management and workers lacked a business orientation. Botelho recalled that when he first joined the company, he asked the acting CEO what Embraer's business was. Reportedly, the reply was, "Our business is to manufacture aircraft." Botelho recalled telling him, "You are wrong. Your business is not to manufacture aircraft. If it is, why not just put a machine to work turning out airplanes? You'll have plenty on the tarmac, and then what? Your business is to serve your customer."[27]

In the past, as a government-owned company, Embraer had been largely insulated from the competition in the highly dynamic global aviation industry. However, Botelho understood that the post-privatization Embraer had to be distinctly customer-oriented. To this end, he started making several changes at the company to bring about a market-focused approach to business.

To emphasize the importance of being customer-oriented, Botelho pointed to the example of the ill-fated Vector, the Embraer aircraft that had failed to sell despite its technical superiority. According to Botelho, the Vector was a plane "designed by engineers for pilots" while ignoring the customer. He said that it exemplified the danger of giving engineers so much free rein that they forgot to focus on customer needs. Reportedly, after he took over, Botelho insisted on having a picture of the Vector in Embraer's offices, as a constant reminder of the dangers of forgetting the customer.[28]

Botelho also reorganized Embraer, creating five new 'profit centers'. Three of these profit centers focused on specific geographic regions; the fourth was for light aircraft; and the fifth for government sales. Botelho put an 'entrepreneur' in charge of each profit center with the specific task of improving customer relationships.

However, Botelho did not make any drastic personnel changes. For example, instead of bringing in new marketing professionals, he trained the existing engineers to direct their skills towards customer needs and expectations in every project they undertook. He also launched a program to provide onsite training in business administration for all managers, and announced that all lower level workers would be brought up to a high school level of education. Botelho also made very few changes in the top management, retaining most of the senior managers and bringing in only three new top executives from outside.

---

[26] Edvaldo Pereira Lima, "Flying high: Embraer's Mauricio Botelho has taken a flagging, state-owned company and turned it into the fourth-largest aircraft maker in the world—Profile," *The Chief Executive*, January–February, 2003.

[27] Russ Mitchell, "The Little Aircraft Company That Could," *Fortune*, November 14, 2005.

[28] David J. Lynch, "Comeback Kid Embraer has Hot Jet, Fiery CEO to Match," *USA Today*, March 7, 2006.

Focus on Regional Jets

When Botelho became the CEO of Embraer, with projects running behind schedule, most of the company's new product development initiatives were in a shambles. Consequently, Embraer had few products that showed commercial potential. An exception was the ERJ-145 project,[29] which had been launched in 1989. The ERJ-145 was a 50-seat regional passenger jet, which was being designed to compete against Bombardier's comparable CRJ-200[30] aircraft.

In 1995, Botelho cancelled all other projects and staked Embraer's future on the ERJ-145. This was an extremely risky move for Embraer, as Bombardier clearly dominated the market for regional jets at that time. Besides, Embraer had little experience in manufacturing jet passenger aircraft. Turboprop aircraft (which the company had considerable experience in designing and manufacturing) were cheaper to build, but were not very popular with passengers and airlines as they were noisy and the ride bumpy. Therefore, Botelho believed that regional jet planes were a better option for the company.

Subsequently, the development of the ERJ-145 was carried out in a very systematic manner. Embraer studied the regional jet market carefully to understand the needs and requirements of airlines that used regional jets. Funds to develop the ERJ-145, however, were not easy to come by. Embraer took a $98 million loan from the Brazilian government to fund the project, with more money being provided by Embraer's new owners—The Bonazo Group, Previ and Sistel. In addition to this, Embraer also entered into partnerships and technical alliances with companies like Parker Hannifin Corporation,[31] Allison Engine Company,[32] and Honeywell Space and Aviation Control (Honeywell),[33] who collaborated on producing the parts for the plane.

The ERJ-145 flew for the first time in August 1995, and Embraer made the first delivery of the aircraft to ExpressJet Airlines (the regional division of US-based Continental Airlines) in December 1996. More orders soon followed, and the ERJ-145 went on to become a major commercial success. During the second half of the 1990s, as the market for regional jets expanded, market leader Bombardier did not have the capacity to meet the increased demand. Embraer moved in to take advantage of the situation. Embraer's planes were also cheaper than those of Bombardier, because of the lower cost of labor in Brazil.

Between 1995 and 1997, the revenue per employee at Embraer rose from $75,000 to $185,000. Embraer returned to profitability in the third quarter of 1997, and in fiscal 1997, the company posted a net income of three million dollars on revenues of $764 million. In 1998, this increased to a net income of $145 million, from revenues of $1.3 billion.

The success of the ERJ-145 prompted the company to focus on making regional jets to take advantage of the expanding market. Over the late 1990s, Embraer added new models to the ERJ-145 family, launching the ERJ-135 and the ERJ-140, which were modified versions of the ERJ-145. By the end of the 1990s, a total of 192 aircraft[34] from the ERJ-145 family were delivered to various commercial airlines.[35]

The E-Jet Era

The success of the ERJ-145 demonstrated the potential for regional jets and prompted Embraer to consider manufacturing a full range of regional jets to tap more segments of the market. For a better understanding of the regional jet market, Embraer surveyed more than 60 airlines around the world. The survey indicated that the segment for mid-sized regional jets was greatly under-served.

Bombardier was the leader in the 50-seat jet segment, while Boeing and Airbus competed in the 130-seat segment. However, no aircraft were available in the 70 to 110-seat segment. This also seemed to be the segment with the maximum potential. (According to analyst estimates, more than 60 percent of all flights in the US had been taking off with passenger headcounts in this range.)[36]

Although some of the smaller Boeing and Airbus aircraft could be (and were being) used to serve this segment, analysts said that these planes came with the same avionics and engineering as the larger planes, and hence were not cost effective. "Airlines are operating with the wrong aircraft, and they're making a loss," said

---

[29] ERJ stood for Embraer Regional Jet.

[30] CRJ stood for Canadair Regional Jet. At that time, in addition to the CRJ-200, the Bombardier regional jet family included the CRJ-100 and the CRJ-440.

[31] Parker-Hannifin Corporation manufactures fluid power systems, electromechanical controls, and related components. Its aerospace segment offers hydraulic and primary flight control systems that include hydraulic, electrohydraulic, and electromechanical components used for control of aircraft rudders, elevators, ailerons, and other aerodynamic control surfaces and utility hydraulic components. The company is based in Ohio in the US.

[32] Allison Engine Company was a US based manufacturer of aircraft engines. It was acquired by Rolls-Royce Plc. in 1995 to become a subsidiary, Rolls-Royce Corporation.

[33] Honeywell Space and Aviation Control was a part of Honeywell International Inc., a major US based conglomerate with interests in aerospace, automation and control systems, specialty materials and transportation systems.

[34] This number does not include the ERJ-140 as the commercial deliveries for this aircraft started in 2001.

[35] Embraer Annual Report 2000.

[36] Jonathan Wheatley, Diane Brady and Wendy Zellner, "Brazil's Embraer Hits the Stratosphere," *BusinessWeek*, April 19, 2004.

Botelho.[37] So, Embraer decided to concentrate on this segment. It was decided that the new Embraer planes would fill the gap between 50-70 seat regional jets and larger jets.

The project was announced at the Paris Air Show in 1999. Embraer said that it would introduce four aircraft in what was to be known as the Embraer Jet or more commonly, the 'E-Jet' family. The four new planes—the E-170, E-175, E-190 and E-195—were to span the 70–110 seat market. The aircraft shared several features, with only minor differences. For instance, the wings and engines of the E-170 and E-175 were the same, and they only differed in fuselage length and maximum take-off weight. The same applied to the E-190 and E-195. Reportedly, the four aircraft had 89 percent commonality. The prices of the aircraft were to start from $20 million[38] (Refer to Table 1 for the seating capacity of the E-Jets vis-à-vis that of Bombardier's regional jets).

The E-Jets were designed to allow airlines to operate short haul flights and to fly between secondary cities where it was not cost effective to operate larger planes. Usually, on secondary routes the passenger traffic was not enough to make the operation of a 150-seat aircraft viable, and many of the aircraft on these routes often took off with empty seats. Because of this, airlines either avoided serving secondary routes, or risked increasing costs by flying half-empty planes. The E-Jets were designed to address this problem by providing an aircraft that would allow airlines to serve these routes in the most cost effective way possible.

Embraer's engineers developed a new design for the aircraft, with an innovative fuselage design, which the company called the 'double bubble'. (The aircraft's top half was wide and tall like a big jet, while the lower half was narrow like a small plane.) This design gave passengers more head and shoulder space in the cabin, while retaining most of the efficiencies of a smaller aircraft body. The cabin was configured for a single aisle with two seats on each side, which meant that every passenger had either a window seat or an aisle seat, doing away with the unpopular middle seat. This was aimed at making flying more comfortable for passengers, who reportedly disliked the cramped design and narrow fuselages of small regional planes.

Embraer estimated that the development costs for the E-Jets would be around one billion dollars. Funds to meet a part of the project cost were raised through an issue of American Depository Receipts (ADRs), which were listed on the New York Stock Exchange in June 2000.[39] Embraer issued 52.8 million new shares and raised $244.2 million. The syndicate of Brazilian investors in Embraer also sold a part of their stake raising $202.6 million.

In addition to this, Embraer enlisted 16 cost sharing partners for the project, including the General Electric Company (GE) to develop the engines, and Honeywell to make the cockpit information system. The partners were to bear about one-third of the total project cost, and according to the contract they signed with Embraer, would share in the profits if the project succeeded.

Most of Embraer's partners in the E-Jets project were international firms operating from outside Brazil, but as the project evolved, many of these companies set up subsidiaries and offices in Brazil to achieve production and logistic efficiencies. For instance, in the early 2000s, US-based C&D Aerospace built a plant in Brazil to supply Embraer with cabin interiors for its jets. Another American firm, Pilkington Aerospace also built a factory in

Table 1	Seating Capacities: Embraer and Bombardier Aircraft		
Embraer		**Bombardier**	
Aircraft	**Seating Capacity**	**Aircraft**	**Seating Capacity**
E-170	70–80	CRJ-440	40–44
E-175	78–88	CRJ-100/200	up to 50
E-190	98–114	CRJ-700	64–75
E-195	108–122	CRJ-900	86–90

Source: Compiled from various sources

[37] Jonathan Wheatley, Diane Brady and Wendy Zellner, "Brazil's Embraer Hits the Stratosphere," BusinessWeek, April 19, 2004.
[38] Russ Mitchell, "The Little Aircraft Company That Could," Fortune, November 14, 2005.
[39] The company had previously been listed in Brazil, on the Sao Paulo Stock Exchange (Bovespa) in 1989.

Brazil to supply Embraer with aircraft windows. Other examples were ENAER, a Chilean firm that supplied the rear fin and other parts, and Gamesa, a Spanish firm that made engine parts, who built manufacturing facilities near Sao Jose dos Campos.

However, despite its partnerships with some of the leading aerospace companies in the world, Embraer retained the development of the aircraft's fuselage (thought to be one of the most critical and technically complex aspects in aircraft design) with itself. (Previously, to obtain greater technological expertise, Embraer had invited Thales Avionics (Thales),[40] Dassault Aviation (Dassault)[41] European Aeronautic Defense and Space Company (EADS),[42] and SNECMA,[43] all of whom were leaders in various aspects of electronic systems and industrial electronics in the aerospace industry, to become shareholders in the company. The consortium formed by these four companies acquired 20 percent of Embraer's shares in 1999. Thales, Dassault and EADS acquired 5.67 percent of the shares each, while SNECMA acquired 2.99 percent.[44])

The E-Jets project was one of the most technologically advanced projects undertaken by Embraer. For this project, the company used virtual mockups (instead of physical ones) and 3D modeling technology for the first time, to evaluate designs and improve the time-to-market of the new aircraft. Virtual mockups allowed Embraer to visualize the aircraft and correct design problems without having to go through the cumbersome process of building multiple physical models.

Among the E-Jets, the E-170 was the first to be flight-tested in February 2002, followed by the E-175, the E-190 and the E-195. The aircraft made an impact on the aviation market very soon after their launch. They were popular mainly because of the element of passenger comfort they brought to the regional jet market. Additionally, they were also reported to be cheap to operate and maintain, and could achieve break-even even on routes where they had to fly half-full. This was an important consideration for airlines, which were facing a decline in passenger numbers after the September 11, 2001 attacks.[45]

Embraer also marketed the E-Jets aggressively. In 2001, even before the E-Jets were flight tested, Botelho reportedly sent a DVD to Robert Milton (Milton), the then CEO of Air Canada, asking him to take a look at the mock-up of the interiors of the new planes, which were being trucked around North America at that time.

Air Canada's headquarters were located next to those of Bombardier, and the airline had had a long standing relationship with the Canadian aircraft manufacturer. Milton was hesitant to consider 'unproven' Brazilian aircraft. But he said that the DVD whetted his curiosity, and he went to check out the planes. Apparently, one look at the cabin and interiors convinced him that the new aircraft had immense potential. Eventually, Air Canada ordered 15 E-175 planes.[46]

The biggest order for the E-Jets came in mid-2003, from US based low cost airline JetBlue Airways Corp. (JetBlue), which placed an order for 101 E-190s, with another 100 on option, in a deal valued at approximately six billion dollars (including the options).[47] This order was particularly significant, as JetBlue, like most other low cost airlines, had stuck to flying a uniform fleet of aircraft until then. At the time of the order, JetBlue had a fleet of Airbus A320s. Most analysts had expected the airline to opt for the Airbus A318 if it expanded its fleet to include smaller aircraft. The Airbus A318 shared many features with the A320, and would contribute to the operational efficiency of the airline.

But JetBlue's CEO David Neeleman (Neeleman) said that when the company's management evaluated the new E-Jets family, they were quite impressed. "When they looked at it, it was like, 'Not only is this not a risk, it's probably a risk if we don't do this,'" he said.[48]

The success of the E-Jets made Embraer a competitor to Boeing and Airbus, as the E-Jets were comparable to some of the smaller models manufactured by the two majors. Analysts said that the regional jets manufactured by Bombardier and Embraer were suddenly making a huge impact on the aviation industry, which until the late 1990s had been dominated by Boeing and Airbus.

---

[40] A part of the France-based Thales Group, Thales Avionics is a leading international aircraft avionics manufacturer supplying complete aircraft avionics systems and customized products for all types of aircraft. Before 2000, the Thales Group was known as Thomson-CSF.

[41] A major French manufacturer of civil and military aircraft.

[42] EADS is a global leader in aerospace, defense and related services. The group includes the aircraft manufacturer Airbus, the world's largest helicopter supplier Eurocopter and the joint venture MBDA, the international leader in missile systems. EADS emerged in 2000 from the link-up of the German DaimlerChrysler Aerospace AG, the French Aerospatiale Matra and CASA of Spain.

[43] SNECMA was formed as Société Nationale d'Étude et de Construction de Moteurs d'Aviation in 1945. The name is roughly translates as "National Company for the Study and Construction of Aviation Engines." In 2005 Snecma merged with Sagem, a major French conglomerate with interests in defense and consumer electronics and telecommunications, to form SAFRAN.

[44] www.wikipedia.com

[45] On September 11, 2001, terrorists hijacked four planes in the US. Two were flown into the twin towers of the World Trade Center while one was flown into the Pentagon. One aircraft crashed into a wooded area in Pennsylvania.

[46] Russ Mitchell, "The Little Aircraft Company That Could," *Fortune*, November 14, 2005.

[47] Jeff Fischer, "JetBlue Changes Planes," www.fool.com, June 10, 2003.

[48] Jonathan Wheatley, Diane Brady and Wendy Zellner, "Brazil's Embraer Hits the Stratosphere," *BusinessWeek*, April 19, 2004.

The increasing demand for regional jets could be attributed to the growing number of low cost airlines around the world in the late 1990s and early 2000s. Low cost airlines tried to work with maximum efficiency so as to cut costs and keep fares low. Therefore, on some routes they did not find it economical to fly large aircraft. The regional jets allowed airlines to match capacity with passenger demand. They were also more efficient than larger jets on short or medium haul flights and allowed for faster turnarounds,[49] which allowed the aircraft to spend more time in the air.

The Embraer–Bombardier Face-off

Competition in the market for regional jets intensified in the late 1990s. Until the launch of the ERJ-145, Bombardier had been the dominant player in the regional jet market, with its family of CRJ aircraft. (Bombardier's CRJ-100, delivered to Lufthansa in 1992, had been the first 50-seat jet aircraft in aviation history.)

At the end of 2005, Bombardier had more orders and deliveries than Embraer. But Embraer had more orders on hand. Besides, the net increase in the number of orders over the previous year was higher for Embraer than for Bombardier. The regional jet market had also been growing very rapidly since the mid 1990s (According to *Fortune*, a prominent business magazine, the market for regional jets had grown by 1,000 percent in Europe and around 1,400 percent in the US between 1995 and 2005).[50]

Bombardier had an established reputation in the aviation industry, while Embraer tended to be viewed as an upstart from the developing world. Bombardier's planes were also thought to be technologically more advanced than those of Embraer. However, Embraer's lower manufacturing costs gave it an advantage in the market. Assembling an aircraft is a labor-intensive process. Being based in a developing country, Embraer had access to cheap labor, which translated into lower manufacturing costs.

Moreover, Embraer had access to a large pool of skilled engineers and technicians. As of mid 2006, nearly 35 percent of Embraer's employees had at least a graduate level education (nearly 4000 employees were engineers). In addition to this, 63 percent of the employees had high-school level education. The company recruited regularly from the several technology institutes in the

Sao Paulo region, and the ITA too was an important source of potential recruits.

Embraer also invested in developing the education infrastructure in Brazil. In the early 2000s, Embraer launched an intensive, 18-month aeronautical engineering program. The graduates from the program were recruited to work at Embraer. The first batch of 164 students graduated in August 2002.

In 2002, Embraer set up a school in Sao Paulo to provide quality education to poor students in that region. The school, named after Juarez Wanderley, a former head of Embraer, took in 200 students every year for the 10th Grade slot as of the early 2000s. The quality of education at the school (which had cost Embraer $2.7 million[51] to set up) was top notch, and the company also assisted the students in pursing higher qualifications by providing stipends. It was reported that more than 40 percent of the students from the school went on to become engineers. In 2006, the company upgraded the laboratories at the school at a cost of $16,000 each, to provide students with a foundation in engineering subjects at high school level.

While Embraer did not promise employment with the company to the students it sponsored, it did rely heavily on local talent for its workforce. Reportedly, employees at the company felt a sense of pride in working for Embraer.

But rival Bombardier said that Embraer was taking advantage of cheap labor and government subsidies to undercut its prices in the regional aircraft market. It said that Embraer's planes were inferior to Bombardier planes, and that the former was able to survive in the industry only because of government support and lower manufacturing costs.

According to Embraer it needed the subsidies and government support because it did not have access to developed capital markets as Bombardier did. It also said that the CEOs of innovative airline companies had understood the value of Embraer's planes and were willing to buy them because of the efficiencies they offered.

The Dispute Goes to the WTO

In the late 1990s, Bombardier filed a complaint against Embraer at the World Trade Organization (WTO), alleging that the latter was using the Brazilian government's export subsidies to gain a price advantage in the

---

[49] Turnaround time is the time that an aircraft that has just landed needs to spend on the ground before it is ready to take off again.
[50] Russ Mitchell, "The Little Aircraft Company That Could," *Fortune*, November 14, 2005.
[51] Geri Smith, "Embraer Helps to Educate Brazil," *BusinessWeek*, July 31, 2006.

international market. Embraer received direct loans from BNDES[52] at subsidized interest rates under the bank's PROEX Scheme (Programa de Financiamento as Exportacoes) which was set up to promote exports. (Under PROEX, Brazilian companies engaged in export were eligible for interest subsidies.) In addition to this, the purchasers of Embraer aircraft were also eligible for interest subsidies if they took loans from the BNDES to finance the purchase.

According to Bombardier, these subsidies allowed Embraer to undercut competitors' prices in the international aviation market. In early 2000, the WTO's Dispute Settlement Body ruled that Embraer stop the BNDES subsidies. In late 2000, Bombardier made the allegation that the export subsidies under the PROEX program were continuing despite the WTO's ruling earlier that year, and appealed to the government of Canada to impose trade sanctions on Brazilian imports into the country.

Subsequently, Canada was permitted by the WTO to impose trade sanctions to the tune of $1.4 billion against Brazilian imports over a period of five years, as the WTO's Dispute Settlement Body found that Brazil's export subsidies program did contravene the 1994 WTO Subsidies Agreement. Brazil appealed against this decision at the WTO's Appellate Body, but the ruling was upheld.[53]

In 2001, Brazil filed a complaint against Bombardier saying that Canada's Technology Partnership Program and its export credit program provided subsidized government loans to Air Wisconsin, allowing Bombardier to win a 75-plane $1.68 billion contract from the airline. The WTO ruled against Canada in this dispute, permitting Brazil to impose $248 million in counter-trade measures against the former, which then agreed to make modifications to its export programs.

Analysts said that Bombardier's decision to take the matter to the WTO showed its determination to defend its turf in the face of the increasing popularity of Embraer's aircraft. Doug Abbey, the executive director of the Regional Air Service Initiative, an industry advocacy group based in Washington said, "Embraer is the risk-taking company that Bombardier used to be."[54]

Embraer for its part said that its rivals were attempting to obstruct a technologically advanced product for fear that it would be more popular than their own products. "The problem is that there is no level playing field," said Embraer spokesman Henrique Rzezinski.[55]

Business Jets and Microjets—The Emerging Trend

In the early 2000s, analysts were predicting a growing market for microjets—small aircraft with a takeoff weight between 5000 and 10,000 lbs, seating less than 20 passengers. These aircraft were usually bought by companies for their higher level executives, or by operators of air taxi services, although some were bought for personal use as well. Business jets, on the other hand, were not necessarily small, although they too were used for similar purposes.

In the early 2000s, Embraer announced the launch of several models of microjets and business aircraft, including the Legacy 600, the Lineage 1000, and the Phenom 100 and Phenom 300.

The Legacy 600 aircraft, a business jet launched in 2000, was based on the ERJ-145 platform. It was a 16-seat aircraft and had a range of 3,250 nautical miles. The Legacy 600 was pitted against Bombardier's Canadair Challenger in the mid-to-upper end of the market. Embraer also launched another version of the Legacy 600 called the Legacy Shuttle, which was designed as a regular commercial passenger plane with the same range and size as the Legacy 600. The Phenom 100 and Phenom 300 projects were announced in New York in May 2005. The Phenom 100 was to be designed as a 'very light jet,' while the Phenom 300 was categorized as a 'light jet.' Both would have the capacity to carry eight or nine passengers.

The Phenom family of aircraft would also be designed with the "double bubble" fuselage, giving passengers more room in the cabin. The interiors of the cabin would be designed by BMW DesignWorks USA, and according to Embraer, would have a 'sleek, modern look'. The Phenoms were to be priced between $2.75 million and $6.65 million.[56] The Phenom 100 aircraft was expected to enter service in mid-2008, and the Phenom 300 in mid-2009.

In May 2006, Embraer announced that it had received orders for 50 Phenom 100 aircraft, with an option on another 50, from Geneva-based airline JetBird. (The options could later be converted into additional orders for the Phenom 300 as well.) The order was valued at around $140 million. The first planes were to be delivered to JetBird in 2009.

---

[52] Banco Nacional de Desenvolvimento Econômico e Social, Brazil's state-owned development bank provided medium and long term financing to industries.

[53] Canada however, never imposed the sanctions against Brazil, but started subsidizing aircraft purchase loans to match those offered by Brazil.

[54] Tim Padgett, "Dogfight," *Time*, April 28, 2003.

[55] "Americas Jet Trade Row escalates," bbc.co.uk, April 17, 2001.

[56] Brian Gorman, "Embraer Thinks Small," www.fool.com, May 6, 2005.

Embraer's management said the market potential for business jets was good in the early 2000s. The market for light and very light jets was also thought to be expanding in both the US and Europe at this time. According to the company's estimates in 2005, demand for microjets would increase by 3,000 units by 2015.[57]

However, the competition in this segment was likely to be intense. In the early 2000s, microjets were being developed by several other companies. Some of the companies manufacturing microjets as of 2006 were Eclipse Aviation,[58] Cessna Aircraft,[59] Adam Aircraft[60] and Honda Motors.[61]

The Outlook for Embraer

Embraer was one the largest and most successful companies in Brazil. In the years 1999, 2000 and 2001, it was Brazil's largest exporter. According to the company's website, between 1995 and 2005, Embraer had accounted for eight billion dollars of Brazil's trade balance. Analysts acknowledged that Embraer contributed significantly to Brazil's economic development and had had a positive impact on the country's international image. "The international press often refers to Brazil with the perception that we burn our forests, we kill our children, we do not pay back our debts, we steal their patents. I don't deny some of those things happen, but they are not the fundamental Brazil. We feel we represent another side of Brazil that is not very well perceived," said Botelho.[62]

However, although Embraer's performance since its privatization has been remarkable, some doubts have been expressed as to whether the going will continue to be smooth. One of the biggest obstacles to Embraer's growth in the aviation market came from the 'scope clauses' that were a part of the pilot contracts of most large, unionized airlines around the world (particularly in the US). Scope clauses prevented airlines from operating regional carriers, as pilots were paid higher salaries for flying bigger planes. If regional planes became more common, then pilots would either be paid lower

salaries, or the airlines would have to employ new pilots willing to fly regional planes, thus reducing the flying hours for the pilots of the larger aircraft.

In the early 2000s, most of the airlines were negotiating with their pilots to remove some of the restrictiveness of the scope clauses, but not much progress had been made. The only airlines that were not burdened by scope clauses were non-union airlines, chiefly low cost airlines like JetBlue.

Another potentially troublesome development for Embraer was the resurgence in the popularity of turboprops in the wake of the fuel price rise in 2003–2004. In 2004 the deliveries and order backlogs for turboprops rose after declining for several years (*Refer to Exhibit 5*). In 2005, the orders for the turboprops manufactured by Bombardier and ATR[63] rose 240 percent to 151 aircraft, while the new orders for small regional jets (30 to 80 seats)[64] numbered 25.

The biggest beneficiary of the revival of turboprops was ATR, which recorded a total of 90 net orders[65] in 2005 for its ATR 42 and ATR 72 turboprops. Bombardier's Dash 8 'Q' family of aircraft also saw an increase in net orders in 2005. On the other hand, most of the small regional jets of both Bombardier and Embraer recorded zero or negative net orders in 2005, the exception being the CRJ-440 (*Refer to Exhibit 6 for more details on the order and delivery positions for regional aircraft*). Bombardier suspended the production of the CRJ-200 in January 2006. (Production was restarted in April 2006, when the CRJ-200's fuselage was used as the platform for Bombardier's Challenger 850 business jet.) Embraer also announced that it would cut the production of its small regional jets significantly.

The increasing interest in turboprops was expected to have a greater impact on Embraer than on Bombardier, as the latter manufactured both turboprops and jets. Embraer, on the other hand, had stopped manufacturing turboprops after its privatization. Orders for Embraer's ERJ-145 family declined drastically in 2004–2005, and the company recorded positive net orders only for its E-Jets in 2005.

---

[57] Brian Gorman, "Embraer Thinks Small," www.fool.com, May 6, 2005.

[58] Eclipse Aviation, a US-based company, was launching a six-seater jet called Eclipse 500. The aircraft was expected to be fully certified by late 2006.

[59] Cessna was based in Kansas, USA, and was one of the oldest aircraft manufacturers in the industry. The Cessna Citation Mustang was a six-seat microjet which was certified in mid 2006. Commercial deliveries of the aircraft were expected to start in 2007.

[60] Adam Aircraft was a Colorado, USA-based aircraft manufacturer. The company's eight seat AdamJet A700 was launched in the early 2000s, with the prototype flying in 2003. The first commercial delivery was made in early 2006.

[61] Honda Motors was a Japanese car manufacturer. In early 2006, the company announced that it would start taking orders for a very light jet called the HondaJet by the end of the year. In 2005, Honda had unveiled a prototype of the HondaJet, but predicted that it might not get the necessary certification to start commercial delivery until 2008–2009.

[62] Russ Mitchell, "The Little Aircraft Company That Could," *Fortune*, November 14, 2005.

[63] Italian-French consortium Aerei da Trasporto Regionale or Avions de Transport Régional (ATR), manufactured short haul turboprops. ATR had two main models as of mid 2006—the ATR 42 and ATR 72, with passenger seating capacities of up to 60 and 74 respectively.

[64] Includes CRJ440, CRJ100/200, ERJ135, ERJ140 and ERJ145.

[65] Increment of total orders over the previous year.

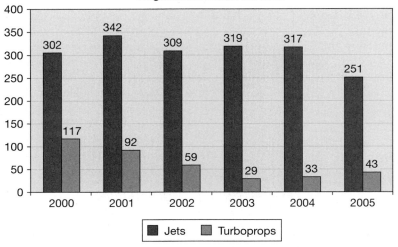

Regional Aircraft Deliveries

Regional Aircraft Backlog

Source: Max Kingsley-Jones "Turboprops Bounce Back," *Flight International*, February 03, 2006.

But the E-Jets had their own share of problems. The E-170 took almost two years to be certified, because of the complications involved in integrating its avionics with its other systems. JetBlue, the largest customer for the E-Jets, also announced that it faced some technical problems with the E-190s that Embraer had started delivering to the airline in mid 2005. In February 2006, JetBlue reported its first quarterly loss after its 2002 IPO.[66]

Analysts said that at least some of JetBlue's financial problems could be attributed to the lower than expected utilization rates of the E-190 aircraft. The problems with the E-Jets prompted some analysts to comment that, in its hurry to occupy the large regional jet niche, Embraer had failed to conduct adequate quality checks on the planes. However, as of mid 2006, most of the problems with the E-Jets had been rectified,

[66] Gregory Polek, "Final E-Jet Cleared for August Service Entry," *Aviation International News*, August 2006.

Exhibit 6 Orders and Deliveries of Regional Aircraft

Deliveries	Total Units	Units 2005	Units 2004	Seats 2005*	Seats Gross 2004*	Orders Gross Units 2005	Gross Units 2004	Total Orders Dec. 31, '05	Orders Dec. 31, '04	Net Change	Total Undelivered Orders
ATR 42	382	5	5	210	210	17	1	398	381	+17	16
ATR 72	307	10	8	720	576	73	11	380	307	+73	73
ATR	689	15	13	930	786	90	12	778	688	+90	89
CRJ440	86	12	33	528	1,452	11	0	86	75	+11	0
CRJ100/200	931	35	75	1,750	3,750	7	104	950	1,019	−69	19
CRJ700	240	64	52	4,555	3,640	52	16	304	261	+43	64
CRJ900	39	14	15	1,260	1,350	14	20	59	45	+14	20
Challenger 800	25	5	1	0	0	5	0	29	24	+5	4
Q100	299	0	0	0	0	0	0	299	299	0	0
Q200	96	1	1	0	0	2	2	98	96	+2	2
Q300	220	9	8	450	400	10	19	241	231	+10	21
Q400	106	18	10	1,260	700	49	12	163	114	+49	57
BOMBARDIER	2,042	158	195	9,803	11,292	150	173	2,229	2,164	+65	187
ERJ135	108	2	1	74	37	0	2	123	123	0	15
ERJ140	74	0	0	0	0	0	0	94	94	0	20
ERJ145	667	46	87	2,300	4,350	6	29	677	684	−7	10
EMBRAER 170	92	46	46	3,220	3,220	42	35	198	158	+40	106
EMBRAER 175	14	14	0	1,120	0	4	15	22	15	+7	8
EMBRAER 190	12	12	0	1,200	0	36	45	191	155	+36	179
EMBRAER 195	0	0	0	0	0	14	0	29	15	+14	29
EMBRAER	967	141†	148†	7,914	7,607	102	126	1,334	1,244	+90	367

* Estimate; excludes freighter/corporate variants

† Includes delivery of 21 Legacy/Military Derivatives in 2005 and 14 in 2004.

Source: Commercial Aircraft (>30-Pax) Orders and Deliveries – December 31, 2005 Aircraft Currently In Production/Development. www.speednews.com, (accessed on September 29, 2006).

Case 13 / Embraer: The Brazilian Aircraft Manufacturer's Turnaround and Growth

and the airlines using them were reportedly satisfied with their performance.

Competition in the regional jet market was expected to increase with the entry of manufacturers from Russia, the Commonwealth of Independent States (CIS), and China. In 2005, the Antonov An-148 70-seat regional jet, manufactured by Ukrainian aircraft manufacturer Antonov ASTC, received its first firm orders from Ilyushin Finance Co., a Russian aircraft leasing company. KrasAir, the fourth largest domestic airline in Russia, also signed a $270 million lease agreement for ten An-148 aircraft with an option on five units.

The Sukhoi SuperJet 100 (formerly known as the Russian Regional Jet and produced by Russian aerospace firm Sukhoi Corporation), and the ARJ21 (China's first indigenously designed passenger jet, manufactured by the Chinese government owned consortium AVIC I Commercial Aircraft Company), were also gaining momentum and were expected to enter the market in 2008 and 2009 respectively.

In August 2006, Embraer signed a deal with the HNA Group of China. The deal, valued at $2.7 billion, was for 50 ERJ-145 aircraft and 50 E-190 aircraft. Embraer had a regional jet production facility in China known as the Harbin Embraer Aircraft Industry Company Ltd. (set up in 2002 as a joint venture with Harbin Aircraft Manufacturing Corp. (Harbin), China's fourth largest aircraft manufacturer), which it would use to manufacture half of the 100 jets.[67]

Analysts were of the opinion that having a production facility in China helped Embraer gain easy access to the Chinese market, which was growing at a rate of 8 to 10 percent annually in the early 2000s,[68] and also avoid the six percent value added tax that China imposed on imported planes.[69] It would also provide a good base for Embraer to manufacture aircraft for other airlines in the rapidly growing Asian region. They said Bombardier would have to cut prices drastically if it had to beat Embraer in China. (Bombardier had earlier turned down an offer of a joint venture with Harbin, because it believed that demand for 50-seat planes in China was weak.)

Some industry observers were of the opinion that, having ventured into mid-sized regional aircraft with some success, Embraer might well consider developing large passenger jets (like those made by Boeing and Airbus) in the future. However, most analysts felt that Embraer still had a long way to go before it could be considered to be in the same class as Boeing and Airbus. For one thing, designing and manufacturing large passenger jets required huge investments, which Embraer would find difficult to obtain as the capital markets in Brazil were not well developed.

Embraer could not look to its existing investors for infusion of fresh capital as the two pension funds Previ and Sistel had already invested the maximum they could under Brazilian law.[70] The company could also not raise funds through the equity market by issuing new shares without additional capital injections from existing shareholders.[71] Foreign investment would be subject to the approval of the Brazilian government, and it was unlikely that the government would allow foreign investors to acquire a majority stake in the company, as Embraer also manufactured military planes for the Brazilian Air Force.[72]

As the company's production was strongly skewed towards exports, Embraer was vulnerable to changes in the global economy. In 2005, only 7.9 percent of the company's revenues came from Brazil. After the WTO's ruling against Brazil's export subsidies, there was a possibility that Embraer might no longer be able to compete in the international market on the basis of low prices.

In 2006, Embraer announced that two Brazilian airlines—Varig and TAM—had expressed an interest in buying Embraer planes. At the time of the announcement, Varig's fleet consisted of 19 Boeing jets and four McDonnell-Douglas aircraft. TAM's fleet consisted of 66 Airbus jets and 22 Fokker aircraft.

A large part of Embraer's revenue (more than 70 percent) also came from commercial aviation. This too could be considered a weakness as commercial aviation was very sensitive to changes in the international economic scenario. Another problem was that commercial airlines generally made large one-time purchases only when they upgraded their fleets. Consequently, there was the possibility of large fluctuations in sales from year to year. However, in 2005–2006, Embraer had announced that it would systematically increase its focus on defense aircraft and government contracts, to expand the contribution of defense from 11 percent to 20 percent of sales (*Refer to Exhibit 7 for the breakup of Embraer's revenue by region and segment*).

---

[67] As of mid 2006, Embraer had five plants in Brazil in three different locations in that state, as well as subsidiaries, offices, technical assistance and supply parts distribution centers in China, Singapore, the United States, France and Portugal.

[68] "Aerospace Industry Market Brief 2005—China Summary," www.buyusainfo.net (accessed on October 10, 2006)

[69] Since 2001, China has imposed an import-stage value added tax of 6 percent on aircraft weighing more than 25 tons, and a 17 percent import-stage VAT on aircraft weighing less than 25 tons to protect the domestic regional jet suppliers. "Aerospace Industry Market Brief 2005—China Summary," www.buyusainfo.net

[70] According to Brazilian law, the funds could invest a maximum of five percent of their net worth or 20 percent of the company's capital. Previ and Sistel had already touched these levels. www.embraer.com

[71] www.embraer.com.br/institucional/download/2_Embraer-AI-Meeting-Corporate-Overview-2006.pdf

[72] Robert Plummer, "Embraer shows Brazil's Aviation Flair," bbc.co.uk, December 6, 2005.

Exhibit 7

Exhibit 7 — Embraer: Revenue by Region and Segment

Revenue by Region (%)	
Americas	67.5
Europe	14.6
Brazil	7.9
Others	10.0

Revenue by Segment (%)	
Commercial Aviation	70.6
Defense Aviation	11.0
Executive Aviation	7.3
Customer Support and Others	11.0

Source: Adapted from "Building a Globally Competitive Company," www.embraer.com

In 2005, Embraer signed a Memorandum of Understanding with the Defense Research and Development Organization (DRDO) of India to support the development of the Indian Air Force's new Airborne Early Warning & Control (AEW&C) system. The new asset would be based on the EMB 145 Intelligence, Surveillance and Reconnaissance (ISR) platform, which was one of the best selling ISR platforms in the world. Analysts said that this represented a return to its roots for Embraer, which had originally started out with military contracts.

In early 2006, Embraer announced that the company would be restructured to improve its access to capital markets and to enhance the quality of corporate governance and standards of transparency at the company. The proposal was approved by a majority of the company's shareholders on March 31, 2006. Under the restructuring, Embraer was merged with Rio Han, a company specifically created for the purpose. Embraer ceased to exist after the merger, and all its shareholders (preferred as well as common) received common shares from Rio Han (which was renamed (EMBRAER— Empresa Brasileira de Aeronáutica S.A.) to replace their old shares. The government also received a golden share (*Refer to Exhibit 8 for more information on Embraer's restructuring*).

Botelho also announced that he would step down as the CEO of the company in April 2007, and would be

Exhibit 8 — Embraer's Restructuring

A: Embraer's Shareholding Pattern as of December 30, 2005

Shareholders	December 30, 2005		
	Common shares (%)	Preferred shares (%)	Interest (%)
Caixa de Previdência dos Funcionários do Banco do Brasil—Previ	23.35	12.32	16.03
Fundação Sistel de Seguridade Social	20.00	0.03	6.74
Cia Bozano	20.00	3.92	9.32
Bozano Holdings, Ltd.	–	1.86	1.23
BNDES Participações S.A.—BNDESPAR	1.44	9.02	6.47
Dassault Aviation [1]	5.67	0.41	2.17
Thomson CSF/Thales [1]	5.67	0.41	2.17
EADS [1]	5.67	0.41	2.17
Safran [1]	3.00	0.22	1.15
Federal Government	0.75	0.10	0.33
Other	14.45	71.30	52.22
Total	100%	100%	100%

Note: Total common shares were 242,544,448; Total preferred shares were 479,287,609; Total shares were 721,832,057
(1) European shareholders
Source: "NM Project: Descriptive Memorandum of the Transaction, January 13, 2006 www.embraer.com, (Accessed on October 04, 2006).

(continued)

Exhibit 8 Embraer's Restructuring (continued)

B: Embraer's Shareholding Pattern after the Restructuring

Shareholder	Shareholding %
Brazilian Government	0.3
BNDESPAR	6.3
Sistel (Pension Fund)	7.4
Previ (Pension Fund)	16.4
Bonazo Group	11.1
Shares listed on Bovespa	17.9
Shares listed on NYSE	40.6
Total	100%

Note: Total shares were 738,611,820

Source: "Company Overview: Building a Globally Competitive Company," July 2006, Embraer Investor Relations Kit, www.embraer.com, (Accessed on October 04, 2006).

C: Embraer's Capital Structure after the Conclusion of the First Stage of Restructuring

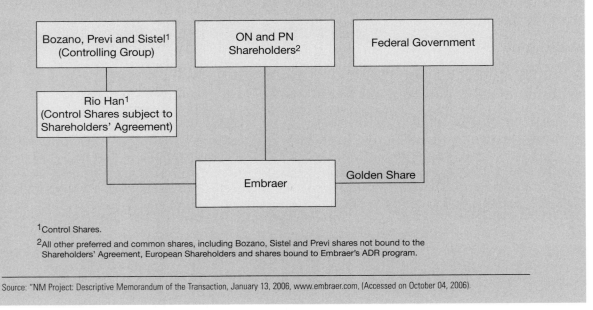

[1]Control Shares.

[2]All other preferred and common shares, including Bozano, Sistel and Previ shares not bound to the Shareholders' Agreement, European Shareholders and shares bound to Embraer's ADR program.

Source: "NM Project: Descriptive Memorandum of the Transaction, January 13, 2006, www.embraer.com, (Accessed on October 04, 2006).

(continued)

Exhibit 8 Embraer's Restructuring (continued)

D: New Embraer's Structure after the Merger

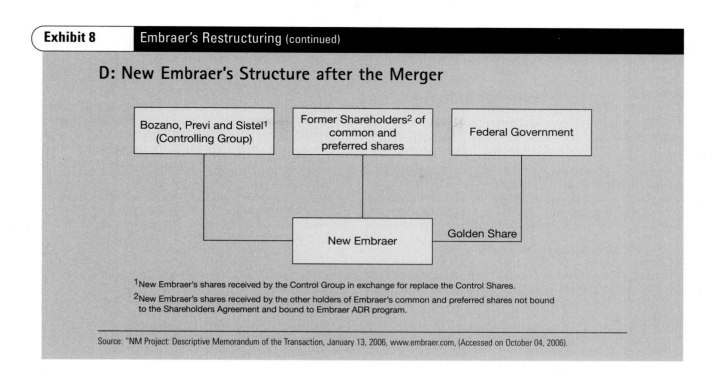

Bozano, Previ and Sistel[1] (Controlling Group)

Former Shareholders[2] of common and preferred shares

Federal Government

New Embraer

Golden Share

[1]New Embraer's shares received by the Control Group in exchange for replace the Control Shares.

[2]New Embraer's shares received by the other holders of Embraer's common and preferred shares not bound to the Shareholders Agreement and bound to Embraer ADR program.

Source: "NM Project: Descriptive Memorandum of the Transaction, January 13, 2006, www.embraer.com, (Accessed on October 04, 2006).

succeeded by Fred Curado, the Executive Vice President of the regional aircraft business at Embraer. Botelho however, would remain as chairman until April 2009.

According to analysts, Embraer was a showpiece of the benefits of privatization. They said that the company's experience demonstrated that firms from developing countries could compete and grow even in technology-intensive and highly competitive international markets.

References and Suggested Readings

1. **"A Very Big Deal,"** *The Economist,* December 4, 1997
2. Lawrence L. Herman, **"Brazil versus Canada—A Primer in WTO Dispute Settlement,"** Legal Alert, July 2000, www.casselsbrock.com (accessed on September 22, 2006)
3. Lorenz Winter, **"Embraer Successfully Expands its Regional Jet Family,"** *Flug Revue,* www.flug-revue.rotor.com, September 2000 (accessed on September 28, 2006)
4. **"Small Is Beautiful,"** *The Economist,* March 15, 2001
5. **"Americas Jet Trade Row Escalates,"** bbc.co.uk, April 17, 2001
6. **"WTO Issues Final Report in Aircraft Dispute,"** http://w01.international.gc.ca, January 28, 2002 (accessed on September 28, 2006)
7. Edvaldo Pereira Lima, **"Flying High: Embraer's Mauricio Botelho Has Taken a Flagging, State-owned Company and Turned it into the Fourth-largest Aircraft Maker in the World—Profile,"** *The Chief Executive,* January–February, 2003
8. Tim Padgett, **"Dogfight,"** *Time,* April 28, 2003
9. Jeff Fischer, **"JetBlue Changes Planes,"** www.fool.com, June 10, 2003
10. Fred Reed, **"Embraer Takes off with Sale to Jetblue,"** *The Washington Times,* June 25, 2003
11. Jonathan P. Doh, **"The Bombardier-Embraer Dispute and its Implications for the Western Hemisphere,"** Policy Papers on the Americas Volume XIV, Study 12, December 2003, http://www.ciaonet.org/wps/doj06/doj06.pdf, (accessed on September 22, 2006)
12. Jonathan Wheatley, Diane Brady and Wendy Zellner, **"Brazil's Embraer Hits the Stratosphere,"** *BusinessWeek,* April 19, 2004
13. Brian Gorman, **"Embraer's Bigger Plans,"** www.fool.com, July 20, 2004
14. Tim Hepher and Jean-Michel Belot, **"Airbus Claims Top Spot over Boeing in 2004,"** news.yahoo.com, January 12, 2005 (accessed on September 26, 2006)
15. Sean Silcoff, **"Embraer Jettisons its 'Jungle Jet' Roots,"** *Financial Post,* March 26, 2005
16. Rick Aristotle Munarriz, **"When the Sky Really Is the Limit,"** www.fool.com, April 18, 2005
17. Brian Gorman, **"Embraer Thinks Small,"** www.fool.com, May 6, 2005
18. Rich Smith, **"Embraer Hits Turbulence,"** www.fool.com, May 19, 2005
19. Stephen D. Simpson, **"Something's in the Embraer,"** www.fool.com, August 15, 2005
20. Stephen D. Simpson, **"Flying the Profitable Skies,"** www.fool.com, November 4, 2005
21. Rich Smith, **"Foolish Forecast: Embraer on the Radar,"** www.fool.com, November 11, 2005
22. Russ Mitchell, **"The Little Aircraft Company That Could,"** *Fortune,* November 14, 2005
23. Stephen D. Simpson, **"Headwinds at Embraer,"** www.fool.com, November 14, 2005
24. Joe Sharkey, **"Air Taxi Anyone?"** *The New York Times,* November 15, 2005
25. **"Embraer Reveals the Phenom 100 and the Phenom 300 at Nbaa,"** www.defesanet.com.br, November 10, 2005 (accessed on September 18, 2006)

26. Robert Plummer, **"Embraer shows Brazil's Aviation Flair,"** bbc.co.uk, December 6, 2005
27. Stuart. F. Brown, **"The Light Jet Age,"** *Fortune,* December 26, 2005
28. **"Commercial Aircraft Orders and Deliveries – December 31, 2005,"** www.speednews.com, (accessed on September 29, 2006)
29. **"NM Project: Descriptive Memorandum of the Transaction,"** January 13, 2006 www.embraer.com, (Accessed on October 04, 2006).
30. Max Kingsley-Jones **"Turboprops Bounce Back,"** *Flight International,* February 03, 2006.
31. **"Embraer Bullish on Asia-Pac Jet Market,"** *The Business Times,* February 20, 2006
32. Gregory Polek and Elizabeth Johnson, **"Reorganization proposed for Embraer,"** *Aviation International News,* February 2006
33. David J. Lynch, **"Comeback kid Embraer has Hot Jet, Fiery CEO to match,"** *USA Today,* March 7, 2006
34. Stephen D. Simpson, **"Uplifted on Embraer,"** www.fool.com, April 3, 2006
35. **"6th U.S. Analyst and Investor Meeting,"** www.embraer.com, April 12, 2006 (accessed on September 28, 2006)
36. **"Embraer wins $400m Saudi Jet Deal,"** bbc.co.uk, March 28, 2006
37. **"Embraer Receives First Fleet Order in Europe for 50 Phenom 100,"** PRNewswire, www.airportbusiness.com, May 3, 2006
38. Christopher Plameri, **"Snarl in the Sky,"** *BusinessWeek,* June 5, 2006
39. Chad Trautvetter, **"Embraer Thinks Big with the Lineage 1000,"** Aviation International News, June 2006
40. **"Falling Demand for Airbus Planes,"** bbc.co.uk, July 11, 2006
41. Tim Beyers, **"Will Embraer Fly?"** www.fool.com, July 19, 2006
42. **"Taking the Taxi to Higher Heights,"** *New York Times,* July 26, 2006
43. Del Quentin Wilber, **"Little Jets Poised To Alter Business Travel,"** *The Washington Post,* July 28, 2006
44. Geri Smith, **"Embraer: An Ugly Duckling Finds Its Wings,"** *BusinessWeek,* July 31, 2006
45. Geri Smith, **"Embraer Helps to Educate Brazil,"** *BusinessWeek,* July 31, 2006
46. **"Company Overview: Building a Globally Competitive Company,"** July 2006, Embraer Investor Relations Kit, www.embraer.com, (Accessed on October 04, 2006)
47. **"Embraer's Board of Directors appoints Mauricio Botelho's successor,"** PRNewswire, www.reuters.com, August 4, 2006
48. Time Beyers, **"Embraer Takes Off,"** www.fool.com, August 14, 2006
49. **"Embraer Announces First Latin American Charter Customer for the Phenom 100 and Phenom 300 Business Jets,"** *PRNewswire,* August 18, 2006
50. **"Embraer Wins Bumper Chinese Order,"** bbc.co.uk, August 31, 2006
51. Sandra Arnoult, **"Interview: Embraer's President and CEO Mauricio Botelho,"** Air Transport World, August 2006
52. Gregory Polek, **"Final E-Jet Cleared for August Service Entry,"** *Aviation International News,* August 2006.
53. **"2006 CIA World Fact Book,"** (accessed on October 4, 2006 from www.theodora.com
54. **"Aircraft Prices and Values,"** AirGuideOnline.com, www.airguideonline.com/ aircr_ prices.htm (accessed on October 4, 2006)
55. **"High Flyers: Brazil,"** Volume One, Science and Technology, tcdc.undp.org (accessed on September 15, 2006)
56. **"Embraer's New Capital Structure,"** Investor Relations, www.embraer.com (accessed on September 19, 2006)
57. **"Brazilian Companies Stake their Ground at the NYSE,"** www.brazilinfocenter.org, (accessed on September 27, 2006)
58. **"Aerospace Industry Market Brief 2005—China Summary,"** www.buyusainfo.net (accessed on October 10, 2006)
59. **Embraer Annual Report 2000,** www.embraer.com
60. **Embraer Annual Report 2005,** www.embraer.com
61. **Bombardier Annual Report 2005,** www.bombardier.com
62. **Airbus Annual Report 2005,** www.airbus.com
63. http://biz.yahoo.com
64. www.hoovers.com
65. www.boeing.com
66. www.airbus.com
67. www.bombardier.com
68. www.britannica.com
69. www.wikipedia.com

Entrepreneurial Search: Growing from a Monopoly Situation— Med-Eng Systems Inc.

Prescott Ensign
(University of Ottawa)

Nicholas Robinson
(McGill University)

A World of Terror

On July 7, 2005, people worldwide sat in horror as unprecedented events unfolded on television screens. For many, the London transportation system bombings were more than news drama—it was a morning of loss and devastation permanently changing many families and terrifying others (unaware of the whereabouts of their loved ones). The human tragedy of violent incidents was remarkable and provided impetus for governments throughout the world to take measures necessary to discourage or prevent future occurrences.

A year later on July 11, 2006 a series of seven explosions within 11 minutes tore through commuter trains in Mumbai, India. The death toll reached 200 with hundreds more injured—four suspects were eventually apprehended. Were these bombings a precursor to the coming G8 summit? Was this '7/11' event tied into others?

9/11, Bali, Madrid, 7/7, Istanbul, Riyadh, and numerous other bombings by fundamentalist organizations increasingly against Westerners caught the attention of the media and changed the mood of the world.[1] Oddly enough, countless other bombings occurred (see Exhibit 1) throughout the world daily never making the news in the West. Events in Israel and other parts of the Middle East were often simply too commonplace to strike a chord with Western media. In the explosive post-9/11 environment, police forces and militaries had an extraordinary new need to deal with the threat of explosive ordnances.

Proven Protection for a Dangerous World™

Fortunately, many firms were actively attempting to address the need for better security and had developed products aimed at protecting police and civilians from the growing threat of global terrorism. One such enterprise was Med-Eng Systems Inc. based in Ottawa, Ontario; the world leader in the research, design, and manufacture of a plethora of personal protective systems aimed at helping police forces and militaries confront explosive ordnances in a way that ensured the safety of their personnel. This meant selling products, such as bomb disposal suits, that employed 'advanced engineering solutions' to protect people and infrastructure from hazardous threats.

> Med-Eng has tackled aggressive R&D programs in conjunction with the Royal Canadian Mounted Police as well as Canadian, US, and other international military and academic research establishments . . . two decades of simulated and live testing have yielded significant breakthroughs in protective technologies to safeguard against the injurious effects of explosive devices, blunt impact, and physiological heat stress.[2]

For this privately held venture the key to developing cutting-edge products and staying on top was to "do the right things right every time, through the collaboration of its clients, vendors, and employees."[3] This

---

[1] There were earlier bombings: US Embassy and Marine barracks in Lebanon (1983), US and French embassies in Kuwait (1984), Pan-Am flight 103 Scotland (1988), World Trade Center (1993), Oklahoma City (1995), Atlanta Olympic Park (1996 to 1998) in which the "bomber placed secondary bombs designed to kill and maim rescuers, paramedics, firefighters . . . which set in motion new training requirements for first responders" (Joseph L. Smith, Vice President, Director of Security Consulting Services), US Embassies in Kenya and Tanzania (1998), USS Cole in Yemen (2000) the first '10/12' event, Bali was the second. See Exhibit 1 for US data.

[2] <http://www.med-eng.com/>

[3] <http://www.med-eng.com/>

Exhibit 1 US Bombing Statistics

"The United States Twenty-Year Experience with Bombing Incidents: Implications for Terrorism Preparedness and Medical Response"

by Bobby G. Kapur MD, MPH; H. Range Hutson MD; Mark A. Davis MD, MS; Philip L. Rice MD

Journal of Trauma-Injury Infection & Critical Care, December 2005

Abstract: Background: Terrorist bombings remain a significant threat in the United States. However, minimal longitudinal data exists regarding the medical and public health impact because of bombings.

Methods: We conducted a retrospective analysis of the number of incidents, injuries, and deaths because of explosive, incendiary, premature, and attempted bombings from January 1983 to December 2002. Morbidity and mortality by motives, target locations, and materials used were evaluated.

Results: In the United States, 36,110 bombing incidents, 5,931 injuries, and 699 deaths were reported. There were 21,237 (58.8%) explosive bombings, 6,185 (17.1%) incendiary bombings, 1,107 (3.1%) premature bombings, and 7,581 (21.0%) attempted bombings. For explosive bombings with known motives, 72.9% of injuries and 73.8% of deaths were because of homicide. For incendiary bombings with known motives, 68.2% of injuries were because of extortion and revenge, and 53.5% of deaths were due to homicide. Private residences accounted for 29.0% of incidents, 31.5% of injuries, and 55.5% of deaths. Government installations accounted for 4.4% of incidents but were the site of 12.7% of injuries and 25.5% of deaths. In bombings with known materials, nitrate-based fertilizers accounted for 36.2% of injuries and 30.4% of deaths, and smokeless powder and black powder accounted for 33.2% of injuries and 27.1% of deaths.

Conclusions: Illegal bombings and related injuries commonly occur in the United States. Because of the easy availability of bombing materials, government agencies and healthcare providers should prepare for potential mass-casualty bombings.

stakeholder-driven approach to product development and marketing led Med-Eng to be on the receiving end of numerous awards, both for the company's competitive strength and international posture.[4] Superior technologies had also led to superior profit margins. Although at inception the firm manufactured protective helmets solely, today Med-Eng held over 95 percent of the bomb disposal suit market worldwide—a market that the firm was forced to enter in 1991 after Med-Eng fought off a takeover attempt from a US-based competitor. At the time Med-Eng's only product was a protective helmet that went with another manufacturer's bomb suit.

"In an effort to weaken Med-Eng's bargaining position, the US firm bought the suit maker, then cut off supply. They bought the company thinking they could put

us out of business," says Med-Eng's co-founder, Vince Crupi. "We either had to get in bed with them, or come up with our own suit."

Med-Eng chose the high road. Crupi and president Richard L'Abbé took the resulting prototype—a less cumbersome, more protective suit and helmet combination with two-way radio technology—on a three-month tour to clients in 45 countries. "We asked them what they thought of it, what needed to be done and asked them for input," explains Crupi. Involving potential clients in the design process helped Med-Eng develop a superior suit and created immediate buy-in among their "consultants," most of whom placed orders. Moreover, Crupi explains, the integrated suit gave Med-Eng new sales leverage: "It made us much more competitive. I don't think we would have survived without the whole package."[5]

---

[4] Med-Eng won Department of Foreign Affairs and International Trade's Canada Export Award in 1989, 1995, and 2001 thus earning "Lifetime Achievement Status." Med-Eng won a "Canada's 50 Best Managed Companies" in 1999, 2000, 2001, and 2003, ensconcing CEO Richard L'Abbé as a judge in subsequent awards. In 2004, Richard L'Abbé won the "CEO of the Year Award" from the *Ottawa Business Journal*. Med-Eng won Ontario Global Traders Awards in 1998, 1999, and 2000. In 1999 the firm picked up an Exporter of the Year Gold Medal from the Ottawa region's Board of Trade. Aside from these commercial distinctions, Med-Eng received numerous honors from customers and clients. These ranged from police forces to military units. Plaques and letters came from generals, battalion commanders, presidents, etc. These awards were associated with names, faces, and carried touching stories including testimonials from combat survivors. Badges and patches from uniforms adorned the corporate boardroom and most corridors in their Ottawa facility. There were photos of ceremonies with prime ministers, presentations of foreign country flags, and even a few showing Med-Eng equipment in Hollywood movies.

[5] Bruce Livesay, "Great moments in marketing." *Profit Magazine.* May 1998.

Med-Eng emerged victorious stealing away the acquiring firm's market and wiping out their bomb disposal business. This type of gusto was practically a trademark of the Med-Eng culture, where management believed in the product so much that they actually tested their suits with live bombs. Richard L'Abbé was surely the only CEO in the world to "blow himself up" for his company and 260 employees. L'Abbé had tested his product 19 times with the use of explosives such as C4 and dynamite—often enough to destroy a car.[6] His tests and the faith he displayed changed public opinion that bomb suits were "little more than just body bags."[7]

Even today, after giving up on testing Med-Eng suits himself—after a noteworthy call from his life insurance agent—L'Abbé's attitude toward the company and its products was steadfast. What had changed, however, was the security environment internationally. Terrorism and escalating conflict in many parts of the world led Med-Eng equipment to markets in over 140 countries worldwide.

The high-quality and specialized nature of Med-Eng products made them a natural choice for organizations looking to bolster preparedness for use in counterterrorism operations—and many forces were in fact upgrading or building up on their stocks of bomb disposal equipment. Only days following the attacks on London, Sir Ian Blair, Metropolitan Police Commissioner, requested an increase of £150 million per year for spending on equipment and personnel in the anti-terrorist branch of the city's police department.[8] The US responded similarly (Exhibit 2).

Background

Richard L'Abbé graduated from the University of Ottawa with a degree in mechanical engineering in 1979. He went to work briefly at Biokinetics (<http://www.biokinetics.com/>), with which Med-Eng still maintained a relationship for product testing. The *Ottawa Business Journal* (CEO Profile, October 20, 2003) recounts that in 1980:

> He was busy studying the mechanics of bodily injury when the company received a contract from the Royal Canadian Mounted Police to design a bomb-disposal helmet. When the president of the company approached L'Abbé to ask for some fresh ideas, L'Abbé sat down for three hours and drew a basic blueprint of what he thought the prototype should look like. After seeing the drawing, his boss replied, "That's pretty cool, why don't you build it?"

In 1982 Med-Eng sold one helmet to the German Federal Police for C$4,000. In 1983, L'Abbé secured their first major sale to "a rude and arrogant gathering of potential clients in France"—6 suit and helmet combos

---

Exhibit 2   **U.S. Department of Justice Anti-Crime Funding Now Available**

According to a U.S. Department of Justice press release issued March 28, 2006, more than $200 million in anti-crime funding will be provided through the Edward Byrne Justice Assistance Grant (JAG) Program. The funding is for use by state and local governments to support a broad range of activities aimed at preventing and controlling crime and improving the criminal justice system. The JAG program allows states, tribes and local governments to support criminal justice activities based on respective local needs and priorities. Funds through the JAG program may be used for training, personnel, equipment and information systems for law enforcement programs. Funding may also be used for prosecution and court programs, drug treatments programs, corrections programs and technology improvement programs.

Awards through the JAG program are determined by a formula that includes a minimum allocation to each state. Additional funds, based on a state's population and crime statistics, are included in the state's award. JAG requires that states sub grant a variable amount of funds to local units of government, such as a city, county, township, town or tribe. Faith-based and other community organizations are eligible to receive pass-through funding from the state.

For more information about this program, please visit www.ojp.usdoj.gov.

---

[6] *Ottawa Business Journal.* October 20, 2003.
[7] *Ottawa Business Journal.* October 20, 2003.
[8] Stewart Tendler, "Police want extra £150m to boost anti-terror manpower." *Times.* August 22, 2005.

for C\$66,000.[9] From that point on, things looked up in subsequent years (Exhibit 3). The First Gulf War led to "spectacular" sales in 1991. L'Abbé remarked:

> *We were a one-product company for the first 10 years of our existence and we've now diversified into new fields . . . the company is very different. Each year the company devotes a full four days to strategic planning to evaluate their current strategic direction, assess what's working and what's not working, discuss what's looming on the horizon and make decisions about whether to shift direction or stay the course.* [10]

L'Abbé credits an executive seminar he attended where Clayton Christensen spoke as the impetus for Med-Eng's disciplined progress. A few follow-up phone calls with the Harvard Business School professor eminent for his insights into innovation and disruptive technology furthered L'Abbé's resolve toward strategic planning and entrepreneurial search for growth.

Products

Med-Eng Systems did not just produce equipment for the war on terrorism. Med-Eng produced a variety of interrelated wares that were used for other purposes; however, most purchases were for police forces and defence organizations.[11] The firm produced most of its 'gear' with a mix of sourced and in-house components and tried to integrate the ideas and concerns of stakeholders into the process. Med-Eng was reputed for its top-notch research activities (often conducted with the input of customers, suppliers, and users of its equipment). Products sold by Med-Eng were subdivided into six main areas of application (see Exhibits 4–9):

(1) Med-Eng's explosive ordnance disposal products were used by bomb squads worldwide. This product line represented the firm's core competency and the firm had upwards of 95% of global market share in this area. Ordnance disposal equipment included bomb suits and helmets used to work with an explosive device. From the period 2002 to 2005, this segment moved from 80% of Med-Eng's overall sales revenue to a mere 20%. While sales for this segment had remained steady, efforts to diversify into other realms were proving fruitful.

(2) Med-Eng manufactured remote handling devices known as 'hook and line kits' to move explosive devices. These tools limited the amount of human contact that would be necessary to manage potentially deadly materials, such as ordnances.

(3) Unexploded ordnance equipment was used by Med-Eng customers in demining; separate suits were offered for landmine reconnaissance and clearance.

Exhibit 3   Med-Eng Systems Inc.'s Revenues

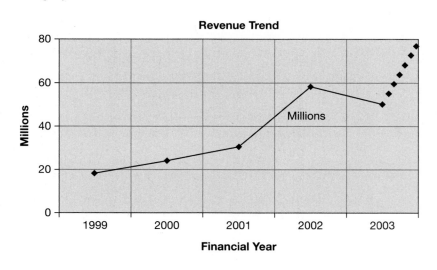

Note: These figures are approximations from public sources.

---

[9] Catherine Morrison "Protective dress spells success for Med-Eng." *Summit Magazine.* November 1998.
[10] Queen's School of Business "Managing for Growth Report." Kingston, Ontario. 2003.
[11] Med-Eng products could be ordered by a government body for official use; no products were available to the public. This was in contrast to companies that 'cashed in' on the public's fear to sell bullet-proof vests, stab-proof clothing, and armour plating for residences and vehicles.

Exhibit 4 | Bomb Suits and Helmets

The EOD 9 Bomb Suit and Helmet Ensemble provides the next generation of modular protection and operational flexibility for EOD and CBRNE missions. This modular Explosive Ordnance Disposal protective platform can be configured in the field by an EOD or IEDD technician based on their threat assessment. Please contact your authorized Med-Eng representative for full details of the more than 15 types of live testing, including extensive live blast test series, such as fragmentation testing.

- Includes Jacket, Integrated Groin Protector and Trousers (including boot covers) for a complete blast protection ensemble
- Integrates with a Chemical Protective Undergarment (CPU) to provide a level of Chem Bio Blast Protection
- Accommodates EOD 9 Helmet Remote Control Module to better control helmet functions
- Integrates with the BCS 4 Personal Climate System to provide personal cooling and mitigate risk of heat stress
- Groin plate retracts for easier kneeling
- Integrated carrying pouch to hold the optional BaquaPak for hydration
- Available in olive drab (standard colour), navy blue or desert tan, each with black webbing trim
- Highly flexible to allow an operator to use Med-Eng EOD Tools

EOD 9 Suit Primary Features The EOD 9 Bomb Suit builds upon the protective strengths of the EOD 8 Bomb Suit with the physical flexibility of the SRS 5 IEDD Search Suit.
EOD Technicians are encouraged to consider the GS1 or GS2 EOD Hook and Line Kit for use with the EOD 9 Bombsuit.

EOD 9 Helmet Primary Features The EOD 9 Helmet uses two interchangeable visors to enable technicians to configure their CBRNE protective platform in the field, based on their threat assessment. This combines operational flexibility with superior EOD and Chem Bio Blast protection.

With millions of antipersonnel landmines still buried and thousands falling victim each year to landmines left from past wars—Med-Eng made it a priority to save human lives from unnecessary catastrophe by manufacturing suits to safeguard those removing landmines.[12] Visors, helmets, hand protection, and footwear—including the company's trademark Spider Boots—were all products in this category. This line of business arose when a C$2million injection of venture capital in 1997, the year of Princess Diana's treaty to ban landmines, was used to "develop equipment for the global crusade to remove land mines."[13]

(4) Force protection outfits were used to equip soldiers facing the threat of being hit by blast, fragmentation, flame, ballistics, and electronic (radio wave) weaponry. These suits were engineered to provide military personnel the best possible protection when faced with serious threat. This segment was pursued as it showed great promise in fulfilling US military need.

(5) Crowd management solutions included gear for prison riots and public demonstrations where items such as Molotov cocktails, stones, and glass bottles posed a threat to the safety of a security force. Gloves, shinguards, helmets, and suits were tailored to this

---

12 This goal carried over toward the causes it supported (Exhibits 10–11).
13 Bruce Livesay, "Great moments in marketing." *Profit Magazine.* May 1998.

Exhibit 5   Remote Handling, Hook and Line Kits

The GS1 features a variety of innovative ropes and pulleys, bars and rods, hooks, clamps and pivot points. New hooks have been designed to allow clinical application with the minimum risk to the operator. The Self Opening Pulleys have a new locking mechanism that optimizes their opening for exacting use. The GS1 also integrates with the Clamp Kit for building and vehicle clearance operations.

The GS2 includes a variety of innovative ropes and pulleys, bars and rods, hooks, clamps and pivot points. New Suction Cups can be deployed in tandem on uneven surfaces or alone in small spaces. The redesigned Reel Stand can be deployed on its side to eliminate the risk of it being tipped over.

The Backpack Hook and Line Kit features a variety of innovative ropes and pulleys, bars and rods, hooks, clamps and pivot points. The new Hook Setter ensures precise deployment of hooks by the technician. The Backpack Hook and Line Kit also integrates with the Clamp Kit for building and vehicle clearance operations. It also contains components commonly used in post-blast investigation.

The Booby Trap Kit is intended for the search, neutralization and removal of booby traps and/or UXOs. It has been configured with consideration for a wide cross-section of field applications. The Kit's unique and innovative set of components are robust and reliable to meet the rigors of field operations. The Booby Trap Kit also contains many custom designed components specially fitted to a tactical assault pack.

The Clamp Kit specialized components integrate with the Med-Eng Hook and Line Kits to attach to and remotely open vehicle doors, windows and trunks. The Clamp Kit's components may also be used in building clearance operations.

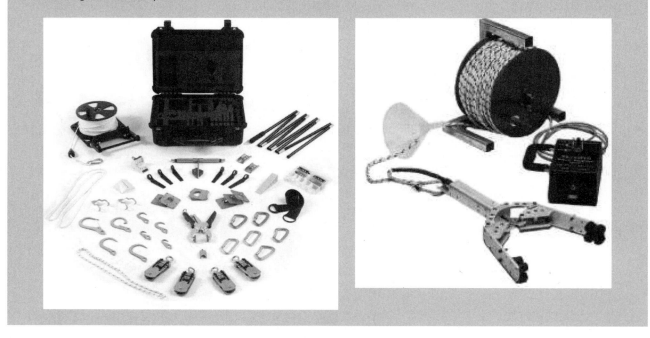

purpose. The outfits came in a variety of configurations and colours—depending on application. They could we worn 'armour out' to look tough or could be covered by loose clothing to look less intimidating.

(6) Personal climate systems such as cooling vests, specialized garments, and chillers were designed and built for use in high temperatures, but field reviews were mixed (Exhibit 12).

The Politics of Bombs

Prior to September 11th, 2001 Med-Eng took a variety of steps to diversify its business outside of conventional bomb suits and into other areas that might provide a more stable flow of revenues. Orders for bomb suits often fluctuated greatly and were sporadic in nature, so the company chose to look at areas of expansion that

Exhibit 6   Demining Suits, Helmets, and Accessories

Med-Eng offers a full range of personal protective equipment for Unexploded Ordnance (UXO), Mine Clearance and Demining operations. This PPE includes modular suit and helmet ensembles, foot protection systems and hand protectors.

Every piece of demining equipment has undergone live blast testing. Each demining suit and demining helmet provides an optimal balance between protection and comfort, and takes into consideration climate and operational demands.

The Spider Boot is truly a revolutionary new design for protecting a deminer's feet and legs against blast-type antipersonnel mines. It can be worn in difficult terrains during reconnaissance, detection and victim assistance operations.

The basic principle of the Spider Boot is remarkably simple and effective: distance the foot from the source of the blast. This enables the blast energy and fragments to be dispersed and deflected away from the foot. Residual blast energy and fragments are absorbed by the hull.

The Spider Boot secures the user's combat boot to a platform with 4 pods: two forward and two rear, and all four extend slightly to the sides.

Primary Features

Provides significant protection for the full range (M14 to PMN) of blast-type anti-personnel mines.

Proven through extensive live blast testing to provide 4 to 5 times the protection of conventional mine boots that put the source of blast in almost direct with the foot.

Exhibit 7 Force Protection for Today's Warfighter

Developing an effective Force Protection solution means saving lives. Med-Eng understands the relationships between threats, operational requirements and practical solutions to help protect today's warfighter against:

Blast, Fragmentation, Impact, Ballistic, Flame, Heat, Electronic/RF

The CPE is designed to provide protection for Cupola Gunners and vehicle crews against blast overpressure and fragmentation from roadside IEDs and RPGs. The ensemble is modular and scalable. It integrates with the Interceptor body armor, but can accommodate other vests. The CPE supplements the body armor's ballistic protection by providing extremity blast and fragmentation protection of the arms, legs, neck and face. The ensemble can also be used in conjunction with the CCS-1 Cupola Cooling System, an LCG Cooling Vest and vehicle-powered 24 Volt DC Vapor Compression Cooling (VCC) Unit.

Modular Components include:
- Visor CPE 450 and Rear Neck Protector
- Vest and Sleeves (with Rear Blast Plate)
- Chest and Groin Plate Carrier
- Trousers
- Integrated Groin Protector (IGP)
- Ballistic Glove Cover
- Front Collar
- Rear Collar

(continued)

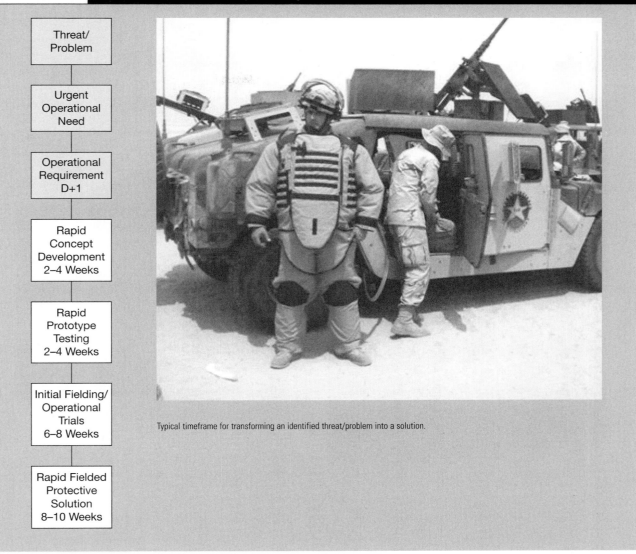

| Threat/Problem |
| Urgent Operational Need |
| Operational Requirement D+1 |
| Rapid Concept Development 2–4 Weeks |
| Rapid Prototype Testing 2–4 Weeks |
| Initial Fielding/Operational Trials 6–8 Weeks |
| Rapid Fielded Protective Solution 8–10 Weeks |

Typical timeframe for transforming an identified threat/problem into a solution.

could smooth revenues while remaining within the firm's core competencies.

After a healthy influx of cash from US policing groups concerned with the possibility of a major bombing at the Salt Lake City Olympics in 2002, the firm invested in the development of body cooling systems to be used in conjunction with bomb suits and riot gear in the hopes of securing a source of stable revenue. Furthermore, the company firmly believed that it could sell the cooling gear to industry at large[14]—thereby further diversifying the firm's target market.

Until this point, Med-Eng's primary customer base consisted of government organizations such as police forces and armies. The opportunity to sell outside of these groups, Med-Eng thought, would help the company weather future political storms and stabilize otherwise unpredictable cash flows. According to L'Abbé, large fluctuations in cash flow had pushed Med-Eng to adopt a policy whereby the company had "enough staff to supply a spike in demand, but not enough to satisfy that level of demand continually." Selling other products to new markets year-round, he expected, would ease the stress arising from revenue swings that often "doubled or halved the firm's output for a particular product over the course of a year."

Surprisingly, however, the company's choice to enter the riot gear market in 2001, when it acquired a

---

[14] There was evidence that corporations—particularly outside North America—were interested in guarding the health and safety of employees routinely exposed to substantial heat.

Heat stress can bring fatigue or even fatal injury to the most highly trained and fit people in military and law enforcement operations.

Med-Eng Liquid Circulating Garments (LCG) and Chillers are essential in reducing the effects of heat stress as a result of environmental conditions, physical work rate and required protective clothing. By removing internally generated metabolic heat and reducing the effects of environmental heat, users are better able to achieve their goal of mission success.

For best results, consider pre-duty, active-duty and post-duty personal cooling.

DC250 Chiller installed in a Humvee.

manufacturer by the name of Rovex V-Top was a failure. Despite having received numerous orders prior to the Summit of the Americas in Québec City (2001) from Canadian police forces of all ranks, and receiving even more orders for gear in preparation for the Battle of Seattle (World Trade Organization meeting riots) in 2000, the firm's sales in riot gear very quickly dried up for a number of reasons. First, only months after the conclusion of the meetings in Quebec City, the events of September 11, 2001 sent the world into a state of panic. Though one might assume that this new political mood of fear and terror would spur on sales of equipment such as riot gear—the exact opposite occurred.

After 9/11, public protests experienced a sharp decline as people chose not to involve themselves for two reasons. First, large public gatherings on US soil were seen as potential targets for terrorists seeking to take the lives of 'innocent Americans' and second, protesting was regarded as 'un-American' or 'anti-American.' Dissenters defying government order were thought to weaken the stance of the US and destroy the solidarity needed to confront the threat posed by extremism. Altogether this meant fewer protests and far fewer orders of riot gear by police forces in the US (the biggest consumer of the product) and throughout the world.

Competition and New Entrants

In addition to the public mood shift leading to lower sales, the number of companies offering riot-type protective gear exploded, with many firms offering suits of varying degrees of quality throughout the world. Given the comparably low degree of technological complexity involved in manufacturing and building riot gear,

Rocks launched from slingshots. Hand to hand combat. Molotov cocktails. These are just some of the threats faced by front line officers at public protests and prison riots.

This is why Med-Eng has engineered the V-Top line of Personal Protective Equipment, or riot gear, to provide an industry leading balance between protection and flexibility.

firms from South America, China and other regions of Asia, and Eastern Europe all competed in the market.[15] Whereas the development of a bomb suit required a notable amount of R&D investment and advanced materials engineering,[16] in contrast, designing and building a riot suit was an accomplishable task for a company without the same degree of technological sophistication as Med-Eng.

Med-Eng's problems were further compounded as competitors chose to copy the company's superior product design. This was a sizable issue in countries where local authorities wanted to buy suits from local

---

[15] V-Top's guards for ankles, shins, knees, hips, and thighs had even been marketed to crashprone downhill mountainbikers prior to Med-Eng's acquisition of the company. It remained to be demonstrated what separated Med-Eng's crowd management product from others' protective sporting goods equipment marketed to police, military, correctional services, and special tactical squads.

[16] Certainly Med-Eng's R&D efforts had put the company sufficiently ahead that competitors were barely recognizable for much of the company's product offerings. And Med-Eng did not rest on its laurels, more and more money was ploughed into product development every year. On several occasions Med-Eng has availed itself of help from the National Research Council's Industrial Research Assistance Program.

companies, and also had little respect for the concept of intellectual property. Resultantly, Med-Eng's design was replicated and sold throughout the globe—illegally, under different brand names. Roughly seven or eight clones of Med-Eng's product emerged on the world market and the firm twice successfully challenged and won injunctions against companies that stole Med-Eng's product design.

The firm held the Czechoslovakian government at ransom when they decided to order product from a local Czech company that had cloned Med-Eng suits; the government was then forced to order from Med-Eng after its courts recognized that the product had been reverse engineered from Med-Eng. Also, in Ecuador, the firm managed to protect its proprietary ideas after it hired a prominent local lawyer and law professor (with political connections) to take Med-Eng's case. Despite these success stories in protecting the firm's new riot gear suits, some major set backs also occurred as a result of foolishly filling one order.

Med-Eng accepted an order of about 150 suits from China in 2001—which Chinese officials reassured would not be reverse engineered or copied in any way. This order L'Abbé mused, "represented a good order, but it was not huge—maybe a couple percentage points of annual sales for that product." Within six months of delivering the product, a Chinese company began marketing an exact replica of the Med-Eng equipment. "They had obviously taken moulds of our gear," remarked L'Abbé, "but there's no way to know what the integrity of their stuff is." After investing millions of dollars in research and development the firm had lost a good chunk of the market in a mere matter of months.

Ultimately, lagging sales, intense competition, and copycat products led Med-Eng to believe that their entry into this market would prove to be relatively unprofitable. The firm's attempts to diversify its product line by entering the body temperature control market yielded similar lessons. After buying Delta Temax Inc.—a Pembroke, Ontario body cooling system maker—in January of 2001, Med-Eng focused on marketing its new acquisition's line of refrigerated vests to industrial workers by presenting the idea to unions, management, and workers themselves. Med-Eng believed that this approach would open up considerable opportunity and lead to new orders from an entirely new market—thereby diversifying the company and steadying sales.

Closing One Door, Opening Another

The firm's sales in the industrial sector flopped and by the summer of 2004, Richard L'Abbé decided to "pull the plug" on selling cooling apparel to the industrial market.

Coinciding with this let down was a spark—the US Army began to face a dilemma in Iraq: troops located there were having difficulty tolerating the extreme heat of the Middle Eastern climate while driving often un-air conditioned vehicles and wearing several pounds of thick body armour and other heavy gear that acted as insulators trapping body heat.

"This was expected to be a very profitable new market for Med-Eng," remarked L'Abbé, "we hoped to see sales of our cooling devices to the US Armed Forces go into the stratosphere." Med-Eng put to use some of Delta Temax's sewing facilities to start manufacturing different items such as the bomb disposal suits. On the redeployment of resources L'Abbé commented, "so, despite an unsuccessful bid at selling cooling systems in the industrial market, we managed to acquire a new skill set that could be used more generally in the manufacture of other products."

Selling "Made in Canada" in the USA

Med-Eng's Canadian identity had several interesting impacts on the firm's ability to sell its products in the US and elsewhere internationally. The fact that Canada, under the leadership of Prime Minister Jean Chrétien, had decided in 2002 not to join the US-led 'Coalition of the Willing' to invade Iraq made the company an obvious target for criticism that it was not playing on the right team to do business with the US. In the past, the Canadian aura had generally served Med-Eng well; Med-Eng benefited from the popular conception worldwide that Canadians were peacekeepers, polite, friendly, and a good dependable neighbour.

US defence contractors from countries supporting the Iraq invasion were generally given preferential treatment whereas Canadian defence contractors were in many ways left out. Med-Eng's position as a contractor that sold mainly to non-defence markets meant that the firm did not bear the full brunt of the Bush administration's retaliation. Med-Eng did, however, get labelled with the stigma that it came from a country that did not support the US position on the 'War on Terrorism.' This label, L'Abbé lamented, "had a huge effect" on Med-Eng's ability to sell itself in the US, where government and police forces were clamouring for bomb disposal gear. The fact that the firm controlled 95% of the market and was the internationally recognized leader in this market meant that US military and government agencies had little choice but to buy from the firm while at the same time Med-Eng scrambled to come up with a solution that was patriotism-proof.

Med-Eng needed to formulate a way to meet requirements of a US law known simply as 'the Berry

Amendment,' which stated that "funds made available to the Department of Defense" may not be spent on apparel items (clothing and other fabricated materials) "unless it is grown, reprocessed, reused, or produced in the United States." In order to satisfy this law, in the spring of 2005 Med-Eng established a branch plant in Ogdensburg, New York, quite literally a stone's throw from the Canadian border.

The Med-Eng facility, located on the shore of the St. Lawrence River, could be reached from Med-Eng's Canadian headquarters in Ottawa, Ontario by car in less than an hour as the city is immediately south of Ottawa. According to L'Abbé, "the move was of strategic importance since the Ogdensburg facility could now supply US military demand for goods 'made in the USA' by Med-Eng." The firm had previously attempted to get exempted from the Berry Amendment by seeking a signoff from the US Department of Defense and its then head, Secretary of Defense Donald Rumsfeld, but failed to receive this. L'Abbé remarked, "we almost got the waiver back in 2002, but even with it—as a Canadian company—you really need somebody down there [in the US] fronting your product."

After contemplating several bids for substantial contracts, Med-Eng discovered that, for the most part, lucrative US Government contracts were awarded to large US companies with good connections and a strong presence in the US. This meant that, as a medium-sized Canadian company with revenues below the US$100 million mark, chances of single-handedly succeeding in a bid for a sizable US contract were slim. For this reason, the company pursued partnering with large US firms for larger contracts (over US$20 million). These contracts for military equipment for the US foray into Iraq were often widely publicized and criticized by political pundits; fearful of this, few elected officials wanted to hand out a contract of this nature to a foreign company. Avoiding this dilemma through partnerships while securing big contracts with US defence contractors in need of equipment was a promising avenue for Med-Eng. Furthermore, according to CEO Richard L'Abbé, "getting with the right partner could mean receiving additional support in other areas—it could be a new source of knowledge and skills."

IPO Potential

As Med-Eng grew, those on both the outside and inside began to ask whether a company with revenues in excess of C$50 million would be better served as a publicly held firm. L'Abbé and many others in the firm were convinced that the volatility of the company's revenues would disappoint analysts and create an element of instability. L'Abbé knew that because of their client base and trends in police and defence spending, revenues could not be steadied to the extent that investors would tolerate and that fickle investors would not appreciate the company's business structure. According to L'Abbé, "sometimes, you have to have a bad year before you can have a great year." Besides, L'Abbé felt Med-Eng would not want to have to "drop its pants in front of analysts every quarter just to make them happy." The firm's CEO was convinced that being privately held meant that the company could operate free of the rhetoric and pressures of investors looking for a steady return. The nature of the company's product also meant that publicly announcing new innovations and strategies would be infeasible. Altogether, despite the firm's size, being privately held meant freedom from undue scrutiny coupled with better control over the company's direction and secrets.[17] In some instances, Med-Eng had to conceal certain information from employees so disclosing these secrets to the public would never be an option.[18]

On top of that, thus far Med-Eng had been successful in getting enough private venture capital to grow. The firm received one round of venture investment in 1997, and received a second round in 2000 when upper management had a run-in with the board of directors. Management's vision for Med-Eng (see Exhibits 10 and 11) conflicted with that of the board. So in early 2000, Schroders & Associates Canada Inc., a buyout group from Montreal (<http://www.schroders.ca/>) was, according to Schroders, approached by Med-Eng management "to buy out the equity participation of a group of four inactive private investors who sought to realize their investment." Med-Eng received the venture capital it needed while ridding itself of directors who were critical of CEO Richard L'Abbé. Less than four years later, Mr. L'Abbé was named 'CEO of the Year' by the *Ottawa Business Journal* as revenues skyrocketed.

---

[17] This is not to say the company received little critical feedback. On the contrary, a board of advisors was often scathing, asked serious questions, and kept L'Abbé and the entire organization in check. L'Abbé was quick to give credit to the advisors for their positive influence, "this was certainly not a group of 'yes men'."

[18] Many business directories listed Med-Eng as a manufacturer of "surgical appliances and supplies," "clothes," or "safety helmets." Little effort was made to correct these inaccuracies, even the company website listed the names of no employees, only job titles; email addresses contained neither first names nor last names merely job descriptions (e.g., sales, R&D, recruiting, etc.).

Exhibit 10   Vision and Values

Vision

To be a world leader in providing advanced engineering solutions to protect people and infrastructure from hazardous threats.

Values

- Focused on leading products, technologies and applications that have major impact in target markets.
- Striving to provide a great customer experience.
- Entrepreneurial spirit in each product line.
- Aspiring to be adaptive, flexible, nimble—Built for change.
- Fiercely competitive in our targeted market segments.
- Deliver, and be accountable for, what we promise.
- Our high level of integrity, ethics and fair dealings with all stakeholders.
- Committed leadership at every level of the organization.
- Responsible Corporate citizens.

Exhibit 11   Social Responsibility

Community Relations

Since 1981, Med-Eng has been a proud supporter of the end user and local communities in many ways.

Give of Your Time

One of the most important commodities anyone can give is their time. This is why Med-Eng and its people have consistently shared their experiences with members of the local business, academic, scientific and non-profit communities.

It is a memorable experience to see Med-Eng President Richard L'Abbé wear a bomb suit as he enters to deliver a career motivational speech in either official language to a graduating class from the University of Ottawa's School of Management or La Cité Collégiale, or to budding entrepreneurs attending a Ministry of Industry conference. In turn, he and other Med-Eng speakers have met people who make the Ottawa valley such a vibrant place to live and work.

Protecting Humanitarian Deminers

Med-Eng has contributed extensive humanitarian demining protective equipment to some the world's most heavily mined areas. These contributions have been co-ordinated through the Canadian Landmine Foundation.

Med-Eng has also donated equipment for auction towards the CLF's Night of a Thousand Dinners program.

Pursuit of Safety in Bomb Disposal

Ron Purvis was a highly respected member of the RCMP and Med-Eng families who dedicated his professional life to relentlessly increasing the safety of bomb disposal technicians worldwide. In 2003, Med-Eng created the Ron Purvis Memorial Award to honour the bomb technician or

(continued)

Exhibit 11   Social Responsibility (continued)

investigator who best exemplifies what Ron stood for. This year, Mr. Bobby Nye of the United States was presented the award.

To nominate someone for this international award, please contact your Regional IABTI representative.

Ottawa Hospital Foundation

Med-Eng has been a strong financial supporter of this important foundation. At a recent fundraising event, former patients explained in their own heartfelt words, why the OHF is so important to so many.

Please visit the OHF and consider the importance of their efforts.

Peaceful Conflict Resolution

Med-Eng has been an active participant and lead sponsor in supporting the St. Paul's University Conflict Resolution symposium. This effort brought together social activists, union leaders, police, politics, and First Nations to share their ideas on alternatives to violence in public protests.

This is directly in keeping with Med-Eng's adherence to developing only defensive equipment, and a recognition that violence from protests can be avoided.

United Way Campaign

The annual United Way Campaign marks a fun time at Med-Eng. Prizes, challenges, bake sales and pot luck lunches all help generate higher levels of support each year. Med-Eng has long conducted a program based on matching employee donations, making the company and its people true fundraising partners.

This multi-faceted organization assists the citizens of Pembroke, Ottawa and beyond.

Ottawa Food Bank

The Social Committee directs its energy into creating a fun workplace and its fundraising into food for those in need, through the Ottawa Food Bank.

Ottawa–Carleton Independent Living Centre

Med-Eng employees have enjoyed many weekends at the ballpark as a company sponsored team in the Centre's annual baseball tournament.

Take Our Kids to Work Day

Med-Eng is proud to support this national program that offers grade nine students a chance to spend a day at workplaces across Canada. Each year, students shadow Med-Eng employees in their jobs to learn about the variety of career opportunities that await them.

Afghanistan, Iraq, and Beyond

Leaning back at his desk in his Ottawa office, Richard L'Abbé, CEO and a co-founder of Med-Eng Systems, looked out the window as employees streamed into the parking lot this cold autumn morning. It was now October 2006 and maple leaves were changing colour from green to yellows, oranges, and reds. The United States Department of Homeland Security threat advisory colour schema was currently at the midpoint of the scale: Yellow "Elevated: Significant risk of terrorist attacks." The next higher level of terrorist threat was Orange, which was divided into two degrees of severity and had been activated eight times in the four years since the scale was introduced. The first Red alert—the highest likelihood of terrorist attack—occurred in mid-August 2006. Military operations in Afghanistan and Iraq

Exhibit 12　News Stories

"Reactions Mixed to Humvee Turret Gunner's Safety Suit"

by Monte Morin, *Stars and Stripes* May 8, 2006

Sure, he may look like an alien astronaut in that bulky blast suit, but turret gunner Bryce Harrison said he feels a little safer from roadside bombs.

The 21-year-old specialist from Satellite Beach, Fla., is one of a number of military police Humvee turret gunners who are testing the U.S. Army's new Cupola Protective Ensemble, or CPE—a heavily armored, liquid-cooled bomb disposal suit adapted for patrols in Iraq.

The CPE features a heavy face shield and protective neck collar. It fits over a soldier's flak vest and is one of a number of methods the Army is experimenting with to reduce the threat of roadside bombs—the biggest killer of U.S. soldiers in Iraq. Turret gunners with the Hanau, Germany-based 709th Military Police Battalion and the Fort Stewart, Ga.-based 549th Military Police Company began testing the suits in January and commanders say that they've already proven their mettle.

Capt. Larry Bergeron, commander of the 549th, said the suits have probably saved the lives of three soldiers who were sprayed by shrapnel from exploding roadside bombs . . .

Despite their protective qualities, the suits have earned mixed reviews from soldiers, who complain that the cooling systems frequently break down and that they "look goofy," wearing the equipment. They say, too, that the extra layer of protection limits their mobility . . .

Soldiers wearing the CPE look and move something like small children wearing heavy winter snowsuits. Heavy ballistic plates line the sleeves and chest. Before shrugging into their armor, soldiers put on a special cooling vest that fits over their T-shirt. The vest is lined with plastic tubing. The tubing is connected to a large "chiller" unit in the rear of the vehicle, which pumps cool water through the vest and reduces the soldier's body temperature—or at least that's what's supposed to happen . . .

As the U.S. military has sought to beef up vehicle armor on Humvees in the battle against roadside bombs, turret gunners have remained the most vulnerable since they stand partially out of their vehicles. Some military police and convoy security units have also adopted the use of the M1117 Guardian Armored Security Vehicle, or ASV—a fourwheeled armored vehicle with an enclosed, rotating turret that protects the gunner.

Several turret gunners who were interviewed recently said that while they had mixed feelings about the suit, they did say they were very happy to have the face shields that were fitted onto their helmets. The shields flip up and down like a welder's mask.

"Everybody likes the face shield," Bergeron said. "It's hot, but they all like it."

"Armoured suits are 'too goofy' say US troops"

by Francis Harris, *Telegraph* May 9, 2006

American troops have complained that a new armoured body suit designed to be worn in Iraq makes them look "goofy".

The water-cooled "alien spacesuits" are being handed out to turret gunners in their notoriously vulnerable Humvee vehicles.

The protective suit, based on those worn by bomb disposal officers, was intended to cut spiralling casualties for one of the most dangerous jobs in modern warfare.

But some troops have complained that the armour and headgear is inelegant. Others say the water-cooling system, designed for the soaring temperatures of an Iraqi summer, regularly breaks down.

Nonetheless, the suits being tested in combat by US military police units in northern Iraq have produced good results.

"One soldier's visor stopped a piece of shrapnel that hit dead centre," said Capt. Larry Bergeron. "If he had not had that suit on, the effects could have been catastrophic."

Gunners on Humvees have high casualty rates. While newly installed armour protects those inside, the gunner stands with the upper half of his body exposed, making him far more vulnerable to roadside bombs and gunfire. Others have been crushed as vehicles overturn.

But Specialist Michael Floyd, 19, said: "I am not a big fan of this thing. It is really hot and hard to move around in. I do feel safer, but only in an explosion. I would not feel safer in a rollover or in small-arms fire."

seemed likely to continue. Med-Eng products were increasingly playing a protective role in active combat.

A number of defence contractors were working on personal microclimate cooling systems. There were those worn by the dismounted warfighter—as such, the cooling vest was typically a heat activated cold pack that would absorb the wearer's heat; alternatively there might be a source of power circulating air around the torso to provide cooling. For the mounted warfighter—weight and power were less of a concern. The soldier could be hooked up to a system that cycled refrigerated fluid through a vest. According to one soldier returning from Iraq, "You kind of get used to being shot at but you never get used to being hot."[19]

Med-Eng's cupola protective ensemble (CPE) was an integrated system combining both personal safety and cooling. The CPE was worn by the gunner exposed on top of an armoured HUMVEE. The CPE's cooling system might also serve in other settings. Dave Hatcher, manager of strategic business development at Med-Eng commented, "we're looking at numerous other applications. If you look at the Abrams, the Stryker, or the Bradley, any one of the vehicles could take that type of cooling system to cool the individuals inside of the vehicle."[20]

While the cooling system portion of the ensemble had multiple applications and competitors; the defence portion of the CPE seemed to have at least one more competitor than it did applications.

A CROW (common remotely operated weapons station) could replace the exposed gunner. A turret with camera and weapons permitted the soldier to remain inside a vehicle to view a computer screen with one hand on a joystick. At US$200,000 or US$250,000 per fitting, they were an expensive alternative.

What Next?

Med-Eng needed to increase its markets and find new ways of ensuring sustained revenue growth. The simple fact was that the world had a finite number of police

departments and new growth would have to emerge from somewhere. War was becoming a foreseeable constant. There would likely always be a need for manned weapons and the CPE could play a role in protecting gunners in Stryker interim armoured vehicles and up-armoured trucks. Because the CPE was derived from the EOD suits the product met US Department of Defense approval in just 10 weeks in 2005 (see Exhibit 5), including blast tests at Aberdeen Proving Ground. Med-Eng's CPE had been in service with US troops in Iraq since January 2006. With much on his mind, L'Abbé reclined in his chair and pondered the future.

The company had been through 'growing pains.' A decent cadre of middle managers was in place and L'Abbé was confident that his marketing and sales teams were taking initiative. It took some time for them and him to get used to changing roles and responsibilities—things were now smooth and freedom, independence, experimentation, and exploration were the norm. While these had always been strengths of engineering and design within Med-Eng Systems, moving these characteristics from the lab to the market had taken effort. Cutting edge science was not enough, there needed to be similar thinking in approaching the marketplace. Get entrepreneurial traits to migrate was not easy; sometimes the solution had been to replace rather than remould an employee. L'Abbé recognized that he no longer hold onto everything, but he still knew about—even if not first hand—everything that was going on. If he had to go on holiday, the place could run without him. He had given his teams room to fail—and they had—but they got it right most of the time. The 'Midas touch' had spoiled them in the past, but at this point only hard work and logic was responsible for their ongoing success.

[19] Scott R. Gourley "Chill Out" <http://www.special-operations-technology.com/>
[20] Scott R. Gourley "Chill Out" <http://www.special-operations-technology.com/>

The Global Luxury Hospitality Industry and the Four Seasons Hotels and Resorts[1]

Shamsud D. Chowdhury
School of Business Dalhousie University

Four Seasons Hotel and Resorts (FS) is considered as the most prestigious hotel chain in the world. FS has experienced rapid expansion in both domestic and international markets over a relatively short period of time. This case illustrates how entrepreneurial risks, combined with a set of sound strategies and their effective execution, can offer endless opportunities to a firm in both Canada and overseas. While competition is intensifying in the global market, FS has signed 12 more letters of intent with an additional room capacity of 2320 beyond 2006. Isadore Sharpe, the CEO of FS and its Chairman of the Board, is assessing the strategic direction for FS so that its leadership position remains unmatched in the global luxury hotels and resorts industry.

> *"Four Seasons Hotels Inc. is regarded as the most prestigious and opulent hotel chain in the world. Hotel lobbies typically feature Venetian chandeliers, antique tables, and Kirman rugs. Management at each hotel keeps meticulous records of hotel guests, and on return visits, guests are greeted by name, booked into the room with their favourite view, and provided with their preferred type of pillow and shampoo."[2]*

The above quote says it all. Over a period of less than fifty years, Four Seasons Hotels and Resorts (Four Seasons), of Toronto, Canada has established itself as an exemplary corporate name, a name synonymous with exponential growth and enviable prestige. It is true that very few companies can boast of such success, pride, and recognition in the industry as does Four Seasons. The entrepreneurial flair of its founder, Isadore (Issy) Sharp, coupled with the selection and execution of the right assortment of strategies, has placed Four Seasons at the forefront of the global luxury hospitality industry.

Isodore Sharp, Chairman and CEO, founded the first Four Seasons hotel in 1960, as a mid-priced hotel in downtown Toronto. In keeping with his entrepreneurial flair, professional intuition, leadership skills, penchant for uniquely tailored customer service, and rich experience in home renovation for about a decade, Sharp developed a formula for the Four Seasons brand as an assortment of luxury hotels and resorts. Ever since, every move Sharp has made to turn Four Seasons from obscurity to the prestige of being the largest luxury hotel management company in the world reflected his passion for customer focus. Apart from properties of exceptional design and unique finish, Four Seasons is well known for its superb personal service, catering to the needs of the discriminating, affluent customers. Four Seasons employs 30,000 employees, has 64 properties in 28 countries, and enjoys revenue earnings of about $3 billion (Canadian).[3] With revenues and net earnings growth of 12% and 515%, respectively, over 2003 (See Exhibit 1) Four Seasons is in the midst of its largest expansion effort to date: adding "new and exciting markets, including Moscow, Beijing, and Dubai. With 12 new letters of intent signed and more than 20 projects already in development, it's clear that (Four Seasons') momentum has never been stronger."[4]

This case is intended to chronicle the entry of Four Seasons into the global luxury hospitality industry in the 1970s and afterwards; to identify the assortment of strategies it pursued for its rapid global expansion; to

[2] Derdak, T. "Four Seasons Hotels Inc." In P. Kepos (ed.) *International Directory of Company Histories*, Vol. 9, pp. 237–238 (London: St. James Press, 1988).
[3] Four Seasons Hotels and Resorts, 2004 Annual Report.
[4] Four Seasons Hotels and Resorts, 2004 Annual Report, p. 2.

Exhibit 1   Financial Highlights

All amounts referred to in this document are in Canadian dollars unless otherwise noted.

(in millions of dollars except per share amounts)	2004	2003[5]	2002
Revenues under management	$ 2,912.0	$ 2,600.4	$ 2,845.4
Earnings before other operating items[6]	$ 79.4	$ 49.5	$ 62.4
Net earnings	$ 33.2	$ 5.4	$ 21.2
Basic earnings per share	$ 0.93	$ 0.15	$ 0.61
Diluted earnings per share	$ 0.89	$ 0.15	$ 0.59
Cash and cash equivalents	$ 272.5	$ 170.7	$ 165.0
Long-term obligations	$ 309.1	$ 120.1	$ 129.1
Working capital provided by management operations	$ 103.3	$ 81.0	$ 83.8

highlight how it positioned itself against its main competitors; and finally, to assess its strategic direction for sustaining its industry leadership position.

Isadore (Issy) Sharp and Four Seasons

Isadore Sharp is the son of Polish immigrants. He began his career working for his father's construction company, building houses and small apartment buildings.[7] After high school, he received training as an architect at Toronto's Ryerson Polytechnic Institute, now Ryerson University, and formally joined his father's firm after graduation. Soon his interests turned to the hotel industry, and he opened the first Four Seasons Hotel on Jarvis street in Toronto. At that time, it was a very run-down area, giving the Four Seasons much less than the luxury image it enjoys today. It cost Sharp $1.5 million to build the hotel. However, because of its upscale and casual look, coupled with an inner courtyard surrounding

a swimming pool, Four Seasons was able to draw relatively wealthy patrons, some even celebrities, right from its inception.[8] Therefore, the Four Seasons Motor Hotel was a surprise success.

Four Seasons' second property seemed equally unusual in terms of location. In 1963, Sharp developed 17 acres of land on the outskirts of Toronto, opening Toronto's Inn on the Park, where the only neighbourhood business was a local garbage dump. Despite the peculiarity of this location at the time, the 569-room hotel proved successful.[9]

It was on a trip to Europe with his wife that Sharp first began to consider the luxury segment of the hotel industry. They had stayed at The Dorchester, one of London's most prestigious hotels, and Sharp realized that its longevity must have been due to its style and quality. Long-lasting hotels maintained a certain degree of excellence, and he realized companies must aim for the top if they want to succeed for any great length of time. Thus, for the years to come, luxury hotels became

---

[5] In December 2003, the Canadian Institute of Chartered Accountants ("CICA") amended Section 3870 of its Handbook to require entities to account for employee stock options using the fair value-based method, beginning January 1, 2004. In accordance with one of the transitional alternatives permitted under amended Section 3870, we prospectively adopted the fair value-based method to all employee stock options granted on or after January 1, 2003. Accordingly, options granted prior to that date continue to be accounted for using the settlement method, and results for the year ended December 31, 2002 have not been restated. The prospective application of adopting the fair value-based method effective January 1, 2003 resulted in a decrease in net earnings of $0.9 million and a decrease in basic and diluted earnings per share of $0.03 and $0.02, respectively, for the year ended December 31, 2003.

[6] Earnings before other operating items is equal to net earnings plus (i) income tax expense plus (ii) interest expense less (iii) interest income plus (iv) other expense less (v) other income plus (vi) depreciation and amortization. Earnings before other operating items is not intended to represent cash flow from operations, as defined by Canadian generally accepted accounting principles ("GAAP"), and it should not be considered as an alternative to net earnings, cash flow from operations or any other measure of performance prescribed by GAAP. Our earnings before other operating items may also not be comparable to earnings before other operating items used by other companies, which may be calculated differently. We consider earnings before other operating items to be a meaningful indicator of operations and use it as a measure to assess our operating performance. It is included because we believe it can be useful in measuring our ability to service debt, fund capital expenditures and expand our business. Earnings before other operating items is also used by investors, analysis and our lenders as a measure of our financial performance.

[7] Goneau, M. "Issy Sharp: Never a Dull Moment with Canada's Leading Hotelier." In *Business Life*, Vol. 10, No. 11, 1982, p. 45.

[8] Derdak, T.

[9] Derdak, T. & Woodward, A. "Four Seasons Hotels Inc." In T. Grant (ed.) *International Directory of Company Histories*, Vol. 29, pp. 198–200 (London: St. James Press, 2000).

his hobby and focus. Inn on the Park, in London's historic Hyde Park, was Sharp's first hotel outside of Canada. The 227-room hotel, which featured amenities quite modern to the time, was opened in 1970. In an overcrowded market with better established, more powerful rivals, such as Claridge, Dorchester, and Savoy, Inn on the Park became an instant success, claiming to be one of the most profitable hotels in the world.[10]

From the time Sharp dreamed of building his luxury hotel empire, he showed a flair for thoroughness in planning, always refusing to skim on details. Sharp believed in a working climate that fostered professionalism and devotion among his employees. True to his beliefs and values, following the founding of the first Four Seasons hotel in Toronto, Sharp initiated a profit-sharing plan, scheduled two stress-breaks every day, and paid his front desk clerks twice the average rate. For Sharp, front desk clerks provide the public with their first impression of the hotel.[11] Over the years, the three hallmarks of Four Seasons—its small/medium size (200–450 rooms), its luxurious appointments, and its impeccable service commitments—combined into what came to be regarded as the personal values of Issy Sharp himself. And without any question, these values have guided, and likely will continue to guide, the expansion and growth of Four Seasons in the decades to come.

In crafting his vision for Four Seasons' competitive strategy and market positioning, Sharp focused on four key components:

1. Operating high quality, small/medium-sized hotels.
2. Redefining luxury as constituting not only lavish decor, but also as unprecedented service quality. This definition of luxury is consistent with the provision of many unprecedented amenities, such as non-smoking floors, fitness rooms, and free shoe shines, which Four Seasons pioneered.
3. A strong service-oriented corporate culture that emphasized "The Golden Rule". This culture would be supported and maintained through rigorous recruitment and training policies.
4. A low-risk investment strategy that would see Four Seasons transition from both property development and management to a property management firm contracted with several different property developers across the globe.[12]

Strategies

In the hospitality industry, where Four Seasons competes, hotel marketers no longer depend on broadly defined market segments, such as corporate travelers, tourists, and convention business; rather, they target a select group of very affluent and famous customers who care about nothing but the very best of service that money possibly can buy.[13] The potential reward from such a market focus is great in that a very small fraction of frequent super-rich travelers means substantial revenues to the hospitality industry. It is an "unobtrusive personal service" that brings those travelers back to the industry.[14] Because super-rich customers make up only a minuscule percentage of the total population of even a very rich country, such as the U.S., rapid global expansion seems to be the most viable strategy for survival and growth for luxury hotels and resorts. Since its inception in 1961, Four Seasons has pursued an effective two-prong strategy to expand—both locally and overseas—at an accelerated pace. The phenomenal increase of its number of properties from 2 to 64 (See Exhibit 2) over a period of slightly more than four decades bears testimony to this. At its business level, the company has pursued a strategy of *differentiation*—a strategy based on unparalleled customer service—at its utmost form. The story of Roy Dyment, a bellboy at Four Seasons Toronto, who, without any authorization, hopped on an airplane for Washington D.C. to return a lawyer's briefcase before the latter's important morning meeting became an epic for his devotion to customer service. A key component of Four Seasons' differentiation strategy is to provide a high level of standardized service throughout the world. Brands also play a very crucial role in the establishment of differentiation in the luxury resort industry. There is no alternative to brand equity in this industry, because existing incumbents, in order to capture global market share, must capitalize on established reputations and carry over the positive image of brand names from country to country.[15] What is critical is reputation, a global brand name that sells. A global brand name is like a stock. A stock incorporates its customer's perceptions of value, signifying for investors a company's understanding of the new business criteria for market strength.[16]

Four Seasons has combined a variant of what is referred to as *multidomestic* strategy to expand into overseas

[10] Derdak, T.

[11] Derdak, T.

[12] Kardonne, R. "JNF New Leaders Get a Sharp Lesson From the Master." *Jewish Tribune*, June 9, 2005.

[13] Mann, I.S. "The affluent: A look at their expectations and service standards." *Cornell Hotel and Restaurant Administration Quarterly*, October 1993; 34 (5): 55–58.

[14] Mann, I.S.

[15] Go, F., Choi, T. & Chan, C. "Four Seasons-Regent: Building a global presence in the luxury market." *Cornell Hotel and Restaurant Administration Quarterly*, August 1996; 37 (4): 58–65.

[16] Sharp, Isadore. "Managing for Global Market Leadership." *Business Quarterly*, Summer 1991; 56 (1): 16–19.

Exhibit 2   Four Seasons Portfolio

	Approximate number of rooms/units	Approximate equity interest (1)
United States		
Four Seasons Hotel Atlanta, Georgia	244	—
Four Seasons Hotel Austin, Texas	291	—
Four Seasons Resort Aviara, California	329	7.3% (2)
Four Seasons Residence Club Aviara, California	120	7.3% (2)
The Regent Beverly Wilshire (Beverly Hills), California	395	—
Four Seasons Biltmore Resort (Santa Barbara), California	213	—
Four Seasons Hotel Boston, Massachusetts (3)	272	—
Four Seasons Hotel Chicago, Illinois	343	—
The Ritz-Carlton Hotel Chicago, Illinois	435	—
Four Seasons Hotel Houston, Texas (3)	404	—
Four Seasons Resort Hualalai at Historic Ka'upulehu, Hawaii	243	—
Four Seasons Resort Jackson Hole, Wyoming (3)	146	10% (2, 5)
Four Seasons Residence Club Jackson Hole, Wyoming	164	10% (2)
Four Seasons Resort and Club Dallas at Las Colinas, Texas	357	—
Four Seasons Hotel Las Vegas, Nevada	424	—
Four Seasons Hotel Los Angeles, California	285	— (5)
Four Seasons Resort Maui at Wailea, Hawaii	377	—
Four Seasons Hotel Miami, Florida	221	4.7% (2)
Four Seasons Hotel Newport Beach, California	295	—
Four Seasons Hotel New York, New York	362	—
Four Seasons Resort Palm Beach, Florida	210	—
Four Seasons Hotel Philadelphia, Pennsylvania	364	—
The Pierre in New York, New York	2016	100% (7)
Four Seasons Hotel San Francisco, California (3)	277	—
Four Seasons Resort Scottsdale at Troon North, Arizona	210	3.9% (2, 5, 8)
Four Seasons Residence Club Scottsdale at Troon North, Arizona	44	14.2% (2, 5)
Four Seasons Hotel Washington, District of Columbia	211	—
Other Americas/Caribbean		
Four Seasons Hotel Buenos Aires, Argentina	165	—
Four Seasons Resort Carmelo, Uruguay	44	—
Four Seasons Resort Costa Rica at Peninsula Papagayo, Costa Rica (3)	165	11.4% (7)
Four Seasons Resort Great Exuma at Emerald Bay, The Bahamas (3)	183	—
Four Seasons Hotel Mexico City, Mexico	240	—
Four Seasons Resort Nevis, West Indies (3)	196	—
Four Seasons Resort Punta Mita, Mexico (3)	140	—
Four Seasons Hotel Toronto, Ontario, Canada	380	—
Four Seasons Hotel Vancouver, British Columbia, Canada	376	100% (7)
Four Seasons Resort Whistler, British Columbia, Canada	273	— (5)
Asia/Pacific		
Four Seasons Resort Bali at Jimbaran Bay, Indonesia	147	—
Four Seasons Resort Bali at Sayan, Indonesia (3)	60	—
Four Seasons Hotel Bangkok, Thailand	340	—
Four Seasons Resort Chiang Mai, Thailand	80	—
Four Seasons Hotel Jakarta, Indonesia (3)	365	2% (2, 10)

(continued)

| Exhibit 2 | Four Seasons Portfolio (continued) |

	Approximate number of rooms/units	Approximate equity interest (1)
The Regent Kuala Lumpur, Malaysia	468	—
Four Seasons Resort Maldives at Kuda Huraa, Maldives	106	—
Four Seasons Hotel Shanghai, People's Republic of China	439	21.2% (2, 5, 9)
Four Seasons Hotel Singapore, Singapore	254	—
The Regent Singapore, Singapore	441	—
Four Seasons Hotel Sydney, Australia	531	15.2% (7)
Grand Formosa Regent Taipei, Taiwan	538	—
Four Seasons Hotel Tokyo at Chinzan-so, Japan	283	—
Four Seasons Hotel Tokyo at Marunouchi, Japan	57	—
Middle East		
Four Seasons Hotel Amman, Jordan	193	1.6% (2)
Four Seasons Hotel Cairo at The First Residence, Egypt (3)	269	—
Four Seasons Hotel Cairo at Nile Plaza, Egypt (3)	365	7.8% (2)
Four Seasons Hotel Riyadh, Saudi Arabia	249	—
Four Seasons Resort Sharm el Sheikh, Egypt (3)	136	—
Europe		
Four Seasons Hotel Gresham Palace Budapest, Hungary	179	18.3% (2)
Four Seasons Hotel Dublin, Ireland	259	—
Four Seasons Hotel Hampshire, England	133	— (5)
Four Seasons Hotel Istanbul, Turkey	65	— (11)
Four Seasons Hotel The Ritz Lisbon, Portugal	282	—
Four Seasons Hotel Canary Wharf, England	142	— (12)
Four Seasons Hotel London, England	220	12.5% (5, 7, 13)
Four Seasons Hotel Milan, Italy	118	—
Four Seasons Hotel George V Paris, France	245	—
Four Seasons Hotel Prague, Czech Republic	161	— (5)
Four Seasons Resort Provence at Terre Blanche, France (3)	115	—

1. In the ordinary course, we make investments in, or advances in respect of or to owners of, properties to obtain new management agreements or to enhance existing management agreements where we believe the overall economic return to us will justify the investment or advance. We generally seek to limit our total long-term capital exposure to no more than 20% of the total equity required for a property. For a description of our investments in, or advances made in respect of or to owners of, properties and other commitments in respect of existing properties, including the equity investments listed in this chart, see "Balance Sheet Review and Analysis" and "Liquidity and Capital Resources".
2. Freehold interest.
3. This project includes, or is expected to include, a Four Seasons Residence Club or a Four Seasons branded residential component.
4. Four Seasons Residence Club Jackson Hole, Wyoming may have up to 40 units at full build out.
5. In addition to providing management services to this property, we have a guarantee or other commitment in respect of this property. See "Off-Balance Sheet Arrangements – Guarantees and Commitments".
6. Includes approximately 30 cooperative suites leased from individual owners and operated as hotel rooms.
7. Leasehold interest.
8. We have a preferred profits interest derived from previously existing subordinated loans to the resort of approximately US$17.4 million in aggregate plus a loan in the amount of US$6.0 million to an entity that owns approximately 85% of the entity that owns the hotel.
9. We anticipate that we will reduce our equity interest through a sale to a third party.
10. The Regent Jakarta was re-branded as Four Seasons Hotel Jakarta effective July 14, 2004.
11. Subject to satisfaction of certain conditions, we may acquire an 18% leasehold interest in conjunction with a proposed expansion and renovation of Four Seasons Hotel Istanbul.
12. We have made a loan of £3 million to the owner of the Four Seasons Hotel Canary Wharf, which is convertible into an equity interest in the hotel on the occurrence of certain events.
13. Four Seasons Hotels Limited ("FSHL") is the tenant of the land and premises constituting Four Seasons Hotel London. FSHL has entered into a sublease of the hotel with the entity on whose behalf we manage the hotel. The annual rent payable by FSHL under the lease is the same as the annual rent that is payable by the sub-tenant pursuant to the sublease. Indirectly, we now hold a 12.5% ownership interest in the sub-tenant.

Source: Four Seasons Annual Report, 2004

markets. Because costs are not all that important to the affluent luxury resort customers, they are not an important consideration for the company as well, for its entry and operations in the global market. Four Seasons always ensures that each of its properties is unique. It takes local conditions seriously into consideration in the design and architecture of its properties. For example, in 2002, when Four Seasons opened its property in Sharm El Sheikh, the famous Egyptian resort city, the property captivated indigenous features so immaculately that it looked like a "village of hotel rooms, like a Mediterranean hill town in an Islamic vernacular."[17] Four Seasons' Hotel Budapest, which opened in 2004, is also a good example of this individualization.

Moreover, contrary to what appears to be the case, the management of hotels for Four Seasons is not that capital intensive. "The vast majority of capital to fund our growth comes from strong, local capital partners who bring opportunities to Four Seasons. Our 64 hotels and resorts belong to more than 40 different owners, who contribute their local political sensibility and market knowledge."[18] Four Seasons has taken advantage of this partnership—a variant of traditional franchising—to make its expansion happen.

Because quality lies at the heart of outstanding customer service, Four Seasons had to ensure that its stellar reputation for customer service remained uniform across its foreign properties. It is true that a luxury traveler would expect utmost customer service at any Four Seasons property, independent of its location. In order to live up to such expectations, Four Seasons had to make special arrangements with different owners, who assumed the rights and obligations to oversee the quality and marketing of the property under the Four Seasons brand name. The proximity of such owners to a much smaller number of Four Seasons properties in a foreign country reduced quality control problems. Moreover, because of the expertise of these strong local partners, Four Seasons could place its own managers in the foreign property (which would be quite akin to a subsidiary owned by a foreign partner or a master franchisee in a foreign country or region)[19] to help ensure that it is doing a good job of monitoring other properties in the country. This organizational arrangement has proven very satisfactory for the company in terms of further value creation.[20] This arrangement, in addition, has enabled Four Seasons to transfer its distinctive competencies in customer service management to other properties in a foreign country, leading to differentiation, premium pricing, and increased demand. Therefore, rapid globalization through the creation of such partnerships has resulted in enormous economic returns to Four Seasons.

Expansion and Growth

The pattern of Four Seasons' growth is what may be referred to as a bit unusual by strategy theorists in general. The Four Seasons Motor Hotel and the Inn on the Park, both opened in Toronto in 1961 and 1963, respectively, were successful for different reasons. Given this, it would be natural for Issy Sharp to look for additional hotels in other large Canadian cities, such as Montreal, Vancouver, Edmonton, Calgary, Ottawa, and Winnipeg. The reputation and success of the first two hotels in Toronto would possibly help Sharp establish other hotels in those Canadian cities. Then in the next bout, it would be usual for him to look for expansion in large U.S. cities. The history of large Canadian multinationals suggests this Canada–America sequence for their expansion and growth. Four Seasons, however, followed a totally different sequence in the pursuit of its expansion. After establishing the first two hotels in Toronto, Sharp took a pause for about a decade to embark on his first truly overseas venture in London. Moreover, Sharp's attempts at Four Seasons' expansion seemed to be disparate and ad-hoc, driven mainly by opportunities. As the following sequence of growth would reveal, it took Four Seasons about 15 years to enter the first U.S. market in San Francisco.

Four Seasons' first step into international luxury markets was its third hotel, the Inn on the Park, in London in 1970. Located in London's historic Hyde Park, many sceptics argued that the property would be unsuccessful as it would be competing against established, well reputed hotels, such as the Savoy and the Dorchester. Much to the surprise of such sceptics, Sharp's opening of the 227-room property became an immediate success. The property enjoyed a 95% occupancy rate,[21] despite room rates approximately 25% higher than the established rivals.[22] The Inn on the Park became very profitable and helped build a solid financial foundation for further expansion.

Four Seasons strived for more international presence, but its initial attempts were not very successful. A luxury condo hotel in Israel was marginally profitable but

[17] Kaise, L.F. "Four Seasons, five continents." *Interior Design*, March 1, 2003, p. 1.
[18] Four Seasons Annual Report, 2004, p. 15.
[19] Hill, C.L. & McKaig, T. "*Global Business Today*" (Canadian edition), 2006. Toronto: McGraw-Hill Ryerson.
[20] Ibid.
[21] Derdak, T. & Woodward, A.
[22] Weber, J. & Rossant, J. "The Whirlwind at the Four Seasons; Luxury hotel chain founder Issy Sharp is on a global tear." *Business Week*. October 13, 1997., Iss. 3548, p. 82.

could not maintain staff; plans for European hotels were postponed after disagreements with potential partners; construction in Rome, unearthed Roman artefacts halting further construction.[23] The company's next successful step in international expansion was its entry into the U.S. market with the 1976 acquisition of The Clift in San Francisco, and more notably, the acquisition of Chicago's Ritz-Carlton in 1977.[24] Slowly, throughout the late 1970s and on through the 1980s, the company continued its North American expansion, opening up new hotels in several major urban centres, including Washington, New York, Houston, and Los Angeles. Expansion into the U.S. definitely helped solidify its global presence. In the late 1980s, Four Seasons began recognizing the world's financial centres as desirable locations for growth. Expansion lagged as Sharp insisted on only premium locations. From 1988 onward, however, the acquisition, development, and building of properties were rapid.[25] By this point, Four Seasons had a considerable North American presence and needed to move across other regions of the globe.

The company had previously maintained a controlled growth strategy, only pursuing expansion when it was in a secure position. Four Seasons was expanding very carefully so that it was able to manage effectively what it was buying. Unlike many of its competitors in the 1980s, Four Seasons did not want to grow beyond its speed. "We've always grown on the premise that our latest hotel to open is the best and kept ourselves in check by never compromising on existing operations."[26] However, in 1992 the company had an opportunity to acquire the Regent hotels in Asia, after the original ownership collapsed.[27] This acquisition provided a golden opportunity for Four Seasons, as the firm needed to expand into a truly global brand. By swallowing Regent, Sharp nearly doubled his management holdings. Regent hotels were well known with luxury travellers in Asia and Australia. The brand was well established, although the ownership was financially shaky. The sellers wanted a buyer that had the resources, as well as the reputation and expertise, to maintain the quality established by the original Regent brand. Four Seasons fit the bill.

As both Four Seasons and Regent were well known in their home regions, this was the opportunity to establish a name that would be recognized by luxury travellers all over the world. A strong brand in one region would lead to recognition in the other. The acquisition gave Four Seasons 100% ownership of the Regent hotels, including 15 management contracts covering properties in such diverse locations as New York, Milan and Bali, its trade names and trademarks, plus a 25% ownership stake in the Regent property in Hong Kong.[28] These properties were quickly re-branded under the name Four Seasons-Regency. This acquisition move had almost doubled the company's holdings in one swift move. This momentum led to further global expansion. 1994 saw the expansion into further global markets, such as Mexico City and Singapore, with properties opening up in Istanbul, Berlin, and Prague in the late 1990s.

The 1990s brought with it one other strategic acquisition as well—that of a minority partner. In the early 1990s, real estate and high-end hotels were hit hard by a global recession. Four Seasons suffered substantial losses, and Sharp realized that managing hotels rather than building them would be a far less risky strategy.[29] He began a series of property divestments, selling off the company's ownership of most of its hotels. Future expansion would focus on management services instead. Share prices also dropped over this period, propelling the company to sell off a portion of the company to raise funds. In 1995, Sharp agreed to sell a portion of shares to His Royal Highness (HRH) Prince Alwaleed bin Talal bin Abdulaziz Alsaud of Saudi Arabia. The deal provided the Prince with 25% of the company, but curiously left significant voting control with Sharp. Said Alwaleed, "What I wanted was Sharp himself, his expertise, the brainpower within Four Seasons."[30]

In December 1996, Four Seasons formed an alliance with Carlson Hospitality Worldwide (Carlson) to enhance the future development of Regent hotels globally. Four Seasons believed that the growth potential for the Regent brand would be better reached through this joint venture than under Four Seasons' direction alone.[31] Carlson is a hospitality management and marketing firm that oversees various hotels, restaurants, and travel agencies. Some of the brands under its control are Radisson, TGI Fridays, and Carlson Wagonlit Travel.[32] Carlson acquired the rights to the Regent name for any new

[23] Derdak, T. & Woodward, A.

[24] Derdak, T. & Woodward, A.

[25] Derdak, T. & Woodward, A.

[26] Newman, P.C. "Building the World's Largest Luxury Chain." *Maclean's*. Aug 3, 1992. Vol.105, Iss. 31, p. 36.

[27] Go, F., Choi, T. & Chan, C.

[28] Go, F., Choi, T. & Chan, C.

[29] Anonymous. "The Prince and the Pauper." *Maclean's*, Oct 10, 1994. Vol.107, Iss. 41, p. 37.

[30] Weber, J. & Rossant, J.

[31] Four Seasons Annual Report, 1996, p. 16.

[32] http://www.carlson.com/aboutus.cfm accessed on February 23, 2006.

development, agreed to create a luxury hotel division to expand the chain of Regent hotels through new franchise arrangements and management contracts. Four Seasons continued to manage the existing nine Regent hotels, and was able to provide management services to new Regent hotels. The goal of the alliance was to maximize the global value of the Regent brand name to create a larger chain of Regent properties throughout the world.[33]

The terrorist attacks in 2001 and the SARS epidemic left an adverse effect on the travel industry. As travel and occupancy rates plummeted, many leading firms began to slash rates in a panic to attract customers. Four Seasons steadfastly refused to do this. During September 2001, the chain's roughly 30 U.S. hotels were only half-full, and in some hard-hit markets occupancy rates plummeted to 30% and lower. This was a significant drop from the over 75% occupancy rates enjoyed the previous year. The low occupancy rates were attributed largely to a decrease in business travel across the entire sector. "The business travel side is not an individual decision. Companies have negotiated rates for certain hotels and that is where the employee is going to stay, in an environment of cost containment, companies look at things like travel as discretionary expenditures that can be cut."[34]

While waiting for better times to return, Four Seasons is continuing expansion plans (See Exhibit 3). Development financing has proved abundant for Four Seasons' projects. Kathleen Taylor, president of worldwide business operations, said in a published interview: "In general, it is the marginal projects, from an economic perspective, that are not getting done in the current environment. But we have found that finding equity and debt capital for good quality projects in the right locations is not a problem. Generally speaking, our pipeline is as busy as it has ever been."[35] Four Seasons growth is fueled mainly by external developers that choose to work with the management company. The firm has little financial involvement in development, and will wait for appropriate opportunities to arise, rather than go looking. According to Taylor, "Because we are working with third-party development groups, our efforts tend to be a bit more reactive than other firms. They might be able to buy a site and develop it themselves. But we're not, for instance, going to buy a plot of land in Paris and then figure out how to build a hotel. Rather, we would wait for a call from, or know someone, who wants to build such a property."[36] The focus is on selectivity of opportunities and strategic partnering for location expansion.

Exhibit 3	Four Seasons Expansion Plans			
Hotel/Resort/Residence Club and location (1, 2)	Approximate number of rooms/units	Total capital commitment as at March 14, 2005 (in millions)	Capital commitment not yet funded as at March 14, 2005 (in millions)	
Scheduled 2005/2006 Openings				
Four Seasons Hotel Alexandria, Egypt (3)	125	—	—	
Four Seasons Hotel Damascus, Syria	305	US$ 5	—	
Four Seasons Hotel Doha, Qatar (3)	230	US$ 4 (4)	US$ 4	
Four Seasons Hotel Florence, Italy	120	10 (4)	10	
Four Seasons Hotel Geneva, Switzerland	100	US$ 19	US$ 15.4	
Four Seasons Hotel Hong Kong, People's Republic of China (3)	395	—	—	
Four Seasons Resort Lanai at Koele, Hawaii, USA	100	—	—	
Four Seasons Resort Lanai at Manele Bay, Hawaii, USA	250	—	—	

(continued)

[33] Four Seasons Annual Report, 1996, p. 16.
[34] Daniels, C. "A room for all seasons. The leading provider of lodging for the rich and famous from the Champs Elysées in Paris to the jungles of Bali, Four Seasons Hotels is a rare Canadian global branding success story." *Marketing Magazine*, Feb 4, 2002, Vol.107, Iss. 5, p. 6.
[35] Selwitz, R. "Four Seasons Stays on Course." *Hotel and Motel Management*, Jul 21, 2003, 218, 13, p. 3.
[36] Ibid.

Exhibit 3   Four Seasons Expansion Plans (continued)

Hotel/Resort/Residence Club and location (1, 2)	Approximate number of rooms/units	Total capital commitment as at March 14, 2005 (in millions)	Capital commitment not yet funded as at March 14, 2005 (in millions)
Four Seasons Resort Langkawi, Malaysia	90	—	—
Four Seasons Resort Maldives at Landaa Giraavaru, Maldives	115	US$ 4	US$ 4
Four Seasons Hotel Mumbai, India	235	—	—
Four Seasons Residence Club Punta Mita, Mexico (5)	35	US$ 36.8	US$ 35.7
Four Seasons Hotel Silicon Valley at East Palo Alto, California, USA	200	US$ 6.7	US$ 0.8
Four Seasons Private Residences Whistler, British Columbia, Canada (6)	35	—	—
Beyond 2006			
Four Seasons Hotel Baltimore, Maryland, USA (3)	200	US$ 5	US$ 5
Four Seasons Hotel Beijing, People's Republic of China	325	US$ 1	US$ 1
Four Seasons Hotel Beirut, Lebanon	235	US$ 5	US$ 5
Four Seasons Resort Bora Bora, French Polynesia	105	US$ 6.5 (4)	US$ 6.5
Four Seasons Hotel Dubai, United Arab Emirates (3)	250	—	—
Four Seasons Hotel Istanbul at the Bosphorus, Turkey	170	US$ 12 (7)	US$ 10.5
Four Seasons Hotel Kuwait City, Kuwait	225	—	—
Four Seasons Hotel Moscow, Russia (3)	210	US$ 10	US$ 10
Four Seasons Hotel Moscow Kamenny Island, Russia (3)	80	US$ 5	US$ 5
Four Seasons Resort Puerto Rico, Puerto Rico (3)	250	US$ 10	US$ 10
Four Seasons Hotel Seattle, Washington, USA (3)	150	US$ 5	US$ 5
Four Seasons Resort Vail, Colorado, USA	120	US$ 6	US$ 6

1) Information concerning hotels, resorts and Residence Clubs or other residential branded components under construction or under development is based upon agreements and letters of intent and may change prior to the completion of the project. We have estimated the dates of scheduled openings based upon information provided by the various developers. There can be no assurance that the dates of scheduled openings will be achieved, that estimated capital commitments will not change or that these projects will be completed. In particular, where a property is scheduled to open near the end of a year there is a greater possibility that the year of opening could be changed.

2) We have made an investment in Orlando, Florida, which we expect to include a Four Seasons Residence Club and/or a Four Seasons branded residential component. The financing for this project has not yet been completed and therefore a scheduled opening date cannot be established at this time.

3) We expect this project to include a Four Seasons Residence Club and/or a Four Seasons branded residential component.

4) All or a portion of the capital commitment is to be provided by way of an operating deficit loan that may or may not be required to be funded. In the case of Four Seasons Hotel Doha, Four Seasons Hotel Florence and Four Seasons Resort Bora Bora, we do not expect the operating deficit loans that we are to provide to exceed US$4 million, US$10 million and US$4 million, respectively, if they are funded.

5) Four Seasons Residence Club Punta Mita remains under development adjacent to Four Seasons Resort Punta Mita.

6) Four Seasons Private Residences Whistler are under development adjacent to Four Seasons Resort Whistler.

7) This capital commitment relates to our purchase of an equity interest in Four Seasons Hotel Istanbul at the Bosphorus as well as the existing Four Seasons Hotel Istanbul.

Source: Four Seasons Annual Report, 2004

Four Seasons' current geographic expansion focuses primarily on China and the Middle East. With these two emerging wealthy economies there are many attractive opportunities. Expansion into the Middle East has some skeptics. Threats of impending political unrest and terrorism may make it a difficult market for a luxury service provider. However, Four Seasons chooses to see opportunities, not problems. Four Season's partnership with the Saudi Prince will be of use in this market. The Prince is not only able to provide substantial cash infusion, but can also serve as an envoy for the company, to help it navigate the foreign system. As of 2004, Four Seasons global expansion plans that included new construction in Beijing, Mumbai, Moscow, Alexandria, Damascus, Dubai and Kuwait City. According to the company "An international profile for the brand name enhances both internal and unit growth, attracting guests to new destinations and increasing our attractiveness as a partner for additional opportunities."[37] Four Seasons' strong global presence further fuels its global growth.

Global Luxury Hospitality Industry

The North American Industrial Classification System (NAICS) classifies the hotel industry as one that comprises "establishments primarily engaged in providing short-term lodging in facilities known as hotels. These establishments provide suites or guest rooms within a multi-storey or high-rise structure, accessible from the interior only, and they generally offer guests a range of complementary services and amenities, such as food and beverage services, parking, laundry services, swimming pools and exercise rooms, and conference and convention facilities."[38] As such, the global luxury hotel industry panders to two key consumers: upscale leisure and business travellers. The needs and travel habits of these two groups are each quite different.

"Luxury" denotes a degree of superiority over more traditional offerings. This superiority is not only in terms of tangible elements, such as architectural features, décor and furnishings, but also in terms of the intangible elements of atmospherics and service delivery. Competition is based on some key dimensions of differentiation, such as quality of both service and facilities, attraction of location, price, and the availability of a global distribution system. Luxury hotels anticipate a client's every need, and ensure that every expectation is not only met, but surpassed. In the luxury segment, quality service is of paramount importance. Although luxurious surroundings are a must, it is equally crucial that unfailingly superior service be inherent in the hotel, if a firm wants to establish consumer trust and loyalty. Hotels must instinctively understand and anticipate the needs, wants and behaviour of their guests. The success of a property in the luxury segment rests on its ability to offer a consistent and believable "personal touch" to its customers. Whether it be a leisure or business traveller, the feeling of being "at home" while staying in a hotel is key. Guests expect conscientious personal service that is not oppressive or overtly familiar.

The luxury hotel industry has become increasingly consolidated. Because of consolidation, the competition among the rivals in the industry is intense. The global landscape is dominated by several internationally known brand names that are controlled by a small number of corporations (See Exhibit 4). Large hotel conglomerates are acquiring smaller hotel chains in order to expand their holdings and international reach. The strategic acquisition of complementary chains allows many firms to enter new markets on an immediate and large scale. This trend makes formal entry through greenfield projects in the global luxury hotel industry very difficult, if not impossible. However, new developments are always a top priority. Most hotel corporations have long-range expansion plans that focus primarily on new

---

Exhibit 4   Corporate Holdings of Competitors in the Global Luxury Hotel Industry

Four Seasons: All holdings compete exclusively in the luxury segment

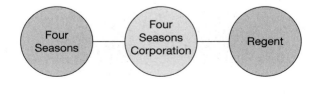

(continued)

---

37 Four Seasons Annual Report, 2006, p. 17.
38 http://stds.statcan.ca/english/naics/2002/naics02-class-search.asp?criteria=721111 accessed on February 08, 2006.

Cendant Corporation: Major competitive holding in luxury segment is Wyndham

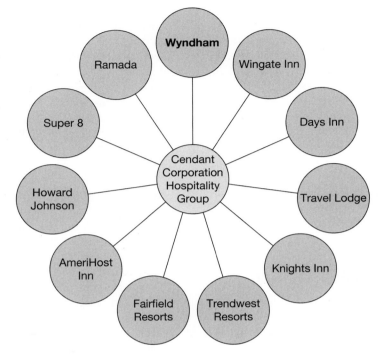

Starwood: Major competitive holdings in luxury segment are St. Regis & Luxury Collection, Westin, and W Hotels

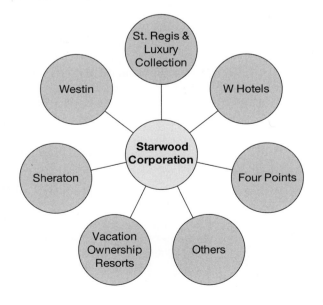

(continued)

Fairmont: All Fairmont affiliates compete in the luxury segment

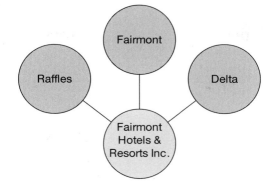

Marriott: Major competitive holding in luxury segment is Ritz–Carlton

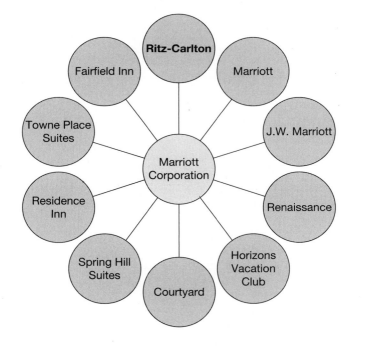

(continued)

Hyatt: Most Hyatt holdings compete in the upscale and luxury segment

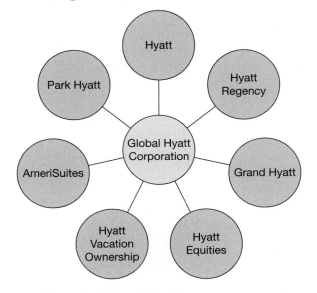

Hilton: Major competitive holdings in luxury segment are Hilton, Conrad, and Doubletree

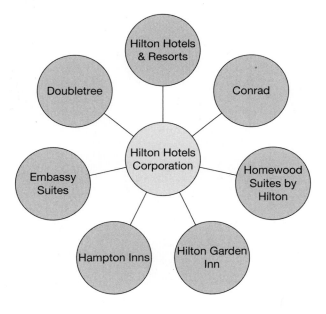

development, and can only consider strategic acquisitions, as opportunities arise.

The global luxury hotel industry is comprised of both property developers and hotel management firms. In the past, hotel properties were traditionally built and owned by the company that managed the location. Properties were corporately owned. However, over the last few decades, there has been an increasing trend in the industry towards purer management services with little to no direct investment in property development or ownership (See Exhibit 5). New properties are usually built by outside developers, and many firms are selling off a significant percentage of existing properties while establishing management contracts with the new owners. There is no uniformity of property ownership, even within a specific hotelier's portfolio, as the precise ownership of each hotel will vary from building to building. Each major competitor has a different proportion of ownership in its portfolio, varying along a continuum of very high to very low (See Exhibit 6), but the trend in property divestment is pervasive throughout the industry.

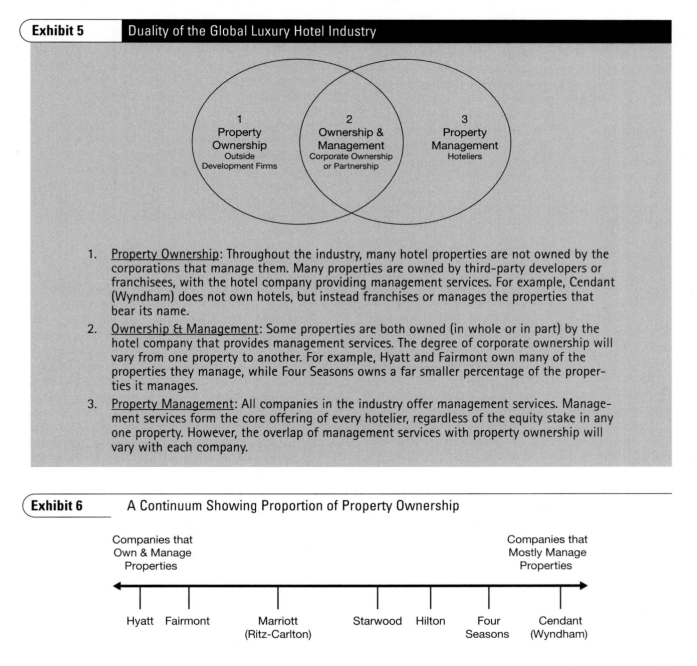

| Exhibit 5 | Duality of the Global Luxury Hotel Industry |

1
Property
Ownership
Outside
Development Firms

2
Ownership &
Management
Corporate Ownership
or Partnership

3
Property
Management
Hoteliers

1. <u>Property Ownership</u>: Throughout the industry, many hotel properties are not owned by the corporations that manage them. Many properties are owned by third-party developers or franchisees, with the hotel company providing management services. For example, Cendant (Wyndham) does not own hotels, but instead franchises or manages the properties that bear its name.

2. <u>Ownership & Management</u>: Some properties are both owned (in whole or in part) by the hotel company that provides management services. The degree of corporate ownership will vary from one property to another. For example, Hyatt and Fairmont own many of the properties they manage, while Four Seasons owns a far smaller percentage of the properties it manages.

3. <u>Property Management</u>: All companies in the industry offer management services. Management services form the core offering of every hotelier, regardless of the equity stake in any one property. However, the overlap of management services with property ownership will vary with each company.

| Exhibit 6 | A Continuum Showing Proportion of Property Ownership |

Companies that
Own & Manage
Properties

Companies that
Mostly Manage
Properties

Hyatt   Fairmont   Marriott   Starwood   Hilton   Four   Cendant
                      (Ritz-Carlton)   Seasons   (Wyndham)

Under a typical management contract, the management firm is responsible for all operating activities, such as human resources recruitment and training, marketing and sales functions for the property, facilities maintenance and repair, as well as accounting and finance duties, all on behalf of the property owner. In return, the hotel management services firm will earn a pre-arranged base fee, which is typically a small percentage of gross revenues for the property. In addition, contracts can include provisions for additional incentive fees paid out for exceeding expected revenues or some other performance target. The trend towards hotel management services is a reflection of the changing nature of the global economy as well as the travel and tourism industry. With increased threats of terrorism and fears of emergent epidemics, the travel industry is volatile. For many hotel management firms, focusing on management services reduces long-term financial commitments and risk that remain associated with traditional hotel ownership.

Within the property development and ownership segment of the industry, there are various groups. Property ownership can be in the hands of new property developers or owners of existing buildings. Developers can range from large-scale, well-financed international development corporations and real estate investment trusts (REITs) to small-scale, regionally focused developers that establish only a few properties. Developers will take an attractive site location and be responsible for construction of the property. Strategic site selection and building design are done in consultation with the hotel management company, in order to ensure success. Hotel management firms will not contract to manage properties that are not consistent with their brand image or located in declining or saturated markets. Developers may have full ownership of the buildings, or may share ownership with the management firm. Ownership profiles will vary from property to property and from brand to brand. In addition to the developer segment of property owners, but more rare, are owners of existing properties that look to re-brand existing hotels under a new management firm. If an existing hotel is underperforming with one brand name, the owner may not renew the management contract and switch to another management firm. This poses a great risk for the hotel management firms. Also, property owners include those who convert an alternate-use property to hotel use. Historic factories and warehouses are often popular targets for conversion as they are large-scale buildings with historic charm, and may often be the only entry into an architecturally protected neighbourhood. An overview of the major global luxury hotel management firms follows.

Hilton Hotels Corporation

American-based Hilton Hotels Corporation (HHC) is one of the largest hotel management firms in the U.S., with an empire that includes 2300 locations. Unlike Fours Seasons, HHC offers a wider range of accommodations, from low-end budget hotels to high-end luxury properties. Although the bulk of properties are mid-market, HHC does compete directly with Four Seasons through the Hilton and Conrad brands. The Hilton name is well known, with the younger Conrad banner growing in recognition as well. The Waldorf Astoria, a well-known name in the world of luxury, is one of HHC's premier prestige locations. Like Four Seasons, HHC has more involvement in the management side rather than property ownership. In fact, HHC has ownership stakes in only 160 properties, and merely manages or franchises the others. HHC had been more North-American centric than some others in the segment, but in 2006 acquired UK-based Hilton International, expanding the firm's global presence with an additional 400 properties.[39]

Global Hyatt Corporation

Global Hyatt Corporation (Hyatt) is a global operator of a wide range of hotels, from mid-range to upscale and luxury hotels. The Hyatt name can be found on over 200 hotels in 40 locations around the world. Brand names include The Hyatt, Hyatt Regency, Grand Hyatt, and Park Hyatt.[40] The Hyatt Regency banner, in particular, competes against Four Seasons for a share of the business upscale leisure market. Hyatt focuses on higher-end properties with facilities geared towards the business professional, and locates itself in both primary and secondary markets. Initially, Hyatt's operating strategy modeled that used by many hoteliers today—revenue streams based on management fees paid by third party developers and property owners. However, the company soon began to turn towards developing its own properties.[41] As of 2006, the company had plans to open an additional 35 properties globally over 18 countries, with the bulk of current expansion being underway in China.[42]

[39] http://cobrands.hoovers.com/global/cobrands/proquest/overview.xhtml?COID=10733 accessed on February 27, 2006.
[40] http://www.hyatt.com/hyatt/about/overview/index.jsp accessed on February 23, 2006.
[41] http://cobrands.hoovers.com/global/cobrands/proquest/history.xhtml?COID=40231 accessed on February 15, 2006.
[42] http://www.hyatt.com/hyatt/about/press/future.jsp accessed on February 26, 2006.

Fairmont

Fairmont is a hotel management company focused solely on the luxury market segment. Brands include the Fairmont, Raffles as well as Delta, which is a Canadian chain of first-class properties. In terms of rooms under management, it leads the competition in North America. Fairmont manages a total of 87 properties under the Fairmont banner in North America, the United Kingdom and Monaco, and 38 properties under the Delta name. Like many of its competitors, Fairmont has an ownership stake in only a portion of the properties it manages. A significant portion of Fairmont's growth has been based upon the acquisition of under-performing properties, refining their operations and repositioning them before selling them to third party owners, but maintaining lucrative management contracts.[43] In January 2006, Fairmont entered in to an acquisition agreement with Kingdom Hotels International and Colony Capital, transferring 100% ownership of Fairmont to the two firms.[44] Kingdom Hotels is a hotel development company owned by HRH Prince Alwaleed bin Talal bin Abdulaziz Alsaud of Saudi Arabia, who is also a minority partner in rival Four Seasons Hotels.

Wyndham

Wyndham Hotels and Resorts is a subsidiary of Cendant Corporation, which is a global travel and hospitality firm.[45] Other hotel brands in the Cendant portfolio are Super 8, Howard Johnson, Travelodge and Ramada.[46] In addition to hotels, Cendant operates in many segments of the travel industry, such as airline tickets sales and car rentals. As a competitor to Four Seasons in the luxury hotel segment, Wyndham's motto is "Luxury accommodations wherever the winds may blow you." In 2006, it was the fastest growing upscale hotel brand in North America. Wyndham caters to both business and leisure travellers with over 100 locations in North America, the Caribbean, and Europe. Unlike many of its competitors, Wyndham's parent Cendant Corporation neither owns nor operates any of its hotels. It is purely a fee-for-service franchising firm.[47]

Ritz-Carlton

Ritz-Carlton is a subsidiary of global hotel industry giant Marriott. Other brands in the Marriott portfolio are Renaissance Hotels and several lower-end brands with variations of the Marriott name. The Ritz-Carlton in particular competes directly with Four Seasons in the luxury segment. There are 60 luxury hotels operating under the Ritz-Carlton banner in more than 20 countries across the globe. For many people, the name Ritz-Carlton is synonymous with luxury. This is evidenced by the firm partnering up with Mercedes-Benz as a marketing partner to cross-promote their products to their shared market segments. For years, the firm was favoured by older consumers, yet in recent years Ritz-Carlton has been trying to reposition itself as the hotel of choice for younger, wealthy travelers as well.[48] Proof of Ritz-Carlton's superiority in luxury operations is the establishment of its "leadership centre". This centre attracts management from various industries to come and learn about Ritz-Carlton's systems and standards, and benchmark their own firms against many of Ritz-Carlton's practices.[49]

Starwood

Starwood is a global hotelier, operating under several brand names. The company manages a range of upscale and luxury hotels. The company owns or leases 140 properties, and an additional 300+ are owned and operated by franchisees. The firm draws the bulk of its revenues from management and franchise fees. Its upscale and luxury properties include the Four Points, Sheraton, Westin, St. Regis and the Luxury Collection.[50] It is the Luxury Collection that is the direct competitor to Four Seasons. Established in 1995, the Luxury Collection is a grouping of Starwood properties that target the luxury travel consumer. Some of the properties are centuries old and internationally recognized. All eight of the St. Regis locations fall within this grouping, with the balance made up of select properties under the other corporate brands. Starwood's expansion is focused on increasing its management contracts with third-party property owners and searching out undervalued properties to re-brand, locating in areas with favourable demographic trends.[51]

---

[43] http://cobrands.hoovers.com/global/cobrands/proquest/overview.xhtml?COID=40897 accessed February 15, 2006.
[44] http://www.fairmont.com/FA/en/CDA/Home/PressRoom/CDPressRoomDetails/0,1099,
code%25255Ftype%253PRESS%2526article%25255Fseq%253D77910729%2526brandCD%253DFA%2526pr%25255Fflag%253D1,00.html accessed February 21, 2006.
[45] http://cobrands.hoovers.com/global/cobrands/proquest/factsheet.xhtml?COID=141920 accessed February 15, 2006.
[46] http://www.cendant.com/about-cendant/travel-content/hospitality-services/hotel-group.html accessed February 21, 2006.
[47] Cendant Annual Report, 2004, p. 7.
[48] http://cobrands.hoovers.com/global/cobrands/proquest/overview.xhtml?COID=41695 accessed February 15, 2006.
[49] http://www.ritzcarlton.com/corporate/leadership/vision_mission.asp accessed February 23, 2006.
[50] http://cobrands.hoovers.com/global/cobrands/proquest/ops.xhtml?COID=10747 accessed February 2, 2006.
[51] http://www.starwoodhotels.com/corporate/company_info.html accessed February 22, 2006.

Four Seasons' Distinctive Competencies

Four Seasons enjoys a competitive advantage over its rivals, most of which boast of much larger size and economic prowess. This competitive advantage, which could be safely characterized *durable*, stems from the following four distinct, but interrelated, distinctive competencies.

Leadership

Isadore Sharp has had a long and successful tenure at the helm of Four Seasons. It is Sharp's instinctive vision throughout the decades that has helped fuel Four Seasons' rise to global leadership in the luxury hotel industry. Often going against the herd in the past, Sharp refused to look short-term during the down-turn in travel after the September 11 attacks in the U.S. With other competitors nervously dropping rates to encourage sales, Sharp foresaw the dangerous long-term effects of such a move. Dropping rates would imply an inferior product, and it would be difficult to raise rates again once the market returned to normal. He advocated maintaining the status quo, and strived to retain as many employees as possible. Decreasing staffing levels would have diminished service and reputation. Sharp remained committed to the bigger picture of quality service and long-term growth. Once again, Sharp is ignoring the general fears of the marketplace by expanding into the Middle East. Time will tell whether his instincts will again prove correct. Sharp has shown himself to be a visionary both in entrepreneurship and management. A long-standing advocate of effective and progressive human resource strategy, Sharp has strived to build a people-centric organization.

Human Resources

Four Seasons has a highly selective recruitment and training program, ensuring that staff are sufficiently prepared to give unfailingly superior service to its guests. The company's recruiting efforts rest on the belief that a service-focused organization must hire employees based on their inherent attitude, and train them in proper procedures to establish skill. Sharp's view on service is that "service errors happen through a lack of knowledge or a lack of attention. Lack of knowledge is a training problem and lack of attention is an attitude problem."[52] Viewing superior staff as a valuable resource, Four Seasons also tries to ensure that staff stays with the company as long as possible. The company offers above industry-average compensation to its workers, as well as a supportive working environment. The company is known for treating its employees with respect. Superior compensation and treatment establishes excellent management-employee relations. This, in turn, is reflected in employee performance and customer service.

Strategic Partnerships

Four Seasons' move towards decreasing its real estate holdings and partnering with outside developers has established a greater degree of flexibility for the company. The company is able to expand much more quickly and build its global presence at an increasing rate. Management contracts are long-term, and many long-standing, mutually advantageous partnerships have developed. In particular, the partnership with Prince Alwaleed bin Talal bin Abdulaziz Alsaud has been significantly valuable. The Prince's large cash infusion and extensive business relationships has opened many doors for the company. As the North American and Western European luxury hotel markets become increasingly saturated, other markets, such as the Middle East, become extremely attractive. With little presence of large global firms, Four Seasons could have a solid first-mover advantage in that region. Partnership with the Saudi Prince could open doors that might not be open to other global players that do not have such a local connection.

Market Focus

Four Seasons has maintained a very strict focus on operating only small to medium size hotels specifically in the luxury segment. Its focus on smaller size properties and manageable growth enables the firm to maintain a consistency in service and customer intimacy. This is rare in the industry, as many competitors are large corporations with several hospitality divisions or brand names. While other firms may hold within their portfolio brands that cater to every segment of the market, Four Seasons' single-minded approach to the industry niche strengthens its credibility with its core market. Four Seasons' brand name has become synonymous with luxury, and this reputation is difficult to match overnight. According to Sharp, this is fundamental to success. "We would create a reputation for service so clear in people's minds that the Four Seasons' name would become an asset of far greater value than bricks and mortar."[53] New competitors would be challenged to rival Four Seasons

[52] Sharp, Isadore. "Quality for All Seasons." *Canadian Business Review*, Spring 1990; 17 (1): 21.

[53] Sharp Isadore. "The Unseen but Decisive Factor in Entrepreneurial Success." *Transcript of Speech Given to the Canadian Club of Toronto*, May 25, 2004.

Exhibit 7	Isadore Sharp's Seven C's of Quality[54]

At Four Seasons, our approach to achieving quality is based on seven basic principles, called the seven C's

1. **C is for Comprehension:** Some managers fail to comprehend what quality is. Quality is not what a company puts into a product; it is what customers get from the product. Quality isn't a function, it's a value.

2. **C is for Culture:** Quality can not be imposed or taught through a program. It is a process that involves emotions. It is not functional—it is attitudinal—a view of life that grows out of corporate culture. The key to having committed troops on the service front is having management committed to value and focused on a goal that employees feel is worthwhile, that they can take pride in helping to build. To get excellence at the bottom, you have to start at the top.

3. **C is for Commitment:** Commitment to quality without compromise. We reasoned that our growth should be based on our strength: the quality service we provide. If your edge is your quality, you shouldn't compromise it.

4. **C is for Credibility:** Most service sector horror stories stem from a lack of management credibility. Our communications effort is designed to build enthusiasm for the company's goals and a team spirit among employees. The communications process helps to teach employees that what is bad for business is bad for them, and the incentive plan gives them a reason to speak up.

5. **C is for Control:** Too little organization brings chaos but too much smothers initiative. We have a centralized framework of policy, planning, systems and standards, but our structure is not rigid.

6. **C is for Creativity:** It has to flow up as well as down. Achieving quality is a continuous process. Our successful anticipation of trends and changing lifestyles gave us the lead in innovation, but we can't patent a service innovation. To stay ahead, we try to tap the creative ideas of everyone in the company.

7. **C is for Continuity:** We must take the long-term view if we are to achieve quality. Unless we pay as much attention to what our customers want and our employees need as we do to our shareholders and bankers; unless we understand that quality improvement starts at the top; and unless we put quality first; ahead of profits and growth, we can not achieve quality.

as the company is firmly established in every developed market and is aggressively pursuing expansion in developing markets as well. Prime locations are a premium, even for the most established competitor in the market.

Corporate Culture

"Developed over more than 40 years, Four Seasons' service culture represents a unique asset and our single most valuable resource."[55] At Four Seasons, the number one goal is a satisfied guest. To all employees in the company, quality is a goal, not a destination. This goal has permeated through the organization so much so that everyone through all rungs has come to embrace customer satisfaction as the unifying glue for everything Four Seasons offers. Superb, highly personalized

customer service cannot be imposed or taught, it is a process that grows out of a uniquely rich culture built around the essence of the company's core values. The essence of this culture is so fundamental to Four Seasons' operations that Sharp has codified what he calls "The Seven C's" of quality (See Exhibit 7).

Future Outlook

This is not the empire building period of the late conglomerate era, this is the corporate world re-enacting Darwin's theory, which has very special ramifications for the global luxury hospitality industry. Business is evolving at a speed never seen before, and the fittest to survive will be those who adapt quickest and best.[56] It is true that Four Seasons has been, and still is, quick in

[54] Sharp, Isadore. "Quality for All Seasons." *Canadian Business Review,* Spring 1990; 17 (1): 21.
[55] Four Seasons Annual Report, 2004, p. 4.
[56] Sharp, Isadore. "Managing for Global Market Leadership." *Business Quarterly,* Summer 1991; 56 (1): 16–19.

hitting the opportunities at propitious times, and its leading position in the industry supports this. From day one, Sharp has been striving to expand and improve on his properties. His goal has been to transform "the name Four Seasons into a common phrase for high-quality hotels,"[57] and it is obvious that his dreams are largely realized. However, this realization does not necessarily guarantee Four Seasons' uninterrupted survival, let alone its dominant industry position. A few challenges, which follow, need to be addressed.

Macro-environment

Following the September 2001 terrorist attack of the World Trade Center, the geo-political situation of the world has changed drastically. The aftermath of the attack seems more damning for the luxury hospitality industry than the material consequences of the attack itself. Four Seasons has a total of 11 properties in the Middle East, and seven more are scheduled to open in the near future. This is indeed a risky expansion move, as general public, but not necessarily the government, are hostile to Western interests and properties in the Middle East. The success of both existing and new properties in this region could be easily jeopardized in the event of political and social unrest.

Industry Structure

The global luxury resort industry is becoming increasingly competitive, both for guests and for the acquisition of new management agreements. The industry is dominated by several internationally known brand names that are controlled by a small number of corporations. Large hotel conglomerates are acquiring smaller hotel chains in order to expand their international reach and market share, thus making the industry more concentrated. In a consolidated industry, competitors are interdependent. The interdependence, in turn, creates some problems for the relatively weaker rivals. The strategic acquisition of complementary chains allows many firms to enter new markets on an immediate and large scale. Competition for guests arises from other luxury hotel chains, individual luxury hotels and resorts, and luxury properties operated by larger hotel chains. This poses significant take-over risks for Four Seasons. Other much large chains, such as Marriott, is so well-entrenched in the industry that it might decide to include Four Seasons, which is essentially a niche player, in its corporate portfolio. Fairmont's acquisition of Kingdom Hotels,

which used to be owned by the Saudi Price Alwaleed bin Talal bin Abdulaziz Alsaud (who holds 25% of Four Seasons' ownership) also signals a telling acquisition possibility in the future.

CEO Succession

In the luxury resort industry, Four Seasons and Issy Sharp are interchangeable names. Over the years, Four Seasons started, thrived, and prospered under Sharp's insight, influence, and charisma. No one in Four Seasons stands tall enough to fill Sharp's shoes. This is indeed a problem for Four Seasons. Sharp, 71, has announced a few times that he would retire, but has held on instead. This sends confusing signals to Four Seasons' external stakeholders, especially property owners for both existing and future management contracts. Although it is a practice in Four Seasons to develop senior managers from within, it can be conjectured that either of the two presidents—Wolf Hengst and Kathleen Taylor—might take over as the CEO following Sharp's retirement. This has not been announced yet, but Four Seasons needs an heir-apparent for stability and growth.

Conclusion

Rooted in his own itinerant childhood, Issy Sharp's commitment to a unique concept—a memorable customer experience—has definitely withstood the test of time. His flair for combining customer service and efficiency with the finest traditions of hospitality has transformed a single motor inn in 1961 to a coveted brand name in the world that embodies the essence of comfort, luxury, and prestige.[58] Over a sojourn of more than forty years, Sharp has emphasized a set of common values around the retention of employees and holding onto the same price structure during both the worst and best of economic times. These value-driven decisions run counter to conventional wisdom and the prescriptions of many strategy pundits. In addition, his pursuit of smart strategies, such as acquisition of promising but smaller competitors in key locations and partnership with parties with complementary resources and capabilities, has contributed to Four Seasons' continued success. Whether this success continues in the future will depend on the degree to which Four Seasons' unique culture, its visionary management, its strategic choices, and its bundle of resources and capabilities remain unmatched by its existing and potential rivals.

---

[57] Dardek, T.
[58] Four Seasons Annual Report, 2004.

GVM Exploration Limited

Michael Rouse

Guo-Liang Frank Jiang

On Monday morning June 27, 2005, Matt Roberts, the engineering manager of GVM Exploration Limited, was preparing for a meeting with the company's CEO and VP Finance. He wondered what action to recommend regarding the weekend blockade by a small group of protesters, consisting mainly of local First Nations people, of the only accessible road to the company's Grizzly Valley coal site in British Columbia, Canada.

Canada's Mineral Industry and Coal Mining

Canada's rich natural resources and the industries they supported were a vital part of the country's economy and society. This sector was the lifeblood of hundreds of communities throughout Canada—many of them rural, remote, northern and aboriginal. Forestry, energy, minerals, metals, earth sciences and allied industries accounted for 13 per cent of Canada's GDP and more than 40 per cent of total Canadian exports. Natural resources companies directly employed almost one million Canadians and just as many were employed indirectly.

The mineral industry was a pivotal part of Canada's natural resource economy, representing 3.9 per cent of Canada's total GDP of $1,045 billion[1] in 2004. An improving global economic environment, especially the rapid growth of China and India, had resulted in a period of high commodity prices since 2003. The strong commodity cycle gave a boost to the Canadian mining industry. According to Natural Resources Canada, preliminary estimates for the value of production for all sectors of the Canadian mining industry (excluding crude oil and natural gas) totaled $24.2 billion in 2004, up from $20.1 billion in 2003 and $19.9 billion in 2002. Of this, metal production increased by 29.6 per cent to $12.5 billion and nonmetallic production increased by 12.6 per cent to $10.0 billion. The value of coal increased by 7.1 per cent to $1.6 billion.

Coal had been mined in Canada on a massive scale. It was Canada's single-most valuable export to Japan. Most coal mining activities took place in Alberta, British Columbia, Saskatchewan and Nova Scotia. The majority of the electricity in Alberta, Saskatchewan and Nova Scotia was generated from coal and the industry created jobs across the country, directly enriching Canada's economy by $5 billion a year.

---

[1] All funds in Canadian dollars unless specified otherwise.

Guo-Liang Frank Jiang wrote this case under the supervision of Professor Michael Rouse solely to provide material for class discussion. The authors do not intend to illustrate either effective or ineffective handling of a managerial situation. The authors may have disguised certain names and other identifying information to protect confidentiality.

GVM Exploration Limited

Based in Toronto, Ontario, GVM Exploration was a junior mining company listed on the Toronto Stock Exchange with interests in seven mineral deposits and a number of exploration projects in Canada. A junior mining company was a company that undertook exploration and/or mine development activities. Juniors might also have production interests. GVM had five full-time employees and one part-time bookkeeper.

Exploration was the first stage in the coal mining industry. At this stage, new coal deposits and existing coalfields were identified and assessed for quality and quantity of the resource. Though the direct economic impact of exploration activities was quite modest, its long-term potential was high when the future value of new deposits, mining operations and revenues were considered. The second stage was development. Social, economic, logistical and environmental plans were prepared and reviewed by various stakeholders at this stage. These plans were designed with input from local residents, environmental agencies, government departments, corporate managers and consultants. This input helped ensure that the construction and operation of mines were sensitive to stakeholders' needs. Successful exploration and development led to the production stage, which included coal mining and processing. Almost all of the jobs, much of the investment, and most of the operating costs occurred at this stage. Production was the economic heart of the coal industry.

A junior mining company operated primarily on the basis of funding its activities by selling shares on a stock market. Juniors lacked the self-sustaining cash flow of major mining companies. Investors who bought shares of a junior hoped that the company would find a deposit or make a deal with a major company, which might increase the share price. A junior company also offered an opportunity for investors to profit if the company transformed itself into a mid-tier or senior mining company. A senior mining company generally had much larger market capitalization and had the capability to take over viable projects and to develop major mines.

GVM Exploration's principal assets were the "world class" Grizzly Valley anthracite coal deposits in southeast British Columbia, and the Dovik Creek gold-cobalt-bismuth deposit in northern Quebec. These two major projects were undergoing various technical, environmental and feasibility assessments by hired contractors and consultants. Commercial production had not begun at either the Grizzly Valley or Dovik Creek projects and

GVM was making the transition from an exploration company to a producer. Grizzly Valley was scheduled to begin production in 2008 and Dovik Creek in 2009. GVM completed a $20 million equity financing in December 2004 (see Exhibit 1). Its market value was approximately $119 million at the end of June 2005, with 34 million shares outstanding and no debt.

Grizzly Valley Project

GVM owned a 100 per cent interest in the Grizzly Valley anthracite coal project in southeast British Columbia. The Grizzly Valley lease was purchased in 2002 from a Canadian subsidiary of a large oil company which conducted exploration and test mining programs, spending approximately $65 million developing the project. The Grizzly Valley project straddled a rail right-of-way and roadbed which provided road access to a provincial highway. However, due to extreme weather conditions, the Grizzly Valley site was only practically accessible between May and early November. A new road was proposed by GVM to connect the mine site to the closest town along the highway. The potential mine site was located within the territory of a First Nations group.[2]

The Grizzly Valley site included four major deposits which collectively contained coal resources of 108 million tonnes classified as Measured, 123 million tonnes classified as Indicated, 2.57 billion tonnes in the Inferred and Speculative classes. Grizzly Valley contained one of the world's largest undeveloped resources of high rank anthracite coal.

Anthracite is a "hard coal" with the highest rank, carbon and energy content, and lowest moisture and volatile content of all coals. Only about one per cent of world coal reserves were anthracite grade. Unique properties made anthracite suitable for use in a broad range of metallurgical, thermal, water purification and composite materials applications. The most important new market for Grizzly Valley anthracite was pulverized coal injection (PCI) coal used in the steel industry. Anthracite was also a preferred fuel source for new "clean coal" technologies for power generation that reduced greenhouse gas emissions. In addition, the high cost of oil was making coal-to-oil liquification technologies economically attractive. World annual production of anthracite was in excess of 350 million tonnes. Prices ranged between US$50 and US$250/tonne with metallurgical products selling for between US$70 and US$130/tonne, and filter media at US$250/tonne.

---

[2] The name of the First Nation is not provided to maintain the company's confidentiality.

Exhibit 1 | Consolidate Balance Sheets

As at December 31	2004	2003
ASSETS		
Current assets		
Cash and cash equivalents	$ 24,642,774	$ 3,348,384
Short-term investments	268,872	1,269,154
Accounts receivable	446,629	132,173
Prepaid expenses	17,865	13,275
	25,376,140	4,762,986
Reclamation bond	225,900	210,000
Investment in and advances to affiliated company	379,440	370,661
Capital assets, net	19,355	9,420
Interests in mining properties	3,153,280	3,153,280
Deferred exploration expenditures	11,296,536	9,156,715
	40,450,651	17,663,062
LIABILITIES AND SHAREHOLDERS' EQUITY		
Current liabilities		
Accounts payable and accrued liabilities	676,405	113,919
Income taxes payable	83,235	60,938
Total current liabilities	759,640	174,857
Future income taxes	4,000,000	2,660,000
Total liabilities	4,749,640	2,834,857
SHAREHOLDERS' EQUITY		
Share capital	36,179,828	14,804,848
Contributed surplus	1,348,840	522,146
Deficit	(1,837,657)	(498,789)
	35,691,011	14,828,205
	40,450,651	17,663,062

Source: GVM Exploration Limited, 2005 Annual Report.

Dovik Creek Project

GVM Exploration's 90 per cent-owned Dovik Creek project in northern Quebec was a significant deposit of cobalt, containing approximately one million ounces of by-product gold and it was one of the largest known resources of bismuth in the world. Cobalt was a high-strength, magnetic metal and it was in increasing demand for a variety of chemical and metallurgical applications. The largest growth in the cobalt market was in the chemicals industry for the manufacture of rechargeable batteries, catalysts, audio recording tape,

pigments and food additives. The global cobalt market was about 49,500 tonnes per year. Annual growth in the cobalt market had averaged between five and six per cent for the past two decades. Prices had generally been in the range of US$15 to US$25/pound for the past two years.

Bismuth was a relatively uncommon metal with unique properties, including very high density and low melting temperature. Bismuth was also quite inert and scientifically recognized as one of the safest metals, making it ideally suited for numerous pharmaceuticals, medicines, cosmetics and medical devices. Significant growth in the bismuth market was accelerating because it had physical properties similar to lead but was non-toxic. Bismuth was replacing lead in a number of applications due to increasing concern for the environment. Current worldwide consumption of bismuth was approximately 7,000 tonnes per year and had been growing at approximately 10 per cent per year. The market was constrained by supply and, ironically, most bismuth was sourced as a by-product from lead mining, which suggested that further decreases in lead consumption would also have an impact on bismuth supply. The long-term price of bismuth had averaged approximately US$4/pound. According to a 2005 research report the in-ground value of the metal content of Dovik Creek resources totaled $2.0 billion.

GVM had recently entered into an agreement to purchase a used mill from another Canadian mining company. The mill was well-suited for use at Dovik Creek and would significantly reduce projected capital costs for the development. GVM would purchase the buildings, major equipment and approximately $2 million in inventory for $3.3 million. A revised feasibility study reflecting the acquisition of this equipment was expected to be completed in mid-2006. Upon the expected closing of the deal in 2006, GVM would have three years to remove the assets to Dovik Creek. Meanwhile, GVM was working on a second transaction to acquire additional equipment. GVM was also planning to conduct a $9.5 million underground bulk sampling program at Dovik Creek in 2006.

First Nations

First Nations refers to any of the numerous aboriginal groups formally recognized by the Canadian government under the federal Indian Act of 1876. First Nation was a legally undefined term that came into common usage in the 1970s to replace the term "Indian band." A band was defined as a body of aboriginals for whose collective use and benefit lands had been set apart or money had been held by the Canadian Crown; alternatively, such a group was declared to be a band for the purposes of the Indian Act. There are over 600 First Nations governments or bands in Canada. Roughly half of these are located in the provinces of Ontario and British Columbia.

In general, the Canadian government provided a strong legislative and political framework for indigenous rights protection. The government's aboriginal policy evolved over the years from an effort to acculturate and assimilate indigenous peoples to one supporting indigenous self-determination and cultural expression. Since 1763, First Nations had ceded their lands to the Crown in return for other benefits. However, British Columbia had adopted different land rights policies. Most of the

lands the B.C. First Nations inhabited had never been ceded. No treaties had been signed. Claims to land title were ambiguous in many First Nations areas.

Canada had a strong record of protecting the environment and the interests of native people while developing the natural resources sector to achieve economic and social benefits. Increasingly, mining companies were taking into account their impact on society through the products they made, the people they employed and the communities in which they worked. However, First Nations issues remained a salient challenge in the mining industry. There were many land access issues. On one hand, the industry and government were making efforts to involve aboriginal peoples. On the other hand, the companies, especially junior firms, continued to feel pressures dealing with native issues. Lack of guidance was attributed to the continuous disputes. The following comment was made by a mining executive at a meeting organized by the Finance and Economic Affairs Committee of the Legislative Assembly of Ontario:

> There doesn't seem to be a set process to work with the First Nations communities and to make a determination of whether or not there are land issues, so it would definitely be beneficial to get some clarification and guidance on how we can walk through the process. We definitely want to do that. We are very interested in making sure all the stakeholders are taken care of, but without guidance it's difficult to determine what is adequate for our permitting and consultation.

Grizzly Valley First Nations

The Grizzly Valley area First Nation refers to a group of aboriginal people whose traditional territories are in southeast British Columbia. Historically, they were a nomadic people, traveling around their area with the seasons and their food supply. Each spring and summer, they traditionally returned to the Grizzly Valley area to fish. Today, they are a small nation of approximately 6,000 persons with all but 800 of their members living outside the traditional territory.

They are comprised of two bands, each with an elected council which comes under the jurisdiction of the local Central Council (CC). The CC was comprised of representatives of 10 families from each band. The CC linked the Grizzly Valley bands and had represented them on issues of joint concern, specifically on asserting inherent rights and title. The CC was a registered society under the B.C. Society Act. The government of British Columbia had been engaged in negotiations with the CC and local bands on a consultation and accommodation agreement on forestry, mining, oil and gas.

However, the CC faced challenges from a small group within the nation. Grizzly Valley Hereditary Chiefs (Elders) had been holding a protest against their leadership for several months and had occupied the office of the elected chief. The Elders also questioned the pace of development. They claimed that the proposed development of a number of resource projects was too fast. The CC was perceived by the Elders to be overly pro-business. The Elders insisted that they participate in the decision-making process.

On January 13, 2005, in response to news that a 160-km industrial road would be built in the area, 35 Elders occupied the band office and asserted their right to speak for their people. They were responding to information that the CC had signed a deal with the province to facilitate mining, logging and hydroelectricity projects in exchange for $250,000 per year for the Council. For many, it was the first time they had received official information about so many industrial projects. Their principal concern was that their land, resources and rights were being sold without their knowledge. The Elders agreed to stand strong to protect the land for future generations. They demanded the resignation of the elected CC leader. He was accused of abusing his elected position in order to promote his own businesses. They demanded that the CC reconsider the agreement with the B.C. government, which they feared would fast-track numerous major projects in the region. These projects included two copper-gold mine projects; a coal bed methane project, and GVM Exploration's Grizzly Valley coal mine project.

On Saturday February 12, the Elders announced a moratorium that prohibited any resource development on local lands until more representative and accountable leadership and governance was achieved. At a meeting on March 10, the Elders delivered the moratorium to representatives of a major oil company. The next day, in support of the moratorium, one of the First Nations bands, along with its Hereditary Chiefs Council and band council, dressed in traditional regalia and formally requested the oil company to leave their territory. The company subsequently cancelled their 2005 field exploration program.

Road Blockade

On Saturday June 25, a group of Elders, and First Nations' families blockaded the entrance to the road which connected the Grizzly Valley site and the rail roadbed and eventually led to the main highway (Exhibit 2). The blockade prevented GVM and other exploration companies from sending in heavy industrial equipment. It also disrupted the business of local tour companies.

The protesters claimed that GVM's project infringed upon Aboriginal Title and Rights when the company was

---

Exhibit 2   The Road Blockade

Source: GVM Exploration Limited, Corporate Archive.

granted tenure without honorable consultation with the family on whose traditional territory the tenure was located. They felt that, because of the breakdown in band leadership, it would be appropriate for GVM to engage directly with the people who would be most affected by the proposed development. A leader of the protest noted,

The GVM Exploration project in the area would directly impact our traditional lifestyle, a lifestyle we've maintained for tens of thousands of years and to date we continue to use this area on a regular basis. Matter of fact a few of our campsites are set to be flooded with waste dumps. However, no one will destroy our world without first consulting with us.

Although the Elders had demanded the resignation of the elected leader since January 2005, some protestors and supporters asserted that the blockade had nothing to do with their resignation demands. They stated that the issue was not just about mining or resource extraction either. Rather, the issue was the protection of the traditional territory, heritage sites and lifestyle from the destruction of non-renewable resource extraction. It was about sustainable development. It was about the inherent rights of traditional peoples to govern their territories as they had for millennia.

Matt Roberts

Matt Roberts started to work at GVM Exploration after he earned an MBA degree from a leading Canadian business school. He had significant experience in energy, metals and industrial minerals projects, having held positions in mine operations and engineering with multiple firms.

Roberts was deeply concerned about the blockade because GVM was unable to mobilize its camp to support a $2 million environmental assessment project. Roberts was worried about the lack of time available to complete the work if the blockade was not lifted. Due to extreme weather conditions, the Grizzly Valley site was really only accessible between May and early November. It would take five months to complete the 2005 work program, gathering baseline data to support the project's application to the B.C. environmental agency. If GVM could not enter the site to perform environmental tests that summer, they would have to wait until May 2006. Their commercial production would be delayed for at least nine months and possibly an entire year (see Exhibit 3). Unlike major mining companies which often had separate departments dedicated to native issues, a junior company like GVM usually could not afford the time and lacked the depth of experience of the majors. The process could last several years. Roberts wondered what the financial implications of the blockade would be, both on the work program and on the company's share price. The valuation of GVM largely hinged on the Grizzly Valley coal project. Thanks to the strong demand from Asian markets, metallurgical coal was selling for record prices in 2005 (see Exhibit 4). Any delay of the project was going to send a negative signal to its shareholders and the investment community.

Roberts wondered if the company should fight for an injunction in court. However, he felt uncomfortable

---

Exhibit 3   Grizzly Valley Project Activity Schedule

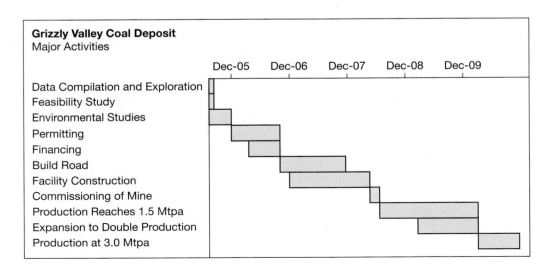

Source: GVM Exploration Limited, Corporate Archive.

Exhibit 4   Average Metallurgical Coal Price

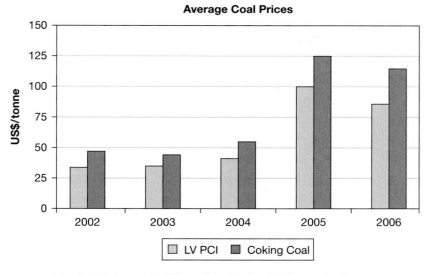

Average Coal Prices

Note: LV PCI = Low-volatile PCI coal. Data of 2005 and 2006 were estimation.

Source: GVM Minerals Limited, 2005 Annual Report.

about the idea. The police might make arrests if the protestors did not cooperate and the possibility of violence and the threat to public safety was a concern. In addition, GVM had been quite cautious in the negotiations with the Central Council and promised to develop a constructive relationship with local communities. Roberts was concerned that a confrontation might undermine these prior efforts. Further complicating the issue was the growing internal dispute amongst the First Nations peoples, leaving GVM in a difficult position.

Roberts doubted that the B.C. government would directly intervene in this incident. He felt that the B.C. government had generally stepped away from native issues and left them up to the companies to work out, although it was trying to create a business-friendly environment for the mining industry. Many thought the previous government's policies had discouraged resource development in the province. Roberts knew that lack of communication might be a contributing factor to the current situation. He was wondering if additional communication and negotiation would help solve the problem.

Roberts did think, however, that GVM was not in a completely passive position. The CC had always been supportive of the coal mine project. GVM planned to enter into an Impact and Benefits Agreements with the Grizzly Valley and other First Nations where operations might impact their traditional territories. The protesters were supported by a relatively small group of people within the

Grizzly Valley First Nation. Many others did not support the blockade. Actually, local First Nations' companies had been directly engaged in environmental studies at Grizzly Valley. GVM retained two local First Nations environmental service companies to collect environmental data and to assist the company with permitting of the project. If the blockade continued, 60 jobs could be lost, along with a $1.5-million contract. Down the road, commercial production would generate a significantly larger number of employment opportunities in the region.

All along, GVM's strategy was to develop the Dovik Creek project independently into production stage and to secure partners to develop the Grizzly Valley project. Production at Dovik Creek would immediately increase GVM's workforce by 300. More importantly, GVM would need approximately $200 million to finance the transformation of the Dovik Creek project. The Grizzly Valley project was on an even larger scale. It had been estimated that GVM would spend $275 million to put the largest Grizzly Valley deposit into production to produce an initial 1.5 million tonnes of ultra-low volatile PCI coal. In the second year of production, a further $158 million would be spent to expand the production to 3.0 million tonnes per year. Some companies had expressed interest in the Grizzly Valley project but there had been no serious negotiations.

Roberts knew he would have to consider GVM's options carefully and present a reasonable plan at the afternoon's meeting.

Haier—The Chinese Global Competitor

Vivek Gupta

Joel Joseph

"In an era of globalization, you can't separate domestic and international markets. We've got to learn how to compete with General Electric and Whirlpool on their home turf. Otherwise, we'll lose the Chinese market."[1]

—*Zhang Ruimin, President, Haier Group.*

"Four years ago, nobody could even pronounce Haier. Today, there is not one retailer in the U.S. who doesn't know us."[2]

—*Michael Jemal, President, Haier America.*

Introduction

On June 21, 2005, the China-based Haier Group (Haier) made a bid of US$ 1.3 billion to acquire Maytag Corporation (Maytag), the third largest manufacturer of household appliances in the US in terms of number of units sold per annum. Industry analysts pointed out that Haier's acquisition bid was an attempt to gain direct entry into the premium segment of the US household appliances market. On June 27, 2005, backed by equity firms—Bain Capital Partners[3] and Blackstone Capital Partners[4]—Haier decided to take on Maytag's debt worth $975 million, thus increasing its bid to $2.275 billion.

According to a Chinese media report,[5] if Haier succeeded in acquiring Maytag, it would be able to leverage upon Maytag's brand in the US market. Haier would also gain access to Maytag's technology and its extensive sales & distribution network. This would strengthen its ability to compete with the three big players of the US household appliances market—GE, Whirlpool, and Electrolux (See Exhibit 1 for detailed information on the leading home appliances companies in the US).

Appreciating Haier's move, Lu Renbo, an analyst at the Development Research Center of the Chinese State Council, commented, "Haier is looking for a new way to achieve its globalization. Purchasing of a local, big name

[1] Mark Landler, "In China, a Management Maverick Builds a Brand," *New York Times,* July 23, 2000.

[2] David J. Lynch, "CEO Pushes China's Haier as Global Brand," *USA Today,* January 03, 2003.

[3] Boston, MA-based Bain Capital is a private equity investment firm that manages private equity, high-yield assets and public equity with over $25 billion in assets under management.

[4] New York-based Blackstone is a private investment and advisory firm with business interests in private equity, real estate, corporate debt investing, mergers and acquisitions, restructuring and reorganization advisory services.

[5] "Haier Group Bids US$1.3b for Maytag," www.beijingportal.com.cn, June 22, 2005.

| Exhibit 1 | Haier's Competitors in the US Market |

Whirlpool

Whirlpool is the biggest manufacturer of domestic appliances in the US. The company product range includes washing machines, refrigerators, freezers, cooking appliances, air-conditioners, mixers, dishwashers and other small household appliances. Whirlpool sells its products under four major brands in the US markets namely, Whirlpool, KitchenAid, Roper and Estate. Whirlpool is also a major supplier of home appliances to retailers like Sears and Roebuck & Co. Sears sells Whirlpool's products under the Kenmore brand. Whirlpool has divided its worldwide business into four regions viz. North America, Europe, Latin America and Asia. The company reported revenues to the tune of $12.1 billion for the year 2003 with a net income of $414 million.

GE Appliances

GE Appliances is the second largest US appliance maker. The company manufactures refrigerators, freezers, electric cookers, microwaves, dishwashers, air-conditioners and other small appliances. GE sells its appliances under Profile, Monogram, Spacemaker, Triton, Hotpoint and GE brands in the US markets. GE Appliances is a part of GE Consumer and Industrial, a $13 billion business unit under the GE fold.

Maytag

Maytag is the third largest US appliance maker. The company's product range includes washing machines, driers, dishwashers, vacuum cleaners and refrigerators. The company has two business segments viz. Home appliances and Commercial products. Maytag sells its products under the Maytag, Amana, Hoover, Jenn-Air and MagicChef brands in the Home Appliances segment. The Commercial Products segment caters to restaurants, hotels and eateries with commercial cooking equipment segment sold under the Jade brand. Maytag sells its products through independent retailers in the US and selected markets abroad. Maytag also owns stores through which it sells its products. For the fiscal year 2004, Maytag reported revenues of $4.7 billion and a net loss of $9 million.

Electrolux

Based in Stockholm, Sweden, Electrolux is the fourth largest manufacturer of appliances in the US. The company has divided its business under two categories—indoor products and outdoor products. The company sells refrigerators, dishwashers, washing machines, vacuum cleaners, floor cleaning equipment and cooking equipment under brands like Electrolux, Eureka, Frigidaire, Partner and Poulan. The company reported worldwide revenues of SEK 120,651 million for the year 2004 with net profits of SEK 4,435 million.

Source: Compiled from various sources.

company may be the best and fastest way for Chinese home appliance makers' global expansion."[6]

From being a small manufacturer of refrigerators in the Chinese town of Qindao in the early 1980s, Haier had grown to become one of the largest manufacturers of domestic appliances in the world with annual sales of RMB[7] 152.99 million by 2005. Haier's growth was attributed to a significant improvement in the quality of its products, which enabled it to establish itself as a leading home appliance brand in the Chinese market. Haier made a number of acquisitions in the mid-1990s, which allowed it to expand its range of products and become a household name in China. Haier's acquisitions mostly involved bankrupt Chinese companies in the

[6] Zhang Lu, "Haier Group Bids US$ 1.3 billion for Maytag," *China Daily*, June 22, 2005.
[7] 1 US $ = 8.27 RMB. After the revaluation of the RMB on July 21, 2005, 1 US $ = 8.11 RMB.

consumer electronics industry that the company managed to turn around. Haier used a three-pronged strategy to turn these companies around—absolute regard for consumer needs and preferences, collaboration with foreign companies, and the inculcation of Haier's work culture in the acquired company. Another important factor that contributed to Haier's success was the OEC management model that created a company-wide commitment to quality.

To seek new markets for its products, Haier began globalizing in the late 1990s. Haier made its first major foray into the global markets by establishing a refrigerator manufacturing facility at Camden, US, in 1999. The localization of product design helped the company gain a foothold in the US market. By 2005, Haier had 18 design institutes, 10 industrial complexes, 22 production facilities, and 58,800 sales agents around the world. Commenting on Haier's globalization strategy, Zhang Ruimin (Zhang), president, Haier Group, said, "We go to easier markets after we first penetrate difficult markets such as the United States and Europe. These are much bigger markets. They are also the home markets of our largest global competitors, and we believe that if we can succeed there we can succeed in easier markets."[8]

Background Note

In 1949, China embraced socialism. The state exercised absolute control over the economy; it owned the large industries, controlled supply, and set prices. Businesses and industrial houses were taken over by the state and managed by state-appointed officials. All industrial activity came under the purview of the government with state-owned enterprises (SoEs) taking center stage in the new centrally planned and controlled economy. The focus of the SoEs was on producing large quantities without much regard for customer preferences. By 1978, the SoEs accounted for roughly 78% of the country's total industrial output and they became the driving force of the Chinese economy.

The SoEs employed millions of Chinese workers and became the primary provider of social welfare and security. Jobs in the SoEs were considered a fundamental right with entitlements that included pensions, medical insurance, and housing. Worker unions became very powerful within the SoEs and that led to widespread indiscipline. The workers refused to work and used the factory facilities for their own businesses. Management control was largely ineffective with workers threatening to physically harm managers who tried to assert any

authority. Inefficient managers also turned toward corruption to make money. All these factors resulted in the SoEs becoming largely unproductive, loss-making bodies that were heavily dependent upon the government for survival. In the early 1980s, the sorry state of affairs at the SoEs forced Deng Xiaoping (Deng), head of the Communist Party of China (CPC), to introduce reforms in the Chinese economy to turn over control of the SoEs to local governments, thereby allowing them greater operating autonomy. These reforms also envisaged a greater role for the private sector in the Chinese economy and the setting up of Collective Enterprises.

Collective Enterprises (CEs) were formed by groups of skilled laborers or small entrepreneurs who wanted to commercialize their skills. These enterprises grew in the aftermath of the economic reforms initiated by Deng in the early 1980s and they began playing a pivotal role in China's significant economic growth in the 1980s and the early 1990s. The SoEs, however, continued to flounder as a result of their inability to adapt to the increased competition in the reformed economy. By the mid-1990s, the CEs accounted for nearly 40% of China's industrial output, and employed a workforce in excess of 100 million.

Even though the ownership of the CEs was in the hands of worker members, the local government exerted full control over all major decision-making pertaining to issues like labor policies and investments. Widespread corruption and constant government interference drove many of the CEs to bankruptcy. The Qingdao General Refrigerator Factory (Qingdao General) was one of the CEs manufacturing refrigerators for sale in China. The company had no funds to invest in new product development or pay employee salaries when Zhang, a bureaucrat with the local government, was asked to take over the reins of the company in 1984.

Zhang realized that Qingdao General was bothered about neither the quality of its products, nor about customer satisfaction. Realizing that he would have to take quick steps to set matters right, Zhang began importing technology from German company Liebherr in 1985 in order to manufacture refrigerators that were technically superior to the ones being manufactured in China. Zhang was particularly concerned about the quality of the company's products and urged the workers to be equally conscious of it. On one occasion in April 1985, he gathered all the employees on the factory floor and before their eyes, smashed a faulty refrigerator with a sledgehammer. He found another 76 faulty refrigerators and ordered the workers themselves to destroy them, adding, "If we pass these 76 for sale, we'll be continuing

---

[8] Yibing Wu, "China's Refrigerator Magnate," *McKinsey Quarterly*, Issue 03, 2003.

Table 1 — Haier Group Financials (1992–1999)

(In hundred million RMB)

Particulars	1992	1993	1994	1995	1996	1997	1998	1999
Main Business Income	5.89	6.84	9.26	15.3	26.4	38.26	38.23	39.74
Net Profit	0.59	0.70	0.96	1.17	1.78	2.45	2.74	3.11
Shareholder Interests	1.24	5.68	6.65	6.14	9.06	15.95	18.60	25.83
Capital Stock	1.70	1.70	2.21	2.21	4.22	4.22	4.22	4.70
Net Assets Earning Rate (%)	48.0	12.2	16.4	19.1	19.7	15.34	14.74	12.03

Source: www.haier.com.

a mistake that has all but bankrupted our company."[9] All 76 faulty refrigerators were then destroyed by the very same employees who had helped to make them. A valuable lesson was learnt—that poor quality would just not be tolerated. The workers realized that quality was of only two types—acceptable and unacceptable. Under Zhang's leadership, the company broke even within a year.

In 1989, Qingdao General changed its name to Qindao Refrigerator Company Limited. It underwent financial restructuring using funds raised from banks and government agencies. Raising funds from banks was easier for Zhang due to his background as a bureaucrat in the local government. In 1991, the company once again changed its name to Qindao Haier Group Company (Qindao Haier) and in the same year, it merged with the Qingdao air-conditioner plant and Qingdao freezer general plant. In 1992, Qindao Haier established the Qingdao Freezing Equipment Company. In the same year, it merged with another previously state-owned enterprise Qingdao Condenser Factory, which manufactured refrigerator condensers. In 1992, Qindao Haier became the first company in China to get the ISO 9001 certification, and the company's name was changed to the Haier Group. In 1993, Haier went in for an initial public offering (IPO) of RMB 50 million and got its shares listed on the Shanghai Stock Exchange (SSE).

Most of the acquisitions that Haier made were of CEs on the brink of bankruptcy but had good manufacturing facilities and well-trained employees. A majority of the CEs acquired were in Qingdao, which allowed Zhang the comfort of negotiating with the same set of government bureaucrats. These acquisitions helped Haier register a spectacular growth in revenues in the mid-1990s (Refer to Table 1 for Haier's financials between 1992 and 1999). In 1995, Haier acquired the Red Star Electric Appliance Company (Red Star) that manufactured washing machines. Red Star had accumulated huge unsold inventories and its debts amounted to $300 million. After acquiring Red Star, Zhang introduced the new work culture, emphasizing quality and discipline, in the firm. The new culture coupled with the new technology acquired from Merloni, an Italian white goods manufacturer, turned Red Star around. Through Red Star, Haier managed to capture more than a third of China's washing machine market by 1998.

Another important acquisition that Haier made was the Huangshan electronics company (Huangshan), based in the Chinese province of Anhui. The company faced the same kind of problems that most of the SoEs in China did. Huangshan manufactured televisions and was quite successful in the local markets but political intervention forced the management to get into unrelated businesses such as real estate. The company began losing money and had accrued debts amounting to $3.65 million by the end of 1997.

Huangshan was controlled by the Hefei city municipal administration. The administration approached Zhang at a time when he was planning to enter the television market. Haier took over the company in December 1997 and immediately began introducing its work culture in Huangshan. The workers started creating problems when they realized that they would now have limited freedom. An instance of the workers' agitation was the march to the city hall by 200 Huangshan workers protesting against the tough stance taken by Haier on discipline. However, both city officials and Haier officials took a no-nonsense approach toward

[9] Anthony Paul, "Companies: China's Haier Power," *Fortune*, February 15, 1999.

these agitations, sending a clear signal to the workers that they could either work for the new management or not work at all. Faced with no choice, the workers agreed to begin production. Huangshan achieved a drastic increase in production volumes from just 200 to 300 televisions per month to 30,000 televisions per month in 1998.

Haier turned around many more loss-making companies after acquiring them and began building a reputation for itself in bringing sick companies back to profitability. Toward the end of 1998, Haier had grown into a conglomerate comprising 50 units, 18 of which were fully owned. With 20,000 employees, the company posted total sales of $2.3 billion for 1998. With assets worth $1.1 billion, Haier emerged as one of the largest companies in China and a serious threat to multinationals who operated in the country. Commenting on the rise of Haier, Ming-Jer Chen, a business professor at the University of Virginia said, "Because of its size and large range of products it sells, Haier is going to be at or near the center of what's happening in China's economy. In other words, what they do will have a big impact on foreign companies that are looking to succeed in China. With Haier, they will find a company whose approach is sophisticated and whose leadership is energetic."[10]

Turning around Sick Companies—The Haier Way

Haier's success was built upon a strategy that comprised three elements. The company extended this recipe of success to the bankrupt companies that it acquired in order to turn them around. The first element of the strategy was paying close attention to customer needs and preferences. An instance of this was the observation made by Haier in 1989 pertaining to the sales of one of its refrigerator models. The model sold well in Beijing but showed disappointing sales in Shanghai. Haier realized through research that the people in Shanghai did not have the space for large refrigerators, living as they did in congested houses. Recognizing the Shanghai residents' need for smaller refrigerators, Haier designed models specifically for that market. This sensitivity to customer preferences allowed Haier to shore up its sales in the city. Another example of Haier's receptiveness to customer preferences was seen in rural China. Haier's employees discovered that people in the rural areas used washing machines for cleaning vegetables, apart from laundering clothes. The company modified its washing machines in

order to cater to this requirement and became a leader in the rural markets.

The second element was collaborating and building alliances with foreign companies. Haier was able to gain access to advanced western technology through these alliances and this enabled it to produce appliances of higher quality. The companies that Haier had alliances with included Liebherr, Philips, Motorola, Merloni, and Mitsubishi. These alliances helped Haier in overcoming a major handicap that most Chinese companies suffered from—the lack of adequate R&D. For instance, Haier's collaboration with Merloni enabled the company to acquire technical know-how in dishwashers and washing machines.

The third and the most important element of Haier's strategy was the work culture that distinguished the company from its rivals in China. Haier's work culture promoted discipline, quality, personal responsibility, and customer service. Top management commitment was also given high priority. The management was held 80% responsible for employee mistakes. A 10/10 principle was also put in place that required 10% of the company's top performers to help the bottom 10% in order to improve the overall productivity of the company. This promoted teamwork among employees and allowed them to have a sense of ownership.

As compared to most of the companies in China, managers at Haier did not face labor problems and ran the business with absolute authority. Commenting on the need for a tough work culture, Zhang said, "If you observe Chinese people's behaviors at the traffic lights, when the red light is on, people simply ignore it and cross the street anyway. At the workplace, Chinese people also tend to ignore rules and do not pay enough attention to details. We need a tough management system with fair rewards and penalty features to help our workers get things done properly."[11]

In order to overcome worker apathy toward their jobs, Haier introduced worker contracts that tied job security to performance, forcing workers to change their ways. Workers were even fired for being resentful of Haier's work methods. These measures helped inculcate discipline into the workers who began reporting for work in time. Group meetings were held in order to sensitize workers to the importance of quality and good work methods. These meetings focused on examples set by workers and managers in quality and production process improvement. Discussions would then follow and the conclusion posted on walls for all to see. Haier also devised policies that introduced competition among

[10] Russell Flannery, "China Goes Global," *Forbes*, August 06, 2001.
[11] Thomas W. Lin, "China Haier Group," *Strategic Finance*, May 2005.

managers. Workers were promoted to managerial positions depending upon their performance. This policy helped Haier to get good employees in key managerial positions. Managers who failed to perform the tasks assigned to them were demoted.

Haier followed a carrot and stick policy in worker management. Workers were rewarded for good work and penalized for bad work. This policy was implemented at various Haier facilities through the SST (Suochou, Suopei, and Tiaozha) wage system that tied worker wages to the quality of their work. The first component of the SST wage system called Suochou was obtained by multiplying the number of well-done jobs with a fixed rate per job. The Suopei component of the wage system was used by Haier to inculcate quality consciousness among workers. This component was arrived at by multiplying the number of defective pieces found by workers by ten times the fixed rate per job. For instance, if a worker found five defective pieces, assuming that the fixed rate per job was 0.05 RMB, the Suopei component would be calculated as 5*(10*0.05) = 2.5 RMB. The third component of the wage, Tiaozha, was aimed at penalizing workers for badly done jobs. This component was calculated by multiplying the number of defective jobs done by a penalty rate per job. For instance, if the penalty rate was 0.06 RMB, the Tiaozha component would be calculated for 10 defective jobs as (10*0.06) = 0.6 RMB. This component was then deducted from the workers' salaries. The final SST wage would be arrived at by adding the Suochou and Suopei components and deducting the Tiaozha component (SST wage = Suochou + Suopei − Tiaozha).

An analysis of the SST wage system brought out three noteworthy features that helped Haier get maximum productivity out of its workers. The Suochou component gave incentives to workers for producing more, thereby improving productivity. The more jobs a worker completed, the more he earned. The Suopei component helped Haier to weed out defective jobs from its manufacturing process and the Tiaozha component, by allowing it to penalize workers for sub-standard work, forced them to be quality conscious.

The OEC management system put in place at Haier during the late 1990s also played an important role in improving the quality of the company's products. The system aimed at encouraging workers to find innovative solutions to manufacturing problems. Every worker was supposed to finish his work on time, on a day-to-day basis. Wang Yingmin, director of Human Resource Management at Haier explained the OEC model, "O stands for Overall; E stands for Everyone, Everything, and Everyday; C stands for Control and Clear. OEC means that every employee has to accomplish the target work every day. The OEC management-control system aims at overall control of everything that every employee finishes on his or her job every day, with a 1% increase over what was done the previous day."[12]

The OEC process began with the supervisor briefing his team before the work began every day. Workers then began their tasks keeping the seven OEC parameters in mind, viz., job quantity, job quality (in terms of defects), raw material consumption, equipment condition, workplace safety, workplace attitude, and discipline. White-collared employees also had a similar set of parameters. Supervisors conducted inspection tours of production sites every two hours in order to detect and solve problems and give an on-the-spot appraisal of worker performance based upon the seven OEC parameters. At the end of the workday, workers filled out their 3E (Everyone, Everything, and Everyday) forms (See Exhibit 2 for 3E form) and submitted them to their supervisors. The 3E forms allowed employees to evaluate themselves on the seven OEC parameters (See Exhibit 3 for 3E evaluation parameters). These forms were then submitted to their respective supervisors for them to review the workers' performance. A more elaborate appraisal of worker performance was then made by the supervisors who awarded A, B, and C grades to them on a daily basis. If a worker received an A grade, 5 RMB was added to his daily wage. The same amount was subtracted if the worker got a C grade.

A comprehensive evaluation form was then submitted by the supervisors to the work area manager, who in turn, submitted the 3E cards to the factory director. The factory director then collated the information from these cards, reviewed them, and prepared a comprehensive report for the deputy divisional general manager. This report detailed various difficulties faced during the course of the day and how the problems were solved. The report also described problems that were not solved along with suggested solutions. A review report was then sent to the divisional general managers for feedback. Discussions were held among the concerned persons to work out solutions for problems that could not be solved.

The results of the evaluation process were then put up on the bulletin boards in the factory for all workers to see. Workers who topped the evaluations for three consecutive days shared their experiences with their fellow workers at group meetings. Haier also had a pair of yellow feet painted on the factory floor for underperformers to stand on and confess their mistakes. Workers

---

[12] Thomas W. Lin, "China Haier Group," *Strategic Finance*, May 2005.

Exhibit 2 — 3E Daily Evaluation Sheet

Front Page

Name: Position: Employee Number: Plant: Team:

Item \ Date	27	28	29	30	31	1	2	3	4	5	6	7	8	9	10	11	12	13	14	15	16	17	18	19	20	21	22	23	24	25	26	Total	Confirm
Production Quantity — Target / Actual																																	
Salary																																	
Quality — Market Chain																																	
Quality — Value Coupon																																	
Quality — Customer Feedback																																	
Quality — Technique																																	
Defective Product Material Used																																	
Equipment Evaluation																																	
Safe Operation																																	
On-Site Evaluation																																	
Other Rewards and Penalty																																	
Self-Calculated Wage																																	
Review																																	
Daily Evaluation																																	
Employee Signature																																	

Back Page

Item \ Date	27	28	29	30	31	1	2	3	4	5	6	7	8	9	10	...	24	25	26	Total
Production Completed — Kind / Point / Price																				

Item	Date		Subtotal	Review	Item	Date		Sub-total	Review	Routine Checks — Name	Quant	Maint. Frequency	Endorsement				
Inventory Check	Time				Equipment Check	Time				Equipment							
	Price					Price				Instrument							
	Amount					Amount				Tool							
On-site Check	Time				Other Check	Time				Desk			Review				
	Price					Price				Lamp			Re-exam				
	Amount					Amount				Air Condition							

Source: Thomas W. Lin, "OEC Management-Control System Helps China Haier Group Achieve Competitive Advantage," *Management Accounting Quarterly*, Spring 2005.

who underperformed frequently were demoted to temporary workers.

The OEC management system enabled Haier to improve the quality of its products, operating efficiency, innovation, and speed to market. In the Chinese market, the Haier brand began to be associated with high quality and superior customer service. However, constant threat from foreign home appliance manufacturers operating in China and increased competition due to China's entry into the World Trade Organization (WTO) in 2001 forced Haier to look at international markets in order to remain profitable (See Exhibit 4 for a note on Chinese home appliances industry). Commenting on the compulsion to go global, Zhang remarked, "Globalization, especially China's anticipated entry into the WTO will make the country wide open to foreign competition. Only by actively taking part in global competition can we seize a chance to survive."[13]

---

[13] "Chinese Entrepreneur Striving to Create Global Brand Name," *People's Daily*, December 24, 2000.

Exhibit 3   3E Card Evaluation Criteria

Production Plan Evaluation Criteria
- If less-than-plan production occurs because of external factors, production plan should be achieved by nonpaid overtime.
- If an employee causes workshop/team overtime of less than 10 minutes, the employee should be fined ¥10 (U.S. $1 =8.27Yuans). If the employee causes workshop/team overtime of more than 10 minutes or whole factory overtime of more than five minutes, the employee's daily wage should be confiscated, unless the cause of the overtime was an unexpected act of God.

Quality Target Evaluation Criteria
- Daily defective-product costs should be fined according to the defective-product prices announced by the Quality Inspection department. The monthly quality target is evaluated by the Technology department.
- Cash-equivalent coupons should be priced daily by the Quality Inspection department.
- Responsibility cost occurred in disposing of defective products should be accounted for according to "Defective-Product Disposal Rule."

Technology-Level and Production-Discipline Evaluation Criteria
- Employees who work without an appropriate technical credential should be fined ¥50.
- Employees who fail to follow the technical production requirements should be fined ¥20.
- Employees who do not follow the company's technical rules in production to record information or who do not record on time should be fined ¥10.
- Employees who have no clear self- and peer-review contents and targets should be fined ¥10.

Equipment Evaluation Criteria
- Employees who fail to check equipment daily should be fined ¥5.
- Employees who fail to lubricate equipment should be fined ¥5.
- Employees who fail to record the condition of equipment properly and in a timely fashion should be fined ¥5.
- Employees who violate equipment operation procedures should be fined ¥50.
- Employees who operate equipment without an appropriate credential should be fined ¥100.

Material Evaluation Criteria
- Employees who produce defective products should be fined an amount of up to 10% of the material price.
- Employees who overuse raw materials should be fined an amount of up to 15% of the materials price.
- Employees who save raw materials should be awarded an amount of up to 5% of the materials price.
- Employees who fail to make timely and exact inventory checks and reports should be fined ¥10.
- Employees who fail to report that there is an insufficient amount of materials 12 hours ahead should be fined ¥300.

Labor Discipline Evaluation Criteria
- Employees who fail to place equipment in the proper area or fail to attach clear and matching tags on the equipment should be fined ¥2.
- Employees who fail to clean and clear their work environment should be fined ¥2.
- Employees who are late for work should be fined ¥2; those who leave early should be fined the daily wage.
- Employees who leave work because of sickness or other personal reasons and who do not have appropriate approval should be fined the daily wage.

(continued)

Exhibit 3 | 3E Card Evaluation Criteria (continued)

- Employees who gather for fun or chat during work time should be fined ¥2.
- Other violations will be handled by related rules and regulations.

Production Safety Evaluation Criteria
- Employees who operate without following proper procedures should be fined ¥10.
- Employees who operate without knowledge of safety operation rules and procedures should be fined ¥10.
- Employees who fail to deal with dangerous factors in time—and effectively—should be fined ¥10.
- Employees who lose safety signs or who have unclear and damaged signs should be fined ¥10.
- Employees who fail to wear uniforms or gloves or wear untidy uniforms should be fined ¥2.

Other Awards and Penalties
- This section will handle actions not mentioned above.

Endorsement
- Additional explanations from the operators or inspectors will be recorded in this section.

Inspection and Review
- Inspectors, known as team chiefs, are required to schedule inspections of the 3E card and give comments on evaluation and endorsement results.
- Reviewers are required to schedule reviews of the 3E card and release a review opinion.

Source: Thomas W. Lin, "OEC Management-Control System Helps China Haier Group Achieve Competitive Advantage," *Management Accounting Quarterly,* Spring 2005.

Exhibit 4 | A Note on Chinese Home Appliances Market

With a population of more than 1 billion, China is one of the largest consumer markets in the world. By the late 1990s, China had emerged as a global manufacturing base. The consumer appliances industry in the country reported healthy revenue growth rates since early 2000s. The industry's production capacity exceeded market demand, especially in the product categories of color TV sets, refrigerators, air conditioners, washing machines and microwave ovens. There was surplus capacity of 20,000,000 TV sets, 8,000,000 air-conditioners, 10,000,000 refrigerators and 11,000,000 washing machines. This surplus brought about price wars in the industry. Since there were more than 100 manufacturers of televisions, they resorted to heavy price-cutting to get rid of their surplus, eroding industry profit margins. Several companies tried to differentiate their products by acquiring new technology. Initially, they imported technologies from abroad, but later on they began to build up their own R&D capabilities.

China became a member of the WTO in 2001. This made its domestic market open to multinational companies. The Chinese consumer appliance companies required technological innovations to compete with multinationals. The Chinese urban markets were saturated with the local products and the rural markets were difficult to penetrate. With the entry of multinationals, competition increased further. So, several Chinese manufacturers shifted their focus to global markets. Most of them acted as OEMs to the big multinational companies. At the same time, several companies started diversifying into manufacturing mobile phone handsets and computer peripherals.

Source: Compiled from various sources.

The Globalization Efforts

Haier began exploring the global markets in the mid-1990s but the company's activities were largely restricted to exports. In 1996, Haier entered the Indonesian market through a joint venture (JV) route. This was the company's first JV outside China. In 1997, Haier entered Malaysia and the Philippines through the greenfield[14] mode of investment. These efforts in the Southeast Asian region focused on building volume and gaining international experience.

Haier's first major effort to globalize was in 1999, when it made a greenfield investment worth $30 million in Camden, South Carolina, US. Haier's decision came at a time when the US home appliance industry was on a downturn and most appliance manufacturers in the US were moving their manufacturing bases to China, Mexico, and other low-cost countries. Analysts were, therefore, surprised when Haier decided to set up its own manufacturing facilities in the US. Zhang explained Haier's decision, "You can't be an international company if you only make things at home and export them."[15]

Localization was Haier's mantra to succeed in the US market. It opened a design center in Los Angeles and hired local talent for designing its products for the US market. Explaining the importance of local talent, Zhang said, "When we enter into overseas markets, if we don't use local resources, we cannot design and produce the products that satisfy the local consumers' needs. In the past we tried to design our products in Qingdao and sell them to the US. These products looked like American products, but once they were released on the market we discovered that there were minor details that didn't meet the needs of American consumers."[16]

The Camden plant workforce was predominantly American with Chinese employees constituting a very small percentage. The Haier work culture was retained in the American plant and used effectively to capture the US market. However, integrating the Chinese management style with the American way of working was not easy. Initially, the American workers were shocked by the autocratic management style of the Chinese, while the Chinese were surprised by the participative management style of the Americans. Zhang said, "In China the leader decides, and the staff do. Here, the leader decides, and the staff responds with questions and suggestions."[17] In order to inject the Haier culture into the mindset of American workers, the management put banners all over factory walls with messages in both Chinese and English. These messages conveyed the importance of defect-free products and innovation. Haier also implemented the 6-S principle on its US workforce. This comprised the Japanese 5-S[18] quality control characteristics plus one more S, added by the company—Safety.

Haier's work culture helped it to gain a competitive advantage in the US market. A case in point was Haier's introduction of compact refrigerators that became a major success and established the Haier brand in the US market. Haier's culture required employees to be sensitive to the customer needs. The company quickly sensed the need for compact refrigerators among college and university students, who could not afford normal size refrigerators. In 1999, Haier launched a compact refrigerator that had two wooden flaps on either side that could be folded out and used as a computer table. This innovation became an instant hit among college students. Of the 1,500,000 compact refrigerators sold in the US in 2002, 670,000 were made by Haier. Commenting on Haier's strategy, Zhang said, "We want consumers to feel that Haier is the one company that comes closest to satisfying their needs."[19]

Speed to market also helped Haier gain market share. Zhang explained the speed to market strategy with an example, "Speed is also important; you win the hearts of consumers by satisfying their needs in the quickest manner possible. In the United States, we also sell wine storage cabinets. A large international manufacturer would spend 18 months developing a new wine storage cabinet, but for Haier it took only five months. Because we can identify and meet consumer needs quickly, we have won more than 50 percent of the total US market; Haier made 55,000 of the 100,000 units sold last year. Usually, those large appliance manufacturers are not as flexible, so their response to the market is slower. This is why we can compete with them."[20]

Haier faced two major obstacles in its entry into the US market. One was the lack of an established brand and the other was the absence of an effective distribution system. It was difficult for the Americans to associate quality with a Chinese brand. Commenting on the problem faced in distributing products, Zhang said, "When Chinese companies go into a new market, they

---

[14] In a greenfield mode of investment, a company designs and builds its own manufacturing facility in a new market.

[15] "Chinese Entrepreneur Striving to Create Global Brand Name," *People's Daily,* December 24, 2000.

[16] "Haier: Local Resources Are Key Overseas," *BusinessWeek Online,* November 08, 2004.

[17] Jonathan Sprague, "China's Manufacturing Beachhead," *Fortune,* October 28, 2002.

[18] 5-S is a Japanese quality program focusing on five aspects—Seiri (discard the unnecessary), Seiton (arrange tools in the order of use), Seisoh (keep the worksite clean), Seiketsu (keep yourself clean) and Shitsuke (follow workshop discipline).

[19] "Haier's Aim: Develop Our Brand Overseas," *BusinessWeek,* March 31, 2003.

[20] Yibing Wu, "China's Refrigerator Magnate," *McKinsey Quarterly,* Issue 03, 2003.

must first find someone to sell their products. Because Chinese products aren't well recognized by local retailers, they must try hard to penetrate new markets."[21]

Haier got over this problem by entering into agreements with leading retail chains such as Wal-Mart, Target, and BestBuy to push its products in the retail market. In 2001, Wal-Mart started selling Haier's chest freezers and compact refrigerators. Haier also studied the consumer profiles of the retail chains that sold its products. The company analyzed the consumer profile of Wal-Mart in order to understand what kind of products would sell there. It found that Wal-Mart attracted many young college students and accordingly decided to sell its compact refrigerators through it. Commenting on the success of Haier's refrigerators, Wal-Mart sources said, "It's not about whether they're made in China. They're an exceptional value. They're popular and beating our expectations on sales."[22]

Haier built its brand in the US market through product innovations and quality. It posted revenues of $250 million in the fiscal 2002. However, Haier's products catered to the lower end of the US home appliance market. The company planned to enter the high-end market leveraging upon the brand image it had built.

Haier also aimed at expanding its operations in the European markets. In 2001, Haier acquired Meneghetti's refrigeration business in Italy. Haier first entered Italy due to the competitive market there and the availability of skilled manpower. The company then expanded its operations in other European markets by opening four distribution centers. These centers were located in Holland, Italy, Spain, and the UK and catered to 17 European countries.

Entering the major Asian countries was equally important for Haier in its globalization efforts. In 2001, Haier opened an industrial park in Lahore, Pakistan. After the US, this was Haier's second major international manufacturing facility. The company manufactured localized products for the Pakistani market. Haier's sales increased by 80% in the second year of its operations in the country. In 2002, Haier entered the Japanese market through an agreement with Sanyo Electric Company. The agreement resulted in the setting up of a JV, Sanyo-Haier Company, that sold Haier's range of refrigerators, freezers, and washing machines. In return, Sanyo's products were sold in China through Haier's sales and distribution network.

Haier proactively globalized its R&D activities. The company established six product design centers in Los Angeles (US), Silicon Valley (US), Amsterdam (The Netherlands), Montreal (Canada), Lyons (France), and Tokyo (Japan). Haier's design centers were situated in highly industrialized nations, enabling the company to access advanced technology. Haier aimed at gathering the technical know-how from the advanced countries, refine them, and adapt them for developing markets. In late 2004, Haier announced its plans to set up its seventh design center in New Delhi, India, with the aim of adapting its technical know-how and designing highly localized products for the booming Indian home appliance market. TK Banerjee, President and CEO of Haier India, remarked, "To start with, we will be investing about Rs 3 to 5 million in this R&D unit of the company which will come up near New Delhi where we will concentrate on Indianising the products and make it in accordance with the needs of Indians."[23]

In fiscal 2004, Haier posted global revenues of 15.299 billion RMB (See Table 2 for Haier's financials between 2000 and 2004). Apart from higher revenues, Haier's globalization efforts helped it to build a global brand

Table 2	Haier Group Financials (2000–2004)				
(In hundred million RMB)					
Particulars	**2000**	**2001**	**2002**	**2003**	**2004**
Main Business Income	48.28	114.42	115.54	116.88	152.99
Net Profit	4.24	6.18	3.97	3.69	3.69
Shareholder Interests	28.90	49.32	50.90	53.89	57.19
Capital Stock	5.65	7.98	7.98	7.98	11.96
Net Assets Earning Rate (%)	14.67	12.53	7.80	6.85	6.46

Source: www.haier.com.

[21] "Haier: Local Resources are Key Overseas," *BusinessWeek Online*, November 08, 2004.
[22] "China Appliance Maker Haier Seeks Cool US Image," www.thestandard.com, August 02, 2001.
[23] "Motorola, Haier on Indian R&D Drive," *Financial Express*, July 14, 2005.

Exhibit 5 | Haier's Global Presence

Country	Year of Entry
Indonesia	1996
Philippines	1997
Malaysia	1997
Yugoslavia	1997
Iran	1999
United States	1999
Jordan	1999
Bangladesh	2001
Australia	2001
Pakistan	2001
Italy	2001
Japan	2002
New Zealand	2002
Germany	2003
Spain	2003
France	2003
India	2004

Source: Compiled from various sources.

(See Exhibit 5 for Haier's global presence). The World Brand Laboratory ranked Haier 95th in its listing of the world's 100 most recognizable brands. Haier was the only Chinese brand on that list.

The Road Ahead

Haier had set ambitious targets for expanding its operations in the international markets. The company aimed at achieving a sales turnover of $1 billion from its operations in North and South America by the end of 2005. It planned to achieve this target through selling high-end products in the American markets, particularly in the US. Most analysts were, however, of the opinion that Haier lacked the brand image to make any serious inroads in the high-end segment of the US market, dominated by giants like GE Appliances, Maytag, Whirlpool and Electrolux.

Brands like GE and Whirlpool had high brand recognition and a worldwide service network that Haier may take a long time to match. These companies also possessed and continued to develop cutting-edge technologies for the US market. Analysts doubted Haier's ability to take on these competitors in the high-end segment in spite of its efforts to gain advanced technical know-how. Haier planned to differentiate its products in the markets in order to overcome this problem. Commenting on this, Michael Jemal, President and CEO of Haier America, said, "We can't just do me-too products. The competition is much more established, with great brands and distribution, so if we're like them, we'll be crushed."[24]

Another major factor that could hinder Haier's ambitious growth plans was the company's lack of transparency and an opaque ownership structure. Being a collective enterprise, ownership lay in the hands of its workers but no dividends were paid to them. Zhang himself admitted the problem, "It belongs to the employees, but no one knows who owns how much."[25]

Chinese governmental interference also caused a few problems for Haier. Local governments in China constantly pressured profitable companies to buy loss-making firms. For instance, Haier was pressured to buy a loss-making pharmaceutical company and a bicycle factory. The government also created obstacles in the form of regulations. Restrictions of various kinds hindered the company's globalization efforts. Zhang explained, "Currently we have too many restrictions in doing overseas businesses. When we have to pay foreign currency to our foreign partners, for example, the procedures are very complicated. So these procedures should be simplified."[26]

Another hurdle that Haier faced in its globalization plans was in the shape of the increasingly suspicious US government that considered China's growing economic clout a threat. There was strong opposition voiced in that country against proposed deals that involved acquisitions of American firms by Chinese companies. Chinese oil company CNOOC's attempts to acquire the US oil company Unocal was a case in point. Most Chinese companies, being government controlled, had access to the huge foreign currency reserves (expected to be $1 trillion by mid-2006) accumulated by China. Attempts by Chinese companies to acquire US businesses using China's foreign currency reserves therefore raised concerns regarding fair competition. Alan Tonelson, a research fellow at the US Business & Industry Educational Foundation, wrote in an article on the Chinese threat, "What Washington needs to consider is why American

---

[24] Jonathan Sprague, "China's Manufacturing Beachhead," *Fortune*, October 28, 2002.

[25] Sarah Schafer, "A Jack Welch of Communists," *Newsweek*, May 09, 2005.

[26] "Haier: Local Resources Are Key Overseas," *BusinessWeek Online*, November 08, 2004.

companies should have to compete with such rivals, which are supported by foreign government treasuries. How would such practices ensure the fairest and most productive competition within the US market? How would they help spread market forces and practices worldwide? The obvious answer: They shouldn't, and they don't."[27]

Despite being faced with many difficulties, Haier's strategy of entering mature markets with low-end products and moving up to offer premium products as the Haier brand became popular among consumers managed to jolt its competitors out of their complacency. Taking note of Haier's challenge, David L. Swift, executive vice-president of Whirlpool's North American region, remarked, "Haier is a good company and somebody we've got to pay a lot of attention to."[28]

Assignment Questions

The following questions can be given as an assignment to students. Each student is supposed to write the answers individually and submit the same to the moderator/concerned faculty for evaluation.

1. Haier's priorities kept changing during its evolution. From quality improvement in the 1980s, the company's priorities moved to acquisition and product line diversification and finally globalization. Critically analyse the role played by Haier's culture and Zhang's management style in the company's success.

2. In 2004, a joint Financial Times/Pricewaterhouse Coopers study ranked Haier number one among the most admired global companies in China. Describe the various stages in Haier's globalization process. Examine the role played by alliances and acquisitions in a company's globalization strategy, with specific reference to Haier.

3. Many Chinese companies are making efforts to globalize in order to tap lucrative markets for their products. However, these companies face serious challenges in their efforts to globalize. Examine the various internal and external factors that hinder Chinese firms in their efforts to globalize.

Additional Readings and References

1. **China and the Chaebol,** The Economist, December 18, 1997.
2. McGonigle, Bill, **State Owned Enterprises in China,** www.andover.edu, November 1998.
3. Anthony Paul, **Companies: China's Haier Power,** Fortune, February 15, 1999.
4. Prasso Sheri, **'We Want to Become a Global Company'**—Interview with Zhang Ruimin, BusinessWeek, June 14, 1999.
5. **Out of the Shadows,** The Economist, August 26, 1999.
6. **Production in the United States—Haier looking to the Future,** www.ultrachina.com, April 8, 2000.
7. McDonald Joe, **China Sends the United States Jobs,** www.asiaweek.com, May 25, 2000.
8. Landler Mark, **In China, a Management Maverick Builds a Brand,** www.bebeyond.com, July 23, 2000.
9. **Chinese Entrepreneur Striving to Create Global Brand Name,** People's Daily, December 24, 2000.
10. Flannery Russell, **China Goes Global,** Forbes, June 8, 2001.
11. Biers Dan, **Taking the Fight to the Enemy,** Far Eastern Economic Review, March 29, 2001.
12. Biers Dan, **A Taste of China in Camden,** Far Eastern Economic Review, March 29, 2001.
13. Landreth Jonathan, **China Appliance Maker Haier Seeks Cool U.S. Image,** www.thestandard.com, August 29, 2001.
14. **Haier Group Ranks Second in Global Fridge Markets,** www.fpeng.peopledaily.com, January 13, 2002.
15. **Internationalized Strategy Bears Rich Fruit,** www.fpeng.peopledaily.com, February 19, 2002.
16. **China's Haier Group Fits US Factory into Global Strategy,** www.lionhrtpub.com, February 22, 2002.
17. **Haier Eyes Overseas Markets,** www.francais.cri.com, March 2002.
18. Roberts, Dexter, Arndt, Michael, & Zammert, Andrea, **Haier's Tough Trip from China,** BusinessWeek, April 1, 2002.
19. Arndt, Michael, **Can Haier Freeze Out Whirlpool and GE?,** BusinessWeek, April 11, 2002.
20. Dougherty Sean M., Mcguckin Robert H., Radzin John, **Don't Underestimate China,** Executive Action, May 2002.
21. **Qingdao Haier Sales Decline,** www.appliancemagazine.com, July 30, 2002.
22. Sprague, Jonathan, **Haier Reaches Higher,** Fortune, September 5, 2002.
23. Sprague, Jonathan, **China's Manufacturing Beachhead,** Fortune, October 28, 2002.
24. Lynch J, David, **CEO Pushes China's Haier as Global Brand,** www.usatoday.com, February 1, 2003.
25. **Chinese Fridge Maker to Tap Markets,** www.news.bbc.co.uk, February 27, 2003.
26. Roberts, Dexter, **Haier's Aim: "Develop Our Brand Overseas,"** BusinessWeek, March 31, 2003.
27. Wu, Yibing, **China's Refrigerator Magnate,** McKinsey Quarterly, March 2003.
28. **Appliances that Read,** Appliance Manufacturer, September 2003.
29. Zeng, Ming, Williamson Peter J., **The Hidden Dragons,** Harvard Business Review, October 2003.
30. Bonnema, Lisa, **Haier: Working its Way up,** Appliance Magazine, October 2003.
31. **Haier's Purpose,** Economist, March 20, 2004.
32. Chen Jin, **Chinese Whispers,** Brand Strategy, May 2004.
33. Dolan, Kerry A., **Taking it Haier,** Forbes, May 10, 2004.
34. Babyak, Richard J., **Adapting to Change,** Appliance Manufacturer, June 2004.
35. **Haier: Local Resources Are Key Overseas,** BusinessWeek Online, November 08, 2004.
36. **How China's Most Valuable Brand Found its Niche,** Managing Intellectual Property, April 2005.
37. Hunt, Lindsay, **Haier Group Company,** www.marketbusting.com, April 29, 2005.

---

[27] Alan Tonelson, "Takeover Bid Reveals Washington's Lack of Strategic Thinking on China," www.americaneconomicalert.org, July 25, 2005.

[28] Michael Arndt, "Can Haier Freeze Out Whirlpool and GE?" BusinessWeek, April 11, 2002.

38. Lin, Thomas W., **China Haier Group**, *Strategic Finance,* May 2005.
39. Schafer, Sarah, **A Jack Welch of Communists,** *Newsweek,* May 09, 2005.
40. **Haier Group Bids US$1.3b for Maytag,** www.beijingportal.com.cn, June 22, 2005.
41. Lu, Zhang, **Haier Group Bids US$ 1.3 billion for Maytag,** *China Daily,* June 22, 2005.
42. Bremner, Brian, Roberts, Dexter, **The Chinese Are Coming**, *Business-Week Online,* June 23, 2005.
43. **Motorola, Haier on Indian R&D Drive,** *Financial Express,* July 14, 2005.
44. **Suds Law**, *Economist,* July 23, 2005.
45. Tonelson, Alan, **Takeover Bid Reveals Washington's Lack of Strategic Thinking on China,** www.americaneconomicalert.org, July 25, 2005.
46. www.twice.com.
47. www.applaincemagazine.com.
48. www.haier.com.
49. www.haieramerica.com.
50. www.ultrachina.com.

Innovation at Cirque du Soleil

Vivek Gupta

Manasi Pawar

"The circus is an unlikely place to find a paragon of innovation, but Cirque du Soleil isn't your garden-variety circus. And that's the point. The Montreal-based performing art group reinvented the circus as a popular entertainment and reinvents itself with each daring new stage show. Its approaches to finding, training and retaining talent, unleashing creativity, and building a beloved brand look like elaborate tricks right out of one of Cirque's shows. But they are calculated risks, the result of intense planning."[1]

—Linda Tischler, Senior Writer and Former Managing Editor of New Media, **Fast Company, in July 2005.**

"One of the successes of Cirque du Soleil, and most certainly Guy Laliberte, is to have made possible the coexistence of business and art within the same company. When Cirque du Soleil began to be successful, Guy Laliberté wanted to reinvest the profits to diversify and plan for the future. Innovation and risk-taking proved to be the solution."[2]

—Chantal Cote, Senior Publicist, Cirque du Soleil, in December 2005.

Introduction

On June 02, 2007, Guy Laliberte (Laliberte), CEO and founder of Canada-based circus company Cirque du Soleil (Cirque)[3] received 2007 'Ernst and Young Entrepreneur of the Year'[4] award. The award was given to entrepreneurs, who with their vision, achievement and leadership, provided inspiration to the corporate world. Commending Laliberte for the work he had done at Cirque, Joseph Schoendorf, Chairman of the judging panel, said, "Guy has changed the face of entertainment and had a huge global impact. The shows that Cirque du Soleil creates and performs have brought joy to millions. All of this year's entrepreneurs were exceptional, but Guy's commitment to his artistic vision and the passion he has for his work were what swayed the judges in his favor."[5]

Cirque was founded in 1983. Since its first performance, the company strove to be different from other circuses, by constantly coming up with innovations. Till August 2007, Cirque's estimated revenues for the year were more than US$ 600 million with over a dozen shows running across the world at any point of time. Every show presented by Cirque was based on a central theme with a supporting storyline, amalgamating

---

[1] Linda Tischler, "Join the Circus," *Fast Company,* July 2005.

[2] Christopher Hogg, "Cirque du Soleil and the Future of Entertainment," *Digital Journal,* December 24, 2005.

[3] Headquartered in Montreal, Quebec, Canada, Cirque du Soleil, which means "Circus of the Sun" in French, is a privately held entertainment company.

[4] 'Ernst & Young Entrepreneur of the Year' is considered to be the most prestigious business award for entrepreneurs all over the world. It recognizes the contribution of those people who have inspired others with their vision, leadership and achievement.

[5] Anastasia Khutko, "Cirque du Soleil's Guy Laliberte Named Ernst & Young 2007 World Entrepreneur of the Year," www.ey.com, June 05, 2007.

Blue Ocean Strategy, a best-selling book released in 2005, was authored by two professors from INSEAD (a management institute in France and Singapore), W. Chan Kim (Chan) and Renee Mauborgne (Mauborgne). They coined this term for a corporate strategy whereby businesses tapped uncaptured market space and thereby made competition irrelevant. In the book, Chan and Mauborgne suggested that businesses should go where there was profit and growth and no competition. To write the book, the authors considered over 150 strategic moves made in 30 industries, in a span of around a century.

The 'ocean' in the title referred to the market and 'blue oceans' to untapped markets which resulted in almost zero competition for anyone who wanted to enter such markets. On the other hand, 'red oceans' referred to markets, where the competition was severe due to presence of several players. The authors proposed that companies entering such blue markets required to be innovative with their products and services in order to create value for the customers. The cornerstone of the Blue Ocean Strategy was value innovation, and rather than slow, incremental value added improvement, an equal amount of value and innovation were applied to raise the product above the average industry standard. This strategy moved away from the traditional belief that the customer could get more value at higher cost or a reasonable value at lower cost. The manufacturer and the customer had to choose between cost and value. The Blue Ocean strategy propounded that the companies needed to bring in valuable innovations along with low costs at the same time.

The authors cited several examples of companies which were pioneers in their industries and had successfully created 'blue oceans'. For example, Cirque brought in a new meaning in the field of circus entertainment. It targeted the sophisticated ballet and opera audience by combining acts that would tickle the intellectual bent of mind, as well as be enjoyable for the children, rather than concentrating on children alone, as traditional circuses were doing. Cirque, by redefining circus, brought in the audiences, who otherwise avoided circus, into its fold. Thus, it was able to avoid the red-ocean and step into blue-ocean.

Another example is Starbucks, the U.S. based coffeehouse chain, which was founded in 1971. Starbucks was the first to provide good quality coffee along with snacks and other beverages in an enjoyable ambiance, thus attracting those customers who frequented restaurants for coffee as there were no coffee shops which would provide them space for a wholesome conversation over a cup of coffee. Hence, Starbucks was also able to create a 'blue ocean' for itself.

Source: Compiled from various sources.

different circus styles from across the world. The shows were presented by more than 800 performers, who were a part of Cirque's 3,000 strong work force. Starting from the recruitment of employees till the production of the shows, it had introduced many innovative processes.

Cirque was cited as one of the companies to have implemented 'Blue Ocean Strategy' by creating demand, by developing a new market space, where competition was non-existent (Refer to Exhibit 1 for information on Blue Ocean Strategy). Instead of being considered as just another circus company in a declining industry, it redefined its market by fusing art and entertainment (Refer to Exhibit 2 for the history of Circus). The company was successful in creating a new form of art by combining circus art, theater and ballet. Subsequently, Cirque also introduced its line of apparel and accessories. About 85 percent of Cirque's revenues were from the sale of show

tickets and the rest from the sale of audios, videos, books, and licensing agreements for products like T-shirts, jewelry, hats, shoes, masks etc.

Apart from touring and permanent shows in places like Las Vegas, Orlando, and Walt Disney World, Cirque had also produced a number of movies and television shows. Some of the shows like 'Cirque du Soleil Fire Within,' Coreto and Dralion had won the popular Emmy awards in various categories. Commenting on the success that Cirque has achieved, Linda Tischler, Senior Writer and Former Managing Editor (of the 'New Media' section), *Fast Company*, wrote, "At a time when audiences for all performing arts are declining, Cirque du Soleil has taken a particularly moribund segment of the market— the circus—and created an entertainment juggernaut, with a burgeoning record label, a retail operation and a deal with Carnival Cruise Lines."[6]

[6] Linda Tischler, "Join the Circus," *Fast Company*, July 2005.

| Exhibit 2 | History of Circus |

A circus typically comprised of several performing artists like jugglers, clowns, trapeze artists etc., who performed to entertain the audience. Most of the circuses included animals trained to perform certain acts. The origins of the circus can be traced back to ancient Rome, where chariot races and horse races were held in an arena. The modern circus was spearheaded by the Briton Philip Astley who established several permanent and traveling circuses in Europe in the late 18th century. The history of the circus can be studied in three parts: ancient, development, and modern.

Ancient Circus: Circus during the ancient roman period featured races, wrestling, jugglers, acrobats apart from trained animals. This circus was influenced by the Greek and Egyptian spectacles of chariot racing and exhibition of animals. The first Roman circus was Circus Maximus which was located in the valley between the Aventine and Palentine hills in the Roman empire. Once the Roman empire fell, the Roman circus ended. However, the animal trainers from these circuses are believed to have toured Europe performing at local fairs in the towns and cities across Europe. In the 14th and 15th centuries there were bands of gypsies which roamed about in Britain and the rest of Europe, performing in the fairs along with their trained animals. The acrobatic art, however, is believed to be primarily a Chinese contribution to the modern circus.

Development of Circus: The modern circuses are usually performed in a circular arena, with seats all around the circle. Such circus was believed to have been popularized by a horse trainer, Philip Astley, in London. He staged the first performance of his circus on January 09, 1768. Astley initially performed in a ring of the diameter 62 meters. Subsequently, the diameter was changed to 42 feet, which went on to become the international standard. His circus company prospered across many generations. In the year 1900, the London Hippodrome was built for both circuses and theater performances. Animals also performed in the arena. It also showcased spectacles such as earthquakes, volcanoes, floods, etc. by creating special effects on the stage. Between 1800 and 1820, the Circus of Pepin and Breschard and Prudy, Welch & Company gave wide popularity to the circus in the U.S. The concept of performing under a big tent was popularized by the American circus led by the juggler Joshua Purdy Brown in 1825. Other major contributors to the development of American circus were PT Barnum and William Cameron Coup. During the late 19th century, they came up with PT Barnum's Museum, Menagerie and Circus.

The three performers Giuseppe Chiarini (Chiarini) from Italy, Louis Soullier (Soullier) and Jacques Tourniaire (Tourniaire) from France were considered to be the first to include international performers and acts in their circuses. They were responsible for introducing circus in the Latin American countries, some of the Asian countries, Russia and South Africa. While Soullier introduced Chinese acrobatics to the European circus, Soullier took the acrobatic art form to Russia. With the arenas becoming larger to accommodate more and more people, dialogue-based performances gave way to action-based performances such as acrobatics. The stage props also changed to more exhibitive and expensive machinery and equipment. In the mid-20th century, following protests from animal activists, circuses changed their focus from animal-based shows to those showcasing human skills and strengths.

Modern Circus: With the advent of movies and television, in the 1960s and 1970s, circuses began to lose popularity. Moreover, animal rights activists started protesting strongly against the cruelty toward animals, especially in circuses. As a result, circuses which did not use any animals evolved. Examples of such circuses are the San Francisco-based The Pickle Family Circus founded in 1975, the Australia-based Circus Oz formed in 1977, the Canadian Cirque du Soleil founded in 1984, and the Cirque Eloize founded in Quebec, Canada in the late 1990s.

Notwithstanding protests from the animal rights activists, several circuses continue to perform with animals like the Ringling Brothers and the Barnum and Bailey Circus, the Moscow State Circus, the Munich-based Circus Krone, the New York-based Big Apple Circus etc.

Source: 'Circus,' www.circushistory.org.

Background Note

In 1980, Gilles Ste-Croix (Ste-Croix), with skills in stilt-walking, along with some performers founded Les Echassiers de Baie-Saint-Paul (Les Echassiers), and began street performances. Soon Laliberte and Daniel Gauthier (Gauthier) joined the group. In the same year, Gauthier and Ste-Croix planned to turn Le Balcon Vert, a performing artists' youth hostel that they managed, into an organized performing troupe. To raise funds for this purpose, Ste-Croix stilt-walked[7] between Baie-Saint-Paul[8] and Quebec City.[9] This attracted the attention of the Quebec Government and it provided the trio with the necessary funds. Their maiden tour was that of Quebec in 1980.

However, initially Les Echassiers was a commercial failure and suffered substantial losses. In late 1980, the trio formed the Club des Talons Hauts, a troupe formed by bringing together many street performers like fire eaters, mime artists,[10] jugglers and stilt walkers. The venture, known as 'High-Heels Club,' started making profits by 1981.

By September 1981, Les Echassiers had broken even. The trio decided to organize a fair, where they could exchange ideas with other performers and also learn new tricks. The fair, which first toured in July 1982, was called the "La Fete Foraine de Baie St-Paul" (La Fete Foraine). La Fete Foraine also held workshops to teach the circus arts to anyone interested in learning them. These people could then take part in the performances.

In 1984, during 450th anniversary of Jack Cartier's discovery of Canada, the troupe convinced the organizers of the celebrations in Quebec to provide them with a grant running to C$ 1.2 million. This led to the subsequent formation of Cirque. The company performed shows across Quebec. Laliberte chose the name Cirque du Soleil for his company as he saw the sun as a symbol of youth, energy, power, and light.

From the very beginning, Cirque's shows were quite different from the shows of a traditional circus. Cirque's shows had much more to offer compared to the traditional circus, as Cirque had artists from several countries performing in the show. It created a new circus experience with amazing light effects, own music, and radically different costumes. To attract audience, traditional circuses, often included performances by well known and famous artists. Cirque did not employ noted performers to pull crowds. Laliberte believed that no performer could be bigger than Cirque itself. Cirque did not include animals in its acts, and by not including animals, the company avoided attacks from animal rights activists and the huge costs involved in maintaining and moving the animals. Cirque also avoided loud background music which was common in traditional circuses.

After its first tour in 1984, Cirque received an additional grant from the Quebec government. With these funds, Cirque carried out a major renovation organizing itself into a formal circus. For this purpose, Laliberte met with Guy Caron (Caron), founder of Canada's National Circus School. Caron began working as Cirque's artistic director. Both Laliberte and Caron played a major role in redesigning Cirque. There was a live band that played strong, emotionally charged music from the start till the end. The performers themselves moved the props and the equipment on and off the stage, blending the process into their performance. This way, the main storyline of the performance was not disrupted.

In 1985, the troupe performed outside Quebec for the first time when it held a show in the neighboring province Ontario. The positive response from the audience encouraged Laliberte to expand Cirque's operations outside Quebec. In the next year, Cirque performed at the Children's Film Festival in British Columbia and at a world fair in Vancouver. By this time, Cirque had a seating capacity to 1500. However, some of the shows failed, leaving Cirque in a financial mess. In late 1985, the performance in Toronto received a poor response from the audience with just 25 percent of the seats being filled. A subsequent show at Niagara was also a failure. As a result, Cirque went deep into debt—to the tune of US$ 750,000. However, the company did not go bankrupt as Cirque's financial institution, the Desjardins Group, postponed Cirque's debt payment of US$ 200,000. The Quebec government granted sufficient funds to the company so that it could sustain itself for another year. At that time, Daniel Lamarre, then President and CEO of largest TV broadcaster in Quebec, joined Cirque. Earlier, Lamarre worked with public relation firms like National Public Relations and Burson-Marsteller.

In 1987, the status of Cirque was changed from nonprofit to a for-profit entity. That year, the troupe was invited to the Los Angeles Arts Festival. Although the company was facing financial problems, Laliberte

---

[7] Stilt walkers attach themselves to very high poles and walk while elevated above normal heights. Stilts are poles made of wood, about five feet in length, provided with a shoulder and strap to support the foot, on the upper part and the lower part is enlarged to enable walking while maintaining balance on the ground.

[8] Baie-Saint-Paul is a city in the province of Quebec and is located on the Saint Lawrence river.

[9] Quebec City is the capital of the Canadian Province Quebec and is the second largest city in the province after Montreal.

[10] Mime is a performance act in which the artist performs a story through body motions and facial expressions without the use of speech.

decided to take a chance and his troupe performed at the festival. The performance was a huge success. The show got noticed by Columbia Pictures,[11] which got into talks with Laliberte and Gautier for making a movie about Cirque. However, Laliberte did not allow the deal to materialize as Columbia Pictures tried to control the production. This experience left him with the conviction that Cirque should be privately held so that he could have all the freedom needed to operate the company.

The company could seat 2,500 people by the year 1990, and the tickets sold for as high as US$ 33.50.[12] By this time, Cirque had different troupes touring several parts of the world and normally halting in cities for about four to five weeks. A new production named Nouvelle Experience which toured 13 major cities in the US and Canada over 19 months enjoyed an excellent response and by the end of its tour, 1.3 million people had seen it.[13]

By mid-1991, Cirque was able to convince Fuji Television Network (Fuji) to sponsor Cirque's tour of Asia and Fuji agreed to give US$ 40 million for the purpose. Cirque performed across eight cities beginning with Tokyo. At the same time, Cirque partnered with Circus Knie[14] for a tour of Switzerland. The company also conducted a tour of North America with its production Saltimbanco ('Street Performer' in Italian) in 1992. Saltimbanco was a major success in North America and it then toured Tokyo for six months.

Cirque also entered into a year-long agreement with Mirage, a Las Vegas hotel, to perform Nouvelle Experience. This was Cirque's first engagement of the kind. The fact that this was a huge success encouraged it to launch another production called Mystère, which began its performance at Mirage. Subsequently, Cirque entered into a ten-year contract with Mirage for the production. Steve Wynn (Wynn), owner of Mirage, also built a permanent facility for Cirque at the cost of US$ 20 million at his new resort, Treasure Island, which opened in 1994. This provided Cirque with a major and steady source of revenue. In addition to the revenues obtained by the company in terms of ticket sales, it was also earning a significant amount from the merchandise that it sold at the performances. There was also a considerable market for Cirque's CDs as the company had created quite a fan following for itself over the years.

In 1995, Cirque established its first European headquarters at Amsterdam. The same year, Saltimbanco went on its first extensive European tour. In 1997, Saltimbanco presented its last performance in London. Cirque's next production was Alegria, which was performed all across Europe for over two years. Cirque's sales had increased manifold from US$ 30 million in 1994 to US$ 110 million in 1996. This growth was mainly because of the production Mystere, a permanent production in Las Vegas. Mystère's revenues were at US$ 40 million. In 1997, Wynn constructed a US$ 60 million theater for Cirque at Bellagio, Las Vegas. Walt Disney also constructed another permanent theater to house Cirque at Walt Disney World, near Orlando, California. The same year, a US$ 22 million facility for rehearsals and costume designing activities called 'Creation Studio' was created by Cirque in Montreal. This also served as the company's headquarters.

In October 1998, Cirque's new production 'O' (after 'eau', which means water in French) debuted at Bellagio. This production was unique with the performance being conducted in, above, and around an Olympic-sized 1.5 million gallon swimming pool that had been created for the purpose.[15] The production cost was a whopping US$ 90 million and the tickets were priced at US$ 100 each. Another production La Nouba debuted at the newly constructed theater at Walt Disney World. Dralion, yet another new production, embarked on a three-year tour of North America in January 1999. Thus, Cirque concluded the 1990s with seven productions and performances in 22 countries in Asia-Pacific, North America, and Europe.

In October 2004, Cirque entered into an agreement with the Beatles[16] stars to create a production to be staged at the Mirage hotel in Las Vegas. The project called Love, recreated the life of the Beatles before they became famous. In November, the same year, there was another permanent production, KA, which played at MGM Grand, Las Vegas. Mirage Resorts was acquired by MGM[17] in 2000 and KA was created specially for MGM. KA was unique in the sense that it was more clear and

---

[11] Columbia Pictures Industries, Inc. is an American film and television production company, owned by Sony Pictures Entertainment, a subsidiary of Japanese electronics corporation Sony. It has produced popular movies such as *Kramer vs. Kramer, Charlie's Angels, Hollow Man,* and the more recent *Spider-Man* Series.

[12] Jeffery L. Covell, "Cirque du Soleil Inc.," www.answers.com, June 02, 1997.

[13] Jeffery L. Covell, "Cirque du Soleil Inc.," www.answers.com, June 02, 1997.

[14] A Switzerland based circus company which was formed in 1803.

[15] Jeffery L. Covell, "Cirque du Soleil Inc.," www.answers.com, June 02, 1997.

[16] The Beatles, an English musical group from Liverpool, was one of the most commercially successful and critically acclaimed bands in the history of popular music. Its members were John Lennon, Paul McCartney, George Harrison and Ringo Starr.

[17] Metro-Goldwin-Mayer Inc. (MGM) is an American media company which is mainly involved in the production and distribution of films and television programs. It was acquired by Sony Corporation of America and Comcast in partnership, in association with the Texas Pacific Group in April 2005. After this acquisition, MGM Mirage was no longer affiliated to MGM.

straightforward unlike other Cirque productions which were quite abstract. The total cost of KA, US$ 220 million, was borne by MGM.

The Innovative Strategies

When Cirque began its operations, it functioned with around 73 employees. By 2007, there were 3,000 people working in various areas like art direction, production, stage settings, lighting and special effects, IT, marketing and public relations, and as trainers, physiotherapists, fitness specialists, musicians, cooks and the kitchen staff, technicians, and performers. The team at Cirque had to constantly be on their toes, always trying to be different. For example, in addition to training the performers, the studio was responsible for developing new acrobatic equipment and techniques; coaches, costume designers, and engineers were always conducting research. Cirque also had an interesting process of developing the acts in a show. Against the usual practice of composing music for the act, in Cirque, the acts were put together based on the music. Almost each new production had a new director (known as guest directors).

Cirque's management claimed that the mission and values that had led to the formation of the company in the 1980s were still alive. Commenting on the values and Cirque's commitment to excellence, Mario D'Amico, Global Vice President, Marketing, at Cirque, said, "As long as Cirque du Soleil stays true to its original mission and values, it will continue. All those things that tend to be on a poster in an office in a lot of companies—those are the things that we live and breathe."[18]

From the very beginning, Cirque tried to establish itself as a circus which was quite distinct from the others in the business. And to maintain this reputation, it kept constantly innovating and adding new acts in its kitty. Cirque strived to deliver best possible performance to provide novel experience to the audience. The company aimed at providing an enriching experience to its customers in every performance that it delivered. Creativity was evident when it came to costume designing, sets and props, HR policies, the way the employees were kept motivated and, most importantly, in the way the shows were developed.

Sets and Costume Design

Cirque invested an enormous amount of time and money in preparing unique sets and costumes. Sometimes, the amount spent on creating a theater for a Cirque production was exorbitantly high. For instance, Cirque spent US$ 165 million to build a theater for KA at the MGM Grand in Las Vegas. The theater's stage had two huge moving platforms which were controlled by a crane which weighed 260,000 pounds and used 4,000 gallons of hydraulic fluid.[19] It could tilt the platform to 110 degrees, rotating and lifting it as well. Cirque could showcase high energy action sequences which worked very well on such a stage. For example, in a chase sequence, as the stage tilted at the speed of twelve degrees per second, the artists would be seen being thrown sixty feet into air bags placed below. This, along with high tech cameras and computer generated special effects, transformed the set into a live cinema screen.

There were two audio speakers in every seat at the KA's theater, placed near the ears, which would give the audience a surround sound experience. Beneath the stage, an infrared motion detecting system was placed.[20] Touch sensitive panels also formed a part of the system which could detect the location of the individual artist and manipulate the video content accordingly.

There was a great amount of technical innovation involved in creating the sets for 'O' too. To make the Olympic-sized swimming pool stage comfortable for the artists, a temperature of 88 degrees Fahrenheit (31.1 degrees Celsius) was maintained at all times. Lower temperature was maintained at the audience area through a virtual separating film between the pool and the audience. Numerous temperature sensors were placed in the audience area to ensure that a comfortable temperature was maintained at all times. Glass enclosures were created for the musicians, so that damage to the musical instruments was minimized. The pool also had an underwater communication system to facilitate communication among the artists and underwater air tanks to help the artists breathe underwater. A team was always present underwater to refill these tanks.

Much thought also went into creating the costumes for the artists. For example, in Dralion, which revolved around the four elements of air, water, fire, and earth, the

---

[18] Marc Henricks, "Bigger than the Big Top," www.americanwaymag.com, October 01, 2004.

[19] Hydraulic fluids are a large group of mineral oil, water, or water-based fluids (such as castor oil, glycol, silicone, etc.) used as the medium in equipments such as brakes, power steering, excavators, garbage trucks and industrial shredders.

[20] InfraRed motion sensors are electronic devices which detect the infrared radiations (invisible to the human eye) that are emitted by the objects in the field of view. The motion is detected when the infrared emitting source with one temperature such as the human body passes in front of another source with another temperature such as a piece of furniture or a wall ("Passive InfraRed Sensors," en.wikipedia.org).

various performers wore different colored costumes for different elements. The Chinese female acrobats, for example, who represented water, were seen in green. The artists representing air wore blue costumes; those representing earth and fire were in brown and red costumes respectively. A production like Quidam[21] used a wide array of fabrics like wool, linen, velvet, lycra, leather, jute, different types of silk, and of cotton.[22] Great effort was put into creating some of the costumes such as the swimsuits for the artists in 'O.' Each one took 40 hours to create and there was a lot of trial and error before the costume designers were able to come up with ways to make the fabric withstand damage due to the chemicals in the water.

A novel way was devised to keep track of the inventory of costume material such as the fabrics, garments, shoes, wigs, masks, hats, buttons, zippers and other material. They were all sent for sewing as kits and marked with the show name for which the costumes needed to be prepared. Manuals and catalogs, also known as 'bibles,' were maintained for each show which described every costume in detail.[23]

As soon as new artists joined Cirque, they were asked to submit plaster casts of their heads so that if their wigs got worn out while they were on tour, the costume shop in Montreal could make a new one immediately without having to bring the artist to the shop. The costume shop at Cirque, which had 30 people working in it in 1989, had 300 people in 2004.[24] At any point of time, more than 3,000 costumes and over 1,000 costume designs were present at the costume house. Cirque's costume workshop utilized twelve miles of fabric every year.

Target Audience and Value Innovation

Cirque differentiated itself from the traditional circus in all business aspects. The company created a niche market of live entertainment within the entertainment industry. Rather than providing a product for which demand already existed, it used its innovativeness and creativity to create a demand for live entertainment. Children formed the target customer segment for traditional circuses. However, in the 1980s and 1990s, this target group preferred television rather than a visit to a circus. The circus industry was losing its market quite rapidly. At this time, Cirque made efforts to change its target market completely rather than vie for the shrinking child audience.

Cirque targeted the adult audiences—those who visited the theater and opera. Once Laliberte had defined the target market Cirque wanted to address, he started to mold the entertainment provided by his circus to suit audience expectations. Cirque, rather than being loud and pompous, was elegant and rich. The shows highlighted artistry rather than the thrills that the traditional circus presented. They blended original music with impressive performances which became Cirque's key attraction. Instead of putting some unrelated acts together, the shows were centered on a main theme, giving them a feel of a story or a message being conveyed. Thus, instead of fighting the competition, Cirque made it irrelevant. Commenting on Cirque, John Fleming, the Performing Arts critic with *St. Petersburg Times*, wrote, "It's a circus for people who think they hate circuses."[25]

Cirque started innovating with a focus on the customers. Innovation and creativity were at the core of the company's business. Each person played an important part in the creative team at Cirque. Lyn Heward (Heward), Executive Producer and Senior Advisor, Cirque, explained, "Creativity is fostered in work groups where people first get to know each other and then learn to trust one another. And in this playground we recognize that a good idea can emerge from anywhere in the organization or from within a team. We make our shows from this collective creativity."[26]

Cirque aimed to provide more and more value to its customers through such focused innovation. Value and innovation were given equal emphasis. For Cirque, customer was of prime importance and strategic thinking revolved around the customer. Each new innovation at Cirque resulted in major advancements rather than mere incremental benefits over the competition. Since Cirque did not employ star performers or animals in its shows, it was able to keep the costs low and to provide customers with a value-for-money-experience.

As a result of the unprecedented value offered by Cirque, the company was able to build brand recognition. This led to a win-win situation for Cirque as well as its Cirque's customers. Heward explained, "We need to take into consideration the needs and expectations of our consumers. Our spectators want to be amused, surprised, if not astounded, and to escape from their daily lives if only for a short while, or to be moved or touched, or somehow changed by the experience. Creativity is first

---

[21] Quidam is a touring show from Cirque which premiered in 1996. It is Latin for "a nameless passerby".

[22] "Quidam," www.cirquedusoleil.com.

[23] Mark Henricks, "Bigger Than the Big Top," www.americanwaymag.com, October 01, 2004.

[24] Mark Henricks, "Bigger Than the Big Top," www.americanwaymag.com, October 01, 2004.

[25] John Fleming, "Cirque du Soleil," www.sptimes.com, November 03, 2002.

[26] Arupa Tesolin, "Business at the Big Top: Four Rings for Creativity and Innovation," www.trainingmag.com, August 08, 2007.

and foremost all about courage—a willingness to take risks, to try new things, and share the experience with others. In fact, as an individual or as a company, complacency is the biggest risk you will ever take, and most often the least productive. Risk-taking can be defined as the balance of power between success and fear of failure. So the moral of this story is that we all need to practice risk taking! Our fears hold us back, make us cautious . . . instead we need to forge ahead and make a few mistakes . . . and hopefully learn from them. Here, we call this research and development!"[27]

Marketing

Typically, when Cirque planned any shows in new markets, a five- to six-member team would reach the new market about eighteen months before the event. They would start the groundwork by locating an alliance to represent the company locally. This alliance or the 'local promoters', as Cirque called them, would introduce Cirque to the important people of the city and help the company get sponsorships and permits. The local promoters would also help Cirque find a venue for setting up their tent. These promoters also publicized about Cirque before it came to the town. Thus, even before the shows were performed in the town, there would be some gossip about it and the 'buzz' would have already been created. This would attract enough of a crowd for the press conferences that Cirque gave prior to their performances. For example, Cirque struck up a deal with the American Electric Power[28] to promote them in North America. Cirque got access to the funding from AEP that would come from the sponsorship. The marketing and positioning for Cirque's shows were taken up by AEP. AEP at that time was striving to change people's perception of it as just a regional energy company and to reposition itself as a diversified energy leader. This campaign increased AEP's visibility in North America. BMW became the sponsor for Quidam's performance in Dubai.

Commenting on marketing the company, D'Amico said, "That is actually our biggest challenge. We are so well known for the creative product that we put on stage that I've got to find ways to be just as creative with the way that I portray the image of this company to the public."[29] According to D'Amico, the premiers of the shows were spectacular events and care was taken on the day the shows opened to invite important people like Hollywood actors, performing arts critics, international sportsmen, and distinguished people from the political world so that they would go back and spread positive reviews about the show by 'word of mouth.' According to him, even in this age of high tech advertising and marketing, word-of-mouth worked best for the company. Cirque also tried to integrate itself with the local community by giving a few tickets to charitable organizations which would in turn help them raise money.

In order to advertise its shows, Cirque came up with several innovative and inexpensive methods. For example, the artists of the adult-themed show Zumanity entertained the guests at bars in American cities like Miami, San Francisco, and New York. On many occasions, a team would be sent to a local venue to perform stunts and to challenge the locals to match them. D'Amico said that such techniques not only spread the word that something unique was coming to town, but also gave the Cirque artists an opportunity to unwind and have a good time.

According to D'Amico, the web was a creative medium of advertising as it could provide a virtual experience of Cirque. Cirque's website won Best Design and Realization award from Suxess, an advertising agency in Austria. Cirque redesigned its website in 2002 to make it much more creative and interactive. For this purpose, the Canada-based advertising agency, Diesel Marketing was selected out of 23 agencies worldwide. Speaking at the launch of the new website, Joanne Fillion, Brand Director, Cirque, said, "We wanted our website to be an extension of the experience people have when they come to our shows. And for those who have never had the opportunity to see one of our shows, the site will be an effective means of introducing them to the Cirque du Soleil experience, by giving them virtual access to our unique universe."[30]

Cirque also launched an email program in order to maintain and strengthen its relationship with its viewers spread across the world. This campaign was unique because it tried to be as personal as possible. For example, the members were invited to "join a fan club" instead of "signing up for an email list". Joining the fan club was made extremely easy with easy links and user-friendly language. Signing up for the fan club took just a few minutes. Double confirmation of membership was taken whereby the potential members would have to reply to a membership confirmation email. If they failed to do this, they would be sent a second reminder after seven days. If they still did not confirm, they would be deleted from the database. This ensured that the database remained effective.

[27] Arupa Tesolin, "Business at the Big Top: Four Rings for Creativity and Innovation," www.trainingmag.com, August 08, 2007.
[28] American Electric Power is a Columbus, Ohio-based electric utility and is largest electricity generating utility in the USA.
[29] "Interview with Mario D'Amico," www.reviews.com, July 2002.
[30] "Cirque du Soleil Officially Launches its Website," www.cirquedusoleil.com, May 16, 2006.

The emails sent to the members were also made very creative. For example, virtual letterheads were used and the emails would be written in the first person, from one of the staff members. Sometimes, specific emails would be signed by the respective character from a show. For example, the show's character 'Madame' would sign off the email for the Zumanity brand fan club, with a virtual red lipsticked kiss.

Interestingly, Cirque never undertook any market research for any of its shows. According to D'Amico, if the shows were driven by market research, they would lose their very essence. He said, "It's very much artistic driven in the same way a painter paints for himself—the way he'll put all of his pre-occupations on a canvas. It's very much the same way here. That's why marketing here isn't about identifying a trend and then speaking to a bunch of creative people to do a show to fulfill that need. We don't do exit interviews on different endings for our show (or) what color should that contortionist be wearing."[31] There was also no effort to update any show. Commenting on this, D'Amico said, "The culture of this company is not to fix a show to meet market demands. We'd rather produce a new show than fix an old one."[32]

The Road Ahead

In April 2001, Laliberte announced that he wanted to make Cirque the entertainment capital of the world. Cirque's future plans included building entertainment complexes in major cities including London, New York, Singapore, Hong Kong, Tokyo and Sydney, in the next 15 years. These complexes would house Cirque-inspired restaurants, hotels, art galleries, spas and movie theaters. A Cirque hotel would subtly showcase the Cirque talent, for example, by making a trapeze artist perform her stunts in the waiting area or the reception. Also, a restaurant would have artists performing while guests were dining. Such a hotel could also have clowns delivering room service and mime artists appearing in elevators. This was Laliberte's idea and commenting on this, D'Amico said, "Guy broke the rules with Cirque. Now with hotels and dinner theaters, he wants to build an experience around the customer."[33] He further elaborated on Laliberte's inspiration behind such a brand extension saying, "When you come to our show,

especially in the big top, we control the environment 100 percent. As soon as you walk onto that site, you're in a magical world. What we learned from our Vegas model is that when people step into our theater, they're ours all the way through the show until they step out of our theater. Then they're in someone else's world; they're in the casino world; they're in somebody else's restaurant. Guy thought, 'I'd really like to control the environment of our patrons beyond just the show. Perhaps we can do this by designing a hotel where we are the creative directors.'"[34]

Cirque also planned to transform Montreal into a world center for circus arts. Montreal already had the National Circus School of Canada, Cirque Eloize (another circus company formed by Cirque veterans), En Piste (the Quebec Circus Association), and many individual jugglers and street performers. Cirque aspired to bring these groups together to form a world circus capital. Cirque would place it at the center of a hub for training, creating, and performing the circus arts. This hub would be called the Cité des Arts du Cirque.

Since each production of Cirque was radically different from the other, the customers who saw the previous productions always visited the new shows mainly out of curiosity. Although the company never gave out its attendance numbers, it was believed that the ticket sales for a touring production kept increasing for each show, as positive word-of-mouth spread across the community. Talking about the occupancy, D'Amico said, "Our average occupancy levels go from 80 to 95 percent. Anything below 80 percent we see as a failure."[35]

Though hotels and nightclubs were natural brand extensions for Cirque, industry experts questioned the success of such a proposition. Commenting on this, Robin Rusch, Director, Interbrand Online and Editor-in-Chief, brandchannel.com, said, "The area that may trip up Cirque will be that, unlike McDonald's or Britney—both highly commercial brands that do not pretend to offer high art—a hotel or spa tips the balance from art to business. Cirque risks alienating its audience if it appears too blatantly to be involved in selling its art."[36]

[31] Robin D. Rusch, "Cirque du Soleil," www.brandchannel.com, December 01, 2003.

[32] Mark Henricks, "Bigger Than the Big Top," www.americanwaymag.com, October 01, 2004.

[33] James Brooke, "Arts Abroad; It's a Circus Out There, But Cirque's Still Not Satisfied," www.nytimes.com, April 11, 2001.

[34] John Fleming, "Cirque du Soleil," www.sptimes.com, November 03, 2002.

[35] John Fleming, "Cirque du Soleil," www.sptimes.com, November 03, 2002.

[36] Robin D. Rusch, "Cirque du Soleil," www.brandchannel.com, December 01, 2003.

Additional Readings and References

1. Jeffrey L. Covell, **Cirque du Soleil Inc.**, www.answers.com, June 02, 1997.
2. Brian D. Johnson, **Cirque du Soleil**, *Maclean's* magazine, July 27, 1998.
3. James Brooke, **Arts Abroad; It's a Circus out There, But Cirque's Still not Satisfied,** www.nytimes.com, April 11, 2001.
4. **Interview with Mario D'Amico,** www.reviews.com, July 2002.
5. John Fleming, **Cirque du Soleil**, www.sptimes.com, November 03, 2002.
6. **Galafilm Wins Emmy for Cirque du Soleil Fire Within,** www.galafilm.com, September 15, 2003.
7. Robin D. Rusch, **Cirque du Soleil**, www.brandchannel.com, December 01, 2003.
8. Marc Henricks, **Bigger than the Big Top**, www.americanwaymag.com, October 01, 2004.
9. **Beatles Teaming Up with Circus**, *The Saturday Morning Herald*, October 15, 2004.
10. M. Rashid Khan, Al—Ansari Mohammed, **Sustainable Innovation as a Corporate Strategy**, www.triz-journal.com, January 02, 2005.
11. **Blue Ocean Strategy for Innovation**, www.tatler.typepad.com, March 02, 2005.
12. Linda Tischler, **Join the Circus**, *Fast Company*, July 2005.
13. Christopher Hogg, **Cirque du Soleil and the Future of Entertainment**, *Digital Journal*, December 23, 2005.
14. **How Cirque du Soleil Uses Email to Sell out Shows at Local Cities,** www.marketingsherpa.com, June 01, 2006.
15. Nancy E. Schwartz, **Follow Cirque de Soleil's Marketing Footsteps for Big Top Success,** www.gettingattention.org, June 08, 2006.
16. Larry Mullins, **Blue Ocean Marketing Can Make Your Competitors Irrelevant—Part 1,** www.furninfo. com, August 08, 2006.
17. **"The Spark" of Creativity at Cirque du Soleil**, www.kentblumberg.typepad.com, September 29, 2006.
18. Peter Fisk, **Cirque du Soleil**, http://innoeurope2.cma.ee, September 30, 2006.
19. **BMW to Sponsor Cirque du Soleil**, www.ameinfo.com, November 15, 2006.
20. **Cirque du Soleil and the Problem of Too Much Innovation**, www.endlessinnovation.typepad.com, February 05, 2007.
21. **Cirque du Soleil**, www.metropolis.co.jp, February 09, 2007.
22. Anastasiya Khutko, **Cirque du Soleil's Guy Laliberte Named Ernst & Young 2007 World Entrepreneur of the Year,** www.ey.com, June 05, 2007.
23. Arupa Tesolin, **Business at the Big Top: Four Rings for Creativity and Innovation,** www.trainingmag.com, August 08, 2007.
24. W. Chan Kim, Mouborgne Renee, **Strategy, Value Innovation, "Marketspace,"** www.smlxl.com.
25. **Cirque du Soleil Has a Secret, and it's Big**, www.greystoneguides.com.
26. **Profile: Cirque du Soleil Grows to a Global Brand by Mario D'amico**, www.internationalistmagazine.com.
27. www.cirquedusoleil.com
28. www.blueoceanstrategy.com.
29. en.wikipedia.org.

Books

1. W. Chan Kim, Renée Mauborgne, **Blue Ocean Strategy: How to Create Uncontested Market Space and Make the Competition Irrelevant,** Harvard Business School Press, 2005.
2. **Fast Company's Greatest Hits: Ten Years of the Most Innovative Ideas in Business,** Edited by Mark N. Vamos and David Lidsky, Portfolio, Penguin Group, 2006.

The Interbrew–AmBev Merger Story

K. Prashanth

"Joining with AmBev, Latin America's leading brewer, and its world class management team is great news for our consumers, employees, distributors and shareholders. The combination preserves the best of both companies, while enhancing our profitability and prospects. For Interbrew, it also represents an opportunity to enter some of the fastest growing beer markets in the world."[1]

—*John Brock, CEO, Interbrew in March 2004.*

"The agreement offers AmBev a unique opportunity to combine with Interbrew and establish a truly global powerhouse, with strong positions in the world's best markets. A unified operation for the Americas, from Canada to Argentina is a very exciting prospect. More broadly, we can now achieve the long-term goal of opening up the world's largest markets for AmBev's brands."[2]

—*Marcel Hermann Telles, Co-Chairman, AmBev in March 2004.*

The Announcement

On March 03, 2004, the world's third largest brewery company—the Belgium-based Interbrew—and the world's fifth largest brewery company—the Brazil-based AmBev announced plans to merge their operations. In a mega deal valued at US$ 12.8 bn, the merger created the world's largest brewing company in terms of volumes produced. The combined entity was expected to generate revenues of € 9.5 bn (US$ 11.9 bn) and command a 14% market share in the global beer market.

Interbrew had a presence in over 140 countries, with a dominant position in Europe and North America. The company had registered a compounded annual EPS growth rate of 24.6% over a decade. AmBev had a nearly two-third share in the Brazilian market and was market leader across the Latin American region. Commenting on the benefits of the deal, Axel Gietz, Senior Vice-President, corporate communications and public affairs at Interbrew said, "The complementary deal will give AmBev a chance to expand into North America and Europe and give Interbrew an opportunity to expand into South America, the world's highest growth beer market after China. This reduces the competitions' ability to expand into South America."[3]

While company officials were optimistic, there was mixed reaction from different sections of the industry. Analysts expressed doubts whether the merger would really create the world's largest brewer. In terms of revenue, the new entity lagged behind the current world

---

[1] Interbrew, AmBev to merge. *Beverage Industry*, March 2004.
[2] Interbrew, AmBev to merge. *Beverage Industry*, March 2004.
[3] Kepp Michael, The Brewmasters, *Latin Trade (English)*, July 2004.

leader, Anheuser-Busch (A-B), which generated US$ 14.1 bn in 2003. Further, given the trend of consolidation in the global brewery industry, industry observers felt that even in volume terms, the new entity might not continue as the world's biggest brewer for long (Refer to Exhibit 1 for a note on the global brewery industry). The stock markets too were not impressed. On the day the deal was announced, AmBev's shares fell by 18%, while Interbrew's witnessed a minimal change (Refer to Exhibit 2 and Exhibit 3 for the stock price charts of Interbrew and AmBev). Analysts felt it would take a long time for the merger to yield the expected returns.

AmBev's competitors in Brazil expressed concern that the deal would result in a price war that would lead to

---

| **Exhibit 1** | **A Note on the Global Brewery Industry** |

The history of beer production can be traced back to the 4000 BC, when it was first made in the Middle East. This marked the beginning of one of the first serious manufacturing activities ever. The global beer industry, in its current shape, comprises several mature markets and only a few emerging or fast growing markets. On the whole, growth in terms of volumes has been fluctuating around the 1–3 percent over the past couple of years.

Japan, Western Europe and North America, Australia and parts of the Asia Pacific are considered the most developed markets in the world for beer production and consumption. In the recent past, these markets have been showing signs of maturity, with volumes stagnant or receding. Factors like decreasing confidence of consumers (mainly in Japan and the US) and changing consumption patterns (mainly in younger consumers, who are shifting towards other drinks like FAB) are responsible for this development.

At the same time, the Latin American, East European, Asia Pacific (outside Japan) and Russian markets have been identified as regions with good potential for volume growth. Major beer consuming countries in these regions include China, Russia, and Brazil. Several factors like rising disposable incomes, improving living standards, enhanced interest shown by the global players through acquisitions and mergers have contributed to this trend. In 2002, China had emerged as the largest beer producing country in the world (Refer Table 1 for the world's top ten beer producing countries). Within a couple of years, China emerged as the world's largest market for beer consumption. Beer sales rose at a rate of 41% between 1998 and 2003 in the country.

Geographically, Europe is the largest market for beer production and consumption. In 2002, Europe accounted for 35.7% of total beer sales, followed by the Asia-Pacific region (29.9%), North America (23.1%), Latin America (8.5%) and other parts of the world (2.7%)

| **Table 1** | **World's Ten Largest Beer Markets by Volume Produced (2002) (In mn hectoliters)** |

Rank	Country	Shipments	World Market Share (%)
1	China	238.0	16.9
2	US	233.6	16.5
3	Germany	100.4	7.1
4	Brazil	86.7	6.1
5	Russia	69.5	4.9
6	Japan	69.3	4.9
7	UK	58.2	4.1
8	Mexico	51.4	3.6
9	Spain	29.5	2.1
10	Poland	26.0	1.8

Source: Impact–Global News and Research for the Drinks Executive, Vol. 33, October 2003.

(continued)

Exhibit 1   A Note on the Global Brewery Industry (continued)

The market for beer can be divided based on the variety of beers as well as on a geographical basis. There are broadly four types of beer including Lager,[4] Dark Beer,[5] Non/Low Alcohol[6] and Stout.[7] Of these, Lager is the most popular and widely brewed beer variety. As per 2002 figures, it accounted for 90.2% of total beer consumption.

The global beer market is highly fragmented, with no company having a dominating market share. Before the Interbrew-AmBev merger, the two leading players in the world in terms of volumes produced were Anheuser-Busch and SABMiller (Refer Table 2 for top eight beer companies in the world in terms of volumes produced in 2002).

Table 2	Market Shares of Beer by Volume (2002)

Company	Market Share
Anheuser-Busch	9.50%
SABMiller	6.60%
AmBev	4.6%
Heineken	4.5%
Interbrew	4.5%
Grupo Modelo	2.3%
Coors	2.1%
Kirin	2.1%
Other	63.8%

Source: Global Brewers. Brewers Industry Profile: Global, 2003.

The US-based Anheuser-Busch is the world's largest producer of beer. Key brands include Budweiser and Michelob, exported across the world. Headquartered in London, SABMiller was formed from the merger of South African Breweries and Miller Brewing Company in July 2002. It operates in 24 countries in four continents—US, Africa, Europe and Asia. Rather than building global brands, the company has concentrated on becoming one among the top two brands in markets where it had a presence. The Dutch company, Heineken, operates in 150 countries with several brands like Astel and Tiger. It has over 110 breweries in over 50 countries.

Several companies in mature markets are making attempts to expand through acquisitions in the emerging markets. Large brewing companies purchase relatively smaller, regional companies and in the process acquire local brands, improve production facilities and use regional markets as a channel to distribute their premium brands. Some instances of such deals include Heinekens US$ 2.4 bn purchase of the Austrian company, BRAG in 2003, the US$ 785 mn purchase of the Italian company, Peroni by SABMiller, and the acquisition of the China-based Harbin Brewery Group by Anheuser-Busch for US$ 720 mn in 2004.

It is very likely that more mergers and acquisitions are on the anvil. It is predicted that Asia's brewery market will expand, led by China. Further, with time, the extent of fragmentation is likely to reduce and the market should get more organized.

Compiled from Various Sources.

---

[4] Beer produced using the bottom fermentation process, where the yeast cells sink to the bottom of the tank during fermentation, and are then drawn off when fermentation is complete. Most lagers are of the pils type. Other examples are Dortmunder, bock, dark lager and Vienna.

[5] A bottom-fermented dark beer. The dark colour is produced by the use of caramelized malt. Dark lagers are popular in Germany and Eastern Europe.

[6] Beer with an alcohol content of no more than 0.5% in volume. The beer is produced by removing the alcohol or arresting the process before fermentation is complete.

[7] This dark beer tastes strongly of malt and hops.

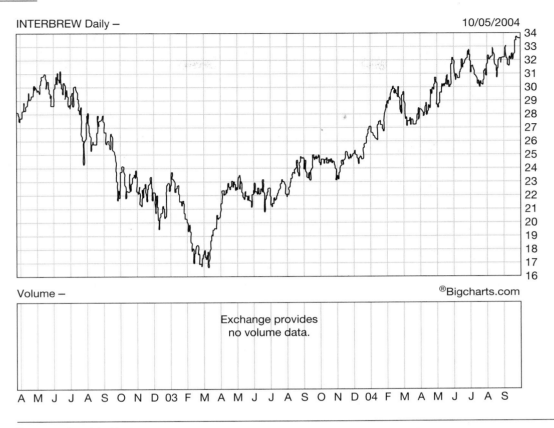

INTERBREW Daily –

10/05/2004

Volume –

®Bigcharts.com

Exchange provides
no volume data.

A M J J A S O N D 03 F M A M J J A S O N D 04 F M A M J J A S

Source: www.cbsmarketwatch.com.

monopolistic practices by the newly formed company. Commenting on this, Vinicius Camargo Silva, the lawyer for Schimcariol, Brazil's second largest brewer said, "The deal will cause the merged company to either arbitrarily increase profits or use its increased margins from economy of scale or purchasing power advantages to wage a price war. A price war's immediate effect might be good for the consumers but the long term effect would be to force competitors out of a market, and then, once the merged company dominates the market, set a price that the consumer is forced to accept."[8]

About Interbrew

Interbrew was founded in the 14th century as Den Hoorn, located on the outskirts of Brussels, Belgium. In 1717, following its acquisition by master brewer Sebastien Artois, Den Hoorn was renamed as Brasseries Artois. By the late 1980s, the company was the second largest brewing house in Belgium. To further consolidate its position in the market, in 1987, Brasseries Artois merged with Belgium's largest brewer, Brasseries Piedboeuf. This resulted in the creation of Interbrew. The two companies owned some key beer brands including Stella Artois, Leffe, and Juniper. Soon, Interbrew started acquiring specialty breweries in Belgium, like Hoegaarde in 1989 and Belle-Vue in 1990.

The spate of acquisitions intensified in the 1990s with the company expanding rapidly across the world. It acquired over 30 breweries, of which the most high profile in terms of size included Labatt (Canada), Oriental Breweries (South Korea), Sun Interbrew (Russia and Ukraine), Bass Brewers (UK), Whitbread Beer Company (UK) and Beck & Company (Germany). In 2004,

---

[8] Kepp, Michael, The Brewmasters, *Latin Trade (English)*, July 2004.

Exhibit 3 AmBev—Stock Price Chart
(November 2003–October 2004)

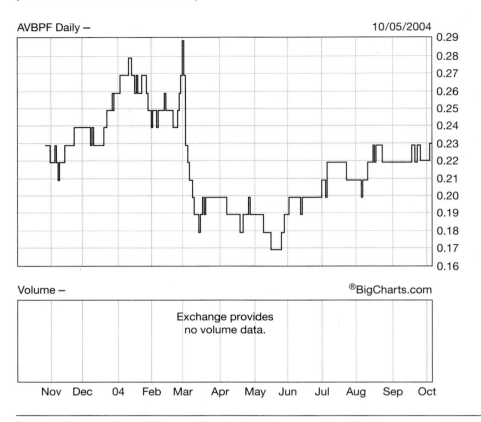

AVBPF Daily –   10/05/2004

Volume –   ®BigCharts.com

Exchange provides
no volume data.

Nov   Dec   04   Feb   Mar   Apr   May   Jun   Jul   Aug   Sep   Oct

Source: www.cbsmarketwatch.com.

Interbrew acquired the Malaysian Lion Group (China) and Apatin Brewery (Serbia). The deal to acquire Germany's Speten Brewery (Gabriel Sedlmayr Spaten-Franziskaner Bräu KGaA) was expected to close in the fourth quarter of 2004.

Interbrew's operations were dispersed across five regions—The Americas, Western Europe, Central & Eastern Europe and the Asia/Pacific. Two of the company's premium brands—Stella Artois and Beck's were globally recognized. While Stella had a significant presence in 16 countries, primarily Europe, Beck was marketed in around 120 countries. Interbrew also had two specialty brands—Hoegaarden[9] and Leffe—and several other brands were introduced in Belgium. Interbrew's focus on expansion contributed to its steady growth, especially over the past couple of years.

About AmBev

AmBev was founded in 1885. However, the company in its present shape was set up in 1999, when two leading Brazilian brewers—Companhia Antarctica Paulista and Companhia Cervejaria Brahma were merged to create AmBev. Like Interbrew, AmBev also expanded its operations through acquisitions. The company acquired 95.4% of the Uruguay-based company—Cerveceria Malteria Paysandu, thereby gaining 48% market share of the country's beer market. In 2001, the company bought over the assets of Cerveceria International, a brewery in Paraguay; increasing its market share in that country. In 2002, the company achieved a higher revenue growth by distributing two of the world's famous soft drink brands of PepsiCo—Pepsi Twist and Mountain Dew.

---

[9] A wheat beer with a cloudy appearance, which is re-fermented in the bottle.

Exhibit 4	AmBev's Market Share in Latin America (2002)

Country	Market Share (%)
Argentina	99
Bolivia	99
Brazil	64
Chile	12
Ecuador	6
Guatemala	10
Paraguay	94
Uruguay	99
Venezuela	7

Source: AmBev Annual Report, 2003.

The company expanded further in 2003 by spending US$ 40 mn on a brewery in Peru. In December 2003, AmBev acquired Cervecería SurAmericana, the second largest brewery in Ecuador.

By early 2004, AmBev had a 65% share in the Brazilian beer market and a 17.2% share in the country's soft drinks market. The company's production facilities were located in Brazil, Uruguay, Argentina, Paraguay and Venezuela. Apart from Latin America, AmBev's products were exported to Bolivia, Colombia, Chile, the US, the UK, France, Germany, Italy, Portugal, Spain, Switzerland, Japan and Angola.

AmBev's major brands in the Brazilian beer market included Skol, Brahma and Antarctica. The soft drinks division not only produced the company's own brands of carbonated soft drinks (like Guarana Antarctica), but also PepsiCo's brands through a license agreement. The company also manufactured mineral water, isotonic beverages and ice tea. Key brands in this category included Marathon, Gatorade, Lipton Ice Tea and Fratelli Vita mineral water. The international beer division manufactured AmBev's beer brands for the global market.

The Rationale

Both Interbrew and AmBev had strong reasons to merge. For Interbrew, it would mean access to the Latin American beer market, identified as a potential region for high growth, where AmBev had a dominant market share (Refer to Exhibit 4 for AmBev's share in the various Latin American countries). Two countries in the region—Argentina and Brazil—were particularly promising as beer consumption there had been growing at an annual rate of 5% over the past 10 years. Compared to this, the average beer consumption in Interbrew's major markets—Europe and the US—was growing much slower. Further, given the trend of rapid consolidation in the beer industry, it was all the more important for Interbrew to firm up its position. Commenting on the deal and its benefits to Interbrew, James Williamson, beverage analyst at SG Securities,[10] said, "There are very few targets of this size so although I think you will see consolidation continue in the brewing sector, it will be bolt-ons, nothing of this size. AmBev is an interesting target with good growth prospects. And South America is an interesting market; as it seems to be at the bottom end of its cycle, I think they can anticipate strong growth in the future. What Brock [CEO of Interbrew] did in terms of timing was quite good."[11]

For AmBev, the deal meant the creation of an American multinational company. Interbrew's strong international presence would give AmBev a strong presence in the mature and therefore less risky US and European markets. Commenting on this, Giovanni Fiorentino, an analyst at Bain, a consultancy firm said, "If you join with an international player, your risk premium falls dramatically."[12] Further, the merger would give AmBev an easy and less expensive means to expand without much risk.

The Merger Deal

According to the merger deal's terms and conditions, Interbrew would purchase a controlling interest in AmBev, by issuing its shares. For its part, AmBev would purchase the Labatt Brewing Company Limited (Labatt)—Interbrew's brewery in North America and Interbrew's 30% stake in Femsa Cerveza, one of the two leading brewing companies in Mexico. AmBev would compensate for this by taking over Labatts' debt of US$ 1.3 bn and by issuing additional shares to Interbrew. Though, it appeared on the surface that Interbrew was losing a minority stake to acquire a majority stake in AmBev, this was offset by the shareholders of both companies being provided equal importance in the functioning of the merged entity. This was named InBev. Thus, the deal seemed an alliance or partnership rather

---

[10] SG is the investment banking division of Société Générale, the world's largest warrants issuer, with 14 years experience of providing a warrant trading service. Société Générale is one of Europe's largest banks, with assets of £ 268 bn at the end of 2002.

[11] Merger creates brewery giant. *Corporate Finance*, April 2004.

[12] An awful lot of brewing in Brazil, *The Economist*, March 06, 2004.

than an acquisition. After the merger, AmBev would have sufficient autonomy in its day-to-day business, the power to influence critical decisions in the group's affairs and the opportunity to further expand its business, domestic as well as geographic.

AmBev's ownership structure, however, made it difficult to integrate the two companies. AmBev's ordinary shares were held with three independent entities—Tinsel Investments SA (Tinsel), which through its subsidiaries Braco Investimentos SA and Empresa de Administraçãoe Participações SA (ECAP), owned 8.25 bn ordinary shares in the company. This accounted for 22.5% of AmBev's equity share capital and 52.8% of voting interests at AmBev. On the other hand, Interbrew was controlled by Stichting Interbrew, a Dutch foundation working on the behalf of the families of Interbrew's founders.

To simplify the merger, the acquisition deal was divided into several parts. InBev first acquired 100% stake in Tinsel by issuing 141.712 mn shares. Following this, it merged Labatt with AmBev. For this, AmBev issued its 7.9 bn ordinary shares and 11.4 bn preference shares. On August 27, 2004, the deal was formally closed and received the approval of Interbrew's shareholders. Commenting on the closure, Victório Carlos de Marchi, Co-Chairman of AmBev, said, "We are pleased to have finalized the combination with Interbrew and are excited about its prospects. Labatt is an ideal North American complement to AmBev's existing businesses, and our team brings the proven skills and experience to enhance its brands and operations, generating significant value and synergies. We are confident that our new global platform will also present significant opportunities to leverage AmBev's brands, particularly Brahma, in new and attractive markets."[13]

In October 2004, it was planned that InBev would issue a Mandatory Tender Offer (MTO) for the remaining common shares of AmBev. If the MTO was fully subscribed, InBev would own an estimated 31.1 bn shares of AmBev, accounting for around 55.6% economic interest and 83.9% voting interest in AmBev. The third major stakeholder in Ambev—Fundaçao Antonio e Helena Zerrenner—decided to continue being a common shareholder of AmBev.

After closing the deal, a new management structure for InBev was announced, in which John Brock was made CEO (Refer to Exhibit 5 for the organization structure of InBev). He would head an Executive Board of Management (EBM), consisting of officers from InBev and AmBev. The EBM comprised five zonal presidents and five global functional heads. The zonal presidents headed five geographical regions—North America, Latin America, Western Europe, Eastern Europe and the Asia Pacific. The global functional heads handled the functional disciplines of finance, information systems, HR, technical and commercial aspects. John Bock's immediate subordinates were the Senior Vice Presidents—Alex Gietz (Corporate Affairs), Gauthier de Biolley (SVP—External Growth) and Jo Van Biesbroeck (SVP—Strategy and Business Development).

Commenting on the structure, Bock said, "The structure we have put in place today ensures that InBev has a management team with highly complementary skills, giving the combined company world-class capabilities across all aspects of the business. Working with one unified vision, each unit will maintain its focus, while at the same time sharing best practices, capturing synergies, and avoiding duplication of resources wherever possible. This structure will enable us to come together quickly and efficiently, and to maximize the core competencies of our worldwide brewing operations."[14]

The Benefits

Several synergies and benefits were expected from the merger (Refer to Table 1). These broadly included financial benefits, a good growth platform and cost synergies.

Table 1	Expected Benefits from the Interbrew-AmBev Deal

- Sell 215 mn hectoliters (hl) in total volume, of which beer would form 190 mn hl and soft drinks 25 mn hl on a pro-forma (2003) basis.
- Combine Interbrew's strength in Europe, Asia and North America with AmBev's unrivalled position in Latin America.
- Rank number one or number two in more than 20 beer markets.
- Have the financial strength to extend its lead in the evolution of the global beer industry.

Source: Interbrew and AmBev Establish InterbrewAmBev, the World's Premier Brewer, www.inbev.com, March 03, 2004.

---

[13] Interbrew and AmBev complete combination to establish InBev, www.inbev.com, August 27, 2004.
[14] Newly Created Inbev Announces Management Structure, August 30, 2004, www.beverageworld.com.

Exhibit 5   Organization Structure of InBev

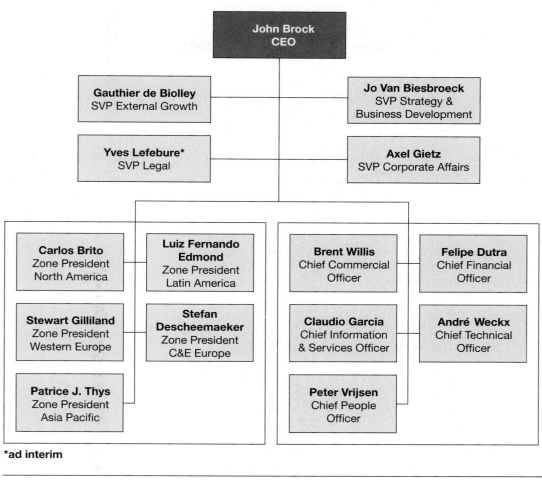

*ad interim

Source: www.inbev.com.

On the pro-forma 2003 basis, Interbrew and AmBev were expected to jointly earn revenues of € 9.5 bn and combined earnings before interest, taxes, depreciation and amortization (EBITDA)[15] of € 1.271 bn. Interbrew's market capitalization at the time of merger was 9.977 bn and had been showing steady growth. In the past couple of years, Interbrew had reported an increase in revenue, net income, volume of beer produced and EBITDA. AmBev's market capitalization was € 8.293 bn. By combining the two companies, the new entity's financial position was expected to improve significantly. The combined net debt as on December 31, 2003, was € 3.3 bn. (Refer to Exhibits 6, 7, 8 and 9 for consolidated statements of income and balance sheets of Interbrew and AmBev).

Apart from creating the world's largest brewer in terms of volumes and market share, both companies could now explore each other's geographical territories and achieve brand leadership in lucrative beer markets in Asia, Europe and America (Refer to Exhibit 10 for the volume sales of leading breweries in the world). The new company could market the three global flagship brands—Brahma, an already established #9 brand in the world, Stella Artois and Beck's—two brands becoming popular (Refer to Exhibit 11 for the top twenty brewery brands in the world in 2002). The merged entity was expected to be either market leader or number two in 20 countries across the world including Brazil, Canada, Russia, Ukraine and Germany. The company could

---

[15] Also known as operating cash flow, EBITDA is calculated by subtracting costs of sales and operating expenses from revenues. Depreciation and amortization expenses aren't included in the costs. EBITDA is a useful measure of cash flow for companies that have low earnings because of large restructuring, capital build-out or acquisition costs.

Exhibit 6

For the year ended December 31	2003	2002
Net Turnover	7,044	6,992
Cost of Sales	(3,385)	(3,418)
Gross Profit	3,659	3,574
Distribution expenses	(778)	(758)
Sales and marketing expenses	(1,377)	(1,317)
Administrative expenses	(615)	(593)
Other operating income/expenses	(50)	(70)
Profit from operations, pre restructuring charges	839	836
Restructuring charges	–	(108)
Profit from operations	839	728
Net financing costs	(131)	(134)
Income from associates	35	71
Profit before tax	743	665
Income tax expense	(185)	(162)
Profit after tax	558	503
Minority interests	(53)	(36)
Net profit	505	467
Weighted average number of ordinary shares (mn shares)	432	431
Fully diluted weighted average number of ordinary shares (mn shares)	434	435
Year-end number of ordinary shares (million shares)	432	432
Basic earnings per share	1.17	1.08
Diluted earnings per share	1.16	1.07
Earnings per share before goodwill and restructuring	1.45	1.51
Diluted earnings per share before goodwill and restructuring	1.44	1.50
Earnings per share before goodwill and after restructuring	1.45	1.33
Consolidated Statement Of Recognized Gains And Losses		
Foreign exchange translation differences	(342)	(431)
Cash flow hedges: Effective portion of changes in fair value	10	6
Transferred to the income statement	(8)	(6)
Other items recognized directly in equity	–	(1)
Net profit recognized directly in equity	(340)	(432)
Net profit	505	467
Total recognized gains	165	35
Effect of changes in accounting policy	–	(32)

Source: www.inbev.com.

Exhibit 7

Interbrew—Consolidated Balance Sheets
(In mn euro, except per share figures)

Year ended December 31	2003	2002
ASSETS		
Non-current assets		
Property, plant and equipment	3,342	3,512
Goodwill	3,744	3,658
Intangible assets other than goodwill	228	133
Interest-bearing loans granted	9	10
Investments in associates	443	625
Investment securities	247	277
Deferred tax assets	169	199
Employee benefits	31	32
Long-term receivables	324	345
	8,537	8,791
Current Assets		
Interest-bearing loans granted	2	1
Investment securities	–	31
Inventories	460	444
Income tax receivable	30	92
Trade and other receivables	1,509	1,572
Cash and cash equivalents	445	215
	2,446	2,355
TOTAL ASSETS	10,983	11,146
EQUITY AND LIABILITIES		
Capital and reserves		
Issued capital	333	333
Share premium	3,215	3,212
Reserves	(232)	108
Retained earnings	1,404	1,041
	4,720	4,694
Minority interests	410	463
Non-current liabilities		
Interest-bearing loans and borrowings	2,200	1,433
Employee benefits	300	329
Trade and other payables	40	45
Provisions	200	252
Deferred tax liabilities	251	242
	2,991	2,301
Current liabilities		
Bank overdrafts	85	122
Interest-bearing loans and borrowings	612	1,320
Income tax payables	122	224
Trade and other payables	1,956	1,940
Provisions	87	82
	2,862	3,688
TOTAL LIABILITIES	10,983	11,146

Source: www.inbev.com.

Exhibit 8

AmBev—Consolidated Statements of Income
(In mns of reais, except for net income per thousand shares)

Year ended December 31	2003	2002
Gross Sales		
Product sales	17,143.5	14,279.9
Sales deductions (Sales taxes, discounts and returns)	(8,459.7)	(6,954.6)
Net sales	8,683.8	7,325.3
Cost of products sold	(4,044.2)	(3,341.7)
Gross profit	4,639.6	3,983.6
Operating income (expenses)		
Selling	(847.1)	(687.2)
Direct distribution	(648.6)	(537.4)
Administrative	(412.0)	(350.5)
Tax, labor and other contingencies	(187.9)	(123.7)
Management and directors' compensation	(5.9)	(23.0)
Depreciation and amortization	(420.0)	(334.6)
Financial income	601.8	2,530.3
Financial expenses	(508.7)	(3,277.3)
Equity in results of investees	(6.2)	–
Other operating income (expenses), net	(240.1)	199.4
	(2,674.7)	(2,604.0)
Operating profit	1,964.9	1,379.6
Other non-operating expenses, net	(100.7)	(72.2)
Income before income tax and social contribution on net income	1,864.2	1,307.4
Income tax and social contribution benefit (expense)	(426.1)	280.6
Income before profit sharing and contributions	1,438.1	1,588.0
Profit sharing and contributions to employees and management	(23.6)	(112.3)
To Zerrenner Foundation		(12.8)
Income before minority interest	1,414.5	1,462.9
Minority interest	(2.9)	47.4
Net income for the year	1,411.6	1,510.3

Source: AmBev Form 6-K, www.ambev.com.

explore two kinds of markets—those, which had experienced strong growth in the recent past in terms of volumes like Brazil, Argentina, Russia, Ukraine and Central Europe; and mature markets like Germany, Canada, UK and Belgium, where organic growth could be achieved through market segmentation and efficiency.

Both Interbrew and AmBev had experienced and highly competitive management teams. The deal enabled the companies to complement each other's capabilities in diverse areas such as costs, sales and distribution, brand building, operational efficiencies (like purchasing cans together), management compensation and incentives, apart from integrating new businesses.

In terms of costs, it was estimated that by merging, an estimated € 280 mn ($ 350 mn) in synergies could be realized annually from 2007 onwards. Of this, an annual savings of € 140 mn would be generated through procurement, technical, general and administrative cost

Exhibit 9	AmBev—Consolidated Balance Sheets (In mns of reais)

Year ended December 31	2003	2002
Assets		
Current		
Cash and cash equivalents	1,196.1	1,131.6
Marketable securities	1,338.1	2,158.4
Unrealized gain on derivatives	258.7	214.9
Trade accounts receivable	725.7	679.0
Inventories	954.6	837.4
Taxes recoverable	771.4	410.3
Other	255.9	139.8
Total	**5,500.5**	**5,571.4**
Long-term receivables		
Compulsory and judicial deposits	365.9	256.9
Loans to employees for purchase of shares	234.7	324.8
Deferred income tax and social contribution	1,831.8	1,558.4
Properties for sale	144.1	121.6
Other	616.1	444.3
	3,192.6	**2,706.0**
Permanent Assets		
Investments		
Holdings in direct subsidiaries, including goodwill, net	1,687.3	626.9
Other investments	24.1	10.4
Total Investments	1,711.4	637.3
Property, plant and equipment	4,166.3	3,330.6
Deferred Charges	259.3	136.2
	6,137.0	**4,104.1**
Total Assets	**14,830.1**	**12,381.5**
Liabilities and Shareholders' Equity		
Current		
Suppliers	800.3	789.1
Financings	1,976.1	607.4
Unrealized loss on derivatives	11.7	3.7
Salaries, profit sharing and social security charges	94.1	59.7
Dividends payable	293.9	345.7
Income tax and social contribution	543.2	74.4
Other taxes and contributions	758.3	619.4
Accounts payable to related parties	0.8	76.8
Other	241.6	257.5
	4,720.0	**2,833.7**

(continued)

Exhibit 9   AmBev—Consolidated Balance Sheets (continued)

Long-term liabilities		
Financings	4,004.3	3,879.3
Deferrals of Taxes on sales	235.2	306.9
Liabilities related to tax and other claims and provision for contingencies	1,232.9	989.3
Other	133.1	163.6
	5,605.5	5,339.1
Minority interest	196.4	79.1
Shareholders' equity		
Subscribed capital stock	3,124.1	3,046.2
Capital reserve	16.6	16.6
Revenue reserves		
Legal	208.7	138.1
Future capital increase	26.1	1,033.9
Statutory	1,271.2	75.4
Treasury stock	(338.5)	(180.6)
	4,308.2	4,129.6
TOTAL LIABILITIES AND SHAREHOLDERS' EQUITY	14,830.1	12,381.5

Source: AmBev Form 6-K, www.ambev.com.

Exhibit 10   World's Leading Brewer's by Volume Sales (2004)

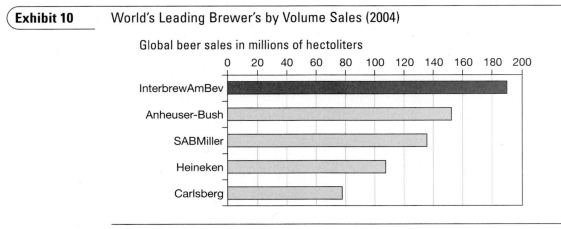

Source: Interbrew.

savings. The remaining € 140 mn annually was expected to be generated through commercial tax savings from 2007 onwards. This would be done by distributing Interbrew's Beck's and Stella Artois brands in Latin America and, similarly, by distributing AmBev's Brahma brand through Interbrew's network. All this was expected to be made possible through appropriate cross-licensing arrangements between the two companies.

The Drawbacks

Despite the optimism from company officials, analysts criticized the Interbrew-AmBev deal on several accounts. The deal was based on the principle of growth through acquisitions. Analysts felt that pursuing growth at any cost was not always beneficial. They felt Interbrew was keen to go ahead with the deal more because of

Exhibit 11

Exhibit 11 | Top Twenty Beer Brands in The World (2002)
(In mns of barrels)

Rank	Brand	Company/Brewer	Shipments[1]
1	Budweiser	Anheuser-Busch, Inc.	38.4
2	Bud Light	Anheuser-Busch, Inc.	37.8
3	Skol	AmBev	27.0
4	Corona	Grupo Modelo	22.8
5	Heineken	Heineken NV	19.5
6	Asahi Super Dry	Asahi Breweries, Ltd.	17.5
7	Coors Light	Coors Brewing Co.	17.0
8	Miller Lite	Miller Brewing Co. (SAB)	15.7
9	Brahma Chopp	AmBev	13.0
10	Polar	Cerveceria Polar CA	12.3
11	Amstel	Heineken NV	9.2
12	Kaiser	Cervajarias Kaiser (Molson)	9.0
13	Carlsberg	Carlsberg A/S	9.0
14	San Miguel Pale Pilsen	San Miguel Corp.	8.8
15	Natural Light	Anheuser-Busch, Inc.	8.4
16	Kirin Tanrei	Kirin Brewery Co. Ltd.	8.4
17	Guinness Stout	Guinness Brewing Worldwide Ltd.	8.2
18	Castle Lager	The South African Breweries Ltd.	7.8
19	Baltika	Baltic Beverages Holding AB	7.8
20	Stella Artois	Interbrew	7.6
Total[2]			304.9

Source: Impact: Global News and Research for the Drinks Executive, Vol. 33, October 1 & 15, 2003.
1—Includes exports and license volume; and 2—Addition of columns may not agree because of rounding

compulsion to maintain its position in the industry. The company's financial performance had deteriorated significantly in the fiscal year 2002. While the company's revenues had fallen by nearly 4%, from € 7.303 bn to € 6.992 bn, its net income was down by a whopping 33%, from € 698 mn to € 467 mn in the fiscal year 2002. Though the financials improved in the fiscal year 2003, they were less than 2001 levels. Some analysts believed that given this deteriorating financial status, Interbrew had to save face, and hence the merger was proposed.

Analysts also wondered about the valuation of the deal, which they felt was very expensive for both parties. It was estimated that Interbrew would be spending US$ 9.2 bn for a 57% equity stake in AmBev. AmBev would be spending an estimated US$ 7 bn for purchasing Labatt (Refer to Exhibit 12 for a comparison of Interbrew-AmBev key financial figures). For both, it seemed too high, given the overall slow global industry

growth, decreasing margins and the long time it would take for returns on investment.

Some analysts felt the deal favoured AmBev. As a result of the merger, Interbrew's existing brands like Stella Artois, Bass and Beck's might suffer, they said. The profits from these brands might get squeezed with the addition of top AmBev brands like Brahma and Antarctica into the portfolio.

Dismissing these concerns and justifying the expenditure, John Brock said, "In terms of the amount paid, I think that when all is said and done, the total amount that Interbrew will have invested in this transaction and, similarly, the total amount that AmBev will have invested as part of buying Canada, the US and Mexico, there are very reasonable multiples that are being paid. If you compare these multiples, which are in the range of 10.5–11.5 and compare them to the kind of multiples that are being paid, and have been paid by other

Exhibit 12   Comparison of Interbrew—AmBev Key Financial Figures

	AmBev 2003 (In mn euro)	AmBev 2003 (In mn R$)	Interbrew 2003 (In mn euro)	Labatt Americas 2003 (In mn euro)
Net Turnover	2502	8684	7044	1659
EBITDA	885	3072	1498	386
Profit from operations	664	2306	839	282
Net profit from ordinary activities	407	1412	505	
Net Profit	407	1412	505	
EPS before goodwill	10.7	37.23 (per thousand shares)	1.45	
Dividend per share	6.7	23.14 (per thousand ordinary shares)	0.36	
		23.45 (per thousand preferred shares)		
ROIC	17.7%	17.7%	10.6%	
Net Capex	273	945	595	
Cash Flow from Operations	728	2528	1151	
Cash interest coverage	13.5X	13.5X	7.6X	
Net Financial Debt	919	3188	2434	
Debt Equity ratio	0.74X	0.74X	0.52X	

Source: Interbrew and AmBev Establish InterbrewAmBev, The World's Premier Brewer, www.inbev.com, March 03, 2004.

international brewers often for minority stakes in Latin American bottlers and brewers, I think what you'll see is that these are very reasonable and fair deals."[16]

Interbrew had reportedly promised its investors that it would attempt to consolidate past acquisitions, before striking any new deal. In this context, analysts felt this merger might have come a bit too early and Interbrew had gone back on its promise.

Analysts also expressed fears of a cultural mismatch. Interbrew was known for its traditional bureaucratic culture. In contrast, AmBev had a more aggressive and ambition-driven culture, which emphasized efficiency through cost cutting. Analysts felt this might result in conflict.

However, both Interbrew and AmBev viewed the cultural differences positively. Commenting on the positive side of the deal and how AmBev would manage, Milton Seligman, Director of Corporate Affairs at AmBev said, "They really are different cultures. That's a reality. Where the experience of one company is better in the sense of the common good, that is what will prevail, and that is the route in terms of culture that we plan to use to deal with the differences."[17]

Fears were also expressed that with this merger, several breweries across the world would be forced to shut down, resulting in massive unemployment and other problems. John Brock did not run away from this possibility. He said, "We don't need 75 breweries. We have got to get a more integrated business that is far more cost-effective than it is today. All options are open. We have a good idea of where we are, and we want to be as good as Anheuser-Busch."[18] Analyst felt that in the name of factors like cost cutting, expansion and competition, social responsibility might take a back seat.

[16] Interbrew and AmBev establish Interbrew AmBev, www.inbev.com, March 03, 2004.
[17] Gilles Castonguay, Nicholas Winning, Shareholders Toast Brewers' Merger, biz.yahoo.com, August 27, 2004.
[18] Interbrew weighs brewery closures, news.bbc.co.uk, May 03, 2004.

Analysts predicted that given the kind of acquisitions going on among top brewery companies in the world, the industry might have only five major brewery companies in the next couple of years. This might dampen competition and leave consumers with few choices.

Additional Readings and References

1. **Global Brewers**, *Brewers Industry Profile: Global*, 2003.
2. **Huge Brazil Deal for Stella Firm**, news.bbc.co.uk, March 03, 2004
3. **Interbew, Ambev to Merge,** *Beverage Industry*, March 2004.
4. **Interbrew and AmBev Establish InterbrewAmBev, The World's Premier Brewer**, www.inbev.com, March 03, 2004.
5. **Largest beverage company in Latin America joins hands with Interbrew**, *World IT Report*, March 03, 2004.
6. Ewing, Jack, **Big Beer's Global Takeover Binge,** *Business Week Online*, March 04, 2004.
7. Kemp, Shirley, **Size Counts. Or Does It?,** m1.mny.co.za, March 05, 2004.
8. **An Awful Lot Of Brewing In Brazil,**. *Economist*, March 06, 2004.
9. **Interbrew Confirms The Press Release Issued On Friday, March 5th, 2004 Providing Additional Information On The Transaction Announced On March 3rd, 2004**, www.inbev.com, March 08, 2004.
10. **What's New in Your Industry**, *Business Latin America*, March 08, 2004.
11. **AmBev's Americas Mandate**, *Business Latin America*, March 08, 2004.
12. **Interbrew—Still Managing to Infuse Private Market with Action**, *Private Placement Letter*, March 08, 2004.
13. Holloway, Andy, **Heady Times**, *Canadian Business*, March 15, 2004.
14. **Hopping**, *Economist*, March 27, 2004.
15. Kirkman, Alexandra, **Beer Buddies**, *Forbes*, March 29, 2004.
16. **Company Spotlight: Interbrew**. MarketWatch, *Global Round-up*, April 2004.
17. Woodley, Monica, **Merger Creates Brewery Giant** *Corporate Finance*, April 2004.
18. Freitas, Claudio Luis, **AMBEV—Was The Ambev Interbrew Merger Good? To Whom?**, www.yeald.com, April 20, 2004.
19. **Interbrew 'Needs Fewer Breweries,'** news.bbc.co.uk, April 30, 2004.
20. **Interbrew Weighs Brewery Closures**, news.bbc.co.uk, May 3rd, 2004.
21. **Interbrew/Ambev: Mixed Blessings**, *MarketWatch: Global Round-up*, May 2004.
22. *Industry Update, MarketWatch: Drinks*, May 2004.
23. **Ambev Says Further Definitions Achieved Regarding Combination with Interbrew**, *World IT Report*, May 25, 2004.
24. Cazin, Natasha, **Beer goes from strength to strength**, www.euromonitor.com, June 25, 2004.
25. Kepp, Michael, **The Brewmasters**, *Latin Trade (English)*, July 2004.
26. **Ambev Announces the Closing of Transactions with Interbrew**, www.beverageworld.com, August 27, 2004.
27. **Interbrew and Ambev Complete Combination to Establish InBev**, www.inbev.com, August 27, 2004.
28. **Shareholders Approve Union of Interbrew, Ambev**, www.cbc.ca, August 27, 2004.
29. **Interbrew: World's No.1 Beer Maker**, www.cnn.com, August 27, 2004.
30. **InBev Announces New Management Structure and Composition**, www.inbev.com, August 30, 2004.
31. **Belgians and Brazilians Create World's Largest Beer Brewer**. *Emerging Markets Economy*, September 02, 2004.
32. **The Shape of Things to Come: Developments in the Global Brewing Industry**, www.harnisch.com, September 2002.
33. Popp, Jamie, **2004 Beer Report, Slow Going In a Variable Market**, www.bevindustry.com
34. **Top 10 Global Brewers**, *Beverage World*, June 15, 2003.
35. **Interbrew And Ambev Face Market Critics**, *Modern Brewery Age*, March 15, 2004.
36. Gilles Castonguay, Winning, Nicholas, **Shareholders Toast Brewers' Merger**, biz.yahoo.com, August 27, 2004.
37. Geitner, Paul, **InBev Brewer Reports Rise in Profits**, www.allheadlinenews.com, September 09, 2004.
38. www.foodsubs.com.

L'Oréal's Business Strategy

Neeraj Kumar Singh

Srikanth G
ICFAI University Press, Business School Case Development Centre

The success of new products, the international break-throughs made by our brands and our spectacular progress in the emerging markets have enabled L'Oréal to achieve another year of strong sales growth. This momentum, combined with the tight control of costs, led to an important improvement in profitability, despite an exceptionally unfavourable economic and monetary environment.[1]

—*Lindsay Owen-Jones, Chairman and Chief Executive Officer of L'Oréal Group*

Introduction

Founded in 1909, L'Oréal had become the world leader in the cosmetics market by 2003. Providing a variety of beauty products, it has transformed from a French company in the early 1900s to a global titan in the 2000s. Its product range included makeup, perfume, and hair and skin care products, which were tailored according to the consumer needs. The company believed in the strategy of innovation and diversification. L'Oréal's growth depended on the global brand, which helped in sustaining the mature consumer-products market even in times when global markets themselves were shaky. High profile, celebrity-driven marketing campaigns and Web-enabled information and customization sites as well as aggressive expansion and acquisition enhanced its global brand image. The cosmetic market as a whole had been slightly on the decline since the late 1990s. But the L'Oréal products were becoming popular due to their uniqueness and catering to the beauty needs of different

ethnic groups and gender. In 2003, the group was number one in the U.S. cosmetic market, but it faced tough competition from Estée Lauder and Procter & Gamble. This made the group refocus its business strategies.

Background

L'Oréal, the world's largest cosmetic company, was established in 1909 by a French chemist, Eugene Schueller. After manufacturing and selling the cosmetic products in Paris for a few years, Schueller started exporting to other European countries like Holland, Austria, and Italy. Gradually the L'Oréal products were distributed to the United States, South America, Russia, and the Far East. By 2003, the L'Oréal group had entered 130 countries, through its 290 subsidiaries and around a hundred agents. More than 80 percent of group sales were generated outside France, with operations in every major territory.

In the 1970s, it acquired Laboratories Garnier of Paris, and this group became one of L'Oréal's largest divisions. The heart of L'Oréal's strategy was the cosmetic and dermatological research department. The group earmarked 3 percent of its turnover (sales) to the research and development work. Since the 1980s, the group had particularly focused its attention on North America with a series of smart launches, clever acquisitions, and dynamic marketing causing problems for domestic rivals.

Since its establishment, the L'Oréal group had marketed over 500 brands, consisting of more than 2,000 products. It provided products for all sectors of beauty business, such as hair color, permanents, styling aid, body care and skincare, cleansers, and fragrances.[2] Its general cosmetics portfolio contained many of the world's biggest beauty products. It owned numerous brands, including Kerastase, Garnier, Maybelline, Helena Rubenstein, Giorgio Armani, Vichy, and La Roche Posay.

The company believed that diversification and innovation were its critical success factors. L'Oréal's concern for offering products that were adaptable to the demands of its clients showed its passion for innovations. Thus, it invested heavily in research and development and recovered its investment by globally launching its new products. All research was centered in France. As finished products were developed, they were offered to subsidiaries across the world. Because brand life cycles for cosmetics could be very short, L'Oréal tried to introduce one or two new products every year in each of its worldwide markets. L'Oréal marketed products under its own name as well as under a number of other individual and family brand names. For example, it marketed Anaïs Anaïs perfume, the high-end Lancôme line of cosmetics, and L'Oréal brand haircare products.

L'Oréal's strategy was to trickle down technology over time from high-end outlets like department stores to mass markets, such as drugstores. The mass-market brand Plenitude had become the market leader in France, but sales in the United States had not been promising. With innovations and diversifying strategies L'Oréal overcame all these hurdles to an extent. In 2001, the Group, headed by CEO Lindsay Owen-Jones, had a turnover (sales) of €13.7 billion. In 2003, L'Oréal was the world's largest skincare company, with revenues of US$17 billion, and employed 50,000 people.[3]

Product Categories

Since its beginning, the L'Oréal Group had developed products in the field of cosmetics. It had four product categories: consumer, luxury, professional, and active (Exhibit 1). These products catered to the needs of hair, skin, makeup, and so on. The consumer products encompassed all the brands distributed through mass-market channels, ensuring that L'Oréal quality was available to the maximum number of consumers. The consumer division accounted for more than half of the sales in 2003. The luxury division offered a range of prestigious international brands selectively distributed through perfumeries, department stores, and duty-free shops. The professional division, the market leader in its sector, offered specific hair care products for use by professional hairdressers and products sold exclusively through hair salons. The active division created and marketed brands of cosmetics and dermatological products for selective distribution through pharmacies and specialty health and beauty outlets. The major brands in

these divisions were L'Oréal Paris, Biotherm, Giorgio Armani, Lancôme, Shu Uemura, Polo Ralph Lauren Blue, and L'Oréal Professional.

Innovations from the research laboratories and a large number of initiatives ensured growth for the group's core brands. The company achieved major market share in all of its product divisions. The Professional Products Division achieved 8.8 percent growth in the first half of 2003. The division took new initiatives in all business segments, particularly in colorants with the launch of Luo (a new translucid colorant) and Equa (a formula developed specifically for the needs of the Japanese market). The Consumer Products Division achieved 9.3 percent growth for the first half of 2003 over that of the previous year, which was well ahead of the growth rate for mass-market products. This growth could be attributed in particular to the launch of innovative products such as Couleur Experte colorants and Double Extension mascara. The Luxury Products Division, operating in markets that were more sensitive to the economic slowdown and the reduction in air travel, managed to maintain growth of 0.2 percent. This performance came from the success of new products such as the Résolution facial skincare from Lancôme, a brand that at the end of 2002 became the world's number one in the selective retailing channel. In perfumes, the successful European launch of Polo Blue by Ralph Lauren confirmed the excellent results achieved in the United States. The Active Cosmetics Department continued its international rollout, while improving its market shares in Europe. It thus achieved a growth rate of 10.9 percent, in line with the figure for the first half of 2002.

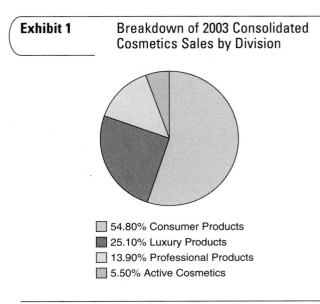

Exhibit 1 — Breakdown of 2003 Consolidated Cosmetics Sales by Division

- 54.80% Consumer Products
- 25.10% Luxury Products
- 13.90% Professional Products
- 5.50% Active Cosmetics

Source: www.loreal.com.

This was boosted especially by the successful Myokine facial skincare from Vichy and the skin redensifier Innéov Fermeté, launched in five European countries, heralding the group's first move into the cosmetic nutritional supplement market. Dermatology achieved sales of €139 million, representing like-for-like growth of 7 percent. Galderma performed well on the acne and rosacea markets. In geographic terms, Galderma continued to achieve sustained growth in North America and made strong advances in Latin America (growth in Brazil was 8 percent and in Mexico 22 percent) and Asia (growth in South Korea was 23 percent).

New Worldwide Markets

L'Oréal was surging in markets from China to Mexico (Exhibit 2). Its secret was conveying the allure of different cultures through its products. Whether it was selling Italian elegance, New York street smarts, or French beauty through its brands, L'Oréal was reaching out to more people across a bigger range of incomes and cultures than just about any other beauty-products company in the world.[4]

The success of L'Oréal cosmetics had been built on the promotion of different brands in different nations, the choice of which was based on views of the local culture. For people interested in finding the most American product possible, the French company used the name Maybelline. Those preferring the most French were given the L'Oréal brand. All the different lines were sold in all of the markets, but only one was excessively promoted, depending on the market.

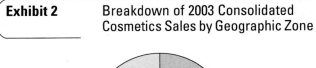

| Exhibit 2 | Breakdown of 2003 Consolidated Cosmetics Sales by Geographic Zone |

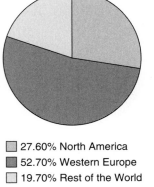

- 27.60% North America
- 52.70% Western Europe
- 19.70% Rest of the World

Source: www.loreal.com.

L'Oréal was number one in the cosmetic industry but competition in the U.S. market as well as international markets such as Japan, China, etc., was growing. In the United States, L'Oréal and Estée Lauder were head to head and Procter & Gamble was slightly behind them. Internationally L'Oréal was facing competition from global as well as local players. Germany's Beiersdorf had stolen a march on L'Oréal by beating it to the market with its Nivea Kao brand of strips used to clean pores. Worldwide, Nivea ranked number one in mass-market face cream, with 11 percent share, slightly ahead of L'Oréal's Plenitude. Procter and Gamble's Oil of Olay skin cream was on par with L'Oréal's Plenitude around the globe.

By tailoring its products to the demands of a specific marketing group with the backing of the international brand name, L'Oréal achieved profitable results for the year 2000, in countries such as Japan (up 46 percent), Korea (70 percent), Brazil (44 percent) and Russia (47 percent) to name but a few. The growth continued in 2003 also. It was very strong in Central and Eastern Europe (up 26.2 percent), particularly in the Russian Federation, where sales advanced once more (up 38.8 percent) after three years of extremely fast growth.

The group made important breakthroughs in the newer markets in 2003. It ventured into the Chinese market, which was crowded with 3,000 domestic cosmetic manufacturers. More than 450 foreign companies had invested in excess of US$300 million in China over the last decade, further stimulating the rapid growth of this sector. L'Oréal, Procter & Gamble, Unilever, and Shiseido ranked among notable international competitors in China. Total sales of cosmetic products in 2000 exceeded RMB30 billion (US$3.66 billion). Since economic reform started 20 years ago, China's cosmetics market had grown an average of 23.8 percent a year from 1982 to 1998. Although this growth slowed down to about 12.9 percent a year after 1998, cosmetic sales in China were expected to reach RMB80 billion (US$9.76 billion) by 2010.[5] L'Oréal wanted to cash in on this opportunity.

Achieving success in the Asian market was a goal for L'Oréal in 2000, an aim the company saw as "internationalization" as opposed to "globalization." Beatrice Dautresme, vice-president in charge of strategic business development, commented, "L'Oréal sees the world as a mosaic of different cultures."[6] In China, where the group's core brands are now fully installed, the growth rate was 69.3 percent, largely thanks to the emblematic success of Maybelline, the country's number one makeup brand. Alongside L'Oréal Paris, which reinforced its luxury brand image, Garnier successfully extended its product offering, particularly in the skincare market. Vichy strengthened its number one position in the 2,500 pharmacies that sold the brand's products across the Russian Federation. In Japan the growth was maintained due to the acquisition of Shu Uemura, cosmetics giant in Japan, and the launch of L'Oréal Paris skincare and makeup lines in Japan, which marked a major advance in establishing the brand in the Japanese market. In India too, growth was extremely rapid at 33.4 percent. This strong performance reflected the breakthroughs achieved by the Garnier brand, which had managed to launch modern colorants that met women's needs at affordable prices. To help fulfill the growth potential in India, the group had started a new factory near the city of Pune (in Western India), which benefited from the most advanced production quality standards.

Changing Strategy

L'Oréal was gradually turning marketing efforts to the ethnic beauty industry, and reaping profits. L'Oréal was working hard to grab a portion of the estimated $14 billion[7] (by 2008) ethnic beauty industry by focusing product lines and marketing on African-American and Asian-American communities. Since 1998, L'Oréal had purchased Soft Sheen and Carson, two black-centered beauty companies, and rolled them into one megacompany. The company had also been busy in acquiring Asian-centered companies, such as Mininurse of China and Shu Uemura of Japan.

L'Oréal had also tuned its research work for developing products specific for the ethnic groups. L'Oréal opened a new research center in Chicago in 2003, to research and study the skin and hair of different ethnic groups. The Institute's first major project was centered on characterizing the chemical and physical properties of African hair. The goal of this research was to better classify hair according to fiber structure so that the performance of hair relaxers currently in the market could be improved. Other projects would investigate skincare problems such as pigment and scarring disorders. Chicago was chosen for a number of reasons. Soft Sheen had long been headquartered in the city; Chicago had historically been a center of black American culture and learning; and there were a number of renowned universities in the area that provided opportunities for synergy with L'Oréal's new research institute. The needs and requirements of consumers of different ethnic origins were different. They had specific skin and haircare needs that required products especially formulated for them. L'Oréal's acquisition of the Soft Sheen–Carson brand, a world leader in skin and haircare for black women, had

greatly expanded the Group's activities in this market sector. Jean-Paul Agon, president and CEO of L'Oréal USA, says about the new research center, "The knowledge and insights that we gain through research conducted at the Institute will ultimately allow us to develop innovative new products that better serve the beauty care needs of the global ethnic market."[8]

As the cosmetic market for women was becoming somewhat saturated, the cosmetic companies shifted their target. The male cosmetic market, a slow burner in beauty, was predicted to take off in the future. The overall market for men's cosmetics grew by 9 percent in 1999, according to NPD Beauty Trends (source: Euro RSCG report).[9] Research showed that men were far more brand loyal in this market than women, mainly because they disliked shopping around.[10] An industry insider commented, "The global male cosmetics market is growing 30 percent annually."[11] L'Oréal had some of the most popular male cosmetics brands in Europe and the United States—including Biotherm Homme, a high-end brand with more than 50 percent market share in Europe. The company began introducing its Biotherm Homme skincare products in China in 2002. The firm had targeted young and fashionable male customers. L'Oréal saw the potential of the cosmetics market for men, although cosmetics for men in 2003 accounted for a very small portion of L'Oréal's sales in China.

In 2003, for the 19th consecutive year, the L'Oréal group showed a double-digit profit growth rate. The net operational profit rose by 13.5 percent to €1.65 billion ($2.1 billion) (Exhibit 3). But its consolidated sales (Exhibit 4) had fallen by 9 percent, mainly due to currency fluctuations. In 2003, L'Oréal battled economic slowdown and adverse currency moves, while war in Iraq forced it to cram product launches into the first and fourth quarters of the year. In 2003, L'Oréal was number one in the United States with a market share of 21.2 percent. Comparatively, its competitors Estée Lauder and Procter & Gamble held market share of 19.6 percent and 13 percent respectively.

In 2004, L'Oréal climbed 10 places to the 20th position in the annual *Financial Times* survey of the "World's Most Respected Companies," compared to the 30th position it held in 2003's ranking. L'Oréal Group CEO Lindsay Owen-Jones also made a very strong impression for his leadership qualities; he was ranked number 16 on the list of the "World's Most Respected Business Leaders," climbing 14 positions in only three years. In the sector rankings, L'Oréal was placed fourth on the list of some of the world's largest consumer goods manufacturers.[12]

Exhibit 3   Ten Years of Consolidated Financial Data of L'Oréal Group

(€ millions)	1994	1995	1996	1997	1998	1998 (1)	1999 (1)(2)	2000 (2)	2001	2002	2003	2004
Results of Operations												
Consolidated sales	7,260	8,136	9,200	10,537	11,498	9,588	10,751	12,671	13,740	14,288	14,029	14,534
Pre-tax profit of consolidated companies	816	897	1,011	1,183	1,339	979	1,125	1,322	1,502	1,698	1,870	2,063
As a percentage of consolidated sales	11.2	11.0	11.0	11.2	11.6	10.2	10.5	10.4	10.9	11.9	13.3	14.2
Income tax	256	285	328	422	488	375	429	488	536	580	629	696
Net operational profit	520	579	644	722	807	722	833	1,033	1,236	1,464	1,661	1,659
As a percentage of consolidated sales	7.3	7.1	7.0	6.9	7.0	7.5	7.7	8.2	9.0	10.2	11.8	11.4
Net operational profit after minority interests	476	515	568	641	719	719	872	1,028	1,229	1,456	1,653	1,656
Total dividend	114	125	144	165	191	191	230	297	365	433	494	554
Balance Sheet												
Fixed assets	3,306	3,550	4,687	5,346	5,590	5,299	5,918	7,605	8,140	8,130	8,136	11,534
Current assets	3,182	3,617	4,048	4,512	4,937	4,229	5,139	6,256	6,724	6,843	6,876	6,645
Of which cash and marketable securities	844	685	810	825	903	762	1,080	1,588	1,954	2,216	1,303	1,981
Shareholders' equity (3)	3,642	3,938	4,429	5,015	5,428	5,123	5,470	6,179	7,210	7,434	8,136	10,564
Borrowings and debts	979	848	1,598	1,767	1,748	1,718	1,914	3,424	2,939	2,646	1,941	2,175
Per Share Data (notes 4 to 6)												
Net operational profit after minority interests per share (7) (8) (9)	0.70	0.76	0.84	0.95	1.06	1.06	1.22	1.52	1.82	2.15	2.45	2.46

Net dividend per share (10) (11)	0.82	0.73	0.64	0.54	0.44	0.34	0.28	0.28	0.24	0.21	0.18	0.17
Tax Credit	–	0.37	0.32	0.27	0.22	0.17	0.14	0.14	0.12	0.11	0.09	0.09
Share price as of December 31 (10)	55.85	65.00	72.55	80.90	91.30	79.65	61.59	61.59	35.90	29.79	18.17	15.09
Weighted average number of shares outstanding	673,547,541	676,021,722	675,990,516	676,062,160	676,062,160	676,062,160	676,062,160	676,062,160	676,062,160	676,062,160	614,601,970	614,601,970

(1) For the purpose of comparability, the figures include:

- in 1998, the pro forma impact of the change in the consolidation method for Synthélabo, following its merger with Sanofi in May 1999,
- the impact in 1998 and 1999 of the application of CRC Regulation no. 99–02 from January 1, 2000 onwards.

This involves the inclusion of all deferred tax liabilities, evaluated using the balance sheet approach and the extended concept, the activation of financial leasing contracts considered to be material, and the reclassification of profit sharing under "Personal costs."

(2) The figures for 1999 and 2000 also include the impact on the balance sheet of adopting the preferential method for the recording of employee retirement obligation and related benefits from January 1st 2001 onwards. However, the new method had no material impact on the profit and loss account of the years concerned.

(3) Plus minority interests.

(4) Including investment certificates issued in 1986 and bonus share issues. Public Exchange Offers were made for investment certificates and voting right certificates on the date of the Annual General Meeting on May 25, 1993 (see Commission des Operations de Bourse information note of June 3, 1993).

The certificates were reconstituted as shares following the Special General Meeting on March 29, 1999 and the Extraordinary General Meeting on June 1, 1999.

(5) Figures restated to reflect the one-for-ten bonus share allocated decided by the Board of Directors as of May 23, 1996.

(6) Ten-for-one share split (Annual General Meeting of May 30, 2000).

(7) Net earnings per share are based on the weighted average number of shares outstanding in accordance with the accounting standards in force

(8) In order to provide data that are genuinely recurrent, L'Oréal calculates and publishes net earnings per share based on net operational profit after minority interests, before allowing for the provision for depreciation of treasury shares, capital gains and losses on fixed assets, restructuring costs, and the amortization of goodwill.

(9) At December 31, 2004, 8.5 million subscription options have been allocated in group executives, and could lead to the issue of the same number of shares.

(10) The L'Oréal share has been listed in euros on the Paris Bourse since January 4, 1999, where it was listed in 1963. The share capital was fixed at €135,212,432 at the Annual General Meeting of June 1, 1999: the par value of one share is now €0.2.

(11) The dividend is fixed in euros since the annual General Meeting of May 30, 2000.

Source: www.loreal-finance.com.

1) Breakdown of consolidated sales by branch

	2003		Growth (as %)		2003		2001	
	€ millions	% of total	Published figures	Excluding exchange effect	€ millions	% of total	€ millions	% of total
Cosmetics	13,704.3	97.7	−1.8	7.1	13,951.8	97.6	13,394.2	97.5
Dermatology	306.5	2.2	−4.5	10.5	321.1	2.3	292.2	2.1
Other	18.3	0.1	21.2	21.2	15.1	0.1	54.0	0.4
Group	14,029.1	100.0	−1.8	7.2	14,288.0	100.0	13,740.4	100.0

Group Share, i.e. 50%

2) Breakdown of consolidated sales by geographic zone

	2003		Growth (as %)		2003		2001	
	€ millions	% of total	Published figures	Excluding exchange effect	€ millions	% of total	€ millions	% of total
Western Europe	7,309.7	52.1	3.8	5.0	7,044.6	49.3	6,667.2	48.5
North America	3,981.4	28.4	−10.3	6.8	4,438.7	31.1	4,450.5	32.4
Rest of the World	2,738.0	19.5	−2.4	14.3	2,804.7	19.6	2,622.7	19.1
Group	14,029.1	100.0	−1.8	7.2	14,288.0	100.0	13,740.4	100.0

3) Breakdown of cosmetics sales by geographic zone

	2003		Growth (as %)		2003		2001	
	€ millions	% of total	Published figures	Excluding exchange effect	€ millions	% of total	€ millions	% of total
Western Europe	7,221.7	52.7	3.7	4.9	6,962.8	49.9	6,580.6	49.1
North America	3,783.7	27.6	−10.4	6.6	4,224.8	30.3	4,256.9	31.8
Rest of the World	2,698.9	19.7	−2.4	14.3	2,764.2	19.8	2,556.7	19.1
Cosmetics branch	13,704.3	100.0	−1.8	7.1	13,951.8	100.0	13,394.2	100.0

Notes

1. "Strong increase in 2003 net operational profit*: +13.5 percent," www.loreal.com, February 20, 2004.
2. "Brands," www.chamberoman.com, 2002.
3. "L'Oréal—World's Largest Skin Care Company—Licenses Tissue-informatics Automated Pathology Slide Screening Software," www.tissueinformatics.com, November 12, 2003.
4. Edmondson, Gail, and Ellen Neuborne, "L'Oréal: The Beauty of Global Branding (int'l edition)," www.businessweek.com, June 28, 1999.
5. "China's Booming Cosmetic Market," www.prorenata.com, February 14, 2002.
6. O'Reilly, Deirdre, "L'Oréal Conquers Asia with Tailored Products," www.archives.tcm.ie, April 22, 2001.
7. "L'Oréal Turns to Black and Asian Communities," www.racerelations.about.com, January 25, 2004.
8. L'Oréal Press, "The Diversity of Beauty," www.loreal.com, August 19, 2003.
9. Lyons, Kate, "Beauty make over," www.bandt.com.au, August 23, 2001.
10. Ibid.
11. Jingjing, Jiang, "Male Cosmetics Consumers Smell Trend's Scent," www.chinadaily.com.cn, March 2, 2004.
12. "L'Oréal Moves Up among World's Most Respected Companies," www.financialtimes.com, January 27, 2004.

MTV Networks International: Localizing Globally

Shirisha Regani

S.S. George

Hema M

"MTV is a global brand which thinks and acts locally. We reflect the taste and demands of our viewers and this differs in each market. Thus the need to create specific channels (in each country) that meet the needs of our target audience."[1]

—*David Flack, Senior Vice President of MTV Asia's Creative and Content Division, in 2003.*

"We came out of the gate intuitively thinking that you have to be local to connect with the audience. That it wasn't only about the language and the music, but sensibility . . . even though the brand can be the same everywhere."[2]

—*Bill Roedy, President of MTV Networks International, in June 2005.*

MTV Networks—Globetrotting

On August 18, 2006, MTV Networks International (MTVI) launched a 24-hour music channel called MTV New Zealand at an event held at Aotea Square in Auckland, New Zealand. The event also marked the re-launch of Nickelodeon[3] in a localized format in New Zealand. Both the channels were to be available on Sky Television.[4] The localized MTV New Zealand channel (which was expected to reach an estimated 650,000 homes) was to be a platform for musicians from the country to showcase their talent.[5]

MTVI, launched in 1987 in Europe, was the international arm of MTV Networks (MTVN), the largest media network in the world. MTVI, which included MTVN's core channel MTV and its sister channels outside the US, was growing at a rate of 20% annually, as of mid-2006. It was also the first international television network to broadcast channels in local languages with localized content in various countries around the world.[6]

In the 1990s, MTVI realized that to be successful globally, it had to adopt a 'region-centric' approach. Therefore, the network began operating localized versions of its channels in addition to acquiring local channels in many regions.

As of mid-2006, MTVI catered to an audience of more than one billion, and had a presence in 179 countries across Europe, Asia, Latin America, and Australia.[7] Apart from its flagship channel MTV, it had a number of other

---

[1] Kenny Santana, "MTV Goes to Asia," www.yaleglobal.yale.edu, August 12, 2003 (Accessed on September 23, 2006)

[2] Greg Lindsay, "Viacom 2.0," *Fortune*, June 23, 2005.

[3] Nickelodeon, a part of MTVN, is a children's entertainment channel. Before the re-launch as a fully customized channel in New Zealand, the Asian version was aired on SKY Channel 42.

[4] Sky Television is New Zealand's leading Pay TV operator, offering sports, movies, and general content in more than 80 channels across the country.

[5] David Eames, "MTV Promises Wealth of NZ Music," *The New Zealand Herald*, August 19, 2006.

[6] Dirk Smillie, "Tuning in First Global TV Generation," *The Christian Science Monitor*, June 4, 1997.

[7] www.viacom.com/cable.jhtml (Accessed on October 3, 2006)

channels in its portfolio. The network operated around 130 channels in more than 25 languages worldwide. In addition, it operated some broadband services and more than 130 websites.[8]

Background

MTV (short for Music Television), the first ever cable music channel, was launched on August 1, 1981, by Warner Amex Satellite Entertainment Company, a joint venture between Warner Communications and American Express. Its launch was said to have marked the beginning of the cable TV revolution. In 1984, the company was renamed MTV Networks (MTVN).

From the time of its launch, MTV's target audience had typically been people in the 12 to 24 age group. However, to cater to the other age groups, MTVN launched several new channels over the years. As MTV aired a lot of heavy-metal and rap music, another channel VH1 (short for video hits one) was formed in 1985 to play light popular music, Rhythm and Blues (R&B), jazz, country music, and classics aimed at the 18 to 35 age group.

From the beginning, MTV encouraged emerging musical talent. Little known musicians became popular after their songs were aired on MTV. Over the years, MTV was credited with the success of many musicians and groups, like Madonna, Michael Jackson, Van Halen, The Police, Def Leppard, and Nirvana. Many artistes also created music videos especially for MTV. The channel also offered exclusive on-air time to popular artistes by staging 'acoustic concerts' in its show 'MTV Unplugged'.

In 1986, MTVN was acquired by Viacom Inc. (Viacom) (Refer to Exhibit 1 for a note on Viacom Inc.). MTVN embarked on its international expansion by launching its first overseas channel in Europe in 1987. Soon after, it established MTVI, to manage all its overseas channels, which included MTV, VH1, and Nickelodeon.

Exhibit 1	A Note on Viacom Inc.

Viacom was established as a public company in 1971. In 1985, it acquired a 65% stake in MTV Networks, which included MTV, VH1 and Nickelodeon, and purchased the remaining interest in 1986. In 1991, Viacom completed its purchase of MTV Europe by acquiring a 50% stake from British Telecommunications and other parties. In 1994, the Viacom Entertainment Group was formed through a merger with Paramount Communications Inc. In 2000, CBS Corporation, a major media network in the US, merged with Viacom, as a result of which TNN (re-named as Spike TV in 2003) and CMT (Country Music Television) joined the MTV Networks. The BET (Black Entertainment Television) channel was acquired by Viacom in 2001. In the early 2000s, Viacom launched many channels worldwide under MTV Networks and BET.

In 2005, Viacom Corporation split into Viacom Inc. and CBS Corporation. In 2006, Viacom Inc. was one of the world's leading media companies operating in the Cable and Satellite Television Networks (C&S) and film production divisions.

Viacom Inc. Brands*
Cable Networks & Digital Media

- MTV Networks (Comedy Central, CMT, LOGO, MTV, MTV 2, MTV U, MTV Networks Digital Suite, **MTV International**, MTV Networks online, Nickelodeon, Nick @ Nite, The N, Noggin, Spike, TV Land, VH1)
- BET Networks

Entertainment (Film & Music Publishing)
- Paramount Pictures
- Paramount Home Entertainment
- DreamWorks SKG
- Famous Music

---

* The list is not exhaustive
Source: www.viacom.com

---

[8] MTVI operated more than 130 websites of its international channels while MTVN, totally, operated more than 150 websites, which included online representations of channels broadcast in the US.

In the 1990s, MTVN launched other new channels like VH1 Classic, MTV 2, MTV U, MTV Hits, etc. to cater to specific demographics (Some of these channels were also launched worldwide by MTVI). Despite its audience comprising various age groups,[9] MTVN primarily targeted the 12–24 age group as MTV had been considered a youth brand right from the beginning.

While the other MTVN-owned channels played different types of music, the core channel, MTV, began playing less music and started airing programs, some of which were based on unusual concepts. The early 1990s saw the launch of one of the first TV reality shows, 'The Real World'. Another show 'MTV Fear' was launched in 2000. Animated cartoon series were also introduced, the most popular of them being 'Beavis and Butthead'.

In the early 2000s, popular reality shows like 'The Osbournes' and 'The Newly Weds' were produced by MTVN to be aired on MTV and some of its sister channels. A few of these programs were also aired over some of the international channels but they met with limited success.

In 2004, MTVN launched MTV World, specifically aimed at the English-speaking Asian community in the US. The channels MTV Desi, MTV Chi, and MTV K were launched for people from South-Asia (especially India, Pakistan, and Bangladesh), China, and Korea respectively, who resided in the US.

Over the years, MTVN became Viacom's core network, bringing in most of the company's revenues. In the US alone, it reached 87.6 million homes.[10] In 2005, Viacom's total revenues (including cable network and entertainment divisions) were $9.6 billion[11] of which the revenues of the cable network channels (which included MTVN) was $6.8 billion.[12] In mid-2006, MTVN accounted for about 85% of Viacom's operating profits.[13]

MTV Network's International Expansion

When MTVI was formed in 1987, the executives at Viacom reportedly believed that anything that worked in the US would work anywhere in the world. Consequently, MTVI began by airing programs similar to those broadcast in the US. However, it soon realized that the audience in various regions preferred localized content, which included music videos and shows by performers from those regions.

MTVI adopted the policy of 'Think Globally, Act Locally', in the mid-1990s and began to launch separate channels in its different regions. Although many programs were adapted from American originals, the channels were presented in a localized format. MTVI tried to establish MTV as a 'global brand' with a 'local outlook'.

MTVI built its base outside the US by not only launching the MTV channel but also by acquiring local music channels. It followed the practice of tying up with a local company for the initial launch and acquiring the channel from the company after some time. For example, in the early 2000s, Viacom acquired MTV Australia, which had initially been set up as a joint venture between Austereo (a national commercial radio network in the country) and MTVN (All the international networks under MTVI were considered direct subsidiaries of Viacom and came under the purview of MTVN).

MTVI's success was also attributed to the growth in the number of people in its target age groups. In the early 2000s, the global population in that age group was estimated to be around 2.7 billion.[14] The purchasing power of this age group was also growing. This led to advertisers choosing MTVI to promote their products at the international level.

Initially, analysts were skeptical about whether MTVI would succeed internationally because of latent and overt anti-American sentiments in some parts of the world. However, the channel did not face too many difficulties. Commenting on this, Bill Roedy (Roedy), President of MTVI, said, "We've had very little resistance once we explain that we're not in the business of exporting American culture."[15] According to some analysts, Roedy was instrumental in taking MTVI across many countries worldwide. To gain an entry into difficult markets like China, Israel, and Cuba, Roedy even met the political leaders of those countries to explain the network's initiatives to them.

Though MTVI experienced some initial hiccups in terms of adapting to local preferences, it spread rapidly to 179 countries, and was launched in about 25 languages (Refer to Exhibit 2 for the channels under MTVI). MTVI comprised MTV Networks Europe (MTVN Europe), MTV Networks Asia-Pacific (MTVN Asia-Pacific), and MTV Networks Latin America (MTVN Latin America).

---

[9] The age-group of MTVN's target audience depended on the channels and their program content. The various channels of MTVN targeted the 12–24, 18–34, and the 18–49 age groups.

[10] "MTV to Launch Music TV Channels in Three Baltic States," www.eubusiness.com, March 6, 2006. (Accessed on September 26, 2006)

[11] Dollars ($) refers to US dollars in this case study

[12] "Viacom Fact Sheet," www.viacom.com (Accessed on October 3, 2006)

[13] Dominic Rushe, "MTV Struggles To Keep the Attention of Young Audience," *The Sunday Times*, August 20, 2006.

[14] Kerry Capell, Catherine Belton, Tom Lowry, Manjeet Kripalani, Brian Bremner, and Dexter Roberts, "MTV's World," *BusinessWeek*, February 18, 2002.

[15] Kerry Capell, Catherine Belton, Tom Lowry, Manjeet Kripalani, Brian Bremner, and Dexter Roberts, "MTV's World," *BusinessWeek*, February 18, 2002.

Exhibit 2   Channels under MTVI

Channel Name	Description	Countries
MTV	Launched as a 24-hour music channel in the US, MTV spread all over the world with exclusive MTV channels for various regions.	Viewed in Asia, Australia, New Zealand, Latin America, parts of Africa, and about 50 countries in Europe.
Nickelodeon	Children's entertainment channel.	Viewed in Asia, Australia, New Zealand, Latin America, and about 20 countries in Europe.
VH1	Plays music videos, programs on artists, pop culture, series, and live events. The channel was launched as an alternative to MTV.	Brazil and other parts of Latin America, India, Indonesia, Thailand, The Middle-East, North Africa, Australia, and in more than 30 countries in Europe.
TMF (The Music Factory)	Launched as a music and lifestyle channel in Holland in 1995, and was acquired by MTVN in 2002. TMF had three channels under MTVN Europe: TMF NL, TMF UK and TMF Vlaanderen.	Holland, the United Kingdom and Belgium.
Paramount Comedy	Launched in 1995, the channel brought popular American shows to UK. The Spanish version was launched in 1992.	The United Kingdom, Spain and Italy.
VIVA	Originally, launched in 1993 as a German pop channel, it was acquired by MTVN in 2004. Another channel VIVA Plus was launched in 1995.	Austria, Germany, Hungary, Poland and Switzerland
The Box	An urban music TV channel	Holland
FLUX	A mobile entertainment subscription-based service	Japan and Italy
Game One	An interactive game channel	France and Israel

Note: This list is not exhaustive
Source: Compiled from various sources

MTV Networks Europe

MTVN Europe was formed in 1987 when the MTV Europe channel (MTV's European version) was launched. In the mid-1990s, MTV Europe, a single channel aired throughout the continent, faced stiff competition from local channels in countries like Germany, Denmark, and the United Kingdom, which provided regional programs in local languages. In a bid to counter the competition, MTVN Europe began offering versions of its channels in local languages throughout Europe. By the early 2000s, MTV Europe had reached about 100 million homes across the continent.

MTVN Europe launched MTV Italia as a separate channel in 1997. MTV Italia became one of MTVI's biggest channels in terms of advertisement revenues and reach. Reportedly, MTV Italia's popularity among the youth was due to the fact that earlier, there had been only one Italian channel that played music and that too only for a few hours every day.[16]

MTV Europe played some of the best and most popular music videos through the night, a programming practice later adopted by MTV Italia. Apart from music programs, MTV Italia also aired lifestyle shows like 'MTV Kitchen,' 'Loveline,' and 'Stylissimo'. In the early 2000s, three more channels were launched in the country— MTV Hits Italia, which played hit music and classics, MTV Brand New, a channel that played the latest music, and MTV Flux, which delivered video programming and music through mobile phones.

MTV Europe was aired in Russia in 1993, but MTV Russia was launched as a separate channel only in 1998.

[16] Kerry Capell, Stephanie Savariaud, "How MTV Conquered Italy," *BusinessWeek*, February 18, 2002.

It was the first international channel to have been customized for the Russian audience. On March 5, 2006, MTVN Europe announced the launch of three new channels—MTV Eesti, MTV Latvijas, and MTV Lietuva—in the Baltic states of Estonia, Latvia, and Lithuania, respectively. Vilnius, the capital of Lithuania, was the broadcasting center for all the three channels.[17] In the same year, MTVN Europe also announced plans for a new channel in Ukraine. The other core MTV channels in Europe were MTV Polska (Poland), MTV Adria, MTV Espana (Spanish), and MTV Holland.

In 2004, MTVI acquired the German pop music channel VIVA, which had been one of MTVN Europe's biggest competitors in Europe in the 1990s. Later, regional versions of VIVA were aired in Germany, Austria, Poland, and Switzerland. Although some critics averred that MTVI was trying to monopolize the music channel market, such acquisitions were instrumental in MTVI's success in Europe.

Some of the channels launched by MTVN Europe were specific to a particular country, while others were aired in two or more countries. For example, MTV Europe was aired in countries like Norway, Denmark Sweden, Finland, Hungary, Belgium, etc., while countries like Spain and Switzerland had their own versions of MTV channels.

MTVN Europe was present in 48 countries in Europe and Africa in 2006. The channels that were broadcast under this network were MTV, MTV 2, MTV Base VH1, VH1 Classic, Nickelodeon, MTV Hits, and TMF. Twelve countries had their own versions of MTV, MTV Adria was aired in five countries, and MTV Europe was aired in the remaining countries. These were the localized versions of the original MTV. European versions of Nickelodeon, VH1, VH1 Classic, MTV 2, and TMF were aired in about 20 countries. Some of these were localized versions pertaining to specific regions. For example, Nickelodeon was aired as Nickelodeon Germany, Nickelodeon UK, etc.

MTV Networks Latin America

MTV Latin America was launched in 1993 to air MTV in Mexico, Venezuela, Argentina, and other Latin American countries. The channel broadcast programs in Spanish and played Spanish and international music videos. The channel was owned by MTVN Latin America, a subsidiary of MTVN headquartered in Miami in Florida, USA.

MTV Brasil, the Brazilian version of MTV, was launched in 1990, as a wholly owned subsidiary of Abril,

Brazil's largest publisher of books and magazines. The channel, which aired programs in Portuguese, operated as a separate entity. In 1996, MTVN acquired 50% of MTV Brasil from Abril. However, in 2005, Abril acquired 20% back from MTVN as, according to Brazilian regulatory requirements, non-Brazilian companies could own only up to 30% of a terrestrial network. As of 2005, MTVN Latin America held 30% in MTV Brasil through its Brazilian subsidiary, Viacom Networks Brasil.

MTV Networks Asia-Pacific

MTVN Asia-Pacific consisted of MTV's Asian and Australian operations. It was established in 1994 with its headquarters in Singapore. The three MTVN branded channels that were available through this subsidiary were MTV, Nickelodeon, and VH1. Each of the three channels had their localized versions in many countries in the region. By 2006, MTVN Asia-Pacific was airing about 20 channels, which included regionalized versions of MTV, VH1, and Nickelodeon.

MTV Australia

MTV Australia was one of MTVI's earliest channels and was launched in 1987. Initially, it was launched as a program produced by Viacom on Nine Network, a free-to-air channel. In 1993, Nine Network discontinued the program after it decided not to renew its contract with Viacom because of high licensing costs. In 1996, MTV re-entered Australia by forming a joint venture with Austereo. In the early 2000s, it moved out of the joint venture to become a wholly owned subsidiary of MTV International.

The program content on MTV Australia was localized only in 2005. Until then, the channel sourced its programs from the US and Europe. Programs like 'Pimp My Ride,' 'Laguna Beach,' and 'Room Raiders,' which were popular in the US, were aired on MTV Australia. Because of this, in the first few years of its launch, the channel was criticized for broadcasting American programs. However, MTV Australia also adapted programs from other regions in addition to those from the US. 'MTV Most Wanted', a request show adapted from MTV Asia, became MTV Australia's most popular show, garnering a sizeable audience.

In 2005, MTV Most Wanted was replaced by Total Request Live (TRL),[18] a popular program on MTV America. The TRL show was so popular that MTV UK had introduced its own version of it in 2003. MTV Australia

---

17 "MTV to Launch Music TV Channels in Three Baltic States," www.eubusiness.com, March 6, 2006. (Accessed on September 26, 2006)
18 TRL was produced on a large yacht, called the 'MTV Cruiser'. The show featured local and international celebrities, and popular bands who performed in front of a studio audience, the 'studio' here being the yacht.

adopted the MTV UK version. In 2005, MTV Networks Australia, which included MTV Australia and the VH1 channels, was established.

MTV Asia

MTVI entered Asia in the early 1990s partnering with STAR TV.[19] However, the initial launch was not successful and the alliance broke up over disputes regarding channel content. While STAR TV wanted to broadcast more local content, MTVI wanted to stick to its international programs. MTVI then wound up operations in Asia. It re-entered the region in 1995 and after its re-launch, it changed its strategy of broadcasting only international programs, as Asia was a diverse region with many languages.

For its re-entry in 1995, MTVI tied up with PolyGram NV[20] to launch an exclusive Mandarin[21] channel for Taiwan. Another channel called MTV Asia was launched in English for India and a few other countries. According to MTV officials, Asian youth preferred songs and videos from their own regions. Also, Asia was considered to be one of the biggest youth markets for music. Analysts felt that MTVI's move to localize channel content would reap long-term benefits for the network.

Initially, MTV Asia was a single channel across India, China, Japan, Indonesia, Malaysia, and other Asian countries. However, keeping in mind viewer preferences, the network began beaming localized content for specific regions from the late 1990s. These channels aired shows hosted by Video Jockeys (VJs) from those regions. Some programs were also hosted by a digitally animated virtual VJ called LiLi. These programs were aired in six countries with LiLi speaking in five Asian languages.[22]

In the late 1990s, MTV Asia was split into regional channels like MTV India, MTV China, MTV Taiwan, MTV Japan, etc. In 2001–02, MTVI, which had been broadcasting a single channel to most South Asian countries, launched new sub-divisions of MTV in Indonesia, the Philippines, and Thailand. Commenting on this, Frank Brown, president of MTVN Asia, said, "It's very important that what we're going to market in each country fits with the local culture."[23]

In November 2006, MTVI launched MTV in Pakistan. It was the 57th MTV channel to be launched worldwide.

MTV India

MTVI entered India in the early 1990s in a tie-up with STAR TV but exited the country in 1994 after differences erupted between the partners in the tie-up. By the time it re-entered India in 1995, STAR TV had launched Channel [V], a 24-hour music channel, which was available in many parts of South-Asia. Channel [V] became very popular, especially in India, because it aired programs in Hindi, and played songs from Bollywood films.[24]

On its re-entry, MTV Asia tied up with India's national television service Doordarshan (DD). Initially, MTV Asia was aired for two hours every day on DD Metro, one of the channels of DD, before becoming a 24-hour channel. MTV India was later launched as a separate channel in 1996.

Taking its cue from Channel [V], MTV India began broadcasting Hindi film songs. Officials at MTV Asia were confident that the channel would become successful in India. MTV Asia's President Peter Jamieson said, "No other channel in the world has the image or connection to young people that we have."[25]

By the late 1990s, MTV India had launched a variety of programs with India-specific content. Most of the programs were film based and were targeted at the youth. The VJs, many of whom were picked through VJ hunts conducted across the country, became very popular. Some 'Indianized' programs like MTV Bakra (a reality prank show), 'Fully Faltoo' (a spoof show on Hindi films and songs), and MTV Roadies (based on the US reality show 'Road Rules') also gained popularity. "Everyone who has a TV knows there's something called MTV," said one college student from Mumbai.[26]

MTV India also co-sponsored many music events and also began merchandising products like clothes and perfumes under the MTV banner in 2001.

Though the programming format of MTV India was more or less similar to that of MTV in America, the content was localized to suit the preferences of Indian viewers. By 2004, MTV India had become the leading Indian music channel in terms of advertising revenues, with a 35% market share.[27] MTV Asia also launched VH1 and Nickelodeon in a localized format in India.

---

[19] STAR TV was set up in 1990 by Hutchinson Whampoa and commenced broadcast in 1991. It was initially launched with five TV channels—Star Plus, Prime Sports, BBC World Service TV, Star Chinese Channel, and MTV Asia. In 1993, Rupert Murdoch's News Corporation purchased 63.6% of STAR TV and the remaining in 1995.

[20] PolyGram NV produced, marketed, and distributed recorded music. The company also produced films and was involved in music publishing.

[21] Mandarin is a Chinese dialect spoken in Northern and South Western China. Standard Mandarin is the official spoken language in the People's Republic of China, Taiwan, and Singapore.

[22] Kerry Capell, Catherine Belton, Tom Lowry, Manjeet Kripalani, Brian Bremner, and Dexter Roberts, "MTV's World," *BusinessWeek*, February 18, 2002.

[23] Kenny Santana, "MTV Goes to Asia," www.yaleglobal.yale.edu, August 12, 2003. (Accessed on September 23, 2006)

[24] Bollywood refers to the Hindi film industry in India. Bollywood films have a huge following not only in the Indian sub-continent but also in the Middle-East and South-East Asia.

[25] Alexandra A. Seno, "And the Beat Goes On," *Asiaweek*, November 8, 1996.

[26] Kerry Capell, Catherine Belton, Tom Lowry, Manjeet Kripalani, Brian Bremner, and Dexter Roberts, "MTV's World," *BusinessWeek*, February 18, 2002.

[27] Nithya Subramanian "Channel [V] to extend brand to merchandise," *The Hindu Business Line*, June 21, 2004.

MTV China

According to MTVI executives, China was one of the toughest markets for the network because of the government's stringent control over the media. Television programming too was controlled by the state. In the late 1990s, MTV had been made available in hotels as a 24-hour channel, and MTV programs were aired for a few hours every day over some terrestrial and cable channels in Guangdong, one of China's wealthiest provinces. However, it took MTVN executives six years to convince Chinese authorities to allow them to broadcast their channels independently. According to analysts, Chinese parents were also restrictive when it came to the choice of TV programs for their children, as they felt that some American programs were unsuitable for children.[28]

However, MTVI began making inroads into the Chinese market with the launch of MTV China and Nickelodeon in the early 2000s. In 2005, MTVN became the first global brand to launch a 24-hour channel in China. Nickelodeon was also launched subsequently.

MTV Japan

MTV Japan was formed in 2001 as a joint venture between MTVN and a private equity firm H&Q Asia Pacific (H&QAP). MTVI also operated Nickelodeon in the country. In 2005, MTVN launched Flux in Japan, which delivered video programming and music through mobile phones (MTVI later adapted the programming content of Flux for use in other countries like Italy). The reason for launching the service in Japan was that the country was a leader in the digital media market.

Subsequently, in 2006, MTVI launched localized versions of Flux in the UK and Italy. In August 2006, MTV Networks announced that it would acquire the remaining stake in MTV Japan from H&QAP. This marked MTVN's largest acquisition in the Asia-Pacific region.

Commenting on the acquisition, the Chairperson and CEO of MTVN, Judy McGrath said, "Through our global network of 130 channels and more than 150 digital media properties, we are uniquely positioned to share innovation throughout our worldwide operations. We will continue to look to Japan as a center of influence that will inform our global digital media strategies."[29]

Other Localization Moves

MTVI, like MTVN, was known for providing a platform for new musicians. Many musicians, who were unknown outside their regions earlier, became global names after having been featured on MTV and its sister channels. For example, Shakira, a Columbian singer, went on to win the Grammy[30] and Latin Grammy[31] awards after she was featured on MTV Unplugged. This established her as one of the leading singers on music charts all over the world. Other singers and music groups like Adnan Sami (Pakistan and India), The Colonial Cousins (India), and t.A.T.u (Russia) became popular after their music videos were aired on MTV.[32]

MTVI also tried airing some programs from the American networks on its channels. However, these programs met with limited success, either because the viewers did not understand the content or because some programs were unacceptable in some countries. For example, MTV Grind, an American show on the annual spring break (a week-long vacation from studies in the early spring in universities and schools in the US and some other countries) was considered unsuitable to Indian culture and had to be removed from MTV India's program list.

However, in February 2002, MTVN produced a show called 'Be Heard,' in which US Secretary of State Colin Powell spoke to a live teenage audience on issues like terrorism, global peace, AIDS, etc. This program was aired on about 33 MTV channels worldwide and was watched by an estimated 375 million households.[33] It was considered to be a landmark program as it reinforced MTVN's international presence.

In 2005, MTVN launched its 100th channel with the airing of MTV Base Africa. MTV Base was a UK-based channel, which was launched in 1999. MTV Base played Hip-Hop music, and MTVI expected to cash in on the growing number of pop-music followers in Africa by launching it in Africa. The channel was operated by MTV Networks Europe.

Apart from localizing the entertainment content, MTVI also ensured that the programming on its channels was sensitive to the traditions and culture of the country in which it operated. For example, in Indonesia, calls for prayer were aired on MTV every day.

In the mid-1980s, MTVN launched the MTV 'Video Music Awards' (VMA), which was touted to be an

[28] David Baroza, "Nickelodeon's Cultural Revolution Reaches China," *The San Diego-Union Tribune,* December 29, 2005.

[29] "Viacom's MTV Networks Reaches Agreement to Take Full Ownership of MTV Japan From Joint Venture Partner H&Q Asia Pacific," www.marketwatch.com, August 29, 2006. (Accessed on October 3, 2006)

[30] The 'Grammy' is a major music awards show held in the US every year. The awards are presented to outstanding performances in the recording industry.

[31] Latin Grammy Awards was launched in 2000 to award achievements in the Latin music industry.

[32] Kerry Capell, Catherine Belton, Tom Lowry, Manjeet Kripalani, Brian Bremner, and Dexter Roberts, "MTV's World," *BusinessWeek,* February 18, 2002.

[33] Kerry Capell, Catherine Belton, Tom Lowry, Manjeet Kripalani, Brian Bremner, and Dexter Roberts, "MTV's World," *BusinessWeek,* February 18, 2002.

alternative to the Grammy awards. The awards show was broadcast live on MTV. As the network began expanding internationally, MTVI introduced versions of the VMA in Europe, Latin America, Asia, and Africa. By the 2000s, MTVI had about 20 locally produced award shows, which included separate shows for music, style, video music, and movies.

To encourage creativity in its international channel operations, MTVI adopted the policy of '70% local content,' which also increased the popularity of the channels. For example, shows like "Twelve Angry Viewers" of MTV Russia and "Rockgol" aired on MTV Brasil were locally produced.

Reportedly, MTVI rarely interfered in the operations of its local channels. According to analysts, this policy of providing creative and commercial autonomy helped in innovation and rapid expansion of its regional channels. MTVI's structure was also decentralized to give the local staff complete control over operations. Commenting on this, Roedy said, "Something we decided early on was to not export just one product for the world but to generate a very different experience for our brands depending on the local cultures."[34]

Outlook

According to some analysts, the biggest advantage that MTVI had over its competitors was that it was one of the early entrants on the international music scene. Therefore MTVN was able to make inroads into international markets before other networks. After MTVI was launched, several regional music channels began sprouting up in many countries. Though this increased MTVI's competition internationally, it also provided the network with a means to understand audience needs and change its programming content accordingly.

However, MTVN had its share of challenges, globally. For one thing, despite being a global player with a vast network, it was unable to enjoy significant economies of scale. To become successful across regions, MTVI had launched many localized channels that were managed by local staff. Also, the global operations contributed only about 20% of MTVN's total revenues. The concept of 'pay-channels' was in its early stages in many regions in Asia, and in some countries, MTV was aired as a program on free-to-air channels, leading to low subscription revenues.

Another problem was that, owing to the growth of the Internet and the availability of online video-sharing websites like 'YouTube'[35] and 'MySpace,'[36] people in MTVN's target age group were spending less time watching television. To counter this challenge, MTVN began sprucing up its online content by launching 'Overdrive,' a broadband Internet video-on-demand service to provide video streams. MTVN provided live videos of its shows through this service.

By 2006, MTVN had more than 150 websites, some broadband services, and more than 25 mobile services. According to the network, these online services were very well received. Officials at MTVN were also optimistic about the changes in audience preferences. According to them, MTVI had built a strong base across countries through its localization policies, and the emergence of digital television and the Internet provided an opportunity to extend their reach to the international audience. Commenting on this, Michiel Bakker, Managing Director of MTV- UK and Ireland, said, "The decline of television hasn't happened. People SMS (text), surf the net, and message each other while they are watching television. The two are happy to coexist."[37]

On August 1, 2006, MTV (the core channel) completed 25 years of broadcasting. Some critics were of the view that MTVN had lost some of its sheen because of MTV's shift to non-music programs, and the emergence of other channels and the Internet. They also said that MTV was struggling to retain its 'youthful' outlook. Though MTVN had pioneered the music television industry, the rise in competition from both television and online channels had become a serious challenge over the years. Critics averred that the popularity of the MTV brand was fading globally, and added that the network would have to make sure that it continued to innovate to stay ahead of the competition.

References and Suggested Readings

1. Alexandra A. Seno, **"And the Beat Goes On,"** *Asiaweek*, November 8, 1996.
2. Dirk Smillie, **"Tuning In First Global TV Generation,"** *The Christian Science Monitor*, June 4, 1997.
3. Bruce Einhorn, **"MTV Cranks Up the Volume in Asia,"** *BusinessWeek*, June 23, 1997.
4. **"Marketing in Latin America,"** *BusinessWeek*, February 9, 1998.
5. Brian Bennett, **"101 Pixels of Fun,"** *Time*, June 4, 2001.
6. **"Localization begins to pay off for MTV Europe,"** www.kagan.com, June 10, 2001. (Accessed on September 4, 2006)

---

[34] Brad Nemer, "How MTV Channels Innovation," *BusinessWeek*, November 6, 2006.

[35] YouTube, which is based in San Mateo, California, USA, is a website that allows users to upload and share videos that include TV clips, movies and music videos. It was founded in February 2005. In October 2006, it was acquired by Google for $1.65 billion.

[36] MYSpace, based in Santa Monica, California, USA, is a website that allows users to submit personal profiles, photos, blogs, music, and video clips, and form an online social network. It was founded in July 2003 and was acquired by News Corporation in July 2005.

[37] Dominic Rushe, "MTV Struggles To Keep the Attention of Young Audience," *The Sunday Times*, August 20, 2006.

7. Kerry Capell, Catherine Belton, Tom Lowry, Manjeet Kripalani, Brian Bremner, and Dexter Roberts, **"MTV's World,"** *BusinessWeek,* February 18, 2002.

8. Kerry Capell, Stephanie Savariaud, **"How MTV Conquered Italy,"** *BusinessWeek,* February 18, 2002.

9. Kenny Santana, **"MTV Goes to Asia,"** www.yaleglobal.yale.edu, August 12, 2003. (Accessed on September 23, 2006)

10. Nithya Subramanian **"Channel [V] to extend brand to merchandise,"** *The Hindu Business Line,* June 21, 2004.

11. Johnnie L. Roberts, **"World Tour,"** *Newsweek,* June 1, 2005.

12. Greg Lindsay, **"Viacom 2.0,"** *Fortune,* June 23, 2005.

13. George Szalai, **"Cultural Exchange,"** *The Hollywood Reporter,* October 25, 2005.

14. David Baroza, **"Nickelodeon's Cultural Revolution Reaches China,"** *The San Diego-Union Tribune,* December 29, 2005.

15. Tom Lowry, **"Can MTV Stay Cool?"** *BusinessWeek,* February 20, 2006.

16. **"MTV to Launch Music TV Channels in Three Baltic States,"** www.eubusiness.com, March 6, 2006. (Accessed on September 26, 2006)

17. **"Viacom Fact Sheet,"** www.viacom.com (Accessed on October 3, 2006)

18. Louis Hau, **"Is MTV ageing well?"** www.forbes.com, July 27, 2006.

19. Dominic Rushe, **"MTV Struggles To Keep the Attention of Young Audience,"** *The Sunday Times,* August 20, 2006.

20. David Eames, **"MTV Promises Wealth of NZ Music,"** *The New Zealand Herald,* August 19, 2006.

21. **"Viacom's MTV Networks Reaches Agreement to Take Full Ownership of MTV Japan From Joint Venture Partner H&Q Asia Pacific,"** www.marketwatch.com, August 29, 2006. (Accessed on October 3, 2006)

22. Brad Nemer, **"How MTV Channels Innovation,"** *BusinessWeek,* November 6, 2006.

23. www.viacom.com

24. www.mtv.com/international

25. www.mtv-media.com

The Nintendo Wii:
A 'Revolution' in Gaming?

S.S. George

Namratha V. Prasad

Sachin Govind

"Our competitors are both going down the same path. Both believe that more and more performance with a higher and higher price tag are their keys to success. So what do I see? I think our two competitors will trade share between them, while we go off and grab share in a completely different way."[1]

—*Reginald Fils-Aime, President and Chief Operating Officer, Nintendo of America, in 2006.*

"By letting Sony and Microsoft split the hardcore teenage/twenty-something video game marketplace, the Wii could end up number one in market share for the next generation."[2]

—*David Cole, Game analyst at San Diego-based DFC Intelligence,[3] in 2006.*

"If it's just the same pointing and shooting all the time, it won't be particularly attractive."[4]

—*Hiroshi Kamide, analyst, KBC Securities,[5] commenting on the Wii, in 2006.*

Introduction

On November 19, 2006, Nintendo Co. Ltd (Nintendo), a Japan-based game console manufacturer, launched the Wii, a video game console which came with a unique wireless controller called Wii Remote, in the US. The Wii made its debut in a highly charged gaming market. Sony had launched the Playstation 3 (PS3), a game console with a Blu-ray[6] player, on November 17, 2006 in the US; Microsoft's game console, the Xbox 360, had been launched in November 2005 and had sold around five million units by June 2006.

Nintendo, which started out as a manufacturer of playing cards in Japan, had gradually shifted to making toys and video games. It was in the 1980s that it launched its first game console, the Nintendo Entertainment System (NES), which went on to become a huge success. The NES was followed by the Super Nintendo Entertainment System (SNES) in 1991, the Nintendo 64 in 1996, and the GameCube in 2001. However, in the early 2000s, Nintendo's fortunes in the game console

---

[1] "Nintendo hopes Wii spells wiinner," www.usatoday.com, August 15, 2006.

[2] "Can Nintendo's Wii end up number one in market share?" www.macdailynews.com, July 18, 2006.

[3] DFC Intelligence is a strategic market research and consulting firm. It publishes in-depth strategic market reports and offers subscription-based research services for companies in the video game, online game, interactive entertainment and interactive television (ITV) market.

[4] "Analysts: Success of Nintendo's Wii hinges on games, not hardware," www.foxnews.com, October 12, 2006.

[5] KBC Securities, created in 1989 is the integrated European Equity House of KBC Group. It had industry expertise in the field of Equity Capital Markets, Mergers & Acquisitions and advisory services.

[6] Blu-ray is the name of next generation optical disc format. It enables playback, recording and rewriting of high definition video. (Source: www.blu-ray.com)

---

market saw a gradual decline. The sales of Sony Playstation 2 and Microsoft Xbox far outpaced that of the Nintendo GameCube. With Nintendo's market share falling, industry observers expected it to exit the game console industry.

Nintendo, however, had other plans. In 2004, it announced that it had begun work on developing a new console. A few months into the development, Nintendo realized that the continuous technological upgradation in each succeeding generation of consoles was increasing hardware costs but discouraging innovation[7] in the games industry. Therefore, it chose to tread a different path. It decided to develop a console that would offer gamers unique gameplay,[8] even though it would not have the latest processor or graphics. For this purpose, it designed a completely new console called the Wii with a unique controller. Apart from the usual gamers, Nintendo wanted to attract casual gamers and people who had never played video games before. To widen the appeal of its console, Nintendo priced the Wii low and provided online capabilities, backward compatibility (with GameCube games), and several multimedia features. The Wii generated a lot of buzz because of its unique design and gameplay, and this was expected to translate into good sales.

The Wii, however, faced several challenges. Analysts were skeptical about whether Wii's unique gameplay would be reason enough for serious gamers to accept a technologically inferior product, especially when the competing consoles (PS3 and Xbox 360) boasted of cutting-edge graphics and HD capabilities. In addition, the fact that games developed for the Wii could not be replicated for PCs or competitor's consoles was expected to reduce the number of prospective game developers for the system, resulting in fewer game titles being available for the Wii.

Background Note

In 1889, Fusajiro Yamauchi (Fusajiro) founded Nintendo Koppai in Kyoto, Japan, to manufacture special hand-made playing cards called "Hanafuda."[9] In 1907, the company started manufacturing ordinary playing cards. In 1929, Fusajiro retired and his son-in-law, Sekiryo Yamauchi (Sekiryo), became the company president. At that time, the company was the largest manufacturer of playing cards in Japan. The company grew rapidly in the 1930s and 1940s. In 1949, Sekiryo was succeeded by his grandson, Hiroshi Yamauchi (Yamauchi), as president.

In 1951, the name of the company was changed to Nintendo Playing Cards Co. Ltd. In later years, Yamauchi modernized the card-making process. In 1959, the company entered into a deal with Walt Disney Company[10] to produce cards with Disney characters, and these became quite popular. In 1962, Nintendo was listed on the Osaka and the Kyoto Stock Exchanges. In 1963, the name of the company was changed to Nintendo Co. Ltd. Yamauchi established a research and development department called "Games" in 1964. In the 1960s, the company launched several toys like Rabbit Coaster, Ultra Hand, Ultra Machine, Love Tester, etc.

In the late 1960s, Nintendo entered into a deal with Sharp Electronics to use their light sensor technology for developing toys. It made a toy called the "Beam Gun" using optoelectronics[11] in 1970, the first time that electronic technology was used to make toys in Japan. Through the 1970s, Nintendo made several toys like laser clay shooting systems, image projection systems, etc.

In 1972, Nintendo distributed the Odyssey video game consoles developed by Magnavox, a video game company. Nintendo's first game system—Color TV Games 6—was launched in the mid-1970s. The company also sold arcade games[12] in this period. However, they were not very successful. In 1980, Nintendo launched Game & Watch—a hand-held electronic gadget with embedded games. The same year, it formed a subsidiary, Nintendo of America Inc., headquartered in New York, to sell the "Game & Watch"[13] series. In 1981, Nintendo developed and distributed the "Donkey Kong", a coin-operated video game that became a huge success. In the early 1980s, Nintendo began selling an 8-bit home video game console called "Family Computer" (Famicom in Japan), which was later renamed the Nintendo Entertainment System (NES).

---

[7] Innovation here refers to development of new games with new interfaces instead of the practice of releasing sequels or presenting the same games with improved graphics.

[8] Gameplay, in the context of video games, indicates the fun quotient. It excludes factors like graphics, sound, and storyline.

[9] Hanafuda is a Japanese card game. The cards that are used in the game are also referred to as Hanafuda and come in twelve designs (each of a different flower) representing the twelve months in a year. Nintendo still produces the cards. The popularity of the game has fallen in Japan. However, it remains quite popular in Hawaii and Korea.

[10] The Walt Disney Company, formed in 1923 by brothers Roy and Walt Disney, is one of the largest entertainment companies of the world. The company is famous for the creation of several cartoon characters such as Mickey and Minnie Mouse, Donald Duck, Chip & Dale, Bambi, etc.

[11] Optoelectronics is a sub-field of photonics. It involves the study of interconversion of electricity and light (gamma rays, X-rays, infrared, and ultraviolet). Its applications include optical communications, optical data storage, and optical sensing.

[12] Arcade games refer to coin-operated games, shooting games, ball toss games, etc. Nintendo launched several arcade games using the light sensor technology.

[13] The Game & Watch series was a product line of about 59 electronic hand-held game devices created by Gunpei Yokoi and made by Nintendo from 1980 to 1991. Each device featured a single game that could be played on an LCD screen with buttons that denoted a clock and an alarm.

The NES included the games 'Super Mario,' 'The Legend of Zelda,' and 'Duck Hunt' that became very popular. In the 1980s, the number of game titles offered by Nintendo gradually grew to 65. In the late 1980s, Nintendo opened several "World of Nintendo" showrooms across the US to market its products. In 1989, it launched the world's first portable, hand-held game device called the Game Boy. In 1991, Nintendo introduced the 16-bit Super Nintendo Entertainment System (SNES). In 1995, a new game, Pokémon,[14] created by Nintendo's in-house game development team, was launched. The Pokémon series went on to become one of Nintendo's best sellers.

In 1996, the Nintendo 64, a 64-bit home video game system with a range of games,[15] and Game Boy Pocket were released. The Game Boy Pocket was 30% smaller than the Game Boy. In 1998, Nintendo launched the Game Boy Color that was backward compatible with games developed for the earlier devices. In 2001, Nintendo released the Game Boy Advance and the 128-bit Nintendo GameCube, an advanced home video game console. Nintendo launched a slew of games[16] at the same time as the new console was launched.

In 2002, Yamauchi, after being at the helm of the company for 52 years, named Satoru Iwata (Iwata) as his successor. In 2003, Nintendo launched the Game Boy Advance SP, an improved version of the original Game Boy Advance. The new version sported a stylish flip-flop design and came with a rechargeable battery. In 2004, Nintendo launched a new dual screen hand-held video game device called the Nintendo DS with touch screen controls and backward compatibility with Game Boy Advance games. In 2005, Nintendo also launched a new hand-held games console, the Game Boy Micro and in January the next year, it launched Nintendo DS Lite, a sleeker and more lightweight version of the Nintendo DS (*See Exhibit 1 for some statistics on Nintendo products*).

Nintendo's Slide in the 2000s

Nintendo's hand-held game devices were hugely popular and were a major source of revenue for the company. However, the company's stationary consoles were not as successful. In fact, Nintendo's console sales declined with the release of every new generation of consoles.

In the 1980s, when Nintendo launched the NES, its only major competitor was Sega Corp. (Sega),[17] which launched the Sega Master System, a not-too-successful game console. However, in 1991, when Nintendo launched the SNES in the US, Sega's Mega Drive/Genesis was the most popular game console in the market. The SNES was not able to dislodge Genesis from its preeminent position, partly because the Genesis, unlike the SNES, offered backward compatibility. The SNES was also incompatible with several US-made TVs, resulting in image distortion. This too proved to be a dampener on sales. However, sales of the NES and the hand-held devices were still strong, which meant that Nintendo was still the biggest player in the gaming (hardware) industry.

Sony ushered in the CD era in gaming. Its first game console, the PlayStation, launched in 1995, used a CD-based format. The PlayStation games had high quality images. Also, newer game genres like role-playing[18] and the introduction of 3D[19] games raised the bar for video games. Nintendo, however, was slow in adapting to the latest technology. The Nintendo 64, launched in 1996, retained the cartridge-based format. While CDs could store around 700 MB of data, cartridges could store only 64 MB. Therefore, the games on CDs were longer and more sophisticated than the ones on cartridges. The cartridges were also more expensive to produce. With the PlayStation proving to be a runaway success, game developers started developing games in the CD format. While Nintendo owned several well-known games, developed by its in-house game development team, it did not have much of third-party game publisher support for its consoles. This was partly because of its reluctance to work with third-party game developers and to allow the use of its iconic characters. This had an impact on the variety of games available for Nintendo consoles. With a wider choice of games in the CD format, customers started favoring PlayStation, making it the largest selling console. Consequently, Nintendo lost its number one position in the gaming industry (*See Exhibit 2 for the history of video game consoles*).

Also, Nintendo games tended to appeal more to children than to teenagers or adults. The company failed to recognize the changing trend in the video game industry, where the share of the kids segment was contracting and that of the teenagers and young adults was growing. The

---

[14] Pokémon games were role-playing games first launched with the Game Boy in 1995. The game involves catching and training creatures (150 in the first version) to fight each other to build up their strength. As of 2006, there were four generations of Pokémon.

[15] N64 titles included Mario Golf, Super Smash Bros., Donkey Kong 64, Mario Party 2, Mario tennis, etc.

[16] The games were Super Mario Sunshine, Mario Party 4, Animal Crossing, Eternal Darkness, Metroid Prime and the online game, Phantasy Star Online.

[17] Sega Corp. was founded in 1940 in Hawaii as Service Games (Sega). Sega's Genesis, a game console, directly competed with Nintendo consoles. In 2001, with Dreamcast, another game console, failing to click in the market, Sega exited the video console industry and became a third-party games developer.

[18] A role-playing game (RPG) is a kind of game in which players assume the roles of characters in a game's storyline and play out the roles.

[19] A 3D appearance was given to games using computer graphics that display three-dimensional objects in two-dimensional space. This aspect gave not only depth to objects in a game but also enabled one object to hide behind another.

Exhibit 1 | Cumulative Sales of Nintendo Products

Product	Worldwide Sales (as of March 31, 2006)	Worldwide Software Sales	(In millions units) Price at launch in the US
NES (1985–1995)	61.9	500.0	US$ 200
SNES (1991–1999)	49.1	379.1	US$ 200
Nintendo 64 (1996–2002)	32.9	225.0	US$ 200
Game Boy (1989–2004)	118.7	501.0	US$ 90
Game Boy Advance* (2001–)	75.1	327.7	US$ 100
Nintendo GameCube (2001–)	20.9	189.1	US$ 200
Nintendo DS^ (2004–)	16.7	60.4	US$ 150

*Game Boy Advance sales figures include that of Game Boy SP and Game Boy Micro.
^Nintendo DS sales figures include that of Nintendo DS Lite.
Source: www.nintendo.com.

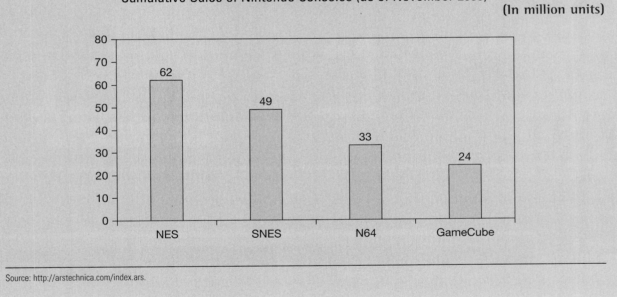

Cumulative Sales of Nintendo Consoles (as of November 2006)
(In million units)

Source: http://arstechnica.com/index.ars.

youth preferred first-person shooter games, action games, etc., and this reduced the appeal of Nintendo consoles among a major section of gamers.

By the time Nintendo launched its CD-based Game-Cube in 2001, competition had intensified, with Sega's Dreamcast (1999), Sony's Playstation 2 (2000), and Microsoft's Xbox (2001) already in the market. Even though the GameCube was launched after the other consoles, it did not have the latest technology. Unlike the competition, it did not have a DVD drive and its online capabilities were very basic. Even though the GameCube was priced lower, the PlayStation (1 & 2) and Xbox became the leading consoles in North America and East Asia—the two largest markets for gaming products. The saving grace for Nintendo was that the company continued to make money on its consoles, even when its console sales lagged behind that of the PS2 and the Xbox (*See Exhibit 3 for five year financial information about Nintendo*). This was primarily because of low manufacturing costs.

Exhibit 2 — History of Video Game Consoles

Particulars	Time Period	Some Products
First Generation	1972–1979	Magnavox Odyssey (1972) PONG (Atari) (1975) Coleco Telstar (1976) APF TV Fun (1976)
Second Generation	1976–1984	Fairchild Channel F (1976) Mattel Intellivision (1980) Sega SG-1000 (1983) RCA Studio II (1977) Magnavox Odyssey^2 (1978)
Third Generation (8-bit era)	1983–1989	Sega Master System (1986) Atari 7800 (1984) **NES (1985)**
Fourth Generation (16-bit era)	1989–1997	Sega Mega Drive/Genesis (1988) NEC PC Engine/TurboGrafx-16 (1987) **SNES (1991)**
Fifth Generation (32-bit/64-bit era)	1993–2004	Atari Jaguar and Atari Jaguar CD (1993) Sega Saturn (1994) Sony PlayStation (1994) **Nintendo 64 (1996)**
Sixth Generation (128-bit era)	1998–2005	Sega Dreamcast (1998) Sony PlayStation 2 (2000) Nintendo GameCube (2001) Microsoft Xbox (2001)
Seventh Generation	2004–present	Microsoft Xbox 360 (November, 2005) Sony PlayStation 3 (November, 2006) **(Nintendo) Wii (November, 2006)**

Source: http://experts.about.com.

Exhibit 3 — Nintendo—Five Year Financial Summary

(in million Japanese Yen)

Year	2006	2005	2004	2003	2002
Net Sales	508,827	514,988	514,409	503,746	554,413
Operating Income	91,223	113,458	110,223	100,252	119,607
Net Income	96,378	87,416	33,194	67,267	106,445

Source: www.nintendo.com.

With the GameCube recording poor sales and Nintendo being reduced to a marginal player in the video game console market, most gaming analysts expected the company to quit the market and become a third-party games developer like Sega.

Making the New Console

Nintendo, however, soldiered on. Immediately after launching the GameCube, the company started work on its next console. Initially, Nintendo aimed to make its new console "faster and flashier" so that it displayed great graphics at high speeds. However, one year into the development of the new console, the company started to rethink its approach.

Faced with rising game console development costs, Nintendo was forced to reconsider whether it wanted to continue in the race to build consoles which had greater processing speeds or which supported improved graphics. "Give them (gamers) one, they ask for two. Give them two, and next time they will ask for five instead of three. Then they want ten, thirty, a hundred; their desire growing exponentially. Giving in to this will lead us nowhere in the end. I started to feel unsure about following that path about a year into development,"[20] said Genyo Takeda (Takeda), General Manager, Integrated Research and Development Division, Nintendo.

In the game console industry, it had become an accepted practice for the console manufacturers to lose money on the hardware and to recover the loss by charging high licensing fees to game publishers and developers. This, however, increased the costs and risks for the publishers and developers. Game developers therefore played it safe by releasing new versions of existing games rather than developing new ones. Also, with console development and game development costs rising, hardware and software prices were also increasing, and this was not very conducive to the growth of the gaming industry. Therefore, Nintendo decided that instead of spending millions on console development and losing money on the hardware, it would focus on creating new and exciting gameplay. "Cutting-edge technologies and multiple functions do not necessarily lead to more fun. The excessively hardware-oriented way of thinking is totally wrong, but manufacturers are just throwing money at developing higher-performance hardware,"[21] said Yamauchi.

In Nintendo's analysis, people were becoming weary of the old forms of gaming and the limited number of unique games. The fact that in 2002 and 2003,[22] the game market in Japan was contracting while the US market was stagnant seemed to bolster Nintendo's view. "We have learned that people get tired of any entertainment form. In Japan, the gaming market is shrinking. If we continue down the same path as we have in the past, people may become tired of gaming,"[23] said Iwata.

According to Nintendo, game consoles did not really need more technological innovations. The graphics processing capabilities of existing consoles were adequate and the way to a more immersive game experience was not through higher quality graphics but through better gameplay. It planned to improve the gaming experience by making it more real so that the players would become more physically involved in the game.

Further, the top management at Nintendo felt that games with unique gameplay experience would revitalize the market, and bring in new customers. On the strategy adopted by Nintendo, Iwata later said, "For some time, we have believed that the game industry is ready for disruption, not just from Nintendo but from all developers. It's what we all need to expand our audience and to expand our imaginations."[24] Nintendo planned to attract 'nongamers' and 'lapsed gamers' through new gameplay experiences and new forms of interaction.[25]

For this purpose, Nintendo planned to make use of technology to develop a new gaming interface rather than pursue faster processing. "Using state-of-the-art technology in unprecedented ways is far more complex, difficult, and requires more technological know-how than simply using the technology to improve performance,"[26] said Takeda.

Nintendo's earlier consoles generally came in bright colors and had a toy-like appearance that seemed to put off older gamers. Therefore, Nintendo decided to design its new console to appeal to gamers of all ages. It also wanted to make the new console as compact as possible, and also incorporate online capabilities into the machine.

The Nintendo design team finally came up with a sleek rectangular system with a slot-loading drive, placed on a stand. The system was made robust with extra metal support plating around the outside of the console. "So we've created something that maintains the functionality and durability of a toy, without looking like one,"[27] said Kenichiro Ashida, Nintendo Product development department and design group member.

After much deliberation, Nintendo decided that, instead of the traditional gamepads,[28] the new console

20 "Wii—Iwata asks," wii.nintendo.com, 2006.

21 "Interview: Hiroshi Yamauchi," http://cube.ign.com/articles/492/492253p1.html, February 13, 2004.

22 According to Yano Research Institute, a Japan-based market research and consultancy firm, the Japanese video game market shrank by 20% in 2003.

23 "Innovate or die," http://money.cnn.com, May 21, 2004.

24 "Breaking: GDC—Detailed Nintendo keynote coverage," www.gamasutra.com, March 23, 2006.

25 Game Interaction refers to the interface between the user and the system. It is generally enhanced through audio-video. It could also include avatars, facial expressions, Artificial Intelligence, etc.

26 "Wii—Iwata asks," wii.nintendo.com, 2006.

27 "Wii—Iwata asks," wii.nintendo.com, 2006.

28 A gamepad is an input device for controlling video games. It is generally connected to the video game console.

would have a completely new design for its controller. The design team strove to incorporate approachability, sophistication, wireless connectivity, and a revolutionary look and feel, in the design of the controller. Approachability and sophistication meant that the controller had to be easy for non-gamers to use, while at the same time providing enough options for veteran gamers. Later, commenting on the specifications for the controller, Iwata said, "We must give players freedom to move. Second, it must be simple, non-threatening. But it should be sophisticated to serve the needs of complex games. And yes, we wanted it to be 'revolutionary.'"[29]

In May 2004, at the E3 conference[30] in Los Angeles, Nintendo unveiled the new console, codenamed 'Revolution.' It revealed the salient features of the new console, including its unique wireless controller.

Wireless Controller

Over the next year, Nintendo further refined the design of the wireless controller and in September 2005, at the Tokyo Game Show,[31] gave out more details on the controller.

Nintendo's new wireless controller looked like a TV remote. Instead of buttons or an analog stick,[32] gamers needed to simply move the controller; the movement would be translated into onscreen action. A motion-detection sensor, placed somewhere around the TV/monitor, detected the signals sent by the controller and determined its position in 3-D space. The sensor, which used Bluetooth, detected depth as well as lateral movement and helped players control the game by swinging the device like a tennis racket or wielding it like a sword. The new controller also served as a central unit to which several peripherals like the nunchuck controller[33] (which featured an accelerator and an analog stick) could be attached. Customers could also play GameCube games by connecting the "classic controller" to the wireless controller.

Nintendo spent a lot of money not only on research and development but also in manufacturing the control system. Iwata later said, "Some people bet their money on the screen [being the most important innovation], but we put our money on the experience. This is an investment in market disruption."[34] Nintendo expected the supposedly "revolutionary" way of playing video games to create a buzz among gamers as well as in the media.

Online Capabilities

The new console was the first among Nintendo consoles with full online capabilities. It was expected to have several services like a virtual console, round-the-clock connectivity, and a browser. The virtual console allowed customers to download games, some of which could be played online. Commenting on Nintendo's online strategy, Reginald Fils-Aime (Fils-Aime), President and COO, Nintendo of America, later said, "We will offer online-enabled games that the consumers will not have to pay a subscription fee for. They'll be able to enjoy that right out of the box. It won't have hidden fees or costs."[35] The virtual console would make the entire game library[36] of Nintendo available on the new console, giving game developers an opportunity to earn money even on 'obsolete' titles.

However, Nintendo itself was expected to benefit the most from the virtual console, as most of the game titles for the previous consoles were owned by the company. It had a large catalog of iconic characters like Super Mario, Link, Donkey Kong, Metroid, Pokémon, etc., that were recognized by gamers across the world. Also, Nintendo had a very loyal fan base that preferred to buy Nintendo titles rather than third-party titles. Downloads would cost between US$ 5 and US$ 10 for a single game. Iwata later said, "In the long run, I think the virtual console could become one of the most significant revenue streams for Nintendo."[37]

The Wii

In May 2006, Nintendo unveiled the new console and the much talked about wireless controller at the E3 conference in Los Angeles. At the conference, Nintendo announced that its new console would be called 'Wii'. It also gave a 150-word explanation as to why it had chosen the name. Nintendo said that the name was in accordance with its philosophy of creating a gaming world without boundaries, attracting new gamers, and

[29] "GDC: Satoru Iwata's Nintendo keynote," www.wonderlandblog.com, March 23, 2006.

[30] The E³ or Electronic Entertainment Expo is an annual trade show for the computer and video games industry. It is organized by the Entertainment Software Association in May each year in Los Angeles, USA. Video game developers unveil their forthcoming games and game-related hardware at the event.

[31] The Tokyo Game Show is the second largest games convention in the world after the E³. The general public is allowed to attend the convention on the last two days.

[32] An analog stick or thumbstick is an input device in the controller and is used for two-dimensional input.

[33] The nunchuck controller contained the same motion-sensing technology found in the Wii Remote. It also includes an analog stick to assist in character movement.

[34] "GDC: Satoru Iwata's Nintendo keynote," www.wonderlandblog.com, March 23, 2006.

[35] "Nintendo exec talks Wii online, marketing," www.cnet.com, August 17, 2006.

[36] The library was to include games made for NES, SNES, N64 and GameCube consoles. In addition, some Sega Genesis and Turbo Graphic 16 games were also to be included.

[37] "Iwata: Virtual console biggest money maker for Nintendo," www.kotaku.com, October 10, 2006.

making a fun product for everyone. Nintendo's press release explained, "Wii sounds like 'we,' which emphasizes this console is for everyone. Wii can easily be remembered by people around the world, no matter what language they speak. No confusion. No need to abbreviate. Just Wii."[38] The unique spelling was also expected to be easy to search on the Internet as well as to serve as a trademark.

Nintendo was successful in creating interest in its new console. The company had been giving details of its new strategy even before the E[3], and when the Wii was finally unveiled, gamers waited in line for hours to get a glimpse of the console and the controller. Alfred Hermida, the BBC News website technology editor, reported that the Wii overshadowed Sony's much anticipated PS3 at the expo.[39]

At the unveiling, Nintendo gave out more information on the Wii. One feature of the console was the WiiConnect24 service, which allowed users to send and receive SMS messages, exchange pictures, etc., even while the console was in the stand-by mode. "Let's say your Wii is connected to the Internet in a mode that allows activation on a 24-hour basis. This would allow Nintendo to send monthly promotional demos for the (Nintendo) DS during the night to the Wii consoles in each household. Users would wake up each morning, find the LED lamp on their Wii flashing, and know that Nintendo has sent them something,"[40] said Iwata. The Wii contained smaller chips, which used very little power (8 watts). Because of its low power consumption, the console could be kept switched on for long periods of time without running up huge power bills, or causing any harm to the machine.

Nintendo announced that the Wii would have the Opera browser. Players who wished to surf the Internet could do so even in the middle of gaming sessions by putting the Wii on standby mode. When compared to other WebTV[41] products, the new console, compatible with Macromedia Flash,[42] was considered to be a superior system to browse the Internet. Using the Nintendo Wi-Fi Connection,[43] users could also play games with their friends over the Internet.

The Wii Remote came with a mini-speaker and had memory to store sound clips which could be heard while playing games. It also had a built-in rumble feature to make games seem more realistic.

The Wii also had a unique multimedia feature called Wii Channels. On one of the channels, called Mii, players could make simplified cartoon-like avatars using face sculpting tools that could be inserted into some games played on the Wii. On another channel, users could edit photos using photo editing tools. There were channels for weather, shopping, and news as well.

The Target Market

Nintendo expected the Wii to appeal to people who had never played video games before, including women and older people, segments which till then had been ignored by the video game industry. It was also meant to attract lapsed gamers. If Nintendo succeeded in its efforts, it was expected to considerably expand the video gaming market.

Nintendo hoped that its strategy of creating simpler games would appeal to ordinary people. Over the years, video games had become longer and more complicated, requiring players to spend a lot of time mastering complex controllers and moves. This was cited as one of the main reasons why many people stayed away from video games. Nintendo believed that simple games that were fun to play, lasted a few minutes, and required only easy-to-use controls, would make more people take up gaming. "Most of the game business is going down a similar path toward hyper-realistic graphics which recreate sports or movies. We want to put a little more art into it and do it in a way that casual consumers can enjoy the games,"[44] said Shigeru Miyamoto, senior managing director at Nintendo.

With the Wii, Nintendo hoped to "put fun back into gaming."[45] A new gamer was expected to take to the new controller naturally. At the same time, because of its novelty, it was also expected to appeal to the serious gamer.

The Wii virtual console would also provide lapsed gamers, who had quit because the games had become too complicated, an opportunity to play previous generation games. The virtual console was also expected to attract hardcore gamers who would be able to download classic Nintendo games from the previous 20 years.

[38] "The Revolution has a name: Nintendo Wii," www.mtv.com, April 27, 2006.

[39] "Nintendo shares see Wii benefits," http://news.bbc.co.uk, May 15, 2006.

[40] "Nintendo President speaks, WiiConnect24, more," www.codenamerevolution.com, June 01, 2006.

[41] WebTV products enable users to surf the Internet through their TVs.

[42] Macromedia Flash is an animation software program used to integrate video into web pages. Consoles with Flash support enable users to view animation.

[43] A Wi-Fi enabled device can connect to the Internet when in proximity to an access point. The Nintendo Wi-Fi Connection was first launched in November 2005 for Nintendo DS users. Wii users can also avail of the service.

[44] "Nintendo Wii celebrates gesture interactions," www.macqueen.com, November 04, 2006.

[45] Kenji Hall, "Wii want to expand games' appeal," www.businessweek.com, September 14, 2006.

Nintendo priced its Wii console, which included the Wii Remote, a nunchuck attachment, the sensor bar, and Wii Sports[46] (*See Exhibit 4 for screenshot of Wii Sports-Tennis*), at US$ 249 in the US—much lower than the PS3 (US$ 599 for the 60 GB Wi-Fi model), and the Xbox 360 (US$ 399 for the 20 GB detachable hard drive/wireless controller model). The relatively low price was made possible by the fact that, unlike the PS3 and the Xbox, the Wii did not use the latest processor, and also did not have a high definition video disc player. Nintendo's R&D and manufacturing costs were reportedly much lower than that of its competitors. Wii game titles, whether offered by Nintendo itself or by third-party publishers, were to sell for around US$ 40–50 (most seventh generation games on the other consoles were expected to cost US$ 60 and above).

Attracting Game Developers

In the video game industry, the prevalent view was that games had to get longer and more complex with each new generation of consoles, if they were to succeed. This meant larger development teams. Also, new games required large marketing budgets. This exposed developers to huge risks and therefore, most of them were comfortable with doing sequels to existing games, using improved graphics. This restricted innovation in the gaming industry. With the Wii, Nintendo was set to change all that.

According to estimates from analysts and game publishers, the development cost for a typical advanced game for the Wii was about US$ 7 million—about half the cost of a new game for the Xbox 360 or the PS3 (some PS3 games were reported to cost as much as US$ 25 million to develop). Nintendo felt that with the Wii not having the graphics capabilities of its competitors, developers would be forced to develop new games that made use of its unique controller. Game developers could also look to recreate popular PS and Xbox games to suit the unique interface of the Wii.

The Wii's virtual console was expected to simplify the game distribution process. Game developers could develop games for the Wii and after the requisite documentation, make the games available on the virtual console, thus cutting distribution costs.

Many game developers were attracted to the Wii Remote and expressed an interest in developing games for the Wii. In August 2006, Electronic Arts Inc., the world's biggest video-game publisher, announced that it was working on seven Wii titles, two more than it had originally planned, in order to capitalize on the buzz that the Wii had been able to create. "There is more excitement among third-party publishers about the Wii than there was for the launch of the GameCube,"[47] said

---

Exhibit 4   A Screenshot—The Wii Sports (Tennis) Game

Source: Tracy Yan

---

[46] A pack-in game featuring five different sports—baseball, tennis, bowling, boxing, and golf.
[47] "En Garde! Fight foes using a controller like a sword," www.nytimes.com, October 30, 2006.

Exhibit 5 | Some Wii Games

Sno	Title
1	The Legend of Zelda: Twilight Princess
2	Raymond Raving Rabbids
3	Red Steel
4	Far Cry: Vengeance
5	Splinter Cell: Double Agent
6	GT Pro Series
7	Monster 4 × 4 World Circuit
8	Call of Duty 3
9	Blazing Angels: Squadron of WW II
10	Trauma Center: Second Opinion
11	Disney Pixar's Cars
12	Need for Speed: Carbon
13	The Grim Adventures of Billy & Mandy
14	The Ant Bully
15	Super Monkey Ball: Banana Blitz

Source: www.thewiire.com.

David F. Zucker, the president and chief executive of Midway, a company which was developing four games for the Wii. As of August 2006, 27 launch titles had been confirmed for the Wii with another 111 titles in development (*Refer to Exhibit 5 for a list of Wii games*).

Marketing the Wii

The Wii was launched on November 19, 2006 in the US and almost simultaneously in Japan, Europe, and Australia. The console was expected to ride high on the intense buzz it had created in the gaming community. Nintendo was depending heavily on word-of-mouth to popularize the Wii. It also expected to have several product demonstrations across stores to showcase the unique gameplay experience. "We're going to create advocacy. We're going to make it so that everyone who tries the Wii experience talks to their friends and neighbors,"[48] said Fils-Aime.

Nintendo planned to promote the Wii heavily for the 2006 Christmas season. It planned to spend around US$ 200 million on marketing the console. The Wii was expected to be the biggest product launch in the company's history. The Internet was to be a major channel for marketing the Wii. The tagline 'Wii Move You' was to be used. "We're just in the final stages of putting our media plan together for Wii, but in terms of online our spend is way more than anything we've ever done before. Particularly over the launch week we'll completely take them over—you'll go online and see Wii everywhere,"[49] said Robert Lowe, Nintendo's product manager for home consoles.

In the middle of November 2006, Nintendo launched the TV and cinema advertisements for the Wii. "The advertising and marketing is for casual gamers. We want to get them excited when they can actually go out and get something,"[50] said Fils-Aime. It also planned in-store advertisements. Nintendo planned to advertise more in the US market as most of the 4 million consoles Nintendo planned to ship worldwide were expected to reach US stores (*See Exhibit 6 for information about the US games industry*).

The Wii vs. the PS3 & the Xbox 360

The November 2006 launches of the Wii and the PS3 were set to spark a battle in the US$ 30 billion world gaming market.[51] Microsoft's Xbox 360, launched in November 2005, had a one year lead over the other two consoles (*See Exhibit 7 for photographs of the Wii, the PS3 and the Xbox 360*). Microsoft planned to re-launch the Xbox 360 again in November 2006 with some minor tweaking and a separate US$ 200 HD DVD drive.[52] However, Nintendo believed that its target market was entirely different from that of Sony and Microsoft (*See Exhibit 8 for a comparison of the features of the Wii, the Xbox 360, and the PS3*).

Both the Xbox 360 and the PS3 provided sharper images because of their HD video capability. The Wii was not HD-capable and offered a resolution of only 480p,[53] with the result that the graphics were suited to regular TVs rather than HD TVs. On the other hand, consumers had to have HD TVs to view the PS3's and Xbox 360's HD images at their best. In other words, customers without

---

[48] "Nintendo exec talks Wii online, marketing," www.cnet.com, August 17, 2006.

[49] "Nintendo announces biggest ever online spend," http://news.spong.com, September 25, 2006.

[50] "Mysteries of the PS3 and Wii launch—solved!" http://money.cnn.com, November 10, 2006.

[51] www.yahoo.com.

[52] The external HD DVD drive connected to the Xbox 360 through an USB port and was priced at US$ 200. The drive would play movies on HD DVD format as well as DVD, VCD formats. As of November 2006, Microsoft had no plans to release an Xbox 360 with an internal HD DVD player or HD DVD games.

[53] 480p refers to the video display resolution. While 480 stands for 480 vertical scanning lines, 'p' stands for progressive scan, which is superior to interlaced (or 'i'). The horizontal resolution is usually 720 pixels. HDTVs typically have a resolution of 1080p.

Exhibit 6 | Some Statistics on the US Games Industry

The three largest markets for computer and video games are the United States, Japan, and the United Kingdom, in that order. Other major markets are Australia, Canada, Spain, Germany, South Korea, Mexico, France, and Italy.

In the US, the average age of a game player is 33 years. Among those who play games frequently, adult males, on an average, have been playing video games for 10 years, while adult females have been playing for 8 years.

Age of Game Players

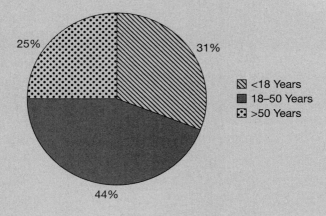

25%   31%   44%

- ⊠ <18 Years
- ■ 18–50 Years
- ⊡ >50 Years

In the US, women aged 18 or older represent a significantly greater portion of the game-playing population (30%) than boys aged 17 or younger (23%). On an average, gamers in the US spend 6.8 hours per week playing games.

Gender of Game Players

38%   62%

- ■ Female
- ⊠ Male

Parents are involved when games are purchased 89% of the time. Around 49% of parents said they played computer and video games with their children at least once a month.

(continued)

Exhibit 6 Some Statistics on the US Games Industry (continued)

Best-Selling Console Game Genres (in 2005)

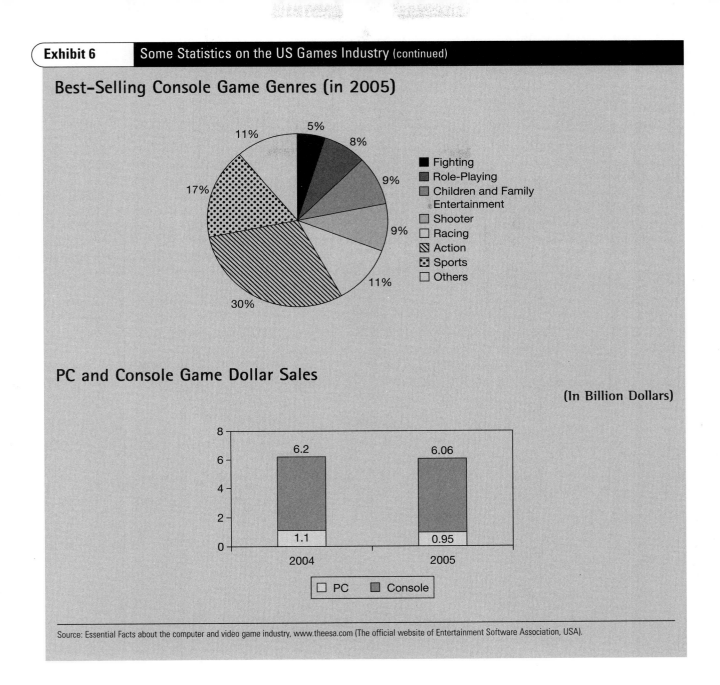

Legend:
- ■ Fighting
- ■ Role-Playing
- □ Children and Family Entertainment
- □ Shooter
- □ Racing
- ▨ Action
- ▦ Sports
- □ Others

PC and Console Game Dollar Sales

(In Billion Dollars)

	2004	2005
Console	6.2	6.06
PC	1.1	0.95

□ PC ■ Console

Source: Essential Facts about the computer and video game industry, www.theesa.com (The official website of Entertainment Software Association, USA).

HD TVs had to invest several hundred dollars more to enjoy the HD capability of the Xbox 360 and the PS3.

Both Microsoft and Sony were selling their consoles at a loss, expecting to earn money on the games instead, even though both the firms had invested billions of dollars in developing their consoles. In contrast, Nintendo's development costs for the Wii were much lower and it was expected to make a profit of about US$ 50 on each unit. "The interesting thing as people focus on our console-market share is they ignore the fact that we're the only gaming company from a hardware and software standpoint that's making money in this industry. Our financial performance has been better than both of them,"[54] said Fils-Aime.

---

54 "Sony, Nintendo, and Microsoft bank on new offerings," www.canada.com, November 14, 2006.

Exhibit 7 — Comparison of the Wii, the PS3, and the Xbox 360

Particulars	Nintendo Wii	Sony PlayStation 3	Microsoft Xbox 360
Processor	729 MHz IBM Broadway	3.2 GHz STI[55] Cell processor	3.2 GHz IBM XCPU
Graphics card	243 MHz ATI Hollywood	550 MHz Nvidia RSX	500 MHz ATI Xenos
RAM	88 MB	512 MB	512 MB
Launch date	November 2006	November 2006	November 2005
Price	Under $250	$499 basic/$599 premium	$299 basic/ $399 premium
Sales	–	*	6 million as of September 2006.

*PS2 still outsells Xbox 360. From November 2005 to September 2006, 11.25 million PS2s were sold.
Source: www.usatoday.com.

Also, both Sony and Microsoft had not made any significant changes in the controller design. In comparison, the Wii Remote was revolutionary. "Microsoft and Sony spend a lot of time developing cutting-edge technology. Nintendo is not a technology company—it's a toy company. It's not interested in bleeding-edge electronics and graphics,"[56] said In-Stat video game analyst Brian O'Rourke.

To take advantage of the surge in demand expected during the Christmas holiday season, Nintendo enhanced production capacities to make four million Wiis available in the US market. On the other hand, production problems at Sony meant that only 400,000 PS3s would be available at the time of launch. "Nintendo seems to have a good handle on the flow of their goods. Sony has put out signals that they're not getting as many as they would like,"[57] said Brian Farrell, president and chief executive officer of THQ, a prominent games development company. The wide availability of the Wii was set to improve its sales.

Challenges

Even though the Wii had a lot going for it, concerns about its eventual success remained. With the PS3 launch, gamers would now be able to experience true high-definition images and sound on their games, in comparison to which the Wii games would look primitive. Some analysts felt that even casual gamers would find the graphics power of the Wii disappointing in comparison to the other consoles.

The unique gameplay of the Wii also had the potential to cause its downfall. Some analysts felt that playing games with the Wii Remote could become repetitive and tiring over time. Also considering the space constraints in modern living rooms, gamers wondered about the playability of some Wii games which required the player to move around a lot. Moreover, some games required people to stand and play, which could make playing games on the Wii a tiring exercise.

Even though Nintendo claimed that its new controller was easy to adapt to, the Wii Remote did require some time to get used to. In 2003, Square Enix Co. Ltd., a Japanese videogame maker, had developed a game in which gamers had to fight monsters using a toy sword, in front of a motion-sensor attached to the TV. That game had been a failure, prompting skepticism about the wide-scale adoption of the Wii.

Some analysts, like BC Securities analyst Hiroshi Kamide (Kamide), felt that the Wii could reach the decline stage in its life cycle quicker than the PS3 or the Xbox 360, as it was already technically somewhat outdated.

Kamide also believed that the Wii's success would ultimately depend on the variety of games that Nintendo would be able to make available. "The fate of the console comes down to depth and width of game software,"[58] he said. Therefore, it was felt that Nintendo should encourage third-party game developers (apart from its in-house game development team) to develop games

---

[55] STI stands for Sony Toshiba IBM.

[56] "Nintendo chief confident in Wii's long-term success," www.technewsworld.com, July 06, 2006.

[57] "Mysteries of the PS3 and Wii launch—solved!" http://money.cnn.com, November 10, 2006.

[58] "Analysts: Success of Nintendo's Wii hinges on games, not hardware," www.foxnews.com, October 12, 2006.

Exhibit 8   Nintendo Wii with the Wii Remote

Source: PR NEWSWIRE/AP Image

which fully exploited the unique features of the Wii Remote.

Though a number of game developers had announced plans to develop games for the Wii, the competing consoles seemed to be ahead in the game software race. While Nintendo's unique gameplay strategy differentiated its product from those of its competitors, it also made the game developers think twice before making games for the Wii. This was because Wii games could be played only on the Wii, while games developed for the PS3 or the Xbox 360 could be played on either console or the PC. Developing Wii games would also require specialist development teams because of the unique interface, and this could increase costs. Also, analysts expected third-party developers to find it difficult to compete with Nintendo's in-house game development team which would have had more time to design games for the Wii.

Unlike Nintendo's portable handheld systems which enjoyed high visibility because people tended to carry them around, the Wii had to depend primarily on demonstrations at retail outlets. "For the (Nintendo) DS, whoever found it interesting carried it with them and showed it to people around them. That was a great demand driver. We cannot expect that sort of push for a stationary console,"[59] said Iwata. However, demonstrating the Wii at retail stores was also going to be somewhat more difficult because of the unique controller.

Nintendo, with its reputation of being a maker of game consoles for children, was also expected to find it hard to position the Wii as a console for gamers of all ages and tastes.

In addition, some analysts felt that in its endeavor to attract casual gamers, Nintendo might have ignored the needs of hardcore gamers. Over the years, Nintendo had managed to generate a loyal fan base for its products. These fans would have liked to see Nintendo's iconic characters in high resolution graphics. "How is the Wii the only right choice for gamers? Contrary to what you believe, Wii games for the most part ignore 'hardcore' gamers,"[60] said Juan Castro, editor of ign.com, a leading website for games information.

Nintendo was selling its games at $40–50 while the highly advanced games for the PS3 and the Xbox 360 were available at around $60. Most gamers felt that Nintendo was charging too high a price for games with low graphics quality. Some gamers also felt that Nintendo's price, of US$ 5–10, for its old games was also too high.

While everyone seemed to agree that more than graphics, fun was an important factor in games, serious gamers who had played games on the Wii complained that the console fell short on that front too. Some game analysts who played some of the Wii games at the E[3] conference felt that 90% of the titles were not something that people would like to play for extended periods of time.

Analysts also wondered if the Wii's lower quality graphics would become a liability as more customers switched to high-definition television. Another concern was whether the Wii would be able to hold its ground when the prices of the Xbox 360 and the PS3 dropped,

59 "Analysts: Success of Nintendo's Wii hinges on games, not hardware," www.foxnews.com, October 12, 2006.
60 "IGN editor slates the Wii," www.wiiblog.net, September 08, 2006.

as they were bound to do when production stabilized and volumes increased. Most analysts expected PS3 sales to pick up in 2007 with increasing interest in Blu-ray technology. "There are quite a few people out there today who have no idea what Blu-ray is. But a year after its launch, at around this time next year, more people will start recognizing the added value brought by a Blu-ray player, just as a DVD player function helped the PS2 to a flying start,"[61] said Deutsche Securities' Takashi Oya.

In October 2006, Sony announced that the PS3s controller would have some of the functions of the Wii Remote. Sony's controller also used a motion-sensing technology to make games more intuitive to play.

Some analysts even criticized Nintendo's choice of the name Wii for its new console. "Even though Wii meets many of the criteria Nintendo should be going for, it fails at the criteria 'don't pick a silly, awful-sounding name,'"[62] said David Sirlin, a game designer.

Doubts were also raised about the success of the virtual console, as similar initiatives in the past had not been very successful. Sony's online games had had problems with several cheat codes[63] and hacks being used by gamers, and the sales of network adapters for the PS2 were also very low. In spite of its better quality of service, most Microsoft's Xbox owners had also never logged on to Xbox Live, the online service network of Xbox.

Outlook

With more and more households willing to buy more than one game console, the Nintendo Wii stood a fair chance of being included in Christmas and other holiday shopping lists, because of its low price (compared to the PS3 and Xbox 360) and unique interface. Analysts felt that customers would choose between the Xbox 360 and the PS3, but were highly unlikely to buy both, mainly because of their high price and similar features. Not surprisingly, Microsoft officials believed that customers would prefer the Xbox 360. "People are going to buy two (machines.) They're going to buy an Xbox and they're going to buy a Wii . . . for the price of one PS3. People will always gravitate toward a competitively priced product—like what I believe Wii will be—with innovative new designs and great intellectual property,"[64] said

Peter Moore, Corporate Vice President, Retail Sales and Marketing, Microsoft.

Nintendo expected to sell six million consoles and as many as 17 million Wii games (or about three games per console sold) by the end of March 2007. The success of the Wii, as well as the sales of the Nintendo DS system, were expected to contribute to an 18% growth in global sales for the company in the year ending March 31, 2007. The buzz around the Wii and the increased sales of the Nintendo DS boosted Nintendo's share price by 71% between January and September 2006.

It was also believed that the success or failure of the Wii would determine the growth trajectory of the gaming industry. If the Wii proved to be success, gameplay would assume importance in future consoles; its failure would confirm the importance of superior graphics and processor speed. However, Nintendo did not expect to lose money on the Wii. "It is a strange notion that a game console always leads to mounting losses in the beginning. We can't promise we won't even have a one yen loss, but we are not expecting an enormous loss,"[65] said Iwata.

With the Wii, Nintendo also seemed to have brought in a fresh new perspective in gaming. A post-E3 poll organized by *Famitsu*, a popular Japanese gaming magazine, revealed that the Wii had been successful in generating interest among the people. To the question— "What gaming hardware are you looking forward to the most?"—around 69% of the respondents picked the Wii, while only 21% opted for the PS3, 7% for the Xbox 360 and 3% for the Nintendo DS.[66]

Analysts expected Nintendo's gameplay strategy to spark more innovation in the video game industry, which would prove to be beneficial for its long-term growth. "The interesting thing is if you do expand the market, you do both. You grow the category, but you'll also dramatically increase your market share. That's all based on a market expansion strategy. And that's what we're looking to do with home consoles,"[67] said Fils-Aime.

However, industry observers remained doubtful whether any one game console would eventually emerge as the leader. "We absolutely do not see a dominant player in our modeling, like we have in the past,"[68] said Simon Jeffery, Sega's president and chief operating officer.

---

[61] "Analysts: Success of Nintendo's Wii hinges on games, not hardware," www.foxnews.com, October 12, 2006.

[62] "Wii reactions: Developers comment," http://gamasutra.com, May 01, 2006.

[63] Cheat codes can be entered into a video game by a particular player to change the game's behavior. This is done to gain an unfair advantage over other players. For example, cheat codes can be used to skip levels, disable other players, etc.

[64] "Microsoft + Nintendo = Gaming without Sony," www.dailytech.com, May 11, 2006.

[65] "A heretical view on video game consoles," www.hunterstrat.com, April 29, 2006.

[66] "Sony competition not the Xbox 360," www.wii-volution.com, June 20, 2006.

[67] "Nintendo hopes Wii spells wiinner," www.usatoday.com, August 15, 2006.

[68] "Mysteries of the PS3 and Wii launch—solved!" http://money.cnn.com, November 10, 2006.

Nintendo too was aware of the uncertain road ahead. "When I think of what faces all of us (Nintendo) right now I imagine what it must have been like for the new explorers who first set foot on new continents. Our adventure is still ahead of us!"[69] said Iwata.

References and Suggested Readings

1. Kyle Orland, **Analyst: Sony to win big in long run**, www.joystiq.com, November 16, 2006.
2. Phil Slattery, **Wii Controller has new competition**, www.revolutionportal .com, October 20, 2006.
3. Stuart Dinsey, **£11m launch spend for Nintendo Wii**, www.mcvuk.com, October 19, 2006.
4. **Analysts: Success of Nintendo's Wii hinges on games, not hardware,** www.foxnews.com, October 12, 2006.
5. Alex Donaldson, **Is it possible for Nintendo to lose?** www.rpgsite.net, September 26, 2006.
6. Brian Bremner, **Will Nintendo's Wii strategy score?** www .businessweek.com, September 20, 2006.
7. **10 reasons Nintendo's Wii will RULE THEM ALL!** www.mytechlists .com, September 15, 2006.
8. Tim Surette, **Nintendo execs talk Wii online**, marketing, www.cnet .com.au, August 17, 2006.
9. Kevin P. Casey, **Nintendo hopes Wii spells wiinner**, www.usatoday .com, August 15, 2006.
10. Simon Carless, **EA sees larger loss, ramps up Wii production**, www.gamasutra.com, August 01, 2006.
11. Jason Dobson, **Analyst: PS3 to slow industry growth, Nintendo & Microsoft Could Capitalize,** www.gamasutra.com, July 18, 2006.
12. Dean Takahashi, **Nintendo targets Wii price, brightens its outlook thanks to expected warm reception for Wii,** http://blogs .mercurynews.com, May 24, 2006.
13. Alfred Hermida, **Nintendo steals the show at E3**, www.bbc.co.uk, May 14, 2006.
14. Adam Schultz, **Nintendo Wii: The brand of buzz—Buzz marketing at its best/worst,** www.searchenginelowdown.com, May 04, 2006.
15. Shawn Rider, **Why Nintendo gets it, or why Sony should start trying**, www.gamesfirst.com, September 17, 2005.
16. Chris Morris, **Innovate or die**, http://money.cnn.com, May 21, 2004.
17. **Analysts squabble over Nintendo's future**, www.theregister.co.uk, February 27, 2003.
18. www.nintendo.com.
19. www.wii.com.
20. www.nintendowiifanboy.com.
21. www.wiisworld.com.
22. www.nwiizone.com.
23. www.gamespot.com.

---

[69] "GDC: Satoru Iwata's Nintendo keynote," www.wonderlandblog.com, March 23, 2006.

Nokia and the Global Mobile Phone Industry

Shirisha Regani

"We want to be the company that brings this industry to the next phase. And if we have a little bit of a bump in the road in 2004, that's immaterial."

—*Jorma Ollila, CEO of Nokia, in mid 2004.*[1]

"Nokia didn't have the coolness factor. They didn't really do flip phones; they were a little late with cameras, and they didn't push them. Coolness in the consumer space is a big deal, and they were stodgy."

—*Jack Gold, vice president of Meta Group, a Connecticut-based technology consulting firm, in 2005.*[2]

Positive Signs

The announcement of Nokia Corporation's (Nokia) quarterly results in April 2005 was a much awaited event as far as the global mobile phone industry was concerned. The company, which had emerged as an industry leader in the late 1990s, had run into rough weather in 2003–2004, with sales and earnings falling below expected levels. So much so that when the company announced poor results in the first quarter of 2004, several analysts declared that it was the beginning of the end of Nokia's dominance in the industry.

However, Nokia was not ready to throw in the towel quite so easily. The company put up a tough fight over the second half of 2004 to recapture its lost position in the market. It introduced several new models, modified designs, and aggressively promoted products with a view to increasing its market share, which had fallen to a low of around 28 percent in early 2004 from an average of 35 percent over the previous three years.

Nokia's efforts started paying off by late 2004. The company announced satisfactory results for the fourth quarter of 2004 and market share for the year 2004 also stabilized at 32 percent by the end of the year. Jorma Ollila (Ollila), Nokia's CEO, while acknowledging that 2004 had been a challenging year, declared that the company was poised to recover in 2005. Ollila's prediction came true when the company announced better than expected results for the first quarter of 2005, ending March 31.

In the first quarter of 2005, Nokia's sales increased 17 percent over the corresponding quarter of the previous year to $9.65 billion. Net profit rose 18 percent to $1.1 billion. Global handset sales rose 11 percent, prompting Nokia to increase its estimate of the size of the global handset market in 2005 by 100 million to 740 million. Commenting on Nokia's improved

---

[1] Kevin Maney, "CEO Ollila says Nokia's 'sisu' will see it past tough times," *USA Today,* July 20, 2004.
[2] Nelson D. Schwartz, "Has Nokia Lost It?" *Fortune,* January 11, 2005.

performance, Jussi Hyoty (Hyoty), an analyst at securities firm FIM Securities, said, "Nokia's result was definitely better than expected, and it shows that it's a growth company again."[3]

However, despite these positive signs, several analysts wondered whether Nokia would ever be able to dominate the industry as it did in the late 1990s and the first two years of the new century, especially in light of the aggressive competition posed by several new Asian companies as well as more established players like Motorola and Sony Ericsson.

Background

Despite the relatively recent emergence of the mobile phone industry globally, Nokia's company history goes back to the 1800s. The company was first set up on the banks of the river Nokia (after which it was named) in southwestern Finland in 1865 by Fredrik Idestam, who was a mining engineer. The original Nokia was a forest industry enterprise that primarily manufactured paper.

In 1898, Carl Henrik Lampen, a shopkeeper, and J.E. Segerberg, an engineer, set up the Finnish Rubber Works Ltd. (FRW) to manufacture rubber and associated chemicals. In 1912, Konstantin Wikstrom, an engineer, set up the Finnish Cable Works (FCW) to manufacture electrical cables for lighting purposes. These three companies had business dealings with each other through the early 1900s and eventually merged in 1967 to form the Nokia Corporation. The new company had four major businesses—forestry, rubber, cable and electronics.

By 1980, Nokia was a large business conglomerate with several businesses ranging from tires to televisions and computers to telecommunications. Nokia's history of mobile phones started in 1981, when the company manufactured the first car phones for NMT, the world's first international cellular mobile telephone network. The phones were launched in Scandinavia. The company was also the original producer of the first hand portable phones in 1987, which revolutionized the portable phones market that had only seen huge, bulky models until then. Nokia was also instrumental in popularizing GSM technology,[4] which, at that time, was just picking up in Finland.

Over the years, Nokia diversified through acquisitions. The company entered new markets and adopted new technologies by acquiring other companies working in those areas. In the early 1980s, Nokia acquired Mobira, Salora, Televa and Luxor of Sweden to strengthen its position in the consumer electronics and telecommunications markets. In 1987, it acquired the consumer electronics operations of the German company, Standard Elektrik Lorenz, the French consumer electronics company, Oceanic, and the Swiss cable machinery company, Maillefer. In the late 1980s, Nokia acquired the data systems division of Ericsson to become the largest Scandinavian information technology company. This was followed by an expansion of its cable industry into Continental Europe with the acquisition of the Dutch cable company, NKF.

The collapse of the USSR in 1990 put Nokia in a difficult situation. Finland had been heavily dependent on the USSR for trade and the collapse sent it spiraling into a depression. Nokia, which was then operating in such diverse fields as rubber, electronics and communication equipment, decided to change its strategy to adapt to the changed global environment. Under the leadership of Ollila, who was made head of the company's cellular phone operations in 1990, Nokia divested itself of its other businesses and sharpened its focus on telecommunications. The company also made the critical decision to manufacture phones that could be sold anywhere in the world, thus adopting the GSM technology standard, which was at a nascent stage at that time.

The Rise to the Top

Nokia drew on its experience of setting up Nordic cellular networks (which were more advanced than those used by Japan, the rest of Europe, and the US at that time) to successfully adopt the GSM standard. The company was listed on the New York Stock Exchange in 1994. Over the 1990s, Nokia became one of the most successful mobile phone manufacturers in the world and began to enter non-Scandinavian markets as well. Nokia was also one of the first mobile manufacturers to realize the importance of the design element in mobile phones and its phones were more aesthetically designed than those of competitors. In 1998, Nokia overtook Motorola to become the largest mobile manufacturer in the world. In that year, Nokia's workforce increased by almost 30 percent, its sales rose by 51 percent, and its operating profits increased by 71 percent.

Over the 1990s and the early 2000s, Nokia introduced several mobile phone models in quick succession. Most of them went on to become runaway successes (Refer to Table 1 for some of Nokia's popular models).

---

[3] "Nokia Sees Double-Digit Growth in Its 1Q," news.yahoo.com.

[4] Global System for Mobile Communications is an international standard for digital cellular communications.

Table 1	Nokia's Popular Phone Models up to 2000	
Model Number	Year of Launch	Unit sales (in millions)
101	1992	12
2100	1994	20
5100	1998	100+
3200	1999	45
8200	1999	35
3300	2000	70+

Source: Paul Kaihla, "Nokia's Hit Factory," Business 2.0, August 01, 2002.

The company hit its peak between 2000 and 2002, when it held a market share of around 35 percent, which was considerably higher than that of its nearest competitor (Refer to Table 2). By 2003, analysts estimated that Nokia had manufactured about one-third of the mobile phones in use around the world.

However, things changed suddenly for the company in 2003, when it began to experience a spate of problems relating to falling market share and poor financial performance.

Designed for Innovation

Nokia was the first mobile phone manufacturer to realize in the late 1990s that phones no longer played only a functional role; they were also becoming fashion symbols. Until Nokia began emphasizing the design aspect, mobile phones were bulky, bricklike devices with an external antenna and a standard keypad. Manufacturers emphasized functionality over aesthetic appeal.

Nokia broke new ground in 1999, when it launched its 8200 handset on the catwalk at a Paris fashion week. The phone was a tremendous success and for Nokia, there was no looking back. Following up on its success with the 8200 series, the company regularly brought out phones that were considered design marvels and impressed customers with their trendy looks. This helped the company create a cult-like following in the market, which helped it become the top mobile manufacturer in the world.

As greater emphasis began to be laid on design and looks, Nokia's dependence on innovation increased. The company realized that innovativeness was an essential attribute if it was to remain in the forefront as far as design and technology were concerned. Consequently, it made an effort to incorporate creativity and innovation in its operations and encouraged employees to come up with new ideas.

Many of Nokia's most successful innovations came from employees. The employees were free to express their ideas, and many of these ideas were incorporated into phones if they were found functional. Employees rarely faced bureaucratic obstacles in bringing their ideas to the top management. Sometimes, new ideas that involved low risk and few resources were implemented without prior approval from the top management. One instance of this was the feature that allowed users to send text messages to each other in a chat room over their mobile phones. This concept, developed by a researcher called Lone Sorenson, was incorporated in the

Table 2	Market Share of Major Players in Mobile Phones			
Company	2002 sales (in thousands)	2002 market share (%)	2001 sales (in thousands)	2001 market share (%)
Nokia	151421.8	35.8	139672.2	35.0
Motorola	64640.1	15.3	59092.2	14.8
Samsung	41684.4	9.8	28233.5	7.1
Siemens	34618.0	8.2	29752.8	7.4
SonyEriccson	23112.9	5.5	26955.9	6.7
Others	107941.4	25.5	115876.6	29.0
Total market	423418.5	100.00	399583.2	100.00

Source: Gartner Dataquest (March 2003) press.gartner.com

3310 model without the prior approval of the top management, and it became hugely popular with customers.

The implementation of Nokia's *Navikey*, which radically changed user interface systems in Nokia's products, was another example of the kind of support researchers received at Nokia. Christian Lindholm (Lindholm), who was an apprentice with a group studying user interfaces in the 1990s, got the idea of improving the user interface on phones by removing some of the dispensable keys and combining their functions in a single key. Yrjo Neuvo, (head of R&D at Nokia at that time), immediately grasped the essentials of the idea and its potential, and helped Lindholm sell it to the other heads in the organization. Within a year, the feature was included in the 5100 and 6100 models, and received instant customer approval.

In another instance, management support led to the development of phones with internal antennae. In 1996, when Erkki Kuisma (Kuisma) got the idea of developing phones with the antenna concealed inside the body, he met with resistance from some of the executives who felt that consumers would perceive a phone without an antenna as not being powerful enough. However, the head of Nokia's R&D division backed him completely, and this eventually helped to clinch the support of the other executives. Models with internal antennae debuted in 1998 in Nokia's 8800 series and were an instant success. The series went on to become one of the most profitable products in Nokia's history, grossing profit margins of 70 to 80 percent.

To facilitate and promote innovation in the best manner possible, Nokia adopted an un-conservative R&D structure. While most large companies had centralized R&D facilities with tall hierarchical structures to facilitate strict control over processes and research, Nokia's R&D operations were scattered across the world in nearly 70 sites. The engineers, designers and sociologists who manned these centers were given complete freedom to operate and develop their own ideas, over and above their officially designated research projects. The structure was flat and most of the employees reported directly to the head of R&D.

According to company sources, the aim of a dispersed R&D was to ensure that the researchers did not develop 'tunnel vision'. By establishing research centers around the world, Nokia was able to get a wider perspective of the market as well as access to international intelligence. This was eventually reflected in its products.

By 2000–2001, Nokia was firmly established at the top of the mobile phone industry, controlling around 35 percent of the market. The top management was positive about the outlook for the company and believed that Nokia's preeminence would last well into the future. Olli-Pekka Kallasvu (Kallasvu), Nokia's chief financial officer, even remarked, "The complexity [of the new devices] benefits us. We know this industry better than anyone. Complexity improves our competitive position."[5] But even at that time, Ollila remarked that the biggest danger the company faced was its own complacency. Events that immediately followed were to prove Ollila's apprehensions right.

Given Nokia's reputation for cutting edge products and the efforts the company made to remain in the forefront, it came as a shock to see it stumble in 2003–2004. Even more unexpected were the reasons given for the company's troubles, which included misinterpretation of market signals and design backwardness, two factors that had played an important role in the company's initial success.

The Decline

In mid-2004, *The Economist* wrote, "When a firm dominates its market, especially one that is driven by constant technological advances, it risks becoming so fixated with trying to ward off what it reckons to be its most powerful challenger that it leaves itself vulnerable to attack from other directions."[6] Analysts said this statement accurately characterized what happened with Nokia.

In the early 2000s, Microsoft Corp (Microsoft) announced its decision to enter the mobile phones market. The announcement set alarm bells ringing in Nokia as Microsoft had the reputation of being an aggressive competitor. Preoccupied with warding off the possible competition from Microsoft, Nokia totally failed to read market signals like growing demand for 'clamshell' phones, color monitors and camera options, while Asian players like Samsung, LG and Sharp quickly introduced new models at better prices. Companies like Motorola and Sony Ericsson also proved more agile than Nokia in adapting to new market demands. "We read the signs in the marketplace a bit wrong. While Nokia was focused on functional advantages like phone size and ease of use, the competition was emphasizing factors such as color richness and screen size. That's attractive at the point of sale," said Anssi Vanjoki, head of Nokia's multimedia operations.[7]

Although the signs were visible even in 2003, Nokia admitted to slowing sales for the first time only in

[5] "A Finnish fable," *The Economist*, October 12, 2000.
[6] "Nokia fights back," *The Economist*, June 15 2004.
[7] Nelson D. Schwartz, "Has Nokia Lost It?" *Fortune*, January 11, 2005.

April 2004, when it announced disappointing first quarter 2004 results. Gartner, a reputed market research firm, estimated that Nokia's unit sales of handsets had grown by a mere 12 percent, from 39.5 million in the first quarter of 2003, to 44.2 million in the first quarter of 2004 compared to the overall market growth of 34 percent.

Nokia's global market share fell to 28.9 percent in the first quarter of 2004, from 34.6 percent in the first quarter of 2003. This was a significant fall, as Nokia's market share had hovered around 35 percent for almost three years. In contrast, all the company's major rivals recorded an increased market share in that quarter (Refer to Table 3).

This trend continued into the second quarter of 2004 as well as Nokia continued to lose market share to rivals (Refer to Table 4). Nokia's global market share fell to 27.7 percent in the second quarter, although the sales increased 11.8 percent over that of the same period of the previous year. Financial performance, however, was poor as revenue fell five percent from around $8.4 billion in the second quarter of 2003 to $8.0 billion in the second quarter of 2004 and the operating margin of the company's mobile phones unit fell to 19 percent in 2004 from 27 percent in 2003.

The reasons for Nokia's poor performance were many. One of the most discussed factors was the company's excessive investment in high-end phones and complicated software, at a time when the market was more favorable for attractive phones at a reasonable price.

One of Nokia's big disappointments in the early 2000s was the lower than expected performance of its cell phone and gaming device N-Gage. While the N-Gage was a technically superior product and spoke for the technological advancement of Nokia, it did not find favor in the market. There were several reasons for this. First, the N-Gage was priced considerably higher than many other gaming devices in the market (the N-Gage was priced at $299, while competing products like the Gameboy Advance were sold at $99). Second, the N-Gage had certain basic design defects, which made it inconvenient to use. Instead of the traditional horizontal screen, the screen in N-Gage was vertically integrated and many users did not like this. In addition, loading the games' software into the system was a long and complicated process taking nearly one and a half minutes to install. Using the phone feature of the instrument was also inconvenient as the device had to be held at an awkward angle for a person to be able to listen and speak into the phone. (Refer to Exhibit 1 for picture). Consequently, the N-Gage did not live up to the hype it had generated before its launch.

Nokia also invested heavily in the development of advanced software, such as the S60 Operating System, which was designed to bring computing capability to mobile phones. However, in 2003–2004, the market was not yet ready for this technology and the operating

Table 3	Global Market Share of Major Players (in %)	
Company	**Q1 2004**	**Q1 2003**
Motorola	16.4	14.7
Samsung	12.5	10.8
Siemens	8.0	7.6
Sony Ericsson	5.6	4.7
LG	5.3	4.9

Compiled from various sources.

Table 4	Global Market Share of Major Players (in %)
Company	**Q2 2004**
Motorola	14.7
Samsung	13.9
Siemens	6.4
Sony Ericsson	6.4
LG	6.1

Source: Compiled from various sources.

Exhibit 1	The Phone Feature of N-Gage

Source: Money.cnn.com

system did not catch on. At the end of 2004, the S60 was present in only one percent of all the mobile phones in the world. Nokia acknowledged that it had focused too much on technologies that were too advanced for the market, but the company justified its investment by claiming that the market would eventually be ready for such devices, giving it an advantage over competitors in the long run.

Analysts said because of its focus on high-end phones and technologically advanced products, Nokia failed to see some of the trends emerging in the mobile phone industry in the early 2000s. For instance, 'clamshells' or flip phones (phones which were foldable) were becoming very popular in Asia and North America, relative to the traditional 'candy-bar' or non-folding models. Clamshells were thought to be easier to carry and more classy in appearance than the candy-bars. By 2004, Nokia was the only mobile manufacturer that did not offer clamshells. Samsung and LG, on the other hand, had an impressive line-up in this design.

Considering its backwardness in adapting to new trends, analysts began to say that Nokia had lost its edge in design. Nokia's phones were very popular initially because of their trendy design and the regular introduction of new features. In fact, analysts observed that during its peak, Nokia introduced new features in almost each of its new phone models.

However, innovation of this kind tapered off around 2003–2004, as Nokia started focusing more on technological superiority and excellence. Certain analysts claimed that despite seeing the growing popularity of clamshells, Nokia obstinately clung to candy-bars as the company reaped cost advantages by producing large volumes of different phones that were variants of the same basic design. In the bargain, it lost a considerable chunk of the market to competitors, as clamshells accounted for nearly 30 percent of all the mobile phones sold by 2004.

In addition to this, Nokia failed to note the growing popularity of color screens and camera phones and had very few models which offered these features. The few that did were priced higher than competitors' products, which made people wishing to upgrade their mobile phones look to vendors other than Nokia.

Analysts said there were huge gaps in Nokia's product line-up. Nokia had a good variety of entry level models (which offered only the basic voice and text functions), as well as a fair number of advanced phones, but had very little to offer in the mid-price segment of phones, which was also the fastest growing in the early 2000s. As the penetration of mobile phones increased, customers were increasingly upgrading to mid-range phones, which offered the basic telephoning features along with a few additions like color monitors and camera options. (Analysts estimated that around two-thirds of the phones sold in 2004 had color screens and around 44 percent had cameras.) This was the segment in which Nokia was the weakest. "The portfolio was missing the edge it had before," said Carolina Milanesi, an analyst at Gartner.[8]

Another important reason for Nokia's problems was the company's reluctance to introduce customized, operator-specific handsets, which was emerging as a major trend in the industry in the early 2000s. In order to capture a share in a fast saturating market, cellular operators around the world were increasingly striking deals with handset manufacturers (especially those from Asia) to manufacture handsets designed especially for the service provider. For instance, Vodafone, one of the largest mobile operators in the world, launched 'Vodafone live!' data service using handsets made by Sharp, the Japanese firm. Motorola also manufactured a special version of one of its handsets for Vodafone.

This tie-up with operators helped many companies boost their market share. However, Nokia was steadfast in refusing to manufacture operator specific handsets as it believed that it was not feasible to produce small volumes of handsets for specific operators in the light of company costs. It also did not want to be a participant in a battle between the several operators providing cellular service. It reasoned that switching between operators was easy and therefore, customer loyalties would lie with the handset makers. By associating itself with certain operators, the company did not want to lose its standing in the market. Analysts said the company lost considerable market share due to this stand.

In addition to this, Nokia underwent an internal reorganization in late 2003, which caused an upheaval in the company and indirectly resulted in its losing focus of the market. Ollila later acknowledged that the timing of the reorganization was wrong, but maintained that it was necessary to equip the company for its future needs. Nokia was divided into four major business groups in addition to a corporate strategy group, research and development units, corporate-wide sales, manufacturing, marketing, logistics and technology units. The four major business groups were:

- **Mobile Phones**—which offered a global range of mobile phones for large consumer segments. The group was headed by Olli-Pekka Kallasvuo (Kallasvuo).

---

[8] "The giant in the palm of your hand," *The Economist*, February 10, 2005.

Case 23 / Nokia and the Global Mobile Phone Industry

- **Multimedia**—which focused on bringing mobile multimedia to consumers in the form of images, games, music and a range of other attractive content. The group was headed by Anssi Vanjoki.
- **Networks**—which offered network technology and related services based on major wireless standards. The group was headed by Sari Baldauf.
- **Enterprise Solutions**—which provided a range of terminals and mobile connectivity solutions to enterprises based on end-to-end mobility architecture. Mary McDowell was appointed as the general manager for the group.

Efforts at Recovery

Soon after announcing disappointing results in the first quarter of 2004, Nokia realized that it was in trouble and began to take steps to correct matters. The company not only cut prices on certain handsets to increase market share, but also fine-tuned its portfolio to adjust products to meet market needs. It killed some outmoded models and brought forward the launch of several others, including a number of clamshell phones.

In June 2004, Nokia launched five new models of phones, out of which three were clamshells. Nokia's new models were the 6260 model, a clamshell whose cover not only flipped open but also swiveled, the 6630, which Nokia claimed was the world's smallest camera phone, designed for 3G networks, another clamshell, the 6170, and two low end models, the 2650 and 2600. Several other models were also marketed aggressively. For instance, the low end 1100 model for emerging markets and the 6230 mid-range model became very popular in 2004. (The 6230 was so popular in some markets that at times, Nokia was not able to meet the demand).

Analysts said Nokia seemed keen to prove that its dominance of the market was not at an end. "We can make phones that consumers can't recognize are from the same platform. There's more emphasis on new form factors like clamshells, swivels, slides. I'm pushing them as quickly as I can," said Kallasvuo, the head of the mobile-phone division.

The company also postponed until 2005 the launch of the 7700, a much hyped 'media device' that it announced in late 2003. The 7700 was designed to be a phone-cum-media player, featuring a wide color screen and a 'jukebox' shape. The phone had the capability to play FM and MP3 files as well as show digital videos and digital broadcast TV. Announcing the postponement, Nokia said that the 7700 was 'too early for the market'.

Nokia's launch of the five new models received mixed responses in the market. Some analysts were positive about the new models. "The clamshell phones are exactly what's needed so they're filling the right gaps," said Hyoty.[9] Others were skeptical, pointing out that Nokia's new models had to compete with a broader line-up from its rivals. "I wasn't that enthusiastic about the new clamshells, even though the 6260 looked okay. I'm not really sure it can match the competition," said Erkki Vesola, a stockbroker.[10] He also expressed concern over the fact that Nokia had cut the number of new product launches in 2004 to 35 from 40, while smaller rivals planned equal or more new products that year.

The company also gave in to operator customization in late 2004, realizing that it risked losing its market presence if it did not cooperate with powerful operators. However, despite giving in to customization, Nokia stayed with software customization rather than customizing hardware. The company launched software that was compatible with different operators' news, music and gaming services, without having to modify the hardware. Nokia, however, announced that it would also look at hardware customization in the future when it became feasible to do so. Market observers said that giving in to customization was a smart move on the part of the company as it had an immediate impact on market share. By late 2004, Nokia's market share had improved considerably, bringing up the annual market share figure to 32 percent.

Analysts also said that Nokia was making efforts to dilute its Finnish character to help the company adapt to an increasingly global scenario. It was finalizing a plan to open a second headquarters in New York in the future. The company also began hiring non-Finnish employees for top level positions in 2004. Some of them were Rick Simpson, who became Nokia's CFO, and Mary McDowell (McDowell), who headed the enterprise solutions division.

A Challenging Future

Despite Nokia's laudable efforts in the direction of recapturing its lost market position, the opinions of analysts on its turnaround were mixed. While the company's detractors believed that Nokia had lost its competitive advantage in the mobile phone market, its supporters said the company's inherent strengths and stable financial position would help it sail through the difficulties it had faced in 2003–2004 to recover in the future. However, most of them agreed that the mobile phone industry was undergoing a vast change.

[9] "Nokia unveils 5 new phones," www.msnbc.msn.com, June 14, 2004.
[10] "Nokia unveils 5 new phones," www.msnbc.msn.com, June 14, 2004.

In the early 2000s, mobile phones were expected to perform a variety of functions in addition to looking stylish and being easy to operate. Nokia's competitors had understood this and were in the process of launching several models that were style statements in themselves. The most popular and stylish phone model in 2004 was the Motorola RAZR V3, which came with a stylish aluminum shell and became extremely popular for its sleek design.

Sony Ericsson also became the first company to launch a 'swivel phone' with a jackknife style of operation when it announced the launch of the S700 mobile phone based on this design in 2005. The S700 resembled a camera when closed, with lens in front and a large screen at the back. When it swiveled open, it revealed a standard mobile phone. The camera quality was also developed like the Sony digital camera. Other companies like LG were also fast developing 3G mobile phones. Although Nokia believed that the market was not completely ready for a 3G model, in the fourth quarter of 2004, it started shipping the 6630 3G phone, which received a positive initial response. The global mobile industry was also becoming increasingly volatile and several Asian players were entering and making their presence felt in the market. These players were not only the more established ones from Japan and South Korea, but also came from emerging countries like Taiwan and China.

A major challenge for Nokia in the future was to identify new avenues for growth in a market that was becoming increasingly saturated. Analysts said that Nokia would do well to concentrate on developing countries, which still offered good potential for mobile penetration. Nokia had already taken steps in this direction, when it launched models specifically designed for emerging markets, notably the successful 1100 phone. In 2004, the company also strengthened its presence in countries like India, Russia, Africa, and the Middle East.

Mobile phones designed specifically for business users presented another possible option. "We think it's probably the single largest untapped market for Nokia," said McDowell.[11] The company primarily focused on mobile corporate e-mail, where it expected to have the maximum potential for growth. Nokia estimated that less than 10 percent of employees had mobile e-mail and hence, the potential market was large. Nokia had already licensed BlackBerry software[12] for use on some of its handsets and was looking at several other similar options. The teams working on business-user focused projects were also based in New York in order to be close

to Wall Street firms, which were usually the leading adopters of new technologies.

Multimedia and gaming devices were also under consideration. However, before launching new devices in this area, Nokia was concentrating on improving N-Gage and warding off competition in the form of the Sony PSP and the Nintendo DS models. The company was also working on mobile television devices.

Considering Nokia's past performance and its capabilities, analysts said the company had the potential to remain a major presence in the global mobile phone industry in the future. However, few believed that the company would regain the undisputed leadership it enjoyed in the late 1990s and in 2001–2002, despite Nokia's ambitious target of capturing 40 percent of the global market in the future.

Questions for Discussion

1. In the late 1990s, Nokia emerged as the leader of the global mobile phone industry. However, by 2003, the company faced several problems. Discuss Nokia's rise to the top and its eventual decline.

2. In its heydays, Nokia was well known and recognized for its innovativeness and rapidity in introducing new products. However, one of the main reasons for its troubles in the early 2000s was that it had failed to read market signals and lagged behind in product development. What were the reasons for the company's problems? Do you agree that complacency had taken its toll on Nokia?

3. Comment on Nokia's efforts to recover its lost market share. Do you think that the company will be able to recapture its position in the mobile phone market? Discuss in light of Nokia's future plans.

Additional Readings & References

1. **To the Finland base station,** The Economist, October 7, 1999.
2. **A Finnish fable,** The Economist, October 12, 2000.
3. **From forests to phones,** The Economist, May 31, 2001.
4. **Surprise! Nokia Doesn't Walk on Water,** Business Week, June 15, 2001.
5. Paul Kaihla, **Nokia's Hit Factory,** Business 2.0, August 01, 2002.
6. **The fight for digital dominance,** The Economist, November 21, 2002.
7. **Nokia's folly,** money.cnn.com, October 6, 2003.
8. **Nokia Downplays Reports It Is Losing Market Share,** TechWeb.com December 8, 2003.
9. Janet Guyon, **Nokia Tries to Reinvent Itself—Again,** Fortune, March 22, 2004.
10. Scott Moritz, **Turnaround Eludes Nokia,** www.street.com, April 16, 2004.

---

[11] "The giant in the palm of your hand," *The Economist,* February 10, 2005.
[12] An email device manufactured by RIM of Canada.

11. Paul R. La Monica, **Flip-phone flip-flop,** money.cnn.com, April 16, 2004.
12. Mark Milner, **Nokia losing market share,** The Guardian, April 17, 2004.
13. **Battling for the palm of your hand,** The Economist, April 29, 2004.
14. Jason Lopez, **Nokia Share Slides as Cell-Phone Sales Jump,** Wireless NewsFactor, June 8, 2004.
15. Paul R. La Monica, **Saying 'no' to Nokia,** money.cnn.com, June 8, 2004.
16. **Nokia losing mobile-phone market share, Gartner says,** Taipei Times, June 9, 2004.
17. **Nokia unveils 5 new phones,** www.msnbc.msn.com, June 14, 2004.
18. Andy Reinhardt, **Wounded, Nokia Comes Back Firing,** Business Week, June 15, 2004.
19. **Nokia fights back,** The Economist, June 15 2004.
20. Peter J. Howe, **As rivals gain, Nokia hustles to offer cellphones with coveted features,** The Boston Globe, June 16, 2004.
21. **Too many candy bars?** The Economist, June 17, 2004.
22. Robin Arnfield, **Nokia Licenses Blackberry Patents,** Wireless NewsFactor, June 17, 2004.
23. Janice Revell, **Why Nokia's a Buy,** Fortune, July 12, 2004.
24. Beatrice Arnfield, **Nokia Disappoints Investors,** Wireless NewsFactor, July 15, 2004.
25. Andy Reinhardt, **Is Nokia Really So Bad Off?** Business Week, July 15, 2004.
26. Kevin Maney, **CEO Ollila says Nokia's 'sisu' will see it past tough times,** USA Today, July 20, 2004.
27. Robin Arnfield, **Study: Nokia Losing Ground,** Wireless NewsFactor, August 2, 2004.
28. Andy Reinhardt, **Nokia's Goal: Cell-Phone Planet,** Business Week, September 7, 2004.
29. Burt Helm, **Tough Calls at Nokia,** Business Week, October 20, 2004.
30. Nelson D. Schwartz, **Has Nokia Lost It?** Fortune, January 11, 2005.
31. **The giant in the palm of your hand,** The Economist, February 10, 2005.
32. Richard Wray, **Nokia upbeat as it predicts mobile users to reach 3bn,** The Guardian, February 15, 2005.
33. **Nokia Sees Double-Digit Growth in Its 1Q,** news.yahoo.com.
34. press.gartner.com
35. Money.cnn.com
36. www.msnbc.com
37. biz.yahoo.com
38. www.hoovers.com
39. www.nokia.com

Nucor in 2005

Frank C. Barnes
University of North Carolina

Beverly B. Tyler
North Carolina State University

Nucor Corp. took first place in the 2005 *BusinessWeek* 50 list of the best performers of S&P 500 companies. Not bad for a company in an industry often considered unexciting and low tech! In 2004 sales were up 82 percent, from $6 to $12 billion, and earnings went from $0.40 to $7.02 per share. In a little over a year the stock price tripled. Longtime employees with $300,000 in their retirement stock saw it rise to more than $1 million. The tons shipped increased 9 percent with the average selling price up 66 percent. However, scrap prices were up 74 percent. At the beginning of 2005 prices seemed to be holding up because of the mergers in the United States and the state control of supply in China. And Nucor expected the first quarter of 2005 to double the 2004 results. This was a reasonable expectation since Nucor began the year with 70 percent of its flat-rolled steel output for all of 2005 sold, compared to just 25 percent a year earlier. Furthermore, in 2005 Nucor had two joint ventures with global partners to find alternatives to the use of scrap steel. In Brazil the company was working on an environmentally friendly way to produce pig iron. With Mitsubishi and the Chinese steelmaker Shougang, Nucor was building a facility in Western Australia to use the new HIsmelt process to produce iron from iron ore finds and cold fines with less energy and pollution.

The previous three years had been among the worst down cycles in the steel industry's history. During those years Nucor acquired failing competitors, increased its steel capacity, and achieved a profit in every quarter. The world economy and demand had improved recently as prices went from $300 a ton to $640 a ton. Thus, Nucor expected profits to continue to grow for a while. While bankruptcies had eliminated some excess capacity in the United States, and state-controlled China could hold back capacity to maintain prices, global competitors were consolidating, suppliers were raising their prices on iron ore and scrap, and buyers were considering alternatives to steel. Nucor, and its new president Dan DiMicco, faced a challenge in continuing Nucor's reputation for excellence.

Background

Nucor can be traced back to the company that manufactured the first Oldsmobile in 1897 and became the Reo Truck Company. As the company declined into bankruptcy in the postwar years, a 1955 merger created Nuclear Corp. of America. Following the "conglomerate" trend of the period, Nuclear acquired various "high-tech" businesses, such as radiation sensors, semi-conductors, rare earths, and air-conditioning equipment. However, the company lost money continually, and a fourth reorganization in 1966 put 40-year-old Ken Iverson in charge. The building of Nucor had begun.

Ken Iverson had joined the Navy after high school in 1943 and had been transferred from officer training school to Cornell's Aeronautical Engineering Program. On graduation he selected mechanical engineering/metallurgy for a master's degree to avoid the long drafting apprenticeship in aeronautical engineering. His college work with an electron microscope earned him a job with International Harvester. After five years in its lab, his boss, and mentor, prodded him to expand his vision by going with a smaller company.

Over the next 10 years, Iverson worked for four small metals companies, gaining technical knowledge and increasing his exposure to other business functions. He

Nucor in 2005 by Frank C. Barnes and Beverly B. Tyler. Reprinted by permission of Frank C. Barnes, University of North Carolina, Charlotte, and Beverly B. Tyler, College of Management, North Carolina State University.

enjoyed working with the presidents of these small companies and admired their ability to achieve outstanding results. Nuclear Corp., after failing to buy the company Iverson worked for, hired him as a consultant to find another metals business to buy. In 1962, the firm bought a small joist plant in South Carolina (Vulcraft) that Iverson found, with the condition that he would be in charge of the plant.

Over the next four years Iverson built up the Vulcraft division as Nuclear Corporation struggled. The president, David Thomas, was described as a great promoter and salesman but a weak manager. A partner with Bear Stearns actually made a personal loan to the company to keep it going. In 1966, when the company was on the edge of bankruptcy, Iverson, who headed the only successful division, was named president and moved the headquarters to Charlotte, North Carolina, where he focused the company business first on the joist industry and then on steel production.

He immediately began eliminating the esoteric, but unprofitable, high-tech divisions and concentrated on the steel joist business he found successful. The company built more joist plants and in 1968 began building its first steel mill in South Carolina to "make steel cheaper than they were buying from importers." By 1984 Nucor had six joist plants and four steel mills, all using the new "mini-mill" technology.

From the beginning, Iverson had the people running the various plants, called divisions, make all the major decisions about how to build and run Nucor. The original board was composed of Iverson; Sam Siegel, his financial chief; and Dave Aycock, who had been with the South Carolina joist company before Nuclear acquired it. Siegel had joined Nuclear as an accountant in 1961. He had quit Nuclear but in its crisis agreed to return as treasurer if Iverson was named president. Aycock and Siegel were named vice presidents at the time Iverson was named president.

Dave Aycock had been very impressed with the original owner of Vulcraft, Sanborn Chase. Aycock had started his career as a welder there. He described Chase as "the best person I've ever known" and as "a scientific genius." He said he was a man of great compassion, who understood the atmosphere necessary for people to self-motivate. Chase, an engineer by training, invented a number of things in diverse fields. He also established the incentive programs for which Nucor later became known. With only one plant, he was still able to operate with a "decentralized" manner. Before his death in 1960, while still in his 40s, the company was studying the building of a steel mill using newly developed mini-mill technology. His widow ran the company until it was sold to Nucor in 1962.

Aycock met Ken Iverson when Nuclear purchased Vulcraft, and they worked together closely for the next year and a half. Located in Phoenix at the corporate headquarters, Aycock was responsible to Iverson for all the joist operations and was given the task of planning and building a new joist plant in Texas. In late 1963 he was transferred to Norfolk, Nebraska, where he lived for the next 13 years and managed a number of Nucor's joist plants. Then in 1977 he was named the manager of the Darlington, South Carolina, steel plant. In 1984, Aycock became Nucor's president and chief operating officer, while Iverson became chairman and chief executive officer.

Aycock had this to say about Iverson: "Ken was a very good leader, with an entrepreneurial spirit. He was easy to work with and had the courage to do things, to take lots of risks. Many things didn't work, but some worked very well." There is an old saying, "failure to take risk is failure." This saying epitomizes a cultural value personified by the company's founder and reinforced by Iverson during his time at the helm. Nucor was very innovative in steel and joists. Its plant at Norfolk was years ahead in wire rod welding. In the late 1960s it had one of the first computer inventory management systems and design/engineering programs. The company was very sophisticated in purchasing, sales, and managing, and beat its competition often by the speed of its design efforts.

Between 1964 and 1984 the bankrupt conglomerate became a leading U.S. steel company. It was a fairy-tale story. Tom Peters used Nucor's management style as an example of "excellence," while the barons of old steel ruled over creeping ghettos. NBC featured Nucor on television and *The New Yorker* magazine serialized a book about how a relatively small American steel company built a team that led the whole world into a new era of steelmaking. As the NBC program asked: "If Japan Can, Why Can't We?" Nucor had! Iverson was rich, owning $10 million in stock, but with a salary that rarely reached $1 million, compared to some U.S. executives' $50 million or $100 million. The 40-year-old manager of the South Carolina Vulcraft plant had become a millionaire. Stockholders chuckled, and un-unionized hourly workers, who had never seen a layoff in the 20 years, earned more than the unionized workers of old steel and more than 85 percent of the people in the states where they worked. Many employees were financially quite secure.

Nucor owed much of its success to its benchmark organizational style and the empowered division managers. There were two basic lines of business, the first being the six steel joist plants which made the steel frames seen in many buildings. The second line included four steel mills that utilized the innovative mini-mill technology to supply first the joist plants and later outside customers. Nucor was still only the seventh-largest steel company in America. Over its second 20 years, Nucor was to rise to become the second-largest U.S. steel company. A number of significant challenges were to be met and overcome to get there, and once that horizon was reached, even greater challenges would arise. The following are the systems Nucor built and its organization, divisions, management, and incentive system.

Nucor's Organization

In the early 1990s, Nucor had 22 divisions (up to 30 by 2005), one for every plant, each of which had a general manager, who was also a vice president of the corporation. The divisions were of three basic types: joist plants, steel mills, and miscellaneous plants. The corporate staff consisted of fewer than 45 people (25 in the 1990s). In the beginning Iverson had chosen Charlotte "as the new home base for what he had envisioned as a small cadre of executives who would guide a decentralized operation with liberal authority delegated to managers in the field," according to *South* magazine.

Iverson gave his views on keeping a lean organization:

> Each division is a profit center and the division manager has control over the day-to-day decisions that make that particular division profitable or not profitable. We expect the division to provide contribution, which is earnings before corporate expenses. We do not allocate our corporate expenses, because we do not think there is any way to do this reasonably and fairly. We do focus on earnings. And we expect a division to earn 25 percent return on total assets employed, before corporate expenses, taxes, interest or profit sharing. And we have a saying in the company—if a manager doesn't provide that for a number of years, we are either going to get rid of the division or get rid of the general manager, and it's generally the division manager.

A joist division manager commented on being in an organization with only four levels:

> I've been a division manager four years now and at times I'm still awed by it: the opportunity I was given to be a Fortune 500 vice president. . . . I think we are successful because it is our style to pay more attention to our business than our competitors. . . . We are kind of a "no nonsense" company.

The divisions did their own manufacturing, selling, accounting, engineering, and personnel management. A steel division manager, when questioned about Florida Steel, which had a large plant 90 miles away, commented, "I expect they do have more of the hierarchy. I think they

have central purchasing, centralized sales, centralized credit collections, centralized engineering, and most of the major functions."

Nucor strengthened its position by developing strong alliances with outside parties. It did no internal research and development. Instead, it monitored other's work worldwide and attracted investors who brought it new technical applications at the earliest possible dates. Although Nucor was known for constructing new facilities at the lowest possible costs, its engineering and construction team consisted of only three individuals. They did not attempt to specify exact equipment parameters, but asked the equipment supplier to provide this information and then held the manufacturer accountable. Nucor had alliances with selected construction companies around the country who knew the kind of work the company wanted. Nucor bought 95 percent of its scrap steel from an independent broker who followed the market and made recommendations regarding scrap purchases. It did not have a corporate advertising department, a corporate public relations department, or a corporate legal or environmental department. It had long-term relationships with outsiders to provide these services.

The steel industry had established a pattern of absorbing the cost of shipment so, regardless of the distance from the mill, all users paid the same delivered price. Nucor broke with this tradition and stopped equalizing freight. It offered all customers the same sales terms. Nucor also gave no volume discounts, feeling that with modern computer systems there was no justification. Customers located next to the plant guaranteed themselves the lowest possible costs for steel purchases. Two tube manufactures, two steel service centers, and a cold rolling facility had located adjacent to the Arkansas plant. These facilities accounted for 60 percent of the shipments from the mill. The plants were linked electronically to each other's production schedules, allowing them to function in a just-in-time inventory mode. All new mills were built on large enough tracks of land to accommodate collaborating businesses.

Iverson didn't feel greater centralization would be good for Nucor. Hamilton Lott, a Vulcraft plant manager, commented in 1997, "We're truly autonomous; we can duplicate efforts made in other parts of Nucor. We might develop the same computer program six times. But the advantages of local autonomy make it worth it." Joe Rutkowski, manager at Darlington steel, agreed. "We're not constrained; headquarters doesn't restrict what I spend. I just have to make my profit contribution at the end of year."

South magazine observed that Iverson had established a characteristic organizational style described as "stripped down" and "no nonsense." "Jack Benny would like this company," observed Roland Underhill, an analyst with Crowell, Weedon and Co. of Los Angeles. "So would Peter Drucker." Underhill pointed out that Nucor's thriftiness didn't end with its "spartan" office staff or modest offices. "There are no corporate perquisites," he recited. "No company planes. No country club memberships. No company cars."

Fortune noted, "'Iverson takes the subway when he is in New York,' a Wall Street analyst reports in a voice that suggests both admiration and amazement." The general managers reflected this style in the operation of their individual divisions. Their offices were more like plant offices or the offices of private companies built around manufacturing rather than for public appeal. They were simple, routine, and businesslike.

Division Managers

The corporate personnel manager described management relations as informal, trusting, and not "bureaucratic." He felt there was a minimum of paperwork, that a phone call was more common than memos, and that no confirming memo was thought to be necessary.

A Vulcraft manager commented: "We have what I would call a very friendly spirit of competition from one plant to the next. And of course all of the vice presidents and general managers share the same bonus systems so we are in this together as a team even though we operate our divisions individually." He added, "When I came to this plant four years ago, I saw we had too many people, too much overhead. We had 410 people at the plant and I could see, from my experience at the Nebraska plant, we had many more than we needed. Now with 55 fewer men, we are still capable of producing the same number of tons as four years ago."

The divisions managed their activities with a minimum of contact with the corporate staff. Each day disbursements were reported to the corporate office. Payments flowed into regional lock-boxes. On a weekly basis, joist divisions reported total quotes, sales cancellations, backlog, and production. Steel mills reported tons-rolled, outside shipments, orders, cancellations, and backlog.

Each month the divisions completed a two-page (11″ × 17″) "Operations Analysis," which was sent to all the managers. Its three main purposes were (1) financial consolidation, (2) sharing information among the divisions, and (3) corporate management examination. The summarized information and the performance statistics for all the divisions were then returned to the managers.

The general managers met three times a year. In late October they presented preliminary budgets and capital requests. In late February they met to finalize budgets and treat miscellaneous matters. Then, at a meeting in May, they handled personnel matters, such as wage increases and changes of policies or benefits. The general managers as a group considered the raises for the department heads, the next lower level of management for all the plants.

Vulcraft—The Joist Divisions

One of Nucor's major businesses was the manufacture and sale of open web steel joists and joist girders at seven Vulcraft divisions located in Florence, South Carolina; Norfolk, Nebraska; Ft. Payne, Alabama; Grapeland, Texas; St. Joe, Indiana; Brigham City, Utah; and Chemung, New York. Open web joists, in contrast to solid joists, were made of steel angle iron separated by round bars or smaller angle iron. These joists cost less, were of greater strength for many applications, and were used primarily as the roof support systems in larger buildings, such as warehouses and shopping malls.

The joist industry was characterized by high competition among many manufacturers for many small customers. With an estimated 40 percent of the market, Nucor was the largest supplier in the United States. It utilized national advertising campaigns and prepared competitive bids on 80 to 90 percent of the buildings using joists. Competition was based on price and delivery performance. Nucor had developed computer programs to prepare designs for customers and to compute bids based on current prices and labor standards. In addition, each Vulcraft plant maintained its own engineering department to help customers with design problems or specifications. The Florence manager commented, "Here on the East Coast we have six or seven major competitors; of course none of them are as large as we are. The competition for any order will be heavy, and we will see six or seven different prices." He added, "I think we have a strong selling force in the market place. It has been said to us by some of our competitors that in this particular industry we have the finest selling organization in the country."

Nucor aggressively sought to be the lowest-cost producer in the industry. Materials and freight were two important elements of cost. Nucor maintained its own fleet of almost 150 trucks to ensure on-time delivery to all of the states, although most business was regional due to transportation costs. Plants were located in rural areas near the markets they served. Nucor's move into steel production was a move to lower the cost of steel used by the joist business.

Joist Production

On the basic assembly line used at the joist divisions, three or four of which might make up any one plant, about six tons of joists per hour would be assembled. In the first stage eight people cut the angles to the right lengths or bend the round bars to the desired form. These were moved on a roller conveyer to six-man assembly stations, where the component parts would be tacked together for the next stage, welding. Drilling and miscellaneous work were done by three people between the lines. The nine-man welding station completed the welds before passing the joists on roller conveyers to two-man inspection teams. The last step before shipment was the painting.

The workers had control over and responsibility for quality. There was an independent quality control inspector who had the authority to reject the run of joists and cause them to be reworked. The quality control people were not under the incentive system and reported to the engineering department.

Daily production might vary widely, since each joist was made for a specific job. The wide range of joists made control of the workload at each station difficult; bottlenecks might arise anywhere along the line. Each workstation was responsible for identifying such bottlenecks so that the foreman could reassign people promptly to maintain productivity. Because workers knew most of the jobs on the line, including the more skilled welding job, they could be shifted as needed. Work on the line was described by one general manager as "not machine type but mostly physical labor." He said the important thing was to avoid bottlenecks.

There were four lines of about 28 people each on two shifts at the Florence division. The jobs on the line were rated on responsibility and assigned a base wage, from $11 to $13 per hour. In addition, a weekly bonus was paid on the total output of each line. Each worker received the same percent bonus on his other base wage. The Texas plant was typical, with the bonus running 225 percent, giving a wage of $27 an hour in 1999.

The amount of time required to make a joist had been established as a result of experience; the general manager had seen no time studies in his fifteen years with the company. As a job was bid, the cost of each joist was determined through the computer program. The time required depended on the length, number of panels, and depth of the joist. At the time of production, the labor value of production, the standard, was determined in a similar manner. The South Carolina general manager stated, "In the last nine or ten years we have not changed a standard."

The Grapeland plant maintained a time chart, which was used to estimate the labor required on a job. The

Table 1	Tons per Man-Hour
1977	0.163
1978	0.179
1979	0.192
1980	0.195
1981	0.194
1982	0.208
1983	0.215
1984	0.214
1985	0.228
1986	0.225
1987	0.218
1988	0.249
1999	0.251
2000	0.241
2004	0.222

plant teams were measured against this time for bonus. The chart was based on the historical time required on the jobs. Every few years the time chart was updated. Because some of the changes in performance were due to equipment changes, generally the chart would be increased by half the change and the employee would benefit in pay from the other half. The last change, in 2003, saw some departments pay increased by as much as 10 percent. The production manager at Grapeland considered himself an example for the Nucor policy—"the sky is the limit." He had started in an entry position and risen to the head of this plant of 200 people.

Table 1 shows the productivity of the South Carolina plant in tons per man-hour for a number of years. The year 1999 set a record for overall tonnage before a downturn that bottomed in 2002, but had begun to rise again by 2004.

Steel Divisions

Nucor moved into the steel business in 1968 to provide raw material for the Vulcraft plants. Iverson said, "We got into the steel business because we wanted to build a mill that could make steel as cheaply as we were buying it from foreign importers or from offshore mills." Thus, Nucor entered the industry using the new mini-mill technology after taking a task force of four people around the world to investigate new technological advancements. A case writer from Harvard recounted the development of the steel divisions:

> By 1967 about 60 percent of each Vulcraft sales dollar was spent on materials, primarily steel. Thus, the goal of keeping costs low made it imperative to obtain steel economically. In addition, in 1967 Vulcraft bought about 60 percent of its steel from foreign sources. As the Vulcraft Division grew, Nucor became concerned about its ability to obtain an adequate economical supply of steel and in 1968 began construction of its first steel mill in Darlington, South Carolina. By 1972 the Florence, South Carolina, joist plant was purchasing over 90 percent of its steel from this mill. The Fort Payne, Alabama, plant bought about 50 percent of its steel from Florence. Since the mill had excess capacity, Nucor began to market its steel products to outside customers. In 1972, 75 percent of the shipments of Nucor steel was to Vulcraft and 25 percent was to other customers.

Between 1973 and 1981 Nucor constructed three more bar mills and their accompanying rolling mills to convert the billets into bars, flats, rounds, channels, and other products. Iverson explained in 1984:

> In constructing these mills we have experimented with new processes and new manufacturing techniques. We serve as our own general contractor and design and build much of our own equipment. In one or more of our mills we have built our own continuous casting unit, reheat furnaces, cooling beds and in Utah even our own mill stands. All of these to date have cost under $125 per ton of annual capacity—compared with projected costs for large integrated mills of $1,200–$1,500 per ton of annual capacity, ten times our cost. Our mills have high productivity. We currently use less than four man hours to produce a ton of steel. Our total employment costs are less than $60 per ton compared with the average employment costs of the seven largest U.S. steel companies of close to $130 per ton. Our total labor costs are less than 20 percent of our sales price.

In 1987 Nucor was the first steel company in the world to begin to build a mini-mill to manufacture steel sheet, the raw material for the auto industry and other major manufacturers. This project opened up another 50 percent of the total steel market. The first plant, in Crawfordsville, Indiana, was successful, and three additional sheet mills were constructed between 1989 and 1990. Through the years these steel plants were significantly modernized and expanded until the total capacity was three million tons per year at a capital cost of less than $170 per ton by 1999. Nucor's total steel production capacity was 5.9 million tons per year at a cost of $300 per ton of annual capacity. The eight mills sold 80 percent of their output to outside customers and the balance to other Nucor divisions.

By 2005, Nucor had 16 steel facilities producing three times as much steel as in 1999. The number of bar mills had grown to nine mills with capacity of 6 million tons by the addition of Birmingham's four mills with 2 million tons and Auburn's 400,000 tons. The sheet mills grew to four and increased capacity one-third with the acquisition of Trico. Nucor-Yamato's structural steel capacity was increased by half a million tons from the South Carolina plant. The new million-ton plate mill opened in North Carolina in 2000. Ninety-three percent of production was sold to outside customers.

All four of the original "bar mills" were actually two mills operating side by side. One mill concentrated on the larger bar products, which had separate production and customer demands, while the other mill concentrated on smaller diameter bar stock. Throughout Nucor each operation was housed in its own separate building with its own staff. Nucor designed its processes to limit work-in-process inventory, to limit space, to utilize a pull approach to material usage, and to increase flexibility.

The Steelmaking Process

A steel mill's work is divided into two phases: preparation of steel of the proper "chemistry" and the forming of the steel into the desired products. The typical mini-mill utilized scrap steel, such as junk auto parts, instead of iron ore, which would be used in larger, integrated steel mills. The typical bar mini-mill had an annual capacity of 200,000 to 600,000 tons, compared with the 7 million tons of Bethlehem Steel's Sparrow's Point, Maryland, integrated plant.

In the bar mills, a charging bucket fed loads of scrap steel into electric arc furnaces. The melted load, called a heat, was poured into a ladle to be carried by an overhead crane to the casting machine. In the casting machine, the liquid steel was extruded as a continuous, red-hot solid bar of steel and cut into lengths weighing some 900 pounds called billets. In the typical plant, the billet, about four inches in cross-section and about 20 feet long, was held temporarily in a pit where it cooled to normal temperatures. Periodically billets were carried to the rolling mill and placed in a reheat oven to bring them up to 2000°F, at which temperature they would be malleable. In the rolling mill, presses and dies progressively converted the billet into the desired round bars, angles, channels, flats, and other products. After being cut to standard lengths, they were moved to the warehouse.

Nucor's first steel mill, which employed more than 500 people, was located in Darlington, South Carolina. The mill, with its three electric arc furnaces, operated

24 hours per day, 5 1/2 days per week. Nucor had made a number of improvements in the melting and casting operations. The general manager of the Darlington plant developed a system that involved preheating the ladles, allowing for the faster flow of steel into the caster and resulting in better control of the steel characteristics. Thus, less time and lower capital investment were required at Darlington than at other mini-mills at the time of its construction. The casting machines were "continuous casters," as opposed to the old batch method. The objective in the "front" of the mill was to keep the casters working. At the time the Darlington plant was also perhaps the only mill in the country that regularly avoided the reheating of billets. This saved $10–12 per ton in fuel usage and losses due to oxidation of the steel. The cost of developing this process had been $12 million. All research projects had not been successful. The company spent approximately $2 million in an unsuccessful effort to utilize resistance-heating. It lost even more on an effort at induction melting. As Iverson told *Metal Producing*, "That costs us a lot of money. Time wise it was very expensive. But you have got to make mistakes and we've had lots of failures."

The Darlington design became the basis for plants in Nebraska, Texas, and Utah. The Texas plant had cost under $80 per ton of annual capacity. Whereas the typical mini-mill at the time cost approximately $250 per ton, the average cost of Nucor's four mills was under $135. An integrated mill was expected to cost between $1,200 and $1,500 per ton.

The Darlington plant was organized into 12 natural groups for the purpose of incentive pay. Two mills each had two shifts with three groups—melting and casting, rolling mill, and finishing. In melting and casting there were three or four different standards, depending on the material, established by the department manager years ago based on historical performance. The general manager stated, "We don't change the standards." The caster, key to the operation, was used at a 92 percent level—one greater than the claims of the manufacturer. For every good ton of billet above the standard hourly rate for the week, workers in the group received a 4 percent bonus. For example, with a common standard of 10 tons per run hour and an actual rate for the week of 28 tons per hour, the workers would receive a bonus of 72 percent of their base rate in the week's paycheck. In the rolling mill there were more than 100 products, each with a different historical standard. Workers received a 4 percent to 6 percent bonus for every good ton sheared per hour for the week over the computed standard. A manager stated: "Meltshop employees don't ask me how much it costs Chaparral or LTV to make a billet. They want to know what it costs Darlington, Norfolk, Jewitt to put a billet

on the ground. . . . Scrap costs, alloy costs, electrical costs, refractory, gas, etc. Everybody from Charlotte to Plymouth watches the nickels and dimes."

Management Philosophy

Aycock, while still the Darlington manager, stated:

> The key to making a profit when selling a product with no aesthetic value, or a product that you really can't differentiate from your competitors', is cost. I don't look at us as a fantastic marketing organization, even though I think we are pretty good; but we don't try to overcome unreasonable costs by mass marketing. We maintain low costs by keeping the employee force at the level it should be, not doing things that aren't necessary to achieve our goals, and allowing people to function on their own and by judging them on their results.
>
> To keep a cooperative and productive workforce you need, number one, to be completely honest about everything; number two, to allow each employee as much as possible to make decisions about that employee's work, to find easier and more productive ways to perform duties; and number three, to be as fair as possible to all employees. Most of the changes we make in work procedures and in equipment come from the employees. They really know the problems of their jobs better than anyone else.
>
> To communicate with my employees, I try to spend time in the plant and at intervals have meetings with the employees. Usually if they have a question they just visit me. Recently a small group visited me in my office to discuss our vacation policy. They had some suggestions and, after listening to them, I had to agree that the ideas were good."

In discussing his philosophy for dealing with the workforce, the Florence manager stated:

> I believe very strongly in the incentive system we have. We are a non-union shop and we all feel that the way to stay so is to take care of our people and show them we care. I think that's easily done because of our fewer layers of management. . . . I spend a good part of my time in the plant, maybe an hour or so a day. If a man wants to know anything, for example an insurance question, I'm there and they walk right up to me and ask me questions, which I'll answer the best I know how.
>
> We don't lay our people off and we make a point of telling our people this. In the slowdown of 1994, we scheduled our line for four days, but the men were allowed to come in the fifth day for maintenance work at base pay. The men in the plant on an average running bonus might make $17 to $19 an hour. If their base pay is half that, on Friday they would only get $8–$9 an hour. Surprisingly, many of the men did not want to come in on

Friday. They felt comfortable with just working four days a week. They are happy to have that extra day off.

About 20 percent of the people took the 5th day at base rate, but still no one had been laid off, in an industry with a strong business cycle.

In an earlier business cycle the executive committee decided in view of economic conditions that a pay freeze was necessary. The employees normally received an increase in their base pay the first of June. The decision was made at that time to freeze wages. The officers of the company, as a show of good faith, accepted a 5 percent pay cut. In addition to announcing this to the workers with a stuffer in their pay envelopes, meetings were held. Each production line, or incentive group of workers, met in the plant conference room with all supervision— foreman, plant production manager, and division manager. The economic crisis that the company was facing was explained to the employees by the production manager and all of their questions were answered.

The Personnel and Incentive Systems

The foremost characteristic of Nucor's personnel system was its incentive plan. Another major personnel policy was providing job security. Also, all employees at Nucor received the same fringe benefits. There was only one group insurance plan. Holidays and vacations did not differ by job. Every child of every Nucor employee received up to $1,200 a year for four years if they chose to go on to higher education, including technical schools. The company had no executive dining rooms or restrooms, and no fishing lodges, company cars, or reserved parking places.

Jim Coblin, Nucor's vice president of human resources, described Nucor's systems for *HRMagazine* in a 1994 article, "No-frills HR at Nucor: A lean, bottom-line approach at this steel company empowers employees." Coblin, as benefits administrator, received part-time help from one of the corporate secretaries in the corporate office. The plants typically used someone from their finance department to handle compensation issues, although two plants had personnel generalists. Nucor plants did not have job descriptions, finding they caused more problems than they solved, given the flexible workforce and non-union status of Nucor employees. Surprisingly, Coblin found performance appraisal a waste of time. If an employee was not performing well, the problem would be dealt with directly. He had observed that when promotional opportunities became available, the performance appraisals were not much help filling the position. So he saw both of these as just more paperwork. The key, he believed, was not to

put a maximum on what employees could earn but to pay them directly for productivity. Iverson firmly believed that the bonus should be direct and involve no discretion on part of a manager.

Employees were kept informed about the company. Charts showing the division's results in return-on-assets and bonus payoff were posted in prominent places in the plant. The personnel manager commented that as he traveled around to all the plants, he found everyone in the company could tell him the level of profits in their division. The general managers held dinners at least once but usually twice a year with their employees. The dinners were held with 50 or 60 employees at a time, resulting in as many as 20 dinners per year. After introductory remarks, the floor was open for discussion of any work-related problems. There was a new employee orientation program and an employee handbook that contained personnel policies and rules. The corporate office sent all news releases to each division where they were posted on bulletin boards. Each employee in the company also received a copy of the annual report. For the last several years the cover of the annual report had contained the names of all Nucor employees.

Absenteeism and tardiness was not a problem at Nucor. Each employee had four days of absences before pay was reduced. In addition to these, missing work was allowed for jury duty, military leave, or the death of close relatives. After this, a day's absence cost employees their bonus pay for that week and lateness of more than a half-hour meant the loss of bonus for that day.

Safety was a concern of Nucor's critics. With 10 fatalities in the 1980s, Nucor was committed to doing better. Safety administrators had been appointed in each plant and safety had improved in the 1990s. The company also had a formal grievance procedure, although the Darlington manager couldn't recall the last grievance he had processed.

The company had conducted attitude surveys every three years for over two decades. These provided management insight into employee attitudes on 20 issues and allowed comparisons across plants and divisions. There were some concerns and differences but most employees appeared very satisfied with Nucor as an employer. The surveys suggested that pay was not the only thing the workers liked about Nucor. The personnel manager said that an NBC interviewer, working on the documentary "If Japan Can, Why Can't We," often heard employees say, "I enjoy working for Nucor because Nucor is the best, the most productive, and the most profitable company that I know of."

The average hourly worker's pay was over twice the average earnings paid by other manufacturing companies in the states where Nucor's plants were located. In many rural communities where Nucor had located, it provided better wages than most other manufacturers. The new plant in Hertford County illustrated this point, as reported in a June 21, 1998, article in *The Charlotte Observer* titled "Hope on the Horizon: In Hertford County, Poverty Reigns and Jobs Are Scarce." Here the author wrote, " In North Carolina's forgotten northeastern corner, where poverty rates run more than twice the state average, Nucor's $300 million steel mill is a dream realized. . . ." The plant on the banks of the Chowan River in North Carolina's banks coastal district would have its employees earning a rumored $60,000 a year, three times the local average manufacturing wage, upon completion. Nucor had recently begun developing its plant sites with the expectation of other companies co-locating to save shipping costs. Four companies have announced plans to locate close to Nucor's property, adding another 100 to 200 jobs. People couldn't believe such wages, but calls to the plant's chief financial officer got "we don't like to promise too much, but $60,000 might be a little low." The average wage for these jobs at Darlington was $70,000. The plant's CFO added that Nucor didn't try to set pay "a buck over Wal-Mart" but went for the best workers. The article noted that steel work is hot and often dangerous, and that turnover at the plant may be high as people adjust to this and Nucor's hard-driving team system. He added, "Slackers don't last." The State of North Carolina had given $155 million in tax credits over 25 years. The local preacher said, "In 15 years, Baron [a local child] will be making $75,000 a year at Nucor, not in jail. I have a place now I can hold in front of him and say 'Look, right here. This is for you.'"

The Incentive System

There were four incentive programs at Nucor, one each for (1) production workers, (2) department heads, (3) staff people, such as accountants, secretaries, and engineers, and (4) senior management, which included the division managers. All of these programs were based on group performance.

Within the production program, groups ranged in size from 25 to 30 people and had definable and measurable operations. The company believed that a program should be simple and that bonuses should be paid promptly. "We don't have any discretionary bonuses—zero. It is all based on performance. Now we don't want anyone to sit in judgment, because it never is fair." said Iverson. The personnel manager stated: "Their bonus is based on roughly 90 percent of historical time it takes to make a particular joist. If during a week they make joists at 60 percent less than the standard time,

they receive a 60 percent bonus." This was paid with the regular pay the following week. The complete pay check amount, including overtime, was multiplied by the bonus factor. A bonus was not paid when equipment was not operating: "We have the philosophy that when equipment is not operating everybody suffers and the bonus for downtime is zero." The foremen were also part of the group and received the same bonus as the employees they supervised.

The second incentive program was for department heads in the various divisions. The incentive pay here was based on division contribution, defined as the division earnings before corporate expenses and profit sharing are determined. Bonuses were reported to run between 0 and 90 percent (average 35–50 percent) of a person's base salary. The base salaries at this level were set at 75 percent of industry norms.

There was a third plan for people who were not production workers, department managers, or senior managers. Their bonus was based on either the division return-on-assets or the corporate return-on-assets depending on the unit they were a part of. Bonuses were typically 30 percent or more of a person's base salary for corporate positions.

The fourth program was for the senior officers. The senior officers had no employment contracts, pension or retirement plans, or other perquisites. Their base salaries were set at about 75 percent of what an individual doing similar work in other companies would receive. Once return-on-equity reached 9 percent, slightly below the average for manufacturing firms, 5 percent of net earnings before taxes went into a pool, which was divided among the officers based on their salaries. "Now if return-on-equity for the company reaches, say 20 percent, which it has, then we can wind up with as much as 190 percent of our base salaries and 115 percent on top of that in stock. We get both." Half the bonus was paid in cash and half was deferred. Individual bonuses ranged from zero to several hundred percent, averaging 75 to 150 percent.

However, the opposite was true as well. In 1982 the return was 8 percent and the executives received no bonus. Iverson's pay in 1981 was approximately $300,000 but dropped the next year to $110,000. "I think that ranked by total compensation I was the lowest paid CEO in the Fortune 500. I was kind of proud of that, too." In his 1997 book, *Plain Talk: Lessons from a Business Maverick*, Iverson asked, "Can management expect employees to be loyal if we lay them all off at every dip of the economy, while we go on padding our own pockets?" Even so by 1986, Iverson's stock was worth over $10 million dollars and the one-time Vulcraft manager was a millionaire.

In lieu of a retirement plan, the company had a profit sharing plan with a deferred trust. Each year 10 percent of pretax earnings was put into profit sharing for all people below officer level. Twenty percent of this was set aside to be paid to employees in the following March as a cash bonus and the remainder was put into trust for each employee on the basis of percentage of their earnings as a percentage of total wages paid within the corporation. The employee was vested after the first year. Employees received a quarterly statement of their balance in profit sharing.

The company had an employer monthly stock investment plan to which Nucor added 10 percent to the amount the employee contributed on the purchase of any Nucor stock and paid the commission. After each five years of service with the company, the employee received a service award consisting of five shares of Nucor stock. Moreover, if profits were good, extraordinary bonus payments would be made to the employees. For example, in December 1998 each employee received an $800 payment. According to Iverson:

> I think the first obligation of the company is to the stockholder and to its employees. I find in this country too many cases where employees are underpaid and corporate management is making huge social donations for self-fulfillment. We regularly give donations, but we have a very interesting corporate policy. First, we give donations where our employees are. Second, we give donations that will benefit our employees, such as to the YMCA. It is a difficult area and it requires a lot of thought. There is certainly a strong social responsibility for a company, but it cannot be at the expense of the employees or the stockholders.

Having welcomed a parade of visitors over the years, Iverson had become concerned with the pattern apparent at other companies' steel plants: "They only do one or two of the things we do. It's not just incentives or the scholarship program; it's all those things put together that results in a unified philosophy for the company."

Building on Its Success

Throughout the 1980s and 1990s Nucor continued to take the initiative and be the prime mover in steel and the industries vertically related to steel. For example, in 1984 Nucor broke with the industry pattern of basing the price of an order of steel on the quantity ordered. Iverson noted, "Some time ago we began to realize that with computer order entry and billing, the extra charge for smaller orders was not cost-justified." In a seemingly risky move, in 1986 Nucor began construction of a $25 million plant in Indiana to manufacture steel fasteners. Imports had grown to 90 percent of this market as U.S. companies failed to compete. Iverson said "We're going to bring that business back; we can make bolts as cheaply as foreign producers." A second plant, in 1995, gave Nucor 20 percent of the U.S. market for steel fasteners. Nucor also acquired a steel bearings manufacturer in 1986, which Iverson called "a good fit with our business, our policies, and our people."

In early 1986 Iverson announced plans for a revolutionary plant at Crawfordsville, Indiana, which would be the first mini-mill in the world to manufacture flat-rolled or sheet steel, the last bastion of the integrated manufacturers. This market alone was twice the size of the existing market for mini-mill products. It would be a quarter of a billion dollar gamble on a new technology. The plant was expected to halve the integrated manufacturer's $3 of labor per ton and save $50 to $75 on a $400 per ton selling price. If it worked, the profit from this plant alone would come close to the profit of the whole corporation. *Forbes* commented, "If any mini-mill can meet the challenge, it's Nucor. But expect the going to be tougher this time around." If successful, Nucor had the licensing rights to the next two plants built in the world with this technology.

Nucor had spent millions trying to develop the process when it heard of some promising developments at a German company. In the spring of 1986, Aycock flew to Germany to see the pilot machine at SMS Schloemann-Siemag AG. In December the Germans came to Charlotte for the first of what they thought would be many meetings to hammer out a deal with Nucor. Iverson shocked them when he announced Nucor was ready to proceed to build the first plant of its kind.

Keith Busse was given the job of building the Crawfordsville, Indiana, steel sheet plant. The process of bringing this plant online was so exciting it became the basis for a best-selling book by Robert Preston, which was serialized in *The New Yorker*. Preston reported on a conversation at dinner during construction between Iverson and Busse. Thinking about the future, Busse was worried that Nucor might someday become like Big Steel. He asked, "How do we allow Nucor to grow without expanding the bureaucracy?" He commented on the vice presidents stacked on vice presidents, research departments, assistants to assistants and so on. Iverson agreed. Busse seriously suggested, "Maybe we're going to need group vice presidents." Iverson's heated response was, "Do you want to ruin the company? That's the old Harvard Business School thinking. They would only get in the way, slow us down." He said the company could at least double, to $2 billion, before it added a new level of management. "I hope that by the time we have group vice presidents I'll be collecting Social Security."

The gamble on the new plant paid off, and Busse, the general manager of the plant, became a key man within Nucor. The new mill began operations in August of 1989 and reached 15 percent of capacity by the end of the year. In June of 1990 it had its first profitable month and Nucor announced the construction of a second plant, in Arkansas.

In December 1992, Nucor signed a letter of intent with Oregon Steel Mills to build a sheet mill on the West Coast to begin in 1994. This project was later canceled. The supply and cost of scrap steel to feed the mini-mills was an important future concern to Iverson. So at the beginning of 1993 Nucor announced the construction of a plant in Trinidad to supply its mills with iron carbide pellets. The innovative plant would cost $60 million and take a year and a half to complete. In 1994 the two existing sheet mills were expanded and a new $500 million, 1.8 million ton sheet mill in South Carolina was announced, to begin operation in early 1997.

In what the *New York Times* called the company's "most ambitious project yet," in 1987 Nucor began a joint venture with Yamato Kogyo, Ltd. to make structural steel products in a mill on the Mississippi River in direct challenge to the Big Three integrated steel companies. John Correnti was put in charge of the operation. Correnti built and then became the general manager of Nucor-Yamato when it started up in 1988. In 1991 he surprised many people by deciding to double Nucor-Yamato's capacity by 1994. It became Nucor's largest division and the largest wide flange producer in the United States. By 1995, Bethlehem Steel was the only other wide flange producer of structural steel products left and had plans to leave the business.

Nucor started up its first facility to produce metal buildings in 1987. A second metal buildings facility began operations in late 1996 in South Carolina and a new steel deck facility, in Alabama, was announced for 1997. At the end of 1997 the Arkansas sheet mill was undergoing a $120 million expansion to include a galvanizing facility.

In 1995 Nucor became involved in its first international venture, an ambitious project with Brazil's Companhia Siderurgica National to build a $700 million steel mill in the state of Ceara. While other mini-mills were cutting deals to buy and sell abroad, Nucor was planning to ship iron from Brazil and process it in Trinidad.

Nucor set records for sales and net earnings in 1997. In the spring of 1998, as Iverson approached his 73rd birthday, he was commenting, "People ask me when I'm going to retire. I tell them our mandatory retirement age is 95, but I may change that when I get there." It surprised the world when, in October 1998, Ken Iverson left the board. He retired as chairman at the end of the year. Although sales for 1998 decreased one percent and net earnings were down 10 percent, the management made a number of long-term investments and closed draining investments. Start-up began at the new South Carolina steam mill and at the Arkansas sheet mill expansion. The plans for a North Carolina steel plate mill in Hertford were announced. This would bring Nucor's total steel production capacity to 12 million tons per year. Moreover, the plant in Trinidad, which had proven much more expensive than was originally expected, was deemed unsuccessful and closed. Finally, directors approved the repurchase of up to five million shares of Nucor stock.

Still, the downward trends at Nucor continued. Sales and earnings were down three percent and seven percent respectively for 1999 (see Appendix 1 for financial reports and Appendix 2 for financial ratios). However, these trends did not seem to affect the company's investments. Expansions were underway in the steel mills and a third building systems facility was under construction in Texas. Nucor was actively searching for a site for a joist plant in the Northeast. A letter of intent was signed with Australian and Japanese companies to form a joint venture to commercialize the strip casting technology. To understand the challenges facing Nucor, industry, technology and environmental trends in the 1980s and 1990s must be considered.

The U.S. Steel Industry in the 1980s

The early 1980s had been the worst years in decades for the steel industry. Data from the American Iron and Steel Institute showed shipments falling from 100 million tons in 1979 to the mid-80 levels in 1980 and 1981. A slackening in the economy, particularly in auto sales, led the decline. In 1986, when industry capacity was at 130 million tons, the outlook was for a continued decline in per-capita consumption and movement toward capacity in the 90–100 million-ton range. The chairman of Armco saw "millions of tons chasing a market that's not there: excess capacity that must be eliminated."

The large, integrated steel firms, such as U.S. Steel and Armco, which made up the major part of the industry, were the hardest hit. *The Wall Street Journal* stated, "The decline has resulted from such problems as high labor and energy costs in mining and processing iron ore, a lack of profits and capital to modernize plants, and conservative management that has hesitated to take risks."

As of	12/31/04	12/31/03	12/31/02	12/31/01	12/31/00
Assets					
Cash	779.05	350.33	219.00	462.35	490.58
Marketable Securities	n/a	n/a	n/a	n/a	n/a
Receivables	962.76	572.48	483.61	330.86	350.18
Total Inventories	1,239.89	560.40	588.99	466.69	461.15
Other Current Assets	193.26	137.35	157.34	133.80	79.53
Total Current Assets	3,174.96	1,620.56	1,448.94	1,393.70	1,381.44
Net	2,818.31	2,817.14	2,932.06	2,365.66	2,329.42
Gross	2,818.31	2,817.14	2,932.06	2,365.66	2,329.42
Deposits & Other Assets	139.95	54.66	n/a	n/a	n/a
Total Assets	6,133.22	4,492.36	4,381.00	3,759.36	3,710.86
Liabilities					
Accounts Payable	471.55	329.86	247.23	189.24	203.33
Curr. Long-Term Debt	n/a	n/a	n/a	n/a	n/a
Accrued Expense	565.28	299.73	319.36	294.92	354.73
Income Taxes	28.96	n/a	8.95	n/a	n/a
Other Current Liabilities	n/a	n/a	n/a	n/a	n/a
Total Current Liabilities	1,065.79	629.59	575.54	484.16	558.06
Deferred Charges/Inc.	514.57	439.85	371.27	329.39	260.05
Long-Term Debt	923.55	903.55	878.55	460.45	460.45
Other Long-Term Liab.	n/a	n/a	n/a	n/a	n/a
Total Liabilities	2,503.91	1972.99	1,825.36	1,274.00	1,278.56
Shareholder Equity					
Minority Interest	173.31	177.28	216.65	283.89	301.34
Preferred Stock	n/a	n/a	n/a	n/a	n/a
Common Stock	73.75	36.43	36.27	36.13	36.04
Capital Surplus	147.21	117.40	99.40	81.19	71.49
Retained Earnings	3,688.56	2,641.71	2,641.58	2,538.88	2,478.79
Treasury Stock	451.96	453.46	454.26	454.74	455.37
Total Shareholder Equity	3,455.99	2,342.08	2,322.99	2,201.46	2,130.95
Total Liab. & Shdr. Equity	6,133.22	4,492.36	4,381.00	3,759.36	3,710.86

In millions of USD

Source: Data by Thomson Financial, Nucor Web page.

These companies produced a wide range of steels, primarily from ore processed in blast furnaces. They had found it difficult to compete with imports, usually from Japan, and had given market share to imports. They sought the protection of import quotas. Imported steel accounted for 20 percent of the U.S. steel consumption, up from 12 percent in the early 1970s. The U.S. share of world production of raw steel declined from 19 percent to 14 percent over the period. Imports of light bar products accounted for less than 9 percent of the U.S. consumption of those products in 1981, according to the U.S. Commerce Department, while imports of wire rod totaled 23 percent of U.S. consumption.

Appendix 1b Income Statement 2000–2004

Period Ended	12/31/04	12/31/03	12/31/02	12/31/01	12/31/00
Net Sales	11,376.83	6,265.82	4,801.78	4,333.71	4,756.52
Cost of Goods Sold	9,128.87	5,996.55	4,332.28	3,914.28	3,929.18
Gross Profit	2,247.96	269.27	469.50	419.43	827.34
R & D Expenditure	n/a	n/a	n/a	n/a	n/a
Selling, General & Admin Exps.	415.03	165.37	175.59	150.67	183.18
Depreciation & Amort.	n/a	n/a	n/a	n/a	n/a
Non-Operating Income	279.30	212.4	249.57	282.87	2150.65
Interest Expense	22.35	24.63	14.29	6.53	n/a
Income Before Taxes	1,731.28	66.88	230.05	179.36	493.51
Prov. For Inc. Taxes	609.79	4.1	67.97	66.41	182.61
Minority Interest	n/a	n/a	n/a	n/a	n/a
Realized Investment (Gain/Loss)	n/a	n/a	n/a	n/a	n/a
Other Income	n/a	n/a	n/a	n/a	n/a
Net Income before Extra items	1,121.49	62.77	162.08	112.95	310.90
Extra Items & Disc. Ops.	n/a	n/a	n/a	n/a	n/a
Net Income	1,121.49	62.77	162.08	112.95	310.9

In millions of USD

Source: Nucor Web page, data by Thomson Financial.

Appendix 2 Nucor Valuation Ratios 2004

P/E (TTM)	7.38	**Growth (%)**	
EPS Fully Diluted	7.02	5 Year Annual Growth	35.60
Revenue Per Share	71.21	Revenue5 Year Growth	23.19
		Div/Share5 Yr Growth	12.57
Profit Margins		EPS5 Year Growth	32.58
Operating Margin	16.23		
Net Profit Margin	9.86	**Financial Strength**	
Gross Profit Margin	19.88	Quick Ratio	1.63
		Current Ratio	2.98
Dividends		LT Debt to Equity	26.72
Dividend Yield	1.13	Total Debt to Equity	26.72
Dividend Yield5 Yr. Avg.	1.28	Return on Equity (ROE) Per Share	38.57
Dividend Per Share (TTM)	0.52	Return on Assets (ROA)	25.40
Dividend Payout Ratio	6.66	Return on Invested Capital (ROIC)	33.33
		Assets	
		Asset Turnover	1.85
		Inventory Turnover	9.70

Source: Data by Thomson Financial, Nucor Web page

Iron Age stated that exports, as a percent of shipments in 1985, were 34 percent for Nippon, 26 percent for British Steel, 30 percent for Krupp, 49 percent for USINOR of France, and less than 1 percent for every American producer on the list. The consensus of steel experts was that imports would average 23 percent of the market in the last half of the 1980s.

Iverson was one of the very few in the steel industry to oppose import restrictions. He saw an outdated U.S. steel industry that had to change.

> *We Americans have been conditioned to believe in our technical superiority. For many generations a continuing stream of new inventions and manufacturing techniques allowed us to far outpace the rest of the world in both volume and efficiency of production. In many areas this is no longer true and particularly in the steel industry. In the last three decades, almost all the major developments in steelmaking were made outside the U.S. I would be negligent if I did not recognize the significant contribution that the government has made toward the technological deterioration of the steel industry. Unrealistic depreciation schedules, high corporate taxes, excessive regulation and jaw-boning for lower steel prices have made it difficult for the U.S. steel industry to borrow or generate the huge quantities of capital required for modernization.*

By the mid-1980s the integrated mills were moving fast to get back into the game: they were restructuring, cutting capacity, dropping unprofitable lines, focusing products, and trying to become responsive to the market. The industry made a pronounced move toward segmentation. Integrated producers focused on mostly flat-rolled and structural grades; reorganized steel companies focused on a limited range of products; mini-mills dominated the bar and light structural product areas; and specialty steel firms sought niches. There was an accelerated shutdown of older plants, elimination of products by some firms, and the installation of new product line with new technologies by others. High-tonnage mills restructured to handle sheets, plates, structural beams, high quality bars, and large pipe and tubular products, which allowed resurgence of specialized mills: cold-finished bar manufacturers, independent strip mills, and mini-mills.

The road for the integrated mills was not easy. As *Purchasing* pointed out, tax laws and accounting rules slowed the closing of inefficient plants. Shutting down a 10,000-person plant could require a firm to hold a cash reserve of $100 million to fund health, pension, and insurance liabilities. The chairman of Armco commented: "Liabilities associated with a planned shutdown are so large that they can quickly devastate a company's balance sheet."

Joint ventures had arisen to produce steel for a specific market or region. The chairman of USX called them "an important new wrinkle in steel's fight for survival" and stated, "If there had been more joint ventures like these two decades ago, the U.S. steel industry might have built only half of the dozen or so hot-strip mills it put up in that time and avoided today's over-capacity."

The American Iron and Steel Institute reported steel production in 1988 of 99.3 million tons, up from 89.2 million in 1987, and the highest in seven years. As a result of modernization programs, 60.9 percent of production was from continuous casters. Exports for steel increased and imports fell. Some steel experts believed the United States was now cost competitive with Japan. However, 1989 proved to be a year of "waiting for the other shoe to drop," according to *Metal Center News*. U.S. steel production was hampered by a new recession, the expiration of the voluntary import restraints, and labor negotiations in several companies. Declines in car production and consumer goods hit flat-rolled hard. AUJ Consultants told MCN, "The U.S. steel market has peaked. Steel consumption is tending down. By 1990, we expect total domestic demand to dip under 90 million tons."

The U.S. Steel Industry in the 1990s

The economic slowdown of the early 1990s did lead to a decline in the demand for steel through early 1993, but by 1995 America was in its best steel market in 20 years and many companies were building new flat-roll mini-mills. A *BusinessWeek* article at the time described it as "the race of the Nucor look-alikes." Six years after Nucor pioneered the low-cost German technology in Crawfordsville, Indiana, the competition was finally gearing up to compete. Ten new projects were expected to add 20 million tons per year of the flat-rolled steel, raising U.S. capacity by as much as 40 percent by 1998. These mills opened in 1997 just as the industry was expected to move into a cyclical slump. It was no surprise that worldwide competition increased and companies that had previously focused on their home markets began a race to become global powerhouses. The foreign push was new for U.S. firms that had focused on defending their home markets. U.S. mini-mills focused their international expansion primarily in Asia and South America.

Meanwhile in 1994, U.S. Steel, North America's largest integrated steel producer, began a major business process re-engineering project to improve order fulfillment performance and customer satisfaction on the heels of a decade of restructuring. According to *Steel Times International*, "U.S. Steel had to completely change the way it did business. Cutting labor costs, and increasing reliability and productivity took the company a long way towards improving profitability and competitiveness. However, it became clear that this leaner organization still had to implement new technologies and business processes if it was to maintain a competitive advantage." The goals of the business process re-engineering project included a sharp reduction in cycle time, greatly decreased levels of inventory, shorter order lead times, and the ability to offer real-time promise dates to customers. In 1995, the company successfully installed integrated planning/production/order fulfillment software and results were very positive. U.S. Steel believed that the re-engineering project had positioned it for a future of increased competition, tighter markets, and raised customer expectations.

In late 1997 and again in 1998, the decline in demand prompted Nucor and other U.S. companies to slash prices in order to compete with the unprecedented surge of imports. By the last quarter of 1998 these imports had led to the filing of unfair trade complaints with U.S. trade regulators, causing steel prices in the spot market to drop sharply in August and September before they stabilized. A press release by U.S. Secretary of Commerce William Daley stated, "I will not stand by and allow U.S. workers, communities and companies to bear the brunt of other nations' problematic policies and practices. We are the most open economy of the world. But we are not the world's dumpster." In early 1999 the American Iron and Steel Institute (AISI) reported in its Opinion section of its Web page the following quotes by Andrew Sharkey and Hank Barnette. Sharkey said, "With many of the world's economies in recession, and no signs of recovery on the horizon, it should come as no surprise that the United States is now seen as the only reliable market for manufactured goods. This can be seen in the dramatic surge of imports." Barnette noted, "While there are different ways to gauge the impact of the Asian crisis, believe, me, it has already hit. Just ask the 163,000 employees of the U.S. steel industry."

The Commerce Department concluded in March 1999 that six countries had illegally dumped stainless steel in the United States at prices below production costs or home market prices. The Commerce Department found that Canada, South Korea, and Taiwan were guilty only of dumping, while Belgium, Italy, and South Africa also gave producers unfair subsidies that effectively lowered prices. However, on June 23, 1999, *The Wall Street Journal* reported that the Senate decisively shut off an attempt to restrict U.S. imports of steel despite industry complaints that a flood of cheap imports was driving them out of business. Advisors of President Clinton were reported to have said the President would likely veto the bill if it passed. Administrative officials opposed the bill because it would violate international trade law and leave the United States open to retaliation.

The American Iron and Steel Institute (AISI) reported that in May 1999, U.S. steel mills shipped 8,330,000 net tons, a decrease of 6.7 percent from the 8,927,000 net tons shipped in May 1998. It also stated that for the first five months of 1999 shipments were 41,205,000 net tons, down 10 percent from the same period in 1998. AISI president and CEO Andrew Sharkey III said, "Once again, the May data show clearly that America's steel trade crisis continues. U.S. steel companies and employees continue to be injured by high levels of dumping and subsidized imports. . . . In addition, steel inventory levels remain excessive, and steel operating rates continue to be very low."

As the 1990s ended, Nucor was the second-largest steel producer in the United States, behind USX. The company's market capitalization was about two times that of the next smaller competitor. Even in a tight industry, someone can win. Nucor was in the best position because the industry was very fragmented and there were many marginal competitors.

Steel Technology and the Mini-Mill

A new type of mill, the "mini-mill," had emerged in the United States during the 1970s to compete with the integrated mill. The mini-mill used electric arc furnaces initially to manufacture a narrow product line from scrap steel. The leading U.S. mini-mills in the 1980s were Nucor, Florida Steel, Georgetown Steel, North Star Steel, and Chaparral. Between the late 1970s and 1980s, the integrated mills' market share fell from about 90 percent to about 60 percent, with the integrated steel companies averaging a 7 percent return on equity, the mini-mills averaging 14 percent, and some, such as Nucor, achieving about 25 percent. In the 1990s mini-mills tripled their output to capture 17 percent of domestic shipments. Moreover, integrated mills' market share fell to around 40 percent, while mini-mills' share rose to 23 percent, reconstructed mills increased their share from 11 percent to 28 percent, and specialized mills increased their share from 1 percent to 6 percent.

Some experts believed that a relatively new technology, the twin shell electric arc furnace, would help mini-mills increase production, lower costs, and take market share. According to the *Pittsburgh Business Times*, "With a twin shell furnace, one shell—the chamber holding the scrap to be melted—is filled and heated. During the heating of the first shell, the second shell is filled. When the heating is finished on the first shell, the electrodes move to the second. The first shell is emptied and refilled before the second gets hot." This increased the production by 60 percent. Twin shell production had been widely adopted in the last few years. For example, Nucor Steel began running a twin shell furnace in November 1996 in Berkeley, South Carolina, and installed another in Norfolk, Nebraska, which began operations in 1997. "Everyone accepts twin shells as a good concept because there's a lot of flexibility of operation," said Rodney Mott, vice president and general manager of Nucor-Berkeley. However, this move toward twin shell furnaces could mean trouble in the area of scrap availability. According to an October 1997 quote in *Pittsburgh Business Times* by Ralph Smaller, vice president of process technology at Kvaerner, "Innovations that feed the electric furnaces' production of flat-rolled[steel] will increase the demand on high quality scrap and alternatives. The technological changes are just beginning and will accelerate over the next few years."

According to a September 1997 *Industry Week* article, steelmakers around the world were now closely monitoring the development of continuous "strip casting" technology, which may prove to be the next leap forward for the industry. "The objective of strip casting is to produce thin strips of steel (in the 1-mm to 4-mm range) as liquid steel flows from a tundish—the stationary vessel that received molten steel from the ladle. It would eliminate the slab-casting stage and all of the rolling that now takes place in a hot mill." Strip casting was reported to have some difficult technological challenges, but companies in Germany, France, Japan, Australia, Italy, and Canada had strip-casting projects under way. In fact, all of the significant development work in strip casting was taking place outside the United States.

Larry Kavanaph, American Iron and Steel Institute vice president for manufacturing and technology, said, "Steel is a very high-tech industry, but nobody knows it." Today's most productive steelmaking facilities incorporated advanced metallurgical practices, sophisticated process-control sensors, state-of-the-art computer controls, and the latest refinements in continuous casting and rolling mill technology. Michael Shot, vice president of manufacturing at Carpenter Technology Corp. in Reading, Pennsylvania, a specialty steels and premium-grade alloys company, said, "You don't survive in this industry unless you have the technology to make the best products in the world in the most efficient manner."

Environmental and Political Issues

Not all stakeholders were happy with the way Nucor did business. In June 1998, *Waste News* reported that Nucor's mill in Crawfordsville, Indiana, was cited by the U.S. Environmental Protection Agency for alleged violations of federal and state clean-air rules. In addition to the incident in Indiana, concerns were also expressed in North Carolina. Specifically, the Pamlico-Tar River Foundation, the NC Coastal Federation, and the Environmental Defense Fund had concerns about the state's decision to allow the company to start building before the environmental review was completed. According to the *News & Observer* Web site, "The environmental groups charge that the mill will discharge 6,720 tons of pollutants into the air each year."

Moreover, there were other concerns about the fast-track approval of the facility being built in Hertford County. First, this plant was located on the banks of one of the most important and sensitive stretches of the Chowan, a principle tributary to the national treasure Albemarle Sound and the last bastion of the state's once vibrant river-herring fishery. North Carolina passed a law in 1997 that required the restoration of this fishery through a combination of measures designed to prevent overfishing, restore spawning and nursery habitats, and improve water quality in the Chowan. "New federal law requires extra care in protecting essential habitat for the herring, which spawn upstream," according to an article in the *Business Journal*. Second were the concerns regarding the excessive incentives the state gave to convince Nucor to build a $300 million steel mill in North Carolina. Some questioned whether the promise of 300 well-paying jobs in Hertford County was worth the $155 million in tax breaks the state was giving Nucor to locate here.

Management Evolution

As Nucor opened new plants, each was made a division and given a general manager with complete responsibility for all aspects of the business. The corporate office did not involve itself in the routine functioning of the divisions. There was no centralized purchasing, hiring and firing, or division accounting. The total corporate staff was still less than 25 people, including clerical staff, when 1999 began.

In 1984, Dave Aycock moved into the corporate office as president. Ken Iverson was chief executive officer and chairman. Iverson, Aycock, and Sam Siegel operated as an executive board, providing overall direction to the corporation. By 1990 Aycock, who had invested his money wisely, owned over 600,000 shares of Nucor stock, five hotels, and farms in three states, and was ready to retire. He was 60, five years younger than Iverson, and was concerned that if he waited, he and Iverson might be leaving the company at the same time. Two people stood out as candidates for the presidency: Keith Busse and John Correnti. In November, Iverson called Correnti to the Charlotte airport and offered him the job. Aycock commented, "Keith Busse was my choice, but I got outvoted." In June 1991 Aycock retired and Keith Busse left Nucor to build an independent sheet mill in Indiana for a group of investors.

Thus Iverson, Correnti, and Siegel led the company. In 1993, Iverson had heart problems and major surgery. Correnti was given the CEO role in 1996. The board of directors had always been small, consisting of the executive team and one or two past Nucor vice presidents. Several organizations with large blocks of Nucor stock had been pressing Nucor to diversify its board membership and add outside directors. In 1996 Jim Hlavacek, head of a small consulting firm and friend of Iverson, was added to the board.

Only five, not six, members of the Board were in attendance during the board of directors meeting in the fall of 1998, due to the death of Jim Cunningham. Near its end, Aycock read a motion, drafted by Siegel, that Ken Iverson be removed as chairman. It was seconded by Hlavacek and passed. It was announced in October that Iverson would be a chairman emeritus and a director, but after disagreements, Iverson left the company completely. It was agreed Iverson would receive $500,000 a year for five years. Aycock left retirement to become chairman.

The details of Iverson's leaving did not become known until June of 1999 when John Correnti resigned after disagreements with the board and Aycock took his place. All of this was a complete surprise to investors and brought the stock price down 10 percent. Siegel commented, "The board felt Correnti was not the right person to lead Nucor into the 21st century." Aycock assured everyone he would be happy to move back into retirement as soon as replacements could be found.

In December 1999 Correnti became chairman of rival Birmingham Steel, with an astounding corporate staff of 156 people. With Nucor's organizational changes, he predicted more overhead staff and questioned the company's ability to move as fast in the future: "Nucor's trying to centralize and do more mentoring. That's not what grew the company to what it is today."

Aycock moved ahead with adding outside directors to the board. He appointed Harvey Gantt, principal in his own architectural firm and former mayor of Charlotte; Victoria Haynes, formally BF Goodrich's chief technology officer; and Peter Browning, chief executive of Sonoco (biographical sketches of board members and executive management are provided in Appendixes 3 and 4). Then he moved to increase the corporate office staff by adding a level of executive vice presidents over four areas of business and adding two specialist jobs in strategic planning and steel technology. When Siegel retired, Aycock promoted Terry Lisenby to CFO and

treasurer, and hired a director of IT to report to Lisenby (see Exhibits 1 and 2, the organization charts in 2000 and 2004).

Jim Coblin, vice president of human resources, believed the additions to management were necessary, "It's not bad to get a little more like other companies." He noted that the various divisions did their business cards and plant signs differently; some did not even want a Nucor sign. Sometimes six different Nucor salesmen would call on the same customer. "There is no manager of human resources in the plants, so at least we needed to give additional training to the person who does most of that work at the plant," he stated. With these new additions there would be a director of information technology and two important committees, one for environmental issues and the second for audit.

He believed the old span of control of 20 might have worked well when there was less competition. Aycock considered it "ridiculous." "It was not possible to properly manage, to know what was going on. The top managers have totally lost contact with the company." Coblin was optimistic that having executive vice presidents would improve management. The three annual meetings of the general managers had slowly increased from about 1.5 days to about 2.5 days and had become more focused. The new EVP positions would bring a perspective above the level of the individual plants. Instead of 15 individual detailed presentations, each general manager would give a short, five-minute briefing and then there would be an in-depth presentation on the Group, with team participation. After some training by Lisenby, the divisions had recently done a pretty good job with a SWOT analysis. Coblin thought these changes would make Nucor a stronger global player.

To Jeff Kemp, the new general manager of strategic planning and business development, the big issue was how to sustain earnings growth. In the U.S. steel industry there were too many marginal competitors. The U.S. government had recently added to the problem by giving almost $1 billion to nine mills, which simply allowed them to limp along and weaken the industry. He was looking for Nucor's opportunities within the steel industry. He asked why Nucor had bought a bearing company. His experience in the chemical industry suggested a need for Nucor to establish a position of superiority and grow globally, driving industry competition rather than reacting. He argued that a company should protect its overall market position, which could mean sacrifices for individual plants. Aycock liked Kemp's background in law and accounting, and had specifically sought someone from outside the steel industry to head up Nucor's strategic planning. By June 2000 Kemp had conducted studies of other industries in the U.S. market

In 1990

Board: Iverson, Aycock, Cunningham, Siegel, Vandekieft.

Executive Office: Iverson, Aycock, Siegel.

1991 to 1994

Board: Iverson, Aycock, Siegel, Cunningham, Correnti.

Executive Office: Iverson, Siegel, Correnti, Lisenby, Prichard.

1995 to 1996

Board: Iverson, Aycock, Siegel, Cunningham, Correnti, Hlavacek.

Executive Office: Iverson, Siegel, Correnti, Doherty, Prichard.

In 1997

Board: Iverson, Aycock, Siegel, Cunningham, Correnti, Hlavacek.

Executive Office: Iverson, Siegel, Correnti, Lisenby, Prichard.

In 1998

Board: Aycock, Siegel, Correnti, Hlavacek, Browning, Gantt, Haynes.

Executive Office: Aycock, Siegel, Correnti, Parrish, Rutowski, Lisenby, Prichard.

1999 to 2000

Board: Aycock, Siegel, Hlavacek, Browning, Gantt, Haynes.

Executive Office: Aycock, Lisenby, DiMicco, Lott, Parrish, Rutowski, Coblin, Prichard.

2002 through 2003

Board: Browning, Daley, DiMicco, Gantt, Haynes, Hlavacek, Milchovich, Waltermire.

Executive Office: DiMicco, Lisenby, Ferriola, Lott, Parrish, Rutkowski, Coblin, Bowers, Frias, Johns, Laxton, Maero, Rowlan, Eagle (new 2003).

and developed a working document that identified opportunities worthy of further analysis.

"Every company hits a plateau," Aycock observed. "You can't just go out and build plants to grow. How do you step up to the next level? I wouldn't say it's a turning point but we have to get our strategic vision and strategic plans." He stated, "We are beginning Nucor's first ever strategic planning sessions; it was not necessary before." His conclusions were partly the result of an imaging study Nucor had conducted.

In early 2000, Nucor had an outside consulting firm conduct a survey of the company's image as seen by the top 10 to 15 managers, including the corporate office. It also gathered the views of a few analysts and media personnel. In looking at the survey, one saw the managers still agreed that Nucor valued risk taking, innovation, and a lean management structure with aggressive, hard-working employees who accepted the responsibility of failure along with the opportunity for success. They

seemed to see Nucor as a way of doing business—not just a way of making steel—in terms of values and personality, not just business terms. When asked to associate Nucor's persona with a public figure, John Wayne was the clear choice.

The managers in the field seemed to believe the new layer of management was needed and were not concerned about a loss of decentralization. They liked the new management team and the changes so far, particularly the improved communications with the corporate office. However, the corporate managers thought the company was changing much faster than the division managers. They also held a more positive view of the company on such things as how good the company was in their community or with the environment.

The people from the media had positive views of Nucor as hard-working and committed to its employees, an innovative risk-taking economic powerhouse. Some, most familiar with the company, believed the company

Peter C. Browning has been the president and chief executive officer of Sonoco Products Company and senior officer since 1993. He was previously the president, chairman, and chief executive officer of National Gypsum Company. He was elected chairman of Nucor's board of directors in September 2000 and became the non-executive chairman of Nucor when David Aycock retired from the board in 2001.

Daniel R. DiMicco was executive vice president of Nucor-Yamato Steel, Nucor Steel Hertford (plate division), and Nucor Building Systems before becoming president. He graduated from Brown University in 1972 with a Bachelor of Science degree in engineering, metallurgy, and materials science. He received a Masters degree in metallurgy from the University of Pennsylvania in 1975. He was with Republic Steel in Cleveland as a research metallurgy and project leader until he joined Nucor in 1982 as plant metallurgist and manager of quality control for Nucor Steel in Utah. In 1988 he became melting and castings manager. In 1991 he became general manager of Nucor-Yamato and a vice president in 1992. In September 2000 he was elected president and chief executive officer of Nucor. In 2001, when Aycock retired, he became vice chairman, president, and chief executive officer of Nucor.

Harvey B. Gantt was a partner in Gantt Huberman Architects for more than 25 years. He also served as mayor of Charlotte, North Carolina, and was active in civic affairs. He was the first African American graduate of Clemson University. He joined Nucor's board of directors in 1998.

Victoria F. Haynes is the president of Research Triangle Institute in Chapel Hill, North Carolina. Until 2000, she was the chief technical officer of B. F. Goodrich Co. and vice president of its advanced technology group. She started with Goodrich in 1992 as vice president of research and development. She joined Nucor's board of directors in 1998.

James D. Hlavacek is the managing director of market driven management. Mr. Hlavacek was a neighbor and long-time friend of Mr. Iverson. He joined Nucor's board of directors in 1995.

Terry S. Lisenby is chief financial officer and an executive vice president. He graduated from the University of North Carolina at Charlotte in 1976 with a Bachelor of Science degree in accounting. Mr. Lisenby held accounting and management positions with Seidman and Seidman, Harper Corporation of America, and Concept Development, Inc. He joined Nucor in September 1985 as manager of financial accounting. He became vice president and corporate controller in 1991 and assumed the role of chief financial officer on January 1, 2000.

Hamilton Lott Jr. is executive vice president over Vulcraft operations, cold-finished operations in Nebraska, and the Utah grinding ball plant. He graduated from the University of South Carolina in 1972 with a Bachelor of Science degree in engineering and then served in the United States Navy. He joined Nucor in 1975 as a design engineer at Florence. He later served as engineering manager and as sales manager at Nucor's Vulcraft division in Indiana. He was general manager of the Vulcraft division in Texas from 1987 to 1993 and the general manager in Florence from 1993 to 1999. He became a vice president in 1988 and joined the executive office in 1999.

D. Michael Parrish is executive vice president for the four steel plants and Nucor Fastener. He graduated from the University of Toledo in 1975 with a Bachelor of Science degree in civil engineering. He joined Nucor in September 1975 as a design engineer for Vulcraft and became engineering manager at Vulcraft in 1981. In 1986 he moved to Alabama as manufacturing manager and in 1989 returned to Utah as vice president and general manager. In 1991 he took the top job with Nucor Steel Texas, and in 1995 at Nucor Steel Arkansas. In January 1999 he moved into the corporate office as executive vice president.

Joseph A. Rutkowski is executive vice president of Nucor Steel in Indiana, Arkansas, and Berkeley (South Carolina), and of Nucor Bearing Products. He graduated from John's Hopkins University in 1976 with a Bachelor of Science degree in materials science engineering. He held metallurgical and management positions with Korf Lurgi Steeltec, North American Refractories, Georgetown Steel, and Bethlehem Steel. He joined Nucor in 1989 as manager of cold finish in Nebraska and became melting and casting manager in Utah before becoming vice president and general manager of Nucor Steel in Darlington in 1992. In 1998, he moved to Hertford as vice president and general manager to oversee the building of the new plate mill.

needed to do a better job of communicating its vision during a period of transition.

Aycock believed Nucor needed to be quick to recognize developing technology in all production areas. He noted the joint venture to develop a new strip caster, which would cast the current flat-rolled material in a more finished form. The impact could be "explosive,"

allowing Nucor to build smaller plants closer to markets. This would be particularly helpful on the West Coast. Nucor would own the U.S. and Brazilian rights, its partners the rest. He was also looking forward to the next generation of steel mills and wanted to own the rights, this time. He praised Iverson's skill at seeing technology and committing to it.

Exhibit 1   Nucor Organization Chart 2000

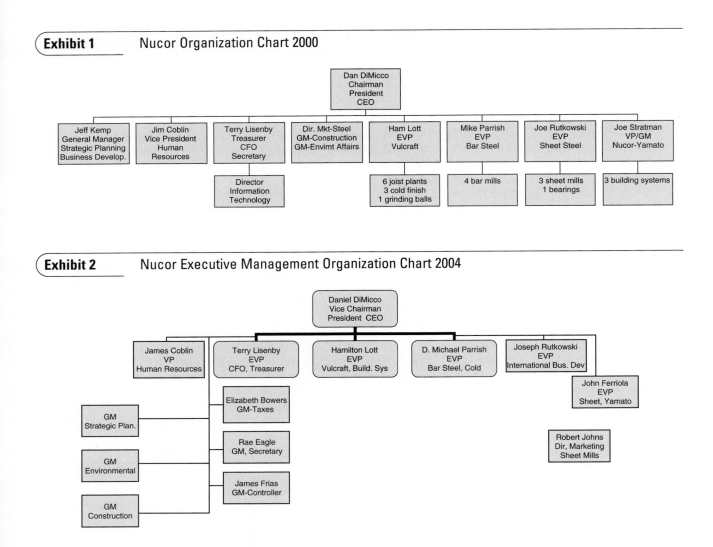

Exhibit 2   Nucor Executive Management Organization Chart 2004

He was very interested in acquisitions, but "they must fit strategically." A bar mill in the upper central Midwest and a flat-rolled plant in the Northeast would be good. A significant opportunity existed in pre-engineered buildings. Aycock intended to concentrate on steel for the next five to six years, achieving an average growth rate of 15 percent per year. In about seven years he would like to see Nucor ready to move into other areas. He said Nucor had already "picked the low-hanging grapes" and must be careful in its next moves.

Daniel DiMicco assumed the role of Nucor's president and chief executive officer in September 2000, when David Aycock stepped down as planned. Peter Browning was elected chairman of the board of directors. Aycock retired from the board a year later.

Sales for 2000 increased 14 percent over 1999 to reach a record level. Earnings were also at record levels, 27 percent over 1999. The year had begun on a strong footing but had turned weak by the year's end. While Nucor remained profitable, other steel companies faced bankruptcy. A Vulcraft plant was under construction in New York. It was the company's first northeastern operation and expanded the geographical coverage into a new region. Nucor was also attempting a break-through technological step in strip casting at Crawfordsville, the Castrip process. Nucor sold its grinding ball process and the bearing products operation because they were not a part of the core business.

In the company's annual report, DiMicco laid out plans for 2000 and beyond: "Our targets are to deliver an average annual earnings growth of 10 to 15 percent over the next 10 years, to deliver a return well in excess of our cost of capital, to maintain a minimum average return on equity of 14 percent and to deliver to return on sales of 8 to 10 percent. Our strategy will focus on Nucor becoming a 'Market Leader' in every product group and business in which we compete. This calls for significant increases in market share for many of our core products and the maintenance of market share where we currently enjoy a leadership position." While pointing out that it would be impossible to obtain this success through the previous strategy of greenfield construction, he added, "There will now be a heavy focus on growth through acquisitions. We will also continue growing through the commercialization of new disruptive and leapfrog technologies."

Steel and Nucor in the 21st Century

In early 2001 the *Wall Street Journal* predicted that all but two of the United States' biggest steelmakers would post fourth-quarter losses. AK Steel Holding Corp. and Nucor Corp. were expected to have profits for the fourth quarter of 2000, while U.S. Steel Group, a unit of USX Corp., was expected to post a profit for the year but not the fourth quarter. By October 1, more than 20 steel companies in the United States, including Bethlehem Steel Corp. and LTV Corp., the nation's third and fourth largest U.S. steel producers, respectively, had filed for bankruptcy protection. Over a dozen producers were operating under Chapter 11 bankruptcy-law protection, which allowed them to maintain market share by selling steel cheaper than non-Chapter 11 steelmakers. On October 20, *The Economist* noted that of the 14 steel companies followed by Standard & Poor's, only Nucor was indisputably healthy. In the fall of 2001, 25 percent of domestic steel companies were in bankruptcy proceedings, although the United States was the largest importer of steel in the world. Experts believed that close to half of the U.S. steel industry might be forced to close before conditions improved.

The world steel industry found itself in the middle of one of its most unprofitable and volatile periods ever, in part due to a glut of steel that had sent prices to 20-year lows. While domestic steel producers found themselves mired in red ink, many foreign steelmakers desperately needed to continue to sell in the relatively open U.S. market to stay profitable. The industry was hovering around 75 percent capacity utilization, a level too low to be profitable for many companies. Three European companies—France's Usinor SA, Luxembourg's Arbed SA, and Spain's Aceralia Corp.—merged to form the world's largest steel company. Two Japanese companies—NKK Corp. and Kawasaki Steel Corp.—merged to form the world's second-largest steelmaker. These new mega-steelmakers could out-muscle U.S. competitors, which were less efficient, smaller, and financially weaker than their competitors in Asia and Europe. At this time the largest U.S. steelmaker, USX-U.S. Steel Group, was only

the 11th largest producer in the world, and continued consolidation in the industry was expected.

In addition to cheap imports, U.S. steel producers faced higher energy prices, weakening demand by customer industries, increasingly tough environmental rules, and a changing cost structure among producers. With the declining economy, energy prices began to drop. However, so did demand for construction, automobiles, and farm equipment. Environmental rules led to costly modifications and closings of old plants, which produced coke along with vast clouds of ash and acrid green smoke. In 1990 mini-mills accounted for 36 percent of the domestic steel market, but by 2000 the more efficient mini-mill had seized 50 percent of the market and the resulting competition had driven prices lower.

The year 2001 turned out to be one of the worst ever for steel. There was 9/11, a recession, and a surge of imports. DiMicco broke with Nucor's traditional opposition to government intervention to make a major push for protective tariffs. He stated, "The need to enforce trade rules is similar to the need to enforce any other law. If two merchants have stores side by side, but one sells stolen merchandise at a vast discount, we know that it's time for the police to step in." In March 2002 President George W. Bush, after an investigation and recommendation by the International Trade Commission, imposed anti-dumping tariffs under section 201 of the Trade Act of 1974. This restricted some imports of steel and placed quotas of up to 30 percent on others. The move was opposed by many, including steel users. Columnist George Will in his editorial on March 10, 2002, criticized Bush for abandoning free trade and pointed out the protection would hamper the necessary actions to restructure the steel industry in America by reducing excess capacity. The European Union immediately threatened reprisals and appealed to the World Trade Organization. In December China imposed its own three-year program of import duties. Steel prices rose 40 percent in 2002 after the tariffs. Within a year hot rolled steel prices increased 50 percent to $260 per ton over the 20-year low of $210 during 2002. The price had been $361 in 1980. In November 2003 the WTO ruled against the tariffs and, under increasing pressure of retaliation, Bush withdrew the tariffs.

While many steel companies floundered, Nucor was able to take advantage of the weakened conditions. In March 2001, Nucor made its first acquisition in 10 years, purchasing a mini-mill in New York from Sumitomo Corp. Nucor had hired about five people to help plan for future acquisitions. DiMicco commented, "It's taken us three years before our team has felt this is the right thing to do and get started making acquisitions." In the challenged industry, he argued, it would be cheaper to buy than to build plants. Nucor purchased the assets of Auburn Steel, which gave it a merchant bar presence in the Northeast and helped the new Vulcraft facility in New York. The company then acquired ITEC Steel, a leader in the emerging load bearing light gauge steel framing market, and saw an opportunity to aggressively broaden its market. Nucor increased its sheet capacity by roughly one-third when it acquired the assets of Trico Steel Co. in Alabama for $120 million. In early 2002, it acquired the assets of Birmingham Steel Corp. The $650 million purchase of four mini-mills was the largest acquisition in Nucor's history.

In addition to making acquisitions to efficiently increase its market share and capacity, Nucor was actively working on new production processes that would provide technological advantages. It acquired the U.S. and Brazilian rights to the promising Castrip process for strip casting, the process of directly casting thin sheet steel. After development work on the process in Indiana, it began full-time production in May 2002 and produced 7,000 tons in the last 10 months of 2002.

Moreover, in April Nucor entered into a joint venture with a Brazilian mining company, CVRD, the world's largest producer of iron-ore pellets, to jointly develop low-cost iron-based products. Success with this effort would give it the ability to make steel from scratch by combining iron ore and coke rather than using scrap steel.

As the year ended Nucor executives were encouraged by the decrease in total steel capacity and what appeared to be a recovery in prices from record lows, and expected slight improvement for 2002.

However, 2002 proved to be a difficult year for Nucor. Revenue increased 11 percent and earnings improved 43 percent over weak 2001, but the other financial goals were not met. Nucor did increase its steelmaking capacity by more than 25 percent. Looking ahead to 2003 the company anticipated a challenging year. However, an executive commented, "Nucor has a long-standing tradition of successfully emerging from industry downturns stronger than ever. It will be no different this time."

During 2003 prices of steel rose in the United States and Asia as global demand outpaced supply in some areas. China, with its booming economy, drove the market. An article in the *Wall Street Journal* on October 15 quoted Guy Dolle, chief executive of Arcelor SA of Luxembourg, the world's largest steelmaker in terms of steel product shipped, as saying, "China is the wild card in the balance between supply and demand." World prices did not soar dangerously because the steel industry continued to be plagued by overcapacity. Still, steel-hungry China and other fast-growing nations added to their steel capacity.

Imports of steel commodities into the United States fell in August 2003 by 22 percent. A weakened dollar, the growing demand from China, and tariffs imposed in 2002 by President Bush drove away imports. Domestic capacity declined, increasing capacity utilization from 77.2 percent to 93.4 percent as producers consolidated, idled plants, or went out of business. Prices for iron ore and energy rose, affecting integrated producers. Mini-mills saw their costs rise as worldwide demand for scrap prices rose. Thus, U.S. steelmakers boosted their prices. By February 2004, a growing coalition of U.S. steel producers and consumers were considering whether to petition to limit soaring exports of scrap steel from the United States, the world's largest producer of steel scrap. The United States had exported an estimated 12 million metric tons of steel scrap in 2003, a 21 percent increase from 2002. Moreover, the price of scrap steel was up 83 percent from a year earlier to $255 a ton. At the same time the price of hot rolled sheet steel rose 30 percent to $360 a ton. One result was that the International Steel Group (ISG) replaced Nucor as the most profitable U.S. steel producer. ISG was created when investor Wilbur Ross began acquiring the failing traditional steel producers in America, including LTV, Bethlehem, and Weirton. These mills used iron ore rather than scrap steel.

When 2003 ended Nucor struck a positive note by reminding its investors that the company had been profitable every single quarter since beginning operations in 1966. But while Nucor set records for both steel production and steel shipments, net earnings declined 61 percent. While the steel industry struggled through one of its deepest down cycles with weak prices and bankruptcies throughout the industry, Nucor increased its market share and held on to profitability. It worked on expanding its business with the automotive industry, continued its joint venture in Brazil to produce pig iron, and pursued a joint venture with the Japanese and Chinese to make iron without the usual raw materials. In February 2004 the company was "optimistic about the prospects for obtaining commercialization" of its promising Castrip process for strip casting in the United States and Brazil. Moreover, Nucor was optimistic because the Bush administration was using its trade laws to curtail import dumping, and Nucor expected higher margins.

Global competition continued. Nucor has good reason to be proactive. According to the *Wall Street Journal*, Posco steelworks in Pohang, South Korea, enjoyed the highest profits in the global steel industry as of 2004. Moreover, *Business Week* reported that the company had developed a new technology called Finex, which turns coal and iron ore into iron without coking and sintering and was expected to cut production costs by nearly one- fifth and harmful emissions by 90 percent. The company had also expanded its 80 Korean plants by investing in 14 Chinese joint ventures. By December 2004 demand in China had slowed and it had become a net steel exporter, sparking concerns of global oversupply.

Global consolidation continued. In October 2004 London's Mittal family announced that it would merge its Ispat International NV with LNM Group and ISG to create the world's largest steelmaker, with estimated annual revenue of $31.5 billion and output of 57 million tons. This would open a new chapter for the industry's consolidation, which had been mostly regional. Although the world's steel industry remains largely fragmented with the world's top 10 steelmakers supplying less than 30 percent of global production, Mittal Steel will have about 40 percent of the U.S. market in flat-rolled steel. Moreover, Mittal, which had a history of using its scale to buy lower-cost raw materials and import modern management techniques into previously inefficient state-run mills, was buying ISG, a U.S. company which already owned the lowest-cost, highest-profit mills in the United States. In January 2005 Mittal announced plans to buy 37 percent of China's Hunan Valin Iron & Steel Group Co.

With output of around 20 million metric tons each, U.S. Steel and Nucor face an uncertain environment as the industry consolidates. Some argue if they don't grow quickly they might be taken over by foreign makers trying to gain entry into the United States. According to *Business Week*, Karlis Kirsis, managing partner of World Steel Dynamics Inc., an information service, said "everybody's in play these days" in the wake of the Mittal's planned merger with ISG. Even as U.S. Steel and Nucor make bids of their own, South Korea's Posco and Belgium's Arcelor might snap them up.

The Print Shop at Eva's Phoenix: "Training Youth for Life"*

Ann Armstrong
University of Toronto

"The Print Shop gave me a chance when no one else would."

Purpose

The Print Shop is a social enterprise designed to train at risk youth and to be a revenue generating social service. It is both a training facility and a commercial print shop. It provides homeless and at risk youth the opportunity to learn fundamental work and life skills. The Print Shop is located at Eva's Phoenix—see Exhibit 1 for a description of Eva Smith and her vision.

The youth are paid entry-level wages and are accountable for duties and responsibilities that mirror those of most printing operations. Even before the youth are hired, they job shadow to get an appreciation of working in the graphic communication industry.

The Print Shop is based on a blended value proposition which entails social, economic and environmental dimensions. It is dedicated to "continuing asset building" so that the youth can become self-sufficient in the long term. Success is achieved if both the youth and the Print Shop develop self-sufficiency.

Operations

The Print Shop specializes in "trainee-friendly" print work, typically small format job printing (11" × 17" and under) in one colour and 2-3 spot colour reproduction. It can work with most graphic design software programs. In-house graphic design work is also available. Commercial projects include business cards, letterhead, forms and brochures. Finishing services include trimming, folding, scoring, perforating and shrink-wrapping.

The Print Shop occupies 800 square feet in Eva's Phoenix. It has four presses: an A. B. Dick 360, an A. B. Dick 9810, a Heidelberg QM-46 and a Multilith 1250, all with colour heads, and other donated equipment.

Michael Rolph joined the Print Shop as its business manager after a long career in advertising. His role is to manage the systems, the people and the business opportunities of the Print Shop. His challenge is "to make sure that the fine line between training needs and business demands is relatively constant."

The Print Shop is supported by an advisory board which includes senior members of the graphic communications industry. The board provides advice on curriculum, employment opportunities and technology. See Exhibit 2 for the members of the advisory board as well as the Print Shop's organizational context. The Print Shop participates actively in the graphic communications industry; for example, it has had booths at trade shows.

Curriculum

The program lasts for 23 weeks and is offered in three stages:

1. Youth get life skills training and counselling for three weeks;
2. They get on-the-job print shop training for 20 weeks; and
3. They make job connections and career development in the last four weeks.

They learn fundamental employability work habits (e.g., team work, attendance, punctuality and safety) as well as a customer service orientation. Youth learn about

---

*Professor Ann Armstrong, Rotman School of Management, wrote this case as a basis for classroom discussion. It is not intended to show effective or ineffective practice. She would like to thank everyone at the Print Shop for giving their precious time to answer her many questions. © 2004.

Exhibit 1 Eva Smith's Vision

Eva Smith (1923–1993) co-founded the North York Emergency Home for Youth, which was later renamed Eva's Place in her honour. Her passion was in helping people, especially urban youth, to use their skills to find solutions to their challenges. Now her passion lives through three shelters in Toronto, known jointly as Eva's Initiatives.

Eva's Initiatives' mission is "[to] work collaboratively with homeless and at risk youth [aged 16 to 24] to actualize their potential to lead productive, self-sufficient and healthy lives by providing safe shelter and a range of services, [and to create] long term solutions for homeless youth by developing and implementing proactive and progressive services."

In the Greater Toronto Area, there are 10,000 homeless and at risk youth. Most are on the streets as they have suffered family breakdown and abuse. Many struggle with substance abuse problems and crime and prostitution are common.

Eva's Place, Eva's Satellite and Eva's Phoenix provide housing for at risk youth. Eva's Phoenix is an innovative 50-bed transitional housing and training facility in downtown Toronto. It was once a fire truck repair garage and has been redesigned as a set of ten townhouse units featuring private and communal living spaces. It has a main street that all the units overlook. Fifty youth apprenticed in the construction trades and helped to build the facility. Forty-one of the youth found work soon after completing the renovation. As one youth puts it, "I used to sleep under a bridge. Now I can build one."

Eva's Phoenix has won many awards for its innovative design. As well, it has been recognized by the Toronto Board of Trade as an outstanding example of public-private partnerships. The approach to designing Eva's Phoenix is being developed for replication across Canada.

In addition to providing secure shelter for one year, Eva's Phoenix provides mentoring and training services. Youth are trained for employment in printing, culinary arts, network administration or film production. "One Day, One Dollar" is a film about the realities of life for youth forced to live on the street because of the abuse they face in their homes.

Photo: Levitt Goodman Architects at www.google.com

the graphic communications industry and go on tours of organizations so that they can see where they might work after graduation. The Print Shop brings in peer mentors to assist both the trainees and the instructors with training and production. The peer mentors are themselves Print Shop graduates. Once the youth graduate, they stay connected to the Print Shop through a two year follow-up program.

They receive training in job planning and organization, prepress using various software programs on both PC and Macintosh platforms, small offset press operation and binding and finishing.

Exhibit 2 | Advisory Board and Organizational Context

Exhibit 3 | Financials—January through September 2004

Mary Black—Ryerson University
Bob Dale—Pilot Graphic Management
Brian Ellis—Heidelberg Canada
David Gibbins—Consultant
Patricia Gloudon—Scotia Capital
Jim Neate—Ernest Green & Son
Brian O'Leary—Kwik-Kopy Canada
Mike Tobias—Ember

Eva's Initiatives
Eva's Satellite
Employment Services
Eva's Place
Housing Services
The Print Shop
Eva's Phoenix

Profit and Loss

Ordinary Income/Expenses	
Income	
Sales	55,528.70
Uncategorized Income	30.00
Social Investment Income	231,973.63
Education Funds	2,978.46
Total Income	290,519.79
Cost of Goods Sold	
Job Expense—COGS	20,755.69
Capital Expense	24,944.29
Total COGS	45,699.98
Gross Profit	244,819.81
Expenses	
Business	69,836.72
Social	82,878.27
	152,715.09
Net Ordinary Income	92,104.72
Net Income	$92,104.72

Summary Balance Sheet

Assets	
Current Assets	
Chequing/Savings	69,876.62
Accounts Receivable	17,707.22
Other Current Assets	8,680.00
Total Current Assets	96,263.84
Fixed Assets	69,297.17
Total Assets	165,561.01
Liabilities & Equity	
Equity	165,561.04
Total Liabilities & Equity	$165,561.01

The program is delivered by two well experienced faculty, Patrick Fisher and Bill Kidd, who work part-time. They have a deep appreciation of the challenges that their students have faced in the past and are patient and flexible in how they deliver the curriculum.

Outcomes

The Print Shop started production in 2002. It trained ten youth in print shop and small business skills—six graduated and four were employed. In 2003, all 11 graduates have gone on to graphic communications programs or to commercial print shops. While four lost their opportunities, two have been re-employed.

Graduates have become press helpers and operators and production assistants, earning between $8.00 and $14.00 an hour. Every year, a graduate is awarded the Toronto Club Printing House Craftsmen's Student Award.

In 2003, the Print Shop had revenues of $50,000, achieving 30 per cent business cost self-sufficiency. It got 80 per cent of its work from other community organizations and 20 per cent from 'caring corporations'. Its clients include Street Kids International, Queen West Community Health Centre, Eva's Initiatives, Royal Bank of Canada, Scotia Capital and the Rotman School of Management.

In 2004, it is on track for revenues of $100,000, achieving 50 per cent of business cost self-sufficiency. Exhibit 3 presents the 2004 financial statements for the Print Shop.

Voices—Graduates

"My training at Phoenix Print Shop helped me get into higher education in visual communications. My Phoenix Print Shop Scholarship Award has helped me stay there."

Rebecca

"I had serious problems with alcohol and was living on the streets. Two months after starting a substance abuse problem, I got a job at the Print Shop. I met great staff who listened to me and taught me the wonders of printing."

David

"I was kicked out of my Dad's house at 19. I had nowhere to live. I now work as a junior pressman and live in a two bedroom apartment and am a peer mentor at Eva's Phoenix."

Reinieire

"At the Print Shop, you get respect and support and the teachers are really patient. . . . The staff advocates for me to employers—just because I'm deaf, it doesn't mean I'm dumb."

Andrea

"It felt like there was family—it was mind-blowing."

Noel

Voices—Advocates

"The real end product is the changed person—it's a very human enterprise. You can't do better than that!"

Michael Rolph, Business Manager, The Print Shop

"I believe that the social enterprise path . . . has integrity as a 'third way' of doing business and delivering social service."

Andrew Macdonald, Manager of Social Enterprise, Eva's Phoenix

"We have a great concern for the lack of entry level staff available to our industry. The Phoenix program is an excellent feeder system providing employers potential staff already knowledgeable in print processes."

Brian O'Leary, Vice President, Kwik-Kopy

"There are few initiatives that encourage young people to consider printing as a career choice. Eva's Phoenix offers this advantage to the industry as well as providing guidance to homeless and at risk youth by giving them structure, education and a path to self-improvement."

Myrna Penny, Managing Director, PrintLink Canada

"This is a win-win partnership for Xerox and the Phoenix Print Shop. The graduate we hired has the right combination of a positive attitude and the critical skills and training necessary to enable him to 'hit the ground running', and instantly contribute to our team."

Robert Wright, Manager of Customer Relations, Xerox

Future Goals

The Print Shop's 2005 social goals are to have 12 participants, ten graduates and eight graduates employed in career-oriented occupations. It also aims to have 75 per cent business cost self-sufficiency. Business costs are defined as "the actions taken by [the Print Shop] to sell

products or services [to] the market." Its longer term growth goals are to achieve 100 per cent business cost self-sufficiency by 2006 without compromising the social mission.

The Print Shop also has social costs which are defined as "the actions and functions that [the Print Shop] takes on in order to enable homeless and at risk youth to work within the enterprise." The Print Shop is working on the assumption that the ratio of business to social costs will be 60:40 in 2005.

At a recent planning session, several factors were identified as critical to the Print Shop's ability to reach its goals. They are (a) high performance work flow, (b) optimizing the sales mix, the equipment and space and (c) high performance outreach and intake, training and production and job development.

Investors

Key investors include the Toronto Enterprise Fund of the United Way of Greater Toronto, Human Resources and Skills Development of Canada, Heidelberg Canada, St. Stephen's Job Connect Program, the Scotia Capital Global Markets Group and the Royal Bank of Canada Foundation.

It has been looking for other sources of funding and participated successfully at the first Canadian Social Investors Forum, held in April 2003. Ten community organizations participated and 100 potential social investors attended. The ten organizations worked for three months with volunteer business coaches to develop their business plans. The forum was described by the Globe and Mail's David Ticoll as "an exciting new charity model that showcased the spectrum of social investment initiatives."

The Forum is a joint initiative between the Tides Foundation and the United Way of Greater Toronto to encourage venture philanthropy. The forum builds on the experience of Social Venture Partners of Seattle, Washington. So far, the Seattle forum has resulted in investments of US\$145,000 of in kind services, US\$300,000 in invited low interest loans and US\$307,000 of cash and stock in various types of community organizations.

Challenges

Several significant challenges lie ahead for the Print Shop and, in particular, for its social enterprise coordinator, Andrew Macdonald. He needs to look at (1) how to financially sustain the Print Shop, (2) how to measure its performance more precisely still and (3) how to advocate for and to diffuse the social enterprise model so that it becomes a more significant "category in current economic analysis."

Ryanair: Flying High at Ryanair

David Dunne
Joseph L. Rotman School of Management
University of Toronto

> *We don't fall over ourselves if they say, "My granny fell ill." What part of no refund don't you understand? You are not getting a refund so fuck off"*
>
> —**Michael O'Leary, CEO, Ryanair**

Loved and hated by Europeans, Ryanair had become one of the most successful airlines in the world. In spite of its exclusive focus on European routes, the airline ranked #11 in the world on operating profit and #2 on operating margin in 2005 (see Exhibit 1). Its CEO, Michael O'Leary, had been rewarded handsomely for his efforts, holding a net worth of €636M[1]—just a shade behind rock band U2 in the *Sunday Times* "Rich List" for Ireland.

Yet Ryanair was a paradox. To quote *The Economist* in 2007:[2]

> *[Ryanair] is hugely successful. It has brought flying within the reach of people of the most limited means. It has helped to change the economic prospects of neglected parts of Europe by bringing passengers and their money to underused provincial airports. But at the same time Ryanair has become a byword for appalling customer service, misleading advertising claims and jeering rudeness towards anyone or anything that gets in its way.*

Brief History[3]

Ryanair was the brainchild of Tony Ryan, a former executive with the Irish national airline, Aer Lingus, who grew wealthy as a broker placing surplus aircraft on behalf of airlines around the world. Ryanair started in 1985 with one 15-seat aircraft ferrying passengers between Waterford, a tiny airport about 90 minutes from Dublin, and London.

In the following year, Ryanair obtained a license to fly from Dublin to London. Aer Lingus, which held a monopoly on this route, protested in vain against the granting of the license, setting the stage for years of bitter competitive conflict.

In 1986 about 800,000 passengers flew on the Dublin–London route, typically paying about £200 for a return ticket[4] for a one-hour flight. With a long history of emigration there were many Irish residents in the UK, but they tended to travel home only for special occasions, such as family weddings or funerals. In May 1986, Ryanair announced that it would charge £99 on its inaugural flight, prompting Aer Lingus to slash its price to £95—and prompting Ryanair, in turn, to drop its price to £94.99.

The ensuing years were turbulent, to say the least, as Ryanair faced fierce competition from established airlines in the form of savage price cuts and lobbying to governments and the emergence of other discount airlines. By 1990, Ryanair's fare on the Dublin–London route had fallen to £59; in 1999, it was £19.99; and in 2005, Ryanair offered a fare of 99p to 100,000 passengers in celebration of its 20th birthday. In May 2007, Ryanair offered a free-seat giveaway to 1m passengers and a guarantee that no other airline could match its fares.

---

[1] €1 = C$1.46 approx.
[2] "Snarling all the way to the bank", *The Economist*, August 23rd 2007.
[3] For more details see http://www.ryanair.com/site/EN/about.php?page=About&sec=story
[4] About €280, or €527 in 2007 currency.

Professor David Dunne prepared this case as a basis for class discussion. It is not intended to illustrate effective or ineffective handling of a managerial situation.

Exhibit 1 | Airline Profitability Ranking

Top 25 Airlines by Operating Profitability, Fiscal Year 2005

(* = Fiscal Year 2004)

By Total Operating Profit			By Operating Margin		
Rank	Airline	US $m	Rank	Airline	%
1	FedEx*	1,414	1	Gol Airlines	23.3
2	British Airways	1,330	2	Ryanair	21.8
3	Air France-KLM	1,200	3	Air Asia	18.9
4	Lufthansa	877	4	COPA	17.3
5	Southwest	820	5	Kenya Airlines	15.6
6	Emirates	786	6	Philippine Airlines	13.7
7	All Nippon	776	7	DHL International*	12.5
8	Qantas*	775	8	Kalitta Air	12.3
9	Singapore Airlines	590	9	Emirates	11.9
10	Cathay Pacific	533	10	Mesa Airlines	11.7
11	Ryanair	459	11	American Eagle	11.3
12	Air China	458	12	SkyWest	11.2
13	Iberia	457	13	Southwest	10.8
14	Air Canada	388	14	Jet Airways*	10.3
15	UPS Airlines	293	15	Air China	9.6
16	Thai Airlines	269	16	Virgin Blue	9.6
17	Gol Airlines	266	17	TAM	9.5
18	TAM	232	18	Singapore Airlines	9.1
19	American Eagle	225	19	Royal Jordanian	9
20	SkyWest	220	20	Qantas*	8.9
21	Korean Airlines	207	21	Atlantic Southeast	8.5
22	Virgin Blue	184	22	British Airways	8.3
23	China Eastern*	179	23	Aer Lingus	8.2
24	LAN Airlines	142	24	Cathay Pacific	8.1
25	Asiana*	136	25	FedEx*	7.2

Source: IATA Economics Briefing, June 2006, "Profitability: Does Size Matter?"

Through this time, Ryanair's passenger traffic grew dramatically (Exhibit 2) and had reached 50m passengers on 571 routes across 26 European countries by 2007. The airline survived the Gulf War in 1991, the aftermath of Sept 11, 2001 and dramatic oil price increases, all of which created severe problems for the industry. By 2007, its route network covered most of Europe and the International Air Transport Association (IATA) reported that Ryanair was the largest international airline in the world in terms of passenger traffic.

Business Model

Ryanair's business model was very simple: it offered the lowest fares possible to passengers. It managed to accomplish this through a relentless focus on costs (see page 308). However, the airline was careful not to compromise safety and as of early 2008 had an accident-free record.

Ryanair was Europe's first discount airline and benefited greatly from the emergence of "open skies" deregulation across that continent. It modeled its strategy on

Exhibit 2   Ryanair Passenger Growth (Millions)

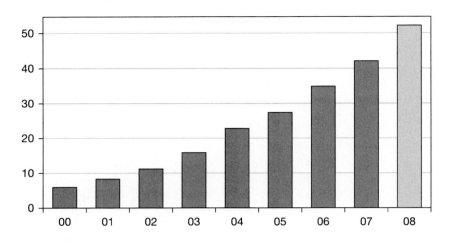

that of Southwest Airlines[5] in the US; O'Leary was one of several airline executives who made the pilgrimage to Dallas in the early 1990's to learn at the feet of Southwest's founder Herb Kelleher.

Cost Control

Ryanair's tight cost control was the backbone of its low-price strategy. As a result of this cost focus, Ryanair had by far the lowest costs in Europe, about 40% lower than its closest competitor. The major elements of its cost-control strategy were:

1. *The Use of Secondary Airports.* Ryanair typically did not fly to the major "hub" airports in Europe, but instead to secondary airports which were often located some distance away from major city centres. For example, Ryanair advertised flights to Frankfurt but flew to Hahn, about 125 km away, and similarly used secondary airports near London, Brussels, Hamburg and Stockholm. In negotiations with secondary airports, often located in economically depressed areas, Ryanair bargained hard for low fees.
2. *Rapid Turnaround.* Ryanair maximized the utilization of its aircraft by turning around its aircraft in 25 minutes, considerably faster than the industry average. This was facilitated by the lower traffic at secondary airports, and allowed Ryanair to keep its planes in the air about 30% longer than the typical carrier.
3. *Point-to-Point Routing.* All Ryanair flights were point-to-point, i.e. did not connect with other

flights. This avoided the costs associated with passenger and baggage transfer.
4. *Aircraft.* Ryanair flew a single aircraft family, the Boeing 737, and thus simplified the maintenance process. Its largest aircraft order was placed in 2001 after September 11, when there were significant bargains to be had. The aircraft themselves were "no-frills": they were ordered without window blinds, reclining seats, headrests or seat pockets.
5. *Fuel.* Fuels accounted for a substantial part (23%) of costs and unlike other carriers, Ryanair had a policy of not applying fuel surcharges. Fuel requirements were typically hedged for 12 to 18 months.
6. *Service.* There were no free snacks or drinks on Ryanair flights. These were supplied by third-party caterers who paid Ryanair a flat per-flight fee for the privilege of selling these items to passengers. Ryanair also charged passengers for checked baggage. Ryanair also had a rigid no-refund ticket policy that helped minimize administrative costs: the airline was also famous for pocketing the fees and taxes paid by "no shows" for its flights—about 8% of passenger traffic—a practice that earned €7.5m in 2003.
7. *Staff and Overheads.* Ryanair's staff were non-union, and subject to tight cost control measures. Pilots and cabin crew received lower salaries than their counterparts in other industries but received significant variable compensation: crew, for instance, received commissions on on-board sales. Staff were forbidden from charging their mobile phones at work, and at

---

[5] Heskett, James, "Southwest Airlines 2002: An Industry Under Siege," Harvard Business School, Case 9-803-133.

one point O'Leary suggested that employees take pencils from hotels rather than use new ones at work.

Service

Flying on Ryanair was truly a no-frills experience. Where traditional airlines provided extensive services on board, Ryanair eliminated snacks, newspapers, food and beverages. There was no business class or frequent flyer club.[6]

However, Ryanair was a pioneer in "unbundling" these services: instead of receiving them free, passengers could buy snacks and newspapers on board. In 2006, Ryanair also introduced a charge of €5.00 (€2.50 if booked in advance) for checked baggage and a further €8/kilo for baggage in excess of the 15-kilo limit. Among the many further revenue-generating services were onboard gaming, rail tickets and travel insurance: see www.ryanair.com for the full range of extra services offered by Ryanair.

On the positive side, several features of Ryanair's operation provided superior service to passengers. Ryanair consistently beat its competition on punctuality and missing bags (Exhibit 3): passengers with Ryanair were almost always assured of getting to their destination on time with their luggage.

On the other hand, Ryanair was notorious for its brash approach to customer service. The airline fought and lost several court cases that made it the poster boy for bad service: one action was brought by a disabled passenger against Ryanair for its policy of charging a fee for wheelchairs; another by Ryanair's millionth passenger, Jane O'Keefe, who received a "free flights for life" coupon, only to find that the airline subsequently restricted the prize to one flight per year. Ms. O'Keefe claimed that she received a torrent of abuse from O'Leary when she called his office to complain.

Ryanair's "no refund" policy also extended to adverse incidents: in the case of delays or cancellations due to weather or equipment problems, passengers could expect to receive no hotel accommodation or meal vouchers, let alone a refund. Ryanair staff had been known to simply close the check-in desk and leave in such situations, and O'Leary himself was known for yelling four-letter words at any passenger who dared ask for a refund.

In a poll of 4,000 travelers by the travel site Tripadvisor, Ryanair was voted the "least liked" airline in the world. The main complaint was unfriendly staff, followed by delays and poor legroom.

Exhibit 3	Customer Service Levels, 2004	
Airline	Punctuality (%)	Missing Bags per 1,000 Passengers
Ryanair	93.0	0.6
SAS	90.6	10.0
Air France	84.7	12.8
Lufthansa	83.6	16.9
easyJet	82.5	n.a.
Iberia	81.9	9.9
British Airways	80.5	16.7
Alitalia	75.5	11.6
Austrian	65.1	22.5

Source: Association of European Airlines, cited in Barrett, S.D. (2004), "The Sustainability of the Ryanair Model," *International Journal of Transport Management*, 2, 89–98.

Competition

Ryanair faced competition from traditional carriers such as Aer Lingus and British Airways, other discount carriers such as easyJet, and charter airlines that focused on package tours. Traditional carriers had tried, for the most part unsuccessfully, to launch their own discount operations. British Airways' discount carrier, Go, was forced to shut down in the face of fierce price cutting from Ryanair, and in 2003, Ryanair acquired KLM's discount operation, Buzz.

Discount operators were closest to Ryanair's business model, but had difficulty matching its low costs. A top executive of easyJet, its primary discount competitor in the UK and Europe, reported in 2005 that profits were below par as a result of fierce competition from Ryanair. Some charter operators were morphing into discount airlines, offering seats independent of holiday packages. One of these, Air Berlin, offered a comprehensive frequent-flier program and hot meals on longer flights.

Ryanair had never pulled its punches in pricing to eliminate competition, and its advertising—developed in-house—reflected a similarly aggressive approach. In what had once been a cozy industry, Ryanair shook up the competitive landscape with publicity stunts and ads that directly attacked competitive airlines. On one occasion, O'Leary arrived at Luton airport in a WW2 tank and

---

[6] A business class and frequent flyer club were launched in 1988, but proved unsuccessful. A Ryanair/MBNA credit card was launched in 2003, offering points that could be redeemed for Ryanair flights.

Case 26 / Ryanair: Flying High at Ryanair

led his "troops" in a chant of "I've been told and it's no lie, easyJet's fares are way too high." Many of these ads shocked both the industry and segments of the public, generating more notoriety for Ryanair. In response to the "Mannekin Pis" ad, Sabena successfully sued and Ryanair was ordered to discontinue the ad immediately and publish an apology. Ryanair used the apology for further price-comparative advertising.

The Future

From its scrappy beginnings as an upstart, Ryanair had become a world aviation leader. It had accomplished this in the face of fierce competition from established players and new discount operators, industry-wide shocks that put several competitors out of business, and a host of bureaucratic obstacles.

In 2006, Ryanair launched a hostile takeover bid for its arch-competitor, Aer Lingus, stating on its website, "In October . . . we made an all-cash offer for the small regional airline, Aer Lingus." The bid was ultimately rejected, but Ryanair continued to hold 25% of the shares in Aer Lingus. In 2007, O'Leary indicated that a new long-haul airline, RyanAtlantic, would be launched in 2009.

As remarkable as Ryanair's meteoric rise was its sheer nastiness with customers, bureaucrats, suppliers and anyone else it dealt with. Yet the airline's success flew in the face of conventional wisdom that customer service was critically important in this industry. In effect, O'Leary adapted everything about the Southwest airlines model except customer service, and there was no sign that this approach was about to change.

Selectpower—Green Energy in Ontario

Robert D. Klassen

Arif Merchant

It was late in the evening as Suzanne Wiltshire finished a long day at Selectpower. She had been working on a business plan that would develop a cohesive strategy for the firm's multiple business units and would provide a framework for future growth. Revenues in 2005 were expected to more than double from last year's level of about $5 million.[1] Wiltshire recalled her recent meeting a few days ago with the Selectpower's board, a small group of community leaders and executives. Their commitment for a cash infusion of $25 million would help to alleviate the current liquidity crunch. However, the limited resources were also forcing her to make some tough decisions about two important opportunities.

New investment could be directed toward either the emerging wind-derived electricity business or the nascent geothermal business. Moreover, Wiltshire believed that Selectpower needed to manage its triple bottom line: balancing economic, environmental and social returns. Both options offered clear environmental benefits to customers, although the strategic and immediate economic benefits to Selectpower were less clear. Significant questions remained given evolving customer expectations, fluctuating energy prices and changing government regulations. Wiltshire knew that the board would be expecting a detailed plan at the next meeting.

Selectpower's Business Strategy

The de-regulation of the electricity industry in Ontario required Guelph Hydro to spin off its non-core businesses. On May 1, 2002, the day the electricity market opened, Selectpower was spun off as a separate, unregulated, for-profit company owned by Guelph Hydro. Wiltshire and her management team, in consultation with the board, determined that Selectpower must pursue revenue growth while moving toward economic self-sufficiency as soon as possible. At the same time, it must contribute to the environmental and social good of the community. After conducting an assessment, Wiltshire implemented a series of changes over several years that yielded four major business units: Retail, Rental, Energy Services and Energy. By 2005, the firm had grown to about a dozen employees.

Selectpower's managers were given considerable latitude in their decision-making, which promoted competition between the business units for further investment. The firm was also viewed as a vehicle to help the city of Guelph achieve its goals around environmental stewardship. For example, the city had set specific goals to reduce its emissions of greenhouse gases, as mandated by the Kyoto Protocol (see United Nations Framework

---

[1] Unless otherwise noted, all financial figures are in Canadian dollars.

Richard Ivey School of Business
The University of Western Ontario

Arif Merchant wrote this case under the supervision of Professor Robert D. Klassen solely to provide material for class discussion. The authors do not intend to illustrate either effective or ineffective handling of a managerial situation. The authors may have disguised certain names and other identifying information to protect confidentiality.

Ivey Management Services prohibits any form of reproduction, storage or transmittal without its written permission. Reproduction of this material is not covered under authorization by any reproduction rights organization. To order copies or request permission to reproduce materials, contact Ivey Publishing, Ivey Management Services, c/o Richard Ivey School of Business, The University of Western Ontario, London, Ontario, Canada, N6A 3K7; phone (519) 661-3208; fax (519) 661-3882; e-mail cases@ivey.uwo.ca.

Convention on Climate Change, www.unfccc.int). Selectpower would help the city to meet these targets by "retailing" wind-generated energy. Wiltshire cautioned:

> You have to differentiate between retailing and distribution. We don't own the grid or maintain the wires which go up on the poles and into residential homes; that's what our regulated sister company, Guelph Hydro Electric Systems, does. Instead, Selectpower buys electricity from wind generators and sells this clean energy to consumers, thereby displacing energy that otherwise would be generated from dirty coal.

As a first step, the firm planned to promote improved energy-efficiency by selling products and services that helped consumers reduce their energy consumption. Customers would then be asked to reinvest some of their savings in green electricity, as greater demand for wind energy would reduce the need for coal-fired generation. To generate additional awareness, Selectpower's managers were also expected to volunteer for various municipal committees, participate in university projects, actively participate in the Ontario Energy Association and the Canadian Wind Energy Association, and promote renewable energy by exhibiting at community festivals, regional energy shows and sustainability conferences. According to Wiltshire, "At Selectpower, we all share a vision. We know what we want the world to look like."

In parallel, Guelph Hydro opened Ecotricity in October 2005, an operation that generated electricity from landfill gas (e.g. biogas or methane). This new affiliate did not have any direct connection to Selectpower. This operation won a 20-year supply contract from the Ontario Power Authority (OPA), the provincial agency that was responsible for supporting the development of adequate, reliable and secure electricity supply, including green energy sources.

Retail

The Retail business unit focused on supplying energy-efficient products for use in homes in the communities of Guelph and neighbouring Cambridge, with a combined population of about 235,000. The product range included electric and natural gas fireplaces, energy-efficient lighting, programmable thermostats and water-saving toilets. These products were sold from three locations: a showroom in its head office; a store in Cambridge; and a large centre-aisle kiosk in a major mall in Guelph.

Rental

Selectpower inherited a fleet of 3,000 electric water heaters which were installed in homes in Guelph. Maintenance was outsourced and monthly rental fees were collected through a fee-for-service arrangement with Guelph Hydro. This allowed customers to receive only one bill each month that included both their electricity and rental charges. "I saw right away that the fleet had been shrinking for many years," observed Wiltshire. "So we added natural gas water heaters to our offering and the fleet stabilized and began to grow again. Rentals provide a very reliable, steady cash flow, but it requires a capital investment of about $150,000 every year and it takes five years to recover that cash. On the other hand, the average life of a water heater is about 13 years."

Energy Services

Draft-proofing, Heating and Cooling
This business unit focused on helping customers reduce the energy consumed in heating and cooling. Households were offered a free energy audit to determine the extent to which draft-proofing would reduce energy use, and to explain the value of upgrading the furnace to a higher efficiency unit that would offer a financial payback to the homeowner. After determining the shortcomings in insulation and the potential cost-saving for heating or cooling, a sales team member would typically make a proposal. Customers could then opt to have Selectpower draft-proof their attics, basements, windows or doors, or replace their heating and/or cooling system. This business enjoyed a great degree of visibility, with a market that extended up to 100 kilometers, serving a total population of over half a million people. Growing at more than 300 per cent per year, Energy Services was a huge success story for the company.

Geothermal Systems
In February 2005, Selectpower Energy Services added geothermal heating and cooling systems to its product mix. In essence, geothermal systems allowed users to extract the heat naturally stored underground to provide low-cost pollution-free heat in winter. If reversed, the system could also cool air in the summer (see Exhibit 1).

Selectpower designed, marketed and installed commercial and residential systems. Because of the necessary marketing expertise and relatively low adoption rates to date, it was worthwhile to market these systems throughout southern Ontario. The success of geothermal systems in both the residential and commercial markets resulted in significant growth for Selectpower. "We started geothermal six months ago, and are already competing for half million dollar contracts," observed Wiltshire.

Operating costs of geothermal systems were very low, as fossil fuels were eliminated for heating and electrical needs were greatly reduced for cooling. However, initial

Exhibit 1   Schematic of a Geothermal System

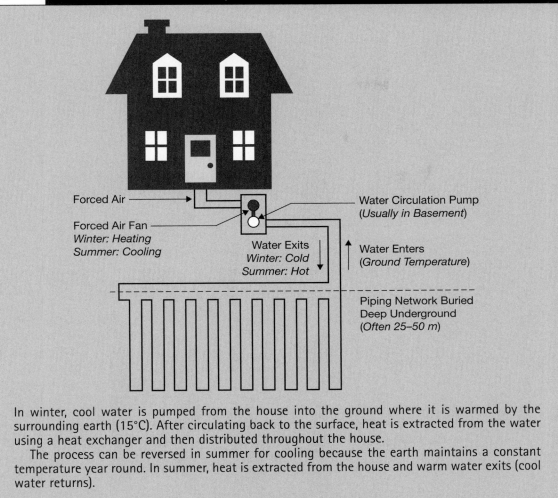

Forced Air

Forced Air Fan
Winter: Heating
Summer: Cooling

Water Circulation Pump
(*Usually in Basement*)

Water Exits
Winter: Cold
Summer: Hot

Water Enters
(*Ground Temperature*)

Piping Network Buried
Deep Underground
(*Often 25–50 m*)

In winter, cool water is pumped from the house into the ground where it is warmed by the surrounding earth (15°C). After circulating back to the surface, heat is extracted from the water using a heat exchanger and then distributed throughout the house.

The process can be reversed in summer for cooling because the earth maintains a constant temperature year round. In summer, heat is extracted from the house and warm water exits (cool water returns).

Source: Selectpower

capital costs to drill and install the ground loops were high, about three times the cost of conventional heating and cooling equipment. As a result, typical payback periods ranged from three to seven years. Life expectancy ranged from 60 to 100 years, or more (see Exhibit 2).

Beyond installation, the system offered another significant opportunity. A number of customers had expressed an interest in renting their system, thereby converting the high capital cost to a monthly fee—money that would have paid for fuel anyway. Wiltshire explained:

> *Some households are not comfortable making the initial investment of $15,000–30,000 because they don't know if they are going to stay in the same house for more*

than five years. We want to be able to tell them: "we'll install it and own it, you rent it from us for a monthly fee and you'll still save."

For Selectpower, this financing option would translate into an enormous upfront capital investment, but it would guarantee a long-term stream of recurring revenues.

Energy

The sale of wind-derived electricity and natural gas also fit well with Selectpower's strategy of providing consumers with choices that help them save money and improve the environment. Both were available through

Comparison of Investment Needed

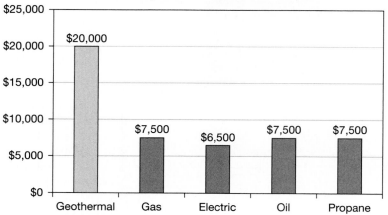

Comparison of Operational Cost

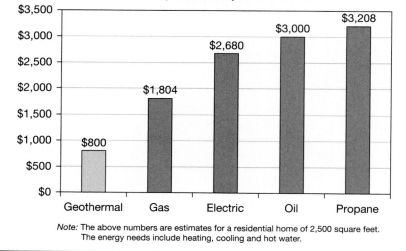

Note: The above numbers are estimates for a residential home of 2,500 square feet. The energy needs include heating, cooling and hot water.

Source: Selectpower

long-term fixed-price contracts where local distribution companies were used to distribute the energy to a broad base of customers throughout Ontario. However, because the electricity and gas utility markets were highly regulated, pricing and marketing efforts engendered a great deal of complexity. "In my business I have to consider not only the economic risk of projects, but also the political and regulatory risks for our shareholder (i.e. elected city council). In particular, a change of provincial government could mean changes to provincial energy policies and electricity regulations."

Natural Gas

The step into natural gas contracts was a difficult decision for Wiltshire. Guelph Hydro had been in the regulated electricity distribution business for a hundred years, but natural gas was a different business and commodity trading was certainly new to the board. However, the learning curve and inherent risks in gas trading made board members nervous. Buying forward contracts and holding them for three to five years would leave Selectpower vulnerable to price volatility and market risk.

After developing a solid risk-management program, Selectpower successfully entered this market by using local natural gas distributors to deliver the product to consumers, first in the southwest region and later throughout most of the province. Here too, a stream of recurring revenues was established, as contracts sold one year continued to pay for up to five years; Wiltshire felt that this growing revenue stream might quickly dwarf other business units.

Green Power: Selectwind

Ontario generated electricity from a mix of resources: hydro, nuclear, natural gas and coal. Sufficient capacity was installed to meet the basic provincial demand of 15,000 megawatts (MW), but during extreme weather when demand could spike to 25,000 MW, electricity was imported from the United States and neighbouring provinces. No new generation capacity had been built in Ontario since the 1970s, with the exception of a few entrepreneurs who had erected 11 wind turbines (40 MW) in recent years.

Electricity power needs fluctuated from hour-to-hour, day-to-day and season-to-season, and could not be effectively stored. As a result, generation was forced to rise and fall to meet demand. Large nuclear generators were the least flexible, typically taking weeks to bring back online if shut down. Hydroelectric generators were more easily adjusted, but within a relatively small range. Natural gas-fired generators were relatively easy to bring online as needed. Finally, coal-fired generators were the last source added to meet peak demand, both because generation levels could be easily adjusted and these generators were the dirtiest source of air pollution.

In Ontario, all electricity generators are connected to the same grid network; thus, customers were not tied to specific generators. So how does a company sell "green" power? The key point was to displace existing fossil fuel-derived electricity with that from wind energy. More specifically, because of very little investment in new generation capacity, coal-fired generators had been used almost continuously since 2002, and currently supplied about 23 per cent of needed electricity. Thus, for each new megawatt of capacity added from wind turbines or other green sources, an equivalent amount of coal generation capacity could be taken out of service, reducing greenhouse gas emissions to zero. In environmental terms, this translated into a reduction of approximately one kilogram of carbon dioxide (CO_2) per kWh of wind-derived energy, in addition to reducing toxic air pollutants. The CO_2 reduction also provided tradable credits in the growing market for emissions trading (e.g. the European Union).

Denmark has demonstrated the potential for wind energy to fulfill the electricity needs of large communities, providing 20 per cent of Denmark's total power. Throughout Europe and even in the United States, huge wind farms supply significant amounts of clean renewable energy to growing economies. That is not to say that these gains have been easy. NIMBY (i.e. not-in-my-backyard) resistance to "unsightly" wind turbines marring the view have significantly slowed a large-scale project off the east coast of the United States near Cape Cod, Massachusetts.

Wind turbines cost about $1.5 million per MW to construct, significantly higher than other forms of electrical generators in Ontario. Combined with maintenance costs, wind-derived "green" power needed to be priced at about $0.10/kWh, much higher than the current regulated rate of $0.043/kWh.

Who would pay this kind of a premium for clean air? Wiltshire thought that the residents of Guelph would. She argued, "For one hundred years people have taken electricity for granted, not knowing how harmful to health and the environment it could be. Educating people to understand the real economic, social and environmental costs of electricity, and changing their behaviour and willingness to pay are huge marketing endeavors." The city also was committed to reducing its emissions as exemplified by its ratification of the Kyoto Protocol.

To enter the market with an affordable product, in 2003 Selectpower designed a unique model. Using the average household consumption of electricity of approximately 750 kWh per month, customers would be offered emissions credits in blocks of 75 kWh, representing 10 per cent of a household's consumption. After running cost estimates, they determined they would charge households an affordable $6.53 per month for 75 kWh. Customers could choose to buy more than one block per month, offsetting up to one hundred per cent of the emissions created by their own electricity consumption. This represented a $0.087/kWh premium, enough to buy the emission credits from the generator with something left over to defer marketing costs for Selectpower.

In order to truly make a difference, customers need to change their behaviour for the long-term. Doing so ensures sufficient demand to encourage the installation of additional wind-derived generation capacity. So Selectpower offered its green energy only for terms of three or five years; it was marketed as Selectwind "clean air." Wiltshire explained, "This level of customer commitment created a significant barrier to initial sales, but over the long term, it has made the program viable economically and environmentally."

"You want me to buy what?" was the typical first reaction to Selectpower's initial sales effort in Guelph. While climate change was constantly in the news media, people tended to view it as remote, long-term or difficult to observe. In contrast, yellow air, smog days and reports of 1,000 premature deaths a year from the Ontario Medical Association were much more immediate and tangible to most of Guelph's residents. Branding also avoided a battle of semantics between the federal and provincial governments. The federal government did not recognize "credits" and the provincial regulatory agency for energy was skeptical of Selectwind's ability to make customers understand that they were not buying electrons. "I was never going to get these two levels of government to agree, but they were both able to accept 'Selectwind' without compromising their positions," said Wiltshire.

In 2003, Natural Resources Canada invited companies to submit a renewable energy marketing plan which, if approved, would be refunded up to 40 per cent by the government. Wiltshire commented, "We won the funding in the first round of bidding, and the second round as well. However, we have barely spent any of it since the 40 per cent rebate means that we would still need to put in the other 60 per cent! We just do not have the funds available." Now the funding is about to expire in 2006 and Selectpower will have no further government support for marketing Selectwind.

Fortunately, as competition was slowly increasing in the emissions trading market, the price of CO_2 was also falling. Over time, Selectpower was able to reduce the cost for emissions and passed this savings along to customers in the form of larger blocks. Thus, the blocks were increased from 75 kWh to 100 kWh per month, still priced at $6.53.

To continue to grow Selectwind, one option was move upstream into wind-derived power generation. Under new provincial regulations, Selectpower could build its own wind farm and sell the power to the OPA under a long-term purchase contract (much like Ecotricity did with methane, described earlier). The project would require an investment of $2 to $5 million or more, but a 20-year fixed-price contract would establish a stable revenue stream without marketing costs. Several large industrial companies were starting to do this, with new farms being sited along the shores of lakes Huron and Erie. Wiltshire wondered if this was the right direction for Selectpower to allocate its limited funds.

Future

While considering various alternatives for Selectpower, Wiltshire was forced to balance the perspectives of multiple stakeholders and its shareholder, the City of Guelph. Moreover, Wiltshire had recently been approached to sell some business units and also was options to obtain funding from the capital markets. She reflected,

> Although we have four separate businesses at work here, we need to focus on one of two key areas: wind-derived electricity and geothermal systems appear to be attractive options for growth. But each also has substantial risks for Selectpower. Strategically, in which part of the value chain should we be investing, and where are we most likely to generate substantial returns, economically, socially and environmentally? With the capital markets, the economic bottom line always takes primary importance, and the triple bottom line can then be seen as ECONOMIC, writ large, and environmental and social in small lettering. I want to see that all three areas get attention in whatever future strategy we adopt.

What should Wiltshire recommend to her board next month? What will her parent company, Guelph Hydro, have to say about it? Should Selectpower relinquish its complex efforts to develop the triple bottom line and focus on profitability?

Target Stores' Differentiation Strategies

Suchitra Jampani

Ajith Sankar R.N.

"What Target did was figure out how to eke out a position on that [retail] landscape that was not about solely playing the cost game, they went a very different direction from Wal-Mart."[1]

—*Nancy Koehn, a Harvard Business School professor and retail historian.*

"Clearly there is a certain drive to be creative. They see ways of doing business that are based on taste and ideas, not just price. Doing that is even more difficult today than in the past because of all of the pressure to perform on both a long- and short-term basis by Wall Street. That Target has been able to proceed the way it has speaks to the company's creativity and vision."[2]

—*Marvin Traub, former chairman and CEO, Bloomingdale's,*[3] *commenting on Target.*

"Branding is one of the things they (Target) do a good job of, and it represents where they want to be in the market"[4]

—*Chris Merritt, principal at Kurt Salmon Associates, commenting on the branding strategies of Target.*

Target the Upscale Discounter

In March 2005, Target Corporation (Target) had 1,330 retail stores in 47 states of the United States. Even though it only had a fifth of the sales and profits of Wal-Mart,[5] it had a loyal customer base that was looking for a trendy, yet, affordable range of merchandise. Target's customers, whom it referred to as 'Guests', were younger and more affluent than that of its rival Wal-Mart.

Target's positioning was based on more than just pricing; it encompassed quality, style, and trend. This

---

[1] Schlosser, Julie, "How Target Does It," www.fortune.com, October 18, 2004.
[2] Arlen, Jeffrey, "Why Is Target So Cool?", www.findarticles.com, April 2, 2001.
[3] Operated by Federated Department Stores, Inc., Bloomingdales is a chain of 36 retail stores in US with sales of $2 billion in 2004.
[4] "Mass Merchants: Aggressive and innovative," www.internetretailer.com, December 2002.
[5] Net sales and net income for Wal-Mart for 2004 was $285,200 million and $10,300 million respectively.

Exhibit 1 Financial Summary of Target Corporation

	2004	2003	2002
Revenues (Million $)	$46,839	$42,025	$37,410
Earnings before Interest and Taxes (Million $)	$3,601	$3,210	$2,861
Net Earnings (Million $)	$1,885	$1,651	$1,407
Net Earnings per share, Diluted	$ 2.07	$ 1.80	$ 1.54

Source: http://www.corporate-ir.net/ireye/ir_site.zhtml?ticker=tgt&script=11906&layout=0&item_id='factcard_39.htm'

was the differentiation strategy that was consistently applied since the launch of the chain. Target positioned itself as an upscale discount chain. It differentiated itself from its competitors by offering trendy merchandise at affordable prices. Target used attractive marketing promotions to communicate this message to customers. By 2002, the company became the second largest discount retailer in US. The differentiation followed by the company and its effective communication programs helped it to continuously increase its revenue and net income (Refer to Exhibit 1).

Background Note

The first Target Store was opened by the Dayton Company in 1962, in Roseville, a suburb of the twin cities Minneapolis-St. Paul, Minnesota. The Dayton Company was started by George Dayton who opened his first store called Goodfellows in Minneapolis in 1902. In 1903, he changed the corporate name to The Dayton Dry Goods Company and in 1910 he changed it to The Dayton Company (Dayton). By the 1940s, it was a thriving family business that operated department stores called Dayton's in the upper Midwest region of the U.S. In 1956, Dayton opened Southdale, the world's first fully enclosed two-level shopping center, in Minneapolis.

In the 1950s, the discount store retail format was taking shape and the pioneers of this format were just establishing themselves. After the success of its department stores, Dayton began exploring the possibilities of starting its own chain of discount stores. John Giesse (Giesse), who was a vice-president at Dayton, was extremely interested in the discount retail format and was even contemplating leaving Dayton to open his own discount stores. Executives at Dayton, who knew about Geisse's ambitions, pointed out to him that he would need capital for the project. Dayton had the capital, they said, and asked Geisse to submit a report on his observations and ideas for a chain of discount stores. Geisse,

who studied the existing discount stores, was of the opinion that there was a place for an upscale discount store. Dayton decided to launch a discount store chain as a subsidiary and named it Target. In 1962, Dayton launched the first Target in Roseville, Minnesota, and three more in Crystal, St. Louis Park, and Duluth, Minnesota, the same year.

The first four stores made about $11 million in sales but did not make any profits in 1962. Slowly, sales began increasing and in 1965, sales were worth about $39 million. In the same year, another Target was opened in Minneapolis. In 1966, Target decided it was time to open stores outside Minneapolis. It opened two stores in Denver. In 1967, Target's parent company, Dayton, went public. The same year, two stores were opened in Minnesota, bringing the total number of stores to nine, and by 1968, Target opened two more stores in St. Louis.

A major change occurred at Dayton in 1969—Dayton merged with the J. L. Hudson Company to form the Dayton Hudson Corporation (DHC). The J. L. Hudson Company operated a chain of department stores called Hudson's in Detroit. Also in 1969, Target decided to open stores without supermarkets. Even though Target believed that providing discount groceries was essential to providing a one-stop shopping experience to the customer, it decided to open its new stores with only general merchandise.

By the end of the 1960s, Target had opened stores in Texas and Oklahoma, and a Northern Distribution Center in Fridley, Minnesota, which had a computerized distribution system. In 1970, it expanded into Wisconsin and the next year into Colorado and Iowa. For its expansion in Colorado, Iowa, and Oklahoma, it acquired 16 Arlans stores and converted them into Target Stores. In addition, it opened six new stores in these states. In 1972, Target started testing electronic point-of-sale terminals with two Minneapolis stores and four stores in Dallas the next year. However, in 1972, the operating income and profits of the Target Stores started declining. Target's top executives had limited experience in the discount retail business and they found the rapid expansion to 46 stores by 1973 difficult to manage. They had problems such as high inventory costs and stale merchandise arising from over-stocking, which in turn led to lower sales and lower operating income. In order to improve Target's performance, Stephen L. Pistner (Pistner), a vice president at DHC, was made the CEO of Target. Kenneth A. Macke (Macke) who had worked with Pistner, was made senior vice president and merchandise manager of soft lines.

In 1973, Target's new management decided to slow down expansion to concentrate on its existing stores' merchandising and operations, so they planned to open only one store the next year. The management also made the decision to make huge markdowns on the excess stock to clean out the existing inventory. In 1974, Target decided to develop Decision Guides, the operating policies and philosophies for the chain's future growth. By 1975, Target's performance had improved and it became DHC's number one chain in terms of revenue. In 1977, Macke became the chairman and CEO of Target and Pistner became the president of DHC. By the end of the 1970s, Target had 80 stores and had crossed the billion mark with $1.12 billion in sales.

In the 1980s, Target rapidly expanded into different markets such as California, Detroit, Tennessee, and Kansas. At the end of 1980, Target acquired the Ayr-Way chain of 40 stores and also got the Eastern Distribution Center in Indianapolis as part of the deal. These 40 Ayr-Way stores were converted into Target Stores in 1981. In the same year, Target opened its Southern Distribution Center in Little Rock, Ark., and ventured into Louisiana. Macke became president of DHC and Floyd Hall (Hall) replaced him as chairman and CEO of Target. In 1982, Target acquired 28 FedMarts[6] in Southern California, four in Arizona, and one in Texas. It also made Los Angeles its regional headquarters and opened a Distribution Center there. By the end of 1982, Target's sales had crossed the two billion mark with $2.41 billion in sales. The FedMarts it acquired were converted to Target Stores by mid-1983.

Bruce G. Allbright (Allbright), who was the vice chairman and chief administrative officer of Target, became chairman and CEO after Hall left the company in 1984. Another major development at DHC that year was the merging of the two department store chains, Dayton's and Hudson's, to become 'Dayton's Hudson's'. Even though Dayton and the J. L. Hudson Company had merged as far back as 1969, the two department store chains were being operated separately. The same year,

Robert J. Ulrich (Ulrich), who was the head of the Dayton Hudson Department Stores (DHDS) group, became the president of Target. By the end of 1984, Target had 215 stores and sales were about $3.55 billion. Target decided to create a new look and layout for its future stores, so it developed a new prototype store and this was introduced in 1985. The new store had three separate merchandising environments: Fashion World of apparel, Home World of home goods, and Basic & Leisure World of hard lines.

Continuing its expansion in Southern California, Target acquired 54 Gemco Stores (Gemcos)[7] in 1986. The acquisition of the Gemcos made it the largest retailer in Southern California. In 1987, Ulrich became the chairman and CEO of Target, while Allbright became the President of the DHDS group. Target continued to drive growth through acquisitions in 1989 by acquiring 31 Gold Circle and Richway stores in Georgia, Florida, and North Carolina.

In September 1990, Target opened Target Greatland, a superstore, which occupied more than 160,000 sq. ft., in Apple Valley, Minnesota. In 1991, Target opened 43 new stores under five different prototypes. Of the five, two of the prototypes with sizes of 135,000 sq. ft. and 120,000 sq. ft. were designed for the Target Greatlands category. Of the other three prototypes meant for the typical Target Stores, a 115,000 sq. ft. prototype was designed for a standard Target Store, a 85,000 sq. ft. prototype designed for smaller county seat markets, while a 90,000 sq. ft. prototype was a scaled-down version of the typical Target Store. In addition, Target updated the retailing technology in its stores. It installed an In-Store Information Systems program that used hand-held scanners in a pull system and started using EDI with vendors that accounted for more than two-thirds of its volume. By the end of 1991, Target had 463 stores with sales of more than $9 billion. (See Table 1 for Target's growth in sales and stores from 1962 to 1991.)

In 1992, Target decided to enter a new area of merchandising—apparel specialty stores. In 1992, Target test marketed its new apparel specialty store, Everyday Hero, in St. Louis Park, a suburb of Minneapolis, Minnesota. Everyday Hero was modeled on mass market specialty apparel retailers such as The Gap, and carried private labels owned by Target. However, after the first store opened, Target scrapped its plans of developing a chain of Everyday Hero stores. In 1994, Target decided to develop its own super center stores[8] like its two major competitors Wal-Mart and Kmart. Target opened its first

---

[6] Headquartered in San Diego, California, FedMart was founded in 1954. The retail chain sold groceries, clothing, and home furnishings.

[7] Target purchased 54 Gemcos from Lucky Stores for $440 million in 1986.

[8] Super centers are discount stores that are larger than the regular discount stores and also sell groceries like a supermarket.

Table 1	Target's Growth in Sales and Stores	
Year	Sales in US $ millions	No. of Stores as of year end
1962	20	4
1968	130	11
1973	375	46
1978	899	67
1983	3,118	206
1988	6,331	341
1991	9,041	463

Source: www.findarticles.com

super center called SuperTarget in 1995, in Lawrence, Kansas. The store covered about 200,000 sq. ft. and Target intended to test different sizes for other SuperTargets. In 1998, DHC acquired Rivertown Trading Company (RTC), a catalog and e-commerce company, and The Associated Merchandising Corporation. By 1999, it had opened 15 SuperTargets and doubled the number by the year 2000.

In 2000, DHC changed its name to Target Corporation (Target Corp.). In addition, it formed Target.direct, a new business unit to oversee its electronic retailing and direct marketing efforts. Target.direct consisted of two subsidiaries of Target Corp.—RTC and Target.direct LLC. RTC managed brands such as Wireless, Signals, Seasons, ILoveADeal and other brands. Target.direct LLC supported Target Stores, Marshall Field's, and Mervyn's e-commerce initiatives. In all, Target.direct operated seven websites: target.com, marshallfields.com, mervyns.com, wirelesstoo.com, signals.com, seasonshop.com, and Iloveadeal.com.

In 2003, Target developed yet another prototype store called P2004. In this prototype, the layout was modified and store space was reallocated to scale back some categories such as men's apparel, automotive, and hardware while expanding better performing categories. The first store of the P2004 prototype was opened in Greeley, Colo., at the end of 2003.

In July 2004, Target sold its department store chain Marshall Field's to the May Department Store Company (May Co.) for $3.24 billion in cash. May Co. acquired all the assets that comprised Marshall Field's, which included 62 stores, inventory, customer receivables, and

distribution centers. As part of the sale, May Co. also acquired the real estate of nine Mervyn's store locations in the St. Paul-Minneapolis area. By the end of 2004, Target had about 1,275 stores, including SuperTargets in 47 states.

Differentiation Strategies

From the very beginning, Dayton's strategy was to position Target as an upscale discount chain at which the prices would be just above the lowest prices. To achieve this upscale image, it offered trendy and stylish goods in an environment that was bright and attractive, unlike other discount stores of the time. To be able to offer the most up to date styles and trends to the customers Target focused on merchandising. Recognizing that just having the goods in the stores was not enough, Target also worked on conveying this image to the customer through its store layouts and displays, and through marketing and promotions. It consistently used its famous Bullseye logo and tag line, 'Expect more. Pay less.' in its marketing and promotions. According to an article[9] in *Advertising Age* in 2003, its logo was recognized by 96% of Americans. Unlike other discounters, Target itself had become a brand because of its successful merchandising strategies, marketing, and advertising.

Merchandising

Target's positioning as an upscale discount chain was reflected in its merchandising strategy as well. Target managers felt that they needed to be constantly in tune with what the customers wanted and anticipate trends and demands. Warren Feldberg, Target's executive vice president of merchandising, tried "looking at the world as our shopping basket and finding ways to bring that basket to the average customer."[10]

Target developed an image and displayed products that matched its customers' lifestyles and created enhanced merchandise displays. It offered a mix of private labels and national brands in creative and innovative layouts and displays. In the early 1990s, Target had several private labels with merchandise at all price points. 'Favorites' was its opening price point label offering basics and its 'Honors' label was priced just above that. The label 'Sostanza', was a better quality, more European look for the younger customer, and was all predominantly ladies' ready-to-wear lines. Target also had 'Pro Spirit', which was an active wear label. Its

---

[9] "Francis' Mission: Shore up Target's Sales by 'Owning Red'."
[10] Lettish, Jill, "A Bloomingdales approach to the discount market," www.findarticles.com, September 17, 1990.

'Greatland' label was positioned as an outdoor wear label. "There's no question we want to continue to take advantage of our own brands. We built some very successful brands that are well identified by our own customers. We also know that we, in the company strategy, believe in brands, so we will obviously balance those two approaches as we go forward,"[11] said Feldberg regarding Target's view of private labels versus national brands.

One of the strategies that most retailers used to create an upscale image was to implement the shop-within-a-shop concept. However, Target had a different approach. In the early 1990s, it decided that it needed to bring in more brands and labels that were associated with department stores and create 'focus areas' for them. These focus areas or 'stripe points' as Target called them would highlight the merchandise, yet be in line with the aesthetics and interiors of the entire store. Target's vendors were appreciative of its merchandising strategies. Charlie Becker, marketing director for E.S. Originals, a footwear company, said E.S. Originals had benefited from the concept of focus areas, which were highlighted through the use of lighting and signage. Alan Silverman, executive vice president of Kid Duds, which manufactured sleepwear for Target, said, "What Target does is purchase long, deep, and narrow. There is a lot of planning at the corporate level, more than in many discounters."[12]

In 1990, Target established a 'Quick Response Task Force' made up of Target officials and vendors. It identified trends and purchasing patterns so that it could quickly develop and implement micro-marketing programs. "The key to success with Target is to be a good listener. They have so much information they are willing to give. There is an unprecedented level of openness and of confidentiality between Target and its vendors,"[13] said Larry Reiner, sales manager for JIK Ltd., an apparel firm that supplied Target with private label knitwear.

Target used a product development team, which was known as one of the best in the industry, to determine what kinds of products to carry and what kind of image to project. In 1996, Louis Padilla, Senior VP and GM Merchandising, soft lines, Target, made a mention of how product development at Target had shifted from being trend-driven to focusing on elements of brand management where each brand had been uniquely positioned for the guests and profiled different product looks. Target applied this approach to all brands, whether national or private. However, it focused more on its private labels as they accounted for over 50% of its apparel and domestics mix. By doing this, Target could more readily offer unique fashions and exert greater control over pricing and the overall look of its stores. Using this approach, it launched several lines of apparel and domestics in 1996. Everything in 'Utility', a line of young men's active apparel, was designed internally at Target while in the case of 'Cherokee' an updated young women's line, Target maintained tight control on its exclusive direct license with Cherokee.

Target applied the same merchandising strategies across all categories of merchandise. "We want to be a leader with the right trends now, not just in apparel, but in home furnishings, home improvements, really across the board", said Ulrich.[14] In the early 1990s, Target developed a house brand of coordinated bedding. It was first called 'Country Estates', then 'Estates', and later 'Garden Estates' as the style and patterns evolved.

With its advertising and in-store presentation Target consistently conveyed the message that the apparel and domestics collections were clean, fresh, and in style, not likely to go out of fashion soon. In addition, it stressed the fact that the goods were priced right, not just in terms of dollars and cents, but in terms of convenience. These messages were clearly conveyed through its circulars, TV ads, point-of-sale signage, and merchandise displays. Thus, Target added more value by reducing the time spent by the customer in trying to figure out where to find what and easily make buying decisions. It was convenient, especially for the time-pressed customer who wanted to spend less time in the stores. Another advantage of efficient communication was an increase in average purchases per visit. An example of this was the 'Destination Sun' theme in spring 1995. It started out as promotions for summer wear especially swimwear, but spread out into other departments. The 'Destination Sun' art and logos were applied to all of Target's summer seasonal items such as swimwear, beach towels, beach toys, tanning lotions, and plastic picnic dinnerware.

Target used point-of-sale tools such as signage on focal fixtures, end caps, ceiling banners, and other visuals to cross-merchandise hard and soft lines across numerous departments without moving products around. Thus, the customer could easily identify and locate all the items needed for the summer or a beach vacation. The same concept was also applied to items related to home decoration across various departments, using a theme called 'Target At Home Collection'.

---

[11] Lettish, Jill, "A Bloomingdales approach to the discount market," www.findarticles.com, September 17, 1990.

[12] Lettish, Jill, "A Bloomingdales approach to the discount market," www.findarticles.com, September 17, 1990.

[13] Lettish, Jill, "A Bloomingdales approach to the discount market," www.findarticles.com, September 17, 1990.

[14] Halverson, Richard, "Target: fighting a two-front war—Target Stores fights national and regional competition," www.findarticles.com, April 18, 1994.

In the late 1990s, Target began using another strategy to reinforce its upscale image and provide quality products to its customers. It began forging partnerships with recognized designers and design houses to bring affordable designer goods to its customers. In 1999, Target introduced the 'Michael Graves collection', a home goods collection designed by Michael Graves exclusively for Target. In the early 2000s, Graves designed the 'Coach's Whistle teapot' priced at $35, a lot cheaper than the expensive kettle he did for Alessi, an Italian design firm. In 2002, Graves followed up with a home office collection that included hardware designed by him, but manufactured by established vendors such as Lexmark. The collection featured a shredder, wireless keyboard and mouse pad, inkjet printer, alarm clock/calculator combination, and a PC speaker system. He also designed a dartboard, poker chips, and a bedding collection in coordinating solids and prints, and kitchenware such as a waffle iron.

In early 2000, Target entered into a licensing agreement with Mossimo, Inc., (Mossimo) a designer and manufacturer of men's and women's sportswear run by the designer Mossimo Giannuli. According to the licensing agreement, Mossimo contributed design services and licensed the Mossimo trademark to Target in return for royalties with substantial guaranteed minimum payments. Target collaborated with Mossimo on design and was responsible for product development, sourcing, quality control, and inventory management. Initially, Target sold women's, men's, and children's clothing under the Mossimo brand. Later on, a line of bath and body products, and men's grooming items was added. A line of maternity wear was also added to the Mossimo brand. Target went on to add product lines exclusively designed for Target by designers such as Isaac Mizrahi[15] (Mizrahi), Liz Lange,[16] and Sonia Kashuk.[17]

One of the most successful designer partnerships made by Target was with Mizrahi. Mizrahi designed women's apparel, footwear, and accessories for Target under the Isaac Mizrahi label. Mizrahi, a recognized designer, was forced to file for bankruptcy in the late 90s when his ready-to-wear clothing lines did not perform well. All his clothing lines were discontinued except for his licensed footwear line. However, his lines for Target, which were considered highly fashionable yet affordable, turned out to be a huge success. An article about his lines was published in *Vogue*, a leading fashion magazine. Mizrahi's success with Target even helped him launch a new line of

couture clothing at Bergdorf Goodman, a department store. In the early 2000s, Target began selling a brand called 'Swell', which was exclusive to Target and target.com. Swell was created by fashion designer Cynthia Rowley (Rowley) and her friend Ilene Rosenzweig[18] (Rosenzweig). The brand encompassed a variety of products such as jewelry, sunglasses, sleepwear, bath, bedding, window coverings, rugs, table linens, and accent furniture.

In 2002, Target also added a line of exclusive kitchenware, and cooking ingredients and specialty foods. The line, called 'Blue Ginger', was created by celebrity chef Ming Tsai, who also owned a restaurant by the name 'Blue Ginger'. The specialty foods and cooking ingredients were East-West, a genre based on the ingredients and cooking techniques of Chinese, Southeast Asian, Korean, Japanese, French, and American culinary traditions.

In 2003, Target added another exclusive designer collection to its stores. The collection called 'Sunny Patch' was designed by David Kirk, author and illustrator of the 'Miss Spider' series of children's picture books. It was a collection of garden products, home décor, and apparel highlighting new and existing characters such as Miss Spider, Lily Ladybug, and Huck Grasshopper.

Advertising and Promotions

In 1975, Target started publishing an ad circular in the Sunday edition of leading newspapers. The circular was bright and colorful with information on the latest offerings from Target. It was very different from the usual coupons of the other discount stores, as it was like a style section of a newspaper. The circular focused on trends and fashion and the must-haves rather than prices. Thus, it was able to project an image of style and sophistication to the consumers.

Target's wide and clean aisles had artful displays. In the late 1990s, Target represented a merchandising style that has been described as Andy Warhol[19] inspired pop art. In contrast to its competitors who focused on price in their advertising, Target attempted to give an impression that there were great finds at Target at great prices. It created a stylish and trendy image for everyday household items, even something as mundane as a lawn mower or a clothes iron. In 2004, Target won the gold, silver, and bronze awards in several categories for advertising and marketing presented by the Retail Advertising and Marketing Association (RAMA) to mass merchandisers. Also in 2004, one of Target's print advertisements used in 2000, was

---

[15] A well-known fashion designer in US who has also appeared in documentaries and movies.

[16] Liz Lange is known for designing maternity wear.

[17] Sonia Kashuk is a make-up artist for Target.

[18] Former Deputy Style Editor for New York Times.

[19] Andy Warhol employed mass-production techniques to create art works that erased the traditional distinctions between fine art and popular culture.

displayed at a design exhibition called "National Design Triennial: Inside Design Now" at the Smithsonian's Cooper-Hewitt, National Design Museum.

In 1999, Target and Collegestudent.com[20] signed an advertising agreement to enhance their online presence. The deal was made to facilitate Target's entry into the college market. A joint marketing campaign was launched, which consisted of an interactive contest, Collegestudent.com promotional events, and an advertising campaign. Target was the sponsor of Collegestudent.com's Housing section and was also featured as a site sponsor for the duration of the marketing campaign. Collegestudent.com links were featured on the Target website. In addition, Target sponsored a contest called "I Need Help!" where students submitted letters online describing why their apartment should be selected as the most in need of decorative help from Target. The winners received free room or apartment makeovers from Target specialists.

In August 2000, Target launched its joint marketing and promotion initiative with America Online, Inc. (AOL). A special edition CD-ROM of the AOL ISP service was co-branded with Target. The service offered 500 free hours of Internet surfing every month, and a free T-shirt. Other features of this service included a customized tool bar and a 'favorites' folder, which had links to target.com and other favorite sites. The co-branded CD-ROMs were available at in-store kiosks. Customers could also order a CD-ROM online at target.com. Customers who subscribed to the AOL service through Target were entitled to a 10 percent discount for up to one year on merchandise purchased at target.com. Other than the co-branded CD-ROM, target.com was made available in the Shop@AOL online shopping destinations and other areas across AOL.

In December 2002, Target did a promotional event in the Manhattan area of New York to assess the feasibility of opening a store there. Its ad agency, Kirshenbaum Bond & Partners, came up with the idea of running a store in a boat at Chelsea Piers. The floating shop was named "U.S.S. Target". Target employees wore red shirts that had "Target crew" written in front and "U.S.S. Target" on the back. The Target crew members were sent out on scooters covered in Target logos to hand out boarding passes in New York City. At the pier where the boat was docked, Target's red-and-white bullseye logo was displayed prominently all over the place. There were several tents, where the Target crew greeted customers and offered them free hot cider to warm up. They also handed out a flyer and "How to Shop" cards, which explained to the customers how to buy the items they liked when they got on the boat.

The store on the boat offered only 92 special holiday items for sale. The items were sealed off behind clear plastic in white structures meant to look like icebergs and printed Post-it notes were placed next to each of these items. When a customer wanted to buy an item, he or she had to take one of the printed Post-it notes next to the item and stick it to the flyer that was given on the way in. After selecting the items customers had to hand their flyers to a Target employee, who would gather the selected items in a basket and give it to them. Thus, Target created a unique shopping experience for its customers. It also took the opportunity to create high visibility for its logo and promote brand recognition.

In 2003, Target organized more temporary stores in New York. Target ran a Mizrahi Target boutique for six weeks in the Rockefeller Center and sold Mizrahi's latest collection for Target Stores. Then in the summer, Target ran a campaign called "Deliver the Shiver". Two bullseye branded trucks were parked at two separate locations in the city to sell air conditioners. Over a thousand of them were sold for $75 each. In 2004, Target opened another temporary shop, this time at Times Square. All the proceeds from sales were designated for breast cancer research. Target ran another promotion in New York in 2004, but did not offer any merchandise for sale. It just sent out thirty-five clones of Target's mascot, a white bull terrier named Bullseye, to the New York City Fashion Week in February. In the same year, it ran a similar promotion in Washington, D.C., where no merchandise was offered. During the Cherry Blossom Festival,[21] rickshaws decorated with Target's bullseye logo roamed around the Jefferson Memorial.

In May 2004, Target opened another temporary store in the state of New York, but this time it was not in the city. It was a special five-week summer store called Bullseye Inn set up at the Bull's Head Inn in Bridgehampton. The store offered various items specially designed for the season. According to John Remington, vice president of events marketing and communications at Target, "With the Bullseye Inn, we want to surprise and delight our guests by bringing everything they need for summer fun directly to them at a favorite summer spot, The Hamptons. The Bullseye Inn represents the best of the best in summer fare and makes Target even more accessible to our guests in New York."[22]

---

[20] Collegestudent.com, which developed localized online campus communities, was online in almost 350 campus communities in 1999. The company shut down its operations in 2000.

[21] The festival marks the celebration of the original gift of the 3,000 cherry trees from the city of Tokyo to the people of Washington, DC in 1912.

[22] "Target at Home in The Hamptons," www.casualliving.com, May 10, 2004.

Partnerships for an Enhanced Shopping Experience

In 2000, Target signed a deal with E*Trade[23] to operate a co-branded website, www.target.etrade.com, which would promote E*Trade to Target and target.com customers and vice versa. As part of the program investors were given a $100 Target gift card when they opened an E*Trade account with $1,000. By January 2001, another agreement was made to open E*Trade financial service centers in SuperTargets. These centers, called E*Trade Zones, offered banking and stock trading services. This agreement was signed after running a test E*Trade Zone in a SuperTarget in Roswell, Georgia (Ga) in September 2000. Said Jerry Storch, vice chairman of Target, "When we launched the Roswell, Ga. test last year, we did so in an effort to complement, strengthen, and enhance the financial services we already offered our guests through the Target Guest Card. The success of that Zone indicates that our guests value Target as a financial services partner and destination."[24] By the end of 2001, there were 22 E*Trade Zones and there were plans to open 43 more in 2002.

In 2001, Target signed an agreement with Visa U.S.A. to provide Target smart Visa cards to its customers. Prior to making it available throughout the country, market tests were conducted in three markets. "The national roll-out of the Target smart Visa card provides a significant opportunity for Target to deepen our relationship with our guests. This revolutionary new card offers our guests a credit vehicle with greater convenience, broader utility, increased value, and expanded rewards programs", said Storch.[25] The Retailers National Bank[26] started issuing the cards at the end of 2001 and installed point of sale terminals that accepted chip payment in all Target Stores in 2002. Target was the first U.S. retailer to introduce smart Visa cards (a new, innovative payment card platform with multi-function capabilities powered by microchip technology). According to Storch, "Adding a smart chip and providing chip readers in our stores underscores our commitment to introduce creativity and excitement to our guests. This innovative new card reinforces Target's differentiated brand image and 'Expect More. Pay Less' promise."[27]

While the Target smart Visa card enhanced the shopping experience of customers when they were in the stores, Target forged another partnership to enhance the online shopping experience of its customers. In 2002, Target moved all of its brands to a common website, Target.Direct, powered by Amazon. The combined site allowed cross shopping in all three Target brands (Target, Mervyns, and Marshall Fields) and on Amazon.com. All purchases, from the Target Corp. brands or Amazon.com, could be made using the same shopping bag. Throughout the site, at the top of every page, the colored logos of all three Target brands and Amazon's appeared prominently next to the shopping bag. There were links for personalized services such as checking order status and viewing recent shopping history at the bottom of every page.

On the website, customers could create a personalized 'My Store' page, which carried the customer's name. For example if the customer's name were Jane, it would become 'Jane's Store'. The page showed products from any brand on the site that the customer viewed. It also provided links to a Gift Reminder and a Wish List for registering gift ideas. A section called 'The Page You Made', gave more details on the most recent items browsed. "We believe this alliance with Amazon will further strengthen our brand and deepen our relationships with our guests," said Storch.[28]

Not Playing the Pricing Game

A major contributor to Target's success was its decision not to compete only on pricing. Target recognized that value was a function of quality, trend, and price, not just price. Many retailers played the pricing game and eventually went bankrupt and/or were acquired by other retailers. Target also recognized the importance of an attractive shopping environment when other retailers were focused on offering goods at the lowest prices, paying little attention to the environment (the stores) they were offered in. The stores had a bright and colorful signage and displays to guide customers through them. According to Target, a pleasant shopping experience would encourage a customer to come back to the stores. When it came to advertising and promotions, Target used creative advertising campaigns and promotions, making customers aware of the latest trends and designs available in all categories of merchandise, from apparel to home goods. Whether it was make-up or kitchen appliances, Target used style and creativity in its promotions. In merchandising, Target applied the concept of 'design for all', which again was in line with its image of a trendy and stylish discounter. It collaborated with many recognized

---

[23] The company, which provides brokerage and banking services, had a net revenue of $1.52 billion in 2004.

[24] Saunders, Christopher, "E*Trade aims at Target shoppers," Click Z News Network, January 26, 2001.

[25] "Target Becomes First U.S. Retailer to Offer smart Visa Card," www.usa.visa.com, June 19, 2001.

[26] Later renamed as Target National Bank. Target National Bank issues Target Visa and Target Card.

[27] "Target Becomes First U.S. Retailer to Offer smart Visa Card," www.usa.visa.com, June 19, 2001.

[28] "Mass Merchants: Aggressive and innovative," www.internetretailer.com, December 2002.

designers to offer exclusive merchandise to its customers. Thus, Target's success could be attributed to its consistent merchandising, marketing, and branding efforts to convey its positioning and image to consumers.

Questions for Discussion

1. "Target positioned itself as an upscale discount chain. Target differentiated itself from its competitors by offering trendy merchandises at affordable prices." Explain in detail how the differentiation strategy helped Target to become one of the leading retailers in the US.
2. "Target began forging partnerships with recognized designers and design houses to bring affordable designers' goods to its customers." Assess the symbiotic relationship that existed between Target and its design partners.
3. One of the key elements in the success of Target has been its ability to effectively communicate the company's unique positioning by coming out with attractive marketing promotions. Analyze how the company conveyed the uniqueness to its customers.

Additional Readings & References

1. Liebeck, Laura, **Mixing discipline with Disney,** www.findarticles.com, September 17, 1990.
2. Lettish, Jill, **A Bloomingdales approach to the discount market,** www.findarticles.com, September 17, 1990.
3. Richard, Halverson, **Target: fighting a two-front war—Target Stores fights national and regional competition,** www.findarticles.com, April 18, 1994.
4. **Target covers its bases with multimedia marketing,** www.findarticles.com, April 1, 1996.
5. Mammarella, James, **Target stays on the hipper side of soft lines: not content with leading the pack, Target refocuses on fashionable house brands,** www.findarticles.com, April 1, 1996.
6. Cox, Beth, **Target Stores Sign Ad deal with Collegestudent.com,** www.clickz.com, July 19, 1999.
7. Lisanti, Tony, **Target: To thine own self be true,** www.findarticles.com, April 19, 1999.
8. Mark, Roy, **AOL, Target Roll Out Marketing Campaign,** www.internetnews.com, August 22, 2000.
9. **MOSSIMO: Enters into Licensing agreement With Target,** www.bankrupt.com, January 2000.
10. Heller, Laura, **Target increases on-line endeavors,** www.findarticles.com, September 4, 2000.
11. **On target,** www.economist.com, May 3, 2001.
12. Heller, Laura, **Target reiterates stable strategy,** www.findarticles.com, June 4, 2001.
13. **Target Becomes First U.S. Retailer to Offer smart Visa Card,** www.visa.com, June 19, 2001.
14. Arlen, Jeffrey, **Why Is Target So Cool?** www.findarticles.com, April 2, 2001.
15. Saunders, Christopher, **E*Trade aims at Target shoppers** www.clickz.com, January 26, 2001.
16. **Target.direct at core of e-commerce strategy,** www.findarticles.com, April 2, 2001.
17. Cox, Beth, **E*Trade Expands Deal With Target Stores,** www.internetnews.com, October 9, 2001.
18. Prior, Molly, **Image is the key to differentiation,** www.findarticles.com, April 8, 2002.
19. Berner, Robert, **Target Takes a Gamble the Markets Don't Like,** www.businessweek.com, April 1, 2002.
20. **New Target stores showcase merchandising exploits,** www.findarticles.com, March 25, 2002.
21. Howell, Debbie, **Exclusive and chic far outpace cheap—Building a Brand the Target Way,** www.findarticles.com, April 8, 2002.
22. **Mass Merchants: Aggressive and innovative,** www.internetretailer.com, 2003.
23. Troy, Mike, **Hardlines stay true to low-SKU strategy,** www.findarticles.com, April 7, 2003.
24. Merchant, Beth, **The Elements of Style; Design that inspires from Cooper-Hewitt's National Design Triennial,** www.avvideo.com, June 2003.
25. Scardino, Emily, **Target touts Mizrahi with NYC debut,** www.findarticles.com, September 22, 2003.
26. **Target introduces Sunny Patch from noted author David Kirk,** www.callaway.com, 2003.
27. **Target Sells Marshall Field's to May,** www.forbes.com, June 10, 2004.
28. Levy, Melissa, **What's in Store: Face-lifts hold key to Target success,** www.startribune.com, September 11, 2004.
29. Heller, Laura, **Target tests new format and dollar-price program,** www.findarticles.com, March 8, 2004.
30. Leonard, Devin, **Why the Scooters Have Polka Dots: Target and others embrace stunts to cut through the clutter,** www.fortune.com, June 28, 2004.
31. **Target at Home in The Hamptons,** www.casualliving.com, May 10, 2004.
32. Heller, Laura, **Target pumps chic into HBC—and mass never looked better,** www.findarticles.com, June 7, 2004.
33. Manning-Schaffel, Vivian, **Target bulls eye,** www.brandchannel.com, October 4, 2004.
34. www.target.com
35. www.ming.com

WorldSpace Satellite Radio: Fading Signals?

Shirisha Regani

S.S. George

Hema M

"People are as developed as the information that they can access. Hence we are committed to creating information affluence. Radio also reaches out to people where other media simply can't."[1]

—*Noah Samara, Chairman and CEO of WorldSpace Corporation, in 2002.*

"If people can pay for superior content on TV, they can do it for radio as well. Those who had heard WorldSpace swore by its content."[2]

—*Farokh Balsara, a senior partner and Media & Entertainment Practice Leader at Ernst & Young India, in 2006.*

Creating a New Identity

In July 2006, WorldSpace India Pvt. Ltd. (WorldSpace India) launched an integrated marketing communications campaign in a bid to strengthen its presence in the country. The campaign included a new series of television advertisements as well as special events like concerts

and award shows. The company also signed on popular Indian music composer A R Rahman (Rahman)[3] as its brand ambassador. Rahman composed a new signature tune for the company, which was to be featured in all the company's television and radio advertisements.

WorldSpace India, which had launched its services in the country in 2000, was a wholly-owned subsidiary of WorldSpace Corporation USA (WorldSpace). WorldSpace, the world's first digital satellite radio service provider, had launched its service (also called WorldSpace) in Africa in 1999. The service was initially launched with the mission of creating 'information empowerment' in Africa and other third world regions, although the company later started offering commercial channels and entertainment as well. At the beginning, WorldSpace offered the same channels in all its markets, but after its launch in India, the company adopted a region-centric approach, and launched several channels with Indian content.

The campaign launched in India in 2006 was a part of WorldSpace's attempt to create a new global brand identity for itself, under which it adopted a new logo and embarked on restructuring its business model. As of mid-2006, the WorldSpace service was available in over

---

[1] Archana Raghuram, "Distance Education Not So Distant," *The Hindu,* September 4, 2002.

[2] Amit Ranjan Rai, "Why WorldSpace Scores over Others," www.rediff.com, August 3, 2006. (Accessed on September 1, 2006)

[3] A.R. Rahman is a popular Indian film music director and has composed music in Indian languages like Hindi, Tamil, and Telugu. He is also popular internationally and had composed music for the successful Broadway musical, "Bombay Dreams." Reportedly, more than 100 million records of his music albums had been sold worldwide by mid-2006.

130 countries around the world, and reportedly covered two-thirds of the world's population. WorldSpace aired a number of channels, which delivered music, news, sports, and other information. As of 2006, the company was the leading provider of digital satellite radio services outside the US and Canada.[4]

Background Note

Noah Samara (Samara), the founder of WorldSpace,[5] was born in Ethiopia, and later migrated to the US for higher education. He founded WorldSpace in 1990 in Washington DC, to provide satellite radio services to the African continent and other third world countries. In Samara's view, there was a distinct need for information in these developing countries, but many of them lacked the infrastructure to receive and disseminate such information. The stated objective of WorldSpace was to provide news, education, and entertainment along with other useful information to the developing regions of the world (Refer to Exhibit 1 for a note on satellite radio).

In the early 1990s, Samara participated in the 'World Administrative Radio Frequency Conference'[6] held in Torremolinos in Spain, which diplomats from 127 countries attended. To provide digital audio broadcasting, Samara required 25MHz of the L-band,[7] which was a slice of the 1000MHz electromagnetic spectrum. This spectrum range was used by countries for communication purposes. After several rounds of negotiations, the International Telecommunication Union[8] agreed to grant Samara the required range in the L-band. Samara also received the US government's approval for the first US Federal Communications Commission (FCC)[9] satellite radio license.[10]

The initial investment of $1.1 billion[11] in WorldSpace was made by two Saudi Arabian businessmen, Khalid bin Mahfouz and Mohammad Hussein Al-Amoudi (Al-Amoudi). Together they held an 80% stake in the company. Another businessman, Saleh Idris bought a 6% stake.

Alcatel Space, a subsidiary of Alcatel Corporation[12] of France, built the geo-stationary satellites,[13] which were to broadcast WorldSpace signals around the world. Samara's objective was to use the satellite coverage to reach the people living in normally unreachable areas.[14]

Each of these satellites transmitted three signal beams. Each beam was capable of delivering about 80 channels. The three signal beams carried the channels to three overlapping coverage areas, each of which was spread over 14 million square kilometers. The channels delivered audio and multi-media content over the 1467–1492 MHz segment of the L-Band. The digital signals beamed by the satellites were received by World-Space receivers. The radio equipment consisted of a receiver and an antenna, which had to be placed in the open in clear view of the satellites. The satellites' broadcast capacity was leased out to the broadcasting stations, which aired programs on WorldSpace.

AfriStar, the first satellite, was launched in 1998 from French Guyana[15] into a geostationary orbit. With this, WorldSpace Corp. became the first satellite radio company to launch its satellites into geostationary orbit. In October 1999, WorldSpace began its services in Africa with the broadcast of thirty channels via AfriStar, thereby marking the launch of the first of such service in the world.

AsiaStar, the second satellite, was launched in March 2000, and its coverage area was spread across parts of Asia, Africa, and Europe. The two satellites together were said to cover almost two-thirds of the earth's surface.

The third satellite AmeriStar, which was to provide services in South America, was not launched because the L-band was used by the US Air Force (Though World-Space agreed that the signal from AmeriStar would not extend beyond the north of Southern Mexico, even as of

---

[4] In the US, the leading satellite radio service providers were XM Radio and Sirius Satellite Radio as of 2006.

[5] He was also the Chairman and CEO of the company as of 2006.

[6] The World Administrative Radio Conference, held once every two years, is part of the International Telecommunications Union-Radio Communications standardization sector.

[7] The L-Band is a part of the electro-magnetic wave ranging from 0.39 to 1.55 GHz. It is used in satellite and terrestrial communications.

[8] The International Telecommunications Union, headquartered in Geneva, Switzerland is an international organization within the scope of the United Nations system. It is a union in which governments and the private sector come together on issues relating to global telecom networks.

[9] The Federal Communications Commission is an US government agency that regulates interstate and international communications by radio, television, wire, cable, and satellite.

[10] Nathan Vardi, "Bird in the Hand," Forbes, April 29, 2002.

[11] Dollars ($) refers to US dollars in this case study.

[12] Alcatel Corporation, headquartered in Paris, France, is a worldwide telecommunications equipment and service provider with revenues of $17.5 billion in 2006. Alcatel Space was renamed Alcatel Alenia Space in 2004.

[13] Geo-stationary satellites are satellites that are launched into geo-stationary orbits. A geostationary orbit is a circular orbit which is directly above the Equator and revolves in the same direction as the earth and with the same orbital period as the earth's period of rotation. Consequently, satellites in the geostationary orbit appear to be stationary with respect to a fixed point on earth.

[14] Kenneth Silber, "Samara: Bringing Satellite Radio to Africa," www.space.com, December 15, 1999. (Accessed on September 4, 2006)

[15] French Guyana is a region of France located in South America.

Exhibit 1   A Note on Satellite Radio

Satellite radios are digital radios that receive signals broadcast by communication satellites. Satellite radio broadcasts are different from the terrestrial radio broadcasts whose reception depends on the power of the broadcasting stations.

A satellite radio signal can reach places that a normal terrestrial radio signal cannot. When calamities strike, the satellite radio helps in providing people with information. Also, the infrastructure remains safe.

Satellite digital broadcasting can disseminate audio and multimedia signals simultaneously. Unlike traditional radio, satellite radio can deliver images, text data and even video. The satellite receiver equipment can be connected to a personal computer or laptop and the Internet can be accessed in an inexpensive manner.

The communication satellites are geo-stationary satellites. The satellites launched into a geostationary orbit appear stationary from a fixed point on the earth. Therefore, the signals can be received by the radio directly from the satellites through antennas placed in the open. Normally two or three satellites can cover an entire continent.

Satellite radio equipment consists of a receiver and an antenna. The antenna has to be placed in an open space and positioned well enough to receive signals from the satellites in orbit. Each receiver has an electronic serial number which is used by the radio to identify signals. Usually an authorization code is used to activate the channels. Without the code the channels are blocked. Usually the service providers allow at least one 'free-to-air' channel to operate without the code to test the signal reception.

As of 2006, there were only three major players in the satellite radio industry. While XM Satellite Radio Holdings and Sirius Satellite Radio broadcast in the US and Canada, the rest of the world was covered by WorldSpace satellite. Each company uses a proprietary technology to receive signals from satellites. WorldSpace and XM receivers use StarMan chipsets to receive and decode signals beamed from the satellites. Each satellite has fuel to stay in service for fifteen years after which they have to be replaced.

Satellite radio offers a host of advantages over terrestrial radio, such as portability, better sound quality, a large coverage area and variety in programming. As of 2006, there were no government regulations in India regarding satellite radio.

Sources: Compiled from www.gare.co.uk, www.howstuffworks.com, www.worldspace.com

2006 the satellite had not been launched). (Refer to Exhibit 2 for WorldSpace's satellite coverage.)

In 2000, WorldSpace was launched in India, with content beamed via the AsiaStar satellite. WorldSpace considered India, with its large base of radio listeners, to be its primary market worldwide. However, the launch initially received a lukewarm response, as the concept of 'paid-radio' was new to consumers in the country. Besides, the price of the receivers was also considered to be very high. (WorldSpace faced the same problem in other developing countries also.)

A Slow Start

In the initial years, WorldSpace did not have a clearly articulated business model as the satellite radio business was still in its infancy. When the company's services were launched, its revenues had come only from receiver sales and from the fees it received from leasing out satellite space to individual channels. All the channels were offered free of cost to those who bought the receivers.

This business model, however, did not work, as the company found it difficult to sell the receivers in some developing countries, where in many cases, the annual per capita income of the population was even lower than the cost of the receivers. Besides, once a receiver was sold, the company had no further avenues of income from the customer.

Also, as the WorldSpace programs were either commercial-free or aired with very few commercials, its advertising revenues were minimal. This approach led to heavy losses. As a result, one of the investors, Al-Amoudi tried to take control of the company. However, Samara raised about $155 million from private investors and restructured the company's debt to become the major shareholder, after which Al-Amoudi exited the company.[16]

In terms of the number of subscribers to the service, WorldSpace had a very slow start. In 2002, three years after the launch of its first satellites, the company had a subscriber base of less than 3000. The revenues were also far less than the forecast (Samara had anticipated sales of one million receivers worldwide by 2001).[17]

---

[16] Nathan Vardi, "Bird in the Hand," Forbes, April 29, 2002.
[17] "WorldSpace Seeks to Become Voice from Home," www.rwonline.com, February 1, 2004.

Exhibit 2   WorldSpace's Satellite Coverage

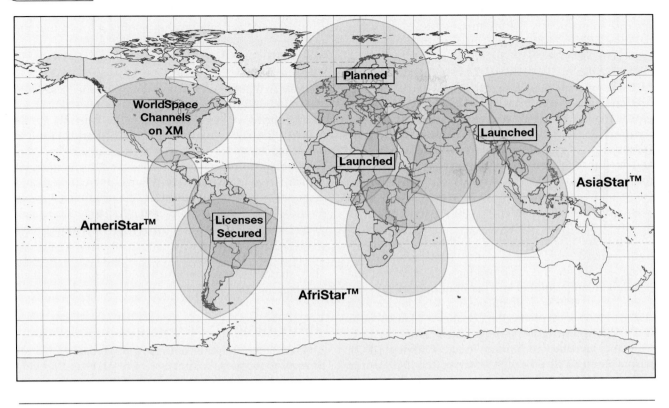

Source: www.whirlwindsales.co.uk

However, despite its lack of commercial success, WorldSpace found takers among expatriates from the US and the UK, and US armed forces personnel. WorldSpace services were said to be of great help to US military personnel who were stationed far from home, but within areas where WorldSpace coverage was available. By providing information and entertainment, the service reportedly boosted the morale of the soldiers. Families and friends of the troops could also send WorldSpace receivers and subscriptions as gifts.[18]

In 2003–04, WorldSpace tied up with UK-based Virgin Radio (Virgin). As per the agreement, Virgin was featured as a premium channel under the WorldSpace service. Virgin provided content for the 'Home Team' radio channel, which targeted US soldiers and expatriates.[19] As of 2006, there were more than 380,000 American troops, coalition forces, and expatriates from the US and the UK

either stationed or living in the Middle-East and Africa, and World Space intended to reach all of them.[20]

However, reliance on expatriate sales did not work out well for the company and it reported losses of $217 million on revenues of $13 million in 2003, and $577 million on revenues of $8.5 million in 2004.[21]

In mid-2003, WorldSpace created a 'Government Sales Unit' (GSU). The GSU was formed to provide services to government agencies that lacked the telecommunication infrastructure for their communication needs.

Launch of a Subscription-based Model

After its losses in 2003–2004, WorldSpace introduced a subscription-based model in all its markets in a bid to improve its business. The prices of receivers were

[18] "WorldSpace Satellite Radio Launches Global Subscription Campaign; Initial Focus on American and British ExPats," www.spaceref.com, March 4, 2004. (Accessed on September 4, 2006)
[19] "WorldSpace Ties up with Virgin Radio," www.agencyfaqs.com, October 29, 2003. (Accessed on September 11, 2006)
[20] "WorldSpace Ties up with Virgin Radio," www.agencyfaqs.com, October 29, 2003. (Accessed on September 11, 2006)
[21] Annys Shin, "XM Invests $25 Million in Rival WorldSpace," *The Washington Post*, July 20, 2005.

reduced and yearly subscriptions were introduced. When this scheme also did not bring in the expected number of subscriptions, WorldSpace introduced special offers to increase subscriptions. For instance, in 2005, it launched a festival offer in India by reducing the entry price for the service and offering quarterly subscription packages. The company also tried to attract subscriptions by providing exclusive Indian channels via AsiaStar.

Apart from WorldSpace, the other players in the global digital satellite radio service industry were XM Satellite Radio (XM)[22] and Sirius Satellite Radio (Sirius).[23] XM and Sirius offered their services in the US and in Canada. WorldSpace had played an important role in the setting up of XM[24] in the US and the two companies had an agreement under which they were to share programming resources and any technological developments in the future.

In July 2005, XM invested $25 million in WorldSpace. It also agreed to co-operate with WorldSpace in developing technology and radio products like receivers, and in strengthening supplier and distribution networks.

The year 2005 was significant for WorldSpace as it added 40,000 subscribers globally, after the launch of its new subscription based model. In the same year, the company launched an Initial Public Offering (IPO), raising about $221 million.[25] However, the IPO was not well received, as people felt that WorldSpace did not have a strong subscriber base like XM and Sirius. Subsequently the share prices fell steeply.[26] One article said, "If you enjoy companies that pay management at a rate of 2.5 times your company's entire revenue, burn cash like crazy, but have a story that sounds good until you listen closely, this may be the stock for you. Knock yourself out. If you're looking for a good investment, look elsewhere."[27]

However, the setbacks after the IPO did not halt WorldSpace's progress in terms of subscription growth, especially in India. In January 2006, WorldSpace received authorization from the FCC to launch another satellite AfriStar II, to expand its services to Western Europe.

After two or three years of its launch, WorldSpace had started focusing more on commercial programming than on its initially stated objective of 'information empowerment'. Though the company was at first involved in some development activities in Africa, by 2004, it was said to have shifted focus and begun concentrating on commercial success. It was felt that the shift in focus was due to the mounting losses that the company was facing, as it struggled to cover the cost of its satellites and the subsequent expansion of its operations across many countries.

In March 2006, WorldSpace commissioned a satellite uplink station in Dubai and launched two Arabic channels beamed via the AfriStar satellite catering to the Middle-East region and North Africa. (WorldSpace had launched its services in the Middle East in 2004).

As of 2006, WorldSpace broadcast 62 channels, of which 32 were provided by national, international, and regional third party broadcasters. The remaining 30 were WorldSpace branded entertainment channels operated from Washington DC (USA), Bangalore (India), and Nairobi (Kenya). Although the two WorldSpace satellites operational in 2006 had different bouquets of channels, they shared several common stations because of their overlapping coverage.

WorldSpace in Africa

One of Samara's initial objectives in launching WorldSpace was to spread awareness about AIDS and provide information on other developmental issues in the developing regions of the world. In his view, many African countries were deprived of important information as they lacked the infrastructure to receive and disseminate such information. According to him, a service like WorldSpace could deliver this information to empower people, particularly in the poorer areas of Africa.

In 1999, WorldSpace launched around thirty channels, including five WorldSpace branded channels, via AfriStar. The other channels were provided by CNN International, Bloomberg LP, African regional radio Kosmos Digital, the Kenyan Broadcasting Company, and Egyptian Radio, among others. In some villages, WorldSpace established 'Telekiosks' which were telecommunication centers set up in rural areas throughout Africa to provide phone, multimedia, and broadcasting facilities to a village or a region. Reportedly, WorldSpace utilized five percent of its satellite capacity in AfriStar and AsiaStar to provide information for developmental activities.[28]

---

[22] XM Satellite Radio, launched in 2001, provides satellite radio services in the US and Canada. XM provided its services through more than 170 channels that included music, entertainment, news, weather, and sports channels.

[23] Sirius Satellite Radio, launched in 1999, provided more than 120 channels that included music, entertainment, news, and sports channels. It provides satellite radio services to the US and Canada.

[24] WorldSpace had partnered with XM's parent company to license broadcasting technology to XM in the mid-1990s. The two companies parted ways in the late 1990s owing to internal disputes.

[25] Peter B. de Selding, "WorldSpace Stock Drops amid Questions about Indian Market," www.space.com, March 27, 2006. (September 11, 2006)

[26] Jerry Knight, "WorldSpace Stumbles," *The Washington Post*, October 10, 2005. (Accessed on September 18, 2006)

[27] Seth Jayson, "A Stellar Way to Lose Money," www.fool.com, September 9, 2005. (Accessed on October 18, 2006)

[28] www.firstvoiceint.org

WorldSpace also associated itself with various organizations to promote development in African villages. In 2002, the company initiated a development program with WOUGNET (short for Women of Uganda Network). Under this, two member organizations of WOUGNET—ALFA (short for Abundant Life for All, an organization for the empowerment of rural women) and Lungujja Women's Association—participated in a one-day demonstration and training program in which the participants were shown how a satellite radio disseminated information to various geographical locations.

During the program, the participants also learned to access the Internet using the radio (the radios when connected to a computer provided the user instant Internet access, doing away with the need for traditional dialup or cable connections).[29] It was thought that this service would be useful to Non-Government Organizations (NGOs), which could buy one radio for all their members. In this way, the NGOs would have the advantage of reaching many communities across regions.

WorldSpace services were also used to provide weather forecasts and other useful information to farmers. In 2004, UNESCO,[30] in association with WorldSpace, conducted a distance education program for rural learners.[31] The project was designed to test the potential of digital satellite services, the effective cost of which was considered to be lower than the cost of an ordinary Internet connection.

However, despite its avowed good intentions, WorldSpace was not able to succeed in its objective of 'information empowerment'. This was attributed to the high cost of its service, which made WorldSpace accessible only to affluent urban people and US expatriates in Africa. These customers were not interested in subscribing to the service for information purposes alone. Hence, the company gradually shifted its focus to commercial content, and started offering more entertainment channels.

WorldSpace in India

India was believed to be a market with great potential for WorldSpace, not only because of the large radio audience in the country, but also because the Indian Government had opened up FM[32] broadcasting to private players in 2000. Until then FM, along with the AM[33] channels, had been broadcast exclusively by the government-owned All India Radio (AIR).[34] Despite the potential competition from local FM channels, the opening up of the market was said to have created opportunities for global players like WorldSpace. According to some analysts, as satellite radio was new to India, WorldSpace was in a position to capitalize on the advantages of the system, which was considered to be superior to that of terrestrial radio.

WorldSpace India, which began its operations in 2000, beamed content via AsiaStar, and was the country's only satellite radio provider. The head office of the Indian operations was set up in Bangalore in South India. For WorldSpace, the Indian market was more challenging than markets in other countries because of the diversity in the languages spoken in the country. The company took up the challenge and introduced channels that were India-specific, broadcasting classical and film music and news. The company initially launched 22 channels[35] including eight Indian channels, of which five were in Hindi,[36] and one channel each in Tamil, Malayalam, and Kannada languages.[37] WorldSpace India struck a partnership with the consumer electronics firm BPL to manufacture and market its satellite receivers.

The WorldSpace launch, however, received only a lukewarm response. When the company entered India it was the country's first 'paid-radio' service provider. Its initial business model in India was similar to that of the WorldSpace model worldwide. The company priced the radio receivers between Rs.5,500[38] and Rs.12,000, and the service was provided free of cost. The revenue depended purely on the sale of receivers.

However, the company's claims of providing superior, commercial-free content could not negate the impact of the high price of the receivers. Commenting on the initial business model, Shishir Lall (Lall), Managing Director of WorldSpace India, said, "In the initial years, we went through our trial-and-error phase. We tried business models that didn't deliver to expectations. But we were able to hang on to the marketplace."[39]

Consequently, the first two years saw very little growth in the number of subscribers. Eventually WorldSpace

[29] "WOUGNET WorldSpace Satellite Radio Program," www.wougnet.org, March 2004. (Accessed on September 4, 2006)

[30] UNESCO, or the United Nations Educational, Scientific and Cultural Organization is a specialized United Nations agency established in 1945 to promote international collaboration through education, science and culture for peace and security between nations.

[31] "WOUGNET WorldSpace Satellite Radio Program," www.wougnet.org, March 2004. (Accessed on September 4, 2006)

[32] FM is short for Frequency Modulation which is used to broadcast hi-fidelity sound through radio.

[33] AM is short for Amplitude Modification. AM radio is broadcast on the Long-wave, Medium-wave, and Short-wave frequency bands.

[34] AIR is a national radio service operated by the Ministry of Information and Broadcasting under the Government of India.

[35] "WorldSpace India Launches 22 Radio Channels in India," www.rediff.com (Reuters), November 23, 2000

[36] Hindi is the official language of India and is spoken mainly in northern and central India.

[37] Tamil, Malayalam, Kannada, and Telugu are languages spoken in south India.

[38] As of September 18, 2006, US$ 1 =Rs. 46.14.

[39] Amit Ranjan Rai, "Why WorldSpace Scores over Others," www.rediff.com, August 3, 2006. (Accessed on September 1, 2006)

India had to change its strategy, and in 2002, subscripztions were introduced for three channels.

In 2004, the company added ten more channels with India-specific content to its bouquet, which had initially consisted mostly of channels with non-Indian content. However, despite these changes, even four years after the launch, WorldSpace India had only around 12,000 subscribers.[40] In 2004, the company revamped its business model completely, by making the service entirely subscription based.[41]

However, even after all these changes, WorldSpace India was able to only add around 9,000 more subscribers by March 2005. According to analysts, this was not adequate to ensure the company's profitability.

As a basis to framing a new strategy for the market, WorldSpace India reportedly identified the following as its potential consumers.[42]

- People who did not know about WorldSpace at all
- People who had heard about the company but did not know about its services
- People who knew about the service but did not know how to access it
- People who knew all these but hesitated to buy the receiver because of the price and because they had not experienced the service

The company's re-positioning strategy strove to address and create awareness among all the consumers.

The Strategy Change

In August 2005, WorldSpace India decided to lower the initial cost of subscribing to the service. This included reducing the cost of receivers from about Rs.5,500 to Rs.1,999, inclusive of the subscription fees for three months. This drop in price led to spurt in subscriptions. In the first month after the new price was announced, the company recorded 12,000 new subscriptions. The increase in subscriptions brought about by the price reduction subsequently helped WorldSpace acquire 100,000 subscribers worldwide, about 65% of whom were from India. The subscription packages were also changed from the usual annual prepaid plans, to three-month promotional packages and half-yearly plans.

The three-month promotional package was critical to the increase in the WorldSpace subscriber base in India. The fourth quarter of 2005 alone saw a jump in subscription by 40,000. In 2005, the number of subscriptions added in India was around 75,000, an increase of 800% over the previous year's subscriptions of around 8,300 (Refer to Exhibit 3 for the subscription base of WorldSpace Corp. over the years).

As the three-month subscription was more a means to introduce customers to the satellite radio experience, the company was faced with the challenge of getting customers to renew their subscriptions at the end of the period. After the launch of the promotional package, WorldSpace India began to offer six-month and annual subscription packages. According to WorldSpace India, by the end of June 2006, only 30% of the subscribers remained in the three-month plan, while the others had renewed their subscriptions. (As of August 2006, the company had a 67% renewal rate and had discontinued the three-month plan.)[43]

The reduction in prices was facilitated by the introduction of a low-priced receiver 'DIVA', a basic model with just a radio receiver and an antenna. The receiver had to be attached to external speakers. Other models, which included built-in speakers and AM and FM radio, were also available, but were priced a little higher. In mid-2006 another inexpensive model called DIVA II was launched (DIVA II had built-in speakers, an audio stereo amplifier, and pre-fixed audio equalizer modes). In addition to the DIVA, other models of receivers were also available.

As of 2006, the Telecom Regulatory Authority of India (TRAI),[44] which laid down the regulations for the other media categories, had not framed any policies for satellite radio. Though WorldSpace India was the only player in the satellite radio services in the country, some analysts suggested that a policy on this issue would remove any future regulatory uncertainties.[45]

Initially, WorldSpace India offered bouquets of channels. Each bouquet, which consisted of a particular set of channels, was priced separately. Sometimes, the subscribers had to choose two or more bouquets to listen to channels of their choice, thereby increasing their subscription costs. To simplify the subscription choices, WorldSpace introduced gold and silver subscription packages in 2005 in place of channel bouquets. The gold package consisted of five more channels than the silver package (which offered 39 channels). (Refer to Exhibit 4 for WorldSpace India's subscription packages.)

[40] Amit Ranjan Rai, "Why WorldSpace Scores over Others," www.rediff.com, August 3, 2006. (Accessed on September 1, 2006)

[41] Ravikumar, R., "Broadcaster WorldSpace Set to go Pay," *The Hindu Business Line*, January 17, 2004.

[42] Ravikumar, R., "Broadcaster WorldSpace Set to go Pay," *The Hindu Business Line*, January 17, 2004.

[43] "WorldSpace Announces Second Quarter 2006 Results," www.worldspace.com, August 9, 2006.

[44] TRAI is the apex regulatory body for telecom, radio, and cable in India.

[45] "Consultation Paper on Issues Relating to Satellite radio Service," www.trai.gov.in, December 29, 2004. (Accessed on October 18, 2006)

Exhibit 3 **WorldSpace Corp. Subscription Base over the Years**

YEAR ENDED DECEMBER 31	2004	2005	2006 (half-year ended)
Net Subscriber Additions	29,287	81,036	44,659
India	8,335	66,239	44923
Rest of World (ROW)	20,952	14,797	(264)
TOTAL SUBSCRIBERS	34270	115306	159,965
India	8,335	74,574	119,497
ROW	25,935	40,732	40,468
ARPU (1)	$6.27	$4.66	$4.00
India	1.95	2.76	2.98
ROW	6.82	6.14	6.54
SAC (2)	$1	$30	$41
India	18	36	42
ROW	0	5	0
CPGA (3)	$66	$173	$133
India	123	188	126
ROW	50	121	225

1. ARPU is the Average Revenue per User derived from the total of monthly earned subscription revenue (net of promotion and rebates) divided by the monthly average number of subscribers for the period reported. ARPU is only a measure of operational performance.
2. SAC is the subscriber Acquisition Cost (SAC) which includes the negative margins from equipment (receiver) sales to end customers.
3. CPGA is the Cost per Gross Addition and it includes SAC as well as advertising, media and other marketing expenses, excluding headcount related to sales and marketing staff.

Source: www.worldspace.com

Exhibit 4 **WorldSpace India's Subscription Rates**

Receiver Model (A)	Cost (in Rs)	One Year Subscription (B)	Total Cost
DIVA	1499	1800	3299
DIVA II	2499	1800	4299
BPL Celeste 2	4990	1800	6790
Polytron	6990	1800	8790

Subscription Packages

Package	6 Months	1 Year	2 Years	No of Channels Provided
SILVER	1000	1800	3250	39
GOLD (C)	1350	2700	NA	44

(A) The DIVA models are the basic models. DIVA II additionally has inbuilt speakers. The BPL Celeste and Polytron come with additional features like built in speakers, cassette player and AM and FM operations.
(B) The Silver package is offered along with the receiver models.
(C) The Gold package includes channels offered in the Silver package plus Bloomberg - Financial News, Fox News—News, Talk Sports—UK Based Sports, Infusion—Information and BBC Global News—International News.

Source: www.worldspace.com

Promotional Campaigns

When WorldSpace India was launched in 2000, it launched a nationwide advertisement campaign, even though the service was initially introduced only in the cities of Bangalore and Chennai. After the adoption of the subscription-based business model in 2004, another print and TV ad campaign was launched in the cities in which the company had a sales presence.

In 2004–2005, WorldSpace India began to move beyond media ads to make the service familiar to the market. (By then, the company was present in ten Indian cities.) The company adopted experiential marketing[46] to promote its services.

Accordingly, the company entered into an arrangement with retail outlets and corporate offices to play music from WorldSpace. The company also tied up with around 200 restaurants, malls, and kiosks to play uninterrupted music from the service.

WorldSpace India also formed alliances with Café Coffee Day[47] and Barista[48] to play music from WorldSpace stations in a bid to target college-goers and young working adults, who visited these places regularly.

Similarly, the company set up 'shop-in-shop' kiosks in music retail outlets Planet M[49] and MusicWorld,[50] both of which had shops spread across the country. It installed WorldSpace receivers at these outlets, thereby giving a chance to people who walked in to get a feel of the service firsthand.

In 2005, 'WorldSpace Lounges' were also set up in retail malls in five Indian cities—Bangalore, Gurgaon, Hyderabad, Chennai, and Kochi—where shoppers could sit and listen to music from WorldSpace stations. The lounges offered comfort and space to customers as they listened to the music. Also, their décor and layout was trendy, to make them attractive to shoppers who visited the malls. Reportedly, in 2006, around 8,000 of WorldSpace India's new subscribers were people who had visited these lounges.[51]

The 'WorldSpace Home Experience' program, launched in 2005, offered a free trial of the service by allowing customers to take home the receivers for about two days and gain a first hand experience of the service. The company also organized road shows and promotional activities at restaurants, colleges, and malls with a view to acquaint people with the satellite radio concept.

In 2005–06, in a program called 'WorldSpace Live,' the company conducted music workshops in which listeners of music interacted with well-known musicians. Under the same program, the company organized and partnered in musical events, including one which featured the American rock group 'Red Hot Chili Peppers'.

When quizzed about the need for experiential marketing, Lall said, "With a concept as new and nebulous as WorldSpace, consumers start comparing it with different offerings in the market, be it FM radio, CDs, or music downloads. It becomes difficult to make them understand that at about Rs. 5 a day for a year, they are actually getting access to rich music of their choice—for a sum they may be spending for a cup of tea."[52]

The various marketing initiatives enabled WorldSpace India to reach a wide audience. The company also advertised on television and in the print media. In July 2005, WorldSpace Corp. announced that it would spend $10 million on advertising in India. Advertisements were featured on television channels to promote the service with the tagline "Over 40 Stations, One Radio". By 2006, the company had expanded to 14 cities. Apart from the big cities, WorldSpace receivers were sold in many small towns across the country through retail outlets. Globally, the brand acquired a new identity and a new logo in 2006.

In July 2006, in a move to attract music lovers from across the country, WorldSpace India signed on film music director A.R. Rahman as brand ambassador, and featured him in a '360 degree' promotional campaign, which included television, print, and multimedia advertisements.

In 2006, WorldSpace India tied up with several companies whereby a WorldSpace receiver along with free subscription was offered to the customers of those companies. These promotions were aimed at making people familiar with WorldSpace service. The company reportedly reasoned that, once customers had a receiver, there was good chance that they would keep renewing the subscription (Refer to Table 1 for the promotional initiatives of WorldSpace India).

Localized Content

WorldSpace India's growth was also attributed to the wide range of content that the company provided on its channels. Channels like "Farishta", Jhaankar (Hindi

---

[46] Experiential Marketing is an approach by which the customer gets to experience a product, brand, or a service before making a purchase decision.
[47] Café Coffee Day is a chain of coffee shops with 326 outlets in 65 cities in India as of 2006.
[48] Barista is a chain of coffee bars with around 100 outlets across India, Sri Lanka, and the Middle-East as of 2006.
[49] Planet M is a chain of music stores and has outlets in more than 14 cities in India as of 2006.
[50] MusicWorld is a chain of music stores spread across nine Indian cities with more than 40 outlets as of 2006.
[51] Amit Ranjan Rai, "Why WorldSpace Scores over Others," www.rediff.com, August 3, 2006. (Accessed on September 1, 2006)
[52] Amit Ranjan Rai, "Why WorldSpace Scores over Others," www.rediff.com, August 3, 2006. (Accessed on September 1, 2006)

Table 1	Some of WorldSpace India's Promotional Initiatives

- In October 2006, WorldSpace announced that it would give away a free diamond pendant along with its receivers.
- In 2006, WorldSpace tied up with Shopper's Stop to give away WorldSpace receivers to all those customers who made a purchase of over Rs. 2500.
- In 2006, *Outlook*, a prominent English magazine, offered free WorldSpace receivers with six-month subscriptions to those who subscribed to the magazine for a term of three or five years.

Source: Compiled from various sources.

Film Music), Shruti, Ghandharv (Indian Classical Music), and KL Radio (Tamil), among others, not only entertained music lovers across the country but also Indians living abroad who received these channels through the AsiaStar satellite, whose footprint covered parts of Asia, Europe, and Africa. The television news channel NDTV India broadcast the audio component of both its English and Hindi news, along with other news providers like CNN International and BBC world (Refer to Exhibit 5 for channels broadcast via the AsiaStar and the AfriStar satellites).

In 2006, WorldSpace Corp. tied up with BBC World Service, TWI,[53] and radio Mid-Day[54] to launch an all sports radio channel, "Play". The channel provided live shows, sports news, and covered all major sporting activities across the world.[55] It was the first radio sports channel in India and as of 2006, no other radio network in India aired a channel dedicated to sports.

The FM radio was gaining popularity in almost all regions of India. The rising popularity was said to be mainly due to the music content and the presentation of shows by radio jockeys (RJ). WorldSpace India roped in some of the popular RJs to present its own shows. As many of the WorldSpace listeners also listened to FM, the channels that were broadcast in Hindi and other regional languages, gained popularity. In fact, 'Spin,' a channel that played international music on WorldSpace, was hosted by an RJ who had earlier been with a private FM channel.[56]

WorldSpace India, with a variety of channels, was able to reach a national audience. A significant aspect of the service was that unlike terrestrial radio, people could listen to the stations of their choice irrespective of where they lived.

By mid-2006, India, with almost 75% of the company's subscribers, was WorldSpace's biggest market.

Community and Educational Services

In the first few years of launch, WorldSpace India had attempted to stay true to its mission of providing education and information via satellite radio. In September 2001, the Bangalore University (BU) signed a Memorandum of Understanding with WorldSpace India to provide distance education.

WorldSpace India also assisted a few community radio[57] initiatives in India. The Hewalvani Community Radio of Uttaranchal (a state in North India) ran a service that provided information related to the region in the local language. The service was run by the local people and addressed issues relating to people of the community in their local language. For this, the company provided radio airtime twice a week.[58]

Vigyan Prasar, an autonomous body of the government of India's Department of Science and Technology utilized the services of WorldSpace with an inaugural broadcast in May 2002 in five schools in Delhi. Three programs based on science and technology were broadcast on an experimental basis. The services were extended to Chennai and Bangalore in 2003.

In 2004–2005, the network provided the Government of India with an exclusive channel during the Asian tsunami disaster.[59] The company also worked toward

---

[53] TWI or Trans World International is a part of the 'International Management Group,' which is a major sports entertainment and marketing company.

[54] Radio Mid-Day is an FM radio channel belonging to Mid-Day Multimedia Ltd, located in Mumbai India.

[55] "WorldSpace Satellite Radio to Deliver 'Play'," www.televisionpoint.com, February 7, 2006. (Accessed on September 4, 2006)

[56] Bhumika K, "Music is Beyond Language," *The Hindu*, August 5, 2006.

[57] Community radio services were initiated for geographically bound territories that had limited infrastructure and were not covered by national and mainstream radio.

[58] Prachi Pinglay, "Reaching out Through the Skies," *Frontline*, May 6, 2005.

[59] A tsunami is a series of waves, usually generated in an ocean, by the occurrences of earthquakes or underwater explosions. The tsunami which hit the coastal areas of many Asian countries on December 26, 2004 was one of the deadliest natural disasters in that region, resulting in the death or displacement of 229,866 persons.

Exhibit 5   List of WorldSpace Channels

Western Music	Fox News	**International Music**
Bob	**NDTV 24 × 7**	Ngoma (African)
Flava	**NDTV India** (Hindi)	Spin
Maestro	NPR I	**Sports**
Orbit Rock	NPR II	Fox Sports
Potion	World Radio Network	Play
Radio Amore	World Radio Network	Talk Sport
Radio Caroline	World Radio Network (German)	**Arabic Channels**
Radio Voyager	**General Entertainment**	BBC Arabic
RIFF	East FM	Channel Islam
The Hop	**Preview Channel**	Min Zaman
The System	**Radio France International**	Radio Monte Carlo Moyen
Top 40 on 40	(French)	Radio Moyen Orient
Up Country	Radio Monte Carlo Moyen	Ranin
Upop	(Arabic)	**Asian Music**
Virgin radio UK	Radio Moyen Orient (Arabic)	**Farishta** (Hindi)
World Zone (Multilingual)	Sunrise Radio (Hindi)	**Ghandharv** (Hindustani)
News	**Lifestyle**	**Jhaankar** (Hindi)
BBS Africa	African Learning Channel	**KL Radio** (Tamil)
BBC Arabic Service (Arabic)	**Art of Living**	**Radio Tara** (Bengali)
BBC Asia West	Channel Islam	**RM radio** (Malayalam)
BBC World Service	**Infusion**	**Spandana** (Telugu)
Bloomberg Radio Asia	**Moksha** (Hindi)	**Sparsha** (Kannada)
CNN International I	**Sai Global Harmony**	**Sruti** (Carnatic)
CNN International II	Sai Global Harmony	**Tunak** (Punjabi)

(Channels beamed via AsiaStar Satellite are indicated in **Bold**)

Source: www.worldspace.com

disseminating information on education and health and launched the 'Asian Development Channel'.

However, there was criticism that these initiatives were far from adequate to fulfill the objectives of 'education and empowerment' and that the company had begun concentrating only on revenues. Commenting on this, WorldSpace India's Director of Network Programming, Velu S. Shankar, said, "We need money to run, and we have to make it somewhere. But that doesn't mean (that) the developmental perspective is not there. For example, we are performing the integral task of pro-

moting musical forms that are under threat of disappearing."[60]

In November 2005, WorldSpace announced a further investment of $150 million in India over the next two years. The company also signed an MOU with Webel Mediatronics, a company owned by the West Bengal government, to explore possibilities of technology transfer to assemble, install, and commission broadcast infrastructure.[61] According to analysts, this co-operation not only brought new technology to India but also opened up more possibilities to reach out to the mass market.

[60] Rakesh Mehar, "Finding Its Own Space," *The Hindu*, April 15, 2006.

[61] "WorldSpace to Invest $150 Million in India," www.rediff.com, November 11, 2005. (Accessed on September 13, 2006)

When asked about WorldSpace's future plans in India, Mehta said, "India is the strongest market for WorldSpace and we feel privileged for this. We are very bullish about our growth in this country. We conduct huge research to better understand our consumer needs and will add more stations to our bouquet if and when there is a consumer demand for this. At the same time, there is a huge untapped market in the existing markets and we will continue to penetrate deep into these markets."[62]

Competition

The greatest competition for WorldSpace India came from the private FM channels that had begun operating in India from 2000. A number of FM channels were launched in this period and they claimed to provide non-stop entertainment to listeners. The success of FM channels was also attributed to the rising number of cars in India. These channels targeted people traveling in cars and became a source of entertainment during travel. They were localized and catered to specific pockets in various regions across India and were usually broadcast in the regional language.

However, WorldSpace India claimed that its services were different from those of FM channels both in content and in technology. Commenting on the competition from FM channels, WorldSpace Corporate Vice President Tedros Lemma said, "WorldSpace is an altogether different medium from FM and is rather complementary to FM channels. Apart from a digital quality sound beam, our subscribers have access to the content 24 hours a day without being interrupted by advertisements."[63]

WorldSpace India also had to compete with the 'direct-to-home'[64] technology that had begun gaining ground in India in the early 2000s. Some analysts predicted that once this technology became more popular, it could pose a potential threat to WorldSpace India.

The Challenges for WorldSpace

WorldSpace Corp.'s total revenue in 2005 was $11.6 million of which $3.4 million (29%) came from WorldSpace India.[65] The first two quarters of 2006 yielded revenues of $7.2 million worldwide. The net losses that WorldSpace had been posting since its initial launch fell substantially from $577 million in 2004 to about $80 million in 2005 (Refer to Exhibit 6 for WorldSpace Corp.'s Financials between 2004 and 2006).

However, while the other two satellite radio service providers, XM and Sirius, made substantial ground in their areas of operation, WorldSpace, which was considered to be the pioneer in digital satellite radio, continued to suffer losses. Its satellites too had completed around half their estimated useful lives.

WorldSpace faced another challenge in the form of mobile radio users. In the US, XM and Sirius tied up with car manufacturers to include satellite radio receivers in their vehicles. WorldSpace's current generation of radio receivers were not compatible with the technology required to receive satellite radio broadcasts in moving vehicles. Although the company planned to bring out mobile receivers in a tie-up with Delphi Corporation, as of mid-2006, there was little progress on the project. Also, in order to make their service available in cars and other vehicles, WorldSpace needed to invest in the creation of substantial terrestrial infrastructure, such as a network of repeaters. However, if WorldSpace could offer its service in moving vehicles, it had the potential to substantially boost its subscriptions and revenues.

As of June 2006, WorldSpace had a subscriber base of around 150,000 while XM and Sirius had over seven million and five million subscribers respectively.[66] XM and Sirius operated only in the US and Canada while WorldSpace covered the rest of the world. According to analysts, the acceptance of satellite radio was closely linked to the spending power in the respective regions. Since WorldSpace Corp. concentrated its operations mostly in Africa and Asia, they felt that WorldSpace's revenues would continue to be much lower than those of XM and Sirius. And if WorldSpace were to expand in India and other Asian countries, it needed to substantially scale up its sales and service facilities in the region.

References and Suggested Readings

1. Kenneth Silber, **"Samara: Bringing Satellite Radio to Africa,"** www.space.com, December 15, 1999. (Accessed on September 4, 2006)
2. Nathan Vardi, **"Bird in the hand,"** www.forbes.com, April 29, 2002. (Accessed on September 1, 2006)
3. Archana Raghuram, **"Distance Education Not So Distant,"** *The Hindu*, September 4, 2002.

---

[62] Asit Ranjan Mishra, "WorldSpace Decoded: Experiential Marketing Does the Trick," www.exchange4media.com, May 23, 2006. (Accessed on September 16, 2006)

[63] "India Our Primary Focus: WorldSpace," *The Hindu*, July 5, 2006.

[64] In the 'direct-to-home' technology, the signals broadcast from communication satellites are received by set-top boxes connected directly to TV sets. It includes both digital and analog radio and TV.

[65] "India Our Primary Focus: WorldSpace," *The Hindu*, July 5, 2006.

[66] www.radiosatellite.org, October 2006. (Accessed on October 18, 2006)

Exhibit 6   WorldSpace Corp. Financials

(All amounts in millions of US dollars $)

Year ended December 31	2004	2005	2006 (Half-year)
Revenue			
Subscription Revenue	1.0	3.7	3.5
Equipment Revenue	2.1	2.8	1.8
Other Revenue	5.4	5.1	1.9
Total Revenue	**8.5**	**11.6**	**7.2**
Operating Expenses			
Satellite, transmission, programming and other expenses	12.29	18.06	13.76
Cost of equipment	2.38	6.72	5.47
Research and development	–	1.04	.49
Selling, general and administrative expenses	32.77	62	39.55
Stock-based compensation	90.32	25.16	7.18
Depreciation and amortization	61.18	61.63	29.45
Total Operating Expenses	**198.94**	**174.62**	**95.91**
Loss from operations	(190.4)	(163.02)	(88.7)
Other Income (Expense)			
Gain on extinguishment of debt	–	14.13	
Interest income	.43	6.59	6.04
Interest expense	(119.3)	(9.88)	(4.62)
Other	(.87)	2.6	(2.81)
Loss before income taxes	(310.1)	(149.5)	(90.09)
Income tax benefit (provision)	(267.27)	69.66	24.22
Net Loss	**(577.4)**	**(79.8)**	**(65.9)**

Source: Adapted from www.worldspace.com

4. **"WorldSpace Launches Government Sales Unit,"** www.satnews.com, May 21, 2003. (Accessed on October 17, 2006)

5. Sam Silverstein, **"Subscription Sales Key to New WorldSpace Strategy,"** www.spacenews.com, 24 June 2003. (Accessed on September 1, 2006)

6. **"WorldSpace ties up with Virgin radio,"** www.agencyfaqs.com, October 29, 2003. (Accessed on September 11, 2006)

7. R. Ravikumar, **"Broadcaster WorldSpace set to go pay,"** *The Hindu Business Line,* January 17, 2004.

8. **"WorldSpace Seeks to Become Voice from Home,"** www.rwonline.com, February 1, 2004. (Accessed on September 1, 2006)

9. **"WorldSpace Satellite Radio Launches Global Subscription Campaign; Initial Focus on American and British ExPats,"** www.spaceref.com, March 4, 2004. (Accessed on September 4, 2006)

10. **"WOUGNET WorldSpace Satellite Radio Program,"** www.wougnet.org, March 2004. (Accessed on September 4, 2006)

11. **"Consultation Paper on Issues Relating to Satellite Radio Service,"** www.trai.gov.in, December 29, 2004. (Accessed on October 18, 2006)

12. Annys Shin, **"WorldSpace sets stock offering,"** www.washingtonpost.com, April 19, 2005. (Accessed on September 1, 2006)

13. Prachi Pinglay, **"Reaching out through the skies,"** *Frontline,* May 6, 2005.

14. **"WorldSpace to Spend $10 Million on Advertisement,"** *The Economic Times,* July 7, 2005.

15. **"WorldSpace Re-launches Services in India,"** www.ndtv.com/money, July 8, 2005. (Accessed on September 11, 2006)

16. Annys Shin, **"XM Invests $25 Million in Rival WorldSpace,"** *Washington Post,* July 20, 2005.

17. Latha Venkatraman, **"WorldSpace Strikes a Chord with Discerning Listeners,"** *The Hindu Business Line,* August 11, 2005.

18. Seth Jayson, **"A Stellar Way to Lose Money,"** www.fool.com, September 9, 2005. (Accessed on October 18, 2006)

19. Jerry Knight, **"WorldSpace Stumbles,"** www.washingtonpost.com, October 10, 2005. (Accessed on September 18, 2006)

20. **"Satellite Radio for the Rest of the World, if they'll Listen,"** www.usatoday.com, October 27, 2005. (Accessed on September 4, 2006)

21. **"Satellite Radio Is Here to Stay,"** www.rediff.com, November 10, 2005. (Accessed on September 1, 2006)

22. **"WorldSpace to invest $150 million in India,"** www.rediff.com, November 11, 2005. (Accessed on September 13, 2006)

23. Asit Ranjan Mishra, **"WorldSpace Adds 12000 Subscribers in First Month of Festive Offer,"** www.exchange4media.com, December 29, 2005. (Accessed on September 1, 2006)

24. **"WorldSpace Music at Coffee Day Outlets,"** *The Hindu Business Line,* January 4, 2006.

25. **"WorldSpace Satellite Radio Unveils New Corporate Brand Identity, Logo and Tagline,"** www.worldspace.com/press/releases, January 6, 2006. (Accessed on September 18, 2006)

26. **"The New Face of WorldSpace,"** www.orbitcast.com, January 7, 2006. (Accessed on September 18, 2006)

27. R. Ravikumar, **"The World's Listening,"** *The Hindu Business Line,* January 12, 2006.

28. **"WorldSpace satellite radio to deliver 'Play',"** www.televisionpoint .com, February 7, 2006. (Accessed on September 4, 2006)

29. **"WorldSpace Launched Fox Sports Radio Channel,"** www .worldspace.ae/english/press, March 6, 2006. (Accessed on September 15, 2006)

30. **"India Drives WorldSpace's Global Growth,"** *Business Standard,* March 29, 2006.

31. Rakesh Mehar, **"Finding its own space,"** *The Hindu,* April 15, 2006.

32. **"WorldSpace Expands to Four More Cities,"** *The Hindu Business Line,* May 9, 2006.

33. Asit Ranjan Mishra, **"WorldSpace decoded: Experiential marketing does the trick,"** www.exchange4media.com, May 23, 2006. (Accessed on September 16, 2006)

34. **"WorldSpace unveils a new signature tune,"** *The Hindu Business Line,* July 4, 2006

35. **"India our primary focus: WorldSpace,"** *The Hindu,* July 5, 2006.

36. "**WorldSpace Unveils Signature Tune by Rahman,"** www.ndtv.com, July 7, 2006. (Accessed on September 11, 2006)

37. Amit Ranjan Rai, **"Why WorldSpace scores over others,"** www.rediff.com, August 3, 2006. (Accessed on September 1, 2006)

38. Arati Menon Carroll, **"Radio from the Skies,"** www.rediff.com, August 13, 2006. (Accessed on September 1, 2006)

39. www.worldspace.com

40. www.worldspace.ae

41. www.worldspace.in

42. www.alcatel.com

43. www.fcc.gov

44. www.firstvoiceint.org

45. www.howstuffworks.com

46. www.radiosatellite.org

47. www.orbitcast.com

The YMCA of London, Ontario

W. Glenn Rowe

Pat MacDonald

As Shaun Elliott, chief executive officer, prepared for the last senior management planning session in 2005, he reflected on what the YMCA of London (the London Y or the association) had achieved in the last four years. Since joining in 2001, Elliott had led the organization from a deficit of $230,000[1] to a projected surplus of almost $1 million by the end of this fiscal year. This turnaround had been accomplished through a careful balance of internal cost cutting and growth through partnering and program expansion. Innovative partnerships with other organizations had allowed the London Y to expand its programs and facilities with minimal capital investment. In addition to its now solid financial performance, the London Y was on track to exceed its targeted participation level of 46,500 individuals by the end of 2005. It was now time for Elliott to turn his attention to achieving the next level of growth: participation levels of 102,000 individuals by 2010. He knew that to achieve an increase of this magnitude, senior management would need to increase their focus and its capacity and that he would need to spend more time on longer term strategic initiatives and community relations. He wondered if this was possible given the current situation.

The YMCA

The Young Men's Christian Association (YMCA) was an international federation of autonomous not-for-profit community service organizations dedicated to meeting the health and human service needs of men, women and children in their communities. The YMCA was founded in London, England in 1844, in response to the unhealthy social conditions resulting from the industrial revolution. Its founder, George Williams, hoped to substitute Bible study and prayer for life on the streets for the many rural young men who had moved to the cities for jobs. By 1851, there were 24 YMCAs in Great Britain and the first YMCA in North America had opened in Montreal. Three years later, in 1854, there were 397 separate YMCAs in seven nations, with a total of 30,400 members.[2]

From its start, the YMCA was unusual in that it crossed the rigid lines that separated the different churches and social classes in England at the time. This openness was a trait that would lead eventually to YMCAs including all men, women and children regardless of race, religion or nationality. In 2005, the YMCA

---

[1] All funds in Canadian dollars unless specified otherwise.

[2] http://www.ymca.net/about_the_ymca/history_of_the_ymca.html. Accessed February 23, 2006.

---

was in more than 120 countries around the world and each association was independent and reflected its own unique social, political, economic and cultural situation. YMCAs worldwide shared a commitment to growth in spirit, mind and body, as well as a focus on community service, social change, leadership development and a passion for youth.[3]

A similar, although separate organization, the Young Women's Christian Association (YWCA) was founded in 1855 in England.[4] It remained a separate organization; however, some YMCA and YWCAs chose to affiliate in order to best serve the needs in their communities.

The YMCA in Canada

The London Y was a member of YMCA Canada, the national body of the 61 Canadian member associations. YMCA Canada's role was to foster and stimulate the development of strong member associations and advocate on their behalf regionally, nationally and internationally. YMCA Canada was a federation governed by a national voluntary board of directors which oversaw national plans and priorities. Volunteer board members were nominated by the member associations. YMCA Canada's President and CEO was accountable to the board for national operations. The national office had only 20 employees in 2005, reflecting the relative autonomy of the member associations.

As in the rest of the world, YMCAs in Canada served people of all ages, backgrounds and abilities and through all stages of life. They were dedicated to helping people attain a healthy lifestyle and encouraging them to get involved in making their community a better place. As charities, the YMCA member associations relied on the support of their communities, the private sector, governments and other agencies. YMCA fundraising campaigns helped to provide better programs and facilities, as well as greater accessibility and financial assistance to include as many people as possible.[5]

Earlier in 2005, YMCA Canada, in conjunction with its member associations, had developed a strong association profile, which comprised a wide range of performance measures similar to a balanced scorecard. Implementation of this measurement tool was voluntary, although YMCA Canada encouraged individual associations to use it to assess their performance and to compare their performance with other associations.

According to the YMCA Canada strong association profile, a strong YMCA position profile is as follows:

- demonstrates that it is having an impact on individuals' spirits, minds and bodies, while building strong kids, strong families and strong communities;
- assists people to participate in the YMCA who otherwise could not afford to be involved;
- is seen as a valued contributor to the community;
- has the capacity to influence the community relative to its strategic priorities;
- has quality programs that help members meet their personal goals;
- demonstrates growth in participation over time;
- offers a variety of programs that are accessible to the community;
- has a culture of involving their members continually by encouraging them to give their time, talent and treasure to the YMCA;
- has identified key audiences and has a communications plan that addresses each audience.

The London Y had piloted an earlier version of the strong association profile and had already set annual targets for 2005 through to 2010 (see Exhibit 1). The London Y planned to implement these targets and measures as part of its 2005 strategic planning cycle.

The YMCA of London

Founded in 1856, the YMCA of London was a multi-service charity that described its mission as providing "opportunities for personal growth in spirit, mind and body for people of all backgrounds, beliefs and abilities."[6] Its articulated values and the principles by which it operates were:

- **Honesty:** to tell the truth, to act in such a way that you are worthy of trust, to have integrity, making sure your actions match your words.
- **Caring:** to accept others, to be sensitive to the well-being of others, to help others.
- **Respect:** to treat others as you would have them treat you, to value the worth of every person, including yourself.
- **Responsibility:** to do what is right, what you ought to do, to be accountable for your behaviour and obligations.

---

[3] http://www.ymca.ca/eng_worldys.htm. Accessed Feb. 23, 2006.
[4] http://www.ywca.org/site/pp.asp?c=djISI6PIKpG&b=281379. Accessed February 23, 2006.
[5] http://www.ymca.ca/eng_abouty.htm. Accessed February 23, 2006.
[6] http://www.londony.ca/. Accessed February 24, 2006.

Exhibit 1 | The YMCA of London Participation Targets

	2005	2006	2007	2008	2009	2010	5 yr inc	avg inc
Childcare								
Infant	70	70	70	70	70	70	0%	0%
Toddler	140	140	140	140	140	140	0%	0%
Preschool	608	672	736	832	928	1,024	68%	14%
School Age	316	316	316	316	316	316	0%	0%
Childcare Total	**1,134**	**1,198**	**1,262**	**1,358**	**1,454**	**1,550**	**37%**	**7%**
Camping and Educational Services								
CQE	1,815	2,215	2,215	2,439	2,471	2,471	36%	7%
Day Camp	5,350	5,457	5,566	5,677	5,791	5,907	10%	2%
Outdoor Education	5,800	6,960	9,048	9,953	10,948	12,043	108%	22%
Children's Safety Village	12,000	13,500	14,000	14,000	14,000	14,000	17%	3%
Community School Programs	1,630	1,880	2,130	2,380	2,630	2,880	77%	15%
Camping Total	**26,595**	**30,012**	**32,959**	**34,449**	**35,840**	**37,301**	**40%**	**8%**
Health Fitness and Recreation								
CBY full fee	5,450	5,580	5,750	5,825	6,000	6,200	14%	3%
CBY assisted	2,210	2,330	2,450	2,500	2,525	2,650	20%	4%
CBY programs	4200	4,580	4,975	5,750	6,875	8,050	92%	18%
BHY full fee	1,500	1,525	1,900	2,100	2,400	2,700	80%	16%
BHY assisted	300	305	380	420	480	540	80%	16%
BHY programs	1,600	7,565	9,100	10,195	11,480	13,125	720%	144%
ELY full fee		1,025	1,050	1,050	1,075	1,200		
ELY assisted		205	210	210	215	240		
ELY programs		4,085	5,010	5,280	5,755	6,225		
SCY full fee	481	865	1,155	1,155	1,155	1,155	140%	28%
SCY assisted	26	74	100	110	110	110	323%	65%
SCY programs	773	826	865	905	925	945	22%	4%
WDY full fee	1,822	1,844	1,879	1,913	2,400	3,040	67%	13%
WDY assisted	373	405	426	449	600	760	104%	21%
WDY programs	4,900	5,680	6,480	6,935	8,140	9,375	91%	18%
New location full fee	n/a	n/a	n/a	5,000	7,000	7,000		
New location assisted	n/a	n/a	n/a	1,250	1,750	1,750		
HFR Total	**18,735**	**31,214**	**35,250**	**49,797**	**57,135**	**63,315**	**238%**	**48%**
Grand Total of Participants	**46,464**	**62,424**	**69,471**	**85,604**	**94,429**	**102,166**	**120%**	**24%**
Volunteers								
Childcare								
Camping								
CBY								
BHY		55	60	65	70	75		
ELY		15	20	25	30	35		
SCY	20	23	27	30	35	40	100%	20%
WD	35	38	42	45	60	80		
Total	**55**	**131**	**149**	**165**	**195**	**230**		

(continued)

Exhibit 1

	2005	2006	2007	2008	2009	2010	5 yr inc	avg inc
Member Retention Rate								
CBY		76%	76%	76%	76%	76%		
BHY		55%	64%	68%	69%	70%		
ELY		55%	64%	68%	69%	70%		
SCY		55%	65%	68%	72%	75%		
WDY		80%	80%	82%	82%	82%		
New Location								

Source: YMCA of London, 2005 Strategic Planning Documents

Exhibit 2   The YMCA of London Growth 2001 to 2005

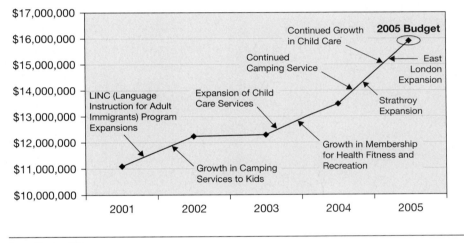

Source: Company files.

The association served almost 28,000 children annually through childcare and camping at 16 childcare locations, two residential camps, one outdoor education centre and numerous summer day camps and after school program locations. In 2004, the London Y had provided 13,025 health, fitness and recreation (HFR) memberships for children and adults at five branches: three in London, one in Strathroy and one in Woodstock. In addition, the St. Thomas YMCA was operated by London Y senior management under contract. To ensure that no one was turned away because of an inability to pay, in 2004, the association provided 2,994 assisted HFR memberships, 1,100 assisted "camperships" and assistance to 310 children in child care. The association had a very positive brand position in the community and its internal research had shown that referrals were the number one source of new members and participants.

The last four years had been a time of renewal and change for the London Y (see Exhibit 2). Revenue had increased by 50 per cent and the association had transformed an operating deficit of $230,000 in 2001 to an expected $1 million operating surplus by the end of 2005 (see Exhibit 3). In 2004, childcare contributed 38 per cent of total revenue, HFR contributed 27 per cent and 16 per cent of revenue came from camping (see Exhibit 4 for The YMCA of London—Revenue). The remaining revenue sources included government programs and contracts, community programs, donations and the United Way. Almost 90 per cent of the London Y's revenue was self-generated through program and participation fees.

Exhibit 3   The YMCA of London Schedule of Operations

REVENUE	2005 Projected	Year ended Dec. 31, 2004	Year ended Dec. 31, 2003	Year ended Dec. 31, 2002	Year ended Dec. 31, 2001
Memberships	3,647,014	3,560,527	3,364,190	3,139,980	3,183,699
Child Care	6,811,401	4,958,138	4,037,612	4,516,214	4,576,632
Camp Fees	2,192,237	2,121,787	2,023,885	2,020,531	1,978,414
Community Programs	260,676	442,927	532,606	863,573	414,659
Program Service Fees	328,495	228,500	342,727	302,069	299,177
United Way	205,999	185,250	169,989	164,619	178,818
Ancillary Revenue	544,748	519,225	458,768	633,102	252,935
Donations & Fundraising	341,701	297,917	371,996	416,779	128,190
Employment Initiatives	989,141	891,815	792,983		
International Contributions & Grants				41,239	46,023
Total Revenue	15,321,412	13,206,086	12,094,756	12,098,106	11,058,547
EXPENSES					
Salaries & benefits	9,550,594	8,525,862	7,663,975	7,718,093	7,288,194
Program costs	973,935	1,357,277	1,237,143	946,329	1,013,640
Facilities	2,060,400	1,830,450	1,746,122	1,918,676	1,878,400
Promotion	165,180	178,053	140,143	183,441	164,600
Association dues	163,543	157,570	137,985	136,795	132,777
Travel & development	214,130	222,013	238,060		
Office expenses	285,302	276,835	284,382		
Professional & other fees	247,592	247,430	302,695		
Miscellaneous	149,741	168,117	128,503		
Administration				840,048	763,095
International development				41,239	46,023
Total expenses	14,399,676	12,963,607	11,879,008	11,784,621	11,286,729
EXCESS (DEFICIENCY) OF REVENUE OVER EXPENSES	921,736	242,279	215,748	313,485	−228,182

Source: The London YMCA Annual Reports 2004, 2003, 2002, 2001.

The responsibility for all development and fundraising activity was in the process of being moved into the YMCA of London Foundation, an affiliated but separate organization which had a strong record of investing and securing grants. In its newly expanded role, the foundation was expected to support capital campaigns, conduct annual campaigns and enhance planned giving.

The London Y's structure included the CEO who was accountable to a volunteer board of directors (the board). Seven general managers and one manager reported to the CEO along with three senior directors and one director. The general managers and manager were responsible for service areas or locations including camping and outdoor education, childcare, community services, London HFR, the Woodstock District YMCA,

Exhibit 4   The YMCA London Revenue 2004

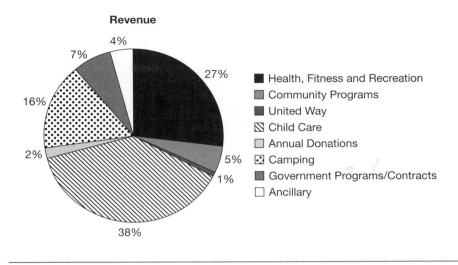

Revenue

- ■ Health, Fitness and Recreation
- ▦ Community Programs
- ▨ United Way
- ▧ Child Care
- ▢ Annual Donations
- ⊡ Camping
- ▩ Government Programs/Contracts
- ☐ Ancillary

4%
7%
16%
2%
27%
5%
1%
38%

Source: The YMCA of London Annual Report 2004

the St. Thomas Elgin Family YMCA, the Strathroy-Caradoc Family YMCA, overall facilities, and employment initiatives. The senior directors and director were responsible for finance, development, human resources and communications, respectively (see Exhibit 5). The number of senior managers had not increased in the last four years.

With the introduction of the strong association profile framework for performance measurement, all senior managers would have performance agreements and work-plans that they had planned together. Measures of participation, program quality and financial performance would be tracked and accountability would be to the group. Once the measures and targets were well established, it was expected that compensation decisions would be based on each senior manager's performance against their plans.

In 2005, the association had over 500 permanent staff with an additional 200 seasonal staff. Full-time employees made up 35 to 40 per cent of the total and the remaining 60 to 65 per cent were part-time employees. Annual staff satisfaction surveys consistently showed high levels of both satisfaction and commitment to the association. However, wages were a persistent issue with staff in the child care centres and finding suitable HFR staff had been particularly challenging.

During the last four years, the board and senior management of the London Y had identified partnering as a key strategy to achieve the association's long term strategic objectives in its three core service areas: HFR, childcare, and camping and outdoor education. Senior management moved quickly to seize opportunities for a number of new partnerships.[7] A new HFR facility in East London was developed in partnership with the London Public Library. Partnerships were established with Kellogg Canada Inc. and John Labatt Ltd. for the London Y to operate their on-site HFR facilities. Childcare services had grown more than 50 per cent, primarily as a result of a partnership with the University of Western Ontario.

Some partnerships were opportunistic or tactical but were nonetheless guided by their fit with the long-term goals and values of the London Y. For example, a partnership with the Children's Safety Village made resources available to pursue a new full service HFR location in an underserved area of the city, thus expanding service and programs. In the absence of a significant capital infusion, senior management believed that new partnerships were critical to the London Y achieving its participation target of 102,000 individuals by 2010.

---

[7] All of the London Y's partnering relationships have approximately the same legal structure which involves a facilities lease and an operating or service provision agreement. There are no fees paid to the partners as all services are provided on a fee-for-service basis and the London Y covers the operating costs of the facility.

Exhibit 5   The YMCA of London Organization Chart

YMCA of London Organization Chart September 2005

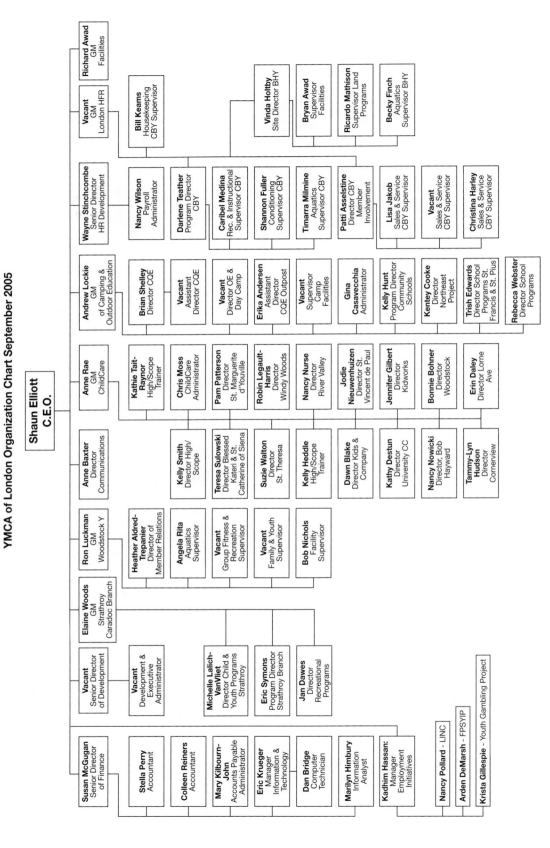

Core Service Areas

Health, Fitness and Recreation

One of the longest standing services that the London Y provided was HFR. These services were offered through five branches each led by a general manager. These included: the London Centre YMCA (CBY), the Bob Hayward (BHY) and East London (ELY) all located in London; The Strathroy-Caradoc Family YMCA (SCY) located 40 kilometres west of London; and The YMCA of Woodstock and District (WDY) located 50 kilometres east of London. By 2005, the London Y had served more than 18,700 individuals through its HFR programs and by 2010 the association had a target of serving more than 63,000 in six locations, an increase of 238 per cent. The St. Thomas Y was located 35 kilometres south of London.

The branches were membership-based and offered health and fitness programs for children, families and adults. Twenty-five per cent of the London Y's members received an assisted membership and paid one third of the cost on average. Programs for children and youth were estimated to cost more than four times the association's programs for adults, yet generated lower fees. Children's programs and services often ran at a loss. The London Y depended on full fee paying adult HFR members to cross-subsidize assisted memberships and children's programs.

The largest challenge to the London Y attracting full fee adult members was the proliferation of fitness facilities for adults. Market-research commissioned by the London Y in 2002, indicated that approximately 30 per cent of the 193,845 adults in London would join a fitness facility and that 25.5 per cent of adults were already members of a fitness club. The potential for market growth was assessed as limited. The research also showed significant penetration of the market by private sector providers with the primary competition in London coming from the Good Life Clubs with 37 per cent market share and The Athletic Club with 22 per cent of the market. The London Y was third in the London market with a share of 12 per cent. The competition had increased recently with the entrance of the Premier/Mademoiselle chain of fitness clubs into the City of London.

The private clubs operated under a very different economic model than the London Y, typically leasing equipment and facilities. They targeted the adult market only and they did not offer pools or as wide a range of programming as the London Y. In contrast to the private operators, the London Y owned relatively large facilities with pools. Only the two newest branches in London and Strathroy (ELY and SCY) did not have pools,

although interest in adding a pool to the SCY had already been raised in the community.

A number of the London Y facilities were aging and required significant capital reinvestment or replacement. The CBY was 25 years old and required ongoing maintenance and refurbishment. The BHY in East London and the WDY were each 50 years old and were not wheelchair accessible. Both buildings required significant capital investment to meet and maintain modern standards. Unfortunately, the BHY was not ideally located so the potential for new members would be limited. More positively, the City of Woodstock had expressed an interest in partnering with the association to develop a new community facility as part of the city's master recreational plan. Replacing the WDY building was considered to be an imperative and partnering with the city was the association's preferred strategy.

Senior management of the London Y believed that to remain relevant in the HFR market as well as meet its targets, the association must develop new facilities in London's north and west ends. The City of London's master recreational plan supported partnership in the delivery of recreational programs and the association had begun discussions with the city regarding development of a new HFR facility in the north end. The city's plan also identified the southwest of the city as a priority site for a HFR facility.

Retention was a key part of membership growth as research showed that two-thirds of new members leave within the first year. Currently, the London Y had relatively high retention rates for members that lasted beyond one year at CBY (76 per cent), WDY (80 per cent) and BHY (75 per cent). ELY and SCY had been in operation less than two years, and retention rates while high were expected to decrease. The association had targeted overall HFR retention rates of 55 per cent at BHY, ELY and SCY next year increasing to more than 70 per cent by 2010. While the association planned to continue its focus on families and to differentiate itself as a values-based organization, it also planned to offer specialized programs targeted at specific groups such as cardiac rehabilitation, weight loss, osteoporosis treatment etc. to enhance both member retention and new member attraction. This would require increased staff with increased qualifications, resulting in increased costs. To offset these expected cost increases HFR management would need to determine ways to increase revenues or fees.

Although the CEO managed most of the HFR facilities, each facility was run as a separate unit by its general manager. Each branch did its own hiring, staff training, uniform purchasing, program development, and sales and promotion materials. This had resulted in inconsistencies in program quality, program delivery, member service, staff management, facility maintenance and house-keeping between branches. There were significant economic and operational inefficiencies as well. Senior management believed that increased consistency would contribute to increased efficiency, allowing the association to serve more members and to retain more of the existing members. However, there were no coordinating mechanisms for HFR other than the CEO. With financial stability and revenue growth as his priorities, he had not had sufficient time to work with each of the HFR general managers. Also, the CEO was not himself an experienced HFR manager, having spent his career in financial services prior to joining the association.

HFR staff tended to be young and at the beginning of their careers. Finding and retaining appropriate HFR staff had been challenging for the London Y. Work had begun on developing relationships with the local Community College and University to establish a placement/apprentice program to identify strong candidates. Also a skill/aptitude profile of HFR staff was in development based on YMCA Canada's standards and training for HFR staff.

The senior management team had developed a number of strategic initiatives for HFR for the coming year. In summary they were:

- develop a new facility in London in partnership with the city of London
- develop a new facility in Woodstock
- manage and promote the Bob Hayward and East London facilities as one branch
- initiate discussions with the town of Strathroy for the development of a pool
- focus on program development and quality, and develop a new revenue structure to support increased quality of service

Childcare Services

Childcare services were the London Y's largest source of revenue. These services were offered through 16 childcare centres located in London (12 locations), Strathroy (two locations), St. Thomas and Woodstock (one location each). The centres were mostly located in leased premises with only the Woodstock centre operating in a facility owned by the association. In 2004, the London Y had served 1139 children in three categories: infant, toddler and preschooler. By 2010, the association planned to serve an additional 415 preschoolers, for a total of 1,554 children. The London Y childcare centres were similar to other providers in offering full-time, part-time and flexible care options and its fees were set between the midpoint and the high end of fees charged in

London. Infants are considerably more expensive to serve due to the higher staff to child ratios required.

Childcare is highly regulated through Ontario's Day Nursery Act (DNA). The DNA prescribes staff to children ratios by age, as well as physical space design, procedures, food preparation and all other aspects of operations. Wage enhancement subsidies were established by the provincial government 10 years ago, as private centres were made public and regulations were established. The subsidies were considered to be necessary for the financial feasibility of centres; however, they had remained at the same levels since their introduction in the early 1990s. Many levels of government were involved with the regulation and funding of childcare, including the Province of Ontario, the Ministry of Community and Social Services, the Ministry of Health, cities and counties, and in some instances, boards of education. It was expected that the landscape of childcare would undergo significant change in 2006 and beyond based on provincial initiatives and programs resulting from proposed increases in federal funding.

Subsidies for child care fees are available to low income families through the cities and counties. These subsidies did not typically cover all of the fees and the London Y absorbed the shortfall as part of its support to the community.

There were two other large childcare providers in London: London Children's Connection with 13 centres and London Bridge with 11 centres. Unlike these service providers, the London Y offered unique programming through its use of the High Scope curriculum and its values-based programming. In fact, the London Y's curriculum and values focus were key reasons that The University of Western Ontario decided to partner with the association. In addition to the High Scope curriculum, the London Y also offered HFR memberships to each full-time child, discounts for HFR family memberships, summer day camp discounts for customers, swimming as part of their programs and family input through parent advisory committees.

The number of children aged zero to four was expected to decline until the year 2012 in the communities the association currently served. However, senior management believed that opportunities for expansion existed in some of the rural communities and counties that were near existing locations. To continue to maintain full enrollment, the association would need to closely monitor local demographics, competitors' expansion and new subdivision development.

The London Y employed a large number of early childhood educators. Wage scales in the industry were lower than in many other industries. While the London Y had made every effort to provide reasonable compensation and reward good performance, staff satisfaction surveys consistently identified wages as an issue. It was now suspected that the London Y was paying slightly below the average childcare wages in the City of London. Management realized that they must carefully balance wage increases and additional managers against their goal of maintaining a surplus.

Communication and consistency among the centres seemed to require constant attention. Some operational processes had been centralized, such as subsidies and collections, while most processes remained with each centre, including the purchasing of supplies and food preparation. Procedures had been standardized with a common operation manual, although there were still many opportunities for greater consistency and standardization.

With more than 50 per cent growth in childcare since 2001, the general manager's scope of authority had become very large. By 2005, she had 18 people reporting directly to her, including all 16 centre directors. This created significant barriers to relationship-building, both internally with staff and externally with parents, potential partners, funding organizations and regulators. It was also a challenge during budget review when the general manager of Childcare had to review 16 centre budgets and the overall child care budget in the same time frame as, for example, a general manager in HFR whose one budget might be smaller than one of the larger child care centres.

While the nature and the extent of the changes in programs and program funding were unclear, senior management believed that the complex regulatory environment gave a distinct advantage to an experienced and competent child care provider. The London Y was confident that it had good working relationships with the cities of London, Woodstock, Strathroy and St. Thomas, the counties in which it operated, and with both the Public and the Roman Catholic School Boards.

Partially in response to the changes expected in the childcare environment, the London Y had begun to explore partnership or merger opportunities with other service providers. In addition to operating advantages, management believed a partnership might also enhance their ability to influence government funding.

The senior management team had developed a number of strategic initiatives for childcare services in the coming year. In summary they were:

- explore partnerships or mergers with other providers
- identify and initiate opportunities in rural areas
- enhance wage structure in balance with budget limitations
- monitor changes in government policy, acquire the best and earliest information and develop appropriate contingency plans.

Camping and Outdoor Education

The London Y expected to serve more than 26,500 participants through camping and education programs in 2005. Residential camping programs were delivered in July and August to almost 2,000 children aged six to 17 at two sites in Northern Ontario, Camp Queen Elizabeth and Camp Queen Elizabeth (CQE) Outpost. Summer day camps served more than 5,000 children aged three to 15 with a variety of programs running from traditional day camps to sports camps and other specialty camps. During the school year more than 1,500 children were served through community school programs delivered in cooperation with school boards. Another 12,000 children were served annually through programs given by police and firefighters at the Children's Safety Village located in the Upper Thames Conservation Authority area near the city of London. Finally, almost 6,000 children and adults participated in outdoor education programs including leadership and team building programs offered at various locations.

Camp Queen Elizabeth had been in operation for 50 years and had an excellent reputation. Each year the Camp was booked to capacity and each year those bookings occurred earlier. Similar to other residential camps, much of the activity was outdoors and programming included water sports, crafts and climbing. Fees were amongst the highest in YMCA camping and the return rate of campers was the highest of all YMCA camps in Ontario. Campers tended to be more homogeneous and from higher income families; however, assisted spots were made available for those unable to afford the fees.

Camp Queen Elizabeth was located on land leased from Parks Canada, a federal department. The current lease was due to expire in 2007 and the London Y had postponed capital investment in the facilities pending renewal of the lease. The association had now received assurance from Parks Canada that the lease would be renewed so a long-overdue refurbishment of the camp's infrastructure could be planned.

The CQE Outpost property had been purchased as a hedge against renewal of the Camp Queen Elizabeth lease as well as for additional capacity to serve older youth with adventure and canoe trips. Service to older youth had not increased as planned and there appeared to be little demand for this type of service. Management was now exploring the possibility of selling the property and using the proceeds towards the renovation of Camp Queen Elizabeth.

The London Y offered a wide variety of day camp and outdoor education programs during all weeks of the summer and, to a limited extent, in the shoulder seasons of spring and fall. During the summer, the association ran a bussing network throughout the City of London to collect and return participants to designated drop-off points. Programming was value-based and emphasized character development more than skill development. Other summer day camp providers included the local University, the City of London, a variety of private businesses and not-for-profit organizations, and churches. The London Y day camps offered the same size groups and staff ratios as other day camp providers and in some cases the offerings were quite undifferentiated. The service needs and selection processes for families and children were not clearly understood by the London Y, although it appeared to management that there were a number of different segments such as skills-based camps, traditional camps and camps that were more like a childcare service.

The association had recently invested some capital dollars in its outdoor education program and developed two new sites in partnership with Spencer Hall, run by the Richard Ivey School of Business and Spencer Lodge, run by the Boy Scouts of Canada. With these new partners and facilities the association hoped to increase the number of its outdoor education program participants by more than 100 per cent by 2010.

The community school program, funded by the United Way and the London Y, was an after school program aimed at improving the academic performance and the social skills of children in higher risk neighbourhoods. The focus was on literacy, social skills and recreation, and the programs were delivered in a number of designated schools. London Y staff worked closely with teachers to identify children who would benefit from participation in the program. This program continued to expand as much as funding and staffing would allow.

Each school year the Children's Safety Village targeted students in grades one to four with its programs on broad safety topics including pedestrian safety, bike safety, fire safety, electrical safety and other household hazards.[8] As a result of their partnership agreement, the London Y's Camping and Outdoor Education operations moved from their dilapidated offices at the association's outdoor education centre to the Children's Safety Village site and the London Y took over management of the site. While the London Y was responsible for the physical operation, the Children's Safety Village Board continued to govern the organization, resulting in some overlapping responsibilities.

Camping and outdoor education offered a wide variety of programs in a large number of locations under a number of different names. Each program produced its own sales and promotion materials and parent communications. A number of programs and facilities were not clearly identified as part of the YMCA, such as Camp Queen Elizabeth or the Children's Safety Village. Management believed that there were a number of opportunities to send a more consistent message to the community and to strengthen the London Y's brand.

The senior management team had developed a number of strategic initiatives for camping and outdoor education in the coming year. In summary they were:

- identify day camp market segments and deliver programs to meet identified needs
- sell the CQE Outpost site and use the proceeds to improve Camp Queen Elizabeth, ensuring that current and expected demand can be accommodated
- negotiate a new governance model and transfer governance of the YMCA Children's Safety Village to the YMCA of London
- ensure that all facilities and programs are clearly identified as part of the London YMCA
- leverage opportunities to serve more individuals in outdoor education programs

Elliott's Consideration of the Situation

Elliott realized that each of the association's three main service areas had very different business models and dynamics and that this created challenges for organizational focus and expertise, resource allocation and communication. He also knew that while the challenges coming from this multi-service approach were abundant and the synergies limited, neither the board of the London Y nor the senior management wished to reduce the range of services that the association provided to the community. Elliott's challenge was how to best manage the association as a whole while appropriately nurturing each of the core service areas. He had a number of concerns.

The recent growth had put significant strain on both the capacity and capabilities of the senior managers. Elliott was concerned that there were simply not enough managers to deliver the targeted growth and, particularly, the new partnership relationships that would need to be established. Over the last few years Elliott felt that he was the "chief business development officer," searching out partnering opportunities with external organizations and developing both the opportunity and the relationship through to the final agreement. The service area leaders had been focusing on operations and

---

[8] http://www.safetyvillage.ca/about.htm. Accessed February 28, 2006.

did not have the time, or perhaps the inclination, to think about innovative ways for their areas to serve more people. He believed that it was now time for the service area leaders to take on the development role and to identify and create their own growth opportunities.

In addition to greater capacity, Elliott believed that the senior management team needed to increase its focus on higher level strategic issues affecting the whole association. With 12 people at the table, senior management team meetings were not as effective as they might have been and in fact some members only contributed when the discussion was about their specific location. Also, the meetings tended to over-emphasize day-to-day HFR operations simply because there were so many HFR general managers at the table. This meant that they were perhaps under-emphasizing the association's other key service areas of childcare and camping.

Along with decreasing senior management's focus on HFR, Elliott knew that he too needed to spend less time on day-to-day HFR operations and more time on strategic initiatives and community relations. However, with four HFR General Managers reporting to him and with HFR representing the biggest operational challenges and the largest growth target, he knew that HFR needed the undivided attention of a capable senior manager. Also, he did not know how the HFR General Managers would respond to any changes that might be perceived as a loss of status or position.

Elliott had real fears about creating a potentially unnecessary layer of management or, even worse, an elite group that became out of touch with the staff and the various locations. He worried about becoming out of touch with the operations himself. One of the first things that Elliott had done when he joined the association in 2001 was to eliminate most of the so called "head office" positions, including the chief operating officer, the head of HFR and the head of development. He did not think that the association could afford those roles at that time and he still believed in carefully balancing expenses and overhead with the need for resources to support expansion. Elliott also had concerns about how the community would perceive a charitable organization that significantly increased its senior management personnel. Finally, he worried about moving too quickly.

Conclusion

Elliott recognized that in trying to determine what was best for the London Y, he must consider the business model and strategy of each of the core service areas while taking into account the overall mission and values of the association. He needed to be confident that any changes would increase the management capacity and focus within each area as well as free him up to focus on longer term strategic initiatives. Elliott was concerned about introducing more overhead expense just when the association's financial performance was stable. He did not have much time left to ponder as he wanted the senior management team to consider any potential organizational changes in the last planning session which was scheduled for next week.